'The *Handbook on Ageing with Disability* is a long-awaited gem of information, research and insights into an area growing in importance but too long ignored. The co-authors are pioneers in this field and they have brought together an impressive international caste of experts. The myriad dimensions and the nuances of aging with a disability, whether intellectual, cognitive, physical, visual, or chronic – are brought together in a masterful collection of prescient chapters. This Handbook is destined to be the "bible" for all of us aging into and with various forms of limitations and disabilities and seeking the latest analysis, data, trends and understanding of this complex yet personal concern.'

Fernando M. Torres-Gil, *UCLA Professor of Social Welfare and Public Policy*

'This Handbook fills a major gap in the knowledge base required to bridge the fields of aging with disability, certainly one of the major challenges for humankind in the XXI Century. The range of topics covered and populations discussed demonstrates the heterogeneity of the aging with disability population and the need for greater attention to common issues in these two areas of research, support and care. This book brilliantly culminates the extensive work the editors have led on this topic over the last 20 years.'

Luis Salvador-Carulla, *Head of the Centre for Mental Health Research at the Australian National University*

HANDBOOK ON AGEING WITH DISABILITY

Mainstream gerontological scholarship has taken little heed of people ageing with disability, and they have also been largely overlooked by both disability and ageing policies and service systems.

The *Handbook on Ageing with Disability* is the first to pull together knowledge about the experience of ageing with disability. It provides a broad look at scholarship in this developing field and across different groups of people with disability in order to form a better understanding of commonalities across groups and identify unique facets of ageing within specific groups. Drawing from academic, personal, and clinical perspectives, the chapters address topics stemming from how the ageing with disability experience is framed, the heterogeneity of the population ageing with disability and the disability experience, issues of social exclusion, health and wellness, frailty, later life, and policy contexts for ageing with disability in various countries.

Responding to the need to increase access to knowledge in this field, the Handbook provides guideposts for researchers, practitioners, and policy makers about what matters in providing services, developing programmes, and implementing policies that support persons ageing with long-term disabilities and their families.

Michelle Putnam is a Professor at the School of Social Work at Simmons University in Boston, Massachusetts. She has studied the experience of ageing with disability, focusing on social care and public policy, for over 20 years. Her work has forwarded efforts to bridge the fields of ageing and disability.

Christine Bigby is a Professor of Social Work and Director of the multidisciplinary Living with Disability Research Centre at La Trobe University, Melbourne, Australia. Her research is focused on building the evidence base for programmes and practice that support the social inclusion of people with intellectual disabilities.

HANDBOOK ON AGEING WITH DISABILITY

Edited by
Michelle Putnam and Christine Bigby

NEW YORK AND LONDON

First published 2021
by Routledge
52 Vanderbilt Avenue, New York, NY 10017

and by Routledge
2 Park Square, Milton Park, Abingdon, Oxon, OX14 4RN

Routledge is an imprint of the Taylor & Francis Group, an informa business

© 2021 selection and editorial matter, Michelle Putnam and Christine Bigby; individual chapters, the contributors

The right of Michelle Putnam and Christine Bigby to be identified as the authors of the editorial material, and of the authors for their individual chapters, has been asserted in accordance with sections 77 and 78 of the Copyright, Designs and Patents Act 1988.

All rights reserved. No part of this book may be reprinted or reproduced or utilised in any form or by any electronic, mechanical, or other means, now known or hereafter invented, including photocopying and recording, or in any information storage or retrieval system, without permission in writing from the publishers.

Trademark notice: Product or corporate names may be trademarks or registered trademarks, and are used only for identification and explanation without intent to infringe.

Library of Congress Cataloging-in-Publication Data
Names: Putnam, Michelle, editor. | Bigby, Christine, editor.
Title: Handbook on ageing with disability / edited by Michelle Putnam and Christine Bigby.
Description: 1 Edition. | New York City : Routledge, 2021. | Includes bibliographical references and index.
Identifiers: LCCN 2020038341 (print) | LCCN 2020038342 (ebook) | ISBN 9781138611498 (hardback) | ISBN 9780429465352 (ebook)
Subjects: LCSH: Older people--Services for. | Older people--Care. | People with disabilities--Services for. | People with disabilities--Care. | Quality of life.
Classification: LCC HQ1061 .H33667 2021 (print) | LCC HQ1061 (ebook) | DDC 362.6/3--dc23
LC record available at https://lccn.loc.gov/2020038341
LC ebook record available at https://lccn.loc.gov/2020038342

ISBN: 978-1-138-61149-8 (hbk)
ISBN: 978-0-429-46535-2 (ebk)

Typeset in Bembo
by KnowledgeWorks Global Ltd.

CONTENTS

List of Figures xi
List of Tables xiii
List of Contributors xiv
Acknowledgments xxi
Preface xxii

PART I
Framing the Ageing with Disability Experience 1

1 Understanding Ageing with Disability 3
   Michelle Putnam, Caitlin E. Coyle, Lydia P. Ogden, and Christine Bigby

2 Rethinking the Concept of Successful Ageing: A Disability Studies Approach 14
   Tove Harnett, Annika Taghizadeh Larsson, and Håkan Jönson

3 Ageing with Lifelong Disability: Individual Meanings and Experiences Over Time 23
   Lieke van Heumen

4 Integrating Critical Disability Studies and Critical Gerontology to Explore the Complexities of Ageing with Disabilities 32
   Hailee M. Yoshizaki-Gibbons

5 Social and Environmental Determinants of the Health of People with Disabilities 44
   Eric Emerson, Zoe Aitken, Hannah Badland, Nicola Fortune, Celia Green, and Jerome N. Rachele

6 Reducing the Shared Burden of Chronic Conditions Among Persons Ageing with Disability and Older Adults in the United States Through Bridging Ageing and Disability 57
   Margaret L. Campbell and Michelle Putnam

7 Segmenting Ageing and Disability Policy: Ethical Concerns 69
   Jerome Bickenbach

PART II
Diverse Experiences of Ageing with Disability 81

8 Understanding the Experience of Growing Older with Cerebral Palsy 83
   Laura R. Moll and Cheryl A. Cott

9 Ageing with Deafblindness 97
   Peter Simcock and Jill Manthorpe

10 Ageing, Serious Mental Illness, and Perceptions of Self Over the Life Course 108
   Lydia P. Ogden

11 Ageing and Brain Injury Long-Term Outcomes in Adults 123
   Angela Colantonio and Melissa Biscardi

12 Ageing with Multiple Sclerosis 138
   Marcia Finlayson, Michelle Ploughman, Julie Pétrin, and Roshanth Rajachandrakumar

13 Ageing when Being Autistic 148
   Hilde M. Geurts, Rebecca Charlton, and Lauren Bishop

PART III
Forwarding Social Inclusion 159

14 Community Participation and Engagement for Persons Ageing with Physical Disability 161
   Rachel Heeb, Courtney Weber, Jessica Dashner, and Kerri Morgan

15 Design for One is Design for All: The Past, Present, and Future of Universal Design as a Strategy for Ageing-in-Place with Disability 169
   Jon A. Sanford and Elena T. Remillard

16 Support for Decision-Making as People Age With a Cognitive Impairment 186
   Terry Carney and Shih-Ning Then

17 Internalised Ageism and the User Gaze in Eldercare: Identifying New Horizons of Possibilities Through the use of a Disability Lens 196
   Håkan Jönson, Annika Taghizadeh Larsson, and Tove Harnett

18 Creating Age and Disability Friendly Communities to Support Healthy and Meaningful Ageing 205
   Friedrich Dieckmann and Christiane Rohleder

PART IV
Intellectual Disability as a Case Example — 217

19 The Emergence of Ageing with Long-Term Disability Populations — 219
    Philip McCallion, Lisa Ferretti, and Mary McCarron

20 Health and Wellness Among Persons Ageing with Intellectual Disability — 229
    Darren McCausland, Philip McCallion, and Mary McCarron

21 Retirement for People with Intellectual Disability: Policy, Pitfalls, and Promising Practices — 240
    Christine Bigby

22 Family Caregiving for Adults Ageing with Intellectual and Developmental Disabilities — 254
    Tamar Heller, Sumithra Murthy, and Catherine Keiling Arnold

23 Ageing with Intellectual Disability In Sweden: Participation and Self Determination — 262
    Mia Jormfeldt and Magnus Tideman

24 Towards Untangling the Ageing Riddle in People with Intellectual Disabilities: An Overview of Research on Frailty and Its Consequences — 273
    Josje D. Schoufour, Dederieke Maes-Festen, Alyt Oppewal, and Heleen M. Evenhuis

25 How to Avoid Early Frailty in People with Intellectual Disabilities? — 287
    Heleen M. Evenhuis, Josje D. Schoufour, Alyt Oppewal, and Dederieke Maes-Festen

26 Dementia Care for Persons Ageing with Intellectual Disability: Developing Non-Pharmacological Strategies for Support — 300
    Karen Watchman and Kate Mattheys

27 End-of-Life Care for Adults With Intellectual Disabilities — 310
    Teresa Moro and Jacqueline McGinley

PART V
Policies to Support Persons Ageing with Disability — 321

28 Responding to Changing Workforce Realities: One Profession's Experience — 323
    Fintan Sheerin, Philip McCallion, and Mary McCarron

29 Ageing in Place in Group Homes: An Australian Context — 337
    Tal Araten-Bergman and Christine Bigby

30 Support, Service Policies, and Programs For Persons Ageing with Disabilities
    in Korea   350
    Kyung Mee Kim and Seung Hyun Roh

31 Trends in Integrating Long-Term Services and Supports in the United States   361
    Michelle Putnam and Caitlin E. Coyle

32 Access to Assistive Technology in Canada   372
    Rosalie H. Wang and Michael G. Wilson

33 Ageing with Disability: Using Financial Mechanisms to Facilitate Intersectoral
    Collaboration   384
    David McDaid and A-La Park

34 Enabling a Good Old Age for People Ageing with Disability: Reflections
    on Progress   392
    Christine Bigby and Michelle Putnam

Glossary   *399*
Index   *404*

FIGURES

6.1	Examples of shared chronic conditions of persons ageing with disability and ageing into disability in later life. *Disability-Related Secondary Conditions*	59
8.1	Defying the odds narrative	86
15.1	ICF model illustrating ageing with disability through the persona of Ralph, an 86-year-old male with Polio, a long-term health condition, who is also experiencing age-related changes in vision and hearing	170
15.2	TechSAge Model of Ageing and Disability	171
15.3	Magnification	173
15.4	Storage of technology	175
15.5	ICF-Based Environmental Intervention Model for Ralph, an 86-year-old male ageing with a long-term mobility disability illustrating how examples of appropriate physical environmental interventions impact body functions and structures, activity limitations and participation restrictions	176
15.6	iPhone user adaption of interfaces	180
15.7	Electronic election ballots	181
18.1	Process model for integrated social planning	212
24.1	Frailty measures in *The Healthy Ageing and Intellectual Disability Study* (HA-ID)	275
24.2	Frailty index distribution (HA-ID study)	277
24.3	Frailty index and the association with age	277
24.4	Kaplan-Meier survival curves stratified according to age categories (a) and frailty subgroups (b)	279
25.1	Frailty index and the association with age	288
25.2	Frailty index vs age in the Canadian Study	289
25.3	Hypothetical model of accumulation of factors threatening health of people with intellectual disabilities during their lifetime Based on Evenhuis (2014)	290
28.1	The roles of the RNID through the life-span	329
30.1	Self-rated perception of good health	351
30.2	Self-reported unmet healthcare need	352
30.3	Household income of persons with disabilities by age	352

Figures

30.4	Household income sources of persons with disabilities by age	353
30.5	Conditions on one-person households for population with disabilities by age	353
30.6	Adults with disabilities' facility experiences (use experiences)	355
30.7	Facility usage of adults with disabilities	355

TABLES

5.1	Percentage of 14-year-old adolescents with and without disabilities growing up in the United Kingdom exposed to childhood adversities	46
6.1	Indicators of the nexus of ageing and disability in the U.S.	62
11.1	Criteria used in diagnosing TBI	124
15.1	The Principles of Universal Design	177
20.1	Logistic regression for self/proxy-reported physical health ($n = 447$)	234
20.2	Logistic regression for self/proxy-reported mental health ($n = 444$)	235
21.1	Traditional models of retirement programs	246
24.1	HA-ID study's frailty phenotype (based on criteria in Fried et al., 2001)	276
25.1	Occurrence rates (%) of most frequent chronic health conditions over age 50 years	295
28.1	Priority areas for future nursing provision	328
28.2	Priority areas for additional education and upskilling	331
32.1	Programs offering funding and services for assistive technology and equity concerns	377
32.2	Key focal areas for bridging ageing and disability to enhance equity of assistive technology access	380

CONTRIBUTORS

Zoe Aitken, MSc is a Research Fellow in social epidemiology with the Centre of Research Excellence in Disability and Health at the University of Melbourne, Australia. Her research focuses on understanding the relationship between disability, socio-economic disadvantage, and mental health.

Catherine Keiling Arnold, PhD is the Director of Community Education at the Institute on Disability and Human Development at University of Illinois at Chicago, Illinois University Center for Excellence in Developmental Disabilities, USA. She is also the Executive Director of the Sibling Leadership Network, a national nonprofit with state chapters that provides information and support to siblings of people with disabilities throughout the lifespan.

Hannah Badland, PhD is a Principal Research Fellow and the Deputy Director in the Centre for Urban Research at RMIT University, Australia. She researches how improving liveable cities through better urban design can improve health and wellness.

Tal Araten-Bergman, PhD is a researcher at the Living with Disability Research Centre, and a lecturer in social work and disability practice in the School of Allied Health, Human Services and Sport at La Trobe University, Melbourne, Australia. Her research investigates policies and practices that aim to support the human rights of adults with intellectual disabilities and their families.

Jerome Bickenbach, PhD, LL.B. is a Queen's University Research Chair and Professor of Philosophy in the Faculties of Law and Medicine. He is also Professor, Department of Health Sciences and Health Policy, University of Lucerne and Leader, Disability Policy Group, Swiss Paraplegic Research, Nottwil, Switzerland.

Christine Bigby, PhD is a Professor and Director of the Living with Disability Research Centre at La Trobe University, Melbourne, Australia. Her research investigates the effectiveness of social programmes and policies that aim to support the social inclusion of adults and older people with intellectual disabilities.

Melissa Biscardi, MSc, RN is a registered nurse, concussion clinician, and doctoral research trainee at the University of Toronto. Her research interests are in persistent symptoms in individual's post-concussion, interventions to support concussion recovery and sex-based differences in recovery and recovery experience.

Contributors

Lauren Bishop, PhD is an Assistant Professor of Social Work and an investigator at the Waisman Center, at the University of Wisconsin-Madison, USA. Her research focuses finding individual and systems-level solutions to help adults on the autism spectrum live long, healthy, and self-determined lives in their communities.

Margaret L. Campbell, PhD is a principal and owner for Campbell & Associates Consulting, located in the Puget Sound area of Washington, USA. She specializes in advising university-based researchers and organization on issues central to ageing, disability, and technology drawing from her more than 30 years career as a university scientist and then as a federal programme officer with the National Institute on Disability Independent Living and Rehabilitation Research.

Terry Carney, PhD is Emeritus Professor of Law at the University of Sydney Law School, Australia, where he was a long-serving Director of Research and past Head of Department. His research interests include mental health law, ageing with disability, and social welfare laws.

Rebecca Charlton, PhD is a Reader in Psychology at Goldsmiths University of London, England. Her research explores cognitive, psychosocial, health, and brain changes in later life including dementia, typical ageing, and how ageing may be similar or different for autistic adults.

Angela Colantonio, PhD is the Director of the Rehabilitation Sciences Institute at the University of Toronto and a Professor in the Department of Occupational Science and Occupational Therapy. Dr. Colantonio leads a programme of research on acquired brain injury with diverse foci on women, sex and gender, work-related traumatic brain injury, and under-served populations.

Cheryl A. Cott, PhD is a Professor Emerita in the Department of Physical Therapy and Rehabilitation Science Institute at the University of Toronto, Canada. A physical therapist and social gerontologist, her research is focused on client-centred rehabilitation services for older adults with chronic illness and disability.

Caitlin E. Coyle, PhD is a Research Fellow and Assistant Professor of Gerontology at the University of Massachusetts-Boston, USA where she conducts applied research on the topics of social isolation and ageing with lifelong disability.

Jessica Dashner, OTD is an Assistant Professor of Occupational Therapy and Neurology at Washington University School of Medicine's Program in Occupational Therapy, St. Louis, Missouri, USA. Her work focuses on improving participation in major life activities for individuals with disabilities.

Friedrich Dieckmann, Prof. Dr., is a Professor of Psychology in Inclusive Education and Director of the Center for Participation Research, Department of Social Services, Catholic University of Applied Sciences North Rhine-Westphalia Münster/Germany. His primary areas of research are ageing of persons with intellectual disabilities and issues of living environments, social inclusion, integrated social planning, ecological psychology, adult siblings, and families.

Eric Emerson, PhD is Emeritus Professor of Disability and Health Research in the Centre for Disability Research, Lancaster University, UK and Honorary Professor in the Centre for Disability Research and Policy, the University of Sydney, Australia.

Heleen M. Evenhuis, MD, PhD worked as a physician in Dutch intellectual disability care, mostly for older adults and a Professor at Erasmus University in Rotterdam. She started the first Dutch university chair in Intellectual Disability Medicine and a specialist education programme on intellectual disability for physicians and developed and led the large-scale Healthy Ageing and Intellectual Disability Study, in collaboration with four care organisations.

Lisa Ferretti, MSW is a Research Assistant Professor at the School of Social Work in the College of Public Health at Temple University in Philadelphia, Pennsylvania, USA. Professor Ferretti is an expert in healthy ageing and ageing services.

Marcia Finlayson, PhD is a Vice Dean of Health Sciences and Professor and Director of the School of Rehabilitation Therapy at Queen's University in Kingston, Ontario, Canada. Her research focuses on generating knowledge to inform the delivery of symptom self-management and rehabilitation programmes and services for people with MS to enable people with MS to exert choice and control in their everyday lives.

Nicola Fortune, PhD is a Research Fellow with the Centre of Research Excellence in Disability and Health at the University of Sydney, Australia. Her research focus is on inequities in the social determinants of health experienced by people with disability.

Hilde M. Geurts, PhD is a Full Professor of Clinical Neuropsychology at the University of Amsterdam, The Netherlands and is a senior researcher affiliated with the Dr. Leo Kannerhuis Autism Clinic. Her research encompasses a broad range of topics as it includes childhood as well as old age and cognition as well as quality of life, focusing mainly on individual differences across the lifespan.

Celia Green is a Research Fellow with the Centre of Research Excellence in Disability and Health at the University of New South Wales, Australia. Her research focuses on policy actions to address the social determinants of health for people with disability.

Tove Harnett, PhD in social gerontology, is an Associate Professor in Social Work at Lund University in Sweden. Her research concerns long-term care, substance abuse, and social rights of older people.

Rachel Heeb, OTD is a PhD student in the Rehabilitation and Participation Science Program at Washington University School of Medicine in St. Louis, Missouri, USA. Her research focuses on people ageing with long-term physical disabilities and how their community participation is influenced by social and physical aspects of their neighbourhood environment.

Tamar Heller, PhD is a Distinguished Professor and Head of the Department of Disability and Human Development, University of Illinois at Chicago, USA where she also serves as Director of the Illinois University Center of Excellence in Developmental Disabilities. Her research focuses on persons with intellectual disabilities, their families, and wide range of health and wellness issues.

Lieke van Heumen, PhD is a clinical Assistant Professor in the Department of Disability and Human Development at the University of Illinois at Chicago, USA. Her scholarship focuses on ageing of individuals with intellectual and developmental disabilities and the application of inclusive research methods with this population.

Håkan Jönson, PhD is a Professor in Social Work at Lund University in Sweden. His research concerns ageism, eldercare, social problems, and social rights of older people.

Mia Jormfeldt, PhD teaches social work at Halmstad University, Sweden. Her research is about older people with intellectual disabilities and their opportunities for self-determination in everyday life.

Kyung Mee Kim, PhD is a Professor in the department of Social Welfare at Soongsil University in Seoul, Korea. Her research focuses on independent living, personal assistance services for people with disabilities, women with disabilities, disability discrimination law, diverse population with disabilities, ageing with disabilities, and the digital divide.

Contributors

Annika Taghizadeh Larsson, PhD is a Senior Lecturer in Social Work at Linkoping University, Sweden. Her research focuses on questions and issues at the intersection of disability studies and social gerontology.

Dederieke Maes-Festen, MD, PhD is a physician for people with intellectual disabilities. She is currently working as Assistant Professor and member of the management team of the Chair of Intellectual Disability Medicine, Department of General Practice at the Erasmus University Medical Center Rotterdam, The Netherlands. Her research focuses on health in people with intellectual disability.

Jill Manthorpe, PhD is a Professor of Social Work and Director of the NIHR Policy Research Unit in Health & Social Care Workforce at King's College London, UK. Her research focuses on the voluntary sector experience in older people's services and policy making as well as ageing care.

Kate Mattheys, PhD served as a Research Fellow during her doctoral studies in the Faculty of Health Sciences and Sport at the University of Stirling, Scotland. She is now an Independent Advocate at Adapt North East, England.

Philip McCallion, PhD is the Director of and Professor at the School of Social Work in the College of Public Health at Temple University in Philadelphia, Pennsylvania, USA. His research interests consider the field of social work, bridging scholarship on ageing populations and those with intellectual disabilities such as Down syndrome.

Mary McCarron, PhD is a Professor of Ageing and Intellectual Disability, School of Nursing & Midwifery and Dean of the Faculty of Health Sciences, and Director of the Trinity Centre for Ageing and Intellectual Disability at Trinity College Dublin, Ireland. She is Principal Investigator of the Longitudinal Comparative Study on Ageing in Persons with Intellectual Disability (IDS-TILDA), a supplement to The Irish Longitudinal Study on Ageing (TILDA).

Darren McCausland, PhD is a Research Fellow, Lead for Social & Community Research at Trinity Centre for Ageing and Intellectual Disability, Trinity College, Dublin, Ireland. He has an investigator with the Longitudinal Comparative Study on Ageing in Persons with Intellectual Disability (IDS-TILDA) leading analysis on the social participation and social connectedness.

David McDaid, PhD is an Associate Professor in Health Policy and Health Economics at the Care Policy and Evaluation Centre at the London School of Economics and Political Science. His work includes a wide range of policy and economic analysis in the field of social care, mental health, and public health, including assessment of approaches to promote intersectoral collaboration.

Jacqueline McGinley, PhD is an Assistant Professor with the Binghamton University Department of Social Work, New York, USA. Her research focuses on improving end-of-life care for people with intellectual disabilities and their families, advance care planning, and decision-making for and with people who have ID.

Laura R. Moll, PhD is an independent research consultant, lecturer, and registered social worker in Ontario, Canada with affiliations to the Rehabilitation Science Institute at the University of Toronto and the Ontario Federation of Cerebral Palsy. Her research focuses on the experience of growing up and growing older with a physical impairment across the life course.

Contributors

Kerri Morgan, PhD is an Assistant Professor for the Program in Occupational Therapy and Neurology at Washington University School of Medicine, St. Louis, Missouri, USA. Her research focuses on how rehabilitation can improve the participation of people with mobility disabilities living in the community.

Teresa Moro, PhD is a Project Coordinator of the STEPS program at Rush University Medical Center, Chicago, Illinois, USA. Her research focuses on exploring larger questions about the health of individuals with intellectual disabilities including health services, chronic illness, disability, and end of life.

Sumithra Murthy, MPH is a PhD student and Project Coordinator at the Department of Disability and Human Development at University of Illinois at Chicago, USA. Her research includes issues of family caregiving and family support for individuals with intellectual and developmental disabilities.

Lydia P. Ogden, PhD is an Assistant Professor at the School of Social Work at Simmons University in Boston, Massachusetts, USA. Her work centres on understanding the stories and developing the potential of persons diagnosed with serious mental illnesses, especially older adults.

Alyt Oppewal, PhD is a human movement scientist and Assistant Professor at the Chair of Intellectual Disability Medicine at the Erasmus MC, University Medical Center Rotterdam, The Netherlands. Her research line focuses on physical activity and fitness in adults with intellectual disabilities.

A-La Park, MSc is an Assistant Professor in Health Economics in Care Policy and Evaluation Centre at the London School of Economics and Political Science. Her work in health economics examines issues of mental health and well-being promotion across the life course.

Julie Pétrin, MSc is a Rehabilitation Sciences Doctoral Candidate in the School of Rehabilitation Therapy, at Queen's University in Kingston, Ontario Canada. Her research examines healthcare service experiences of persons with multiple sclerosis.

Michelle Ploughman, PhD is a neurological physiotherapist and Associate Professor of Physical Medicine and Rehabilitation at Memorial University of Newfoundland, St. John's, Newfoundland and Labrador, Canada. Her research seeks to advance healthy ageing with MS and explore new technologies including use of robust sensorimotor interventions that restore function in MS and stroke.

Michelle Putnam, PhD is a Professor at the School of Social Work, Simmons University, Boston, Massachusetts, USA. Her research focuses on the intersections of ageing and disability, public policy, and persons ageing with disability.

Jerome N. Rachele, PhD is a Lecturer in Public Health in the College of Health and Biomedicine, Victoria University, and Honorary Research Fellow in the Melbourne School of Population and Global Health, The University of Melbourne, Australia. His research focuses on how health inequalities between people with and without a disability can be reduced through urban design.

Roshanth Rajachandrakumar, MSc is a Research Assistant at the School of Rehabilitation Therapy at Queen's University in Kingston, Ontario, Canada.

Elena T. Remillard, M.S. in Gerontology, is a Research Scientist at the Center for Inclusive Design and Innovation, within the College of Design at the Georgia Institute of Technology, Atlanta, Georgia, USA. Her research centres around design and technology for ageing-in-place, technology acceptance among older adults, and ageing with long-term disability.

Contributors

Seung Hyun Roh, PhD is a Professor in the Department of Social Welfare at Luther University in Yongin, Korea. His research focuses on healthy ageing with disability, active ageing with disability, ageing in place with a disability, developmental disability.

Christiane Rohleder, Prof. Dr., holds a Professorship in Sociology, Department of Social Services, Center for Participation Research, Catholic University of Applied Sciences North Rhine-Westphalia Münster/Germany. Her main areas of research include ageing with a severe mental illness and integrated social planning for old age.

Jon A. Sanford, M. Arch is a Professor in the School of Industrial Design and Director of the Rehabilitation Engineering Research Center on Technologies for Successful Ageing with Disability, at Georgia Institute of Technology, Atlanta, Georgia, USA. His research focuses on universal design, accessible design, and design for ageing.

Josje D. Schoufour, PhD is a nutritional scientist and currently working as a Senior Researcher at the Faculty of Sports and Nutrition & Faculty of Health, Center of Expertise Urban Vitality, Amsterdam University of Applied Sciences, Amsterdam, The Netherlands. Her research focuses on the combination of nutrition, exercise and creative technology to prevent frailty across the lifespan.

Fintan Sheerin, PhD is an Associate Professor is Intellectual Disability Nursing and Head of School, School of Nursing and Midwifery Trinity College Dublin, The University of Dublin where he leads the mental health component of the IDS-TILDA research study. His research focuses on mental well-being and issues which impact well-being including human rights, parenting, and sexuality.

Peter Simcock, PhD is a Senior Lecturer in Social Work at Birmingham City University, UK and is the lead of the Deafblind International Acquired Deafblindness Network. His research interests are in dual sensory loss, particularly as experienced by older people.

Shih-Ning Then, PhD is an Associate Professor at the Australian Centre for Health Law Research in the Faculty of Law at Queensland University of Technology in Brisbane, Australia. Her scholarship focuses on health law, supported decision-making, and biomedical ethics.

Magnus Tideman, PhD is a Professor in Disability Research with a focus on Social Work at Halmstad University, Sweden. His research centres on policy and practice related to people with intellectual disability in a range of areas including education, living conditions, self-advocacy, supported decision-making, the transition from school to labour market.

Rosalie H. Wang, PhD is an Assistant Professor in the Department of Occupational Science and Occupational Therapy, University of Toronto, Ontario, Canada and an Affiliate Scientist at Toronto Rehabilitation Institute as a member of their AI and Robotics in Rehabilitation team. Her research focuses on developing and implementing technology to enable daily activity participation and social inclusion of seniors and facilitate rehabilitation with individuals after stroke.

Karen Watchman, PhD is a Senior Lecturer in Ageing, Dementia and Frailty in the Faculty of Health Sciences and Sport at the University of Stirling, Scotland. Her research focuses on post-diagnostic dementia care, intellectual disability, and equality issues and seeks out diverse views of participants less often included in research.

Courtney Weber, OTD/S is a current student in the occupational therapy clinical doctorate programme at Washington University School of Medicine in St. Louis, Missouri, USA. Her doctoral research focused on physical activity and participation of people ageing with physical disabilities, and she plans to pursue clinical work in this realm.

Michael G. Wilson, PhD is the Assistant Director of the McMaster Health Forum, an Associate Professor in the Department of Health Research Methods, Evidence, and Impact (HEI), and a member of the Centre for Health Economics and Policy Analysis at McMaster University, Hamilton, Ontario, Canada. His research focuses on supporting the use of research evidence by health system decision makers, including policymakers and stakeholders such as community-based organizations.

Hailee M. Yoshizaki-Gibbons, PhD is a Postdoctoral Fellow in Biomedical Humanities at Hiram College, Ohio, USA. Her research examines intersections between disability and ageing and analyses how these identities interact socially and culturally to affect people's lived experiences, relationships, opportunities, and participation in society.

ACKNOWLEDGMENTS

We would like to acknowledge the invaluable support in the preparation of the manuscript from Dr David Henderson and Lauren De Losa who are staff from the Living with Disability Research Centre at La Trobe University and Morgan Siska who is a research assistant at Simmons University.

PREFACE

Advancing Knowledge in Ageing with Disability
The Ageing with Disability Phenomenon

In the last 40 years, there has been a growing population of people ageing with a disability in most countries with advanced economies. The term ageing with disability refers to individuals who experience onset of impairment or disability at birth, in childhood or in adulthood prior later life and live with long-term disability (sustained or chronic rather than a single short-term episode) as they grow older. Included in the population of persons ageing with disability are individuals with conditions such as polio, spinal cord injury, cerebral palsy, multiple sclerosis, intellectual disability, traumatic brain injury, autism, deafblindness, and severe mental illness among persons with other conditions. Ageing *with* disability can be contrasted against ageing *into* disability, or experiencing prolonged disability for the first time in later life. Much of what we know about ageing and disability is based on research of persons ageing *into* disability who acquire specific diagnostic impairments or fall within specific disability categories in later life, but who had no prior history of extended disability. The population of persons ageing *with* disability is different. It is a heterogeneous population, but one that shares the common experience of disability intersecting with other aspects of their lives. How and why this matters is the focus of this Handbook. The Handbook is the first to pull together knowledge about the experience of ageing *with* disability with the aim of providing a broad look at scholarship in this developing field, across disability categories, so that readers gain insight into what is unique about the ageing with disability experience.

The study of ageing with disability is relatively new. Research and scholarship on ageing with disability dates roughly back to the 1980s, when trends in ageing among persons with early and mid-life onset of disability began to be noted and ageing-related changes began to be identified for people with certain diagnostic conditions. For example, lifespan among persons ageing with intellectual disability has nearly doubled in the last 40 years; this trend started to gain attention in the mid-1980s. About the same time, unanticipated longevity among persons with severe spinal cord injury and persons with polio and cerebral palsy attracted research attention. Increased life expectancy is due in large part to advances in medical treatment and rehabilitation and the concurrent development of a wide range of public education, employment, income, housing, and social supports. In other segments of the population, like persons with multiple sclerosis (MS), life expectancy has not increased but much more is known about how to reduce its symptoms and impact.

The size of the ageing with disability population has proved hard to discern world-wide due to lack of population level data on disability onset and duration, but its existence is not in question. As awareness of the ageing with disability phenomenon has grown, so too has research in this area; however, the field has remained quite small. Areas of study include accelerated ageing, secondary disability, chronic conditions, health promotion, employment and retirement, social engagement and social networks, caregiving and care receipt, housing and independent living, service delivery and policy development, and gaps in ageing and disability services. An international body of scholarship has developed related to ageing with disability; however, researchers in the United States, Australia, Ireland, the United Kingdom, Sweden, and Austria have produced the largest share to date. In part, this may be related to public funding streams supporting this work as well as the types of social welfare schemes, civil and human rights laws, and the historical patterns of treatment of persons with disabilities that vary across nations, which are linked to growing older with disability. That said, ageing with disability has also been recognised as an important population trend in Asian countries like Korea, Taiwan, Hong Kong, European countries including Germany and Spain, and in South American countries including Brazil and Argentina. Thus, the trend of ageing with disability is becoming a shared international phenomenon and one that requires the development of specialized knowledge and understanding of how to meet the bio-psycho-social needs of this population as they grow older.

Unique Aspects of Ageing with Disability

Ageing with disability is different from ageing into disability. Below, we set out some of the themes that readers will identify across the chapters in this Handbook:

Presence of Chronic Conditions, Ageing-Related Symptoms, and Early or Accelerated Ageing

People ageing with disability, as a population group, experience higher rates of chronic conditions such as osteoarthritis, diabetes, heart disease, and obesity. Persons with conditions such as spinal cord injury or multiple sclerosis, among others, also commonly experience symptoms such as pain, fatigue, muscle weakness, and depression. Persons with intellectual disabilities have higher rates of frailty and cognitive impairment at earlier ages. In many cases, chronic conditions and ageing-related symptoms are undiagnosed, under-treated, or not fully addressed through provision of supports and services resulting in the unnecessary exacerbation of disability in later life. In some cases, they are preventable through life style changes and good support earlier in the life course.

Additional Barriers to Independence and Community Participation

People ageing with disability can face additional hurdles in initially achieving independence and in maintaining independence and community engagement across the life course. Later life is a particular time of vulnerability to social forces that are not supportive of persons with disabilities. For example, persons with intellectual/developmental disabilities may need assistance transitioning from employment or full-time activity programmes to retirement but this may not be available. Persons with intellectual disability who retire may find they become socially isolated and lonely, with few activities to replace their former work life, and limited opportunities to make new friends. Traditional programmes for older adults may not be welcoming to older persons with intellectual disability, further closing off socialisation options. Isolation and loneliness may result in negative health outcomes and in some cases, result in placement in a care home.

Segmentation of Ageing and Disability Services and Policies, Health, and Social Care

Historically, in most nations, social care or public long-term supports and services for persons with disability are divided by age and disability type. Working age individuals receive services under disability and rehabilitation polices and related programmes. In some countries, these are divided further into distinct services for persons with physical, intellectual/developmental, vision and/or hearing impairment, and mental health, or psychiatric disability, although such differentiation by group has diminished in Australia and the Scandinavian countries. Older adults receive services under ageing programmes that are not disability specific. In most cases, services or amount of services received differ, for example older adults are not eligible for the same number of hours of personal attendant services and persons with disabilities not of retirement age. Working-age adults with disability may not be eligible for many of the health promotion, wellness, and socialisation programmes offered to older adults. Often, in the case of persons with developmental/intellectual disability, services are not restricted by age, but age-appropriate or life stage-related adaptations may be difficult to achieve. This same type of division can be found between health and mental health and social care. Mental health care and supports for persons with severe mental illness in particular are often completely absent from traditional ageing and disability social care models. Integrated care in private or public health insurance models often is often poorly equipped to meet the needs of persons with disabilities. In short, the whole person is rarely attended to within an integrated health and social care model. The gaps that persons ageing with disability often fall into due to the segmentation of systems often results in individuals not getting the help and supports they need to live healthy and full lives.

Lack of Expertise Related to Ageing with Disability

Few practice, policy, or research professionals have knowledge or training related to ageing with disability. Although the overall knowledge base is modest, there is much that can be learned from what we currently know and there are evidence-informed interventions and programmes that support positive outcomes for persons ageing with disability. Often, persons with disabilities or their family members are in the position of educating the professionals who provide their health and social about their conditions, needs, and experiences, and even sometimes availability of services: they are the experts rather than the health and social care professional. Professional practitioners and programmes need to build knowledge and expertise themselves in order to adequately and successfully provide care and assistance to and design programmes and policies that meet the needs of persons ageing with disability.

What is in this Handbook

This Handbook brings together a set of international scholars, who review important areas and issues of ageing with disability. Authors range from experts who have devoted decades to building knowledge in order to better support ageing with disability populations to early career scholars who are broadening the field with their work on intersecting and complex issue of ageing and disability. Many of our authors are persons who experience disabilities themselves.

The authors tackle some common issues – such as identifying what is specific to ageing with disability and understanding the role that health and social care play in supporting positive outcomes in later life – as well as discernible variation in the type and depth of knowledge we have for certain disability groups. For example, the knowledge base related to ageing with intellectual disability is much more substantial than it is for persons ageing with serious mental illness or even persons ageing with physical disability. We explicitly note that the knowledge base we are referring to is written in English and our authors in this Handbook write in this language as well (many write in other languages too at other times). Therefore, we are missing research and scholarship published in other languages and voices of non-English speaking contributors. We encourage readers who are interested in exploring the knowledge base for specific disability groups, categories, or topics further to do so, and have indicated at the end of each chapter readings that may be helpful in this.

Authors in this Handbook use varying terminology in referring to groups of persons with disabilities. We have not standardized terminology use as we believe it is important for readers to be familiar with these variations and to consider how and why authors use the terms that they do. For example, authors based in the United States use the term intellectual and developmental disability (I/DD) and while authors from Australia use the term intellectual disability (ID). These differences relate to how persons with cognitive difference are categorized diagnostically in each nation and how they are defined in public policies. All of our authors use person-first language (i.e. persons with disabilities) but each clarifies the groups they are discussing by defining the categories, diagnostic conditions, or impairment group they are writing about. Because the ageing with disability population is heterogeneous, there are fewer chapters that focus on the entire population and more that examine issues for a specific group. This allows not only for variation across chapters but for some authors to discuss issues in greater depth.

The Structure of the Handbook

The Handbook is organized into five sections. Part I has seven chapters that provide conceptual, social-cultural, health, and ethical contexts to frame the ageing with disability experience. Chapter 1, *Understanding Ageing with Disability*, lays out core concepts and ideas that underlie the field of study with the aim of giving readers a starting point into the topic of ageing with disability. Chapter 2, *Rethinking the Concept of Successful Ageing: A Disability Studies Approach*, offers the opportunity to consider how well disability actually fits into the normative model of successful ageing and suggests a revision that is more inclusive. Chapter 3, *Ageing with Lifelong Disability: Individual Meanings and Experiences over time*, looks in depth at how persons with intellectual disabilities perceive growing older and what it means for their own happiness and well-being in later life. Chapter 4, *Integrating Critical Disability Studies and Critical Gerontology to Explore the Complexities of Ageing with Disabilities*, takes a critical look at the ways we think about the complexities of ageing and argues there is a need for deeper analysis into how society and individuals view and understand this experience. Chapter 5, *Social and Environmental Determinants of the Health of People with Disabilities*, turns the lens on larger cultural and structural issues that influence the life course and individual health and wellness over time, indicating that most outcomes in later life are predicated on factors and facets of early life and adulthood. Chapter 6, *Reducing the Shared Burden of Chronic Conditions Among Persons Ageing with Disability and Older Adults in the United States Through Bridging Ageing and Disability*, considers physical health and chronic conditions, focusing on what conditions are most shared with the older adult population in general and which are unique to the ageing with disability population and could be better addressed through targeted interventions. Chapter 7, *Segmenting Ageing and Disability Policy: Ethical Concerns*, presents a case for eliminating categorical labels – ageing and disability – and centring efforts on addressing the needs of persons with functional limitations regardless of how, why, or when a person encounters disability.

Part II aims to give the reader an understanding of the heterogeneity of the ageing with disability population with a set of chapters that look at diversity in experience by the type of impairment or condition an individual has. Chapter 8, *Understanding the Experience of Growing Older with Cerebral Palsy*, offers insights from persons with lived experience of cerebral palsy and a model for understanding how perceptions of self change as individuals develop their own identities and negotiate those externally laid upon them. Chapter 9, *Ageing with Deafblindness*, considers how vision and hearing impairment can be layered over time and what this means for persons as they grow older, commonly in social and physical environments that have not considered their needs. Chapter 10, *Aging, Serious Mental Illness, and Perceptions of Self Over the Life Course*, presents perspectives on life lived with an invisible disability that is often poorly understood by others, and the strategies and approaches individuals take to live their life of choice. Chapter 11, *Ageing and Brain Injury Long-Term Outcomes in Adults*, describes in detail current knowledge about how brain injury intersects with health as persons grow older and the influence of disability related to brain injury has on life experiences. Chapter 12, *Ageing with Multiple Sclerosis*, discusses concerns related to choice, control, and decision-making about community living and social care, as well as fears of institutionalisation, given the lack of public provision of services to ensure individuals remain participants in society as they grow older. Chapter 13, *Ageing when Being Autistic*, overviews the wide range of health and wellness issues persons with autism encounter as they age and the implications disability can have for these individuals over the life course.

Part III looks at issues of social inclusion and exclusion, with particular consideration of factors that act as facilitators or barriers to advancing health and participation. Chapter 14, *Community Participation and Engagement for Persons Ageing with Physical Disability*, discusses individual health-related symptoms of ageing as well as physical environmental features that matter in sustaining community participation and engagement for persons ageing with long-term physical disability. Chapter 15, *Design for One is Design for All: The Past, Present, and Future of Universal Design as a Strategy for Ageing-in-Place with Disability*, reviews the limited adoption of universal design over the past few decades and forwards the concept of design for one in the era of internet technology and individualized solutions as an approach to ageing in place. Chapter 16, *Support for Decision-Making as People Age With a Cognitive Impairment*, reviews the concept of decision-making from ethical, legal, and practical perspectives and argues that personalised and adaptive forms of decision support are most compatible with self-determination. Chapter 17, *Internalised Ageism and the User Gaze in Eldercare: Identifying New Horizons of Possibilities Through the use of a Disability Lens*, considers the satisfaction of persons ageing into disability with social care supports and services and how perspectives on what is acceptable change when a disability lens is applied. Chapter 18, *Creating Age and Disability Friendly Communities to Support Healthy and Meaningful Ageing*, identifies a successful process for integrating persons ageing with disability into their local communities and the implications this can have for positive outcomes in later life.

Part IV considers what is known about ageing with intellectual disability, the subcategory with the longest history of scholarship in the field. Chapter 19, *The Emergence of Ageing with Long-Term Disability Populations*, provides a history of the population trend of ageing with intellectual disability and the scholarship that has accompanied it, establishing a context for current and future work in the field. Chapter 20, *Health and Wellness Among Persons Ageing with Intellectual Disability*, explores trends in health outcomes, identifying areas of preventable health disparities and their cumulative effects over time. Chapter 21, *Retirement for People with Intellectual Disability: Policy, Pitfalls, and Promising Practices*, explores the experiences and perspectives of people with intellectual disabilities on retirement and the challenges retirement has posed for policy and service systems. Chapter 22, *Family Caregiving for Adults Ageing with Intellectual and Developmental Disabilities*, outlines the role the family members play in supporting individuals ageing with intellectual disability as well as the reciprocity of care persons ageing with intellectual disability often provide to ageing parents. Chapter 23, *Ageing with Intellectual Disability In Sweden: Participation and Self Determination*, discusses the extent to which the principles of participation and self-determination are embedded in services for the older people with intellectual disability and what that means for everyday life. Chapter 24, *Towards Untangling the Ageing Riddle in People with Intellectual Disabilities: An Overview of Research on Frailty and its Consequences*, identifies the features of frailty in persons ageing with intellectual disability and summarises current knowledge and future research needs to treat and reduce this common condition. Chapter 25, *How to Avoid Early Frailty in People with Intellectual Disabilities?*, articulates how social, economic, and cultural factors contribute to frailty among persons ageing with intellectual disability and prescribes solutions for preventing and remediating frailty. Chapter 26, *Dementia Care for Persons Ageing with Intellectual Disability: Developing Non-Pharmacological Strategies for Support*, presents alternatives for dementia care tailored to persons with intellectual disabilities that support health and wellness outcomes in later life. Chapter 27, *End-of-Life Care for Adults With Intellectual Disabilities*, argues for greater planning and transparency in care for persons with intellectual disability at the end-of-life so that individuals, families, and care providers are better prepared for decision-making and providing quality care.

Part V, the final collection of chapters, examines the policy context for ageing with disability. Chapter 28, *Responding to Changing Workforce Realities: One Profession's Experience*, looks at the process of deinstitutionalization of persons with intellectual disability in Ireland and how the profession of intellectual disability nursing has responded to it noting the many challenges that remain in moving from institutional to community-based social care. Chapter 29, *Ageing in Place in Group Homes: An Australian Context*, considers the complexities of implementing the ageing in place concept in a living environment of group homes that are not designed for growing older and the promise offered by the National Disability Insurance Scheme to enable flexible support as people age. Chapter 30, *Support, Service Policies, and Programs For Persons Ageing with Disabilities in Korea*, provides an overview of personal assistance and support services for older and younger adults with disabilities and identifies limitations in the policies for persons ageing with disability. Chapter 31, *Trends in Integrating Long-Term Services and Supports in the United States*, briefly overviews the tangle of health and social care insurance schemes and programmes available to persons in the United States and initiatives aimed at closing some of the gaps that persons ageing with disability can fall into. Chapter 32, *Access to Assistive Technology in Canada*, presents an analysis that categorises and synthesises the dozens of programmes and policies that offer assistive technology support to Canadians with disabilities with the aim of identifying what individual access to assistive technology actually is. Chapter 33, *Ageing with Disability: Using Financial Mechanisms to Facilitate Intersectoral Collaboration*, articulates a rationale for policy makers to promote collaboration that bridges ageing and disability support systems that emphasises financial prudency, consumer access, and ability to provide higher quality of care. Chapter 34, *Good Old Age for People Ageing with Disability: Reflections on Progress*, summarises key themes across the Handbook and situates them within broader thoughts about where the field of ageing with disability has been and where it needs to go in the future.

Last Notes for Readers

This idea for this Handbook arose from discussions regarding the need to increase access to knowledge in the field of ageing with disability as well as the need to increase the number of scholars, practitioners, and policy makers with knowledge about ageing with disability. As with any Handbook, choices are made as to what to include and authors availability to contribute varies. We are very pleased that the Handbook includes the collection of high-level contributors that it does. We believe readers will learn much in reading their work. We also strongly encourage readers to use this Handbook as a starting point for their learning and explore the additional work in the field produced by the authors here and by others. Curiosity about ageing with disability is what will move this field forward. We hope this Handbook does indeed, make you curious to learn more and to contribute to this important and developing field of scholarship.

PART I

Framing the Ageing with Disability Experience

PART I

1
UNDERSTANDING AGEING WITH DISABILITY

Michelle Putnam, Caitlin E. Coyle, Lydia P. Ogden, and Christine Bigby

Foundational Concepts of Ageing with Disability

The term *persons ageing with disability* refers to individuals who experience the onset of disability in early life or mid-life and who continue to experience disability over the life course. The nature and/or severity of disability may vary somewhat over time, for persons in this population, but the disability experience is a regular part of their lives prior to, and during, later life. This is different from the experience of *persons ageing into disability*. *Ageing into disability* refers to individuals who experience disability for the first time in later life – whether in short bouts or in a sustained way. An individual who *ages into disability* can be characterised as someone who lives mostly disability-free until they reach an older age. In later life, this person also experiences growing older with disability, but their disability experience is concentrated in later life, a shorter period of their life course than a person ageing with a disability.

This distinction is important as experiencing disability in early and mid-life, particularly substantial functional or cognitive disability, is strongly linked to disadvantageous economic, social, psychological, and health outcomes for individuals. Less positive outcomes for persons with disabilities compared to age-matched peers are demonstrated on all these domains in both cross-sectional and longitudinal research (Clarke & Latham, 2014). However, our empirical knowledge base for understanding and finding solutions to issues and problems encountered over the life course by individuals and populations of persons ageing with disability is fairly modest. Neither does this group generally figure in studies of the general ageing population. We need to increase scholarship and research so that persons ageing with disability are more overtly recognised as a population subgroup and to increase understanding and awareness of how experiences of long-term disability influence the ageing process and outcomes for persons in later life.

Fields of study (disability, rehabilitation, intellectual and developmental disability, gerontology), service systems (health, mental health, public health), and professions (medical allied health, social work) have historically segmented people with disabilities by age – older (60 or 65 and above) and younger (64 or 59 and younger). The resulting research and scholarship has created bifurcated knowledge bases to inform practices and policies to facilitate positive outcomes for persons ageing with disability (Salvador-Carulla, Putnam, Bigby, & Heller, 2012). Scholars focusing on ageing with disability often knit together pieces of knowledge from across fields, literatures, and evidence bases to engage in work that explores how disability matters over time, over the life course. This exercise in knitting has begun to create the fabric of a new field explicitly focused on ageing with disability.

Much less is formally known about the experience of ageing with disability than about either ageing or disability. This may be due, in part, to the rapid increase in life expectancy among persons with disabilities over the past four or five decades and the limited recognition of this trend given the relatively small size of the population ageing with disability compared to the general population. It may also be associated with the diversity of this group, which includes people with lifelong and acquired disabilities as a result of chronic health issues, traumatic injury or genetic predisposition, who have physical, sensory, cognitive impairments. It may also be connected to a lack of awareness and understanding about what makes ageing with disability different – why duration of disability, timing of onset, and changes in disability or an underlying impairment or condition over time matter across the life course. A small but rich body of lived experience literature in the form of auto-biographies, histories, and social accounts has contributed to what we know about ageing with disability and has helped to guide the direction of existing scholarship and research. Alongside this, there is a developing body of professional practice knowledge and expertise guiding work in the health and social care sectors. Much of this practice knowledge has come from empirical research. As scholarship moves forward, we will have a stronger and fuller empirical knowledge base to guide work that supports positive outcome in later life and throughout the ageing process.

In this chapter, we briefly discuss some of the foundational concepts that create a framework for understanding the experience of ageing with disability and the population of persons ageing with disability. These include how the ageing with disability population is defined, its size, why it is considered a relatively new and distinct population group, where this population fits in regard to existing theories and scholarship, and the idea of bridging ageing and disability fields as a way to rapidly advance research, policy, and practice related to ageing with disability. While individual scholars have expertise in different sub-populations of persons ageing with disability, we all tend to cover these same concepts in introducing this population and their experiences in our classes, at conferences, in our writings, and in our community partnerships. We do so because they encompass the initial questions usually posed by our audiences. Presenting this type of information helps listeners and readers to begin their own process of knitting together what they know already about ageing and disability with new knowledge about ageing with disability. Our discussion of these foundational concepts is in no way exhaustive. Rather, it is intended to support readers to think critically about ideas and issues related to ageing with disability and ask complex questions about our current empirical knowledge and our practices related to ageing and disability, including public policy responses to the needs of persons with disabilities across the life course. We also hope to encourage readers to keep learning and help to advance knowledge related to the experience of ageing with disability. We begin with one of the most fundamental questions.

How is the Ageing with Disability Population Defined?

The ageing with disability population is often defined by two parameters – age of disability onset and duration of disability. Age of onset refers to the point in time when an individual first experiences challenges or difficulties negotiating everyday activities common for a particular life stage. The World Health Organization (WHO) understands disability as a complex interaction between the capabilities of the individual and the resources (or lack thereof) of the environment that support their capabilities (World Health Organization, 2011). Thus, the disability onset varies between individuals with similar capabilities, and is based on the match between an individual and their social and physical environment.

According to this understanding of disability, age of onset of impairment or condition is different than age of onset of disability. Onset of impairment refers to when a condition and/or its associated traits start to limit function capacity. Onset of impairment or condition happens prior to disability but does not necessarily result in disability. The level of impairment or intensity of a condition may have minimal or no impact on the individual's ability to do the things they would like to or need to do. Thus, for these reasons, age of onset of disability varies widely among persons within the ageing with disability population.

There are, however, subgroups of the population with common age ranges of disability onset based on condition or impairment – such as persons with intellectual disability who are generally only classified as such if onset occurs in the first two decades of life (National Academies of Sciences, Engineering, and Medicine, 2015). There are also subgroups among whom age of onset varies substantially – for example spinal cord injury can happen at any age. To be included in an ageing with disability study, researchers often specify a disability onset age of 64 or less, but there is no formally defined upper bound of onset age for inclusion in the population of persons ageing with disability. Some scholars are more comfortable using age 60 as a maximum age and often use even lower limits such as age 50 or 55. At times, questions about who is included in the ageing with disability population have been further complicated by decisions of researchers to include people younger than 50 years, to take account of premature ageing experienced by some subgroups. Indeed, some of the early research on people ageing with intellectual disability included people as young as 40 years (e.g. see Seltzer & Krauss, 1989).

Chronological age alone has limited usefulness in defining the ageing with disability population without also knowing information about duration of disability. This is because the amount of time an individual experiences disability during their early and mid-life is important to understanding the experience of ageing with disability. Typically, a duration of disability of at least five or more years *combined* with an age of disability onset prior to age 64 (or below) are generally thought to be necessary included as part of the ageing with population. Although, as noted above, there are no formal guidelines on inclusion or exclusion based on age or duration of disability.

After these two parameters are considered (duration of disability and age of disability onset), a third parameter, diagnostic condition or type of disability experienced (e.g. mobility, sensory, psychiatric), is useful to further refine the ageing with disability population being identified. Sometimes, diagnostic categories are used with age or age of onset alone (without duration of disability). This occurs when there is a presumption that most persons with the identified condition are likely to experience disability given the commonality of both traits of the condition and features of social and physical environments. In these cases, however, it remains important to know or find out if individuals actually experience disability or if they experience impairment or have a diagnosed condition without experiencing disability.

How Big is the Ageing with Disability Population?

There is no clear estimate of the size of the international ageing with disability population. In large part this is because age of onset of disability is not universally asked in surveys or census instruments that collect data on disability on the national level. Some nations have better estimates than others for specific diagnostic groups or persons with certain chronic conditions. For example, Ireland has robust data on the prevalence of I/DD among its residents (Central Statistics Office, 2019) while the United States has very few nationally representative data sources that have the ability to identify persons ageing with disability (Coyle & Putnam, 2017). As noted above, sometimes diagnostic category or condition combined with chronological age is used to identify persons ageing with disability. In the calculation of the size of the ageing with disability population, it is not uncommon to use international and national estimates of the number of persons living with particular diagnostic conditions that typically have onset in early and mid-life in combination or alone with current disability status to calculate a rough approximation of the ageing with disability population.

As an example, international estimates for the prevalence several diagnostic conditions using data reported from the 2016 Global Burden of Disease study reports 2.2 million persons with multiple sclerosis, 55.5 million persons with traumatic brain injury, 27.4 million persons with spinal cord injury, 20.8 million persons with schizophrenia, 18.3 million persons with Autism spectrum disorder, and 114.8 million persons with intellectual/developmental disability (GBD 2016 Disease and Injury Incidence and Prevalence Collaborators, 2017). This small listing suggests that the potential ageing with disability population is sizable – adding up to more than 200 million people in these groups alone. However, we do not know if all of these individual experience disability – it is likely they do not. Additionally, many impairments or diagnostic conditions are not exclusive to a life stage or age group, even if the highest incidence rates are among children or adults of younger ages. Using this approach will likely result in individuals who experience onset in later life being included in the population, which inflates the estimated size.

Disability prevalence, in general, is hard to estimate as measures of disability vary and most surveys rely on self-report. It is not unusual for a measure of functional limitation to be included in surveys collecting data on disability to help clarify severity of disability in terms of its impact on daily life. This distinction is readily seen in WHO data, which estimates the global number of persons with disabilities of any kind is over 1 billion or 15% of the world's population; however, they estimate only about 2–4% of persons globally to have significant difficulty in functioning (between 110 and 190 million) (World Health Organization, 2018). Based on our discussion thus far, it is perhaps not surprising that most people who self-report disability indicate that they experience mild or moderate levels of disability.

This may very well be the case for persons ageing with disability too. Representative datasets do not always tell us the reason for functional limitations or disabilities, just that they exist. Thus, how to estimate the size of the ageing with disability population also involves determining if and how severity of disability or functional limitation will be considered as inclusion or exclusion criteria for membership. Individuals with the same diagnostic conditions and duration of disability can experience different levels of disability severity or functional limitations depending on their unique bio-psycho-social factors. It is also the case that some diagnostic and health conditions are more or less stable over time while others are characterised by cycles or regular changes in symptoms and effects. Being able to identify subgroups of the ageing with disability population, which, compared to the general ageing population, may need greater levels or adjustments to assistance with health and social care, employment, housing and transportation, and other key areas of life will be most useful for developing public policies and support and service programmes. Using a population base that includes persons with a full range of severity (mild, moderate, and severe) may also be useful for understanding differences within the ageing with disability experience.

Why is Ageing with Disability a New Phenomenon?

Living longer and growing older with disability that starts in early or mid-life is still a relatively new phenomenon. It corresponds to continuing improvements in medical, rehabilitation, and social science research-based knowledge and practice; availability of health and social care; recognition of the rights of persons with disability and implementation of laws related to non-discrimination in employment, public education, accessibility, and civil rights; and disability rights advocacy for inclusion and equity (Kemp & Mosqueda, 2007). Increased longevity also corresponds to elimination of eugenics policies, mass institutionalisation, and legalised differential treatment and abuse of individual with disabilities (Pfeiffer, 1994; Tilley, Walmsley, Earle, & Atkinson, 2012). As conditions and factors that contributed to shortened lifespans for persons with disabilities started to be removed in the 1950s 1960s, 1970s, and 1980s, they began to be replaced with those that extended lifespan. This is particularly the case in nations with more advanced economic and social sectors, although the ageing with disability population is also emerging in less developed nations.

In general, persons ageing with disability are living longer than they have in the past although there are substantial variations in life expectancy by diagnostic condition, severity of disability, nation, and global region of residence. For example, an analysis by Dolan, Lane, Hillis, and Delanty (2019) indicates that life expectancy for persons with I/DD has increased in most nations with advanced public and economic sectors, nearly doubling from 30 years in 1970 to 60 years in 2000 (Dolan et al., 2019). However, that same analysis indicated that life expectancy among persons with I/DD varies by severity and continues to lag behind the general population in most nations by roughly 10 years or more. Similarly, there have been substantial gains in life expectancy for persons with spinal cord injury post injury, as demonstrated by Savic et al. (2017). Their analysis of 70 years (1943–2010) of data from spinal cord injury patients admitted to one of two major spinal cord injury centres in Great Britain found that risk of mortality within five years for persons injured between 2010 and 2014 was 83% less than for those injured between 1944 and 1949. Their work also found that for most categories of injury, as ranked on the American Spinal Cord Injury Scale, patient life expectancy post injury nearly, or more than, doubled.

The primary reason that ageing with disability is considered a population trend, or a phenomenon, is that for the first time large numbers of persons who have onset of disability in early or mid-life are now growing older. It has become normative to live long-term with disability that begins in early or mid-life and to experience ageing-related changes. Previously, very little attention was paid to the implications of longevity of disability because it was generally assumed that persons experiencing significant disability would not live to older ages. Additionally, institutionalisation of persons with disabilities meant that ageing-related issues were hidden from the general public in a way that they are not now, given the notable changes in social inclusion and disability rights advocacy that mean more people with disabilities live in the community. This longevity shift is cause for deeper consideration of the heterogeneity of the ageing population in general, and specifically what makes the experience of ageing with disability distinct.

How is *Ageing with Disability* Different Than *Ageing Into Disability*?

Distinguishing between *ageing with* and *ageing into* disability is one aim of scholars and researchers who study ageing with disability. Conceptually and practically, there are both shared and different experiences between ageing with and ageing into disability – identifying and understanding what these are and how much they matter for facilitating positive outcomes in later life is a large part of what scholars are trying to learn more about. Below are a few examples.

> An individual who sustains a spinal cord injury at age 40, Mark, and one who sustains a spinal cord injury at age 70, Ben, may share parts of the ageing with disability experience – particularly those related to initial medical treatment, rehabilitation and use of assistive equipment to navigate home and community environments. However, what may differ substantially is the impact of the injury on the individual's daily life. Mark, the 40-year-old may no longer be able to work or have difficulty finding work the accommodates his disability. This may impact his ability to save for retirement and he then may be financially less secure in later life than he otherwise might have been if he had not incurred the spinal cord injury.
>
> Lisa, a woman with intellectual disability and Down Syndrome lives independently in her community and works at a local supermarket. She never marries or has children. At age 52, Lisa is experiencing early signs of Alzheimer's disease and her employer thinks it is time for her to think about retiring. She is open to the idea but her family worries that if she does, her social network will shrink and there are few programs for older persons with I/DD in Lisa's town to help her make new friends and stay engaged. Her parents are in their early 80s. Her mother cares for her father who has dementia and is unable to engage socially as much as she would like to with her daughter. The woman's 62-year old neighbour Monique, also never married and is retired, has one parent caring for the other, but has a strong social network through her church and a high-school alumni group and drives a car.
>
> David, a 60-year old man with a 40 year history of bipolar 1 disorder severe and lengthy treatment-refractory episodes of depression, has also been diagnosed with heart disease and encouraged by his physician to engage in regular physical exercise, adopt a heart-healthy diet, and participate in an online heart-health support group offered by the local hospital that provides encouragement and social accountability for the recommended exercise and diet plan. Participants in this support group are 60 or older with heart disease none have severe mental illness. The support group leader Luna, notices that David rarely attends the group but other members are at most of online meetings.

In all of these scenarios, disability intersects with ageing. These examples present some of the complexities of attempting to distinguish what is related to disability (the mismatch of personal capabilities to environmental supports), what is related to ageing (the process of growing older), and what is a product of the intersection of these. These examples focus on the experience of ageing with disability and identify just a few of the extensive number of bio-psycho-social elements of living long-term with disability. Distinguishing the process of ageing from the experience of disability can be useful. It can help identify what is typical for someone of a certain age and what is not. In doing so, it provides an indication of where an intervention might be targeted to improve an outcome and what that intervention might be. It also helps us reconsider how we conceptualise ageing and disability theoretically and how current theories of ageing and disability do, or do not, fit our understanding of ageing with disability. Trying to distinguish ageing related from disability-related support needs may be problematic however. It can lead to disputes about funding or irresolvable questions about which services system, disability, or ageing should take responsibility for providing services to persons ageing with disability.

How Do Social Models of Disability Apply to Persons Ageing with Disability?

Most ageing with disability scholarship draws on social models of disability, which view disability as an interaction between the person and their broader environment; between the person's capabilities and the demands of the environment. Social models of disability have varied over time, between cultures and with the emphasis they place on power and structural aspects of environments.

In attempting to bring together different models. Shakespeare (2006) suggested that disability is a

> combination of a certain set of physical or mental attributes in a particular physical environment within a specified social relationship, played out within a broader cultural and political context which combines to create the experience of disability for any individual or group of individuals. (p. 98)

This notion of an interaction between the person and the environment was originally presented by Lawton and Nahemow (1973) in their seminal theory of 'person-environment fit'. This theory posits that a match between the capacities of an older person and the press of their particular environment (home, neighbourhood, workplace, mode of transportation, etc.) creates conditions for overall wellbeing. When there is not a match, an individual will experience difficulty doing the things they need and want to do as the environment offers too many obstacles and is not supportive enough. A classic example is a person with a mobility impairment who needs to reach a high floor in a building without a working elevator. A more complex model of this person-environment congruence developed by Brandt and Pope (1997) demonstrated the ability of environmental supports and increases in the individual's capabilities to reduce disability by improving the person-environment fit. Other models that have built off this work include the International Classification of Functioning (World Health Organization, 2001), which seeks to develop an ontology of factors that support and hinder individual function. In the United Kingdom, the social model of disability developed by writers such as Oliver, Barnes, and Finkelstein in the context of physical disability had a sharper political edge, and understood disability as a form of oppression. As Watson (2004) suggests, it drew a firm distinction between impairment and disability understanding

> impairment as lacking part of all of a limb or having a defective limb, organism or mechanism of the body; and disability as, the disadvantage or restriction of activity caused by a contemporary social organisation which takes little or no account of people who have physical impairments and thus excludes them from participation in the mainstream of social activities. (p. 102)

Social models of disability provide a means of understanding the context of the disability experience for the person in their environment. Frameworks can be applied on their own or used in combination with other theories that attempt to explain an event or experience. For example, researchers have used social models to explore issues of health and wellness (Goering, 2015). Others have considered how the model influences disability identity, social stigma, and public perceptions of persons with disabilities (Grue, 2016). Social models of disability have been applied in studies of ageing with disability as a way of framing the person in the environment but do not address the ageing process itself.

A challenge for advancing social models of disability related to ageing with disability has been the long shadow of the medical or individual model of disability, which still holds a prominent place in the field of gerontology and geriatrics. Within a medical model, disability is inherently a personal trait; disability is viewed as loss of function or ability, and a normative part of growing older. While supports can be provided to the individual and environmental modifications made, there is more emphasis in the medical model on adjusting to reduced capability rather than positing that social and physical environments should be welcoming and accessible to persons of all abilities to begin with so adjustment is not required. The latter is the stance of the social model of disability. Scholars in the field of disability studies have argued vehemently that disability is not an inevitable outcome of cognitive, physical, or psychiatric difference (Oliver, 1990). This perception is slowly reaching the ageing field, which is beginning to promote strategic campaigns to combat ageism and social exclusion of older adults – most notably the WHO's Age-Friendly City initiatives (WHO, 2007). This is a global voluntary community planning effort that individual cities and communities can engage in to support older residents to actively participate in their communities and is perhaps the most visible use of social models of disability in public initiatives related to ageing.

How Do Theories of Ageing Apply to Persons with Early and Mid-Life Disability Onset?

There are a wide range of ageing-related theories addressing societal interaction to psychological development to physiological change. Most theories of ageing tend to focus either on the process of ageing or later life experiences. Later life is usually considered the last third or fourth of a person's lifetime roughly starting around age 60. Many factors influence the ageing process and later life experience at the biological, physiological, social, and structural levels – resulting in substantially different outcomes between individuals and groups of the older adult population. Nearly universally, however, ageing-related theories tend to view disability as a negative factor or outcome in later life (Putnam, 2002) rather than a personal or functional difference, as mentioned earlier. That is, disability is usually seen as ageing-related change or loss. Theories usually start with the assumption that an individual in early or mid-life starts at a 'normal' level of health and function, which declines over time. The aim then is to 'optimise' performance or cope with disability by making selective adjustments and changes so that an individual is still able to do what they want to do, even if the activity or engagement is somewhat different than before disability onset (Carpentieri, Elliott, Brett, & Deary, 2017). In this way, most ageing-related theories do not make room for the diversity of health and function found in the younger population of persons with disabilities and are not well-matched to the experiences of persons ageing with disability. Using the medical model of disability to study ageing processes and experiences stymies our understanding of the ageing with disability. Extending theories of ageing to persons with early and mid-life onset of disability will require starting with a different set of assumptions about growing older and the ageing individual.

Understanding the process and developing relevant theories of psychological and physiological change related to ageing with disability is important. Part of the needed work is distinguishing ageing-related effects (things that happen over time and things that happen because a person is growing older) from the experience of disability (things that happen because a person experiences disability). In addition, there is also the need to understand more about how the process of ageing and experience of disability intersect for persons ageing with disability. For example, bone density may change as people grow older (ageing-related effect) and create greater vulnerability for bone breakage if a person falls (Goltzman, 2019). While physical barriers such as a street with no curb cuts on the sidewalks in a person's neighbourhood can create disability if that person needs a sloped transition between walkways (barrier creates disability) and result in the individual getting less exercise or being less physically mobile than they otherwise might be if there were curb cuts (Twardzik et al., 2019). Reduced mobility can exacerbate bone density loss for anyone (Santos, Elliott-Sale, & Sale, 2017), but persons ageing with disabilities may more likely to encounter barriers to exercise and mobility at younger ages than persons ageing into disabilities and the thus bone health may be effected earlier than might typically be seen in persons growing older without a history of disability in early or mid-life (O'Connell et al., 2019). Rates of poor bone health and thus risk of bone breakage have been shown to be higher among persons ageing with disability than their age-matched peers without disability (Burke et al., 2019; Matsuda, Verrall, Finlayson, Molton, & Jensen, 2015). In this example, being able to identify ageing effects, disability effects, and their interaction is important for finding an effective intervention that improves bone health *and* mobility. Thus, considering both ageing and disability theory together in this example should produce a stronger analysis.

The process of extending theories of ageing will require asking core questions about their assumptions regarding disability and challenging them when they do not seem to apply. Questions for both theories of ageing and social models of disability include how does long-term disability influence the ageing process? And how does the process of ageing influence the experience of disability? These need to be answered at the individual, community, and structural levels in order to better understand the interaction of the ageing process and the disability experience theoretically, which will support all scholarship, but particularly the development of empirical research related to ageing with disability.

What is the Status of Scholarship Related to Ageing with Disability?

At this time, there is a slim body of scholarship, including research-based evidence, focused on ageing with disability. We know from individual lived experience accounts that the experience of ageing with disability has implications for physical and mental health and short- and long-term care needs; education, employment, and retirement; social roles and social networks; housing and transportation; social and physical environmental design; community engagement and participation; financial well-being; and other important areas of life. There are substantial bodies of evidence from the fields of gerontology, disability, rehabilitation, health, mental health, and related disciplines that can help inform our understanding of ageing and disability. However, there is very little research related to these topics that employs study samples of persons ageing with disability. In sum, much more research is needed.

Within the existing body of scholarship, a wide range of questions are asked and topics pursued. For example, researchers focused on ageing with intellectual disability have asked questions such as: How does a person retire from a supported workplace? How do families plan and prepare for caregiver transitions when parents of adult children with intellectual disability become older or are closer to their own end of life? How are the early onset of dementia symptoms best managed in persons with intellectual disability? In exploring issues related to physical disability and ageing, researchers have focused on concerns about accelerated ageing and post-onset or late-life effects of conditions such as polio or spinal cord injury, common ageing-related symptoms including pain and fatigue as well as the high prevalence of depression, and understanding patterns of employment, retirement, and community engagement. Only in the past 10 years or so has ageing with serious mental illness become an area of focus, as the effects of living long-term with mental health symptoms have been linked to reduction in lifespan, development of chronic physical health conditions, and social and economic challenges in later life. These issues are also just beginning to be explored among persons with sensory impairment, traumatic brain injury, and autism spectrum disorder - populations where ageing issues have not previously been extensively considered.

The limited amount of scholarship related to ageing with disability is directly related to the small number of scholars working in this field. Although scholars across the globe engage in this work, there are few dedicated education, training, or long-term research programmes focused on ageing with disability. There is a distinct need to increase the knowledge base to support the development of health and social care, work and family supports, community and environment practices, interventions, and policies that meet the needs of the ageing with disability population. We need more scholars working to build this knowledge base.

Why is it Important to Bridge the Fields of Ageing and Disability?

Segmenting issues of ageing and disability have served the purpose of developing specialised areas of research, policy and programmes, and professional practice that improve the lives of younger persons with disabilities and older adults. However, it has also created a bifurcated way of viewing disability – as a normative physiological experience of loss and decline among older people as they age *or* as mismatch between individual capability and social and physical environmental traits for young and middle-aged people. Bridging the fields of ageing and disability is one way to more quickly advance work in the field of ageing with disability by linking and integrating existing theory and knowledge to inform policy and practice. There is a real need to fill in the gaps that exist in our understanding of the ageing with disability experience and the needs, issues, and concerns of persons ageing with disability. Not all of this can be achieved by the small number of scholars currently working in the field of ageing with disability.

Arguments for bridging ageing and disability have been made internationally (Leonardi, Bickenbach, & Leroy, 2012). Notably, the Toronto Declaration on Bridging Ageing and Disability (Bickenbach et al., 2012) outlined several areas where bridging work is needed including health and well-being, inclusion, participation and community, long-term supports and services, income security, and the science of bridging. As the Toronto Declaration suggests, the work of bridging is wide in scale and global in aim:

> Bridging encompasses a range of concepts, tasks, technologies and practices aimed at improving knowledge sharing and collaboration across stakeholders, organizations and fields of care and support for persons with disabilities, their families, and the ageing population. Bridging tasks include activities of dissemination, coordination, assessment, empowerment, service delivery, management, financing and policy. The overall purpose of bridging is to improve efficiency and equity of care and inclusion and support at all levels, from the person to the society. (p. 2)

Key to any bridging effort, however, is understanding more about the population that is needing those bridges built – persons ageing with disability. Strengthening our knowledge about the experience of ageing with disability is at the centre of ensuring the bridges we build are supportive and lasting.

Conclusion

The ageing with disability population is international, heterogeneous, and comprises individuals living in diverse circumstances. Ageing with disability is not only a personal experience but also a social one as individuals engage with friends, family, and their larger communities. Larger factors including cultural, social, economic, and political forces influence the experience of ageing with disability and outcomes for persons ageing with disability in later life. We have much to learn about the ageing with disability experience and the population of persons ageing with disability. Despite scholarship now stretching back some 40 years, ageing with disability remains a new field of study. We hope that the brief introduction provided in this chapter to core questions that frame the field provides readers with a strong starting point for not only learning more about ageing with disability but also contributing to the growing knowledge base through their own professional work.

References

Bickenbach, J., Bigby, C., Salvador-Carulla, L., Heller, T., Leonardi, M., Leroy, B. ... Spindel, A. (2012). The Toronto declaration on bridging knowledge, policy and practice in aging and disability: Toronto, Canada, March 30, 2012. *International Journal of Integrated Care, 12*, e205. https://doi.org/10.5334/ijic.1086

Brandt, E. N. Jr., & Pope, A. M. (Eds.). (1997). *Enabling America: Assessing the role of rehabilitation science and engineering*. National Academies Press. https://doi.org/10.17226/5799

Burke, É, Carroll, R., O'Dwyer, M., Walsh, J. B., McCallion, P., & McCarron, M. (2019). Quantitative examination of the bone health status of older adults with intellectual and developmental disability in Ireland: A cross-sectional nationwide study. *BMJ Open, 9*(4), e026939. https://doi.org/10.1136/bmjopen-2018-026939

Carpentieri, J. D., Elliott, J., Brett, C. E., & Deary, I. J. (2017). Adapting to aging: Older people talk about their use of selection, optimization, and compensation to maximize well-being in the context of physical decline. *The Journals of Gerontology. Series B, Psychological Sciences and Social Sciences, 72*(2), 351–361. https://doi.org/10.1093/geronb/gbw132

Central Statistics Office. (2019). *Census of population 2016 – Profile 9 health, disability and carers*. Government of Ireland. https://www.cso.ie/en/releasesandpublications/ep/p-cp9hdc/p8hdc/p9tod/

Clarke, P., & Latham, K. (2014). Life course health and socioeconomic profiles of Americans aging with disability. *Disability and Health Journal, 7*(1 Suppl), S15–S23. https://doi.org/10.1016/j.dhjo.2013.08.008

Coyle, C. E., & Putnam, M. (2017). Identifying adults aging with disability using existing data: The case of the health and retirement study. *Disability and Health Journal, 10*(4), 611–615. https://doi.org/10.1016/j.dhjo.2016.12.016

Dolan, E., Lane, J., Hillis, G., & Delanty, N. (2019). Changing trends in life expectancy in intellectual disability over time. *Irish Medical Journal, 112*(9), 1006. https://www.ncbi.nlm.nih.gov/pubmed/31651135

GBD 2016 Disease and Injury Incidence and Prevalence Collaborators. (2017). Global, regional, and national incidence, prevalence, and years lived with disability for 328 diseases and injuries for 195 countries, 1990–2016: A systematic analysis for the global burden of disease study 2016. *Lancet, 390*(10100), 1211–1259. https://doi.org/10.1016/S0140-6736(17)32154-2

Goering, S. (2015). Rethinking disability: The social model of disability and chronic disease. *Current Reviews in Musculoskeletal Medicine, 8*(2), 134–138. https://doi.org/10.1007/s12178-015-9273-z

Goltzman, D. (2019). The aging skeleton. *Advances in Experimental Medicine and Biology, 1164*, 153–160. https://doi.org/10.1007/978-3-030-22254-3_12

Grue, J. (2016). The social meaning of disability: A reflection on categorisation, stigma and identity. *Sociology of Health & Illness, 38*(6), 957–964. https://doi.org/10.1111/1467-9566.12417

Kemp, B., & Mosqueda, L. (2007). Introduction. In B. Kemp & L. Mosqueda (Eds.), *Aging with disability: What the clinician needs to know* (pp. 1–8). Johns Hopkins University Press.

Lawton, M. P., & Nahemow, L. (1973). Ecology and the aging process. In C. Eisdorfer & M. P. Lawton (Eds.), *Psychology of adult development and aging* (pp. 619–674). American Psychological Association. https://doi.org/10.1037/10044-020

Leonardi, M., Bickenbach, J., & Leroy, B. (2012). International initiatives on bridging knowledge, policy and practice. *International Journal of Integrated Care, 12*, e203. https://doi.org/10.5334/ijic.1084

Matsuda, P. N., Verrall, A. M., Finlayson, M. L., Molton, I. R., & Jensen, M. P. (2015). Falls among adults aging with disability. *Archives of Physical Medicine and Rehabilitation, 96*(3), 464–471. https://doi.org/10.1016/j.apmr.2014.09.034

National Academies of Sciences, Engineering, and Medicine. (2015). *Mental disorders and disabilities among low-income children*. The National Academies Press. https://www.ncbi.nlm.nih.gov/books/NBK332877/#:~:text=DSM%2D5%20defines%20intellectual%20disabilities,1.

O'Connell, N. E., Smith, K. J., Peterson, M. D., Ryan, N., Liverani, S., Anokye, N. ... Ryan, J. M. (2019). Incidence of osteoarthritis, osteoporosis and inflammatory musculoskeletal diseases in adults with cerebral palsy: A population-based cohort study. *Bone, 125*, 30–35. https://doi.org/10.1016/j.bone.2019.05.007

Oliver, M. (1990). *Politics of disablement*. Macmillan International Higher Education.

Pfeiffer, D. (1994). Eugenics and disability discrimination. *Disability & Society, 9*(4), 481–499. https://doi.org/10.1080/09687599466780471

Putnam, M. (2002). Linking aging theory and disability models: Increasing the potential to explore aging with physical impairment. *The Gerontologist, 42*(6), 799–806. https://doi.org/10.1093/geront/42.6.799

Salvador-Carulla, L., Putnam, M., Bigby, C., & Heller, T. (2012). Advancing a research agenda for bridging ageing and disability. *International Journal of Integrated Care, 12*, e204. https://doi.org/10.5334/ijic.1085

Santos, L., Elliott-Sale, K. J., & Sale, C. (2017). Exercise and bone health across the lifespan. *Biogerontology, 18*(6), 931–946. https://doi.org/10.1007/s10522-017-9732-6

Savic, G., DeVivo, M., Frankel, H., Jamous, M. A., Soni, B. M., & Charlifue, S. (2017). Long-term survival after traumatic spinal cord injury: A 70-year British study. *Spinal Cord, 55*, 651–658. https://doi.org/10.1038/sc.2017.23

Seltzer, M. M., & Krauss, M. W. (1989). Aging parents with adult mentally retarded children: Family risk factors and sources of support. *American Journal of Mental Retardation: AJMR, 94*(3), 303–312.

Shakespeare, Tom. *Disability rights and wrongs*. Routledge, 2006. https://doi.org/10.4324/9780203640098

Tilley, E., Walmsley, J., Earle, S., & Atkinson, D. (2012). 'The silence is roaring': Sterilization, reproductive rights and women with intellectual disabilities. *Disability & Society, 27*(3), 413–426. https://doi.org/10.1080/09687599.2012.654991

Twardzik, E., Duchowny, K., Gallagher, A., Alexander, N., Strasburg, D., Colabianchi, N., & Clarke, P. (2019). What features of the built environment matter most for mobility? Using wearable sensors to capture real-time outdoor environment demand on gait performance. *Gait & Posture, 68*, 437–442. https://doi.org/10.1016/j.gaitpost.2018.12.028

Watson, N. (2004). The dialectics of disability social model for the 21 century? In Barnes, C., & Mercer, G. (eds). *Implementing the Social Model of Disability: Theory and Research Leeds*. The Disability Press, (pp. 101–117).

World Health Organization. (2001). *International classification of functioning, disability and health (ICF)*. World Health Organization. https://www.who.int/classifications/icf/en/

World Health Organization. (2007). *Global age-friendly cities: A guide*. World Health Organization. https://www.who.int/ageing/publications/Global_age_friendly_cities_Guide_English.pdf

World Health Organization. (2011). *World report on disability*. World Health Organization. https://www.who.int/disabilities/world_report/2011/report.pdf

World Health Organization. (2018). *Disability and health*. World Health Organization. https://www.who.int/news-room/fact-sheets/detail/disability-and-health

Suggested Readings

Bickenbach, J., Bigby, C., Salvador-Carulla, L., Heller, T., Leonardi, M., Leroy, B. ... Spindel, A. (2012). The Toronto declaration on bridging knowledge, policy and practice in aging and disability: Toronto, Canada, March 30, 2012. *International Journal of Integrated Care, 12*, e205. https://doi.org/10.5334/ijic.1086

Dolan, E., Lane, J., Hillis, G., & Delanty, N. (2019). Changing trends in life expectancy in intellectual disability over time. *Irish Medical Journal, 112*(9), 1006. https://www.ncbi.nlm.nih.gov/pubmed/31651135

Oliver, M. (1990). *Politics of disablement*. Macmillan International Higher Education.

World Health Organization. (2018). *Disability and health*. World Health Organization. https://www.who.int/news-room/fact-sheets/detail/disability-and-health

2
RETHINKING THE CONCEPT OF SUCCESSFUL AGEING
A Disability Studies Approach

Tove Harnett, Annika Taghizadeh Larsson, and Håkan Jönson

Introduction

Characterisations of active, 'successful' ageing have been closely related to individual effort and the maintenance of high physical and cognitive functions. While these ideas have gained paradigmatic status in gerontology, proponents of disability studies have argued that the concept of 'successful ageing' is stigmatising and should be abandoned. The question that we pose in this chapter is whether there is a 'third route' to the debate on successful ageing, where researchers, policy makers, and social movements rework the concept rather than just calling for its disappearance.

Several researchers have proposed that adopting successful models developed within the field of disability studies would improve gerontology and the support systems for older people (Krassioukova-Enns & Ringaert, 2012; Naue & Kroll, 2010; Oldman, 2002; Putnam, 2002). In this chapter, we will redirect attention from the – much criticised – normative and individualised character of successful ageing, into an alternative model inspired by disability policies. The model is based on *comparisons of possibilities* as a means to argue for *social rights* and based on those rights, regardless of impairments, to have a 'continued engagement with life, which includes relations with others and productive activity' (Rowe & Kahn, 2015, p. 593).

In Scandinavia, a normalisation principle has expressed the view that society should make available for people with disability *living conditions* and patterns of everyday life that are as close as possible to those of 'others' (Nirje, 1992; Tideman, 2000). By using an approach that is prominent in Scandinavian disability policies, the aim of this chapter is to propose a *Scandinavian Model of Successful Ageing* that focuses on the efforts of society to enable individuals to age successfully rather than on measuring the characteristics of the individual to calculate success. Given that the aim to rework successful ageing may appear as provocative to some readers, we would like to stress that our main objective is to delineate a model that has potential for improving welfare and enhancing social rights of older people.

What the chapter proposes lies in the borderland between vision and reality. It reports on the reality of actual persons who receive support that enables them to live lives that would appear as unimaginable when only looking at the population of frail older persons. These persons are not typical, but what they show us is the potential for society to increase its support efforts to facilitate successful ageing for all people. This chapter demonstrates that it seems possible, even achievable, to provide support that enables older persons with severe disabilities to maintain high functional capacity and an active engagement with life. Their ways of life serve to refute the established idea that limitations and problems during the period defined as old age are caused by the ageing process, and what has not been prevented should be accepted.

Successful Ageing

Successful ageing is one of the most influential concepts in gerontology. It originated in the 1950s (Havighurst, 1961, 1963; Havighurst & Albrecht, 1953) as part of the normative aim of social gerontology 'to help people live better lives in their later years' (Havighurst, 1963, p. 299). In the 1980s, the so called *MacArthur model* introduced 'objective' criteria for the measure of successful ageing (Rowe & Kahn, 1987). This model has not only gained paradigmatic status in the field of gerontology but has also been heavily criticised (Holstein & Minkler, 2003).

Rowe and Kahn (1987) argued that research had come to associate ageing with losses and that the ageing process as such was regarded as a cause for 'age-associated declines' that were in fact caused by life style, habits, diets, and different psychosocial factors extrinsic to ageing. In addition, definitions of normal ageing were based on a division between persons with and without illness and impairment (pathologic and non-pathologic), but the heterogeneity among persons within these categories was not acknowledged. Rowe and Kahn therefore suggested that normal ageing could be divided into two categories – *usual ageing* and *successful ageing*. The first subcategory was associated with the absence of disease and disability but with the presence of age-related alterations such as increase in blood pressure and blood glucose and modest memory decline that are risk factors for ill health. The second category was associated with the absence of these risk factors. Later, Rowe and Kahn (1997) specified the content of the *MacArthur model* as consisting of three main components: (1) Low probability of disease and disease-related disability (2) High cognitive and physical functional capacity and (3) Active engagement with life (specified as interpersonal relations and productive activity). Beyond the fact that choice of particular lifestyles may provide more years and better life, a probable reason for the attractiveness of successful ageing lies in the way that descriptions of people who age successfully refute traditional images of older people as frail, dependent, and essentially different from the non-old.

The individualising focus and normative features of the MacArthur model have attracted a flood of criticism. In a systematic review, Martinson and Berridge (2015) identified such critique from many quarters, including social gerontology (Hooyman & Kiyak, 2011), cross-cultural studies (Romo et al., 2013), anthropology (Lamb, 2014), psychology (Villar, 2012), and queer studies (Van Wagenen, Driskell, & Bradford, 2013). Rowe and Kahn's tendency to polarise ageing in relation to functional capacity and health has been referred to as a 'new ageism' (Angus & Reeve, 2006) or a 'polarised ageism' (Rozanova, Northcott, & McDaniel, 2006). Researchers in disability studies have criticised the absence of subjective measures in the model (Montross et al., 2006). Studies have shown that many older people living with disability view themselves as ageing successfully but the MacArthur model would suggest that they are wrong to do so (Strawbridge, Wallhagen, & Cohen, 2002). The focus on lifestyle, bodily function, and individual choices that are part of the definition of successful ageing reinforces the stigma of disease and disability in older people, and proponents of disability studies have suggested that the entire concept is harmful and should be abandoned (Stone, 2003).

The MacArthur model emphasises how decline and loss should be prevented through individual action, with limited attention paid to how societies could fully include people with disabilities. The absent role of society has been commented on by Katz and Calasanti (2015), who argue that inequalities in social support and income shape individuals' abilities to age successfully. Minkler and Fadem (2002, p. 233) likewise have suggested that the type of social support that has been pivotal for the 'new paradigm of disability' should be applied to the concept of successful ageing. This chapter is a response to those calls. We present a third route – one that is critical of the MacArthur model, but does not advocate abandoning the concept of successful ageing altogether (Butler, Fujii, & Sasaki, 2011; Dillaway & Byrnes, 2009). Rather, we propose to hold society, and not the individual, responsible for providing the appropriate living conditions so that all older people have the same possibilities to live high-capacity lives (with support).

Disability Policies and the Normalisation Principle

The tradition in gerontology and policy has focussed on normative aspects of ageing (Katz, 1996; Lamb, 2014; Tornstam, 1992), expressed in concepts such as active ageing (Foster & Walker, 2015), healthy ageing (Kuh, 2007), and successful ageing (Rowe & Kahn, 2015). The MacArthur model of successful ageing marks a peak in this tradition, with many western European governments mobilising parts of their framing and features. Policies on 'active ageing' appear both on EU level, that is 'The European Innovation Partnership on Active and Healthy Ageing' and on national level in most European countries.

In contrast to the normative character of ageing policies and research, disability policies and research in the Scandinavian countries do not appeal to a conception of self-realisation, but have been mainly directed to social inclusion and the redistributive dimension of social justice (Fraser & Honneth, 2003). Researchers, activists, and policymakers have referred to normal and typical activities and arrangements (mainly with reference to age) as a benchmark when demanding equal rights for citizens (Jönson & Larsson, 2009). For many years, the pursuit of equal living conditions was guided by the *Scandinavian normalisation principle*, which identifies people with disabilities as deprived relative to non-disabled members of society. Like the social model of disability, the normalisation principle is an alternative to a medical model that casts disability as an individual problem associated with abnormal body function – that is, the individual is either normal/healthy or abnormal/sick (Tideman, 2000). Nirje summarises the normalisation principle as meaning:

> ... you act right when making available to all persons with intellectual or other impairments or disabilities patterns of life and conditions of everyday living which are as close as possible to or indeed the same as the regular circumstances and ways of life of their communities (1992, p. 16).

Nirje (1985, p. 97) emphasised that the Scandinavian principle should apply to *living conditions* rather than bodily attributes of people with disabilities: 'the normalisation deals with the realities of life, not with appearances of conformity and passing, hiding what some call deviancy'. Normalisation should not be a matter of individual attempts to live up to societal ideals.

The Scandinavian Model of Successful Ageing

The Scandinavian model of successful ageing is an innovative contribution to the nexus of ageing and disability, offering as it does a new way of thinking about the standard for comparison of and locus of intervention into disabled and ageing people's lives. It shifts the focus of the MacArthur model in two fundamental ways: (1) from normative to comparative standards and (2) from individual to societal responsibility.

The Scandinavian model uses older people without disease and disease-related disability, who are actively engaged in life, and who function at a high level as a comparative reference group to serve as the basis for claims that older people with disabilities are treated unjustly relative to others. According to our model, successful ageing is accomplished if older people with disabilities are:

- Enabled (by society) to have an active engagement in life (component one in the Scandinavian Model); and also
- Enabled (by society) to engage in activities that require a high level of functioning (component two in the Scandinavian Model)

The concept of 'society' should not be equated with the welfare state; rather, it is broader and includes social policy, societal norms, and the elimination of obstacles and different kinds of supportive environments. One issue that needs attention is MacArthur model's reference to 'a high cognitive and physical functional capacity'. It seems possible to enable people to engage in activities that require a high level of physical function with support, but the issue of cognition is exclusionary, and for this reason we have chosen a general reference to a high level of function.

The purpose of our proposed model is to enhance the social rights of a misrecognised group that has been subject to maldistribution (compare Fraser & Honneth, 2003) as well as to shift the focus from individual to societal responsibility. The Scandinavian model of successful ageing can be used by older people with disabilities to claim rights based on comparative references to the living conditions of other non-disabled pensioners, and a fundamental aspect is that 'success' is about making society (not the individual) 'act right'.

A Different Kind of Successful Ageing

In this section, we explore the usefulness of the Scandinavian model of successful ageing by describing personal assistance as an idea and a practice. Personal assistance is a specific form of societal support that has been central to Scandinavian disability policies for implementing the rights of people with profound disabilities to live like others and be self-determining. Similar systems exist in several other countries. Personal assistants serve as the assistance users' 'arms and legs', while the latter determines what should be done and how. In Scandinavian countries, however, policy regimes are such that personal assistance has to be granted before age 65 (Christensen, Guldvik, & Larsson, 2014). Following reforms in 2000, it is now possible to keep – but not increase – the number of hours of personal assistance granted before age 65. As a result, some people who would otherwise have been confined to nursing homes or received extensive home care now age with personal assistance.

The empirical cases that we use in this chapter are based on three qualitative studies (Hellström & Taghizadeh Larsson, 2017; Taghizadeh Larsson, 2013). Living with their disabilities for a long time, many informants in these studies have embraced the principles of access and inclusion advanced by the disability movement and incorporated into official policies. They constitute a crossover population in the sense that they have expectations of the kind of life that have been described as missing among older people with high support needs (Kane & Kane, 2005). From the perspective of the MacArthur model of successful ageing, the informants are plainly not 'successful agers'. All of them have major, permanent disabilities. But what happens if we apply the criteria of the Scandinavian model of successful ageing to these people's lives? Does society enable them to maintain physical and cognitive function, like others in the third age? Are they enabled by society to have an active retirement and be fully engaged with life?

When the informants in the first study (aged 65–73, with physical disabilities for at least 30 years) talked about an ordinary week and day, images of recreationally active and engaged individuals emerged. The women and men, all of whom had extensive support needs, described how they went to the theatre and concerts, were involved in artistic activities, took part in language studies, sports, and gymnastics, and travelled both within and outside Sweden. Several actively volunteered for organisations that work to improve the living conditions of people with disabilities. Thus, to use the wording of the MacArthur model, the interviewees displayed an *active involvement in life* and *high functional capacity*, in the sense of being able to carry out a variety of activities that benefited themselves and others. The support from their personal assistants stood out as crucial for their lives. Some expressed the view that assistance makes it possible to 'manage oneself', which can be interpreted as an indication that one can be relatively dependent on other people, yet perceive oneself as autonomous.

Being Enabled to Engage in Activities that Require a High Level of Functioning

Where the interviewees in the first study gave vivid accounts of active recreational lifestyles and ongoing engagement with disability organisations, those in the second study highlighted the possibility of continued engagement in activities that had been part of their adult life *without* disabilities. One example is Steven, aged 73. Steven had a stroke and was granted personal assistance three months before his 65th birthday. If he had had his stroke after that date, he would have had to receive either home help or nursing home care instead. When Steven talks about an ordinary day or week, he describes an active life: he sings in a choir, he plays boccia, he goes to ice hockey games, and he regularly meets old friends in town for coffee. When the interviewer asks what the personal assistants help him with, Steven says they do everything for him except for chewing his food and shaving.

STEVEN: So we go every other Monday now [for a coffee in town with friends].
I: Yes, so it is a kind of new activity?
STEVEN: Yes, we meet, and we used to ski in the same ski club and play football so we have a lot to talk about. And sometimes in the summer … I play boccia, because PRO [the Pensioners' Organisation] has a boccia court. So we go there. And it's kind of fun because the ladies are the most enthusiastic of us all [—] They swear and roar! They really go for it. But we play for a few hours and then we talk and have a bite to eat and a cup of coffee. And then we play another game. So it's mostly social.
I: Mm and the racetrack?
STEVEN: We go to the racetrack 3 or 4 times in Smallville.
I: A year?
STEVEN: Yes. [—]
STEVEN: And then I have an old schoolmate with a sailboat in Littletown. I have been out on that for a day. We sail. Maybe we start at 10–11 and then we're back at around 3 or 4 and have lunch out at sea. And then I have been up at the Furu Mountain 3 or 4 times. My brother has a cottage there and I go there with my siblings, so then I don't have any assistants with me.
I: No, but for all the other activities you talked about before, then you have your assistants? Or assistant?
STEVEN: Yes, they are with me [—]

Steven continues by talking about his car that the assistants drive so he can visit his daughter and grandchildren and go to the racetrack and ice hockey. Even if he needs help with many tasks, he has a very active life and is able to engage just like other pensioners. He visits friends and family, goes to sporting events, goes sailing, and sings in a choir.

In contrast to Steven, who described being able to pursue hobbies and leisure activities, others described how support from personal assistants could enable them to engage in work-related activities. John, a 71-year-old man from the north of Sweden who had a stroke in 2004, describes how he used to be the head of the regional archives and that he still goes into work three or four times a week:

JOHN: I go there and do research in the archives, and I use the computers to do research on digitalized material from other departments. It enriches my life. And I meet people that I have employed. It is kind of fun. I feel I get extra service from them.
I: Maybe they think it is fun too. So then you have your assistants with you?
JOHN: Yes, they have to carry my [—] and make sure I end up sitting in the right place. [—]
JOHN: But then, after I get to sit down, they can leave and return at the time we have agreed. [—]
JOHN: Usually I settle down on my research chair at ten. And then I usually … normally they return at 12.15. Because then my wife is here at home, cooking … if I've not been invited out for lunch in a restaurant.
I: So you eat out sometimes?
JOHN: Yes.

John and his wife talk about what his life would have been like if he had not been able to continue with his research in the archives, and John says that he would probably be sitting at home watching TV, which in his view would have been bad. The lack of support would have limited his activities and in effect also his functional capacity. Even though John enjoys his research he admits that there is a downside to being a researcher – the stress of deadlines.

The Challenge of Dementia

The two persons with dementia that participated in the third study (Hellström & Taghizadeh Larsson, 2017) were at a phase in the trajectories of their illness when they could no longer use spoken language or move from one place to another without assistance. In relation to any model on successful ageing, they did not meet the criteria of having high cognitive function. Still, their cases are interesting as they were enabled to have an active engagement with life, and the supportive structure of society made extensive attempts to interpret their interests and wishes. For both individuals, a lot of support was provided by the personal assistants and by their spouses in order to meet their needs for food, going to the toilet or change of incontinence pads, stay warm and clean, sleep, medication, transport, or dealing with contacts with health care professionals. In fact – and as told by Monica's husband at a later contact – from a medical perspective, Monica was considered as being at the very last stage of the disease, and of her life. Just a couple of weeks after the researcher (ATL) visited Monica and her husband, Monica's physician had a meeting with the husband aimed at preparing him for the end-of-life phase and to get his views on life sustaining treatment. According to the physician, the disease would soon inhibit vital bodily functions and lead to death.

The case of Monica highlights how technical devices and a flexible and personalised support system such as personal assistance are used to enable an active and relatively independent life inside one's own home and in the local community. Together with her personal assistants, Monica went on daily trips with the adapted car to various destinations, such as cafés or, tourist sights. Monica's daily life also included visiting friends and acquaintances; shopping, coffee on the balcony; accompanying the assistants in the kitchen while cooking; and watching TV. On the weekends, her spouse took on the role of personal assistant and supported Monica and, as a couple, they continued to do things that they had been doing together before dementia entered their life.

As Monica had lost her ability to speak, she could not tell the researcher her preferences and whether she preferred to live this active life at – and outside – her (ordinary) home, or if she would prefer a quieter life in a residential care unit. However, her husband claimed with certainty that his wife still liked to live the way she had previously, before she was affected by the disease – that is, an active and social life. As before, she particularly appreciated going on excursions by car and enjoying the sun. What the researcher witnessed during the days that she followed Monica from morning until night gave no reason to question her spouse's assessment. In line with the daily work performed by Monica's assistants and her husband in interpreting Monica's wishes and preferences by looking at bodily and facial signs of pleasure or discontent, this conclusion was based on Monica's body language. This included observing how happy and relaxed she appeared, how alert and awake she was, and if she smiled or clenched her teeth hard. Monica could be regarded as a person who does not have high functional capacity. Her challenges are great but there are extensive attempts to meet them.

The situation of Monica or other persons with cognitive impairments should not be idealised, and there are numerous ethical problems involved in attempts to interpret the interests of a person with limited capacity to express her will. What we argue is that the Scandinavian Model of Successful Ageing directs attention to the efforts of society to enable people with complex disabilities to be as active and involved in life and have as high a degree of functional capacity as possible.

Conclusion

In this chapter, we used a critical gerontology approach informed by a disability studies perspective to discuss the concept of successful ageing and its appearance in two different models. According to the MacArthur model, it is not possible for people with disabilities to age successfully. Following disability rights' calls to consider the role of social structures in producing or ameliorating disability, we harness the Scandinavian normalisation principle to propose the Scandinavian Model of Successful Ageing. In doing so, we develop the argument that disabled people can age 'successfully', whether they age with or into disability. Our Scandinavian model excludes the first criteria of the MacArthur model – a low probability of disease and disease-related disability – and turns the tables on success: through focusing on transforming the built and social environment. We have described supportive arrangements that seem to enable successful ageing among people with profound disabilities, in the sense that they have an active engagement in life and engage in activities that require a high level of function. Several interviewees contrasted experiences of the home care system (where help was provided by home-care services of the type reserved for older people with support needs) with those of the personal assistance system (where assistance was provided for those who became disabled prior to age 65). Home care meant that the care user had to adapt to the organisation that provided the help, whereas personal assistance was associated by informants with flexibility, autonomy, and independence.

It could be argued that older people with disabilities are better served if society acknowledges that we are all vulnerable and interdependent. Any model of successful ageing may impose a 'coercive standard' on older people, which has a damaging effect on those who fail to live up to the ideal (Holstein & Minkler, 2003; Lamb, 2014). We acknowledge this problem but suggest that it is a challenge that should be addressed through critical reflection and a robust, person-centred policy. Disability policies for younger persons have addressed similar challenges, when for instance demanding support to live independently, even though independence could also be described as a coercive standard. Comparisons to what non-disabled people can access are powerful tools for people with disabilities when it comes to claiming citizenship rights. The MacArthur model of successful ageing is not likely to go away. Could the life that is possible for persons who are judged to age successfully according to this model be used to improve the living condition of others?

The Scandinavian Model of Successful Ageing does not measure individual achievement, but rather redirects attention from normative to comparative standards in order to ensure the fair distribution of social rights. In Sweden, disability activists have used comparisons between people of similar age to confront injustice and discrimination, for instance by demanding that a teenage wheelchair user should be able to study, travel, go to the movies, and party like other teenagers (Jönson & Larsson, 2009). Similar references to persons defined as living in the third age could be used to claim that an older person in a wheelchair should have the right to be enabled to live independently, visit family and friends, study, travel, pursue hobbies and leisure activities, and do voluntary work, just like others of their age (Jönson & Harnett, 2016; Taghizadeh Larsson & Jönson, 2018).

References

Angus, J., & Reeve, P. (2006). Ageism: A threat to "ageing well" in the 21st century. *Journal of Applied Gerontology*, 25(2), 137–152. https://doi.org/10.1177/0733464805285745

Butler, J. P., Fujii, M., & Sasaki, H. (2011). Balanced aging, or successful ageing?. *Geriatrics & Gerontology International* 11(1), 1–2. https://doi.org/10.1111/j.1447-0594.2010.00661.x

Christensen, K., Guldvik, I., & Larsson, M. (2014). Active social citizenship: The case of disabled peoples' rights to personal assistance. *Scandinavian Journal of Disability Research*, 16(sup1), 19–33. https://doi.org/10.1080/15017419.2013.820665

Dillaway, H. E., & Byrnes, M. (2009). Reconsidering successful aging: A call for renewed and expanded academic critiques and conceptualizations. *Journal of Applied Gerontology*, 28(6), 702–722. https://doi.org/10.1177/0733464809333882

Foster, L., & Walker, A. (2015). Active and successful aging: A European policy perspective. *The Gerontologist*, 55(1), 83–90. https://doi.org/10.1093/geront/gnu028

Fraser, N., & Honneth, A. (2003). *Redistribution or recognition? A political-philosophical exchange*. Verso.

Havighurst, R. J. (1961). Successful ageing. *The Gerontologist*, 1(1), 8–13. https://doi.org/10.1093/geront/1.1.8

Havighurst, R. J. (1963). Successful ageing. In *Processes of aging: Social and psychological perspectives* (Vol. 1, pp. 299–320).

Havighurst, R. J., & Albrecht, R. (1953). *Older people*. Longmans, Green.

Hellström, I., & Taghizadeh Larsson, A. (2017). Dementia as chronic illness: Maintaining involvement in everyday life. In L.C. Hydén & E. Antelius (Eds.), *Living with dementia: Relations, responses and agency in everyday life*. Red Globe Press, Palgrave Macmillan.

Holstein, M. B., & Minkler, M. (2003). Self, society, and the "new gerontology". *The Gerontologist*, *43*(6), 787–796. https://doi.org/10.1093/geront/43.6.787

Hooyman, N. R., & Kiyak, A. H. (2011). *Social gerontology: A multidisciplinary perspective* (9th ed.). Pearson.

Jönson, H., & Harnett, T. (2016). Introducing an equal rights framework for older persons in residential care. *The Gerontologist*, *56*(5), 800–806. https://doi.org/10.1093/geront/gnv039

Jönson, H., & Larsson, A. T. (2009). The exclusion of older people in disability activism and policies—A case of inadvertent ageism? *Journal of Ageing Studies*, *23*(1), 69–77. https://doi.org/10.1016/j.jaging.2007.09.001

Kane, R., & Kane, R. (2005). Ageism in healthcare and long-term care. *Generations*, *29*(3), 49–54.

Katz, S. (1996). *Disciplining old age: The formation of gerontological knowledge*. University of Virginia Press.

Katz, S., & Calasanti, T. (2015). Critical perspectives on successful aging: Does it "appeal more than it illuminates"? *The Gerontologist*, *55*(1), 26–33. https://doi.org/10.1093/geront/gnu027

Krassioukova-Enns, O., & Ringaert, L. (2012). Rights and knowledge-based approach to ageing and disability: An overview of issues and approaches. *Social Welfare: Interdisciplinary Approach*, *2*(2), 23–34.

Kuh, D. (2007). A life course approach to healthy aging, frailty, and capability. *The Journals of Gerontology Series A: Biological Sciences and Medical Sciences*, *62*(7), 717–721. https://doi.org/10.1093/gerona/62.7.717

Lamb, S. (2014). Permanent personhood or meaningful decline? Toward a critical anthropology of successful aging. *Journal of Ageing Studies*, *29*, 41–52. https://doi.org/10.1016/j.jageing.2013.12.006

Martinson, M., & Berridge, C. (2015). Successful aging and its discontents: A systematic review of the social gerontology literature. *The Gerontologist*, *55*(1), 58–69. https://doi.org/10.1093/geront/gnu037

Minkler, M., & Fadem, P. (2002). " Successful aging:" A disability perspective. *Journal of Disability Policy Studies*, *12*(4), 229–235. https://doi.org/10.1177/104420730201200402

Montross, L. P., Depp, C., Daly, J., Reichstadt, J., Golshan, S., Moore, D., & Jeste, D. V., (2006). Correlates of self-rated successful aging among community-dwelling older adults. *American Journal of Geriatric Psychiatry*, *14*(1), 43–51. https://doi.org/10.1097/01.JGP.0000192489.43179.31Get

Naue, U., & Kroll, T. (2010). Bridging policies and practice: Challenges and opportunities for the governance of disability and ageing. *International Journal of Integrated Care*, *10*, 1–7. http://doi.org/10.5334/ijic.522

Nirje, B. (1985). The basis and logic of the normalization principle. *Australia and New Zealand Journal of Developmental Disabilities*, *11*(2), 65–68. https://doi.org/10.3109/13668258509008747

Nirje, B. (1992). *The normalization principle papers*. Uppsala University, Centre for Handicap Research.

Oldman, C. (2002). Later life and the social model of disability: A comfortable partnership?. *Ageing & Society*, *22*(6), 791–806. https://doi.org/10.1017/S0144686X02008887

Putnam, M. (2002). Linking ageing theory and disability models: Increasing the potential to explore ageing with physical impairment. *The Gerontologist*, *42*(6), 799–806. https://doi.org/10.1093/geront/42.6.799

Romo, R. D., Wallhagen, M. I., Yourman, L., Yeung, C. C., Eng, C., Micco, G. ... Smith, A. K. (2013). Perceptions of successful aging among diverse elders with late-life disability. *The Gerontologist*, *53*(6), 939–949. https://doi.org/10.1093/geront/gns160

Rowe, J. W., & Kahn, R. L. (1987). Human aging: Usual and successful. *Science*, *237*(4811), 143–149. https://doi.org/10.1126/science.3299702

Rowe, J. W., & Kahn, R. L. (1997). Successful aging. *The Gerontologist*, *37*(4), 433–440. https://doi.org/10.1093/geront/37.4.433

Rowe, J. W., & Kahn, R. L. (2015). Successful aging 2.0: Conceptual expansions for the 21st century. *The Journals of Gerontology: Series B*, *70*(4), 593–596. https://doi.org/10.1093/geronb/gbv025

Rozanova, J., Northcott, H. C., & McDaniel, S. A. (2006). Seniors and portrayals of intra-generational and inter-generational inequality in the globe and mail. *Canadian Journal on Aging/La Revue Canadienne du Vieillissement*, *25*(4), 373–386. https://doi.org/10.1353/cja.2007.0024

Stone, S. D. (2003). Disability, dependence, and old age: Problematic constructions. *Canadian Journal on Aging/La Revue Canadienne du Vieillissement*, *22*(1), 59–67. https://doi.org/10.1017/S0714980800003731

Strawbridge, W. J., Wallhagen, M. I., & Cohen, R. D. (2002). Successful aging and well-being: Self-rated compared with Rowe and Kahn. *The Gerontologist*, *42*(6), 727–733. https://doi.org/10.1093/geront/42.6.727

Taghizadeh Larsson, A. (2013). Is it possible to 'age successfully' with extensive physical impairments? In E. Jeppsson Grassman & A. Whitaker (Eds.), *Ageing with disability* (pp. 55–71). Policy Press.

Taghizadeh Larsson, A., & Jönson, H. (2018). Ageism and the rights of older people. In L. Ayalon & C. Tesch-Römer (Eds.), *Contemporary perspectives on ageism* (pp. 369–382). Springer Open. https://doi.org/10.1007/978-3-319-73820-8_22

Tideman, M. (2000). *Normalisering och kategorisering: Om handikappideologi och välfärdspolitik i teori och praktik för personer med utvecklingsstörning* [Normalization and categorization: On disability ideology and welfare policy in theory and practice for people with intellectual disabilities]. Lund: Studentlitteratur.

Tornstam, L. (1992). *Åldrandets socialpsykologi* [Social psychology of ageing]. Stockholm: Rabén & Sjögren.

Van Wagenen, A., Driskell, J., & Bradford, J. (2013). "I'm still raring to go": Successful aging among lesbian, gay, bisexual, and transgender older adults. *Journal of Aging Studies*, *27*(1), 1–14. https://doi.org/10.1016/j.jageing.2012.09.001

Villar, F. (2012). Successful ageing and development: The contribution of generativity in older age. *Ageing and Society*, *32*(7), 1087–1105.

Suggested Readings

Jönson, H., & Harnett, T. (2016). Introducing an equal rights framework for older persons in residential care. *The Gerontologist*, *56*(5), 800–806. https://doi.org/10.1093/geront/gnv039

Krassioukova-Enns, O., & Ringaert, L. (2012). Rights and knowledge-based approach to ageing and disability: An overview of issues and approaches. *Social Welfare: Interdisciplinary Approach*, *2*(2), 23–34.

Taghizadeh Larsson, A. (2013). Is it possible to 'age successfully' with extensive physical impairments? In E. Jeppsson Grassman & A. Whitaker (Eds.), *Ageing with disability* (pp. 55–71). Policy Press.

Taghizadeh Larsson, A., & Jönson, H. (2018). Ageism and the rights of older people. In L. Ayalon & C. Tesch-Römer (Eds.), *Contemporary perspectives on ageism* (pp. 369–382). Springer Open.

3

AGEING WITH LIFELONG DISABILITY

Individual Meanings and Experiences Over Time

Lieke van Heumen

Introduction

Ageing has increasingly been recognised as a lifelong process that occurs from birth through death (Elder Jr., Kirkpatrick Johnson, & Crosnoe, 2003). The life course perspective has therefore emerged as a key area of scholarship for understanding ageing (Dannefer, 2011; Elder Jr. et al., 2003). In addition, scholars acknowledge that an understanding of how life is experienced and interpreted by individuals is crucial to comprehending what it means to grow old (Schroots & Birren, 2001). These perspectives have methodological implications (Alkema & Alley, 2006; Jamieson, 2002; McAdams, 2001; Victor, Westerhof, & Bond, 2007) and have led to a vast body of theory and research revolving around individual narratives and life stories (McAdams, 2001) often referred to as narrative gerontology. Narrative gerontology uses the metaphor of life as story. This field of study aims to improve understandings of ageing by exploring the stories older people use to express their experiences (McAdams, 2001). Narrative gerontology explores the various ways in which stories operate in our lives, as well as how we ourselves function as stories. Non-gerontologists have contributed to the development of narrative gerontology, particularly disability scholars (Bornat, 2002).

There are at least two purposes in exploring life stories, to advance our knowledge and to improve lives (Schroots & Birren, 2001). With more knowledge about the life experiences of older adults, their current needs can be better understood. This holds important value for the population ageing with lifelong disability. It is the first time in history that many individuals with lifelong disabilities are living into old age (Mosqueda, 2004). Therefore, those who recently aged into older adulthood are the first generation of this population. This means limited knowledge is available about how they age (Kemp & Mosqueda, 2004). This chapter will outline the life course perspective and life story research and explore their application to the experiences of individuals who are ageing with lifelong disability. Additionally, contemporary understandings of individual meanings and experiences with disability over time will be discussed.

Life Course Perspective

Knowledge of the lifelong context in which individuals develop is needed to understand ageing and what it means for individuals to grow old (Cavanaugh, 1999; Elder Jr. et al., 2003). The life course perspective recognises that ageing is a lifelong process that occurs from birth through death. Individuals shape their own life course with their choices and actions. Life courses are also influenced by the opportunities and limitations individuals experience due to their unique historical and social circumstances.

The individual's place in history operates in the shaping of that person's life (Elder Jr. et al., 2003). The life course perspective also acknowledges that circumstances, events, and behaviour earlier in life (and prenatally) impact development as people age (Elder Jr. et al., 2003).

The life course of individuals is shaped by cohort-historical factors (Elder Jr. et al., 2003; Marshall, 1996; Passuth & Bengtson, 1988). These are events or circumstances that many people in the same culture experience at the same time in their lives. This can provide them with a unique generational identity (Cavanaugh, 1999). The life course perspective also proposes that individual consequences of life transitions, events, and behavioural patterns differ based on their timing in the person's life (Cavanaugh, 1999; Elder Jr. et al., 2003). Individuals from the same cohort can age in different ways if they have different experiences at different times in their lives and follow different pathways as a consequence (Elder, 2001). For example, individuals born during the 1920s in Europe had different exposure to WWII than their slightly younger siblings, who were too young to actively remember the difficult circumstances. Additionally, the war might have delayed the older siblings' education and start of their working and family lives, altering the course of their lives.

Finally, people live their lives interdependently in networks of shared relationships. The life course perspective proposes that individual lives and experiences need to be interpreted with consideration of the individual's significant relationships. Individuals can be impacted by large social changes and the influence of these on other people in their lives (Elder Jr. et al., 2003). For example, economic hardship during the U. S. farm crisis in the 1980s in the state of Iowa caused depression among parents. This in turn impacted child development in negative ways (Conger & Elder Jr., 1994).

Life Course Perspective on Ageing with Lifelong Disability

Little is known about what it is like to grow older with a lifelong disability, and what it is like to live with a disability over many years. Most research on ageing has addressed impairments associated with the ageing process rather than the impact of living a long life with disability or the experience of ageing with previous disabilities (Jeppsson Grassman, Holme, Taghizadeh Larsson, & Whitaker, 2012). There is also little research that has examined the experience of lifelong disability from a life course perspective (Jeppsson Grassman et al., 2012; Kelley-Moore, 2010; Parker Harris, Heller, & Schindler, 2012; Priestley, 2003; Yorkston, McMullan, Molton, & Jensen, 2010). The experiences of young adults, adults of middle age, and older adults tend to be considered independently, without acknowledgment of life course processes (Kelley-Moore, 2010).

There are several reasons that can explain the lack of research on disability that is informed by a life course perspective and addresses ageing issues. First, ageing with lifelong disability is a recent phenomenon. Due to improvements in social and health care, individuals with lifelong disabilities live into older age for the first time in history (Jeppsson Grassman et al., 2012; Mosqueda, 2004). Second, disability tends to be seen as a static condition (Kelley-Moore, 2010) that individuals learn to cope with once and for all using their available resources. There is a lack of recognition of the dynamic nature of disability and the lifelong process of adjustment to evolving needs and coping with secondary conditions (Jeppsson Grassman et al., 2012).

Applying the life course perspective to disability issues through various life stages and across generations is complex, but important to further our understanding of disability (Parker Harris et al., 2012). Exploring disabled lives and ageing experiences from a life course perspective creates a focus on the meaning of disability within life as a whole. It considers when individuals became disabled, how long they have lived with disability, how their disability experience impacted different stages of life, and how old they are at the moment of reflecting on their life with disability (Jeppsson Grassman et al., 2012). Disabling barriers impact people with disabilities of different generations in different ways through the life course. Therefore, there are differences in the life experiences of different age cohorts of persons with disabilities. Furthermore, a life course perspective to disability acknowledges that disability can be experienced differently in different stages of life (Irwin, 2001; Parker Harris et al., 2012).

Universal changes occur for all people as they age, but the rates and nature of change are different based on variability in individual circumstances across the lifespan (Heller & Marks, 2006; Kelley-Moore, 2010; Mosqueda, 2004). The resulting heterogeneity or diversity among older persons was recognised in gerontology as early as the 1970s. The occurrence of poverty and inequality in old age is another common theme in the field. These combined observations have led to the formulation of the cumulative advantage/disadvantage theory. This theory defines cumulative advantage/disadvantage as 'the systemic tendency for inter-individual difference in a given characteristic (e.g., money, health, or status) with the passage of time' (Dannefer, 2003, p. S327). Cumulative advantage/disadvantage has been operationalised not for individuals, but as 'a property of populations or other collectivities (such as cohorts), for which an identifiable set of members can be ranked' (Dannefer, 2003, p. S327).

Early challenging life experiences such as institutionalisation, lack of educational and social opportunities, and low income and poverty are prevalent in the lives of older people with lifelong disabilities. These experiences have formative and cumulative effects on their long-term economic, social, psychological, and physical well-being (Grant, 2005; O'Rand, 2009). Insight into such life experiences is needed to understand the lives of this population. A way to get access to these experiences is by retrieving the stories they share about their lives.

Life Stories

Storytelling is a fundamental aspect of being human. We 'story' our lives, who we are and the world around us. The stories produced by this process concern our lives as a whole – past, present, and future – that is, where we have come from, where we are now, and where we are going, providing them with a sense of unity and purpose (Basting, 2009; Gubrium, 2011; Kenyon & Randall, 2001; McAdams, 2001; Meininger, 2001). The life story consists of various scenes and scripts that make up someone's identity (McAdams, 2001) and is ever changing.

Life stories connect and are created within the context of the larger story that persons live within. Lives are affected by the structure of society, such as social policies, power relations, and economic realities. It is important to realise that such structural dimensions can be crucial constraints, effectively stunting stories, silencing voices, and setting limits to persons' sense of possibility. In the United States, disability policy promoting the rights of people with disabilities only started impacting the opportunities of people with disabilities from the 1970s, following fierce advocacy of the disability rights movement. The 1975 federal Education for all Handicapped Children Act (later renamed the Individuals with Disabilities Education Act) guaranteed the right of all children with disabilities to public education in the most integrated setting appropriate (Longmore, 2009). This meant that children with disabilities' right to an education could no longer be dismissed.

Lives are also affected by sociocultural dimensions, namely the social meanings that are associated with ageing and the life course within a given cultural context (Gubrium, 2011; Kenyon & Randall, 2001; McAdams, 2001). Life stories reflect societal norms, values, and power relationships (McAdams, 2001). For example, people with disabilities encounter discriminatory attitudes on a daily basis as negative beliefs about what it means to live with disability are prevalent in dominant society (Fisher & Purcal, 2017).

Additionally, lives are fundamentally interpersonal. This means that stories exist to be told to others and are shaped by and entwined with the life stories of others. Finally, life stories also have an intrapersonal dimension as individuals create and discover meaning and coherence within each of them uniquely (Gubrium, 2011; Kenyon & Randall, 2001; McAdams, 2001; Meininger, 2005).

Life stories are of particular importance to older adults, as the longer life is, the more there is to be told. The importance of remembering and reviewing life to older adults has been widely acknowledged. Older adults' subjective well-being is impacted not only by their present experiences but also by their past experiences, and their retrospective views on those experiences (Westerhof, Dittman-Kohli, & Thissen, 2001). Life review has been described as a means to age successfully (Butler, 1963) and retrieving memories as an important activity in the last stages of life (Erikson, 1997). Talking about their life is a way for older people to make peace with themselves and their accomplishments. It can also provide them with insight into how they became the person they are today (van den Brandt-van Heek, 2011). In addition, older adults have wisdom to share with younger generations by telling their stories. As people grow older the issue of generativity, the need to guide younger people and support younger generations, may increasingly move to the front and centre of the life story (McAdams, 2001).

Life Story Research with Adults with Lifelong Disability

'Life story research' is the umbrella term used in this chapter to refer to work done with individuals to retrieve their life experiences. Life story research includes different methodological approaches that put individual's lives and experiences and their context in the centre of investigation. Though these different approaches may have distinct characteristics and epistemological roots, they ultimately all aim to reveal lives or segments of lives of people. In-depth, qualitative interviews are the most common means by which researchers conduct life story research (Harrison, 2008). In addition to 'life story research', many different terms are used interchangeably and compete for attention within social sciences, such as 'life history work', 'biography', 'oral history', 'reminiscence', 'narrative analysis', and 'life review'.

One way to distinguish these approaches is to determine how they relate to the subject and what the participation of the subject looks like (Bornat, 2002). Within oral history, life history work, reminiscence, and life review, the subject is an active participant in the research process. In contrast to oral history, life history work can also draw on other data sources, such as surveys or public data, to expand the analysis with the goal to understand social processes. Within reminiscence, retrieving memories aims to achieve improved well-being for the speaker or speakers involved. Life review tends to be conducted with an individual by a professional or practitioner who seeks to assist the individual to understand and reflect on their life as a whole, accepting it in all its aspects, as it has been lived. Life review serves more as an intervention than a research method. However, life history work and oral history often have strong life review aspects within them as well (Bornat, 2002).

Life story research has become a prevalent approach particularly in the intellectual disability field in Europe (e.g. Atkinson, Doeser, & Varga, 2000; Atkinson, Jackson, & Walmsley, 1997; Atkinson & Walmsley, 1999; Cadbury & Whitmore, 2010; Goodley, 1996; Gray, 1997; Hreinsdottir, Stefansdottir, Lewthwaite, Ledger, & Shufflebotham, 2006; Husain, 1997; Mee, 2010; Roets, Goodley, & van Hove, 2007; Roets, Reinaart, & van Hove, 2008; Roets & Van Hove, 2003; Van Puyenbroeck & Maes, 2004). There are three approaches to work with the life experiences and stories of people with intellectual disabilities (Meininger, 2003, 2005; Van Puyenbroeck & Maes, 2008). In each of these, the process is more important than the product. First and foremost, the telling of the story should be meaningful to the individual (Van Puyenbroeck & Maes, 2008). The critical approach aims to recover the voices of people with intellectual disabilities. The facilitator serves as a critical educator who coaches persons with intellectual disabilities to claim authorship and ownership of their own life stories. This approach enhances individuals' awareness of their past (Van Puyenbroeck & Maes, 2008). The person-centred approach refers to 'life story work'. It aims to 'retell, study and discuss life stories in contacts between persons with intellectual disabilities, their relatives and friends and caregivers' (Meininger, 2005, p. 108). Life story work aims to inform individuals who provide everyday support to persons with an intellectual disability about their needs (Meininger, 2003, 2005; van den Brandt-van Heek, 2011) and, therefore, resembles strategies for person-centred planning (Aspinall, 2010; Van Puyenbroeck & Maes, 2008). The focus of this approach is not on empowerment, but rather on dialectical understanding and relational intimacy. One activity using this approach is creating a written record of a life story such as compiling a life book (Van Puyenbroeck & Maes, 2008). In the clinical approach, reminiscence is used as a diagnostic instrument and counselling method (Van Puyenbroeck & Maes, 2008).

For individuals with disabilities, creative and accessible methods should be used that do not rely on the individual's ability to communicate verbally. Life stories can be captured using different media such as a photo album, an audio account, a video report, or a 'memory box', which uses physical objects to represent memories. Multimedia life stories that use computer technology are another possibility to convey the life story. After working with a facilitator to retrieve and create the life story, persons with limited or no verbal communication can present it by pressing keys on the computer keyboard or another device. Music and sounds can be included in multimedia life stories to make it an animated and personal experience (Aspinall, 2010).

Individual Meanings and Experiences of Disability over Time

Life story research with adults ageing with lifelong disabilities provides insights into how they experience living with disability over time, as well as how they experience the ageing process. This section briefly discusses findings from a selection of studies in the small but growing body of work using life story research with older adults with lifelong disabilities.

Experiences with institutionalisation have been documented in life story research with older adults with intellectual disabilities. Cadbury and Whitmore (2010)'s project documented the long life of Patricia Collen in an institution, though she moved into her own home in old age. Mee (2010) facilitated individuals with intellectual disabilities sharing their oral histories with nursing students. The individuals with disabilities shared their negative experiences with being institutionalised.

A small number of studies have retrieved experiences of older adults with intellectual disabilities with ageing. In a study of adults with intellectual disabilities age 40 and older conducted in Ireland, most of the adults who were interviewed described their health as very good to excellent but they also expressed negative views of the consequences of ageing (Burke, McCarron, Carroll, McGlinchey, & McCallion, 2014). Brown and Gill (2009) conducted a participatory study with older women with intellectual disabilities. They found that these women experienced getting older in a mostly negative manner. They thought of ageing as a physical process and considered getting ill and dying as part of ageing. The women also experienced the loss of loved ones, such as parents, friends, or siblings. Some women experienced positive aspects of ageing, such as 'getting discounts' and believed that older people 'deserve more respect'. A study conducted with older women with intellectual disabilities in Israel found that these women desired to be active and were reluctant to retire. Furthermore, they also associated ageing with physical deterioration and decline (David, Duvdevani, & Doron, 2015). In their study in Sweden, Kahlin, Kjellberg, Nord, and Hagberg (2015) also found that older adults with intellectual disabilities characterise ageing as a process of bodily change.

Little is known about the lives of older adults who have serious chronic mental illness. Nearly absent from the literature is research reporting on the perspectives of these individuals on their life experiences. A small life story-oriented interview study by Bülow and Svensson (2013), with seven adults aged from 60 to 72 with long-term mental illness, found their reflections lacked positive evaluation of their early stages of life. Memories of abuse or painful events were rampant. Similarly, positive evaluations of work and professional experiences were lacking. Study participants did not describe employment as important components of their life stories. The researchers remarked that the life stories of adults without disabilities tend to be structured in stages or chapters delineating distinct phases in the life course such as childhood, school, marriage and family, work life, retirement, and present life as an old person. In the life stories of the adults with mental illness in this study, this type of clear structure of life course phases was vague or absent. Participants divided their lives in 'before' and 'after' according to events related to their mental illness, such as when they first experienced symptoms or were first hospitalised. The participants' experiences with being ill permeated most of their life experiences. Experiences related to work and family life complemented their experiences with mental illness rather than the other way around. Within the context of long-term experiences with psychiatric care and other supports, participants felt it had been difficult to assert self-determination and control over their own lives. The authors of the study remarked that the illness experience overshadowed other concerns in old age. Participants carried the illness they had lived with for most of their lives into older adulthood and as a result some of the challenging experiences of ageing experienced by others, such as shrinking autonomy were not as noticeable. Their illness did not change in a significant way when they became an older person. The participants shared experiences of loneliness. Finally, they shared concern about the future related to having to receive inpatient care as well as to the use of new medication with more challenging side effects.

Shibusawa and Padgett (2009) completed 44 life history interviews with 25 adults with mental illness in New York City aged from 40 to 62 who had also been homeless. Many of the participants spoke about their lives with a sense of loss and regret about their past. In reflecting on their lives, some participants felt they matured as they entered mid-life and later adulthood. Many had struggled with feelings of being out of sync with their peers without mental illness. Some considered this to be caused by the severe deprivation caused by homelessness and associated survival mechanisms. Others felt that their behaviour set them apart and caused others to worry about them. Additionally, participants experienced the negative impact of stigma, and awareness of their age sometimes increased these feelings. Voluntary or involuntary institutionalisation brought participants the benefit of being temporarily relieved from the deprivations and temptations of life on the street. Being jailed or hospitalised involuntarily was not viewed as desirable by the participants, though they did consider these stays as a time to evaluate their lives. Participants were very aware of high illness and death rates among homeless individuals and they suspected their own life spans were going to be shortened.

A series of studies by Jeppsson Grassman and colleagues (2012) with older adults with physical disabilities in Sweden demonstrated that despite disability policy reforms in their lifetimes, they experienced many challenges to full participation in society. Some respondents said that they felt less concerned about aspects of their lives and bodies compared to their younger years. For example, they were not as concerned with their appearance or what others thought of them. The authors observed that age was of secondary importance in the lived experiences of adults who lived a long life with disability. Many of the study participants expressed concern about their future, particularly the possibility of receiving enough assistance.

Conclusion

Future research should apply the life course perspective to the experiences of adults ageing with lifelong disabilities and needs to take into account the impact of early life experiences on long-term health and well-being. The perspectives of older adults with lifelong disabilities on their lives continue to be a rare topic of investigation. Their lived experiences and those aspects of their lives that bring happiness, joy, and meaning should be examined. Such knowledge is important in designing effective policies and supports to meet the needs of this population.

There is a need for more inclusive approaches to research with adults with disabilities to increase the relevance and quality of research (Walmsley & Johnson, 2003). In inclusive research, adults with disabilities serve as active partners and not only as respondents or subjects. Additionally, research needs to be more accessible to adults with disabilities. Research methods and procedures should fit the population to be studied, and not the other way around. This requires an investment and commitment on the part of researchers, and a dedication to flexible approaches that meet individual needs of research participants with disabilities.

The application of life story work in support practices for older adults with disabilities holds the promise of bringing a meaningful experience to this population. Yet, life story work is not yet widespread in systems of services and supports. As more people age with lifelong disability, the field needs to expand and apply new techniques and methods to promote this population's well-being.

References

Alkema, G. E., & Alley, D. E. (2006). Gerontology's future: An integrative model for disciplinary advancement. *The Gerontologist, 46*(5), 574–582. http://dx.doi.org/10.1093/geront/46.5.574

Aspinall, A. (2010). Creativity, choice and control: The use of multimedia life story work as a tool to facilitate access. In J. Seale & M. Nind (Eds.), *Understanding and promoting access for people with learning difficulties. Seeing the opportunities and challenges of risk* (pp. 43–54). Routledge.

Atkinson, D., Doeser, M. C., & Varga, A. K. (Eds.). (2000). *Good times, bad times: Women with learning difficulties telling their stories*. BILD Publications.

Atkinson, D., Jackson, M., & Walmsley, J. (1997). *Forgotten lives: Exploring the history of learning disability*. BILD Publications.

Atkinson, D., & Walmsley, J. (1999). Using autobiographical approaches with people with learning difficulties. *Disability & Society, 14*(2), 203–216. http://dx.doi.org/10.1080/09687599926271

Basting, A. D. (2009). *Forget memory: Creating better lives for people with dementia*. The Johns Hopkins University Press.

Bornat, J. (2002). Doing life history research. In A. Jamieson & C. Victor (Eds.), *Researching ageing and later life: The practice of social gerontology*. Open University Press.

Brown, A. A., & Gill, C. (2009). New voices in women's health: Perceptions of women with intellectual and developmental disabilities. *Intellectual and Developmental Disabilities, 47*(5), 337–347.

Bülow, P., & Svensson, T. (2013). Being one's illness: On mental disability and ageing. In E. Jeppsson Grassman & A. Whitaker (Eds.), *Ageing with disability. A life course perspective*. Policy Press, University of Bristol/University of Chicago.

Burke, E., McCarron, M., Carroll, R., McGlinchey, E., & McCallion, P. (2014). What it's like to grow older: The ageing perceptions of people with an intellectual disability in Ireland. *Intellectual and Developmental Disabilities, 52*(3), 205–219. https://doi.org/10.1352/1934-9556-52.3.205

Butler, R. N. (1963). The life review: An interpretation of reminiscence in the aged. *Psychiatry, 26*, 65–76.

Cadbury, H., & Whitmore, M. (2010). Spending time in Normansfield: Changes in the day to day life of Patricia Collen. *British Journal of Learning Disabilities, 38*, 120–126. http://dx.doi.org/10.1111/j.1468-3156.2010.00636.x

Cavanaugh, J. C. (1999). Theories of ageing in the biological, behavioural and social sciences. In J. C. Cavanaugh & S. K. Whitbourne (Eds.), *Gerontology: An interdisciplinary perspective* (pp. 46–357). Oxford University Press.

Conger, R. D., & Elder, G. H. Jr. (1994). *Families in troubled times: Adapting to change in rural America*. Routledge.

Dannefer, D. (2003). Cumulative advantage/disadvantage and the life course: Cross-fertilizing age and social science theory. *Journal of Gerontology: Social Sciences, 58*, S327–S337. http://dx.doi.org/10.1093/geronb/58.6.S327

Dannefer, D. (2011). Age, the life course, and the sociological imagination: Prospects for theory. In R. H. Binstock & L. K. George (Eds.), *Handbook of ageing and the social sciences* (pp. 3–13). Academic Press.

David, N., Duvdevani, I., & Doron, I., (2015). Older women with intellectual disability and the meaning of ageing. *Journal of Women & Ageing, 27*(3), 216–236. https://doi.org/10.1080/08952841.2014.933608

Elder, G. H. (2001). Life course. In G. L. Maddox (Ed.), *The encyclopedia of ageing* (pp. 593–596). Springer.

Elder, G. H. Jr., Kirkpatrick Johnson, M., & Crosnoe, R. (2003). The emergence and development of life course theory. In J. T. Mortimer & M. J. Shanahan (Eds.), *Handbook of the life course* (pp. 3–19). Springer.

Erikson, E. (1997). *The life cycle completed*. W. W. Norton.

Fisher, K. R., & Purcal, C., 2017. Policies to change attitudes to people with disabilities. *Scandinavian Journal of Disability Research, 19*(2), 161–174. http://doi.org/10.1080/15017419.2016.1222303

Goodley, D. (1996). Tales of hidden lives: A critical examination of life history research with people who have learning difficulties. *Disability and Society, 11*(3), 333–348. http://dx.doi.org/10.1080/09687599627642

Grant, G. (2005). Healthy and successful ageing. In G. Grant, P. Goward, M. Richardson, & P. Ramcharan (Eds.), *Learning disability: A life cycle approach to valuing people* (pp. 469–490). Open University Press.

Gray, G. (1997). *A long day at the seaside*. Reedprint.

Gubrium, J. F. (2011). Narrative events and biographical construction in old age. In G. Kenyon, E. Bohlmeijer & W. L. Randall (Eds.), *Storying later life. Issues, investigations, and interventions in narrative gerontology* (pp. 126–142). Oxford University Press.

Harrison, B. (2008). Editors' introduction: Researching lives and the lived experience. In B. Harrison (Ed.), *Life story research* (pp. xxii–xlvi). Sage.

Heller, T., & Marks, B. (2006). Ageing. In G. L. Albrecht (Ed.), *Encyclopedia of disability* (Vol. 1, pp. 67–78). Sage Publications, Inc.

Hreinsdottir, E. E., Stefansdottir, G., Lewthwaite, A., Ledger, S., & Shufflebotham, L. (2006). Is my story so different from yours? Comparing life stories, experiences of institutionalisation and self-advocacy in England and Iceland. *British Journal of Learning Disabilities, 34*(3), 157–166. http://dx.doi.org/10.1111/j.1468-3156.2006.00417.x

Husain, F. (1997). Life story work for people with learning disabilities. *British Journal of Learning Disabilities, 25*(2), 73–76. http://dx.doi.org/10.1111/j.1468-3156.1997.tb00014.x

Irwin, S. (2001). Repositioning disability and the life course: A social claiming perspective. In M. Priestley (Ed.), *Disability and the life course: Global perspectives*. Cambridge University Press.

Jamieson, A. (2002). Theory and practice in social gerontology. In A. Jamieson & C. Victor (Eds.), *Researching ageing and later life. The practice of social gerontology* (pp. 7–20). Open University Press.

Jeppsson Grassman, E., Holme, L., Taghizadeh Larsson, A., & Whitaker, A. (2012). A long life with a particular signature: Life course and ageing for people with disabilities. *Journal of Gerontological Social Work, 55*(2), 95–111.

Kahlin, I., Kjellberg, A., Nord, C., & Hagberg, J. E. (2015). Lived experiences of ageing and later life in older people with intellectual disabilities. *Ageing & Society, 35*(3), 602–618. https://doi.org/10.1017/S0144686X13000949.

Kelley-Moore, J. A. (2010). Disability and ageing: The social construction of causality. In D. Dannefer & C. Phillipson (Eds.), *The SAGE handbook of social gerontology* (pp. 96–110). Sage Publishers.

Kemp, B. J., & Mosqueda, L. (2004). Introduction. In B. J. Kemp & L. Mosqueda (Eds.), *Ageing with a disability: What the clinician needs to know* (pp. 1–5). John Hopkins University Press.

Kenyon, G. M., & Randall, W. L. (2001). Narrative gerontology: An overview. In G. Kenyon, P. Clark & B. de Vries (Eds.), *Narrative gerontology. Theory, research and practice* (pp. vii–ix). Springer Publishing Company.

Longmore, P. (2009). Disability rights movement. In S. Burch (Ed). *Encyclopedia of American disability history* (pp. 280–285). Facts on File, Inc.

Marshall, V. W. (1996). The state of theory in ageing and the social sciences. In R. H. Binstock & L. K. George (Eds.), *Handbook of ageing and the social sciences* (4th ed., pp. 12–30). Academic Press.

McAdams, D. P. (2001). The psychology of life stories. *Review of General Psychology, 5*(2), 100–122. http://dx.doi.org/10.1037/1089-2680.5.2.100

Mee, S. (2010). You're not to dance with the girls: Oral history, changing perception and practice. *Journal of Intellectual Disabilities, 14*(1), 33–42. http://dx.doi.org/10.1177/1744629510373053

Meininger, H. P. (2001). Autonomy and professional responsibility in care for persons with intellectual disabilities. *Nursing Philosophy, 2*(3), 240–250.

Meininger, H. P. (2003). Werken met levensverhalen: Een narratief-ethische verkenning [Work with lifestories: A narrative-ethical exploration]. *Nederlands Tijdschrift voor de Zorg aan Verstandelijk Gehandicapten [Dutch Journal on Support for People with Intellectual Disabilities], 29*(2), 102–119.

Meininger, H. P. (2005). Narrative ethics in nursing for persons with intellectual disabilities. *Nursing Philosophy, 6*(2), 106–118. http://dx.doi.org/10.1111/j.1466-769X.2005.00206.x

Mosqueda, L. (2004). Psychological changes and secondary conditions. In B. J. Kemp & L. Mosqueda (Eds.), *Ageing with a disability* (pp. 35–47). Johns Hopkins University Press.

O'Rand, A. M. (2009). Cumulative processes in the life course. In G. H. Elder, Jr., & J. Z. Giele (Eds.), *The craft of life course research* (pp. 121–140). The Guilford Press.

Parker Harris, S., Heller, T., & Schindler, A. (2012). Introduction, background and history. In T. Heller & S. P. Harris (Eds.), *Disability through the life course*. Sage Publications, Inc.

Passuth, P. M., & Bengtson, V. L. (1988). Sociological theories of ageing: Current perspectives and future directions. In J. E. Birren & V. L. Bengtson (Eds.), *Emergent theories of ageing* (pp. 333–355). Springer.

Priestley, M. (2003). *Disability. A life course approach*. Polity Press.

Roets, G., Goodley, D., & van Hove, G. (2007). Narrative in a nutshell: Sharing hopes, fears, and dreams with self-advocates. *Intellectual and Developmental Disabilities, 45*(5), 323–334. http://dx.doi.org/10.1352/0047-6765(2007)45[323:NIANSH]2.0.CO;2

Roets, G., Reinaart, R., & Van Hove, G. (2008). Living between borderlands: Discovering a sense of nomadic subjectivity throughout Rosa's life story. *Journal of Gender Studies, 17*(2), 99–115. http://dx.doi.org/10.1080/09589230802008865

Roets, G., & Van Hove, G. (2003). The story of Belle, Minnie, Louise and the Sovjets. Throwing light on the dark side of an institution. *Disability & Society, 18*(5), 599–624. http://dx.doi.org/10.1080/0968759032000097843

Schroots, J. J. F., & Birren, J. E. (2001). The study of lives in progress: Approaches to research on life stories. In G. D. Rowles & N. E. Schoenberg (Eds.), *Qualitative gerontology: Perspectives for a new century* (pp. 51–67). Springer Publishing Company.

Shibusawa, T., & Padgett, D. (2009). The experiences of "ageing" among formerly homeless adults with chronic mental illness: A qualitative study. *The Journal of Ageing Studies, 23*(3), 188–196. https://doi.org/10.1016/j.jageing.2007.12.019

van den Brandt-van Heek, M. (2011). Asking the right questions: Enabling persons with dementia to speak for themselves. In G. Kenyon, E. Bohlmeijer & W. L. Randall (Eds.), *Storying later life. Issues, investigations and interventions in narrative gerontology* (pp. 338–353). Oxford University Press.

Van Puyenbroeck, J., & Maes, B. (2004). De betekenis van reminiscentie in de begeleiding van ouder wordende mensen met verstandelijke beperkingen. Een kwalitatieve verkenning [The meaning of reminiscence in the support of ageing people with intellectual disabilities. A qualitative exploration]. *Nederlands Tijdschrift voor de Zorg aan Mensen met Verstandelijke Beperkingen [Dutch Journal on Support for People with Intellectual Disabilities]*, *30*, 146–165.

Van Puyenbroeck, J., & Maes,, B. (2008). A review of critical, person-centred and clinical approaches to reminiscence work for people with intellectual disabilities. *International Journal of Disability, Development and Education*, *55*(1), 43–60. http://dx.doi.org/10.1080/10349120701827979

Victor, C., Westerhof, G. J., & Bond, J. (2007). Researching ageing. In J. Bond, S. Peace, F. Dittman-Kohli & G. J. Westerhof (Eds.), *Ageing in society* (pp. 85–112). Sage Publications.

Walmsley, J., & Johnson, K. (2003). *Inclusive research with people with learning disabilities: Past, present and futures*. Jessica Kingsley Publishers.

Westerhof, G. J., Dittman-Kohli, F., & Thissen, T. (2001). Beyond life satisfaction: Lay conceptions of well-being among middle-aged and elderly adults. *Social Indicators Research*, *56*(2), 179–203.

Yorkston, K. M., McMullan, K. A., Molton, I., & Jensen, M. P. (2010). Pathways of change experience by people ageing with disability: A focus group study. *Disability and Rehabilitation*, *32*(20), 1697–1704.

Suggested Readings

Heller, T., & Parker Harris, S. (2012). *Disability through the life course*. Sage Publications, Inc. http://dx.doi.org/10.4135/9781412994217.

Heller, T., & van Heumen, L. (2013). Ageing with disability. In M. Wehmeyer (Ed.), *Oxford handbook of positive psychology and disability* (pp. 409–423). Oxford University Press. http://dx.doi.org/10.1093/oxfordhb/9780195398786.013.013.0025

Jeppsson Grassman, E., & Whitaker, A. (Eds.), (2013). *Ageing with disability. A lifecourse perspective*. Policy Press. http://dx.doi.org/10.1332/policypress/9781447305224.001.0001

Priestley, M. (2003). *Disability. A life course approach*. Polity Press.

4
INTEGRATING CRITICAL DISABILITY STUDIES AND CRITICAL GERONTOLOGY TO EXPLORE THE COMPLEXITIES OF AGEING WITH DISABILITIES

Hailee M. Yoshizaki-Gibbons

Introduction

As the average lifespan of people with lifelong disabilities increases into their seventh decade and beyond, new approaches are needed to understand the social, structural, and cultural factors that influence their experiences and lives. Critical gerontology and critical disability studies are two fields in which scholars and activists seek to critically explore the complexity of ageing and disability and work towards a more just and inclusive society for old and disabled people. Although critical gerontology and critical disability studies have historically been distinct fields, there are a growing number of scholars and activists seeking to integrate these critical perspectives in their work on ageing and disability. There are extensive possibilities for scholarly and activist work that draws from both critical gerontology and critical disability studies, particularly as growing numbers of people are ageing with lifelong disabilities (Yoshizaki-Gibbons, 2018a).

In this chapter, I argue that drawing from critical gerontology and critical disability studies will allow scholars to gain a deeper understanding of the diverse experiences of people ageing with disabilities and the social, structural, political, economic, and cultural factors that influence their experiences. First, I provide a brief overview of critical gerontology and critical disability studies. Then, I elucidate the distinct histories of these two fields of study, highlighting the ways they have often been on parallel paths with limited collaboration or convergence. Next, I employ a narrative methodology to examine the life story of Corbett O'Toole, a queer, old, disabled woman who has aged with disabilities, using critical gerontology and critical disability studies perspectives, contending that this interdisciplinary analysis emphasises the unique ways people ageing with disabilities are marginalised throughout their life course and in ways that often culminate in later life. I contend that integrating critical gerontology and critical disability studies perspectives uncovers the ways that anti-ageing and anti-disability discourses interact in the lives of those ageing with disabilities. Finally, I consider future possibilities for further intersections between critical gerontology and critical disability studies in explorations of ageing with disability.

What is Critical Gerontology?

Gerontology is the study of the ageing process and older adults. According to Bass (2009), 'Gerontology sought to bridge the worlds of life sciences, medicine, and the social sciences in a comprehensive view of the ageing individual within a larger societal context' (p. 349). Since the discipline's beginning in the 1940s, gerontology has been dominated by scholarship that aligns itself with the medical, natural, and social sciences and produces research grounded in positivism, or the epistemological belief that reality can be measured and 'objective' knowledge produced through scientific research (Baars & Phillipson, 2013). Critical gerontology emerged from gerontology as scholars increasingly engaged with critical perspectives and theories to critique constructions of ageing that did not consider researcher subjectivity or the social and structural contexts in which people age. Hence, critical gerontology has critiqued much of the knowledge base in mainstream gerontology due to its alignment with the medical, natural, and social sciences and their claims to produce 'neutral' or 'objective' knowledge about ageing.

Bass (2009) characterised critical gerontology as a broad category of scholars working in the areas of 'political economy, moral economy, feminist theory, cumulative advantage/disadvantage, or structured dependency of ageing' (p. 356). These perspectives share an emphasis on power, privilege, oppression, social structures, social inequalities, and social justice. In alignment with its critical focus, critical gerontology is an interdisciplinary field, drawing from the social sciences and humanities to complicate traditional, medicalised views of ageing and further develop diverse social and cultural perspectives on old age and ageing. Accordingly, Estes and Phillipson (2007) stated that the overall project of critical gerontology is 'to provide alternative theoretical frameworks and emancipatory knowledge' (p. 330). Critical gerontology has thus produced important analyses related to ageing and old age that in mainstream gerontology have been historically ignored or marginalised.

What is Critical Disability Studies?

Disability studies examines disability from social, political, cultural, economic, and structural perspectives. Rather than viewing disability as an individual, pathological, or medical problem, disability studies explores disability as a social and cultural construction, a politicised identity, and a lived experience influenced by capitalism, medicine, law, politics, and cultural discourses (Goodley, Lawthom, Liddiard, & Runswick-Cole, 2019). Disability studies is an interdisciplinary field that draws from the humanities, arts, and social sciences. The field emerged in conjunction with the growing disability rights movement, and as such, is highly concerned with civil and human rights and social justice. As Linton (2005) noted, 'Disability studies' project is to weave disabled people back into the fabric of society, thread by thread, theory by theory' (p. 518). Hence, disability studies has been and continues to be empowering and liberating for disabled people.

Critical disability studies represents a turn in the field of disability studies, as scholars explore disability in progressively complex ways, challenge and enhance existing models and frameworks, and increasingly apply diverse critical social theories to the study of disability (Goodley, 2016; Goodley et al., 2019; Yoshizaki-Gibbons, 2018b). Some scholars view critical disability studies as a paradigm shift, distinct from the field of disability studies (Shildrick, 2012), whereas others conceptualise critical disability studies as the latest wave in the maturation of disability studies (Meekosha & Shuttleworth, 2009). Regardless of one's approach to the field, critical disability studies scholars are united by their commitment to broaden current and traditional understandings of disability.

According to Goodley (2016), critical disability studies is a 'location populated by people who advocate building upon the foundational perspectives of disability studies whilst integrating new and transformative agendas associated with postcolonial, queer and feminist theories' (pp. 190–191). Given critical disability studies' orientation, disability serves as a starting point to analyse and critique wide ranging cultural and social structures and systems. As noted by Yoshizaki-Gibbons (2018b), 'Critical disability studies is concerned with disability but also more broadly with issues connected to disability that affect all people, such as bodily experiences, identity, care, difference, power, and globalization' (p. 149). Consequently, critical disability studies has generated varied and important ways of critically analysing disability in diverse contexts, thereby enhancing the ways disability is understood throughout the world.

The Parallel Paths of Critical Gerontology and Critical Disability Studies

Critical gerontology and critical disability studies share several significant values: (a) emphasising structural, cultural, and social factors, (b) drawing from critical theories and frameworks, (c) centring the lives of old/disabled people, and (d) including the voices and perspectives of old/disabled people. However, despite these commonalities and the growing understanding that disability and ageing interweave throughout the life course, critical gerontology and critical disability studies have historically been distinct areas of study with unique histories, trajectories, and approaches (Gibbons, 2016; Verbrugge & Yang, 2002). As noted by Gibbons (2016), critical gerontology and critical disability studies are 'fields on parallel paths' that 'rarely intersect' (pp. 73-74). Consequently, there has been limited collaboration and integration between these two critical fields.

The divergences between critical gerontology and critical disability studies are partly rooted in dominant cultural discourses that link old age and disability. Due to this strong cultural association, referred to as 'the social construction of causality' by Kelley-Moore (2010), illness, impairment, pain, and frailty are considered 'normal' for old people but 'abnormal' for young or middle-aged people. These deeply embedded assumptions likely influenced critical gerontology and critical disability studies to focus primarily on their 'proper objects of study' (Butler, 1994). Gerontologists sought to challenge the dominant societal ideas that old age is equated with disability and that ageing is solely a process of decline and dependence, while disability studies scholars contested the beliefs that being disabled precludes economic, educational, political, cultural, and social participation (Yoshizaki-Gibbons, 2018a).

As a result, a great deal of critical gerontology and critical disability studies scholarship and activism historically evolved within 'a generational system' (Priestley, 2003), with a particular emphasis on roles associated with being an old person versus roles associated with being a young or middle-aged person, and with old age and disability approached as distinct. As noted by Sheets (2005), 'Ageing agenda priorities have focused on old age and retirement issues. Disability agenda priorities have reflected the needs of a younger constituency and have broadly focused on education, rehabilitation, independent living, and employment' (p. 40). This generational system limited critical disability studies and critical gerontology from examining disability from a life course perspective, which is essential to understand the lived experiences and social structural conditions of people ageing with disabilities. Furthermore, although critical gerontology and critical disability are both deeply concerned with oppression, the delineation of the fields within a generational system has resulted in critical gerontology focusing primarily on ageism and critical disability studies focusing primarily on ableism. These distinct foci hinder understandings of how people ageing with disabilities experience ageism and ableism in varying ways throughout the life course.

In recent years, there have been increasing numbers of scholars and activists calling for and engaging in collaborations between critical gerontology and critical disability studies (Yoshizaki-Gibbons, 2018a). Despite this, ageing with disability is still not a central area of focus in either field. The limited connections between critical gerontology and critical disability studies has had implications on academic, cultural, and societal understandings of the lived experiences of those ageing with disabilities. Molton and Yorkston (2017) observed:

> For able-bodied individuals, significant disability tends to develop late in life, whereas, for individuals with long-term impairments...onset of disability is typically in the first four decades. This variability in onset and trajectory makes for important differences in the developmental life course. (p. 291)

Given that people ageing with disabilities exist at the intersections of age and disability, it is important to draw from critical gerontology and critical disability studies to engage in interdisciplinary explorations of their lived experiences and the cultural and social contexts in which these experiences occur.

'As We Get Older, We Get Poorer': Corbett O'Toole's Story

In order to centre the voices of those ageing with disabilities and to further elucidate the ways anti-ageing and anti-disability discourses and practices intersect for those ageing with disabilities, I employ a narrative methodology to share the life story of Corbett O'Toole, who has been disabled throughout her life and is now navigating old age. I then draw on critical gerontology and critical disability studies to demonstrate how integrating these perspectives provides deeper, more complex ways of understanding the experiences of ageing with disabilities. Analysing Corbett's experiences through critical gerontology and critical disability studies standpoints uncovers the unique forms of oppression people ageing with disabilities experience, particularly in ways that are also racialised, gendered, and classed.

Corbett is a queer, disabled elder in disability communities and a writer, artist, and public speaker. She was born in 1951. Her mother and father are from families of Irish immigrants. When Corbett was two years old, she contracted polio, which resulted in paralysis. She was placed in a full body cast for two years, and then was taken to a rehabilitation centre to learn to walk. As a child, Corbett and her family were told by medical and rehabilitation professionals that she would be walking with mobility aids such as canes and crutches for the rest of her life. However, as Corbett aged, she found that these doctors, nurses, social workers, and therapists had very limited knowledge of what it meant to age with polio and what her experience of ageing might be like over her life course.

> By the time I was twenty, I was walking with a cane. By the time I was thirty, I was using a wheelchair. Because the paediatric people had a paediatric view, they didn't have a life view.

Despite the significant number of people who had polio before it was eradicated and the prominence of people with polio such as President Franklin D. Roosevelt, Corbett quickly learned that there was limited information about what it meant to age with polio, particularly within the medical industrial complex.

> There was a huge patient population, but the information wasn't being captured in a way that communicated from children's medicine to adult medicine. [...] So much about ageing with a disability has been [that] nobody knows, there has been nobody outside of disabled people to tell me what's coming next or what's in the future, and medicine has been wrong and useless most of the time in terms of helping with that.

Although Corbett's future was uncertain, she understood from a young age that she was expected to work, particularly given the prominence of President Roosevelt. As a disabled woman in a working-class family, Corbett was encouraged to focus on working rather than starting her own family.

> The focus for me in my working-class family was my sisters could get married and have a husband, but I was supposed to work. And in those days, it was secretary, teacher, or nurse, for my generation, my class, my race.

Given these options, Corbett elected to become a teacher and earned a Bachelor's degree in Special Education. After college, she ended up in Berkeley, California, where she was suddenly immersed in disability communities and disability rights movements. By the age of 40, Corbett was unable to sustain full time work.

> I ended up stepping out of the paid workforce at the age of forty, because working full time—it became like a 14-hour a day job. To get ready, to get public transportation, to get to work, to do the eight hours, nine hours of work, to get home. [...] My entire life was just keeping me together enough to keep going back to work.

Corbett had been told she would be able to have a 'normal' working life but learned that was not the case for her body and mind. Corbett quit her job and began receiving Social Security Disability Insurance (SSDI) benefits for disabled workers. She had an additional safety net because the job she held prior to receiving SSDI provided long-term benefits, including health insurance and supplemental income, which would cover her until age 65. Corbett then began exploring other ways she could contribute through her disability rights activism.

> As I became less and less able to work—again this is the whole thing of they tell you one thing and it's another—I had to find a new way of thinking about how to be useful, because our society is predicated on people being productive workers.

Ultimately, Corbett drew on her experiences with teaching to begin training others and engaging in public speaking around disability. At the time, she classified herself as at the lower end of the working class, but still felt she was comfortable. During this time period, when she was in her 40s, she also adopted a daughter from Japan, and switched from a manual wheelchair to a power wheelchair so that she could maintain mobility while holding and caring for her daughter.

However, as Corbett aged, her financial precarity increased significantly. The amount of money she received from SSDI each month from the age of 40 on was stagnant. Then, at the age of 65, her 'Cadillac' employer insurance ended, and she had to enrol in Medicare (public health insurance for older adults), which only reimburses her for 80% of her medical expenses. Her supplemental income from her previous employer also ended. At the age of 66, she was transitioned from SSDI to Social Security Retirement Benefits, but found that the monthly amount she received was still low and remained static.

> So, for 25 years, my income didn't rise but...the world around me rose quite a bit. So, when I went out on disability, I was—if you looked at those poverty level charts, I was kind of comfortably working-class. So, I qualified for some programs and not others. Over time, I have literally dropped off the bottom of extremely poor.

To alleviate her cost of living and continue living in the community, Corbett attempted to receive subsidised housing. Over the course of ten years, she continuously tried to obtain a federal Section 8 certificate that would cap the amount of rent she paid, but was unsuccessful as there were inadequate vouchers available for the number of people who qualified for them. She noted that many of the public 'safety nets' were either inadequate or unavailable, contributing to her financial precarity and placing her at risk for homelessness or institutionalisation in a nursing home, which would be fully funded by the State through federal public insurance.

> Yes, on one hand there's sort of this quasi-safety net, but on the other hand, the economy has... shifted so dramatically that the middle and working-class have become poorer and poorer, and as they've been pushed down poorer and poorer, people like me on fixed incomes have literally gone under.

Corbett found her experience of ageing increasingly precarious, in large part due to poverty.

> My income is decreasing, my housing costs are increasing, my medical costs are increasing, I have no ability to get my equipment maintained, and at every juncture, it's like the system is saying, we will be glad to put you in a nursing home. And it's like, it's my fault! You know, I can't get help for the stuff I need help for.

Corbett increasingly felt she was trapped in what she described as a 'poverty to nursing home pipeline', in which she is doing all she can to avoid institutionalisation, but the threat continues to loom, and poverty makes it nearly impossible to avoid.

> I feel like as I've aged, I've become actually more visibly disabled, so I am dealing with more ableism, more often, and also, my fears of institutionalization are becoming much more real, cause now I am in more categories of risk for institutionalization. Like when I could walk, I felt like I was safer…I was less likely to be seen as somebody who should be in a nursing home. Now that I'm not walking anymore and I use a powerchair, I feel like I'm much more easily tracked. I'm moving into more and more demographics…older people, sicker people, people that see the doctors more, people that fall down or have a risk of falling, people that use mobility devices, I feel like the number of ways [the nursing home industry] can get me [is increasing], and then the poverty just makes it all worse.

As a person immersed in disability communities and in connection with many people ageing with disabilities, Corbett was acutely aware that her experiences were not singular. As she lamented, 'For me and for a whole lot of other disabled people…as we get older, we get poorer'.

Integrating Critical Gerontology and Critical Disability Studies

Analysing Corbett's narrative through the lenses of critical gerontology and critical disability studies demonstrates the ways ageing and disability intersect through the life course for those ageing with disabilities. Scholars working from mainstream gerontology perspectives might analyse Corbett's narrative with an emphasis on how her impairments are intensifying as she ages and they might suggest interventions that would assist Corbett in maintaining or improving her abilities and remaining as independent as possible. Likewise, scholars using traditional disability studies perspectives might have focused on how Corbett's experiences were influenced by the medical model of disability – which understands disability as an individual, medical problem – and could be improved through the application of the social model of disability – which understands disability as socially constructed and advocates for environmental and social changes to make society more accessible and inclusive for disabled people. While such analyses are important and needed, using an individualised, medicalised approach or focusing primarily on the social model disregards or obscures the larger economic, political, social, and cultural context in which Corbett is ageing.

Critical disability studies and critical gerontology provide a framework for scholars to interrogate the structural, cultural, and social factors that influence how people age with disabilities. In particular, I argue that integrating critical gerontology and critical disability studies perspectives highlights the ways that neoliberal capitalism has transformed the meanings of ageing and disability by forwarding ideologies of self-reliance and personal responsibility to enforce compulsory able-bodiedness/able-mindedness and compulsory youthfulness. In turn, these systems discipline disabled, ageing bodies into exploitable consumers in need of market-based solutions, rather than state support. For those ageing with disabilities such as Corbett, these forms of marginalisation occur throughout the life course and are often exacerbated in old age. In what follows, I analyse Corbett's narrative using critical disability studies and critical gerontology perspectives to demonstrate the potential of integrating these critical fields.

Neoliberal Capitalism and Political Economy

As Corbett aged with a disability, her economic status and the political context in which she was ageing played a significant role in her life. Her life course was strongly influenced by the political economy – a central framework in both critical gerontology and critical disability studies. According to Kail, Quadagno, and Keene (2009), the political economy comprises 'the social, political, and economic processes involved in the distribution of scarce resources and the ways that the state and market economy participate in shaping the redistribution effort' (p. 555). Hence, the political economy perspective recognises the ways in which aspects of economics, such as distribution and trade, are interconnected with politics, such as governmental laws and policies. Examining the political economies of ageing and disability elucidates the institutional and structural forces that play a significant role in the ways ageing and disability is constructed socially, culturally, and in public policy (Estes, 2001; Russell, 2001). Hence, analysis of political economies requires a systemic viewpoint, predicated on the belief that ageing and disability must be examined in the wider economic, political, and societal context in which they occur.

Critical gerontologists and critical disability studies scholars have particularly highlighted the ways in which neoliberal capitalism influences the political economy of ageing and disability. Neoliberalism has had a profound economic and social impact in the United States and throughout the world. The rise of neoliberalism began in the 1970s and 1980s, during which time falling profit rates and global competition incited politicians and business interests to attempt to revitalise the economies of nation states throughout the world (Duggan, 2003; Harvey, 2005). According to Duggan (2003), the 'architects' of contemporary neoliberalism drew from classic liberalism, which idealised free markets and minimal governments. Harvey (2005) defined neoliberalism as 'a theory of political economic practices that proposes human well-being can best be advanced by liberating individual entrepreneurial freedoms and skills within an institutional framework characterised by strong private property rights, free markets, and free trade' (p. 1). Hence, neoliberalism promotes competitive self-interest, individualism, and the free market as key organising doctrines of society.

According to Soldatic and Meekosha (2012), neoliberalism manifests in various ways through the political economy, state formations, and ideologies. Thus, as an economic, political, and ideological force, neoliberalism is deeply entrenched in various cultural and societal institutions, such as public policy and the media (Douglas, 2014; Estes, 2014). For old and disabled people, as well as other oppressed groups, the effects of neoliberalism have been devastating. Duggan (2003) noted that neoliberalism's emphasis on individualism, competition, and market discipline resulted in 'a vision of national and world order [characterized by]…inequality…public austerity…and "law and order"' (p. x). Thus, neoliberalism disproportionately impacts people marginalised by age, disability, race, gender, class, sexuality, and other social identities.

As the neoliberal political economy supports competition, privatisation, and free and unregulated markets, it has contributed to the economic and social marginalisation of old and disabled people, including those ageing with disabilities (Polivka, 2011; Russell, 2001). One of the key ways a neoliberal political economy has exploited old and disabled bodies is by emphasising private, consumer-based solutions to the 'problems' of old age and disability and minimising or eradicating public, federal and state funded services and supports. At the core of neoliberal beliefs and practices that individuals must consume to avoid or manage the 'problems' of old age and disability is ableism and ageism.

Ageism, Ableism, and Compulsory Systems

Ageism and ableism are systems of oppressive beliefs, values, and practices that hold old age and disability as devalued states of being, thereby concurrently reinforcing youthfulness and able-bodiedness/able-mindedness as ideals (Bytheway, 2005; Campbell, 2009). These oppressive systems have been major areas of focus in critical gerontology and critical disability studies, although critical gerontology has focused primarily on ageism and critical disability studies has focused primarily on ableism. By drawing from both critical gerontology and critical disability studies, scholars can begin to explore the various ways ageism and ableism intersect throughout the life course for people ageing with disabilities.

While some scholars have connected fears of ageing and disability to issues such as psychological concerns over our possible future selves (Robbins, 2015), social structures such as segregation (Hagestad & Uhlenberg, 2005), and cultural anxieties regarding dependence and death (Martens, Goldenberg, & Greenburg, 2005), it is essential to also situate these systems of oppression in the neoliberal era. As Estes (2011) noted, systems of oppression, such as ageism, sexism, and racism, are both ideological and structural in nature, and thus intersect with neoliberal policies and practices. By framing disablement throughout the life course as a personal responsibility, neoliberal ideologies frame disability and old age as the result of individual decisions and actions. As such, youthfulness and able-bodiedness/able-mindedness are transformed in an ageist and ableist society from ideals to compulsions, in which youthfulness and able-bodiedness/able-mindedness are natural, normal, desirable, and obligatory (Gibbons, 2016; Kafer, 2013; McRuer, 2006). Furthermore, neoliberal ideologies position the avoidance or minimisation of disability and old age as within the locus of control of the individual. Under these systems and within a neoliberal context, old and disabled people are cast as abnormal and deviant and held responsible for their 'failure' to remain as youthful and non-disabled as possible. Hence, neoliberalism relies on discourses of ageism/compulsory youthfulness and ableism/compulsory able-bodiedness/able-mindedness to enforce consumption by disciplining ageing and disabled bodies into consumers in need of market-based solutions.

Similar to the role of 'citizen as labourer', the neoliberal state expects individuals to fulfil the role of 'citizen as consumer'. According to Grossman, Solway, Hollister, Estes, and Rogne (2009), 'The designation of the role of citizen as consumer recognizes the vital role of consumption for the maintenance of both national and global economies, and the financing of the state' (p. 122). Mitchell and Snyder (2012) noted that people with disabilities are increasingly becoming their own disciplinary agents. As such, they are fuelled by neoliberal discourses of individualism and personal responsibility to act as active consumers seeking to ameliorate the bodily effects of ageing and disablement. As Watson (1998) argued, 'The rise of "consumer society" and "consumer behaviour", the genesis of "commodity culture" with its focus on the body, can create anxiety in those who do not conform to cultural and social norms' (p. 147). Thus, old and disabled people may seek products of 'normalisation' as their bodies and minds are increasingly pathologised under ageist and ableist compulsory systems. According to Mitchell and Snyder (2012):

> Late capitalism produces bodies as languishing through excessive demands of labor productivity, exacerbated social anxiety and toxic environments in order to exploit new markets. Whereas a prior era celebrated autonomous bodies rich in capacity, our own era turns the corner and proliferates pathologies as opportunities for new product dissemination opportunities. (p. 45)

Hence, neoliberal capitalism seeks to take advantage of its disabling effects by turning old and disabled people into consumers who need devices, technologies, medicine, services, and other products.

Corbett indicated that there were a number of community-based services and supports that would have benefited her, such as assistance with personal care (e.g. showering, skin care), assistance with meal or food delivery, and assistive device repairs. However, the State would not fully fund or provide them for a variety of reasons. For example, Corbett had a leg brace that assisted her in transferring from her wheelchair to her bed or toilet or shower, but the leg brace was broken. Medicare would assist in paying for the repair, but Corbett would have to pay a 20% co-pay, which she could not afford. She explained, 'I'm having worse and worse equipment, which means…I am becoming more disabled even in my home environment, because the lack of healthcare coverage, that doesn't cover what I have to have for my disability. That's [also] true for medications, you know my medication costs have gone up, so [I am] rationing meds, not being able to get my wheelchair fixed so it's like duct tape and whatever, so that's increasing the discomfort in my body'. Hence, Corbett's inability to independently finance and consume the medication, devices, and supports she needed, coupled with the lack of public support, disabled her even more, thereby furthering her precarious situation and increasing her risk for institutionalisation.

Commodification

For old and disabled people unable to consume private, market-based solutions to the 'problems' of old age and disability, the neoliberal capitalist political economy has exploited their old and disabled bodies through the creation of the ageing and disability enterprises, which have resulted in the construction of old and disabled bodies as commodities from which private industries can profit (Estes, 2011, 2014; Grossman et al., 2009; Mitchell & Snyder, 2012; Russell, 2001). The primary beneficiary of the ageing and disability enterprises is the medical industrial complex, which as Estes (2014) noted, 'operates largely in the private (increasingly proprietary) sector and is heavily subsidized by the federal government' (p. 94). These subsidies primarily occur through Medicaid (public health insurance for low-income people), Medicare, and Affordable Care Act policy and financing. Thus, as a result of neoliberal policies in a capitalist system, the primary driver for the medical industrial complex has become profit, rather than the provision of quality healthcare, services, and supports that maintain individual's health and economic security.

One of the primary sectors of the medical industrial complex that benefits from the ageing and disability enterprises is long-term services and supports providers. Rather than approach care and long-term services and supports as a public good, neoliberal policies have required individuals and families to be largely responsible for their own care in the realms of labour provision and funding. Regarding labour, the system mainly relies on informal (i.e. unpaid) caregivers, who are predominately women, to engage in difficult labour without pay or benefits (Estes, 2014). Additionally, the system dictates that individuals and families must finance their own care, with public assistance only becoming an option after a person becomes impoverished (Applebaum & Bardo, 2014). Furthermore, long-term services and supports policies have also created an institutional bias, in which Medicaid predominately funds nursing home and other forms of residential care. Although efforts to rebalance Medicaid towards home- and community-based services have been somewhat successful, for older people and adults with physical disabilities, the nursing home industry still receives approximately 59% of Medicaid funding (Accius & Flinn, 2017).

For Corbett, the threat of institutionalisation was a structural issue. Her income from Social Security was stagnant and insufficient for the rapidly increasing cost of living. She was denied access to affordable housing, despite repeated attempts. She was forced to move to the most economical, non-subsidised housing she could find, which was in a neighbourhood where she could not receive meal delivery or grocery delivery or easily access public transit. Corbett was unable to afford the majority of the co-pays under Medicare, and so she was having to choose between which medical visits, tests, and medications were truly necessary and which she could forgo or delay. She was also unable to have her assistive devices repaired or replaced. For all of these structural challenges Corbett was facing, institutionalisation in a nursing home was forwarded as a primary solution and one that was inevitable due to Corbett's supposed individual 'failure' to remain independent. In other words, when remaining youthful and able-bodied/able-minded enough to live in the community is framed as a personal responsibility within a neoliberal, capitalist political economy, institutionalisation becomes an individual's fault.

Portacolone's (2013) ethnographic work on elders struggling to live alone in San Francisco highlights these discourses. Her participants, many of whom were women, people of colour, disabled, and poor, feared institutionalisation so strongly that they refused to seek help or services, out of fear of being forced into a nursing home. In one striking example, a woman drove a manual vehicle home with a broken foot to avoid asking for assistance. When local media covered how much these elders were struggling to live alone in the city, commentators showed no sympathy and indicated that old people have 'had their entire lives to save' and it's 'unpatriotic and un-American to expect the taxpayer to make up the difference' (Portacolone, 2013, p. 172). The participants' fears of being labelled as 'too old' and 'too disabled' to live in the community reflect Corbett's own fear of institutionalisation.

Corbett's inability to be an independent consumer of disability and ageing service and technologies would justify her confinement and a nursing home. In turn, her body would be commodified, as the nursing home industry could still profit from her needs by providing those services and technologies for her and then seeking reimbursement from the State. According to Russell (2001):

> Nursing homes…have commodified disabled bodies so that the least productive can be made of use to the economic order. Disabled persons contribute to the Gross Domestic Product when occupying a bed in an institution where they generate $30,000 to $82,000 in annual revenues and contribute to a company's net worth. (p. 93)

Thus, commodification within the ageing and disability enterprises serves as a powerful and insidious form of institutional oppression supported by a neoliberal political economy in Corbett's life and the lives of others ageing with disabilities. This form of precarity, which is created by compulsory systems of able-bodiedness/able-mindedness and youthfulness under neoliberal capitalism, is particularly relevant to those ageing with disabilities, whose needs may change or progress as they age, who are more at risk for poverty, and who are marginalised throughout their life course as disabled people.

Examining Corbett's narrative through critical disability studies and critical gerontology perspectives, theories, and frameworks illustrates the potential of integrating these fields to deepen our understanding of the experiences of people ageing with disabilities. While using mainstream gerontology and disability studies to analyse Corbett's story would also produce meaningful analyses, incorporating critical disability studies and critical gerontology uncovers the ways in which Corbett's life course has been affected by a neoliberal capitalist political economy and an ableist and ageist cultural context, in which old and disabled individuals are held personally responsible for remaining independent and avoiding institutionalisation, despite a lack of public services and support and numerous economic and structural barriers. By highlighting these complex social and political formations, scholars and activists can work towards a more just society for Corbett and all people ageing with disabilities.

Conclusion

Historically, people ageing with disabilities have not been a central focus in disability studies or gerontology. However, people in old age who have been disabled throughout their life course exist at the intersections of old age and disability, and thus an interdisciplinary approach is essential to expanding our understanding of their diverse experiences. In particular, integrating critical disability studies and critical gerontology will lend itself to analyses of how social, structural, political, economic, and cultural factors influence the experiences of those ageing with disabilities. Bridging critical disability studies and critical gerontology will also aid scholars and activists in employing critical theories and frameworks, focusing on the lives of people ageing with disabilities, and including the voices and perspectives of people ageing with disabilities. When analysing Corbett's story, I primarily used four core concepts and frames in critical disability studies and critical gerontology: political economy, ableism and ageism, compulsory youthfulness and compulsory able-bodiedness/able-mindedness, and commodification. However, there are numerous other theories and models in critical disability studies and critical gerontology that scholars studying ageing with disability might use, such as precarity (Portacolone, 2013, 2018), debility (Puar, 2017), moral economy (Minkler & Estes, 1991), dependency and interdependency (Johnson, 1993; Wendell, 1996), and complex embodiment (Siebers, 2008). Applying these perspectives to Corbett's narrative, or the experiences of people ageing with disabilities more broadly, would open up numerous possibilities for increasing knowledge about the ways old age and disability intersect for those who experience disability throughout the life course. Furthermore, there are various areas related to ageing with disability in which critical gerontology and critical disability studies may intersect in future research and activism, including political and moral economy, embodiment and bodies/minds, ageism and ableism, and care. There are also diverse contexts to be explored, such as ageing with a disability in communities of colour, in multiply marginalised communities, or in the Global South. Given the growing numbers of people ageing with disabilities in the United States and throughout the world, it is essential to integrate critical disability studies and critical gerontology and the possibilities to do so are interminable.

References

Accius, J., & Flinn, B. (2017). *Stretching the Medicaid dollar: Home and community-based services are a cost-effective approach to providing long-term services and supports.* AARP Public Policy Institute. Retrieved from https://www.aarp.org/content/dam/aarp/ppi/2017-01/Stretching%20Medicaid.pdf

Applebaum, R., & Bardo, A. (2014). Will you still need me, will you still feed me, when I'm 84? Long-term care challenges for an aging America. In R. B. Hudson (Ed.), *The new politics of old age policy* (3rd ed., pp. 221–235). John Hopkins University Press.

Baars, J., & Phillipson, C. (2013). Introduction. In J. Baars, J. Dohmen, A. Genier, & C. Phillipson (Eds.), *Ageing, meaning, and social structure: Connecting critical and humanistic gerontology* (pp. 1–10). Policy Press.

Bass, S. A. (2009). Toward an integrative theory of social gerontology. In V. L. Bengston, D. Gans, N. M. Putney, M. Silverstein (Eds.), *Handbook of theories of aging* (2nd ed., pp. 347–374). Springer.

Butler, J. (1994). Against proper objects. *Differences: A Journal of Feminist Cultural Studies, 6*(2&3), 1–26.

Bytheway, B. (2005). Ageism and age categorization. *Journal of Social Issues, 61*(2), 361–374.

Campbell, F. K. (2009). *Contours of ableism: The production of disability and abledness.* United Kingdom: Palgrave Macmillan.

Douglas, S. J. (2014). Still living with sexism (after all these years): How neoliberalism operats at the intersections of sexism and ageism. *Soundings: A Journal of Politics and Culture, 58*(1), 34–43. https://www.muse.jhu.edu/article/565756.

Duggan, L. (2003). *The twilight of equality: Neoliberalism, cultural politics, and the attack on democracy.* Beacon Press.

Estes, C. L. (2001). Political economy of aging: A theoretical framework. In C. Estes (Ed.), *Social policy & aging: A critical perspective* (1–18). Sage.

Estes, C. L. (2011). Crises and old age policy. In R. A. A. Settersten Jr. & J. L. L. Angel (Eds.), *Handbook of sociology of aging* (pp. 297–320). Springer.

Estes, C. L. (2014). The future of aging services in a neoliberal political economy. *Generations, 38*(2), 94–100.

Estes, C. L., & Phillipson, C. (2007). Critical gerontology. In J. E. Birren (Ed.), *The encyclopedia of gerontology* (2nd ed., pp. 330–336). Academic Press.

Gibbons, H. M. (2016). Compulsory youthfulness: Intersections of ableism and ageism in "successful aging" discourses. *Review of Disability Studies, 12*(2&3), 70–88.

Goodley, D. (2016). *Disability studies: An interdisciplinary introduction* (2nd ed.). Sage.

Goodley, D., Lawthom, R., Liddiard, K., & Runswick-Cole, K. (2019). Provocations for critical disability studies. *Disability & Society, 34*(6), 972–997. https://doi.org/10.1080/09687599.2019.1566889

Grossman, B. R., Solway, E., Hollister, B. A., Estes, C. L., & Rogne, L. (2009). One nation, interdependent: Exploring the boundaries of citizenship in the history of social security and medicare. In L. Rogne, C. L. Estes, B. R. Grossman, B. A. Hollister, & E. Solway (Eds.), *Social insurance and social justice: Social security, medicare, and the campaign against entitlements* (pp. 115–148), Springer.

Harvey, D. (2005). *A brief history of neoliberalism.* Oxford University Press.

Hagestad, G. O., & Uhlenberg, P. (2005). The social separation of old and young: A root of ageism. *Journal of Social Issues, 61*(2), 343–360.

Johnson, M. (1993). Dependency and interdependency. In J. Bond, P. Coleman, & S. Peace (Eds.), *Ageing in society* (pp. 255–279). Sage.

Kafer, A. (2013). *Feminist, queer, crip.* Indiana University Press.

Kail, B. L., Quadagno, J., & Keene, J. R. (2009). The political economy perspective of aging. In V. L. Bengston, M. Silverstein, N. M. Putney, & D. Gans (Eds.), *Handbook of theories of aging* (2nd ed., pp. 555–572). Springer.

Kelley-Moore, J. A. (2010). Disability and ageing: The social construction of causality. In D. Dannefer & C. Phillipson (Eds.), *The SAGE handbook of social gerontology* (pp. 96–110). Sage.

Linton, S. (2005). What is disability studies? *PMLA, 120*(2), 518–522. www.jstor.org/stable/25486177

Martens, A., Goldenberg, J. L., and Greenberg, J. (2005). A terror management perspective on aging. *Journal of Social Issues, 61*(2), 223–239.

Meekosha, H., & Shuttleworth, R. (2009). What's so critical about critical disability studies? *Australian Journal of Human Rights, 15*(1), 47–75. https://doi.org/10.1080/1323238X.2009.11910861

Minkler, M., & Estes, C. L. (Eds.). (1991.) *Critical perspectives on aging: The political and moral economy of growing old.* Baywood Publishing Co.

Mitchell, D., & Snyder, S. (2012). Minority model: From liberal to neoliberal futures of disability. In N. Watson, A. Roulstone, & C. Thomas (Eds.), *Routledge handbook of disability studies* (pp. 42–50). Routledge.

Molton, I. R., & Yorkston, K. M. (2017). Growing older with a physical disability: A special application of the successful aging paradigm. *Journals of Gerontology B: Social Sciences, 72*(2), 290–299. https://doi.org/10.1093/geronb/gbw122

Priestley, M. (2003). Disability and old age. In M. Priestley (Ed.), *Disability. A life course approach* (pp. 143–165). UK: Polity Press.

Polivka, L. (2011). Neoliberalism and postmodern cultures of aging. *Journal of Applied Gerontology, 30*(2), 173–184. https://doi.org/10.1177/0733464810385919

Portacolone, E. (2013). The notion of precariousness among older adults living alone in the U.S. *Journal of Aging Studies, 27*(2), 166–174. https://doi.org/10.1016/j.jaging.2013.01.001

Portacolone, E. (2018). A framework to identify precarity in aging studies. *Innovation in Aging, 2*(S1), 684.

Puar, J. (2017). *The right to main: Debility, capacity, disability*. Duke University Press.

Robbins, L. A. (Ed.) (2015). Ageism in America: Reframing the issues and impacts. *Generations, 39*(3).

Russell, M. (2001). Disablement, oppression, and the political economy. *Journal of Disability Policy Studies, 12*(2), 87–95. https://doi.org/10.1177/104420730101200205

Sheets, D. J. (2005). Aging with disabilities: Ageism and more. *Generations, 29*(3), 37–41.

Shildrick, M. (2012). Critical disability studies: Rethinking the conventions for the age of postmodernity. In N. Watson, A. Roulstone & C. Thomas (Eds.), *Routledge handbook of disability studies* (pp. 30–41). Routledge.

Siebers, T. (2008). *Disability theory*. University of Michigan Press.

Soldatic, K., & Meekosha, H. (2012). Disability and neoliberal state formations. In N. Watson, A. Roulstone, & C. Thomas (Eds.), *Routledge handbook of disability studies* (pp. 195–210). Routledge.

Verbrugge, L. M., & Yang, L. (2002). Aging with disability and disability with aging. *Journal of Disability Policy Studies, 12*(4), 253–267. https://doi.org/10.1177/104420730201200405

Wendell, S. (1996). *The rejected body: Feminist philosophical reflections on disability*. Routledge.

Yoshizaki-Gibbons, H. M. (2018a). Engaging with aging: The "greying" of critical disability studies. In R. Garland-Thomson, K. Ellis, M. Kent, & R. Robertson (Eds.), *Manifestos for the future of critical disability studies* (pp. 179–188). Routledge.

Yoshizaki-Gibbons, H. M. (2018b). Critical disability studies. In T. Heller, S. Parker Harris, C. Gill, & R. P. Gould (Eds.), *Disability in American Life: An Encyclopedia of Concepts, Policies, and Controversies* (pp. 149–152). Santa Barbara, CA: ABC-CLIO.

Suggested Readings

Aubrecht, K., Kelly, C., & Rice, C. (Eds.). (2020). *The aging-disability nexus*. UBC Press.

Gibbons, H. M. (2016). Compulsory youthfulness: Intersections of ableism and ageism in "successful aging" discourses. *Review of Disability Studies, 12*(2&3), 70–88.

Meekosha, H., & Shuttleworth, R. (2009). What's so critical about critical disability studies? *Australian Journal of Human Rights, 15*(1), 47–75. https://doi.org/10.1080/1323238X.2009.11910861

Yoshizaki-Gibbons, H. M. (2018). Engaging with aging: The "greying" of critical disability studies. In R. Garland-Thomson, K. Ellis, M. Kent, & R. Robertson (Eds.), *Manifestos for the future of critical disability studies* (pp. 179–188). Routledge.

5
SOCIAL AND ENVIRONMENTAL DETERMINANTS OF THE HEALTH OF PEOPLE WITH DISABILITIES

Eric Emerson, Zoe Aitken, Hannah Badland, Nicola Fortune, Celia Green, and Jerome N. Rachele

Introduction

Throughout the life course, people with disabilities have poorer physical and mental health, and die sooner, than their non-disabled peers (World Health Organization and the World Bank, 2011). A key question for science, policy, and practice is whether this difference represents an inequity in health. Health inequities are

> avoidable inequalities in health between groups of people ... [that] ... arise from inequalities within societies. Social and economic conditions and their effects on people's lives determine their risk of illness and the actions taken to prevent them becoming ill or treat illness when it occurs.
>
> World Health Organization, 2008, para. 1

Health inequities are avoidable, unjust, and violate human rights. Growing evidence suggests that the inequality in health status between people with and without disability results, in part, from the increased risk of people with disabilities being exposed to some very well-established social and environmental determinants of poor health (Emerson et al., 2011; Emerson et al., 2012; Krahn, Walker, & Correa-De-Araujo, 2015). As such these inequalities represent, at least in part, inequities.

Our aims for this chapter are to illustrate some of the things we know about the: (1) Extent to which people with disabilities are more, or less, likely to be exposed to well-established social and environmental determinants of poor health in childhood and as working age adults and (2) Impact that such exposures have on their health. We focus on earlier stages in the life course, which lays the foundations for healthy (and unhealthy) ageing (e.g. Ploubidis, Benova, Grundy, Laydon, & De Stavola, 2014). Readers, however, do need to keep two caveats in mind when thinking about the material included in the following sections. First, it is not possible within the constraints of a single chapter to provide a comprehensive overview of these two issues. We have been selective in our choice of issues on which to focus and on the evidence we cite. Regarding the latter, we have prioritised evidence derived from studies that have used samples that are likely to be representative of national populations. Second, we have included evidence from several countries. However, great care needs to be taken when making comparisons between countries, especially given the variations between countries in how disability is defined and measured.

Background: Social and Environmental Determinants of Health

For over 150 years, epidemiologists have been studying the association between living conditions and health (Krieger, 2011). Over that time, it has become increasingly apparent that many of the inequities in health that we see (whether between different countries or between different groups within countries)

> arise from the societal conditions in which people are born, grow, live, work and age, referred to as social determinants of health. These include early years' experiences, education, economic status, employment and decent work, housing and environment, and effective systems of preventing and treating ill health'
>
> World Health Organization, 2011, p. 2

It has also become increasingly apparent that making progress in reducing health inequities within countries will depend on reducing the probability that marginalised/vulnerable groups (such as people with disabilities) will be exposed to social and environmental determinants of poorer health (World Health Organization, 2008, 2011; World Health Organization Regional Office for Europe, 2014).

Most approaches to synthesising knowledge about how social determinants impact on health focus on the extent to which social stratification leads to differential: (1) Exposure to material and psychosocial hazards that are detrimental to well-being and (2) Vulnerability or resilience to the impact of such exposures on health and well-being (Diderichsen, Evans, & Whitehead, 2001; Krieger, 2011; Marmot et al., 2008). Social stratification refers to the hierarchies that exist in all societies that are characterised by differences in access to key resources such as wealth, power and prestige. Socioeconomic position (SEP) and socio-economic status are terms commonly used to describe social stratification. Most of the known social and environmental determinants of health show a social gradient in the risk of exposure. The further one moves down social stratification hierarchies, the more likely it is that people will be exposed to these social and environmental determinants of (poorer) health. Social gradients are evident for such diverse risks as exposure to income poverty, poor housing conditions, unemployment, material hardship, social exclusion, discrimination, domestic and community violence, tobacco smoke and outdoor air pollution (Berkman et al., 2014; Marmot & Wilkinson, 2006). Position in the social hierarchy also influences access to resources that build resilience in the face of adversity. We will use this simple framework, described by Public Health England to structure the rest of this chapter.

> resilience is not an innate feature of some people's personalities. Resilience and adversity are distributed unequally across the population and are related to broader socioeconomic inequalities which have common causes - the inequities in power, money and resources that shape the conditions in which people live and their opportunities, experiences and relationships. Those who face the most adversity are least likely to have the resources necessary to build resilience. This "double burden" means that inequalities in resilience are likely to contribute to health inequalities
>
> Public Health England, 2014

Growing Up With a Disability

Overall, children with a disability are more likely than other children to be brought up in families with lower SEP, including families living in poverty (Banks, Kuper, & Polack, 2017; Spencer, Blackburn, & Read, 2015; World Health Organization and the World Bank, 2011). Families supporting a child with

Table 5.1 Percentage of 14-year-old adolescents with and without disabilities growing up in the United Kingdom exposed to childhood adversities

Adversity	Adolescents with disability	Adolescents without disability	p
Income poverty	71.2%	56.1%	<0.001
Material hardship	72.1%	51.3%	<0.001
Household with no adult working	69.6%	52.3%	<0.001
Mother has possible mental illness	55.4%	35.9%	<0.001
Parental substance abuse	22.0%	20.9%	n.s.
Domestic violence	11.1%	9.2%	n.s.
Parental separation or divorce	53.8%	40.8%	<0.001
Death of a parent	2.2%	1.9%	n.s.
Separated from family	3.8%	2.1%	<0.05
Has been homeless	9.5%	6.1%	<0.01
Second hand tobacco smoke in home	67.7%	56.9%	<0.001
Lived in area with high level of social deprivation	38.1%	33.8%	<0.05
Lived in area with high levels of outdoor air pollution	43.3%	43.7%	n.s.
Bullied at school (parental report)	29.0%	11.5%	<0.001
Bullied at school (self-report)	27.5%	15.4%	<0.001
Not exclusively breast fed at 3 months	83.0%	77.3%	<0.01
Childhood accident involving hospital admission	12.0%	8.6%	<0.01

Source: Analysis of waves 1–6 of the UK's Millennium Cohort Survey (For details of some of measures, see Public Health England, 2015).

disability are more likely to become poor, to spend longer living in poverty and are less likely to escape from poverty (Shahtahmasebi, Emerson, Berridge, & Lancaster, 2011). Families living in poverty are more likely to be exposed to a wide range of specific material and psychosocial hazards including: poor housing conditions, parental unemployment, parental mental health problems, family bereavement, family separation/divorce, parental substance abuse, domestic and community violence, second-hand tobacco smoke, and outdoor air pollution (Jones et al., 2012; World Health Organization and the World Bank, 2011). The risk of exposure to a diverse array of adversities is illustrated in Table 5.1 for 14-year-old adolescents with and without disabilities growing up in the United Kingdom.

While different countries measure child disability and poverty in different ways, disabled children are more likely to be growing up in poverty than their peers.

- In the United Kingdom in 2008/9, 40% of disabled children were living in poverty compared with 29% of non-disabled children (The Children's Society, 2011)
- In the United States in 2017, 28% of disabled children were living in poverty compared with 18% of non-disabled children (Fontenot, Semega, & Kollar, 2018)

Why is there a link between family SEP and childhood disability? First, many of the health conditions associated with childhood disability are more likely to affect children of families with lower SEP. This is particularly true for childhood disability associated with intellectual disability, activity-limiting asthma, psychological disorders, and sensory impairments (Spencer et al., 2015). Second, it has been argued that having a child with a disability may lead to downward social mobility, lowering family SEP due to parents (typically mothers) not working or working fewer hours and/or the extra financial costs associated with raising a child with disability. However, evidence from longitudinal studies suggests that, in the United Kingdom at least, these effects are small (Shahtahmasebi et al., 2011).

In addition to the link between childhood disability and low family SEP, children with disabilities are likely to experience discrimination and harassment based on their disability. Specifically, they are more likely to be bullied at school, be socially excluded, and have fewer friends (Arculi et al., 2019; Emerson & Spencer, 2015; Kavanagh, Priest, Emerson, Milner, & King, 2018; Pinquart, 2017; Sentenac et al., 2013). There is abundant evidence that exposure to social and environmental adversities in childhood has significant and potentially long-lasting effects on health (Shonkoff, 2016; World Health Organization, 2008; World Health Organization Regional Office for Europe, 2014). Evidence specific to children with disabilities is much less developed. However, recent research has indicated that, among adolescents with a disability, being a victim of bullying is associated with higher rates of emotional difficulties, poorer self-rated health, lower life, and school satisfaction (Arculi et al., 2019; King et al., 2018; Sentenac et al., 2013).

The Living Conditions of Working Age Adults with a Disability: Poverty and Low Socio-economic Position

Living in poverty has long been known to be associated with increased risk of mortality and morbidity (e.g. Krieger, 2011; Marmot et al., 2008; World Health Organization and Calouste Gulbenkian Foundation, 2014; World Health Organization Regional Office for Europe, 2014). In addition, studies undertaken in high-income countries have consistently reported that working age adults with disabilities are significantly more likely to be living in poverty than their non-disabled peers (e.g. Brucker & Houtenville, 2015; Emerson et al., 2018; Heslop & Emerson, 2017). The link between poverty and disability is also evident in low- and middle-income countries (Banks et al., 2017). Despite these strong associations, surprisingly few studies have investigated the association between poverty and health among working age adults with disabilities. The scant evidence that does exist suggests that exposure to poverty among people with disabilities is associated with poorer self-rated health (e.g. Emerson & Hatton, 2008; Emerson, Hatton, Baines, & Robertson, 2016).

Working age adults with disabilities are more likely to live in poverty than their peers.

- In Australia in 2016, 38% of working age adults with disabilities experienced one or more financial stressor, compared with 18% of non-disabled working age adults (Emerson et al., 2018)
- In the United Kingdom in 2012, 30% of working age adults with disabilities were living in poverty compared with 13% of non-disabled working age adults (Heslop & Emerson, 2017)
- In the United States in 2017, 26% of working age adults with disabilities were living in poverty compared with 11% of non-disabled working age adults (Fontenot et al., 2018)

The association between poverty and health appears to be mediated, in part, by the association between poverty and the probability of engaging in some riskier health behaviours (e.g. smoking, physical inactivity). Given the association between poverty and disability, it is not surprising that smoking rates are higher among people with disabilities than among their non-disabled peers (Australian Institute of Health and Welfare, 2016; Courtney-Long, Stevens, Caraballo, Ramon, & Armour, 2014; Emerson, 2018), and that people with disabilities are more likely to be physically inactive (Australian Institute of Health and Welfare, 2016).

Employment

Employment is an important social determinant of health, with a well-established evidence-base demonstrating negative effects of unemployment, employment insecurity, and poor psychosocial job quality on physical and mental health (Marmot et al., 2008).

Working age adults with disabilities are more likely to be unemployed or not in the labour force than those without disabilities.

- In Australia in 2016, 41% of working age adults with disabilities were not in the labour force compared to 16% of non-disabled working age adults; of those in the labour force, 13% of adults with disabilities were unemployed compared with 5% of non-disabled adults (Emerson et al., 2018)
- In the United Kingdom in 2012, 51% of working age adults with disabilities were not in the labour force compared with 17% of non-disabled working age adults; of those in the labour force 9% of adults with disabilities were unemployed compared with 7% of non-disabled adults (Heslop & Emerson, 2017)
- In the United States in 2017, 58% of working age adults with disabilities were not in the labour force compared with 19% of non-disabled working age adults; of those in the labour force 12% adults with disabilities were unemployed compared with 5% of non-disabled adults (Fontenot et al., 2018)

A comparison of countries in the Organization for Economic Co-operation and Development using data from 2003 to 2006 demonstrated large inter-country variation in employment rates between people with and without disability, ranging from 70% lower for people with disability in South Africa and 62% in Japan, to only 8% lower in Malawi and 19% in Switzerland (World Health Organization and the World Bank, 2011). There is also evidence that people with disabilities are less likely to enjoy optimal working conditions (Milner, Krnjacki, Butterworth, Kavanagh, & LaMontagne, 2015) and more likely to be underemployed (Milner et al., 2017) and underpaid (Hogan, Kyaw-Myint, Harris, & Denronden, 2012).

There is some evidence that poor employment outcomes impact on the health of people with disabilities. The negative mental health effects of becoming unemployed, economically inactive or underemployed have been found to be greater for people with a disability compared to those without (Milner et al., 2017; Milner et al., 2014). For young people who acquired a disability, one of the determinants of poor mental health trajectories was unemployment (Kariuki, Honey, Emerson, & Llewellyn, 2011). Finally, a study examining the association between disability acquisition and mental health found evidence that the deterioration in mental health was predominantly explained by material socioeconomic factors including employment (Aitken, Simpson, Gurrin, Bentley, & Kavanagh, 2018). These findings highlight the importance of employment for the health of people with disabilities.

Housing Conditions

People with disabilities face problems in finding adequate, accessible, and affordable housing. Housing contributes to the disabling or enabling environment experienced by people with disabilities. Inappropriate housing can represent a major barrier to independent living and social inclusion, with consequences to health and well-being. People with disabilities are particularly vulnerable to experiencing poor housing outcomes because of the compounding effects of institutional reform, low employment rates, and low income. In addition, people with disabilities may have specific accommodation requirements, which limit their housing options (Beer & Faulkner, 2009).

Working age adults with disabilities are more likely to live in lower quality housing than their peers.

- In Australia in 2016, 24% of working age adults with disabilities reported that they could not pay their mortgage, rent or bills on time due to a shortage of money, compared with 12% of their non-disabled peers (Emerson et al., 2018)
- In the United Kingdom in 2012, 14% could not afford to keep their home adequately warm compared with 5% of non-disabled working age adults (Heslop & Emerson, 2017)

In Australia, people with disabilities have been shown to be at higher risk of poor housing outcomes. They are more likely to experience homelessness (Beer & Faulkner, 2009), housing insecurity (Kavanagh et al., 2015), housing unaffordability, and poor-quality housing, and live in public housing (Aitken et al., 2019); and there is evidence that housing inequities are increasing over time (Disability Housing Futures Working Group, 2016). Many people with disabilities live in institutions, group homes, or in nursing homes because of lack of appropriate housing (Wiesel et al., 2015). In the United States, households in which one or more household member had a disability were less likely to own their own homes compared with other households (Wang, 2005), and were more likely to experience housing unaffordability, severe housing cost burdens, housing poverty, and housing assistance (White, Peaslee, & LaQuatra, 1994). In the United Kingdom, people with disabilities were more than twice as likely as non-disabled people to live in social housing, less likely to be homeowners, and more likely to report poor suitability and adequacy of housing (Papworth Trust, 2011).

There is little research on the association between housing and health outcomes relative to disability. There is evidence suggesting that, for people with psychosocial disability, choice of housing type is associated with increased quality of life (Welch & Cleak, 2018), and housing insecurity and frequent moves are associated with poorer health (Kyle & Dunn, 2008). There is also evidence that the negative effect of disability acquisition on mental health is greater for people living in unaffordable housing (Kavanagh et al., 2015).

Exposure to Violence

Exposure to violence can have a detrimental impact on an individual's physical and mental health. A growing number of studies have reported that working age adults with disabilities are more likely to be exposed to violence, including sexual and partner violence, interpersonal violence outside of the home and hate crime; violence directed towards a person because of their disability' (Breiding & Armour, 2015; Emerson, Krnjacki, Llewellyn, Vaughan, & Kavanagh, 2016; Emerson et al., 2018; Emerson & Roulstone, 2014; Harrell, 2017; Hughes et al., 2012; Krnjacki, Emerson, Llewellyn, & Kavanagh, 2016). Very few population-based studies have investigated the association between exposure to violence and health among working age adults with disabilities. The limited evidence that does exist suggests that exposure to interpersonal violence is associated with poorer health and more risky health behaviours (Mitra & Mouradian, 2014).

Working age adults with disabilities are more likely to be exposed to violence than their peers.

- In Australia in 2016, 3% of working age adults with disabilities reported having been physically assaulted in the previous 12 months, compared to 1% of non-disabled working age adults (Emerson et al., 2018)
- In the United Kingdom between 2009 and 2011, 5% of working age adults with disabilities were the victims of violent crime, compared to 4% of non-disabled working age adults (Emerson & Roulstone, 2014)
- In the United States between 2011 and 2015, 5% of working age adults with disabilities were the victims of violent crime, compared to 2% of non-disabled working age adults (Harrell, 2017)

Discrimination

A substantial body of research suggests that exposure to overt acts of discrimination may be detrimental to physical and mental health (Krieger, 2014). Most of the evidence is from studies of the association between exposure to racial discrimination and health status in the United States. However, there is some limited evidence that exposure to discrimination based on non-racial characteristics (including disability) may have a stronger association with poor health than exposure to racial discrimination (Alvarez-Galvez, 2016; Du Mont & Forte, 2016). The few population-based studies that have investigated the association between disability-based discrimination and health have reported that exposure to disability discrimination is associated with poorer self-reported health (Alvarez-Galvez, 2016; Du Mont & Forte, 2016; Emerson, 2010; Krnjacki et al., 2018; Sutin, Stephan, Carretta, & Terracciano, 2015), greater psychological distress (Emerson, 2010; Krnjacki et al., 2018; Wamala, Boström, & Nyqvist, 2007) and lower life satisfaction (Sutin et al., 2015).

Working age adults with disabilities are more likely to experience discrimination than their peers.

- In the United Kingdom between 2009 and 2011, 26% of working age adults with disabilities reported being discriminated against in the previous 12 months compared to 9% of non-disabled working age adults (Emerson & Roulstone, 2014)
- In 2015, 14% of Australians with disability reported disability-based discrimination in the previous year (Krnjacki et al., 2018)

Conclusion

Future Research Priorities

In the preceding sections, we have briefly summarised what is known about the: (1) Extent to which children and working age adults with disabilities are exposed to well-established social determinants of poorer health and (2) Associations that such exposures have on health for people with disabilities. Below, we outline three priorities for future research.

Expand the range of social determinants and settings studied

While increasingly robust evidence is becoming available on the extent to which people with disabilities are exposed to some well-established social determinants of health, our knowledge on other social and environmental determinants (e.g. social isolation, aspects of the physical environment) is much more limited.

The physical environment, the scale, form, and function of areas (including the street network, destinations and open spaces), is an important determinant of health due the extent to which it facilitates, or restricts, access to opportunities. How areas are designed influences how people behave, and in-turn, their health. For example, mobility is important for being able to access education, employment, and leisure opportunities (World Health Organization, 2008), all of which are social determinants of health. We have long-written about the importance of a supportive physical environment, for example, through universal design and its principles (Government of Ireland, 2005). However, more work needs to be done to understand whether and to what extent people with disability are differentially exposed to physical environment characteristics needed for health-enhancing opportunities (and whether this differs between and within countries). And while intuitively, it is discernible that people with disability are likely to be differentially vulnerable to physical environments with limited health-enhancing attributes, we need better evidence that quantifies the extent to which these environments limit the social determinants of health of people with disability, and the overall costs to society.

In addition, virtually all the evidence we have cited are derived from cross-sectional population-based studies undertaken in high-income countries. There is a pressing need to expand research in the world's low- and middle-income countries, where the majority of people with disabilities live (World Health Organization and the World Bank, 2011).

Increase Our Understanding of Vulnerability/Resilience

There is abundant evidence from general population-based studies (which are likely to include a significant proportion of people with disabilities) that exposure to the social determinants described in the previous sections has significant and potentially long-lasting effects on health (e.g., Krieger, 2011; Marmot et al., 2008; Shonkoff, 2016; World Health Organization, 2008; World Health Organization and Calouste Gulbenkian Foundation, 2014; World Health Organization Regional Office for Europe, 2014). Evidence that specifically relates to health impacts for people with disabilities is much more limited and all too often is based on cross-sectional studies, which cannot provide evidence of causality.

There is no good reason to think that people with disabilities would be immune to the effects of exposure to such adversities. However, given that people with disabilities are less likely to have access to the kinds of resources that promote resilience in the face of adversity (e.g. wealth, power, social support, access to timely and effective healthcare), it may be expected that exposure to adversities would have a greater impact on the health of people with disabilities (see Emerson & Hatton, 2007).

Increase Our Understanding of Intersectionality

We know relatively little about the extent to which exposure to social determinants (and the impact of such exposure) varies with other potentially important characteristics of people with disabilities (e.g. gender, ethnicity, age, sexual orientation, religion, severity of disability, and the type of health condition or impairment associated with their disability). The limited literature, which has addressed these issues, indicates that both gender and type of health condition/impairment can have marked effects on the probability of exposure to some social determinants, such as particular types of violence and socioeconomic disadvantage (see Hughes et al., 2012; Kavanagh et al., 2015).

Implications for Policy and Practice

Although there is overwhelming research evidence showing that the social determinants of health are more important for health outcomes than access to health services, this research has not necessarily translated into effective policy action. This is evident in disability, where health recommendations and policies typically focus on health services (Stein, Stein, Weiss, & Lang, 2009; United Nations, 2006) and neglect the broader social determinants of health (Emerson et al., 2011). The wider population health literature has identified 'lifestyle drift' as a significant barrier to effective policy action on the social determinants of health (Baum, 2011; Popay, Whitehead, & Hunter, 2010; Raphael, 2008; Whitehead, 2012). This term has been used to describe how policy initiatives aimed at addressing health inequalities often start with a social determinants (upstream) focus but then shift over time to centre mainly on (downstream) individual lifestyle factors, as well as a general trend towards governments investing more in individualistic approaches (Baum, 2011; Hunter, Popay, Tannahill, & Whitehead, 2010). This can be seen in the shift towards personalised funding models for disability (Askheim, 1999; Needham, 2016), such as Australia's National Disability Insurance Scheme, which emphasises 'choice and control' for individuals in the services they use rather than governments implementing policies aimed to address the broader social determinants (Carey, Malbon, Reeders, Kavanagh, & Llewellyn, 2017).

Sociological theories such as the residualistic conversion model have recently been applied to understanding how to manage lifestyle drift (Carey, Malbon, Crammond, Pescud, & Baker, 2017). This model proposes that if health issues are maintained in the social sphere by framing them as affecting the whole of society rather than just certain 'vulnerable groups' (Frohlich & Potvin, 2008; McLaren & McIntyre, 2014), then 'upstream' policy action should happen more easily (Carey, Malbon, Crammond, et al., 2017). Public pressure can ensure governments accept the political nature of a social problem, thereby keeping it in the political sphere and making it more likely that intersectoral attempts will be made to solve it at a government level (Jamrozik, 1998). Policy process theories such as Kingdon's Multiple Streams Approach (Kingdon, 1995) and the Advocacy Coalition Framework (Jenkins-Smith, Nohrstedt, Weible, & Sabatier, 2014) show how groups acting together as policy entrepreneurs to promote a particular idea or agenda are instrumental in shaping such policy outcomes. Disability advocacy groups could connect with each other as well as other social service peak bodies to work together to promote the message frame that social determinants of health affect the whole of society. Coordinated pressure group campaigns using appropriate political messaging could enable governments to view social determinants such as housing and social exclusion as problems, which are larger social issues, rather than just specifically affecting people with disability.

More nuanced approaches, which combine universal (whole of society) and targeted policies that bring together upstream and downstream approaches, could also be utilised and these have direct application for disability and health policy. A framework developed by Carey, Crammond, and De Leeuw (2015) shows how best to strike a balance between universal approaches supporting fairness and equity alongside catering for specific groups with differing levels of risk and need. This keeps upstream (social determinants) action in place but still allows for needs of particular social groups to be met where required (Carey & Crammond, 2017). Action on social determinants becomes the responsibility of federal governments and smaller targeted programmes are run at a community/local level to ensure they are context-specific and do not disturb the implementation of universal approaches (Carey et al., 2015). An example of this would be local governments developing plans to create disability inclusive environments such as local transport infrastructure and accessible buildings.

Finally, as part of a book on ageing and disability, this chapter has provided evidence about the negative impact of multiple adverse social determinants on the health and well-being of people with lifelong disabilities. It has illustrated the poor foundations for healthy ageing laid during the earlier stages of their life course. This evidence helps to explain the disadvantages people with a disability have as they begin to experience ageing, and some of the social actions to address social determinants earlier in the life course that will improve their chances of healthy and active ageing.

References

Aitken, Z., Baker, E., Badland, H., Mason, K., Bentley, R., Beer, A., & Kavanagh, A. M. (2019). Precariously placed: Housing affordability, quality and satisfaction of Australians with disabilities. *Disability and Society*, *34*(1) 121–142. https://doi.org/10.1080/09687599.2018.1521333

Aitken, Z., Simpson, J. A., Gurrin, L., Bentley, R., & Kavanagh, A. M. (2018). Do material, psychosocial and behavioural factors mediate the relationship between disability acquisition and mental health? A sequential causal mediation analysis. *International Journal of Epidemiology*, *47*, 829–840. https://doi.org/10.1093/ije/dyx277

Alvarez-Galvez, J. (2016). Measuring the effect of ethnic and non-ethnic discrimination on Europeans' self-rated health. *International Journal of Public Health*, *61*(3), 367–374. https://doi.org/10.1007/s00038-015-0728-1

Arciuli, J., Emerson, E., & Llewellyn, G. (2019). Adolescents' self-report of school satisfaction: The interaction between disability and gender. *School Psychology*, *34*(2), 148–158.

Askheim, O. P. (1999). Personal assistance for disabled people – The Norwegian experience. *International Journal of Social Welfare*, *8*(2), 111–120. https://doi.org/10.1111/1468-2397.00072

Australian Institute of Health and Welfare. (2016). *Health status and risk factors of Australians with disability 2007–2008 and 2011–2012*. AIHW. https://www.aihw.gov.au/getmedia/6b61cb2e-69d5-4eec-bdc3-412991e33e9e/Health%20status%20and%20risk%20factors%20of%20Australians%20with%20disability%202007-08%20and%202011-12.pdf.aspx?inline=true

Banks, L. M., Kuper, H., & Polack, S. (2017). Poverty and disability in low- and middle-income countries: A systematic review. *PLoS ONE*, *12*(12), e0189996. https://doi.org/10.1371/journal.pone.0189996

Baum, F. (2011). From Norm to Eric: Avoiding lifestyle drift in Australian health policy. *Australian and New Zealand Journal of Public Health*, *35*(5), 404–406. https://doi.org/10.1111/j.1753-6405.2011.00756.x

Beer, A., & Faulkner, D. R. (2009). *The housing careers of people with a disability and carers of people with a disability*. Australian Housing and Urban Research Institute. https://www.ahuri.edu.au/__data/assets/pdf_file/0022/2974/AHURI_RAP_Issue_107_The-housing-careers-of-people-with-a-disability-and-carers-of-people-with-a-disability.pdf

Berkman, L. F., Kawachi, I., & Glymour, M. M. (Eds.). (2014). *Social epidemiology*. Oxford University Press. DOI: 10.1093/med/9780195377903.001.0001

Breiding, M. J., & Armour, B. S. (2015). The association between disability and intimate partner violence in the United States. *Annals of Epidemiology*, *25*(6), 455–457. https://doi.org/10.1016/j.annepidem.2015.03.017

Brucker, D. L., & Houtenville, A. J. (2015). People with disabilities in the United States. *Archives of Physical Medicine and Rehabilitation*, *96*(5), 771–774. https://doi.org/10.1016/j.apmr.2015.02.024

Carey, G., & Crammond, B. (2017). A glossary of policy frameworks: The many forms of 'universalism' and policy 'targeting'. *Journal of Epidemiology & Community Health, 71*(3), 303–307. http://dx.doi.org/10.1136/jech-2014-204311

Carey, G., Crammond, B., & De Leeuw, E. (2015). Towards health equity: A framework for the application of proportionate universalism. *International Journal for Equity in Health, 14*, 81. https://doi.org/10.1186/s12939-015-0207-6

Carey, G., Malbon, E., Crammond, B., Pescud, M., & Baker, P. (2017). Can the sociology of social problems help us to understand and manage 'lifestyle drift'?. *Health Promotion International, 32*(4), 755–761. https://doi.org/10.1093/heapro/dav116

Carey, G., Malbon, E., Reeders, D., Kavanagh, A., & Llewellyn, G. (2017). Redressing or entrenching social and health inequities through policy implementation? Examining personalised budgets through the Australian National Disability Insurance Scheme. *International Journal for Equity in Health, 16*(1), 192. https://doi.org/10.1186/s12939-017-0682-z

Courtney-Long, E., Stevens, A., Caraballo, R., Ramon, I., & Armour, B. S. (2014). Disparities in current cigarette smoking prevalence by type of disability, 2009–2011. *Public Health Reports, 129*(3), 252–260. https://doi.org/10.1177/003335491412900307

Diderichsen, F., Evans, T., & Whitehead, M. (2001). The social basis of disparities in health. In T. Evans, M. Whitehead, F. Diderichsen, A. Bhuiya, & M. Wirth (Eds.), *Challenging inequities in health: From ethics to action* (pp. 12–23). Oxford University Press.

Disability Housing Futures Working Group. (2016). *Final report*. Brisbane: National Affordable Housing Consortium. https://nahc.org.au/

Du Mont, J., & Forte, T. (2016). Perceived discrimination and self-rated health in Canada: An exploratory study. *BMC Public Health, 16*(1), 742. https://doi.org/10.1186/s12889-016-3344-y

Emerson, E. (2010). Self-reported exposure to disablism is associated with poorer self-reported health and well-being among adults with intellectual disabilities in England: A cross-sectional survey. *Public Health, 124*(12), 682–689. https://doi.org/10.1016/j.puhe.2010.08.020

Emerson, E. (2018). Smoking among adults with and without disabilities in the UK. *Journal of Public Health, 40*(4), e502–e509. https://doi.org/10.1093/pubmed/fdy062

Emerson, E., & Hatton, C. (2007). Mental health of children and adolescents with intellectual disabilities in Britain. *The British Journal of Psychiatry, 191*(6), 493–499. https://doi.org/10.1192/bjp.bp.107.038729

Emerson, E., & Hatton, C. (2008). Self-reported well-being of women and men with intellectual disabilities in England. *American Journal on Mental Retardation, 113*(2), 143–155. https://doi.org/10.1352/0895-8017(2008)113[143:SWOWAM]2.0.CO;2

Emerson, E., Hatton, C., Baines, S., & Robertson, J. (2016). The physical health of British adults with intellectual disability: Cross sectional study. *International Journal for Equity in Health, 15*(1), 11. https://doi.org/10.1186/s12939-016-0296-x

Emerson, E., Krnjacki, K., Llewellyn, G., Vaughan, C., & Kavanagh, A. (2016). Perceptions of safety and exposure to violence in public places among working age adults with disabilities or long-term health conditions in the UK: Cross sectional study. *Public Health, 135*, 91–96. https://doi.org/10.1016/j.puhe.2015.10.036

Emerson, E., Llewellyn, G., Stancliffe, R., Badland, H., Kavanagh, A., Disney, G., & Zhou, Q. (2018). *A fair go? Measuring Australia's progress in reducing the disadvantage for adults with disabilities 2001–2016*. Centre for Research Excellence in Disability and Health, University of Melbourne. https://apo.org.au/node/223371

Emerson, E., Madden, R., Graham, H., Llewellyn, G., Hatton, C., & Robertson, J. (2011). The health of disabled people and the social determinants of health. *Public Health, 125*, 145–147. https://doi.org/10.1016/j.puhe.2010.11.003

Emerson, E., & Roulstone, A. (2014). Developing an evidence base for violent and disablist hate crime in Britain: Findings from the life opportunities survey. *Journal of Interpersonal Violence, 29*(17), 3086–3104. https://doi.org/10.1177/0886260514534524

Emerson, E., & Spencer, N. (2015). Health inequity and children with intellectual disabilities. *International Review of Research in Developmental Disabilities, 48*, 11–42. https://doi.org/10.1016/bs.irrdd.2015.03.001

Emerson, E., Vick, B., Graham, H., Hatton, C., Llewellyn, G., Madden, R., … Robertson, J. (2012). Disablement and health. In N. Watson, C. Thomas, & A. Roulstone (Eds.), *Routledge companion to disability studies* (pp. 253–270). Routledge.

Fontenot, K., Semega, J., & Kollar, M. (2018). *Income and poverty in the United States: 2017*. Washington, DC: US Census Bureau, P60-263. https://www.census.gov/content/dam/Census/library/publications/2018/demo/p60-263.pdf

Frohlich, K. L., & Potvin, L. (2008). Frohlich and Potvin respond. *American Journal of Public Health, 98*, 1352–1352. https://doi.org/10.2105/AJPH.2008.141309

Government of Ireland. (2005). *Disability Act 2005*. Found at: http://www.irishstatutebook.ie/eli/2005/act/14/enacted/en/html

Harrell, E. (2017). *Crime against persons with disabilities, 2009–2015 – Statistical tables*. US Department of Justice, Office of Justice Programs, Bureau of Justice Statistics. https://www.bjs.gov/content/pub/pdf/capd0915st.pdf

Heslop, P., & Emerson, E. (2017). A worsening picture: Poverty and social exclusion and disabled people. In E. Dermott, & G. Main (Eds.), *Poverty and social exclusion in the UK* (pp. 173–192). Policy Press.

Hogan, A., Kyaw-Myint, S., Harris, D., & Denronden, H. (2012). Workforce participation barriers for people with disability. *International Journal of Disability Management*, 7, 1–9. https://doi.org/10.1017/idm.2012.1

Hughes, K., Bellis, M. A., Jones, L., Wood, S., Bates, G., Eckley, L., ... Shakespeare, T. (2012). Prevalence and risk of violence against adults with disabilities: A systematic review and meta-analysis of observational studies. *Lancet*, *379*(9826), 1621–1629. https://doi.org/10.1016/S0140-6736(11)61851-5

Hunter, D. J., Popay, J., Tannahill, C., & Whitehead, M. (2010). Getting to grips with health inequalities at last?. *BMJ Open*, *340*, c684. https://doi.org/10.1136/bmj.c684

Jamrozik, A. (1998). *The sociology of social problems: Theoretical perspectives and methods of intervention*. Cambridge University Press.

Jenkins-Smith, H. C., Nohrstedt, D., Weible, C. M., & Sabatier, P. A. (2014). The advocacy coalition framework: Foundations, evolution, and ongoing research. In C. M. Weible & P. A. Sabatier (Eds.), *Theories of the policy process* (3rd ed.). Westview Press.

Jones, L., Bellis, M. A., Wood, S., Hughes, K., McCoy, E., Eckley, L., ... Officer, A. (2012). Prevalence and risk of violence against children with disabilities: A systematic review and meta-analysis of observational studies. *The Lancet*, *380*(9845), 899–907. https://doi.org/10.1016/S0140-6736(12)60692-8

Kariuki, M., Honey, A., Emerson, E., & Llewellyn, G. (2011). Mental health trajectories of young people after disability onset. *Disability and Health Journal*, *4*(2), 91–101. https://doi.org/10.1016/j.dhjo.2010.08.001

Kavanagh, A. M., Krnjacki, L., Aitken, Z., LaMontagne, A. D., Beer, A., Baker, E., & Bentley, R. (2015). Intersections between disability, type of impairment, gender and socio-economic disadvantage in a nationally representative sample of 33,101 working-aged Australians. *Disability and Health Journal*, *8*(2), 191–199. https://doi.org/10.1016/j.dhjo.2014.08.008

Kavanagh, A., Priest, N., Emerson, E., Milner, A., & King, T. (2018). Gender, parental education, and experiences of bullying victimization by Australian adolescents with and without a disability. *Child: Care, health and development*, *44*(2), 332–341. https://doi.org/10.1111/cch.12545

King, T., Aitken, Z., Milner, A., Emerson, E., Priest, N., Karahalios, A., & Blakely, T. (2018). To what extent is the association between disability and mental health in adolescents mediated by bullying? A causal mediation analysis. *International Journal of Epidemiology*, *47*(5), 1402–1413. https://doi.org/10.1093/ije/dyy154

Kingdon, J. W. (1995). *Agendas, alternatives, and public policies* (2nd ed.). Longman.

Krahn, G. L., Walker, D. K., & Correa-De-Araujo, R. (2015). Persons with disabilities as an unrecognized health disparity population. *American Journal of Public Health*, *105*(S2), S198-S206. https://doi.org/10.2105/AJPH.2014.302182

Krieger, N. (2011). *Epidemiology and the people's health: Theory and context*. Oxford University Press.

Krieger, N. (2014). Discrimination and health inequities *International Journal of Health Services*,*44*(4), 643–710. https://doi.org/10.2190/HS.44.4.b

Krnjacki, L., Emerson, E., Llewellyn, G., & Kavanagh, A. (2016). Prevalence and risk of violence against people with and without disabilities: Findings from an Australian population-based study. *Australian & New Zealand Journal of Public Health*, *40*(1), 16–21. https://doi.org/10.1111/1753-6405.12498

Krnjacki, L., Priest, N., Aitken, Z., Emerson, E., King, T., Llewellyn, G., & Kavanagh, A. (2018). Disability-based discrimination and health: Findings from an Australian based population study. *Australian & New Zealand Journal of Public Health*, *42*(2), 172–174.

Kyle, T., & Dunn, J. R. (2008). Effects of housing circumstances on health, quality of life and healthcare use for people with severe mental illness: A review. *Health and Social Care in the Community*, *16*(1), 1–15. https://doi.org/10.1111/j.1365-2524.2007.00723.x

Marmot, M., Friel, S., Bell, R., Houweling, T. A. J., & Taylor, S., & on behalf of the Commission on Social Determinants of Health. (2008). Closing the gap in a generation: Health equity through action on the social determinants of Health. *The Lancet*, *372*, 1661–1669. https://doi.org/10.1016/S0140-6736(08)61690-6

Marmot, M., & Wilkinson, R. G. (Eds.). (2006). *Social determinants of health* (2nd ed.). Oxford: Oxford University Press.

McLaren, L., & McIntyre, L. (2014). Conceptualizing child care as a population health intervention: Can a strong case be made for a universal approach in Canada, a liberal welfare regime? *Critical Public Health*, *24*(4), 418–428. https://doi.org/10.1080/09581596.2013.803035

Milner, A., King, T. L., LaMontagne, A. D., Aitken, Z., Petrie, D., & Kavanagh, A. M. (2017). Underemployment and its impacts on mental health among those with disabilities: Evidence from the HILDA cohort. *Journal of Epidemiology and Community Health*, *71*(12), 1198–1202. https://doi.org/10.1136/jech-2017-209800

Milner, A., Krnjacki, L., Butterworth, P., Kavanagh, A., & LaMontagne, A. D. (2015). Does disability status modify the association between psychosocial job quality and mental health? A longitudinal fixed-effects analysis. *Social Science & Medicine*, *144*, 104–111.

Milner, A., LaMontagne, A. D., Aitken, Z., Bentley, R., & Kavanagh, A. M. (2014). Employment status and mental health among persons with and without a disability: Evidence from an Australian cohort study. *Journal of Epidemiology and Community Health*, *68*(11), 1064–1071.

Mitra, M., & Mouradian, V. E. (2014). Intimate partner violence in the relationships of men with disabilities in the United States: Relative prevalence and health correlates. *Journal of Interpersonal Violence*, *29*(17), 3150–3166. https://doi.org/10.1177/0886260514534526

Needham, C. (2016). The boundaries of budgets: Why should individuals make spending choices about their health and social care? In J. Butcher & D. Gilchrist (Eds.), *The three sector solution* (pp. 319–336). ANU Press.

Papworth Trust. (2011). *Disability in the United Kingdom 2011: Facts and figures*. Papworth Trust. https://www.papworthtrust.org.uk/about-us/publications/papworth-trust-annual-report-and-accounts-2011.pdf

Pinquart, M. (2017). Systematic review: Bullying involvement of children with and without chronic physical illness and/or physical/sensory disability: A meta-analytic comparison with healthy/nondisabled peers. *Journal of Pediatric Psychology*, *42*(3), 245–259.https://doi.org/10.1093/jpepsy/jsw081

Ploubidis, G. B., Benova, L., Grundy, E., Laydon, D., & De Stavola, B. (2014). Lifelong socio economic position and biomarkers of later life health: Testing the contribution of competing hypotheses. *Social Science & Medicine*, *119*, 258–265.

Popay, J., Whitehead, M., & Hunter, D. J. (2010). Injustice is killing people on a large scale – But what is to be done about it? *Journal of Public Health*, *32*, 148–149. https://doi.org/10.1093/pubmed/fdq029

Public Health England. (2014). *Local action on health inequalities: Building children and young people's resilience in schools*. Public Health England. https://assets.publishing.service.gov.uk/government/uploads/system/uploads/attachment_data/file/355770/Briefing2_Resilience_in_schools_health_inequalities.pdf

Public Health England. (2015). *The determinants of health inequalities experienced by children with learning disabilities*. Public Health England. https://assets.publishing.service.gov.uk/government/uploads/system/uploads/attachment_data/file/613182/PWLDIE_2015_main_report_NB090517.pdf

Raphael, D. (2008). Grasping at straws: A recent history of health promotion in Canada. *Critical Public Health*, *18*(4), 483–495. https://doi.org/10.1080/09581590802443604

Sentenac, M., Gavin, A., Gabhainn, S. N., Molcho, M., Due, P., Ravens-Sieberer, U., … Godeau, E. (2013). Peer victimization and subjective health among students reporting disability or chronic illness in 11 Western countries. *European Journal of Public Health*, *23*(3), 421–426. https://doi.org/10.1093/eurpub/cks073

Shahtahmasebi, S., Emerson, E., Berridge, D., & Lancaster, G. (2011). Child disability and the dynamics of family poverty, hardship and financial strain: Evidence from the UK. *Journal of Social Policy*, *40*(4), 653–673. https://doi.org/10.1017/S0047279410000905

Shonkoff, J. P. (2016). Capitalizing on advances in science to reduce the health consequences of early childhood adversity. *JAMA Pediatrics*, *170*(10), 1003–1007. https://doi.org/10.1001/jamapediatrics.2016.1559

Spencer, N., Blackburn, C., & Read, J. (2015). Disabling chronic conditions in childhood and socio-economic disadvantage: A systematic review and meta-analyses of observational studies. *BMJ Open*, *5*(9), e007062. http://dx.doi.org/10.1136/bmjopen-2014-007062

Stein, M. A., Stein, P. J., Weiss, D., & Lang, R. (2009). Health care and the UN Disability Rights Convention. *The Lancet*, *374*(9704), 1796–1798. https://doi.org/10.1016/S0140-6736(09)62033-X

Sutin, A. R., Stephan, Y., Carretta, H., & Terracciano, A. (2015). Perceived discrimination and physical, cognitive, and emotional health in older adulthood. *The American Journal of Geriatric Psychiatry*, *23*(2), 171–179. https://doi.org/10.1016/j.jagp.2014.03.007

The Children's Society. (2011). *4 in every 10 disabled children living in poverty*. The Children's Society. https://www.childrenssociety.org.uk/sites/default/files/tcs/4_in_10_reportfinal.pdf

United Nations. (2006). Convention on the Rights of Persons with Disabilities. Retrieved from https://www.un.org/development/desa/disabilities/convention-on-the-rights-of-persons-with-disabilities.html.

Wamala, S., Boström, G., & Nyqvist, K. (2007). Perceived discrimination and psychological distress in Sweden. *The British Journal of Psychiatry*, *190*(1), 75–76. https://doi.org/10.1192/bjp.bp.105.021188

Wang, Q. (2005). *Disability and American families: 2000*. US Census Bureau. https://www.census.gov/prod/2005pubs/censr-23.pdf

Welch, T., & Cleak, H. (2018). Is housing a predictor of autonomy and quality of life of people with severe mental illness? Implications for social work. *Australian Social Work*, *71*(4), 491–506. https://doi.org/10.1080/0312407X.2018.1498114

White, B. J., Peaslee, J., & LaQuatra, J. (1994). Comparing housing affordability and quality among disability households: The United States and its regions. *Journal of Family and Economic Issues*, *15*(4), 367–380. https://doi.org/10.1007/BF02353811

Whitehead, M. (2012). Waving or drowning? A view of health equity from Europe. *Australian and New Zealand Journal of Public Health*, *36*(6), 523–523. https://doi.org/10.1111/j.1753-6405.2012.00947.x

Wiesel, I., Laragy, C., Gendera, S., Fisher, K. R., Jenkinson, S., Hill, T., ... Bridge, C. (2015). Moving to my home: Housing aspirations, transitions and outcomes of people with disability. *AHURI Final Report*, *246*. https://www.ahuri.edu.au/__data/assets/pdf_file/0014/2165/AHURI_Final_Report_No246_Moving-to-my-home-housing-aspirations,-transitions-and-outcomes-of-people-with-disability.pdf

World Health Organization. (2008). *Closing the gap in a generation: Health equity through action on the social determinants of health. Final report of the Commission on the Social Determinants of Health*. Geneva: World Health Organization. https://www.endfgm.eu/resources/health/who-closing-the-gap-in-a-generation-health-equity-through-action-on-the-social-determinants-of-health-2008/

World Health Organization. (2011). *Rio Political Declaration on Social Determinants of Health*. World Health Organization. http://www.who.int/sdhconference/declaration/en/

World Health Organization and Calouste Gulbenkian Foundation. (2014). *Social determinants of mental health*. World Health Organization. https://www.who.int/mental_health/publications/gulbenkian_paper_social_determinants_of_mental_health/en/

World Health Organization and the World Bank. (2011). *World report on disability*. World Health Organization. https://www.who.int/disabilities/world_report/2011/report.pdf

World Health Organization Regional Office for Europe. (2014). *Report on social determinants and the health divide in the WHO European region: Final report (updated)*. World Health Organization Regional Office for Europe. https://www.euro.who.int/en/publications/abstracts/review-of-social-determinants-and-the-health-divide-in-the-who-european-region.-final-report

Acknowledgment

We would like to acknowledge the contributions made by our colleagues in the Centre for Research Excellence on Disability and Health (https://credh.org.au/) in shaping the ideas expressed in this paper.

Suggested Readings

Emerson, E., Vick, B., Graham, H., Hatton, C., Llewellyn, G., Madden, R., ... Robertson, J. (2012). Disablement and health. In N. Watson, C. Thomas & A. Roulestone (Eds.), *The Routledge companion to disability studies* (pp. 253–270). Routledge.

Krahn, G. L., Walker, D. K., & Correa-De-Araujo, R. (2015). Persons with disabilities as an unrecognized health disparity population. *American Journal of Public Health*, *105*(S2), S198-S206. https://doi.org/10.2105/AJPH.2014.302182

United Nations. (2006). Convention on the Rights of Persons with Disabilities. Retrieved from https://www.un.org/development/desa/disabilities/convention-on-the-rights-of-persons-with-disabilities.html.

World Health Organization. (2011). *Rio Political Declaration on Social Determinants of Health*. World Health Organization. http://www.who.int/sdhconference/declaration/en/

6

REDUCING THE SHARED BURDEN OF CHRONIC CONDITIONS AMONG PERSONS AGEING WITH DISABILITY AND OLDER ADULTS IN THE UNITED STATES THROUGH BRIDGING AGEING AND DISABILITY

Margaret L. Campbell and Michelle Putnam

Changing Demographics of Ageing and Disability

As is well established, the proportion of older adults in the global population is rapidly increasing. According to data from the United Nations, between 2015 and 2030 the number of older persons (those aged 60 years or over) in the world is projected to grow by 56%, from 901 million to more than 1.4 billion. By 2030, older persons are projected to outnumber children and to account for 1-in-6 people worldwide, an increase from 1-in-8 people in 2015. Additionally, life expectancy has increased worldwide— 60% of women and 52% of men born between 2000 and 2005 are expected to survive to their 80th birthdays, compared to less than 40% of the women and men born between 1950 and 1955 (United Nations, 2015). In relation to disability, according to the World Health Organization's (WHO) World Report on Disability, about 15% of the world's population (or 1 billion people) currently lives with some form of disability, and between 2% and 4% experience severe disability (World Health Organization, 2011). Based on WHO projections in the same report, the number of people with disabilities is growing and expected to continue to grow, due to both population ageing and the global increase in chronic health conditions associated with disability, such as diabetes, cardiovascular diseases, and mental illness. In sum, having a disability places a person in one of the world's largest minority groups.

Over the past several decades, the increased longevity among people with disabilities has emerged as an important demographic trend to consider in regards to health promotion and chronic conditions. This phenomenon of increased longevity is often described as *Ageing with Disability* (Campbell, Sheets, & Strong, 1999; Field & Jette, 2007a, 2007b; Treishman, 1987). While there is no empirical standard for defining who is *Ageing with Disability*, the general agreement is that the term refers to people living with the long-term effects of disabilities acquired from birth to middle age who are now surviving into mid- and later life (Field & Jette, 2007a, 2007b; Iezzoni, Kurtz, & Rao, 2014; Verbrugge & Yang, 2002; Verbrugge, Latham, & Clarke, 2017). People who are ageing with a disability include traditional rehabilitation populations (e.g. people with spina bifida, cerebral palsy, neuromuscular disorders, polio, spinal cord injury, traumatic brain injury, multiple sclerosis, etc.), and persons with intellectual and developmental disabilities.

The size of the ageing of the disability population worldwide or for specific nations is largely unknown. Some national estimates are available, but they tend to be imprecise due to differing ways disability is defined and measured (e.g. functional limitation, disease diagnosis, inability to work) as well as incomplete data often related to the omission of questions on age of onset and/or the duration of primary disability (Putnam, Molton, Truitt, Smith, & Jensen, 2016). The most recent inference for the United States (U.S.) suggests that between 12 and 13 million adults 18 years and older are living with an activity limitation acquired before age 40 (Freedman, 2014; LaPlante, 2014). This is a small but significant sub-set of the overall population of persons with disabilities living in the U.S., estimated to be 39.9 million in 2014 based on a self-reported functional limitation, or 12.6% of the community of the living population over 5 years of age (Erickson, Lee, & Schrader, 2017). It is an unknown percentage of the older adult population aged 65 or older, which in 2014 was estimated to be 46 million or 14.9% of the total U.S. population (Colby & Ortman, 2015). While the ageing with disability population may seem modest in comparison to these larger groups, the longevity trends of this sub-population represent significant advances made in medicine, rehabilitation, education, social and employment programs, and disability rights, access, and inclusion over the past 50 years.

This paper focuses on persons ageing with disability in the U.S. as a case example. It articulates distinctions between disability-related secondary conditions and age-related chronic conditions as a first step in identifying shared conditions important to address for both mid-life and older adults with disabilities. It also provides recommendations for bridging activities in the United States by researchers, professionals, and consumer advocates. We argue that these can more efficiently move research and practice than if activities were undertaken separately in each field (ageing and disability/rehabilitation).

Clarifying Understanding of Ageing with Disability and Chronic Conditions

In general people ageing with long-term disability with onset prior to later life in the United States are concentrated among the population ages 40-to-64 (Iezzoni et al., 2014). In our review of the literature, we were unable to identify similar data for other nations; however, we recognise there may be differences in disability trends based on wealth and income patterns, as well as the global burden of disease (Officer & Posarac, 2011) This population is distinguished from people ageing into disability in later life and those who acquire sustained significant disability for the first time at older ages (Verbrugge & Yang, 2002).

It is clear from the research literature that people with an early onset of disability, beginning at approximately age 45, report greater difficulty with independent living than they did at early onset. A challenge clinicians, practitioners, and individuals ageing with disabilities themselves encounter in working with persons ageing with long-term disability is distinguishing the effects of living with long-term disability from the onset of age-related secondary conditions. Difficulty in making this distinction stems from (1) A lack of clear terminology in clinical practice and research; and (2) The need to disentangle the concepts of secondary conditions, related to a primary disability, and chronic conditions, which are generally not related to the primary disability, but to ageing, so that they are not mistaken for each other or conflated. We present a brief distinction between these concepts and show overlap in shared conditions in Figure 6.1.

Research and clinical observations, together, show that as individuals ageing with disabilities continue to live longer there is an increased likelihood of experiencing secondary conditions directly or indirectly. These secondary conditions are typically related to the underlying disability, including the onset of new functional changes and declines, and can threaten independence and participation and lead to secondary disabilities (Marge, 1988). Secondary conditions associated with disability are defined as any additional physical or mental health conditions that can result from a primary disabling condition but are not a diagnostic feature of that condition (Pope & Tarlov, 1991). This includes preventable physical, mental, and social disorders resulting directly or indirectly from an initial disabling condition (Molton et al., 2014) that are generally considered direct secondary conditions. It is not unusual for indirect secondary conditions to be experienced by people living with long-term disability. Indirect secondary conditions are in part due to physical overuse of compensatory limbs (e.g. shoulder injuries

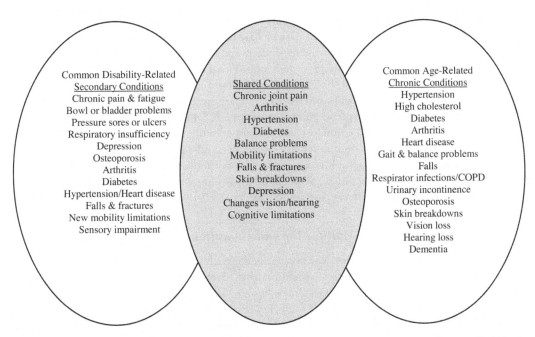

Figure 6.1 Examples of shared chronic conditions of persons ageing with disability and ageing into disability in later life. *Disability-Related Secondary Conditions.*

for manual wheelchair uses), sedentary life styles, environmental barriers to recreational and leisure opportunities, and poor health behaviours. These are frequently the same as the age-related chronic conditions experienced by the ageing population at large (Jensen et al., 2013; Smith, Molton, & Jensen, 2016).

While precise data are not available for the U.S. population, clinical and survey research indicate that the high rates of complications and/or changes experienced by people with long-term disability typically occur about 20–25 years sooner compared to peers without disabilities (Field & Jette, 2007a, 2007b). Specifically, '… as persons with long-term disability reach age 50, many show the kind of functional ages that would *not* be expected until age 70–75 in people without disabilities' (Kailes, 2017). Given the timing of the onset of ageing with disability, typically starting in the mid-40s, and the impact on physical function, secondary conditions have been described in the literature as evidence of *pre-mature, atypical, and accelerated ageing* (Field & Jette, 2007a, 2007b; Verbrugge & Yang, 2002). While the onset and severity of secondary conditions varies by the severity and duration of the underlying disability, research conducted during the last 25 years indicates that the most common conditions include the following: chronic pain and fatigue, bowel or bladder problems, pressure sores or ulcers, respiratory insufficiency, depression, osteoporosis, accelerated arthritis, falls & fractures, new mobility problems, hypertension, heart disease, and sensory and cognitive impairments (Kinne et al., 2004; Molton et al., 2014; Verbrugge & Yang, 2002).

Age-Related Chronic Conditions

Current trends in longevity and population growth are associated with the rise in the prevalence of chronic disease and other chronic conditions and combinations of chronic conditions associated with ageing and growing older, long-term effects of exposure to environmental hazards, and long-term effects of poor health behaviours or the practice of poor health behaviours over time. Although the literature does not support a single uniform definition for chronic conditions, recurrent themes or criteria include: the non-self-limited nature of the condition, requiring ongoing medical attention; the association with persistent and recurring health problems and diseases, and activity limitations; and a duration measured in months and years, not days and weeks. Chronic conditions include both *physical conditions,* such as arthritis, sensory impairments, cancer, and HIV infection, *and cognitive disorders,* such as ongoing depression, substance abuse, and dementia (Goodman, Posner, Huang, Parekh, & Koh, 2013; World Health Organization, 2014). Examples of common age-related chronic conditions include: hypertension, high cholesterol, diabetes, osteoarthritis, heart disease, gait and mobility problems, falls, respiratory infections/chronic obstructive pulmonary disease (COPD), urinary incontinence, osteoporosis, skin breakdowns, hearing and vision loss, and dementia. In the United States, the onset for chronic conditions and diseases begins in midlife for just over half of all adults. Roughly 53% of adults with chronic conditions ages 45–64 have at least one chronic condition and nearly 86% of adults age 65 and older have at least one chronic condition (Ward, Schiller, & Goodman, 2014); and thus, they are generally described as *age-related chronic conditions* (Goodman et al., 2013).

Multiple Chronic Conditions

Similar to the risk of *secondary disabilities* for people ageing with long-term disability, multiple chronic conditions (MCCs) are concurrent chronic conditions that affect a person at the same time (Department of Health and Human Services, 2010; Goodman et al., 2013). The most common MCC dyads are hypertension and arthritis, hypertension and high cholesterol, and hypertension and diabetes. The most common MCC triads are hypertension, high cholesterol, and diabetes, and hypertension, high cholesterol, and arthritis (Goodman et al., 2013). The effects of CCs and MCCs on individuals, families, and healthcare systems are many. For individuals, CCs and MCCs can negatively affect physical and psychosocial functioning, independence, and participation in community life, including work. CCs and MCCs are associated with a greater risk of poor day-to-day functioning. In addition, they can diminish quality of life and add to the demands on family members or others as caregivers. In some cases, MCCs may be simply a cluster of ageing-related chronic conditions found among older individuals, but not all MCCs are age-related. Some individuals may experience MCCs at younger ages such as hypertension and high cholesterol. U.S. data show that just over 7% of adults ages 18–44 have MCCs (19% have a single CC) (Ward et al., 2014). The common CCs and MCCs noted above may also include age-related CCs not commonly found among younger adults such as dementia, urinary incontinence, and gait problems for persons ageing with and ageing into disability.

At a systems level, CCs and MCCs can challenge health care professionals whose education has not prepared them to care knowledgeably for people ageing with long-standing disabilities. CCs and MCCs increase the risk for repeat hospitalisations and of receiving conflicting advice from physicians and other health care providers. They also contribute to frailty, functional limitations, and disability, which further complicate access to health care, interfere with self-management, and necessitate reliance on caregivers. In general, MCCs are associated with substantial health care costs: in the U.S., about 66% percent of the total health care spending is related to care for CCs/MCCs (Kinne et al., 2004).

Understanding the Nexus of Ageing and Disability

As Figure 6.1 demonstrates, persons ageing with disability and older adults share a common set of chronic conditions as a result of experiencing disability-related secondary conditions, particularly indirect secondary conditions, or age-related chronic conditions. In addition, persons ageing with disability may also experience age-related chronic conditions as well as disability-related secondary conditions, making the intersection of shared conditions wider. Based on disease diagnosis or impairment status, there may be some variances between persons ageing with disability and older adults in onset, the specific nature and/or symptoms related to the conditions, or in the way these conditions interact with primary disability or other chronic conditions. That said, there is arguably more potential to advance clinical and program interventions that address these shared chronic conditions through research that develops more universal interventions that have efficacy for both persons ageing with disability and the traditional older adult population than by pursuing two distinct lines of intervention research and practice (one for each population group). In sum, segmenting *people ageing with disabilities* from *people ageing into disability in later life*, those who acquire a sustained disability for the first time at older ages (Verbrugge et al., 2017) (we place persons with CCs/MCCs in this latter group), can be considered inefficient. It would be more relevant to work towards a better understanding of the nexus of ageing and disability (Torres-Gil, 2007), focusing on shared chronic conditions, so that more universal interventions can be developed.

The Shared Burden of Chronic Conditions

Historically, there has been little focus on the shared burden of chronic conditions across persons ageing with disability and older adults in CC practice and research. This may be due to the age targeting of public health research and program interventions or, in some cases, efforts aimed at populations with specific disease and/or diagnostic conditions. The chronic conditions evidence base tends to straddle two substantially separate literatures, gerontology and rehabilitation/physical medicine, which typically focus on older and younger/middle-aged adults, respectively. Public health literature is less age-specific, but it remains rare to find research that attempts to do any of these three things which would help build the evidence base: (1) Understand disability and chronic conditions across the life course (2) Include both persons ageing with and ageing into disability and (3) Attempts to translate evidence, including interventions, from younger persons with disabilities to older persons with disabilities and vice versa. It is also rare to find practice guidelines with any of the above traits. In sum, this approach of segmenting the study of chronic conditions by age group and disability history or diagnosis has substantially limited our understanding of chronic conditions among persons ageing with a disability in particular, creating a shortage of evidence-based practices (EBPs) to promote health and reduce the burden of chronic conditions. For example, to date, there are few empirical studies of ageing with disability for midlife and older persons in general (Clarke & Latham, 2014; Hardy, Allore, Guo, Dubin, & Gill, 2006; Verbrugge & Yang, 2002). Table 6.1 presents indicators of the nexus of ageing and disability in the U.S., highlighting the shared burden of CCs.

The Growing Demand for More Evidence-Based Practices (EBP) to Promote Health and Reduce the Shared Burden of Chronic Conditions in the U.S.

There has been agreement across ageing and disability sectors, and within U.S. federal agencies focused on health, ageing, and disability, that prevention of chronic conditions should be a major component of health promotion for older adults and people with disabilities (American Public Health Association, 2017). In response to the high rates of chronic conditions and diseases observed for middle-aged and older adults with and without disabilities, between 2000 and 2016, the U.S. Congress passed legislation establishing new federal programs and modified administrative regulations to require and encourage the delivery of evidence-based (EB) health promotion and disease prevention programs, as well as services for older adults and populations with greater likelihood of experiencing chronic conditions, including persons with disabilities and individuals within racial and ethnic minority groups. Examples of key legislation include the 2010 Patient Protection and Affordable Care Act (ACA) Title IV: Prevention of Chronic Disease and Improving Public Health. While the primary focus of Title IV is on removing financial barriers and increasing access to preventative healthcare services, it also awards competitive grants to eligible entities for programs that improve health, reduce chronic disease rates, address health disparities, and develop stronger evidence based on effective prevention programming. While there are ongoing calls for revisions and the repeal of the ACA, which may reduce funding or eliminate these programs, the costs of chronic disease at the state and federal level are well documented (Trogdon et al., 2015) and may be persuasive in continuing the emphasis on the health promotion program regardless of any political discord.

Table 6.1 Indicators of the nexus of ageing and disability in the U.S.

Overall disability prevalence is substantial.
- In 2014, 39.9 million or 12.6% of the community of the living population ≥5 years or older reported having a disability (Ward et al., 2014).

Disability prevalence is increasing over time.
- The total number of non-institutionalised civilians ≥age 18 reporting disability increased by 2 million between 2005 and 2010 (Brault, 2010).

Prevalence of disability increases with age.
- Disability rates are 10.7% for persons age 21–64 years; 25.4% for age 65–74 years; and 49.8% for ages 75 and over (Groah et al., 2012).

Prevalence of multiple disabilities increases with age.
- Prevalence of three or more disabilities are 18.2% for persons ages 18–44 years; 27.6% for age 45–79 years; and 45.4% for ages 80 and older.
- Mobility disabilities are most likely to co-occur with other types of disabilities. For example: among persons who report movement difficulties, 27.6% also report sensory difficulties and 42% reported work limitations (Iezzoni et al., 2014).

Persons with early and mid-life significant disability have increased life expectancy.
- Research studies indicate that people with physical disabilities now have nearly normal life spans (Brault, 2010; Groah, 2012).
- People with developmental disabilities now routinely live beyond 50 (Klingbeil, Baer, & Wilson, 2004).

Persons with existing disabilities experience increased disability over time (Iezzoni et al., 2014).
- Between 1998 and 2011, chronic disability rates increased significantly across groups of individuals with six different types of conditions (movement, emotional, cognitive, self-care, social, and work) among civilian, non-institutionalised adults over 18, and older based on data from the NHIS.
- The greatest increase was for movement difficulties, which increased from 19.3 to 23.3% in persons 18 and older (Courtney-Long et al., 2015).

Substantial percentages of individuals report average age of onset of primary disability as before age 65.
- 30% of individuals with disabilities report experiencing onset at age 44 or younger. 13% of 15–64 year olds reported disability onset at birth. Half of all persons age 65 or older reported having activity limitations before age 65 (Department of Health and Human Services, 2010).

There are other legislative and administrative regulation changes, which also support greater use of EBPs that may be more politically durable. For example, beginning in 2016, all funds for disease prevention and health promotion services delivered under the Older Americans Act Title IIID and administered by the Administration on Aging (AoA) within the U.S. Administration for Community Living (ACL) may only be spent on programs that meet the highest-level criteria for EBPs (e.g. use of experimental and quasi-experimental research designs and translation into community settings per a new administrative rule) (Administration for Community Living, 2017a, 2017b, 2017c). Another example is the U.S. Administration on Community Living (ACL) itself, which receives funding from various legislated programs including the ACA, the OAA, and the Rehabilitation Act to achieve its mission to 'maximize the independence, well-being, and health of older adults and people with disabilities across the lifespan' (Administration for Community Living, 2017a, 2017b, 2017c). Key health promotion programs under the ACL include Disease Prevention and Health Promotion Services (DPHPS), Aging and Disability Network of Evidence-Based Programs (ADEPP), and Chronic Disease Self-Management Education Programs (CDSMP). All of these programs support the development of and implementation of evidence-based programs.

Since the change in presidential administration in January 2017, it is not clear what the future of these legislative programs and their administration will be as most reflect the priorities of the prior presidential administration. However, the costs of treating chronic conditions and the premature deaths related to them are well established (Buttorff, Ruder, & Bauman, 2017; Center for Disease Control and Prevention, 2017; Department of Health and Human Services, 2010) and there is substantial interest in programs, interventions, and treatments that bring the best evidence to bear in addressing chronic conditions by other stakeholders including individuals with chronic conditions, practitioners and service providers, and health care organisations that are likely to keep the momentum for the development and implementation of EB health promotion and chronic care intervention programs moving forward. These are positive developments, but they also highlight the substantial gap between the critical need for EBP health promotion programs that have been tested and successfully implemented in community settings (e.g. in real homes, neighbourhoods, and community-based organisations) and their supply, which are notably few. While this imbalance between supply and demand exists for all adults with disabilities and activity limitations, the gap is more pronounced for middle aged individuals with early onset disabilities than for their older counterparts. For example, a scoping review of the National Council on Aging (NCOA) Center for Healthy Aging database containing all the health promotion programs that meet the ACL criteria for EBPs found that only 2 of the more than 150 randomised controlled trials listed included middle-aged individuals with early-onset, long-term disabling conditions in the clinical trial of the intervention. The other 148 studies were based exclusively on older adults with and without chronic conditions, but no significant disabilities (Molton et al., 2014).

Additional evidence of the gap in EB health promotion programs for persons ageing with a disability exists. ACL maintains a webpage entitled Aging and Disability Evidence-based Programs and Practices (ADEPP) that lists the EBPs that are ready for dissemination. Of the three EB health promotion programs with the highest level of evidence under the OAA Title IIID criteria (Stanford's Chronic Disease Self-Management Program (CDSMP), A Matter of Balance for fall prevention, and Health IDEAS for depression management (National Council on Aging, 2017) only the CDSMP has been evaluated for effectiveness with people with disabilities under research conditions. However, it has yet to be implemented for this population in standard practice in community-based settings, so it is unclear how well the intervention will translate to everyday practice. Similarly, of the 12 EB health promotion interventions listed on the ADEPP website (Administration for Community Living, 2017a, 2017b, 2017c), which are maintained by the U.S. ACL, none have been tested and demonstrated to be effective for middle aged individuals with an early onset of long-term disabilities. The net result is that despite ACL's mission, people ageing with long-term disabilities between the ages of 45 and 64 are less likely to receive EB health promotion programs in community settings through their programs compared to older adults with and without activity limitations.

In part, the explanation for the shortage in EBP to reduce the burden of chronic conditions for people ageing with a disability can be explained by differences in research investment. While both ageing and disability fields face the same increased demand for the delivery of effective EB health promotion programs in community settings, the nature of the gap is different. From the ageing perspective, there are a sizable number of EBPs related to chronic care and health promotion. The gap results primarily from a lack of funding for translational and implementation science research aimed at adapting the portfolio of existing EB health promotion interventions for older adults for delivery in community-based settings. Whereas, from the ageing with disability perspective, the gap is more fundamental and results from both (1) A historical lack of national attention to the health and wellness needs of people with disabilities in general, related in part to outdated stereotypes that disability is synonymous with poor health; and (2) A historical lack of government funding for basic intervention development research for middle-aged adults ageing with long-term disabilities, ready to be translated and implemented in community settings, that would create a portfolio of EB health promotion programs for adults with disabilities (Rimmer, 1999). It is possible to close this gap, but focused initiatives and actions will be required to do so.

Closing the EBP Needs and Supply Gap by Bridging Ageing and Disability Research and Practice

To help close the gap in our data and knowledge and increase the availability of evidence-based health promotion programs that reduce the burden of chronic conditions experienced by people ageing with disability in midlife and beyond, key actions are needed both at the systems and the practice levels that work to bridge the fields of ageing and disability. Bridging ageing and disability is noted to be the process of actively promoting the development of mechanisms that create pathways across fields of research and practice, foster interdisciplinary collaboration, and pursue a common knowledge base that can support both sharing and shared evidence (Bickenbach et al., 2012). Engagement in bridging work has the potential to more efficiently work towards closing the gap between the need for EBPs that reduce the shared burden of chronic conditions and the supply of these programs and interventions. Below we outline several recommendations for where and how to begin this bridging work that we believe have considerable potential for success.

At the systems level, ageing, disability, and public health agencies within the government can have a significant impact on the development, implementation, and dissemination of EBPs by taking the following concrete steps. First, advance understanding of the patterns and trajectories as well as increase the ability to study chronic conditions over time by developing and funding new (or providing expanded funding for existing) public longitudinal data systems that include both younger and older individuals ageing with long-term disabilities. Rather than setting an ending or beginning point of a data set at age 60 or 65, the sample base should span the transition from mid-life into later life. Age segmenting data sets with cut-offs of age 60 or 65 do not permit an understanding of the ageing with disability process and its relationship to chronic conditions. A good example of this is the National Health and Aging Trends Study (NHATS), a new longitudinal data set launched in 2011 (National Health and Aging Trends Study, 2017). NHATS includes a wide set of bio-psycho-social domains but the age range of the sample is 65 and older. Some U.S. longitudinal data sets do have wider age ranges, e.g. the Panel Study on Income Dynamics (as early as birth) (Panel Study on Income Dynamics, 2017) and the Health and Retirement Study (age 50 and older) (Health and Retirement Study, 2017), but few contain measures of the age of onset and the duration of onset of disabilities, as well as the age of onset of significant activity limitations and the duration of activity limitations. This limits the possibilities for identifying persons ageing with a long-term disability and the ability to better identify (Coyle & Putnam, 2017) and understand the intersections of age-related chronic conditions and disability-related secondary conditions. That said, it can be argued that data sets that start at age 50 do permit an analysis of persistence of disability over time, regardless of the lack of onset measure (Verbrugge et al., 2017). Depending on the purpose of the analysis, this may be accepted. However, as a second action, we recommend that the new and/or expanded data sets include measures of the age of disability diagnosis, the age of disability onset, and other relevant time variables.

Third, government ageing and disability agencies should work in collaboration with private funders, foundations, and affiliated organisations to bring scientists, policy experts, program administrators, and other stakeholders together in organised events to develop a coordinated research agenda that includes both the traditional older population and persons ageing with disability. This agenda should identify priorities that respond to the challenges of ageing with disability and chronic conditions across the life cycle. At this time, the lack of an agenda hinders strategic, forward progress in creating the supply of EB health promotion programs and chronic condition interventions and limits opportunities to leverage public and private funds. Fourth, in response to this research agenda, government and private sector funders and organisations should consider investing in new joint funding initiatives that support interventions development, efficacy, and effectiveness trials, as well as translational research and scaled up evaluations of evidence-based health promotion programs that include both traditional ageing populations and persons ageing with a long-term disability.

Fourth, and finally, government agencies, as well as private funders, should invest in the development of researchers with knowledge and capacity in bridging ageing and disability to support work across traditional ageing and disability populations. They should also support the development of researchers who have dedicated training related to ageing with disability. This can be done by providing funding for cross-disciplinary training of new and seasoned researchers as well as by supporting pre- and post-doctoral fellowships. This will expand the workforce of scientists available to work on EBPs related to health promotion and chronic conditions for adults with disabilities of all ages.

At the practice level, researchers, educators, providers, and consumer advocates can facilitate and support efforts to bridge the ageing and disability program and practice networks by doing the following. One, seek and develop partnerships and collaborations that cut across the ageing and disability practice and service networks. These partnerships can do many things ranging from helping individuals find resources and support, to providing the resources and platforms necessary to support community-based research, to assisting in the implementation of evidence-based health promotion programs. In the United States, examples of programs where these opportunities for bridge building lie are the Ageing and Disability Resource Centers (Putnam, 2014) which are charged with helping individuals with disabilities of all ages understand and access support and service options. Without these partnerships and collaborations, it is difficult to share existing knowledge or advance a more unified evidence base.

Two, where there is a gap in the evidence base, practice professionals can draw on best practices from both the ageing and disabilities bodies of knowledge when selecting health promotion programs and chronic care intervention approaches until the gap is filled. In sum, practitioners should look across fields of study and practice, as shared conditions between the older adults and persons ageing with disability suggest that within the nexus of ageing and disability, it is possible for practices used with one population to benefit the other.

Three, researchers, educators, providers, and consumer advocates should educate themselves on ageing and disability policy, funding streams, and service delivery systems so that they understand more broadly where chronic condition programs are provided, how they are delivered, and how they are funded. This broad knowledge will help guide persons in need of assistance to potential resources, as well as increase awareness of the gap in the provision of chronic condition interventions and health promotion programs. Among other things, this knowledge can be used by professionals and advocates to advocate for funding changes that help bridge ageing and disability programs, which have historically segmented clients and consumers by age, often providing different sets of benefits to different age and/or diagnostic or impairment groups.

Finally, four, researchers, educators, providers, and consumer advocates should actively advocate for the rights of people ageing with disabilities and older adults ageing into disabilities to receive effective, evidence-based health promotion programs in community settings. This highlights a true bridge between the fields of ageing and disability – the desire to live in the community – that has the potential to overcome historical differences between ageing and disability sectors (Putnam, 2007). In this pursuit, professionals and consumer advocates would be well-served to use inclusive language that reflects a bi-cultural understanding of the similarities and differences in the ageing and disability experience, honouring the history and values of the respective ageing and disability movements, in an effort to advance shared interests.

Conclusion – Reducing the Shared Burden of Chronic Conditions

In the U.S., the divide between ageing and rehabilitation/physical medicine has left a substantial void in our understanding of how best to intervene in real-life settings to improve health by addressing secondary conditions related to ageing and age-related secondary conditions. However, this void is visible internationally as well, as evidenced in the academic literature. The U.S. is just one case example. The growth of the ageing with disability population is a worldwide phenomenon that is under-studied, including the role of CC/MCC's in exacerbating disability and increasing premature mortality. As increased global attention is paid to non-communicable diseases by the World Health Organization and other leading international non-governmental organisations (World Health Organization, 2014), there is a need to consider the most effective and efficient ways of developing and implementing health promotion interventions for persons with disabilities of all ages. The increased longevity experienced by both middle-aged and older adults living with long-term disabilities and significant activity limitations, combined with the high risk of secondary and chronic health conditions, reinforces the importance of bridging knowledge, policy, and practice across ageing and disability fields to better serve the emerging population of persons ageing with disabilities. Recognising the shared burden of chronic conditions and taking steps to reduce the burden as efficiently as possible by recognising this shared interest is critical to closing the gap in the evidence base and developing community-based, health-promotion programs and chronic condition interventions that are readily usable and benefit all adults ageing with disabilities.

References

Administration for Community Living. (2017a). *About ACL*. U.S. Department of Health and Human Services. https://acl.gov/about-acl

Administration for Community Living. (2017b). *Aging and disability evidence-based programs and practices*. U.S. Department of Health and Human Services. https://www.acl.gov/node/619

Administration for Community Living. (2017c). *Disease prevention*. U.S. Department of Health and Human Services. https://acl.gov/programs/health-wellness/disease-prevention

American Public Health Association. (2017). *Prevention and public health fund*. U.S. Department of Health and Human Services. https://www.hhs.gov/open/prevention/index.html

Bickenbach, J., Bigby, C., Salvador-Carulla, L., Heller, T., Leonardi, M., Leroy, B., ... Spindel, A. (2012). The Toronto declaration on bridging knowledge, policy and practice in aging and disability: Toronto, Canada, March 30, 2012. *International Journal of Integrated Care, 12*, e205. https://doi.org/10.5334/ijic.1086

Brault, M. W. (2010). Americans with disabilities: 2010, *Current Population Report* P70-131, U.S. Census Bureau. http://www.census.gov/prod/2012pubs/p70-131.pdf.

Buttorff, C., Ruder, T., & Bauman, M. (2017). *Multiple chronic conditions in the United States*. Rand Corporation. https://www.rand.org/content/dam/rand/pubs/tools/TL200/TL221/RAND_TL221.pdf

Campbell, M. L., Sheets, D., & Strong, P. S. (1999). Secondary health conditions among middle-aged individuals with chronic physical disabilities: Implications for unmet needs for services. *Assistive Technology: The Official Journal of RESNA, 11*(2), 105–122. https://doi.org/10.1080/10400435.1999.10131995

Center for Disease Control and Prevention. (2017). *About chronic diseases*. CDC. https://www.cdc.gov/chronicdisease/about/index.htm

Clarke, P., & Latham, K. (2014). Life course health and socioeconomic profiles of Americans aging with disability. *Disability and Health Journal, 7*(1 Suppl), S15–S23. https://doi.org/10.1016/j.dhjo.2013.08.008

Colby, S. L., & Ortman, J. M. (2015). Projections of the size and composition of the U.S. Population: 2014 to 2060, *Current Population Reports*, P25-1143. U.S. Census Bureau, https://www.census.gov/content/dam/Census/library/publications/2015/demo/p25-1143.pdf

Courtney-Long, E. A., Carroll, D. D., Zhang, Q. C., Stevens, A. C., Griffin-Blake, S., Armour, B. S., & Campbell, V. A. (2015). Prevalence of disability and disability type among adults—United States, 2013. *Morbidity and Mortality Weekly Report, 64*(29), 777–783.

Coyle, C. E., & Putnam, M. (2017). Identifying adults aging with disability using existing data: The case of the health and retirement study. *Disability and Health Journal, 10*(4), 611–615. https://doi.org/10.1016/j.dhjo.2016.12.016

Department of Health and Human Services. (2010). *U.S. multiple chronic conditions: A strategic framework for optimum health and quality of life for individuals with multiple chronic conditions*. U.S. Department of Health and Human Services. https://www.hhs.gov/sites/default/files/ash/initiatives/mcc/mcc_framework.pdf

Erickson, W., Lee, C., & von Schrader, S. (2017). *Disability statistics from the American Community Survey*. Cornell University Yang-Tan Institute. www.disabilitystatistics.org

Field, M., & Jette, A. (2007a). Secondary conditions and aging with disability. In Field, M., & Jette, A. (Eds.), *The future of disability in America* (pp. 136–161), The National Academies of Science Press.

Field, M., & Jette, A. (2007b). *The future of disability in America*. The National Academies Press

Freedman, V. A. (2014). Research gaps in the demography of aging with disability. *Disability and Health Journal, 7*(1 Suppl), S60–S63. https://doi.org/10.1016/j.dhjo.2013.04.009

Goodman, R. A., Posner, S. F., Huang, E. S., Parekh, A. K., & Koh, H. K. (2013). Defining and measuring chronic conditions: Imperatives for research, policy, program, and practice. *Preventing Chronic Disease, 10*, E66. https://doi.org/10.5888/pcd10.120239

Groah, S. L., Charlifue, S., Tate, D., Jensen, M. P., Molton, I. R., Forchheimer, M., ... Campbell, M. (2012). Spinal cord injury and aging: Challenges and recommendations for future research. *American Journal of Physical Medicine & Rehabilitation, 91*(1), 80–93. https://doi.org/10.1097/PHM.0b013e31821f70bc

Hardy, S. E., Allore, H. G., Guo, Z., Dubin, J. A., & Gill, T. M. (2006). The effect of prior disability history on subsequent functional transitions. *The Journals of Gerontology. Series A, Biological Sciences and Medical Sciences*, *61*(3), 272–277. https://doi.org/10.1093/gerona/61.3.272

Health and Retirement Study. (2017). Health and Retirement Study. University of Michigan. http://hrsonline.isr.umich.edu/

Iezzoni, L. I., Kurtz, S. G., & Rao, S. R. (2014). Trends in U.S. adult chronic disability rates over time. *Disability and Health Journal*, *7*(4), 402–412. https://doi.org/10.1016/j.dhjo.2014.05.007

Jensen, M. P., Truitt, A. R., Schomer, K. G., Yorkston, K. M., Baylor, C., & Molton, I. R. (2013). Frequency and age effects of secondary health conditions in individuals with spinal cord injury: A scoping review. *Spinal Cord*, *51*(12), 882–892. https://doi.org/10.1038/sc.2013.112

Kailes, J. I. (February 16, 2017). *Aging with disability*. http://www.jik.com/awdrtcawd.html

Kinne, S., Patrick, D. L., & Doyle, D. L. (2004). Prevalence of secondary conditions among people with disabilities. *American Journal of Public Health*, *94*(3), 443–445. https://doi.org/10.2105/ajph.94.3.443

Klingbeil, H., Baer, H. R., & Wilson, P. E. (2004). Aging with a disability. *Archives of Physical Medicine and Rehabilitation*, *85*(S3), 68–73. https://doi.org/10.1016/j.apmr.2004.03.014

LaPlante, M. P. (2014). Key goals and indicators for successful aging of adults with early-onset disability. *Disability and Health Journal*, *7*(1 Suppl), S44–S50. https://doi.org/10.1016/j.dhjo.2013.08.005

Marge, M. (1988). Health promotion for persons with disabilities: Moving beyond rehabilitation. *American Journal of Health Promotion: AJHP*, *2*(4), 29–44. https://doi.org/10.4278/0890-1171-2.4.29

Molton, I. R., Terrill, A. L., Smith, A. E., Yorkston, K. M., Alschuler, K. N., Ehde, D. M., & Jensen, M. P. (2014). Modeling secondary health conditions in adults aging with physical disability. *Journal of Aging and Health*, *26*(3), 335–359. https://doi.org/10.1177/0898264313516166

National Council on Aging. (2017). *About evidence-based programs*. NCOA. https://www.ncoa.org/center-for-healthy-aging/basics-of-evidence-based-programs/about-evidence-based-programs/

National Health and Aging Trends Study. (2017). *NHATS at a glance*. Johns Hopkins University. https://www.nhats.org/

Officer, A., & Posarac, A. (2011). *World report on disability*. WHO. https://www.who.int/disabilities/world_report/2011/report.pdf

Panel Study on Income Dynamics. (2017). *The Panel Study on Income Dynamics*. University of Michigan. https://psidonline.isr.umich.edu/default.aspx

Pope, A. M., & Tarlov, A. R. (Eds.). (1991). *Disability in America: Toward a national agenda for prevention*. National Academies Press.

Putnam, M. (2007). Moving from separate to crossing aging and disability service networks. In M. Putnam (Ed.), *Aging and disability: Crossing network lines* (pp. 5–17). Springer.

Putnam, M. (2014). Bridging network divides: Building capacity to support aging with disability populations through research. *Disability and Health Journal*, *7*(1 Suppl), S51–S59. https://doi.org/10.1016/j.dhjo.2013.08.002

Putnam, M., Molton, I. R., Truitt, A. R., Smith, A. E., & Jensen, M. P. (2016). Measures of aging with disability in U.S. secondary data sets: Results of a scoping review. *Disability and Health Journal*, *9*(1), 5–10. https://doi.org/10.1016/j.dhjo.2015.07.002

Rimmer, J. H. (1999). Health promotion for people with disabilities: The emerging paradigm shift from disability prevention to prevention of secondary conditions. *Physical Therapy*, *79*(5), 495–502.

Smith, A. E., Molton, I. R., & Jensen, M. P. (2016). Self-reported incidence and age of onset of chronic comorbid medical conditions in adults aging with long-term physical disability. *Disability and Health Journal*, *9*(3), 533–538. https://doi.org/10.1016/j.dhjo.2016.02.002

Torres-Gil, F. (2007). Translating research into program and policy change. In M. Putnam (Ed.). *Aging and disability: Crossing network lines* (245–258). Springer

Treishman, R. (1987). *Aging with a disability*. Demos Medical Publishing.

Trogdon, J. G., Murphy, L. B., Khavjou, O. A., Li, R., Maylahn, C. M., Tangka, F. K., & Orenstein, D. (2015). Costs of chronic diseases at the state level: The chronic disease cost calculator. *Preventing Chronic Disease*, *12*, 150131. https://doi.org/10.5888/pcd12.150131

United Nations. (2015). *World Population Ageing 2015 Highlights (ST/ESA/SER.A/368)*. UN Department of Economic and Social Affairs, Population Division. http://www.un.org/en/development/desa/population/publications/pdf/ageing/WPA2015_Highlights.pdf

Verbrugge, L. M., Latham, K., & Clarke, P. J. (2017). Aging with disability for midlife and older adults. *Research on Aging*, *39*(6), 741–777. https://doi.org/10.1177/0164027516681051

Verbrugge, L. M., & Yang, L.-S. (2002). Aging with disability and disability with aging. *Journal of Disability Policy Studies*, *12*(4), 253–-267. https://doi.org/10.1177/104420730201200405

Ward, B. W., Schiller, J. S., & Goodman, R. A. (2014). Multiple chronic conditions among US adults: A 2012 update preventing chronic disease. *Preventing Chronic Disease*, *11*, E62. http://doi.org/10.5888/pcd11.130389

World Health Organization. (2011). *World report on disability: Summary.* World Health Organization (WHO) and World Bank. http://apps.who.int/iris/bitstream/10665/70670/1/WHO_NMH_VIP_11.01_eng.pdf

World Health Organization. (2014). *Global status report on non-communicable disease.* WHO. http://www.who.int/nmh/publications/ncd-status-report-2014/en/

Acknowledgments

This chapter was previously published in the journal *Healthcare* under Creative Commons license 4.0. The following citation applies:

Campbell, M. L., & Putnam, M. (2017). Reducing the shared burden of chronic conditions among persons ageing with disability and older adults in the United States through bridging ageing and disability. *Healthcare (Basel, Switzerland), 5*(3), 56. https://doi.org/10.3390/healthcare5030056

Suggested Readings

Freedman, V. A. (2014). Research gaps in the demography of aging with disability. *Disability and Health Journal*, 7(1 Suppl), S60–S63. https://doi.org/10.1016/j.dhjo.2013.04.009

Iezzoni, L. I., Kurtz, S. G., & Rao, S. R. (2014). Trends in U.S. Adult chronic disability rates over time. *Disability and Health Journal*, 7(4), 402–412. https://doi.org/10.1016/j.dhjo.2014.05.007

Molton, I. R., Terrill, A. L., Smith, A. E., Yorkston, K. M., Alschuler, K. N., Ehde, D. M., & Jensen, M. P. (2014). Modeling secondary health conditions in adults aging with physical disability. *Journal of Aging and Health*, 26(3), 335–359. https://doi.org/10.1177/0898264313516166

Verbrugge, L. M., Latham, K., & Clarke, P. J. (2017). Aging with disability for midlife and older adults. *Research on Aging*, 39(6), 741–777. https://doi.org/10.1177/0164027516681051

7
SEGMENTING AGEING AND DISABILITY POLICY
Ethical Concerns

Jerome Bickenbach

Introduction: Ageing and Disability

Any exploration of ethical issues arising from social policies, laws, and practices involving the domains of ageing and disability soon becomes enmeshed in the sociological and political complexities of minority group dynamics, identity politics, and political activism. Dangerous as this may be, I want to steer clear of or navigate around these deep and troubling waters. I am not suggesting that ethics can be pulled apart from politics or political activism, or that ethical analysis is detachable from sociological and socio-psychological discussions of the personal and group experience of 'being an older adult' and 'being a person with a disability'. Nonetheless I want to focus on fairly discrete ethical concerns raised – not by the domains of ageing and disability themselves – but by what I take to be the standard response of segmenting or separating these domains when constructing and implementing policy. This standard response assumes, first of all, that there are relatively discrete sub-populations called 'older adults' and 'people with disabilities'; secondly that these sub-populations, in terms of standard policy metrics, are vulnerable, or potentially so, although in different ways; and thirdly that, as a consequence, there needs to be different policy responses to the vulnerabilities, inequities, and needs of these distinct sub-populations. The focus of this chapter is on the revealed ethical concerns of these assumptions as reflected in the standard policy approach of separating and segmenting 'ageing policy' from 'disability policy'.

So that there is no confusion about what my assumptions, I begin by laying all my cards on this table:

- Although I am not going to offer a world-wide summary of national and international ageing and disability policy regimes, I start with the assumption that disability and ageing social policy are standardly thought to be, like the sub-populations they serve, separable and parallel policy regimes (the Standard Approach).

It should be said that increasingly there are some exceptions to this assumption – especially in the overlapping policy concern of individual ageing with a pre-existing disability, for example, ageing with intellectual or developmental disability (Putnam, 2014).

- This Standard Approach raises obvious ethical concerns: inefficiency, ineffectiveness and wastage at the policy level, and invidious distinction, stigma, and discrimination at the personal level.
- These ethical concerns arise because, conceptually, there is a fundamental consilience between ageing and disability, which are neither psychologically distinct nor do they generate discrete sub-populations: everyone ages and everyone experiences disability.

Standard Policy Approach

Generalising about national social policy for groups perceived to be vulnerable is foolhardy as there is simply too much variation, even among similarly high-resourced countries of the world. The International Social Security Association (ISSA), the primary international database for social security programming for 170 countries, has conveniently categorised these policies into *Old Age, Disability, and Survivors*; *Sickness and Maternity*; *Work Injury*; *Unemployment*; and *Family Allowances* (ISSA, n.d.). A glance through the various regional ISSA databases shows a bewildering variety, not only of specific programs, but also of regulatory frameworks (including legislation, regulation, and guidelines), coverage, source of funding, qualifying conditions, and other criteria. Yet, at least among the Organization for Economic Co-operation and Development (OECD), high-resource countries, there are discernible patterns, reflecting historically common sources of these policies – all of which address, roughly speaking, permanently, temporarily, or episodically vulnerable people.

Given that policies tend to develop in idiosyncratic ways – responding to country-specific events or political or cultural shifts – the sequencing of policies innovations, and the levels of coverage and qualifying conditions are highly reactive, *ad hoc*, and generally unpredictable. Yet from the earliest days of these social policies – going back to Bismarck in the 1880s – old age and invalidity (especially for veterans) were unquestioned categories of vulnerability. And from the outset, programming was separated by these categories. In part this was a natural feature of the dynamics of ageing and health status: old-age pensions were explicitly chronologically structured, whereas disability pensions were based on the timing of acquired disabilities during the working life (so that the pension becomes a form of income replacement). Disability financial supports, moreover, were either temporary or permanent and designed for congenital or early onset disabilities or adult-life health problems. Disability benefits were always closely tied to family benefits, often on the assumption that the disabled child would never work, or would not live to old age, or a dependent adult would perforce have to rely on a spouse or child for daily support. Even when some of these assumptions no longer held true, the traditional approach to separating ageing from disability policy held sway.

Over the last couple of decades, especially in light of dramatic trends of population ageing, some of the assumptions about the robustness of chronological definitions of ageing have been questioned (Sanderson & Scherbov, 2005; Sanderson & Scherbov, 2013) and reinforced by the looming economic burden of pensions and other benefits for an increasingly larger retired population (Chatterji, Byles, Cutler, Seeman, & Verdes, 2015). At the same time advancements in medical care – especially increased reliance on rehabilitation to extend a person's functional ability, despite chronic health problems – as well as improved assistive technology, has led policy-makers to wonder whether recipients of 'permanent disability' benefits should be encouraged to enter the workplace, with supports (Bickenbach, Posarac, Cieza, & Kostanjsek, 2015). In the disability space, moreover, increased recognition of the basic human rights of everyone to fully participate in all areas of human life – exemplified by the United Nations *Convention on the Rights of Persons with Disabilities* (CRPD) (UN, 2006) – has shifted public perceptions of the capabilities of persons with disabilities to lived active and productive lives, rather than being sidelined and beneficiaries of social support.

The overall effect of these and other demographic, epidemiological, and cultural shifts is to muddy the hard and fast distinction between 'older adults' and 'people with disabilities'. If an older person requires support to pay for a wheelchair because of lower-body paralysis caused by a tumour, how is that need different from that of an 18-year needing a wheelchair because of a spinal cord injury or a young child born with spina bifida? Clearly the need for the wheelchair is the same, as is the need for financial support to pay for it. Why not create a single policy for whoever needs financial support to pay for a wheelchair? What we find instead, almost universally, are at least three separate policy arrangements: one for older adults, one for adults and one for children. Each program is backed by a different regulatory framework (inevitably arising from different ministries or departments of government), with different coverage and qualifying requirements, funded from different sources (and to different degrees) and supported by different administrative arrangements.

No doubt this is an easy example. Nonetheless very few countries have even attempted to rationalise and consolidate financial support for assistive technology in this universalistic manner. People have different needs that is hardly debatable. But it is not clear how much of these differences are directly linked to chronological age. To be sure, there are well-recognised, age-related health experiences – multimorbidity and frailty, for example (WHO, 2015). Yet the kinds of health services and supports that these needs create are not themselves directly linked to age-related differences. At the level of clinical care, health services should be provided to people in a manner cognisant of age differences; yet their differences are no more problematic than those of language and culture, education, or geography. We want our health services to be client-centred, and to pattern our supporting policy programming to be aware of these differences; but there is no obvious reason why policy programming has to be rigidly siloed by the human difference of chronological age.

The very specific example of financial support for the provision and maintenance of assistive technology may be an easy example, but a quick review of standard ageing and disability policy support categories generated similar issues. In high resource countries, there are policies on pensions and income supports (temporary and permanent); employment and education services and supports; housing, community living, and supportive living supports; transportation and communication services and others. There also basic policy guidelines and laws concerning the general issue of accessibility of public services and buildings (for people with mobility, sensory or cognitive impairments) accommodations at work and school, and, at the highest policy level, enforceable protections of basic human rights. People experiencing impairments and people who are older can benefit from the supports and services that might be offered under all of these policy rubrics. There will be differences in the character or configuration of these supports and services and how they are provided; but that is obvious, people are different. What is less clear is why these various benefits need to be duplicated and separately channelled through administrative categories and regulatory frameworks that are labelled 'Ageing' and 'Disability'.

On the face of it, the complaint here seems to turn on economics – why have two administrative policy regimes to provide similar benefits to people who, already different in age, have similar needs and would similarly benefit? The redundancy seems highly problematic from a purely budgetary perspective. Surely it would be more efficient to merge these programs, eliminate administrative duplication and, perhaps, reap the benefits of economies of scale.

This intuition is undoubtedly correct. Unfortunately, there is not enough reproducible and generalisable empirical evidence to cite to support this intuition, either for a single country or more generally. But the ethical intuition remains if it is unethical to waste scarce economic resources that might be better used to benefit more people in more ways. Inefficient use of resources, without a robust justification, is one kind of ethical concern to the standard approach to ageing and disability policy. Another concern comes into play at a more individual level. Before clarifying both of these concerns, I want to directly address a powerful response to the claim that the standard approach is ethically problematic. That is the claim that the standard approach is inevitable because ageing and disability conceptually distinct human experiences.

The Deep Consilience of Ageing and Disability

Defining multidimensional and complex terms like 'ageing' and 'disability' is difficult in the abstract, in part because how we approach definition depends on our purpose for defining. In the policy domain, our purpose is to define sub-populations in order to 'target' individuals who, because of their membership, are likely to have needs associated with a trait that – for historical, sociological, or psychological reasons – has made them vulnerable. As noted, ageing and disability were the original, and most intuitive, sources of vulnerability. From the start both were characterised as dichotomous traits, in the sense that an individual was either a member or not a member of the relevant sub-population. It was widely acknowledged, however, that this was illogical since it was perfectly clear that both disability and ageing are continuous, not dichotomous traits: people are *more or less* disabled and *more or less* old. Despite this, to create administratively workable eligibility rules a 'threshold' on the continua of disability and ageing had to be arbitrarily drawn. Hence the use of chronology for ageing (65 years of age) and one or another arbitrary cut-off point of 'severity' of disability.

Dichotomising populations raises an ethical conundrum that is both common and seemingly avoidable. Unless everyone is provided with the same benefit equally (in the form of so-called universal policy, such as universal basic income or basic child support lump sum payments), there are bound to be 'borderline cases' of individuals who just miss the cut-off point. A person who is 64 years and 364 days old is in no real sense in a different situation than someone who passed his or her 65th birthday – but from a policy standpoint, they are members of entirely different groups. Similarly, a person who is severely disabled and cannot feed or dress themselves, but who, on some artificial scale of severity, falls just short of the cut-off point of say 66%, will not officially qualify for the support they need. In practice, at least for disability, there may well be unofficial 'recalculating' of severity to push such a borderline case past the cut-off point, and this ad hoc solution can deal with troubling cases of near misses; but such a practice, if it is used too often, will destroy the credibility of the eligibility determination process.

The obvious way out of this problem – created by the administrative necessary of distributing resources by a vulnerable trait-defining category – would be that of objectively determining real need for a service or support. For most policy-makers, the thought of distributing benefits funded by the public purse in terms of scientifically-determine genuine need seems utterly fantastical since the notion of 'need' appears to be unmanageably subjective. After all, what are needs, and how can we possibly adjudicate which needs are legitimate or which are excessive (I need a new BMW!)? Is it fair to satisfy the needs of people who happen to have very high expectations of what they are owed in life, while providing those with lower expectations and modest wants far less? (See discussion of this paradox in Sen, 1999.) This is why, when eligibility requirements for a benefit are conditionalised to include or exclude otherwise qualified individuals, policy makers turn to the objective measure of 'income-testing' rather than the unwieldy 'need-testing'.

The problem of characterising need is common between ageing and disability policy; and if society takes on the task of responding to the needs of its vulnerable populations, dealing with the problem of need is unavoidable. But it is instructive to review how this issue has been handled in the domain of disability policy over the past half century in high resource countries. The path that disability policy has taken is instructive.

In the case of disability, health professionals (especially in rehabilitation) have a long tradition of objectively assessing genuine, disability-related need. They can rely on a measurable, need-creating property – variously called *functional limitation*, *capacity limitation*, or *decrement in functioning*. In the health domain, people with health problems – diseases, injuries or other health issues – usually end up living with one or more impairments (limitations in body function or structure) that limit or restrict what they can do in their everyday lives. People with impairments may have problems walking, climbing stairs, seeing things at a distance, reading a newspaper, doing their housework, making friends, having a family, performing adequately at their job or in school, or participating in community activities. These are all problems in functioning, in one or more domains of life, simple to complex. They are, more specifically, disabilities – problems people have performing activities in their daily live, in interaction with their environment, because of a health condition (WHO, 2001).

But the thing about disabilities, defined the way rehabilitation health professionals tend to (Meyer et al., 2011), is that the health-related problems create both general and specific needs – health care needs, as well as medication, assistive technology and possibly personal assistance – or they may need long-term care, income support, renovation of their homes, and so on. Since these general and specific needs are directly relevant to their functioning problems, and since these problems are objectively measurable, their needs are as well. For a rehabilitation professional, in short, health-related, disability needs are objectively determinable and measurable.

Statistically, disability needs are objectively determined because, first there is an underlying latent trait *functioning* that is a plausible common metric for impairment-based limitations and restrictions in the performance of human activities, and secondly, there is an implicit assumption of a threshold of functioning, for each domain, based on clinical standards (Stucki, Prodinger, & Bickenbach, 2017). Objective health-related, impairment-based need, therefore, is both conceptually and practically possible.

These health-related needs are 'basic' in that sense that they are needs the satisfaction of which would enable a person to perform actions and levels of social participation that are 'normal' or standard for the population. In practice, the policy response to such needs tends to favour some form of financial aid rather than specific 'in kind' supports and services (such as assistive technology or personal assistance). Even when disability-related needs can be precisely defined by health, educational or other social professionals, the reality of cost-variations, market variabilities, and other transaction costs makes a strong administrative case for favouring cash benefits. There is also the consideration, more powerful in politically libertarian cultures that the individual should be given the freedom to decide on how to spend the cash to meet his or her needs.

There is, however, another and broader sense of 'need' that is generated by theories such as Amartya Sen's Capability Theory (Sen, 1999). On this account, need is characterised in light of individual's goals and aspirations, what people want to do with their own lives. In this sense of need (depending on the nature of the goal or aspiration) a social response may require resources far beyond those identified by normal or standard functioning levels. To aspire to be an Olympic athlete, for example one would clearly 'need' resources to support functioning levels in relevant domains that would be beyond statistical norms. An open political question is whether society has the obligation to respond to this broader, and clearly more subjective, sense of need in its population. Setting the bar at responding to basic needs of a person with disabilities is for many countries of the world already too high.

In some high resource countries, disability policy is based on in-kind benefits that address objective needs for goods and services as determined by health, education, labour or other professionals. 'Needs assessment' in these settings will be both individualised and contextualised, since the point is to serve the actual requirements of the individual where he or she lives and works. The professional will be asked about the functioning limitations that require amelioration or augmentation and for what purposes – to attend school, to carry out the requirements of a job, to live independently. Return to work policy, for example is grounded in a determination of 'work capacity', analysed in terms of task-related domains of mental and physical functioning, while return to work benefits include the provision of relevant work-related assistive devices, training and vocational rehabilitation, and in some cases modifications to the workplace. As a general matter, disability policy is moving towards providing goods and services because, given improved survival rates linked to better access to health case and epidemiological increases in chronic health problems, societies are increasingly unable to afford to remove people from the labour market and pay them full disability pensions. Increasingly countries want people to be able to work, or to return to work (Bickenbach et al., 2015).

Are there lessons that can be learned for ageing policy? Asking this question is tantamount to answering it. Obviously, the situation is identical. The bulk of the needs that are relevant to the vulnerability of people who are old, and growing older, are associated with age-related limitations in functioning across domains. This fact has been thoroughly developed in the recent world report by the World Health Organization (WHO), the *World Report on Ageing and Health* (WHO, 2015).

The report begins by asking 'What is ageing?' The answer is two-fold:

> At a biological level, ageing is associated with the gradual accumulation of a wide variety of molecular and cellular damage. Over time, this damage leads to a gradual decrease in physiological reserves, an increased risk of many diseases, and a general decline in the capacity of the individual. Ultimately, it will result in death.

> Beyond these biological losses, older age frequently involves other significant changes. These include shifts in roles and social positions, and the need to deal with the loss of close relationships.
>
> WHO, 2015, p. 25

Noting that age-related biological changes are only loosely associated with chronological age, the report describes the two components of the ageing process in more detail: ageing is, first of all, a matter of *intrinsic capacity* (the composite of all the physical and mental capacities of an individual) in interaction with the person's physical, attitudinal, and social environment. Ageing is, secondly, a matter of *functional ability* (the health-related attributes that enable people to be and to do what they have reason to value). The life course trajectory of intrinsic capacity is modifiable, but only to a limited degree: total intrinsic incapacity, ultimately death, is inevitable. The life course trajectory of functional ability is a different matter. With appropriate health and social interventions, the path of functional ability does not have to mirror that of intrinsic capacity.

From this conceptual basis it is clear what ageing policy is about and what its aim should be. Ageing policy should, first of all, address intrinsic capacity by making available or directly providing those health and social resources that address the downward slope of the intrinsic capacity trajectory. Although the direction of this slope is unavoidable, its configuration is, to some degree, open to human modification. But ageing policy should also address functional ability. Here much more is possible, and the avenues that policy can take are more various and require more innovation. In the health domain, the limitations in functional ability caused by decrements in intrinsic capacity can be ameliorated, repaired or limited; while in the social domain, environmental barriers that restrict what older people can do or become can be removed or adjusted and environmental facilitators can be provided to enabled older people to more fully participate.

The conceptual consilience between disability and ageing – and that of disability policy and ageing policy – should be clear. Disability is a decrement in the performance of activities and social roles that results as an outcome of an interaction between impairments and the person overall physical, human-built, interpersonal, attitudinal, and social environment. Ageing similarly is a process of accumulating limitations in functional ability as a consequence of declining intrinsic capacity in interaction with the physical, human-built, interpersonal, attitudinal, and social environment. Disability and ageing are neither purely biological, nor purely social phenomena: they are rather complex intermixtures of both. The two policy domains simply mirror the conceptual consilience. Hence, in disability policy we aim both to limit the unavoidable impact of health problems over the life course and optimise functioning by providing resources that improve health-related capacity and, through environmental changes and augmentation, enhance the performance of actions and the achievement of desired social roles and personal goals. Ageing policy simply repeated those two aims: where feasible policy will enhance intrinsic capacity, and to the fullest extent possible improve functional ability, in light of what the individual what to do and become.

The overlap is so fundamental that one might be forgiven for thinking that ageing is simply a process of accumulating disabilities, while disability is just a chronologically-neutral state of ageing. Or to put it another way: every human being is either ageing into disability or ageing with disability.

Unarguably, there are salient sociological and psychological differences between ageing and disability. Since all of us absorb social values and beliefs, the experience of being old will tend to be a fairly radically different kind of experience, involving different social responses and social perceptions, than the experience of being a person with a disability. Despite this, however, many of these seemingly fundamental differences are in the end merely manifestations of basic misconceptions about what disability and ageing are. For example most cultures tend to view disability diachronically (as a permanent state that a person is in), and most cultures assume that people with disabilities have very serious impairments and are either children or working age adults. On the other hand, we also tend to think of ageing synchronically (as a process) and assume that whatever impairments older people experience are just 'part of old age'. But despite these assumptions, disability and ageing are actually both continuous rather than dichotomous phenomena. This means that a disability need not be severe and an old person with mild age-related impairments is still disabled.

Nor should we mistake our own cultural assumptions for trans-cultural truths. Although generally people with disabilities have lower social values, in some cultures some forms of disability are highly socially valued (e.g. shaman and seers often have mental or physical impairments). Similarly, while older people in high income, industrial settings are often sidelined and devalued, in some cultures they are highly respect and valued. Since social values and assumption invariably impact self-perception, we need to be aware of them when designing and implementing relevant policies and practices. But, dramatic social changes in the last decades suggest that these differences should never be assumed to be unmodifiable or inevitable.

The standard policy approach: ethical concerns

To recall, the point of dwelling on the conceptual consilience of ageing and disability was to dismiss the argument that the standard siloed approach to disability and ageing policy, although perhaps unfortunate, is nonetheless not ethically problematic because disability and ageing just are fundamentally different. I have argued that conceptually this is nonsense, although the perception of fundamental difference persists for complex historical, sociological, and psychological reasons. At this juncture I definitely do not want to claim that these underlying social and psychological reasons for denying the consilience between ageing and disability are trivial. Quite the contrary, the perception of fundamental difference is not only entrenched but highly consequential. What I want to argue for here is the more modest claim that there are sound ethical reasons for trying to foster an agenda of 'bridging ageing and disability' – a focused agenda to enhance an appreciation for the conceptual consilience of ageing and disability in research, practice and policy (Bickenbach et al., 2012; Leonardi, Bickenbach, & Leroy, 2012). There are two clusters of ethical concerns that I want to develop in this regard: the first concerning the ethical character of social policy, and the second the ethically problematic impact on individuals of the standard policy approach.

The Ethical Requirements of Good Social Policy

Social policy, like any intentional human activity, can be assessed ethically. Abstractly, social policy is a social mechanism – usually taking the form of laws, regulations, rules, and actions implemented by state agencies – for meeting perceived needs of and to ensure fair opportunities for the overall population or some targeted sub-group. The relevant needs and opportunities tend to cluster around the basic needs of security, health, education, housing, social supports and social participation, while the relevant opportunities tend, at least in liberal societies, to involve the provision of means for people to lead the kinds of lives that they themselves value (Williams, 1991). Ultimately the ethical rationale for all social policy is normatively grounded in the value of distributive and procedural justice and empirical grounded in the fact that humans are vulnerable beings dependent on others and crucially, are equally vulnerable and equally dependent. Traditionally, distributive justice is associated with the fairness of distribution of benefits and burdens, while procedural justice involves the fairness of processes to determine, among other things, the distribution of benefits and burdens (Miller, n.d.).

Social policy, whatever form it takes, can be assessed ethically in terms of four straightforward criteria: *relevance* (do the policies have relevant aims, do they identify the right needs and opportunities, benefits and burdens); *effectiveness* (do the policies as implemented accomplish what they are supposed to accomplish); *efficiency* (do the policies as implemented accomplish their aims without wasting resources?); *equity* (is everyone who could benefit from the policy treated equally in relation to the nature and extent of their need). These standard criteria are performance indicators for monitoring and assessing policies in practice. They presume both that social resources (financial, human, and material) are scarce and that every policy incurs operating costs that must be added to the value of the resource that is actually distributed by the policy. In the real world, operationalising these general criteria is far too complicated to go into here. Although individual policies can fail for many reasons, very roughly speaking, the three prominent reasons for failure are these:

- People who need something do not get it
- People who do not need something do get it
- Policies ignore differences between people that matter with respect to their needs or focus on differences between people that do not matter with respect to their needs

When a policy succumbs to one or more of these problems, the result may either be duplication and redundancy (which violates both criteria of effectiveness and efficiency), wastage (violating efficiency and equity), or a failure to benefit people in need (violating relevance and equity). Whatever the diagnosis, bad policy simply does not achieve its aims. Given the (inevitable) scarcity of resources, failure to achieve the aims of policy is an ethical misuse of social resources, since the opportunity cost of bad policy is a failure to use the resources in a manner that would have achieved a better outcome. It is uncontroversial that bad policy is a waste of time and money. But given scarcity and the assumption that society owes a duty to its people to perform optimally, bad policy is also unethical policy.

As mentioned, the standard approach to ageing and disability policy is to design responses to the needs of these sub-populations as if these were discretely different sets of people, with different sets of needs, requiring qualitatively different kinds of policies. The conceptual consilience of ageing and disability demonstrates that the nature of the vulnerability that underlies both people with disabilities and people who age is identical. In both instances, it is a function of functional limitation (impairments and intrinsic incapacities) and, in interaction with the person's environment, a decrement in carrying out those activities and social roles that the person wishes to carry out (disabilities and functional inabilities). In other words, the unquestioned assumption that these are different groups and different needs is mistaken. The two sub-populations will not in practice be identical because different operational qualifying criteria define membership, but diachronically the populations overlap (and synchronically they approach identity). The third assumption is more plausible, simply because the dynamics of the saliency of environmental influences on levels of disability or functional inability are shaped by historical, sociological, and psychological forces tend to differ.

Because of these three assumptions about disability and ageing, the presence of separated and siloed disability and ageing policy entails failures across all these dimensions: they are ineffective, inefficient, and inequitable. Segmenting ageing and disability policies – and in particular not taking full advantage, in a context of scarcity, of the efficiencies that result from the fact of common needs – are ultimately unethical.

No better concrete example of this failure could be conceived than a recent call for a United Nations human rights convention on ageing (see, e.g. Harpur, 2016). The CRPD, now ratified by a vast majority of countries of the world, responded to the genuine concern that persons with disabilities were in many countries not counted as persons who enjoyed human rights. The level of marginalisation of people with severe disabilities, in all areas of life, was such that an explicit reminder that these individuals have the same human rights as everyone else was salutary, and perhaps essential. In the Convention, the population involved is characterises to include those '…who have long-term physical, mental, intellectual or sensory impairments which in interaction with various barriers may hinder their full and effective participation in society on an equal basis with others'. All of the provisions of the CRPD derived from this interaction, and the physical and social and attitudinal barriers that hinder participation. The CRPD addresses concerns of accessibility, the need for facilitating accommodation, guaranteeing dignity and avoiding stigma, discrimination, and inequality. Implementing the CRPD at national level, however ethically essential, demands policy changes that, inevitably, incur social costs.

The question is, however, in what ways would an additional and completely parallel 'convention on the rights of ageing people' – which would of course duplicate these costs – add any protections or human rights guarantees not already protected by the CRPD? Given the consilience between ageing and disability all of the human rights concerns experienced by older populations are created by the same kinds of environmental barriers – physical, built, interpersonal, attitudinal, and social – as create the human rights issues that persons with disabilities face. Given the consilience, protections of human rights for ageing populations will require the need for precisely the same provisions for accessibility, the need for facilitate accommodations, ensure dignity and prevent stigma, discrimination, and inequality that are already provided by the CRPD. Having two, parallel but separate international legal regimes, generating at the national level parallel but separate human rights implementation policy regimes, would not only be wasteful, it would eventually undermine the effectiveness of both of the conventions as countries backed away from the escalating costs of implementation.

Ethically Adverse Impacts of the Standard Approach

One of the less acknowledged difficulties with population-based social activism, highlighted by the extreme example of so-called 'identity politics', is the apparent need to create or solidify group cohesion by emphasising the differences between one identity group and another. There is some evidence of this in both the political approaches and tacit assumptions of disability and ageing activism. It is not uncommon for ageing advocates to vigorously insist that their constituency is perfectly healthy and able-bodied – or that their arthritis is not a disability, merely a feature of ageing. From the other side, it is not uncommon for disability advocates, focused on getting people with disabilities fully involved in employment and educational opportunity, to distance themselves from people who old, retired and excluded from workforce. Both reactions are stigmatising and prejudicial. When these reactions impact individuals directly, they have adverse ethical significance.

A clear example of what undoubtedly is a wholly unintentional form of stigmatisation is the lobbying tool used by ageing advocates that raises the banner of what is variously called 'healthy', 'successful' or 'active ageing'. Although some gerontologists worry about the kind of message that 'successful' sends (Pruchno, 2015), the WHO in particular has long championed the notion of healthy or active ageing as the leading message for ageing policy (see, e.g. WHO, 2002). To be sure, the WHO definition on the face of it merely highlights the basic human rights agenda of full participation and inclusion (WHO, 2015, p. 12):

> Active Ageing is the process of optimizing opportunities for health, participation and security in order to enhance quality of life as people age
>
> Healthy Ageing [is] the process of developing and maintaining the functional ability that enables wellbeing in older age.

Implicit in these definitions is the intimation that a health problem is a failure that undermines an active life and inevitably reduces quality of life and wellbeing. Given that ageing is itself a process of decline of intrinsic capacity associated with health conditions, and given that realistically speaking everyone who ages will experience permanent impairments and multi-morbidities across several body functions, the aspiration of 'healthy ageing' is, if nothing else, ultimately futile. But, more importantly for people, of all ages, who live with permanent or chronic health conditions – people with disabilities in other words – these slogans send a very clear signal: they are failures. Sending such a message, unintentional or not, it is one of the hidden consequences of radically disassociating ageing from disability in particular, and health in general. It is also unethical.

Conclusion

What is the alternative? The gravitation force of history and entrenched assumptions about disability and ageing make fundamental changes in the structure of social policy for the benefit of people with disabilities and older adults extremely unlikely. It is possible that efforts to 'bridge' ageing and disability in scientific work, more practically in truly interdisciplinary clinical team approaches to service delivery, and even administrative attempts to merge agencies, may help in the long term. But what is also needed is a fundamental paradigm shift, and such shifts are not, by definition, everyday events.

Despite this poor prognosis, it is not difficult to imagine what the alternative would look like. What is needed is to ignore or radically downplay the very categories of ageing and disability themselves and focus instead on the genuine, underlying grounds of vulnerability all people experience. This can be assessed in terms of an objective, and common, metric of need, namely experienced levels of functioning, both in terms of intrinsic health capacity and person-environment performance of activities, simple to complex.

This is very likely what the American sociologist Irving Zola had in mind when he spoke of the need for the disability community to 'universalize' disability policy (Zola, 1989). Acknowledging that the political strategy of viewing people with disability as an oppressed minority group had been very successful in raising awareness in the United States and around the world Zola argued that in time it made more sense to understand disability as a universal human phenomenon. In 'Ageing and Disability: Toward a unifying agenda', Zola argues that although people who age and persons with disabilities have 'traditionally been split into opposing camps by providers of services and themselves'. Fundamentally the distinction is both conceptually and factual artificial: '....everyone with a disability will age, and everyone who is ageing will acquire one or more disabilities' (Zola, 1988, p. 265). As a sociologist, Zola was primarily concerned about building a mutual, universalistic, political agenda and rationalising supports and services.

If he had thought through the implication of 'universalism', Zola might have turned his mind to consider what ageing and disability have in common that explains, both the risk of vulnerability and dependence and the characteristics of need (Bickenbach, 2014). I have offered the notion of functioning and its manifestations as a potential conceptual basis for universalisation. The notion has the benefit of being rooted in health, where the basic vulnerabilities of human existence arise, and can be operationalisable for measurement purposes. But, I have tried to argue as well that, getting at the bottom of the need to reform social policy in a way that moves beyond the traditional sub-populations of vulnerability towards a more rational, efficient, and non-stigmatising universalism of functioning, will also address fundamental ethical concerns that are inherent in social policy.

References

Bickenbach, J. (2014). Universally design social policy: When disability disappears? *Disability and Rehabilitation*, *36*(16), 1320–1327. https://doi.org/10.3109/09638288.2014.932447

Bickenbach, J., Bigby, C., Salvador-Carulla, L., Heller, T., Leonardi, M., Leroy, B., ... Spindel, A. (2012). The Toronto declaration on bridging knowledge, policy and practice in aging and disability: Toronto, Canada, March 30, 2012. *International Journal of Integrated Care*, *16*, 12. https://doi.org/10.5334/ijic.1086

Bickenbach, J., Posarac, A., Cieza, A., & Kostanjsek, N. (2015). *Assessing disability in working age population: A paradigm shift from impairment and functional limitation to the disability approach*. Report No: ACS14124. The World Bank. http://documents.worldbank.org/curated/en/272851468164970738/Assessing-disability-in-working-age-population-a-paradigm-shift-from-impairment-and-functional-limitation-to-the-disability-approach

Chatterji, S., Byles, J., Cutler, D., Seeman, T., & Verdes, E. (2015). Health, functioning, and disability in older adults—Present status and future implications. *The Lancet*, *385*(9967), 563–575. https://doi.org/10.1016/S0140-6736(14)61462-8

Harpur, P. (2016). Old age is not just impairment: The CRPD and the need for a convention on older persons. *University of Pennsylvania Journal of International Law*, *37*, 1027. https://scholarship.law.upenn.edu/jil/vol37/iss3/4

ISSA. (n.d.). *Social security country profiles*. Available at: https://www.issa.int/en_GB/country-profiles

Leonardi, M., Bickenbach, J., & Leroy, B. (2012). International initiatives on bridging knowledge, policy and practice. *International Journal of Integrated Care*, *16*(12). httpa://doi.org/10.5334/ijic.1084

Meyer, T., Gutenbrunner, C., Bickenbach, J., Cieza, A., Melvin, J., & Stucki, G. (2011). Towards a conceptual description of rehabilitation as a health strategy. *Journal of Rehabilitation Medicine, 43*(9), 765–769. https://doi.org/10.2340/16501977-0865

Miller, D. J. (n.d.). *Stanford encyclopedia of philosophy.* https://plato.stanford.edu/entries/justice/

Pruchno, R. (2015). Successful aging: Contentious past, productive future. *The Gerontologist, 55*(1), 1–4. https://doi.org/10.1093/geront/gnv002

Putnam, M. (2014). Bridging network divides: Building capacity to support aging with disability populations through research. *Disability and Health Journal, 7*(1), S51–S59. https://doi.org/10.1016/j.dhjo.2013.08.002

Sanderson, W. C., & Scherbov, S. (2005). Average remaining lifetimes can increase as human populations age. *Nature, 435*(7043), 811–813. https://doi.org/10.1038/nature03593

Sanderson, W. C., & Scherbov, S. (2013). The characteristics approach to the measurement of population aging. *Population and Development Review, 39*(4), 673–685. https://doi.org/https://doi.org/10.1111/j.1728-4457.2013.00633.x

Sen, A. 1999. *Development as freedom.* Oxford University Press.

Stucki, G., Prodinger, B., & Bickenbach, J. (2017). Four steps to follow when documenting functioning with the International Classification of Functioning, Disability and Health. *European Journal of Physical and Rehabilitation Medicine, 53*(1), 144–149. https://doi.org/10.23736/S1973-9087.17.04569-5

United Nations. (2006). *Convention on the Rights of Persons with Disabilities.* http://www.un.org/esa/socdev/enable/rights/convtexte.htm.

Williams, F. (1991). *Social policy: A critical introduction.* Wiley.

World Health Organization. (2001). *The International Classification of Functioning, Disability and Health (ICF).* WHO. https://apps.who.int/iris/bitstream/handle/10665/42407/9241545429.pdf;jsessionid=59F4BF70561545AE0C0F933DD9E1A53A?sequence=1

World Health Organization. (2002). *Active aging: A policy framework.* WHO. https://www.who.int/aging/publications/active_aging/en/

World Health Organization. (2015). *World report on aging and health.* WHO. https://www.who.int/aging/events/world-report-2015-launch/en/

Zola, I. (1988). Aging and disability: Toward a unifying agenda. *Educational Gerontology, 14*(5), 365–-387.

Zola, I. (1989). Toward the necessary universalizing of a disability policy. *Milbank Quarterly, 67*(Sup 2, Pt 2), 401–428. https://doi.org/10.1111/j.1468-0009.2005.00436.x

Suggested Readings

Bickenbach, J., Bigby, C., Salvador-Carulla, L., Heller, T., Leonardi, M., Leroy, B., ... Spindel, A. (2012). The Toronto declaration on bridging knowledge, policy and practice in aging and disability: Toronto, Canada, March 30, 2012. *International Journal of Integrated Care, 16,* 12. https://doi.org/10.5334/ijic.1086

Iezzoni, L. I. (2014). Policy concerns raised by the growing U.S. population aging with disability. *Disability and Health Journal, 7*(1), S64–S68. https://doi.org/10.1016/j.dhjo.2013.06.004

Leonardi, M., Bickenbach, J., & Leroy, B. (2012). International initiatives on bridging knowledge, policy and practice. *International Journal of Integrated Care, 16*(12). http://doi.org/10.5334/ijic.1084

Zola, I. (1988). Aging and disability: Toward a unifying agenda. *Educational Gerontology, 14*(5), 365–387.

PART II

Diverse Experiences of Ageing with Disability

8
UNDERSTANDING THE EXPERIENCE OF GROWING OLDER WITH CEREBRAL PALSY

Laura R. Moll and Cheryl A. Cott

Introduction

Typically, we hold the assumption that the experience of disability presents in old age (ageing and disability), after living a relatively healthy life and having fully participated in activities related to school, work, family, and leisure (McPherson, 1998; Tremblay et al., 1997). Less often do we think of persons with early onset disability who then age (ageing with disability). The experience of individuals living with the consequences of congenital or early-onset of physical impairment is not characterised by the same trajectory as individuals who age into disability and/or chronic illness (Bottos, Feliciangeli, Sciuto, Gericke, & Vianello, 2001; Kemp & Mosqueda, 2004; Tremblay et al., 1997). The purpose of this chapter is to describe the experience of growing up and growing older with cerebral palsy (CP) (Moll, 2012).

Overview of Cerebral Palsy

CP is a term given to a lifelong neurological condition that results from damage to the brain due to loss of oxygen prior to or during the birth of a child or during an early period in childhood. It manifests in difficulties with balance and coordination and can impact one or all four limbs. Difficulties with speech and cognition (information processing) may accompany this condition, as well as developmental disabilities. There is extensive research on CP in childhood and adolescence which views CP as a paediatric condition that is stable over time. Most of this literature is based on the assumption that individuals with moderate to severe CP experience the greatest benefits from health care and rehabilitation during childhood and experience little or no improvement during adulthood (Bottos et al., 2001). However, over the past 30 years research has found that individuals with congenital or early-onset physical impairment such as CP experience declines in physical functioning in young or middle adulthood, many years before they reach old age (Hilberink et al., 2007; Kemp & Mosqueda, 2004; Lankasky, 2004; Zaffuto-Sforza, 2005).

Despite advances in health care, the incidence of CP has not declined over the past 30 years. According to the International Cerebral Palsy Society (2011), there are approximately 17 million people living with CP; there are over 60,000 Canadians living with CP (Ontario Federation of Cerebral Palsy, 2010). Many individuals living with CP lead full lives, in the areas of school, work, family, and leisure. However, many are at risk for, and have encountered, problems as adults that interfere with participating in daily living. Despite the emergence of these issues, there is a dearth of research on ageing with CP (Moll, 2012).

Ageing with Disability (Congenital or Early-Onset)

Advances in sanitation, healthcare, rehabilitation, and technology have contributed to increasing the life expectancy for individuals with disabilities (Kemp & Mosqueda, 2004; Strauss, Ojdana, Shavelle, & Rosenbloom, 2004; Tremblay et al., 1997). Individuals with congenital and early-onset physical impairment have benefited from comprehensive rehabilitation that supported achieving independence, community integration, and participating in activities they value (Colantonio, Ratcliff, Chase, & Vernich, 2004; Lutz & Bowers, 2005; Pentland, McColl, & Rosenthal, 1995; Wiley, 2004). However, research has found that 10 to 20 years post injury, many individuals are encountering chronic pain, arthritis, changes in musculoskeletal functioning, and increased fatigue that impinged on their abilities to participate in everyday life (Dean, Colantonio, Ratcliff, & Chase, 2000; Kemp & Mosqueda, 2004).

Expanding our knowledge of ageing with CP is important to gain a better understanding about how adulthood and ageing are experienced by individuals with this condition and the implications for health, education and social services for these individuals. It is important to challenge the assumption that CP is predominantly a paediatric condition and, thus, increase our awareness of the changing needs of individuals with lifelong impairments. CP is a lifelong condition that may be accompanied by improvements early in the lives of individuals, as well as plateaus and periods of declines later in life due to acute and/or chronic conditions that accompany the primary condition. Achieving this recognition could change the ways in which we think about people with CP, and the practices that are used in health care and rehabilitation to treat and manage their condition across the life course.

Our understanding of ageing with CP has primarily focused on the physical challenges that individuals encounter: increased spasticity, pain, fatigue, loss of strength, declining mobility, and musculoskeletal deformities (Bottos et al., 2001; Haak, Lenski, Hidecker, Li, & Paneth, 2009). Other health problems that have been identified include bowel and bladder difficulties, respiratory problems, dystonia and problems with oral hygiene. The experience of individuals with CP is unique from four standpoints: (1) Many of these individuals have received health care and rehabilitation from infancy up to late adolescence but no longer have access to comprehensive and integrated health care and rehabilitation once they transition into adulthood (2) There are very few health care professionals who have training, knowledge, and experience in working with adults with CP (3) Medical environments are typically not accessible to assess and treat the health care needs of these individuals (Bottos et al., 2001; Hilberink et al., 2007; Neri & Kroll, 2003; Tighe, 2001) and (4) Research on adolescents and young adults is finding that declines in functioning in relation to walking and needing assistance with some personal care begin as early as late adolescence and young adulthood (Andrén & Grimby, 2000; Bottos et al., 2001; Hilberink et al., 2007; Kemp & Mosqueda, 2004; Strauss et al., 2004; Zaffuto-Sforza, 2005).

Methods of Recruitment, Data Collection, and Analysis at a Glance

The experience of growing older with CP is depicted in this chapter through the narrative *Defying the odds: Growing up and Growing older with a physical impairment*. This narrative was a product of the PhD study conceptualised and completed by the first author and supervised by the second author (Moll, 2012). The narrative was co-constructed by the first author and nine participants with CP (3 men; 6 women) between 26 and 70 years old, with mild, moderate, and severe forms of the condition. The study took place in Toronto, with ethics approval from the University of Toronto's ethics committee (2006–2012). Participants were recruited by contacting community organisations that provided programs and services to this client group, and through word of mouth (Moll, 2012). The experience of growing older with a physical impairment was co-constructed through a two step process: (1) The co-construction of each individual's narrative and (2) The analysis of the narratives to identify key themes and players. Participants shared their life stories with the first author by meeting with her three and sometimes four times for one to two hours to gain a comprehensive understanding of their lived experience through the lens of a life course perspective (Clausen, 1998; Giele & Elder Jr., 1998; White Riley, 1998). Individual life stories were co-constructed from the interview transcripts (transcribed verbatim). When the life stories of participants were completed, a comparative thematic and narrative analysis was completed on the nine life stories. Consensus of the emerging themes found in Moll (2012) was achieved through member checking, and consultation with the first authors supervisor. The common themes provided the foundation for co-constructing a narrative that captured the experience of growing up and growing older with a physical impairment. After the narrative was written it was analysed for deeper meanings embedded in the text (Moll, 2012; Moll & Cott, 2013). Data were transcribed and qualitatively analysed for themes. The narrative analysis wove together the experiences of participants. More details of data collection and demographic attributes are in Moll (2012).

Theoretical Perspective

This research was undertaken in order to understand the complexities of ageing with a lifelong physical impairment. The life course perspective provides a theoretical framework for studying the influences – individual and environmental – that shape the life experience of an individual, including the transactional relationships that take place between individuals, and individuals and their environments, over time. It looks beyond physiological declines in functioning that is the focus of most research on ageing with disability (spinal cord injury, traumatic brain injury, polio, CP, spina bifida) (Bottos et al., 2001; Krause & Broderick, 2005; Meade, Forchheimer, Krause, & Charlifue, 2011). Furthermore, this perspective is embedded in theoretical pluralism, encompasses human agency (making decisions about one's life and acting upon them), and explains the elements that contribute to the formation of self-identities and adaptation over time (Giele & Elder Jr., 1998; Patton, 2002). This perspective identifies elements at the micro, macro, and mezzo levels of organisation that influence personal biographies, and the meanings that individuals ascribe to significant life events and transitions at a particular point in time (Giele & Elder Jr., 1998; Priestley, 2003).

Defying the Odds: Growing Up and Growing Older with Cerebral Palsy

Growing up and growing older with CP is complex and multifaceted, and changes over time. Having a lifelong physical impairment impacts the unfolding of peoples' lives at many different levels (individual, social, cultural, institutional, political and economic) which influences the kinds of opportunities they have in life. As their lives unfold, many people with CP may not able to achieve 'normal' standards of physical and social functioning at the same pace as nondisabled individuals. Being able to participate in mainstream social life is also hindered by having a body that is difficult to control and regulate, and comes to represent a 'disordered body' (Turner, 1992). People with CP are confronted with functional deterioration and secondary health problems in young adulthood or midlife that impact multiple areas of their lives and threaten their long-term physical and emotional well-being. Functional declines associated with ageing coincide with limitations in activity (ADL and IADL) and threaten their ability to participate in daily life and to continue to fulfil the roles and responsibilities associated with work, social, family and leisure.

Figure 8.1 illustrates the main phases and challenges encountered in the *Defying the odds* narrative as the participants describe the experience of growing up and growing older with lifelong physical impairment. Each of these phases is discussed below as part of this narrative.

The 'defying the odds' Narrative

Defying the odds depicts the inner drive of individuals with CP to create a life for themselves even when faced with the adversity of biomedical and cultural discourses about the 'normal' body and impairment that the institutions of medicine, rehabilitation and education use to manage and regulate

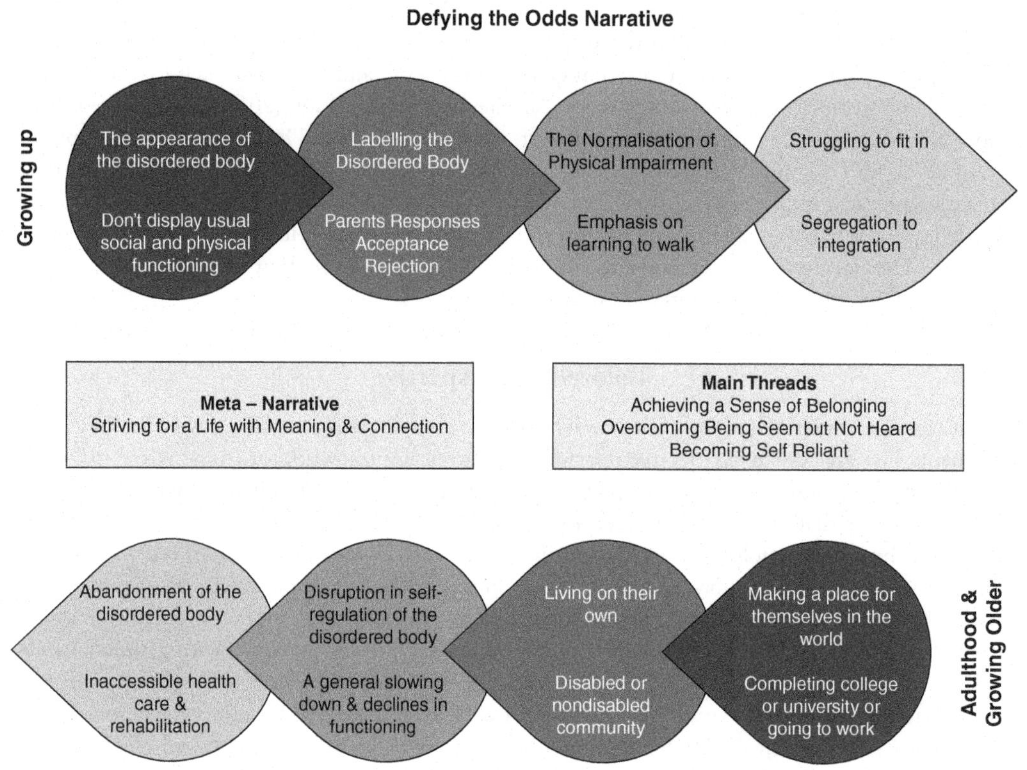

Defying the Odds Narrative

Growing up
- The appearance of the disordered body / Don't display usual social and physical functioning
- Labelling the Disordered Body / Parents Responses Acceptance Rejection
- The Normalisation of Physical Impairment / Emphasis on learning to walk
- Struggling to fit in / Segregation to integration

Meta – Narrative
Striving for a Life with Meaning & Connection

Main Threads
Achieving a Sense of Belonging
Overcoming Being Seen but Not Heard
Becoming Self Reliant

Adulthood & Growing Older
- Abandonment of the disordered body / Inaccessible health care & rehabilitation
- Disruption in self-regulation of the disordered body / A general slowing down & declines in functioning
- Living on their own / Disabled or nondisabled community
- Making a place for themselves in the world / Completing college or university or going to work

Figure 8.1 Defying the odds narrative.

their bodies. *Defying the odds* consists of *Growing up* (when their disordered bodies are labelled and their narratives shaped by the institutions of family, medicine, rehabilitation and education) and *Growing older* (when they attempt to find a place for themselves in the world and manage an ageing disordered body). Throughout these experiences, people with CP are striving for a life with meaning and connection as they try to achieve a sense of belonging, overcome being seen but not heard and become self-reliant.

The meta-narrative that weaves the *Defying the odds* narrative together is *Striving for a life with meaning & connection* which consists of three threads: *Achieving a sense of belonging*; *Overcoming being seen but not heard*; and, *Becoming self-reliant*.

Growing up with Cerebral Palsy

The Appearance of the Disordered Body

The *Defying the odds* narrative begins at birth when participants encounter and survive their first medical crisis due to a high-risk pregnancy or complications during the birthing process. Once the baby's medical condition is stabilised, parents are sent home without knowing or realising that their children may face challenges with respect to their physical functioning as a result of their difficult births. As months passed all participants were confronted with new odds that manifested in failure to begin to display the ability to regulate and control physical abilities characteristic of their age. Parents became concerned when their children did not display abilities such as sitting up without support, rolling over, or beginning to crawl.

Labelling the Disordered Body

The next stage of the *Defying the odds* narrative involves parents searching for answers to their children's challenges through the institutions of medicine and, eventually, rehabilitation. It is here that the thread of *Being seen but not heard* begins as their parents and health care professionals make decisions for the children with CP without their input. This thread follows them throughout their lives.

It is through the professional gaze, knowledge and expertise that the participants are assigned a diagnosis or label for the physical challenges they were displaying (Green, Davis, Karshmer, Marsh, & Straight, 2005). The label that is assigned identifies both the condition and its attributes (e.g. spastic CP). Labelling the disordered body is considered beneficial because the health professional can make recommendations for medical and surgical treatment and/or physical rehabilitation to improve physical functioning so the individual is better able to conform to normal standards of functioning. However, the use of labels establishes parameters on how much and/or how little a person is expected to be able to achieve, what he/she needs, and determines the life which he/she will be able to lead.

The medical gaze perpetuates the feelings of being seen but not heard. The gaze of health care professionals negatively impacts the child's sense of self and devalues their existence through its legitimation of normality. All participants encountered these experiences in different social contexts throughout their lives; however, this experience was profound in health care and rehabilitation settings (see Moll & Cott, 2013).

Putting a name or label to the physical and social delays and difficulties their children were displaying had a significant impact on parents. The diagnosis provided them with an explanation for the difficulties their sons or daughters were experiencing however, at the same time, concerns associated with the long-term outcomes that accompanied the diagnosis were raised. The ways that parents embraced or resisted these medical discourses were key to shaping the participants' narratives.

It is here that we pick up the thread of *Achieving a sense of belonging* that weaves through the *Defying the odds* narrative. Needing and wanting to belong begins and is shaped within the family context, and depends on how families accept or reject the discourse of disability. The need to be loved and accepted – first within the context of their families and later among the people they interact with outside of the home – was very important to all the participants. As the primary characters in their lives at this point in the narrative, the ways in which parents dealt with having a child with a disability, and the decisions they made, significantly shaped their son/daughter's narrative. The paths the participants took throughout life had their origins in the patterns of interactions within the context of the family which was their first social network and primary source of nurturing their sense of self.

Parents had different responses to their children's label. Some parents who accepted the disability discourse and rejection of the child, were only able to deal with their children's medical needs and seemed unable to respond to their needs for love and acceptance. Having a physical impairment influenced how parents related to their son/daughter on an emotional level both physically (hugging and kissing) and verbally (providing encouragement, love and support), and engaging in activities together.

Other parents were resistant to the disability discourse and championed inclusion of the child, participants told stories about their parents embracing and supporting them in being the best they could be despite their impairments. This was not limited to meeting their daily needs, but also seeking community support and resources to enhance their abilities, as well as socialising with others (family and children) so they could experience life like other children their age. They felt loved and accepted from the time they came into the world.

The Normalisation of Physical Impairment

Following diagnosis and labelling, recommendations were usually made by the doctor for the child to receive rehabilitation. At this point, the plot line of all of the participants' narratives changed dramatically, as having CP expands the cast of characters involved in their lives to include rehabilitation specialists who have a strong influence on the shape of their narratives. Entering the disciplines of health care and rehabilitation meant surrendering themselves to the expertise and practices of these health professionals who decided the kind of programs and services from which they may benefit based on the assessment of their physical functioning as measured against standards of normal physical functioning.

The health care professionals that participants and their parents came into contact with were concerned with engaging in medical practices such as orthopaedic surgery that would 'fix' the disordered body so that it would be able to benefit from physical rehabilitation to enhance physical functioning and bring it closer to normal standards. Some participants underwent orthopaedic surgery to correct atypical musculoskeletal structure or reduce spasticity before they reached physical maturity. Following diagnosis almost all parents took their children to receive physical rehabilitation where, once again, the focus was on transforming the body to one that conformed to normal standards of functioning and appearance. Although the participants acknowledged the results, they were able to achieve through rehabilitation, they felt pressured to conform to a notion of 'normal' that they found difficult to achieve (see Moll & Cott, 2013).

The progress that many of the children displayed from the physical rehabilitation they received was encouraging to their parents. These achievements made them believe that their children could have 'normal' lives, especially those with mild to moderate impairments. In contrast, learning about the possible outcomes they could expect from their children sometimes blinded parents from acknowledging their son or daughters' needs and aspirations by either being overprotective and/or discouraging them from achieving due to the difficulties associated with their condition.

Even though participants confronted so many odds at an early time in their lives they still found ways of defying the odds and exercising their agency, as becoming more independent through rehabilitation made other experiences and opportunities possible. Participants wanted more out of their lives than simply managing their physical conditions and they resisted the low expectations and the lives that were constituted for them by the experts. Participants with moderate to severe impairment who could not walk achieved greater independence using a wheelchair which gave them more freedom to move around and manage activities of daily living. Their success and accomplishments in defying the odds challenged the medical assumptions and expectations associated with physical impairment.

Both the successes and challenges participants encountered through the rehabilitation process and their interactions with others contributed to the emergence of the third thread, *Becoming self-reliant*, which is associated with achieving functional independence that goes beyond being able to walk. The desire to become self-reliant was a gradual process that was characterised by multiple achievements that extended beyond the medical management of the participants' conditions. Becoming self-reliant was an integral part of becoming functionally independent, as it included acquiring the abilities, they needed to achieve self-efficacy and make decisions about what they want and need to support them in being able to participate in social life, and live to their full potential.

Struggling to Fit In

The participants' determination to overcome the limitations of their disordered bodies and become self-reliant began to appear when they started school. Their narratives diverge depending on whether they attended segregated schools for children with disabilities or whether they were integrated into mainstream schools. In both cases they encountered new characters in their lives that would support or hinder the acquisition of skills and abilities that extended beyond the mastery of physical functioning emphasised in rehabilitation. The cast of characters expanded to include teachers and other children with/without impairments who would move to the foreground of their lives. These new social worlds to which they were exposed greatly influenced their subjectivity and life direction. Even though they went in different directions, they were all continuing to grapple with overcoming being seen but not heard, continuing to strive to become self-reliant, as well as achieve a sense of belonging.

Prior to the Independent Living Movement, segregation of children with disabilities into separate schools was recommended for some as the best way to improve children's physical functioning and enhance their education. The reasoning attached to segregation was that children with physical impairments would find it difficult to enter a regular school as educators were not trained or experienced to meet their needs and mainstream schools were not physically accessible.[1]

On the one hand, attending segregated schools helped to develop a sense of belonging, in this case, with other children with disabilities. However, many participants who were segregated felt disadvantaged because they felt that they did not learn what they needed to know when they transferred to the public-school system for high school. Participants felt that more time was spent on learning skills that would enable them to manage their ADLs and physical therapy so that that they could achieve functional independence rather than teaching them skills and abilities they would need as they grew up such as being able to live independently, being able to work in the community (proper education and training). Most felt they did not learn the skills they needed to prepare them for life because expectations were low as to what they could accomplish.

In contrast, participants who were integrated into public schools were able to benefit from a more comprehensive education that could potentially support the acquisition of skills and abilities that they would need in life to pursue a higher education and employment. However, they did not achieve a sense of belonging as described by some who attended segregated schools. They were often the only children in the public school with functional difficulties which only served to emphasise their differentness. It was not uncommon for them to be ridiculed and rejected by their peers.

The participants' narratives converged again when they were integrated into the public-school system for high school. Now both groups had to contend with the issue of achieving a sense of belonging with maturing, able bodied classmates. In addition, the previously segregated group had to address issues of academic differences and differing academic expectations. The sense of belonging they had achieved in the segregated school with other children with impairments was lost.

Achieving a sense of belonging within the family, among peers, and within communities spans the life course of all individuals. The fulfilment of these needs during childhood and adolescence provides a foundation for achieving self-confidence and self-affirmation, both of which are necessary for forming and maintaining meaningful relationships with others.

In late adolescence and early adulthood participants encountered significant shifts in the primary and secondary characters involved in their lives. The institution of rehabilitation and the professionals attached to it receded into the background. Even though participants wanted to make their own place in the world, they felt that they were left unprepared for adulthood in two ways: (1) All the care and treatment they received growing up had been done to them and for them without including them in the process and (2) They had limited opportunities to participate in mainstream social life due to their inadequate preparation for adulthood with nowhere for them to go.

Growing Older with Cerebral Palsy

As participants approached late adolescence and the completion of high school, many found themselves with nowhere to go to engage in higher education and pursue a career. Their transition into young adulthood coincided with not being eligible for health care and rehabilitation services and programs they had received during childhood. Many participants found themselves without having an adult health provider as those linkages were not coordinated by their paediatric physician, and/or they did not exist or were difficult to find.[2]

Making a Place for Themselves in the World

The central narrative of participants began to diverge again. Some participants began to pursue a post-secondary education without being able to finish and faced challenges finding employment opportunities and independent living arrangements. Other completed college/university, becoming gainfully employed, and lived on their own from the time they started school or work.

The desire to participate in productive work was important to all participants. However, for some, poor academic competence coupled with the extended time needed to acquire certain skills and complete activities meant that they were not competitive in the job market. Being able to engage in paid work was challenging in part due to the negative attitudes towards hiring people with disabilities and the lack of training for a specific career. Nonetheless, even those participants with more severe impairments were actively engaged in activities focused on increasing awareness about living with a disability, and advancing the rights of people with disabilities in the areas of education, accessibility (transportation, physical environments), and independent living as volunteers, disability activists and educators on a number of disability issues. Achieving these milestones enhanced their self-reliance, their sense of belonging and being able to engage productive activities.

Living on Their Own

Being able to live in the community away from the family home was important to all participants because they wanted to experience life like their able-bodied counterparts as well as being able to actively construct how they lived their lives personally and socially. Moving into a community residence for persons with disabilities was the only option for participants with more severe impairments.

While living in the residence appeared to offer them greater independence, their lives continued to be regulated by the administration and health care professionals managing the institution. Despite these boundaries, the participants who lived there were able to achieve a sense of belonging, resisted the restrictions placed on them by exercising their agency and enhanced their ability to overcome being seen but not heard by voicing their needs and aspirations, as well as learning to become self-reliant within the policies that governed their lives.

Disruptions in Self-Regulation of the Disordered Body

Many participants found that they began to encounter difficulties in physical functioning in young and/or middle adulthood, often many years earlier than traditionally experienced by individuals who grow older without lifelong impairment. The difficulties participants experienced as a consequence of their disordered bodies were overshadowed by having to cope with and adjust to changing life circumstances such as diminishing social networks due to the changing structure and function of the family, the death of loved ones and friends, as well as more limited social and vocational opportunities and financial resources.

Many participants encountered changes in the structure and function of the family with respect to providing care, resources or support, as well as continued companionship where families once were close. What sense of belonging they had been able to achieve in young adulthood was threatened by these losses. There are two issues these participants confronted: who will be there for them when their families are no longer able to care for them? How will they be able to maintain their current lifestyle and have their needs met by people who don't know them?

The physical difficulties participants encountered as they grew older were characterised by a general slowing down that was accompanied by pain associated with changes in their musculoskeletal structure and fatigue. For most participants these changes had a gradual onset in their early 30s or mid 40s with a profound impact on their ability to engage in activities of daily living that they had once completed on their own in a timely manner. They also experienced disruptions with work and being able to participate in activities they valued with friends and family. Most participants felt that they began to experience these changes after many years of pushing their bodies beyond their limits as they tried to maintain a full and busy schedule without having support in the home or workplace or getting the rest they needed.

Abandonment of the Ageing Disordered Body

The changes that participants encountered due to declines in physical functioning were often dealt with in isolation as they did not have access to the same programs and services they had received growing up. They found it challenging to have their health care needs addressed because many health care professionals with whom they came into contact with were not trained or experienced in providing health care services and/or assessments to adults with physical and communication impairments. Consequently, these experiences challenged participant's ability to regulate their bodies, overcome being seen but not heard, and continue to be self-reliant.

It may seem inconceivable that the experiences of individuals with CP under the age of 65 can help us understand the significance and complexities associated with the lived experience of growing older, but they do. What linked the experiences of the nine individuals reflected in this narrative are the following themes:

- The appearance of the disordered body – participants didn't display the usual social and physical capacities
- Normalisation of physical impairment through process of rehabilitation – emphasis was placed on achieving normal physical functioning, especially learning to walk
- Abandonment of the disordered body – didn't have access to health and rehabilitation

Examples of these experiences are as follows:
Normalisation of physical impairment:

> I think it was very good for them to do those things in terms of like it's helped me do very practical things for myself from a medical standpoint. I can do a lot of things physically and I'm physically a very strong person as well. So, I think all of these things are great you know because I can wear a backpack and walk to the post office and things like that. At the same time though I think there's this whole business of normalcy and the idea that we're going to try to make this child walk as close as possible like as close as possible like the normal body or the idea of the normal body. (Marni, 26)

The abandonment of the disordered body:

> I just remember getting the electric wheelchair at 19 or 20, when I first got into college and [my doctor] said to me, okay, this is the last time you're going to see me. Now, if you have any other issues, you'll see Dr. – ..., at ...Hospital. And I saw him once or twice and I thought he was very useless to me, because I wanted to keep continuing on with some form of therapy and he recommended a few places, but the places he recommended me to, as soon as I would explain my situation it was like, sorry we don't deal with people "like you", meaning people with your type of issues. (Vanessa, 35)

Interpretation

The *Defying the odds* narrative describes the challenges that people with CP encounter growing up and growing older and the ways in which they overcome or resist biomedical and cultural discourses about impairment. They challenge and resist the discursive and non-discursive practices that the institutions of medicine, rehabilitation, and education use to manage and regulate their bodies discursive practices refer to the role of knowledge (scientific) and institutions (health care and rehabilitation) and education in constructing the lives of people with physical impairments (along with management and regulation of the disordered body) (Turner, 1992). Non-discursive practices capture the embodied experience of impairment, more commonly known as the lived experience of impairment, which considers how the body and individual subjectivity are constructed and reconstructed through interactions with 'others' (Turner, 1992). Both sets of practices overlap with one another and occur simultaneously as peoples' lives unfold and are reflected by the primary and secondary characters, they encounter at different phases of their lives such as their parents, extended family, health professionals, and educators.

The *Defying the odds* narrative depicts the notion that individuals with lifelong physical impairments possess an inner drive to create a life for themselves even when adversity is confronted on a regular basis. Adversity takes the form of little or no expectations for achievement, being defined by their impairments, growing up without social, emotional, and instrumental support that contributes to developing a positive self-concept, and acquiring the skills and abilities needed in adulthood. It also includes not having access to social and educational, and later, vocational, opportunities that support their development and overall well-being.

There are physical capacities that people acquire as they mature that enable them to control and regulate their bodies in order to perform certain skills and abilities that contribute to society through participation in roles such as student, parent, worker and citizen (Foucault, 1973; Turner, 1992). These basic physical abilities include being able to sit, stand, walk, and regulate and control physiological processes on a day to day basis. These attributes are considered as 'normal' functions or body techniques that people learn to manage as they mature (Merleau-Ponty, 1962; Turner, 1992). A body is considered disordered when an individual has impairments that alter the appearance of the body and interfere with being able to control and manage physical functioning and normal physiological processes. These bodies deviate from the norm and are difficult to control and regulate (Seymour, 1998; Turner, 1992).

The economic, political, social, and cultural contexts in which people with disordered bodies exist impact the ways in which they are treated through biomedical intervention, rehabilitation, and education, as well as the experiences and opportunities within which they engage (Hughes, 2009; Sullivan, 2005). Being labelled disabled or physically impaired carries certain conceptions and assumptions about a given subject that are often not positive and can lead to misconceptions about what they can and cannot achieve. Having a physical impairment is a devalued physical attribute that is stigmatised by able-bodied persons and perceived as being associated with inability and/or lack of potential (Davis, 1995; Goffman, 1963; Green et al., 2005). Being stigmatised coincides with segregation and discrimination, which limits the opportunities of individuals possessing the negative physical attribute to fully participate in mainstream social life. This experience is also accompanied by being perceived as non-human, as incapable of being productive, or as not having the same needs as their able-bodied counterparts.

The participants' early socialisation was fragmented and did not offer them the same experience as their able-bodied counterparts that led to marriage, family, employment and other resources that their able-bodied counterparts could draw from when they grew older and encountered impairment in later life. During young and middle adulthood, the institutions, professionals, and family members which were in the foreground of their early lives receded to the background and in some instances could not be counted on for instrumental and/or social support.

Implications for Rehabilitation Practice

Other studies have identified persistent health and musculoskeletal problems in young adults with CP (Sandström, 2007). Early onset declines are characterised by what many describe as a 'general slowing down' that interferes with and/or disrupts daily living and fulfilling the personal and professional roles and responsibilities they have/desire.

The participants in this study felt that rehabilitation was helpful for enhancing their physical functioning; however, it did not prepare them to achieve capacities that would enable them to manage their condition while navigating life as adults. Similar to other studies, participants in this study encountered declines in functioning in young or middle adulthood changes (Andrén & Grimby, 1999; Bottos et al., 2001; Charlifue, Lammertse, & Adkins, 2004; Harrison & Stuifbergen, 2005; Liptak, 2008). They felt that they did not have the knowledge and resources (personal, financial, health care, or rehabilitation) to deal with these changes. Consequently, by the time they transitioned into adulthood they had begun to slow down without having access to comparable services they received as children and adolescence.

Many found it difficult to find accessible health care and care providers with knowledge and training to respond to the issues that adults with lifelong physical impairments confronted (Darrah, Magil-Evans, & Adkins, 2002; Hilberink et al., 2007; Neri & Kroll, 2003). Over the past 30 years, advances in rehabilitation have enhanced the functional outcomes for people living with impairments from illness and injury. Yet from a rehabilitation perspective, funding and services are mainly available to individuals whose condition is labelled acute since these individuals with acquired impairments are considered to have the potential to achieve a successful recovery and to be reintegrated into their communities (Hammel, 2006; Hilberink et al., 2007).

Experts working with the participants in this study were guided by the same assumptions with one unique difference: individuals with CP were considered to possess the greatest potential for improvements in functional abilities during childhood. As a result, the participants had little or no access to rehabilitation in adulthood. Other studies have also found that the physical improvements that clients/patients made in rehabilitation during childhood are perceived by rehabilitation specialists to support individuals for the remainder of their lives (Bottos et al., 2001; Kemp & Mosqueda, 2004; Lankasky, 2004; Wiart & Darrah, 2002). What is significant about these findings is that they reveal that CP should no longer be considered a stable condition, as individuals living with the condition were informed by their doctors when they were young.

Within biomedical and rehabilitation frameworks the primary focus is on assessing functional abilities that are measured against a normative standard that if achieved and displayed coincides with being granted the right to participate in mainstream social life, or being able to engage in life (Oliver, 1998; Schneidert, Hurst, Miller, & Üstün, 2003). Achieving these norms are unrealistic especially when they are socially constructed and perpetuated by cultural beliefs that serve to legitimate the beliefs of a dominant group of individuals who decide what is normal/abnormal in physical representation, structure and function of the body (Hewitt, 1991).

These findings suggest the need to develop and implement a continuum of care across the life course. A continuum of care is not limited to providing young adults with impairments with the knowledge and skills they need to transition from paediatric to adult care. This approach should be predicated on ensuring that these individuals have access to comprehensive services including access to trained and experienced professionals, resources and technologies they need to engage in meaningful occupations, and manage life with physical (including their general health and emotional well-being) many years following comprehensive paediatric rehabilitation.

Notes

1 The Independent Living Movement coincided with deinstitutionalisation of persons with disabilities in Canada and other nations in the 1960s and 1970s along with the formation of advocacy groups among people with disabilities. They came together advocating for accessible transportation, housing, education, and work opportunities.
2 Pediatric services are comprehensive and well-integrated in Canada, while adult health care is more fragmented. Additionally, rehabilitation has mainly been available to adults with acute conditions, not for individuals living with chronic and/or long-term conditions.

References

Andrén, E., & Grimby, G. (2000). Dependence and perceived difficulty in activities of daily living in adults with cerebral palsy and spina bifida. *Disability and Rehabilitation, 22*(7), 299–307. https://doi.org/10.1080/096382800296656

Bottos, M., Feliciangeli, A., Sciuto, L., Gericke, C., & Vianello, A. (2001). Functional status of adults with cerebral palsy and implications for treatment of children. *Developmental Medicine and Child Neurology, 43*(8), 516–528. https://doi.org/10.1017/s0012162201000950

Charlifue, S., Lammertse, D. P., & Adkins, R. H. (2004). Aging with spinal cord injury: Changes in selected health indices and life satisfaction. *Archives of Physical Medicine and Rehabilitation, 85*(11), 1848–1853. https://doi.org/10.1016/j.apmr.2004.03.017

Clausen, J. (1998). Life reviews and life stories. In Giele, J. Z., & Elder Jr., G. H. *Methods of life course research: Qualitative and quantitative approaches* (pp. 189–212). Sage Publications. https://doi.org/10.4135/9781483348919

Colantonio, A., Ratcliff, G., Chase, S., & Vernich, L. (2004). Aging with traumatic brain injury: Long-term health conditions. *International Journal of Rehabilitation Research, 27*(3), 209–214. https://doi.org/10.1097/00004356 200409000-00006

Davis, L. J. (1995). *Enforcing normalcy: Disability, deafness, and the body.* Verso.

Darrah, J., Magil-Evans, J., & Adkins, R. (2002). How well are we doing? Families of adolescents or young adults with cerebral palsy share their perceptions of service delivery. *Disability and Rehabilitation, 24*(10), 542–549. https://doi.org/10.1080/09638280210121359

Dean, S., Colantonio, A., Ratcliff, G., & Chase, S. (2000). Clients' perspectives on problems many years after traumatic brain injury. *Psychological Reports, 86*(2), 653–658. https://doi.org/10.2466/pr0.2000.86.2.653

Foucault, M. (1973). *The birth of the clinic: An archaeology of medical perception.* Routledge.

Giele, J. Z., & Elder, G. H. Jr., (1998). *Methods of life course research: Qualitative and quantitative approaches.* Sage Publications Inc.

Green, S., Davis, C., Karshmer, E., Marsh, P., & Straight, B. (2005). Living stigma: The impact of labeling, stereotyping, separation, status loss, and discrimination in the lives of individuals with disabilities and their families. *Sociological Inquiry, 75*(2), 197–215. https://doi.org/10.1111/j.1475-682X.2005.00119.x

Goffman, E. (1963). *Stigma and social identity.* Prentice Hall.

Haak, P., Lenski, M., Hidecker, M. J. C., Li, M., & Paneth, N. (2009). Cerebral palsy and aging. *Developmental Medicine & Child Neurology, 51*, 16–23. https://doi.org/10.1111/j.1469-8749.2009.03428.x

Hammel, K. W. (2006). *Perspectives on disability and rehabilitation: Contesting assumptions; Challenging practice.* Elsevier.

Harrison, T. C., & Stuifbergen, A. (2005). A hermeneutic phenomenological analysis of aging with a childhood onset disability. *Health Care for Women International, 26*(8), 731–747. https://doi.org/10.1080/07399330500179689

Hewitt, M. (1991). Bio-politics and social policy: Foucault's account of welfare. In M. Featherstone, M. Hepworth & B. S. Turner (Eds.), *Theory, culture & society: The body: Social process and cultural theory* (pp. 225–255). SAGE Publications Ltd. https://doi.org/10.4135/9781446280546.n9

Hilberink, S. R., Roebroeck, M. E., Nieuwstraten, W., Jalink, L., Verheijden, J., & Stam, H. J. (2007). Health issues in young adults with cerebral palsy: Towards a life-span perspective. *Journal of Rehabilitation Medicine, 39*(8), 605–611. https://doi.org/10.2340/16501977-0103

Hughes, B. (2009). Wounded/monstrous/abject: A critique of the disabled body in the sociological imaginary. *Disability & Society, 24*(4), 399–410. https://doi.org/10.1080/09687590902876144

Kemp, B., & Mosqueda, L. (2004). *Aging with a disability: What the clinician needs to know.* The John Hopkins University Press.

Krause, J. S., & Broderick, L. (2005). A 25-year longitudinal study of the natural course of aging after spinal cord injury. *Spinal Cord, 43*(6), 349–356. https://doi.org/10.1038/sj.sc.3101726

Lankasky, K. (2004). A consumer's perspective on living with a disability: How change in function affects daily life. In B. Kemp & L. Mosqueda. (2004). *Aging with a disability: What the clinician needs to know* (pp. 9–18). The John Hopkins University Press.

Liptak, G. S. (2008). Health and well being of adults with cerebral palsy. *Current Opinion in Neurology, 21*(2), 136–142. https://doi.org/10.1097/WCO.0b013e3282f6a499

Lutz, B. J., & Bowers, B. J. (2005). Disability in everyday life. *Qualitative Health Research, 15*(8), 1037–1054. https://doi.org/10.1177/1049732305278631

McPherson, B. D. (1998). *Aging as a social process: An introduction to individual and population aging*. Harcourt Brace & Company.

Meade, M. A., Forchheimer, M. B., Krause, J. S., & Charlifue, S. (2011). The influence of secondary conditions on job acquisition and retention in adults with spinal cord injury. *Archives of Physical Medicine and Rehabilitation*, *92*(3), 425–432. https://doi.org/10.1016/j.apmr.2010.10.041

Merleau-Ponty, M. (1962). *Phenomenology of perception*. Routledge.

Moll, L. R. (2012). *Defying the odds: Growing up & growing older with a lifelong physical impairment (cerebral palsy)* [Unpublished doctoral dissertation]. University of Toronto.

Moll, L. R., & Cott, C. A. (2013). The paradox of normalization through rehabilitation: Growing up and Growing older with cerebral palsy. *Disability and Rehabilitation*, *35*(15), 1276–1283. https://doi.org/10.3109/09638288.2012.726689

Neri, M. T., & Kroll, T. (2003). Understanding the consequences of access barriers to health care: Experiences of adults with disabilities. *Disability and Rehabilitation*, *25*(2), 85–96. https://doi.org/10.1080/0963828021000007941

Oliver, M. (1998). Theories of disability in health practice and research. *BMJ*, *317*(7170), 1446–1449. https://doi.org/10.1136/bmj.317.7170.1446

Patton, M. (2002). Designing qualitative studies. In M. Patton (Ed.), *Qualitative research and evaluation methods* (3rd ed., pp. 223–246). Sage Publications Inc.

Pentland, W., McColl, M. A., & Rosenthal, C. (1995). The effect of aging and duration of disability on long term health outcomes following spinal cord injury. *Spinal Cord*, *33*(7), 367–373. https://doi.org/10.1038/sc.1995.84

Priestley, M. (2003). *Disability: A life course approach*. Polity Press.

Riley, M. W. (1998). A life course approach: Autobiographical notes. In Giele, J. Z., & Elder Jr., G. H. *Methods of life course research: Qualitative and quantitative approaches* (pp. 28–51). SAGE Publications, Inc. https://doi.org/10.4135/9781483348919

Sandström, K. (2007). The lived body — experiences from adults with cerebral palsy. *Clinical Rehabilitation*, *21*(5), 432–441. https://doi.org/10.1177/0269215507073489

Schneidert, M., Hurst, R., Miller, J., & Üstün, B. (2003). The role of environment in the International classification of functioning, disability and health (ICF). *Disability and Rehabilitation*, *25*(11–12), 588–595. https://doi.org/10.1080/0963828031000137090

Seymour, W. (1998). *Remaking the body: Rehabilitation and change*. Routledge.

Strauss, D., Ojdana, K., Shavelle, R., & Rosenbloom, L. (2004). Decline in function and life expectancy of older persons with cerebral palsy. *NeuroRehabilitation*, *19*(1), 69–78. https://doi.org/10.3233/NRE-2004-19108

Sullivan, M. (2005). Subjected bodies: Paraplegia, rehabilitation, and the politics of movement. In S. Tremain (Ed.), *Foucault and the government of disability* (pp. 27–44). The University of Michigan Press.

Tighe, C. A. (2001). 'Working at disability': A qualitative study of the meaning of health and disability for women with physical impairments. *Disability & Society*, *16*(4), 511–529. https://doi.org/10.1080/09687590120059513

Tremblay, M., Tryssenaar, J., Clark, K., Richardson, J., Watt, S., Rosenthal, C., ... Pentland, W. (1997). Aging with a preexisting disability: Developing a bibliography and curriculum guide for health and social science educators. *Educational Gerontology: An International Quarterly*, *23*(6), 567–579. https://doi.org/10.1080/0360127970230606

Turner, B. (Ed.) (1992). *Regulating bodies: Essays in medical sociology*. Routledge.

Wiart, L., & Darrah, J. (2002). Changing philosophical perspectives on the management of children with physical disabilities – their effect on the use of powered mobility. *Disability and Rehabilitation*, *24*(9), 492–498. https://doi.org/10.1080/09638280110105240

Wiley, E. A. M. (2004). Aging with a long-term disability: Voices unheard. *Physical & Occupational Therapy in Geriatrics*, *21*(3), 33–47. https://doi.org/10.1080/J148v21n03_03

Zaffuto-Sforza, C. D. (2005). Aging with cerebral palsy. *Physical Medicine and Rehabilitation Clinics*, *16*(1), 235–249. https://doi.org/10.1016/j.pmr.2004.06.014

Acknowledgements

This research was funded through TD Grants in Medical Excellence, TD Bank Financial Group, Formerly, Scholarship in Rehabilitation-Related Research for Graduate Students with Disabilities (in association with the Toronto Rehabilitation Institute), 2006–2011; and Toronto Rehabilitation Institute Graduate Scholarship Fund, 2005–2006.

Suggested Readings

Green, S., Davis, C., Karshmer, E., Marsh, P., & Straight, B. (2005). Living stigma: The impact of labeling, stereotyping, separation, status loss, and discrimination in the lives of individuals with disabilities and their families. *Sociological Inquiry*, 75(2), 197–215. https://doi.org/10.1111/j.1475-682X.2005.00119.x

Harrison, T. C., & Stuifbergen, A. (2005). A hermeneutic phenomenological analysis of aging with a childhood onset disability. *Health Care for Women International*, 26(8), 731–747. https://doi.org/10.1080/07399330500179689

Lankasky, K. (2004). A consumer's perspective on living with a disability: How change in function affects daily life. In B. Kemp & L. Mosqueda. (2004). *Aging with a disability: What the clinician needs to know* (pp. 9–18). The John Hopkins University Press.

Moll, L. R., & Cott, C. A. (2013). The paradox of normalization through rehabilitation: Growing up and Growing older with cerebral palsy. *Disability and Rehabilitation*, 35(15), 1276–1283. https://doi.org/10.3109/09638288.2012.726689

9
AGEING WITH DEAFBLINDNESS

Peter Simcock and Jill Manthorpe

Introduction

As a complex impairment with many different causes (Bodsworth, Clare, Simblett, & Deafblind UK, 2011), the term deafblindness has legal, clinical, and functional definitions. Many terms are used to describe the phenomenon, including dual sensory impairment, deafblindness, and combined hearing and vision loss (Wittich, Southall, Sikora, Watanabe, & Gagne, 2013). It affects people in different ways. Owing to its complexity, it is not surprising that deafblindness is described as an 'unrecognised disability' (Alley & Keeler, 2009, p. 3). The term 'deafblind' can be used to describe the continuum of combined hearing and sight loss, irrespective of the age and order of onset of each impairment and the severity of each loss (Ask Larsen & Damen, 2014; Wittich et al., 2013). As such, people who are considered deafblind vary considerably (Simcock, 2017). Nevertheless, what deafblind people have in common is deprivation in use of the distance senses (sound and sight) (McInnes, 1999), resulting in difficulties with communication, accessing information and mobility. The integrated experience of ageing and deafblindness is captured by Pollington (2008, p. 32), who observes that 'getting older is another change that I am living through. I have found old age an ambiguous process. I cannot divorce ageing from deafblindness because that is what I am'.

While establishing the prevalence of deafblindness is challenging because of this definitional complexity, most researchers agree that prevalence rises with increasing age (Wittich & Simcock, 2019). In developed countries, older people with acquired deafblindness form the largest sub-group of the deafblind population (Munroe, 2001; Robertson & Emerson, 2010; Wittich, Watanabe, & Gagne, 2012). However, this chapter considers those older people who are ageing with the impairment, about whom little is known (Simcock, 2017). After discussing the limited literature about this group, we argue that they challenge the division usually drawn between congenital (people who are born deafblind) and acquired deafblindness, before analysing the commonly reported experiences of ongoing change and adaptation. We then describe the concerns that people who are ageing with deafblindness have about the ability of health and social care services to meet their particular needs, before concluding the chapter by recommending next steps in research, policy, and practice. The chapter ends by suggesting further readings on the topic.

Background Literature

Writing in 2001, Rönnberg and Borg (2001, p. 74) observe that '[f]rom an international perspective, the population of deaf-blind [had] received little research attention'. Just as Moll and Cott (2013) note a focus among rehabilitation services on children with cerebral palsy rather than older adults with the condition, the provenance of deafblindness campaigning organisations came from shared concern about the needs of deafblind children; it was not until the 1980s that organisations explicitly highlighted the needs of older deafblind people (Wittich & Simcock, 2019). Wittich, Jarry, Groulx, Southall, and Gagne (2016) report that the research community had a similar approach, initially focusing on the needs of deafblind children, resulting in few studies of the older deafblind population. Particularly little is written about older deafblind people living in low and middle-income nations (Jaiswal, Aldersley, Wittich, Mirza, & Finlayson, 2018; World Federation of the Deafblind, 2018), despite the increased likelihood of early onset impairment in such countries (Westwood & Carey, 2018). Furthermore, there are specific calls for more qualitative research exploring deafblind people's experiences (Jaiswal et al., 2018; Schneider et al., 2011; Tiwana, Benbow, & Kingston, 2016) and for further inquiry into the impact of the impairment on family members (Lehane, Wittich, & Dammeyer, 2016). Consequently, writing over a decade after Rönnberg and Borg (2001), Dammeyer (2015) argues that research in deafblindness remains in its infancy.

The existing research on deafblind older people has been described as being of variable quality (Heine & Browning, 2015; Saunders & Echt, 2007). A particular critique of current research is the failure of study authors to make explicit the specific sub-group of the deafblind population concerned, which makes the synthesis of material, and ability to draw conclusions from it, problematic (Dammeyer, 2015; Rönnberg & Borg, 2001; Simcock, 2017; Tiwana et al., 2016). The majority of literature on older deafblind people focuses on those people with late-life acquired deafblindness (Wittich & Simcock, 2019); this reflects demographic changes of ageing societies which have encouraged research activity with this group (Wittich & Simcock, 2019). Nonetheless, other groups of older deafblind people, who would be considered to be ageing *with* the impairment, are described in English health and care policy (Department of Health, 1997). This policy attention includes: those people living with sight impairment who subsequently acquire hearing loss; deafened or hearing impaired older adults using speech to communicate, who subsequently acquire sight loss; older culturally Deaf people using sign language who subsequently acquire sight loss; and those who have been deafblind for all or the majority of their life. As noted in the introduction, determining the prevalence of deafblindness is complex, and the number of adults ageing with the impairment is not known (Wittich & Simcock, 2019), although contemporary diagnostic and treatment advances may expand any 'ageing with' population (Westwood & Carey, 2018).

Despite the increase in studies on late-life acquired deafblindness, few researchers have involved older people who are ageing with the condition. In a systematically conducted review, Simcock (2017, p. 1703) found 'no studies [that] focus specifically or solely… on the experience of ageing with deafblindness'. What was identified were studies on the experiences of deafblind people, which include people who have aged with the impairment (see, for example, Damen, Krabbe, Kilsby, & Mylanus, 2005; Dammeyer, 2010; LeJeune, 2010; Oleson & Jansbøl, 2005), literature authored by social work practitioners, drawing on practice experience and interviews with deafblind people (see, for example, Miner, 1995, 1997; Wickham, 2011), and personal/autobiographical accounts, written by those ageing with the impairment and published in various journals and other media (see, for example, Bejsnap, 2004; Pollington, 2008; Stiefel, 1991; Stoffel, 2012). This material details particular differences between the needs and experiences of those with late-life acquired deafblindness and those ageing with the impairment (Simcock, 2017). Akin to those people ageing with various impairments, those ageing with deafblindness are reported to experience: ongoing change and the consequent need for adaptation; a particular reciprocal relationship between the ageing process and the impairment; and a sense that while one can learn adaptive strategies, living with an impairment for a long time does not make this easier. As Simcock (2017) contends, these experiences may be considered features of what Putnam (2012, p. 92) defines as the 'uniqueness of ageing with disability'. Drawing on the existing body of work and more recent doctoral study involving adults ageing with deafblindness undertaken by the first author (Simcock, 2020) and supervised by the second, this chapter now turns to explore its first key point:

that those ageing with deafblindness are a hidden population that challenge the division usually drawn between congenital and acquired manifestations of the impairment.

A Hidden Population Challenging the Congenital: Acquired Divide

Although research exploring ageing with a single sensory impairment has been undertaken (Age UK & Royal National Institute of Blind People, 2015; Jeppsson Grassman, Holme, Taghizadeh Larsson, & Whitaker, 2012; Young, 2014), having more than one sensory impairment is rarely researched. This invisibility in the literature is echoed in the exclusion of older deafblind people in international development programmes (World Federation of the Deafblind, 2018). For example, there are only limited references to deafblindness in both the *United Convention on the Rights of Persons with Disabilities* and the WHO *World Report on Disability* (World Health Organization, 2011). Simcock and Wittich (2019) observe that in the UNCRPD particularly, these references largely focus on children.

Older deafblind people face various barriers to participation in research (Jaiswal et al., 2018; Roy, McVilly, & Crisp, 2018; Skilton, Boswell, Prince, Francome-Wood, & Moosajee, 2018) resulting in the ongoing absence of their voices in mainstream gerontological literature. However, for those ageing with deafblindness, invisibility is also apparent in the 'ageing with' literature. Identifying the key physical and sensory disabilities with which people may age in a chapter on 'ageing with impairment', Westwood and Carey (2018) only list the two single sensory impairments (visual impairment and hearing impairment) and omit deafblindness. Furthermore, in a later discussion about the experiences of those ageing with deafblindness in long-term care settings such as nursing homes, they erroneously support the points made with reference to a study concerning those with late-life acquired deafblindness, which specifically excluded those who are ageing with the impairment (see Roets-Merken et al., 2017). In the 'deafblindness literature', Simcock (2017) argues that there is an inherent assumption that 'older deafblind people' are those who have acquired the impairment in later life, noting the broad titles of numerous journal articles that focus exclusively on the late-life acquired population. While in some articles clarity on the population is offered in the abstract or introduction, in others it is merely implied. Simcock (2017) also highlights the exclusion or limited inclusion of older people from research on the experiences of those living with deafblindness (see, for example, Ellis & Hodges, 2013; Kyle & Barnett, 2012; Oleson & Jansbøl, 2005), and limited coverage of the experience of ageing and old age in the autobiographical accounts, which tend to focus on experiences earlier in life, such as education and adolescence (see, for example, Coker, 1995; Murphy, 1991).

Such invisibility may partly be explained by the 'ageing with deafblindness' population's highlighting a key distinction drawn in deafblind research, policy, and practice: that between congenital impairment and acquired impairment (Dalby et al., 2009). Complexity in describing deafblindness was noted in the introduction to this chapter. In seeking to add clarity to descriptions of deafblindness and its effects, Dammeyer (2014) observes the long-standing classification of the impairment into either the congenital or acquired category by the research, policy, and practice communities. Notable differences in experiences and needs between these groups are confirmed in the literature (Dalby et al., 2009). For example, there is wide variation in the communication methods used by those in each category (Dalby et al., 2009) and while communication poses difficulties for all deafblind people, it can prove uniquely challenging for congenitally deafblind people, who may experience difficulty understanding the very concept of language (Hart, 2008). It is interesting to note that the relatively new *Journal of Deafblind Studies on Communication* focuses almost solely on communication among congenitally deafblind people.

Although the distinction can be helpful therefore, those ageing with deafblindness include people across this divide. For example, the population comprises of those ageing with congenital conditions, such as congenital rubella syndrome, but also those for whom one impairment is congenital and one acquired in childhood or early adulthood, and those for whom both impairments are acquired in childhood or early adulthood (Wittich & Simcock, 2019). It also includes those with a congenital condition that results in acquired deafblindness, such as Usher Syndrome. The participants in Simcock's (2020) study illustrate this diversity, although they are all considered to be ageing with deafblindness ($n = 8$): one had congenital deafblindness; one had congenital deafblindness with subsequent trauma resulting in further sight loss; two had congenital profound deafness and acquired sight loss in childhood; three had congenital hearing impairment and acquired sight loss in early adulthood; and one acquired both visual and hearing impairment in early adulthood. The congenital versus acquired distinction is therefore overly simplistic (Wittich & Simcock, 2019) and arguably artificial (Clark, 2014; Moller, 2003). In developing an approach to the description and classification of deafblindness, Ask Larsen and Damen (2014) have thus added, *inter alia*, the onset of each impairment relative to chronological age. However, arguably, it is the ageing with deafblindness population that specifically highlight the inadequacy of this long-standing distinction.

Multiple Changes, Constant Adjustment

Experiences of multiple changes are commonly reported among people ageing with deafblindness (Gullacksen, Göransson, Rönnblom, Koppen, & Jørgensen, 2011; LeJeune, 2010; Oleson & Jansbøl, 2005; Spring, Adler, & Wohlgensinger, 2012), challenging the description of sensory impairments as 'stable' conditions (see, for example, Kelley-Moore, 2010; Shakespeare & Watson, 2001). When ageing with disability, changes in impairment occur concurrently with changes associated with ageing (Westwood & Carey, 2018) and such phenomena are observed among deafblind people (Simcock, 2017). This includes deterioration in hearing and vision, which may be associated with late manifestations of the original aetiology (Laustrup, 2004), the development of additional age-related sensory impairment (Wittich et al., 2012) or indeed both (Barr, 1990). Trauma in childhood or adulthood may also impact on any residual hearing or vision; for example, a participant with congenital deafblindness in Simcock's doctoral study was involved in an accident in early adulthood, which damaged the residual vision left in one eye. Gullacksen et al. (2011) note the increased risk of other physical health problems among congenitally deafblind people as they age; this may include further deterioration in proprioceptive function, as a result of changes in the peripheral and central nervous system (Goble, Coxon, Wenderoth, Van Impe, & Swinnen, 2009).

Changes are not restricted to those of a physical nature. Those ageing with deafblindness have had a life of reduced access to information, communication difficulty and potentially, high levels of social isolation (Gullacksen et al., 2011) and therefore may face old age with a sense of uncertainty (Simcock, 2017). Changes in social networks and loss of friendships and relationships, particularly with those able to use appropriate communication methods, have also been reported (Simcock, 2017). Such changes are largely related to the ageing process, but the associated effects are complicated by the existing deafblindness. Change in employment status, particularly the need for early retirement, was a shared experience for participants in Simcock's doctoral research (Simcock, 2020). It appears that this is a common event for both deafblind people (World Federation of the Deafblind, 2018) and those ageing with other impairments (Westwood & Carey, 2018), resulting in the risk of both financial and social disadvantage. Verbrugge, Latham, and Clarke (2017) maintain that those with impairments may experience such changes associated with ageing sooner; a phenomenon termed 'accelerated ageing'. In her personal account of ageing with Usher syndrome, Stiefel (1991) describes many of her experiences as 'accelerated ageing' and Laustrup (2004) similarly observes early manifestations of ordinarily age-related change in data on deafblind adults with congenital rubella syndrome.

Responding to the various life changes experienced, those ageing with deafblindness report having to make adjustments (Simcock, 2017); the nature of these is described as 'multiple' (Miner, 1995), 'repeated and ongoing' (Göransson, 2008; Gullacksen et al., 2011), and 'constant' (Duncan, Prickett, Finkelstein, Vernon, & Hollingsworth, 1988). Westwood and Carey (2018, p. 229) note that people living with impairments 'lose many of the gains they achieved in rehabilitation' as they age. This experience is evident in the ageing with deafblindness population (Göransson, 2008), particularly in relation to communication and the need to learn new methods of communication over the lifecourse (Erber & Scherer, 1999; Simcock, 2017). For example, age-related reduced sensitivity in the fingers can impact on the accessibility of tactile reading and writing systems such as braille, which may have previously been a format used to access information (Yoken, 1979). For some people ageing with deafblindness, living with the impairment for a long time renders such adjustments easier to manage (Bejsnap, 2004; Yoken, 1979). Nevertheless, for others, such adjustments are not experienced as easier, but rather reported as becoming harder or perceived as such, as the ageing process and impairment combine (Butler, 2004; Damen et al., 2005; Stiefel, 1991), as illustrated by the following:

[A]t the age of 68, I contemplate the future with trepidation. There will be further transitions. They will be harder.

Pollington, 2008, p. 33

Now that I'm of retirement age, the difficulties are closing in.
71-year-old contributor in

Stoffel, 2012, pp. 201–202

Westwood and Carey (2018) argue that research involving those ageing with impairments can enhance our knowledge about resilience and positive adaptation, and our understanding of ageing with deafblindness is impoverished if the positive changes reported are not considered. Some people ageing with the impairment report on improvements in their hearing and/or vision, owing to either changes in their condition or medical intervention (Ellis & Hodges, 2013; Stoffel, 2012; Yoken, 1979). This includes those ageing with congenital deafblindness; for example, one participant in Simcock's study (2020) describes his latest hearing aids as being 'brilliant' and comments that since having them, while 'I still don't hear everything… it is not a problem'. Others ageing with deafblindness describe their active engagement with rehabilitation services and enjoying the opportunity to learn new skills, even in much later life (Bejsnap, 2004; Duncan et al., 1988; Jenson & Christiansen, 2011; Pollington, 2008; Schoone & Snelting, 2011; Stoffel, 2012). An experience noted in Pollington's (2008) personal account is the ability to 'merge into the background' as she gets older, particularly as acquired deafblindness is common in later life (Wittich & Simcock, 2019). Now as an older person, one participant in Simcock's study (2020) jovially describes no longer being the only one of her family to have sensory loss, now that they have all aged: in the words of Pollington (2008, p. 33), for those with impairments, '[a]geing is a leveller'.

Unmet Needs and the Misrecognition of Deafblindness

Westwood and Carey (2018) maintain that an under-developed understanding of the features of ageing with impairment results in the marginalisation of disabled people in ageing policy. While the World Federation of the Deafblind (2018) argue that all deafblind people are at risk of exclusion from national and international welfare policies and development programmes, Simcock & Wittich (2019) contend that those ageing with the impairment are particularly overlooked. However, Westwood and Carey (2018) also maintain that health and social care services are ill-equipped to meet the needs of disabled people in later life, noting that disability organisations are not always able to respond to 'ageing issues', while services for older people often fail to respond to disability related matters. This latter point is illustrated by the observation that the human rights campaigning of organisations for older people has not engaged explicitly with disability rights (Phillips, Ajrouch, & Hillcoat-Nalletamby, 2010). Those ageing with deafblindness are reported to have expressed concerns about the ability of deafblind organisations to meet their needs as older people, and mainstream older people's services' ability to meet their needs as deafblind adults (Simcock, 2017). For example, those living in mainstream older people's accommodation-based care settings describe experiences of unmet need, especially in relation to social inclusion (Göransson, 2008; Spring et al., 2012; Stoffel, 2012). Isolation in mainstream older people's services is not simply a consequence of health and social care staff lacking the relevant knowledge and skills, but also an outcome of being the only deafblind person in the setting, particularly where the deafblind person uses sign language (visually or tactually).

Westwood and Carey (2018, p. 234) also observe that health and social care systems are often designed around 'individual diseases rather than conditions involving multimodality'. Participants in LeJeune's (2010) qualitative study of the experiences of those acquiring a second sensory impairment, in addition to a pre-existing one, report on the inadequacies of single sensory impairment services in meeting their needs. While the experience of comorbid physical and mental health problems among deafblind people has been demonstrated (Bodsworth et al., 2011; Tiwana et al., 2016; Wahlqvist, Möller, Möller, & Danermark, 2013, Wahlqvist, Möller, Möller, & Danermark, 2016), Miner (1995) points out that for those ageing with deafblindness, a life of reduced access to information can result in limited awareness of the healthcare services available for older people.

The World Federation of the Deafblind (2018) reports that from the data available, only 37% of countries ($n = 50$) recognise deafblindness as a distinct disability. Feeling that one's needs or situation have not been recognised or have been misrecognised was a key experience among participants in Simcock's (2020) research, and contributed to their feelings of vulnerability, as the following examples illustrate:

> I knew I was getting in the way, and I just felt quite vulnerable at that particular moment, I, I didn't really know what to do… I don't know what other people thought of me. I'm trying to put myself in their shoes, trying to imagine them looking back at me, seeing this person floundering and not really understanding why I was doing that (52-year-old with Usher Syndrome Type II).
>
> They (Healthcare Workers) often don't know about what's going on with deafblind people, so you have to plan every stage…. You have to give them information, information, tell them all. It takes lots of energy, lots of energy, explaining again and again and again… if you don't have a plan, you get a bit lost really (73-year-old with Usher Syndrome Type I: English interpretation of original contribution given in British Sign Language).

Although a lack of recognition and a paucity of research have resulted in those ageing with deafblindness being *de facto* excluded from welfare policies and development programmes, the tendency of national and international policy on old age to homogenise the ageing experience (Lloyd-Sherlock, 2002; Walker, 2017) also contributes to their invisibility. The need to develop our understanding of the specific needs and experiences this sub-group of the deafblind population, through their increased involvement in deafblind research and mainstream gerontological study, therefore appears evident. Nevertheless, writing from a social model of disability perspective, Oliver (2013, p. 1026) warns against emphasising differences between diverse sub-groups of disabled people, arguing it to be 'impotent in protecting disabled people, [their] benefits and services'. He maintains that such approaches depoliticise the social model, focusing on individual impairment and difference, rather than disabling barriers, which are then used in government policy to ration welfare, care and support. Furthermore, while change and consequent adaptation are common experiences of the ageing with deafblindness population, it can be similarly argued that a model of individual adjustment is an inadequate interpretative tool for understanding the experience. Using the example of communication method adaptations by those ageing with the impairment, Hersh (2013) observes that the corresponding need for communication partners to adapt to such changes is not always acknowledged or explored in the literature. The 'life adjustment model' adopted by Gullacksen et al. (2011) in their exploration of the experiences of deafblind people over the lifecourse more clearly acknowledges the need for the social environment and service providers to adjust as those with deafblindness age.

Next Steps and New Directions

There are clear knowledge gaps about people ageing with impairments (National Institute for Health and Care Excellence, 2015) and there have been associated calls for both further research and the inclusion of those ageing with disability to be involved in the co-production of knowledge (Westwood & Carey, 2018). Establishing the size of the ageing with deafblindness population locally and nationally is an important next step in increasing their visibility and informing resource allocation and health and social care service planning. Such data could also be useful in developing understandings about the importance of social and cultural contexts. Nevertheless, observing a paucity of good practice guidance for the involvement of all deafblind people in research and policy development (Jaiswal et al., 2018; Roy et al., 2018), establishing effective research and consultation approaches to secure meaningful participation is also a priority. Such approaches can inform much needed further qualitative inquiry into the experiences of those ageing with deafblindness to improve practice effectiveness. In enabling the accurate synthesis of research knowledge, study authors must make explicit the specific sub-group of the deafblind population concerned; in relation to particular sub-groups of those ageing with deafblindness, there have been specific calls for further research into the clinical needs of those ageing with congenital rubella syndrome and those with Usher syndrome (Armstrong & O'Donnell, 2004; Dalby et al., 2009; Ellis & Hodges, 2013).

In considering the maintenance of independence for those ageing with impairment, Agree (2014) proposes further exploration of the potential of assistive technologies. Wittich et al. (2016) identify improved assistive technologies as a priority for both the rehabilitation and research communities in the deafblind field, and some older deafblind people have expressed a desire to learn how to use new assistive technologies (Stoffel, 2012). However, those ageing with deafblindness have commented on the lack of available information about assistive technologies (LeJeune, 2010), and the difficulties using such devices owing to age-related changes such as reduced fine motor skills (Cohn, 1998; Göransson, 2008). It is therefore imperative that future research and development involves the 'ageing with' population.

The need for further research to inform, increase competence and capacity in both the policy and practice communities in the deafblind field and more widely is evident. Indeed, allied health and social care professionals working with older people have reported a lack of expertise in relation to supporting those with sensory impairment (Wittich & Simcock, 2019) and this probably extends to wider practitioner groups. Developing our understanding of the experiences and needs of people ageing with deafblindness requires collaboration between researchers and research stakeholders in both the congenital impairment and acquired impairment fields: it is time for deafblind researchers, advocacy and disability groups, policy makers, and practitioners to bridge this long-standing divide.

References

Age UK, & Royal National Institute of Blind People. (2015). *Improving later life for people with sight loss*. Age UK and RNIB. https://www.rnib.org.uk/sites/default/files/ENG091524_JOINT_SENIMAR_REPORT_V3.pdf

Agree, E. M. (2014). The potential for technology to enhance independence for those aging with a disability. *Disability and Health Journal*, 7(1), S33-S39. https://doi.org/10.1016/j.dhjo.2013.09.004

Alley, R., & Keeler, G. (2009). *Kent Deafblind Development Project*. Kent Adult Social Services. https://www.yumpu.com/en/document/view/24338037/kent-deafblind-development-project-kent-county-council

Armstrong, N., & O'Donnell, N. (2004). Rubella: 40 years after the epidemic. *The American Journal for Nurse Practitioners*, 8(4), 51–56.

Ask Larsen, F., & Damen, S. (2014). Definitions of deafblindness and congenital deafblindness. *Research in Developmental Disabilities*, 35(10), 2568–2576. https://doi.rog/10.1016/j.ridd.2014.05.029

Barr, D. (1990). Visiting the land of green ginger (with a little help from my friends). *New Beacon*, 74(880), 336–337.

Bejsnap, O. (2004). An account about being deafblind. In H. Ottesen, & H. Riber (Eds.), *Not quite like the rest. Life seen through deafblind eyes as teenagers, adults, and parents* (pp. 72–76). Herlev, Denmark: Information Center for Acquired Deafblindness.

Bodsworth, S. M., Clare, I. C. H., Simblett, S. K., & Deafblind, U. K. (2011). Deafblindness and mental health: Psychological distress and unmet need among adults with dual sensory impairment. *British Journal of Visual Impairment*, *29*(1), 6–26. https://doi.org/10.1177/0264619610387495

Butler, S. (2004). *Usher 2: How is it for you?* Sense. https://www.sense.org.uk

Clark, J. L. (2014). *Where I stand: On the signing community and my deafblind experience*. Handtype Press. http://www.handtype.com/books/whereistand/

Cohn, H. (1998). Problems experienced by hearing and visually impaired people. *British Journal of Visual Impairment*, *16*(1), 19–22.

Coker, J. (1995). The invisible helmet: A first-person account of deaf-blindness. *Journal of Visual Impairment & Blindness*, *89*(3), 201–208.

Dalby, D. M., Hirdes, J. P., Stolee, P., Strong, J. G., Poss, J., Tjam, E. Y., ... Ashworth, M. (2009). Characteristics of individuals with congenital and acquired deaf-blindness. *Journal of Visual Impairment & Blindness*, *103*(2), 93–102.

Damen, G. W., Krabbe, P. F., Kilsby, M., & Mylanus, E. A. (2005). The usher lifestyle survey: Maintaining independence: A multi-centre study. *International Journal of Rehabilitation Research*, *28*(4), 309–320. https://doi.org/10.1097/00004356-200512000-00003

Dammeyer, J. (2010). Interaction of dual sensory loss, cognitive function, and communication in people who are congenitally deaf-blind. *Journal of Visual Impairment & Blindness*, *104*(11), 719–725. https://doi.org/10.1177/0145482X1010401108

Dammeyer, J. (2014). Deafblindness: A review of the literature. *Scandinavian Journal of Public Health*, *42*(7), 554–562. https://doi.org/10.1177/1403494814544399

Dammeyer, J. (2015). Deafblindness and dual sensory loss research: Current status and future directions. *World Journal of Otorhinolaryngology*, *5*(2), 37–40. https://doi.org/10.5319/wjo.v5.i2.37

Department of Health. (1997). *Think dual sensory: Good practice guidelines for older people with dual sensory loss*. UK Department of Health. http://www.deafblind.com/thinkold.html

Duncan, E., Prickett, H., Finkelstein, D., Vernon, M., & Hollingsworth, T. (1988). *Usher's syndrome. What is it, how to cope, and how to help*. Charles C Thomas Publisher.

Ellis, L., & Hodges, L. (2013). *Life and change with usher: The experiences of diagnosis for people with usher syndrome: Research report prepared for sense*. University of Birmingham. http://www.birmingham.ac.uk/Documents/college-social-sciences/education/projects/final-report-on-life-and-change-with-usher.pdf

Erber, N. P., & Scherer, S. C. (1999). Sensory loss and communication difficulties in the elderly. *Australasian Journal on Ageing*, *18*(1), 4–9.

Goble, D. J., Coxon, J. P., Wenderoth, N., Van Impe, A., & Swinnen, S. P. (2009). Proprioceptive sensibility in the elderly: Degeneration, functional consequences and plastic-adaptive processes. *Neuroscience and Biobehavioral Reviews*, *33*(3), 271–278. https://doi.org/10.1016/j.neubiorev.2008.08.012

Göransson, L. (2008). *Dövblindhet i ett livsperspektiv. Strategier och metoder för stöd* [Deafblindness in a life perspective. Strategies and methods of support]. Mo Gårds Förlag.

Gullacksen, A., Göransson, L., Rönnblom, G., Koppen, A., & Jørgensen, A. (2011). *Life adjustment and combined visual and hearing disability/deafblindness – An internal process over time*. Nordic Centre for Welfare and Social Issues. http://nordisktvalfardscenter.se/PageFiles/5593/168730_Engelsk.pdf

Hart, P. (2008). Sharing communicative landscapes with congenitally deafblind people: It's a walk in the park! In M. S. Zeedyk (Ed.), *Promoting social interaction for individuals with communicative impairments. Making contact*. Jessica Kingsley Publishers.

Heine, C., & Browning, C. J. (2015). Dual sensory loss in older adults: A systematic review. *The Gerontologist*, *55*(5), 13–28. https://doi.org/10.1093/geront/gnv074

Hersh, M. (2013). Deafblind people, communication, independence, and isolation. *Journal of Deaf Studies and Deaf Education*, *18*(4), 446–463. https://doi.org/10.1093/deafed/ent022

Jaiswal, A., Aldersley, H., Wittich, W., Mirza, M., & Finlayson, M. (2018). Participation experiences of people with deafblindness or dual sensory loss: A scoping review of global deafblind literature. *PLoS ONE*, *13*(9), 1–26. https://doi.org/10.1371/journal.pone.0203772

Jenson, D. L., & Christiansen, H. S. (2011). *Development late in life* [Paper presentation]. Inclusion for a lifetime of opportunities, 15th Deafblind International Conference, Sao Paulo, Brazil.

Jeppsson Grassman, E., Holme, L., Taghizadeh Larsson, A., & Whitaker, A. (2012). Long life with a particular signature: Life course and aging for people with disabilities. *Journal of Gerontological Social Work*, *55*(2), 95–111. https://doi.org/10.1080/01634372.2011.633975

Kelley-Moore, J. (2010). Disability and ageing: The social construction of causality. In D. Dannefer & C. Phillipson (Eds.), *The SAGE handbook of social gerontology* (pp. 96–110). Sage. http://dx.doi.org/10.4135/9781446200933.n7

Kyle, J., & Barnett, S. (2012). *Deafblind Worlds*. Deaf Studies Trust and Sense. http://deafstudiestrust.org/wp-content/uploads/2020/04/Deafblind-Worlds-final.pdf

Laustrup, B. (2004). The ageing process and the late manifestation of conditions related to the cause of congenitally deafblind adults in Denmark. *DbI Review, 33*, 4–7. https://www.yumpu.com/en/document/view/40997455/the-ageing-process-and-late-manifestations-deafblind-international

Lehane, C., Wittich, W., & Dammeyer, J. (2016). Couples' experiences of sensory loss: A research and rehabilitation imperative. *The Hearing Journal, 69*(8), 34–36. https://doi.org/10.1097/01.HJ.0000491116.66672.40

LeJeune, B. J. (2010). Aging with a dual sensory loss: Thoughts from focus groups. *AER (Association for Education and Rehabilitation of the Blind and Visually Impaired) Journal, 3*, 146–152.

Lloyd-Sherlock, P. (2002). Social policy and population ageing: Challenges for north and south. *International Journal of Epidemiology, 31*, 754–757. https://doi.org/10.1093/ije/31.4.754

McInnes, J. M. (1999). *A guide to planning and support for individuals who are deafblind*. University of Toronto Press.

Miner, I. (1995). Psychosocial implications of usher syndrome, type 1, throughout the life cycle. *Journal of Vision Impairment and Blindness, 89*(3), 287–296. https://doi.org/10.1177/0145482X9508900317

Miner, I. (1997). People with usher syndrome, type 2: Issues and adaptations. *Journal of Visual Impairment and Blindness, 91*(6), 579–589.

Moll, L. R., & Cott, C. A. (2013). The paradox of normalization through rehabilitation: Growing up and Growing older with cerebral palsy. *Disability and Rehabilitation, 35*(15), 1276–1283. https://doi.org/10.3109/09638288.2012.726689

Moller, C. (2003). Deafblindness: Living with sensory deprivation. *The Lancet, 362*, S46–S47. https://doi.org/10.1016/s0140-6736(03)15074-x

Munroe, S. (2001). *Developing a national volunteer registry of persons with deafblindness in Canada: Results from the study 1999–2001*. Canadian Deafblind and Rubella Association. https://www.cdbanational.com/wp-content/uploads/2016/03/registry_eng.pdf

Murphy, P. (1991). How I live with deaf-blindness. In G. Taylor & J. Bishop (Eds.), *Being deaf: The experience of deafness* (pp. 169–172). The Open University.

National Institute for Health and Care Excellence. (2015). *Older people with social care needs and multiple long-term conditions*. NICE. https://www.nice.org.uk/guidance/ng22

Oleson, B. R., & Jansbøl, K. (2005). *Experiences from people with deafblindness – A Nordic project*. Herlev, Denmark: Information Center for Acquired Deafblindness.

Oliver, M. (2013). The social model of disability: Thirty years on. *Disability & Society, 28*(7), 1024–1026. https://doi.org/10.1080/09687599.2013.818773

Phillips, J., Ajrouch, K., & Hillcoat-Nalletamby, S. (2010). *Key concepts in social gerontology*. Sage. http://dx.doi.org/10.4135/9781446251058

Pollington, C. (2008). Always change – The transitions experienced by an older woman with declining sight and hearing. *Talking Sense, 52*(2), 30–33.

Putnam, M. (2012). Can aging with disability find a home in gerontological social work? *Journal of Gerontological Social Work, 55*(2), 91–94. https://doi.org/10.1080/01634372.2012.647581

Robertson, J., & Emerson, E. (2010). *Estimating the number of people with co-occurring vision and hearing impairments in the UK*. Centre for Disability Research. http://www.research.lancs.ac.uk/portal/en/publications/estimating-the-number-of-people-with-cooccurring-vision-and-hearing-impairments-in-the-uk%28e25a9d72-82c0-4040-aee7-bb43a4bb773b%29.html

Roets-Merken, L., Zuidema, S., Vernooij-Dassen, M., Dees, M., Hermsen, P., Kempen, G., & Graff, M. (2017). Problems identified by dual sensory impaired older adults in long-term care when using a self-management program: A qualitative study. *PLoS One, 12*(3), e0173601. https://doi.org/10.1371/journal.pone.0173601

Rönnberg, J., & Borg, E. (2001). A review and evaluation of research on the deaf-blind from perceptual, communicative, social and rehabilitative perspectives. *Scandinavian Audiology, 30*(2), 67–77. https://doi.org/10.1080/010503901300112176

Roy, A., McVilly, K., & Crisp, B. (2018). Preparing for inclusive consultation, research and policy development: Insights from the field of deafblindness. *Journal of Social Inclusion, 9*(1), 71–88. http://doi.org/10.36251/josi.132

Saunders, G. H., & Echt, K. V. (2007). An overview of dual sensory impairment in older adults: Perspectives for rehabilitation. *Trends in Amplification, 11*(4), 243–258. https://doi.org/10.1177/1084713807308365

Schneider, J. M., Gopinath, B., McMahon, C. M., Leeder, S. R., Mitchell, P., & Wang, J. J. (2011). Dual sensory impairment in older age. *Journal of Aging and Health, 23*(8), 1309–1324. https://doi.org/10.1177/0898264311408418

Schoone, A. M., & Snelting, M. E. (2011). *Creating opportunities for a deafblind elderly person who had no chances in his life* [Paper presentation]. Inclusion for Lifetime of Opportunities, 15th Deafblind International Conference, Sao Paulo, Brazil.

Shakespeare, T., & Watson, N. (2001). The social model of disability: An outdated ideology? *Research in Social Science and Disability, 2*, 9–28. https://doi.org/10.1016/S1479-3547(01)80018-X

Simcock, P. (2017). Ageing with A unique impairment: A systematically conducted review of older deafblind people's experiences. *Ageing & Society, 37*(8), 1703–1742. https://doi.org/10.1017/S0144686X16000520

Simcock, P. (2020). *The lived experience of vulnerability among adults ageing with deafblindness: an interpretative phenomenological analysis*. [PhD thesis], King's College London.

Simcock, P., & Wittich, W. (2019). Are older deafblind people being left behind? A narrative review of literature on deafblindness through the lens of the United Nations principles for older people. *Journal of Social Welfare and Family Law*, *41*(3), 339–357.

Skilton, A., Boswell, E., Prince, K., Francome-Wood, P., & Moosajee, M. (2018). Overcoming barriers to the involvement of deafblind people in conversations about research: Recommendations from individuals with usher syndrome. *Research Involvement and Engagement*, *4*(1), 40–51.

Spring, S., Adler, J., & Wohlgensinger, C. (2012). *Deafblindness in Switzerland: Facing up to the facts. A Publication on the study "The living circumstances of deafblind people at different stages of their lives in Switzerland"*. Swiss National Association of and for the Blind (SNAB). https://www.hfh.ch/fileadmin/files/documents/Dokumente_FE/C.4_e_Deafblindness---Facing-up-to-the-facts---SNAB-Switzerland-Print.pdf

Stiefel, D. H. (1991). *The madness of usher's. Coping with vision and hearing loss (usher syndrome type II)*. The Business of Living Publications.

Stoffel, S. (2012). *Deaf-blind reality: Living the life*. Gallaudet University Press.

Tiwana, R., Benbow, S. M., & Kingston, P. (2016). Late life acquired dual-sensory impairment: A systematic review of its impact on everyday competence. *British Journal of Visual Impairment*, *34*(3), 203–213. https://doi.org/10.1177/0264619616648727

Verbrugge, L. M., Latham, K., & Clarke, P. J. (2017). Aging with disability for midlife and older adults. *Research on Aging*, *39*(6), 741–777. https://doi.org/10.1177/0164027516681051

Wahlqvist, M., Möller, C., Möller, K., & Danermark, B. (2013). Physical and psychological health in persons with deafblindness that is due to usher syndrome, type II. *Journal of Visual Impairment & Blindness*, *107*(3), 207–220. https://doi.org/10.1177/0264619615610158

Wahlqvist, M., Möller, C., Möller, K., & Danermark, B. (2016). Physical and psychological health, social trust, and financial situation for persons with usher syndrome type 1. *British Journal of Visual Impairment*, *34*(1), 15–25. https://doi.org/10.1177/0264619615610158

Walker, A. (2017). Why the UK needs a social policy on ageing. *Journal of Social Policy*, *47*(2), 1–21. https://doi.org/10.1017/S0047279417000320

Westwood, S., & Carey, N. (2018). Ageing with physical disabilities and/or long-term health conditions. In S. Westwood (Ed.), *Ageing, diversity and equality: Social justice perspectives: Social justice perspectives* (pp. 225–244). Routledge.

Wickham, K. (2011). Depression in the deafblind community: Working from a social work perspective. *DbI Review*, *46*, 56–58.

Wittich, W., Jarry, J., Groulx, G., Southall, K., & Gagne, J. P. (2016). Rehabilitation and research priorities in deafblindness for the next decade. *Journal of Visual Impairment & Blindness*, July–August, 219–231.

Wittich, W., & Simcock, P. (2019). Aging and combined vision and hearing loss. In J. Ravenscroft (Ed.), *The Routledge handbook of visual impairment*. Routledge.

Wittich, W., Southall, K., Sikora, L., Watanabe, D. H., & Gagne, J. P. (2013). What's in a name: Dual sensory impairment or deafblindness? *British Journal of Visual Impairment*, *31*(3), 198–208. https://doi.org/10.1177/0264619613490519

Wittich, W., Watanabe, D. H., & Gagne, J. P. (2012). Sensory and demographic characteristics of deafblindness rehabilitation clients in Montreal, Canada. *Ophthalmic and Physiological Optics*, *32*(3), 242–251. https://doi.org/10.1111/j.1475-1313.2012.00897.x

World Federation of the Deafblind. (2018). *At risk of exclusion from CRPD and SDGS implementation: Inequality and persons with deafblindness. Initial Global Report 2018*. International Disability Alliance. http://www.internationaldisabilityalliance.org/sites/default/files/wfdb_complete_initial_global_report_september_2018.pdf

World Health Organization. (2011). *World Report on Disability*. World Health Organization. https://www.who.int/disabilities/world_report/2011/report.pdf

Yoken, C. (1979). *Living with deaf-blindness: Nine profiles*. Gallaudet College.

Young, A. (2014). *Older deaf people and social care: A review*. Royal Association for Deaf People (RAD). https://pdfs.semanticscholar.org/9e87/f91feb2012f77c484e44a8eae387214533f0.pdf

Acknowledgment

Professor Jill Manthorpe is funded by the NIHR (National Institute for Health Research) Health and Social Care Workforce Research Unit; the views expressed in this chapter are the authors alone and should not be interpreted as necessarily shared by the NIHR or Department of Health and Social Care.

Suggested Readings

Gullacksen, A., Göransson, L., Rönnblom, G., Koppen, A., & Jørgensen, A. (2011). *Life adjustment and combined visual and hearing disability/deafblindness – An internal process over time.* Nordic Centre for Welfare and Social Issues. http://nordisktvalfardscenter.se/PageFiles/5593/168730_Engelsk.pdf

Laustrup, B. (2004). The ageing process and the late manifestation of conditions related to the cause of congenitally deafblind adults in Denmark. *DbI Review, 33*, 4–7. https://www.yumpu.com/en/document/view/40997455/the-ageing-process-and-late-manifestations-deafblind-international

LeJeune, B. J. (2010). Aging with a dual sensory loss: Thoughts from consumer focus groups. *AER (Association for Education and Rehabilitation of the Blind and Visually Impaired) Journal, 3*, 146–152.

Pollington, C. (2008). Always change – The transitions experienced by an older woman with declining sight and hearing. *Talking Sense, 52*(2), 30–33.

Simcock, P. (2017). Ageing with a unique impairment: A systematically conducted review of older deafblind people's experiences. *Ageing & Society, 37*(8), 1703–1742. https://doi.org/10.1017/S0144686X16000520

10
AGEING, SERIOUS MENTAL ILLNESS, AND PERCEPTIONS OF SELF OVER THE LIFE COURSE

Lydia P. Ogden

Introduction

A serious mental illness (SMI) is 'a diagnosable mental, behavioral, or emotional disorder ... that has resulted in serious functional impairment, which substantially interferes with or limits one or more major life activities' (Substance Abuse and Mental Health Services Administration (SAMHSA), 2012, p. 9). It is estimated that approximately 5% of adults in the U.S. have an SMI diagnosis (SAMHSA, 2012). While no longer considered invariably lifelong disabling conditions, many persons diagnosed with an SMI will experience differing levels of disability from their age of onset until through later life. For example, schizophrenia-spectrum disorders affect up to 0.5% of the older adult population (Meeks & Jeste, 2008) and as many as 70% of persons with schizophrenia aged 55 and over experience psychiatric symptoms that require ongoing treatment (Bankole et al., 2008). Bipolar disorder, another category of SMIs, affects about 2.1% of the population, continuing into later life. Depressive symptoms increase with age (Coryell, Fiedorowicz, Solomon, & Endicott, 2009), with affected individuals more likely to develop toxicity and experience other negative side effects from the medications in later life (Dols & Beekman, 2018). Over a person's life course, these SMIs and others can contribute to cognitive impairment, problematic alcohol and substance use, relationship and employment problems, medical problems, and social isolation far surpassing that of the general population (Castle & Morgan, 2008; Hafner & Heiden, 2008).

Experiences in early and mid-life can affect an individual's experiences in ageing, perceptions of disability, and perceptions of self after a diagnosis of an SMI. In addition to illness, demographic, and treatment factors, experiences with stigma and self-stigma, social relationships, and barriers to and opportunities for social inclusion interact over time to create perceptions of self and lived experiences of disability in later life. Many of these experiences are negative. However negative experiences are modifiable through practice and policy initiatives, and changes in the areas noted above have the potential to improve the experience of ageing with SMI.

Later Life and Serious Mental Illnesss

SMIs are generally considered disorders of adolescence or young adulthood, with initial onset rarely occurring in later life. As such, for most older adults living with SMI diagnoses, their experience with symptoms, treatments, side effects, and stigma, stretches back decades before they are considered 'older'. Therefore, the impact of SMIs on ageing, and of ageing on SMIs, can best be understood as the result of long-term processes through which lifetime adversities and advantages have interacted. Later life can be seen as a time in the life course when new opportunities or challenges may arise.

The broad picture of adversities for individuals with SMIs includes comorbid psychiatric conditions, compromised cognitive functioning, physical morbidity risks, loss of functioning and decreased quality of life and well-being, as well as increased mortality risks. These combine to create a picture of cumulative adverse later life circumstances. Depression and post-traumatic stress syndrome, SMIs in and of themselves, are among the most common psychiatric comorbidities that accompany other SMIs in later life: as one example, more than 40% of individuals diagnosed with schizophrenia experience clinical depression in later life (Bartels & Pratt, 2009).

Cognitive Factors

The risks of cognitive decline for older adults with SMIs are greater than for those in the general population, since cognitive impairments that accompany SMIs are exacerbated by ordinary age-related cognitive functioning declines, and compounded by lifetime deprivations such as institutionalisation and underemployment (Cohen et al., 2000). Persons with schizophrenia are more than twice as likely as older adults in the general population to develop neurocognitive disorders (Ribe et al., 2015), and there is a statistically significant increase in neurocognitive disorders for persons with other SMIs (da Silva, Gonçalves-Pereira, Xavier, & Mukaetova-Ladinska, 2013; Wu et al., 2013). Such cognitive impairment can contribute in turn to suboptimal healthcare in general, to increased lengths of inpatient hospital stays, and to early nursing home placement (Andrews, Bartels, Xie, & Peacock, 2009; Bartels & Dums, 2003; Bartels & Pratt, 2009). Cognition and its functional and behavioural consequences are thus particular concerns for older adults with SMIs.

Morbidity and Mortality

Ageing for persons living with SMIs presents physical morbidity and mortality risks beyond those faced by the general population. In a groundbreaking 2006 report that analysed multiple state health records in the United States, Parks et al. (2006) found that persons with SMIs in general had substantially increased rates of physical morbidity and mortality, with lifespans 25 years less, on average, than members of the general population. They found as many as 55% of persons diagnosed with schizophrenia were also diagnosed with obesity and among both persons with schizophrenia and those with bipolar disorders, more than 10% were diagnosed with diabetes. Parks, Svendsen, Singer, and Foti (2006) noted that many of the health risk factors faced by these older adults were preventable, stemming from lifestyle factors such as smoking, poor diet, and lack of exercise. They reported that over 50% of persons with SMIs smoked tobacco. Furthermore, approximately 60% of premature deaths were due to preventable and/or highly treatable medical conditions including cardiovascular, pulmonary and infectious diseases, diabetes and respiratory disease (Parks et al., 2006). Although the data in this report is now more than 15 years old, there is no indication in the available data that circumstances have changed.

At all ages the convergence of psychiatric symptoms and physical health issues typically leads to a loss of functioning in more than one important area. Tasks such as sustaining adequate housing through regular rent payment and maintenance, and personal and instrumental activities of daily living such as bathing, cooking, and cleaning, can require training and assistance, and become harder to do. This loss of function can have significant consequences. For example, inability to maintain housing through rent payment and appropriate home maintenance contributes to high rates of homelessness among persons with SMIs. As many as 42% of homeless persons in Western countries have an SMI (Fazel, Khosla, Doll, & Geddes, 2008). In terms of institutionalisation, while the majority of older adults with SMIs live in the community, 85% of institutionalised older adults with SMIs live in nursing homes rather than psychiatric care settings, despite the poor psychiatric care available to them in nursing homes (Andrews et al., 2009).

Social Disability

Social disability is part of the definition of an SMI and is exacerbated or resolved through multiple factors ranging from family involvement in treatment in care at age of onset and in later life (Aldersey & Whitley, 2015) to life course work opportunities, housing circumstances, and chronic medical conditions (Drake & Whitley, 2014). As with all older adults, a lack of close relationships affects the length and quality of life while living in the community (Drake & Whitley, 2014; Lubben & Gironda, 2003), but older adults with SMIs are half as likely as those in the general population to be integrated into their communities (Cohen, Pathak, Ramirez, & Vahia, 2009). The majority of older adults with SMIs have few social contacts and most lack a close family caregiver (Drake & Whitley, 2014; Jeste & Nasrallah, 2003). Social isolation contributes to the loneliness and lower subjective ratings of well-being among this population, and is likely connected to the increased medical morbidity and mortality, reflecting an accumulation of adverse circumstances.

The Impact of Policies on Individuals

An important adversity to consider for many older adults with SMIs involves the history of the treatment of the mentally ill in the United States, and in particular, the institutionalisation and deinstitutionalisation of persons with SMIs. Throughout policy fluctuations dating as far back as 1955, persons who were considered 'chronically mentally ill' were not considered appropriate for community living until as late as the 1980s in many areas (Lamb & Bachrach, 2001). Many older adults with SMIs have personal histories of long-term dehumanising and involuntary hospitalisations and debilitating medication side-effects, perhaps most notably tardive dyskinesia, as the result of treatment efforts (Harvey, 2005; Mechanic, 2008). Although deinstitutionalisation policies were meant to enhance civil rights and quality of lives of persons with SMIs through high-quality community-based psychiatric care, institutional discharge was often followed by homelessness and its accompanying adversities of exposure to violence and lack of access to food, medical and psychiatric care. In 1997, Hopper, Jost, Hay, Welber and Haugland (1997) identified a process whereby persons with SMIs in the United States often ended-up traversing through an 'institutional circuit' that included homeless shelters, acute and long-term psychiatric inpatient units, jails and prisons, and other institutional placements. Accessing housing and effective treatment remains an ongoing challenge for persons with SMIs, and of all age-groups, older adults are least likely to receive any form of mental health services (Drake & Whitley, 2014; Jin et al., 2003).

All told, the multitude of sources of adversity often faced by persons with SMIs across the life course and into later life create a potentially devastating picture of accumulated adversities, setting the stage for a later life defined by further adversities, morbidities, and early mortalities (Parks et al., 2006), as well as decreased resilience, hopefulness, and self-esteem (Wartelsteiner et al., 2014). Despite these myriad challenges, disability in later life is not inevitable for persons with SMI. Informed by the recovery movement, a growing body of research, including narrative and other qualitative research models, have identified specific advantages leading to better outcomes and subjective experiences of self for older adults with SMIs. Domains of these advantages include illness factors, treatment factors, demographic factors, and the nature of the social environment, and of social supports.

Mental Health Recovery and Positive Outcomes

A variety of non-modifiable illness and individual factors are associated with better symptomatic and life course outcomes for persons diagnosed with SMIs. In schizophrenia, for example, these include female gender; later illness onset; acute onset of illness; less prominent negative symptoms; hallucinatory and delusional content; brief duration of the active phase symptoms with good functioning between illness episodes; minimal residual symptoms; absence of structural brain abnormalities; and normal neurological functioning (American Psychiatric Association (APA), 2013). In terms of demographic variables, persons in higher socio-economic status (SES) groups are more likely to experience financial security and social support, continuous insurance coverage, and more consistent higher-quality psychiatric care, which in turn is associated with better symptom and functional outcomes (Seng, Kohn-Wood, & Odera, 2005; West et al., 2005; Wilk, West, Narrow, Rae, & Regier, 2005). In the U.S., White racial identity is associated with increased access to and use of psychiatric services, and higher quality services, than those of other racial/ethnic groups of the same SES status, and leading to better illness outcomes (Bresnahan et al., 2007).

Treatment Factors

Treatment factors provide modifiable and potentially significant advantages to illness courses and outcomes. In the last three decades, the consumer-driven mental health recovery movement has played an important role in the development of a growing foundation of evidence-based treatments and macro- and micro-level policies. Recovery-oriented approaches, and recovery itself, are defined by the prioritising of meaningful activity and positive relationships, the return and maintenance of hope, and ability to achieve personal goals and live a satisfying life, as valued and defined by the individual (Bellack, 2006; Davidson, O'Connell, Tondora, Staeheli, & Evans, 2005; Deegan & Drake, 2006; Drake & Whitley, 2014). This is in contrast to treatment approaches that focus solely on symptom reduction.

To date there is a growing research body on recovery-oriented practices for older adults for SMI. Group-based psychoeducation programs for older adults with SMIs have contributed to measurable improvements in social skills and everyday functional skills, cognitive insight and comprehension, and in access to healthcare and medical problem detection by participants (Cohen, Pathak, Ramirez, & Vahia, 2009; Pratt, Bartels, Mueser, & Forester, 2008). In particular the HOPES psychosocial skills training program (Pratt, Van Citters, Mueser, & Bartels, 2008) has demonstrated improved community living skills and functioning, greater self-efficacy, lower overall psychiatric and negative symptoms, greater acquisition of preventive healthcare services and nearly twice the rate of completed advance directives among older adults with SMIs (Bartels et al., 2014).

Another promising 'treatment' area involves older-adult focused peer supported programs, especially including those that use smart phone technology apps and social media for texting communications (Fortuna et al., 2018; Fortuna et al., 2019). Through technology-based peer support, older adults with SMIs have improved their psychiatric illness management and made health behaviour changes.

Unfortunately, to date, access to these programs, and to recovery-oriented treatment in general, are not widely available for any persons with SMIs, including older adults (Drake & Whitley, 2014), and there are significant workforce shortages in the area of SMIs (Olfson, 2016).

Social Factors

Advantageous social factors include experiences of and opportunities for inclusion in the social environment. Overall, it is well established that meaningful relationships and activities are important to the mental health recovery of persons with schizophrenia of all ages (Bradshaw, Armour, & Roseborough, 2007; Davidson et al., 2001). Lower experience of stigma of mental illness in the social environment has been associated with improved self-esteem and hopefulness (Lysaker, Roe, & Yanos, 2007).

A large body of research examines the importance of family for social support and recovery. In the best-case scenarios, family provides moral and practical support, and motivates individuals to recover (Aldersey & Whitley, 2015). Negative family interactions, such as those that contribute to stigma and act as stressors, are modifiable through family psychoeducation (Aldersey & Whitley, 2015). Positive family relationships can reduce psychiatric hospitalisations and can be fostered through psychosocial interventions (Tomita, Lukens, & Herman, 2014).

Thus, while a host of adversities are associated with SMIs over the life course and in later life, distinct, modifiable advantages contribute to better outcomes. The remainder of this chapter will examine in-depth modifiable factors, proposing that social science policy and practice can address them to improve the experience of ageing for persons with SMI. These three factors are the disabling role of stigma, the healing role of social inclusion, and the importance of social relationships.

Narrative Understanding

Throughout this section, emphasis will be placed on narrative understanding of these three factors. Narrative research explores in-depth meanings attributed to life events, such as the development and role of an SMI over the life course, in retrospective accounts wherein autobiographical memories serve as metaphors, tying together memory and meaning (Randall, 2011). In narrative gerontology, the personal stories remembered are those that contain metaphors most relevant to our identities, reflecting our senses of self, personal values and the meanings we attach to experiences. Resolution of complex stories of self is a narrative one that occurs throughout the meaning-making process of storytelling, and is considered an essential task of later life development (Randall, 2011). Furthermore, improved understanding of individual lives is gained by listening to and observing those who have experienced them first-hand, and this understanding has the potential to improve social service programs designed to address those challenges (Flanagan, Davidson, & Strauss, 2007). Therefore, perceptions of self in later life can best be understood through a narrative lens. Additionally, because narrative research strategies can be especially effective in providing an understanding of the personal impact of these factors which are otherwise only understood from the outside, and often in dehumanising ways (Davidson, 2003), findings from my own narrative research examining the experience of ageing with schizophrenia, often considered the most disabling of psychiatric diagnoses, will be presented. (Methods are described in Ogden, 2014a).

Stigma: A Modifiable, Disabling Factor

Stigma has long been intertwined with mental illness, which was used by Goffman (1963) as the quintessential example of the phenomenon. He defined stigma as the response to perceptions of negative difference, or deviance from a norm, which evokes negative responses (Bos, Pryor, Reeder, & Stutterheim, 2013; Goffman, 1963; Susman, 1994). Stigmatising occurs at the individual level when it is internalised by those with SMIs, but it is created in structural and institutional contexts that define norms and carry the power to assign stigma to identities (Bos et al., 2013). The stigmatising process begins with distinguishing and labelling human differences, followed by linking dominant cultural beliefs to labelled persons that make their differences negative (Link & Phelan, 2001). Subsequently, labelled individuals and groups are categorised in a way that separates an 'us' from a 'them'. Invariably, such stigmatised persons experience status loss and discrimination leading to unequal outcomes, including decreased access to social connections and inclusion, economic power, and political power – all of which are experiences typical of persons with SMI. These losses and discrimination lead to further highlighting of the differentness of the individual, deepening the construction of stereotypes, and further separation of the individual from the normative group, at which point 'disapproval, rejection, exclusion, and discrimination' becomes an inherent part of the individual's existence (Link & Phelan, 2001, p. 367) in a process termed 'structural stigma' (Bos et al., 2013) and places persons with SMIs with other groups of persons who experience stigma and discrimination, including older adults (Corrigan, 2016).

Due to this complex stigmatising process for individuals with SMIs, many feel that the stigma of carrying the label of an SMI diagnosis is as disabling, or more disabling, than the symptoms of SMI itself (Corrigan, 2016). As others respond to someone with an SMI negatively, that person becomes socialised into the role of a mentally ill person and internalises the negative, stigmatised views about himself. For example, as others maintain social distance from someone with an SMI, the person with an SMI receives a message that they are socially undesirable and may avoid contact with others in order to conform to expectations or to avoid unpleasant social interactions. Psychiatric symptom severity, and lack of hope, empowerment, or diminished self-esteem, will increase the likelihood of internalisation of stigma into self-stigma (Livingston & Boyd, 2010).

Stigma is important to consider for older adults diagnosed with SMIs because it is considered a contributor to loss of life opportunities, including housing and employment, beyond what the presence of SMI symptoms would yield (Corrigan, 2016). In fact, longitudinal studies consistently show a wide variety of courses of disability and illness experience for persons with SMIs. As many as 20% of individuals diagnosed with schizophrenia, considered to be the most chronic and disabling SMI, make a full recovery (APA, 2013). Despite the realities of recovery, SMIs and self-stigma frequently coincide.

Self-stigma comes from awareness and acceptance of stigma associated with an SMI, and then application of it to oneself, leading to decreased self-esteem, self-efficacy, and motivation (Corrigan, 2016). For schizophrenia in particular, the diagnosis is so stigmatising that individuals diagnosed with schizophrenia who have strong clinical insight (they understand how the label applies to them and agree with it) have a higher suicide rate than those who reject the label entirely and who may otherwise have poor treatment outcomes, but a more intact sense of self (Lysaker, Roe, & Yanos, 2007). As ageing and 'being old' also carries stigma (Chasteen & Cary, 2015), assaults on identity may be heightened in later life for persons with SMIs. Furthermore, stigma has been found to be a barrier to care seeking and participation in treatment (Clement et al., 2015).

In one of my own narrative research, one participant's self-narrative rejected the label of schizophrenia. He described himself as 'saved', in a Christian, religious sense, and consistently expressed an overall positive self-narrative and self-perception (Ogden, 2012; Ogden, 2014a). This was in stark contrast to a peer with the same age, diagnosis, and symptom profile, who accepted the label of schizophrenia and internalised it (Ogden, 2012). The peer's self-narrative included interpretations of the voices as 'invading' and described feeling unable to take small steps towards his modest goals (these included saving enough money to buy new pants and cooking pasta at home). Functional expressions across the two cases included ability to work even in the face of psychotic symptoms and multiple close relationships for the first man, contrasted with inability to work and no close relationships for the second. While certainly symptoms could have been objectively worse in the second participant, the role of stigma (or lack thereof) in the self-narrative was apparent in both (Ogden, 2014a).

Therefore, improving the later life experience for older adults with SMIs includes addressing the stigma that is attached to individuals with SMIs across the life course, so that barriers of structural stigma and the toll of self-stigma do not lead to an accumulation of life adversities in later life. Application of laws, such as the 1990 Americans with Disability Act, to individuals with SMIs, acknowledges the very really discrimination such individuals have faced and provides a system-based, rather than individual-based, means of fighting stigma (Corrigan, 2016). A number of public health and clinical interventions have demonstrated success in decreasing stigma to date. One of the most successful is 'contact and education', wherein people are taught about mental illness and meet someone with a psychiatric diagnosis (Corrigan, 2016). The only caveat for this to work is, the person must have a just-right level of symptomatology – too symptomatic and the program can increase stigma; not impaired enough and program participants will think the individual is an exception.

Overall, stigma is a modifiable condition that, if addressed, can improve the experience of ageing for older adults with SMIs. It ties closely to social inclusion and relationships, two essential features of a positive ageing experience, and thus progress in either of those areas are dependent on progress in addressing stigma.

The Necessity of Social Inclusion

Social inclusion might be as significant as illness and treatment factors in later life outcomes for persons with SMI. Social inclusion involves having equitable access to resources and opportunities, such as stable and secure housing, and competitive employment, which are often at risk for individuals with SMI. However, access to housing and employment can create significant ripple effects across the life course that improve the experience of ageing.

Housing

There is a strong correlation between homelessness and mental illness in Western countries. Interaction with, response to, and interpretation of housing environments can affect sense of self and contribute to a sense of prestige or self-stigma, and thus experiences of homelessness, housing and home have a deeper meaning than merely 'shelter' (Blasi, 1990; Shaw, 2004; Wardaugh, 1999). Home has been defined as a safe haven and a refuge from social forces and psychological stressors (Blasi, 1990; Shaw, 2004; Wardaugh,1999); a space in which self-esteem, identity, and when needed, a renewed sense of humanity can be developed (Padgett & Henwood, 2012). The concept of ontological security describes the sense of security and control developed by having a home, a setting wherein life's daily routines are enacted, and where, free from surveillance, personal senses of identity are formulated (Dupuis & Thorns, 1998; Shaw, 2004).

Padgett and Henwood (2012) used narrative analysis methodology to examine experiences of formerly homeless persons with mental illness in housing, and found that participant narratives shared appreciation of the benefits of having a home and gratitude for housing. The perceived advantages of housing were connected to those described by ontological security, however, obtaining and maintaining housing did not erase the lifetime of adversity experienced by many of the participants. In an earlier study of the same population, Padgett (2007) used life history narrative interviews and grounded theory analysis finding that homelessness had been experienced as an assault to sense of self and so that in addition to safe and stable shelter, housing was valued as the setting for identity re-construction and repair, and a symbol of having overcome years of adversity. Stigma, social isolation, and uncertainty about the future were ongoing challenges for the participants. Regarding ageing and homelessness among persons diagnosed with SMIs, Shibusawa and Padgett (2009) found that these older adults valued the space and time to evaluate, reflect upon losses, and address ongoing issues.

In my research in this area, four shared core themes ran throughout the narratives of homelessness, housing, and home of older adults with schizophrenia (Ogden, 2014b). The first theme was the interweaving of housing status and sense of self. Participants' narrative identities were connected to and evolved around housing status, and ongoing housing and self-perception challenges lay in the extent to which they felt they were housed, as opposed to home. The closely related second theme was that present-time housing symbolised personal resilience and overcoming adversity. Participants often discussed their current housing in comparison with their episode(s) of homelessness, and their present-time, housed, circumstances were looked on as proof that they had overcome hardships.

I called the third theme, 'waiting to go home'. This was a phrase used by one of the study participants to describe his current living situation, and succinctly summarised the gap between the reality of participants' present housing and their dreams of having a home. Having housing did not necessarily equate to having a home.

The fourth theme was that of conflicted feelings about long-term relationships with housing-based social service providers, with whom participants had complex understandings and experiences. From their narratives it emerged that to provide homes, organisations needed to balance institutional rules with space for autonomy, and adequate internal support with opportunities for community integration. Participants struggled in particular with the extent to which they wanted more autonomous housing. Their narratives evidenced identity repair, gratitude, comfort, and even general satisfaction with housing, and they also evidenced an underlying sense that ongoing involvement with the housing organisations meant they were not 'free'. While they described having been 'saved' by the housing organisations, they also described having been made 'invalids' by them. The participants' conflict between needing and wanting support in housing and their opposing need for more autonomy was central to what made relationships with housing social service providers complicated. Throughout the literature on housing for persons with SMIs, one finds that such persons appreciate support in specific domains of daily life that sustain independent living, such as practical housekeeping and financial help (Gunnmo & Bergman, 2011) and value the feature of security and stability (Padgett, 2007) in their social service provided housing settings. For my participants who had experienced homelessness, the absence of the desired degree of autonomy contributed to a shared sense that they were not yet home, despite their appreciation of stable, comfortable housing, and thus one meaning attached to home was out of reach. As personal stories are interpreted through their telling, the narrators are simultaneously interpreting and representing their senses of selves (Randall, 2011). In my study, the retrospective accounting of experiences of homelessness by participants was interwoven with their accounting of self, and reflected selves who were not quite where they wanted to be.

Evidence around housing for persons with SMIs who have experienced homelessness supports autonomy-building housing programs, such as through Pathways' Housing First Program (Padgett, Henwood, & Tsemberis, 2016), and shorter duration of housing-related social services, such as through Critical Time Intervention, a time limited approach to housing social services (Hanesworth & Herman, 2019). Nursing homes, which appear to be a trend for these older adults, are not suitable as homes and are suboptimal for psychiatric care (Andrews et al., 2009). Overall, research that evaluates optimal housing environments and housing-based social services specifically for older adults with SMIs is needed.

Work

Meaningful activities, including employment, are central to mental health recovery for persons of all ages with SMIs (Bradshaw et al., 2007; Drake & Whitley, 2014). Past interpretations of the stress-diathesis model of schizophrenia suggested that persons living with SMIs should refrain from work, because the stress from work was believed to exacerbate psychiatric symptoms. But the recovery movement has successfully reframed discussion of working with SMI as an antidote to psychiatric symptoms and a less stressful alternative to poverty, boredom, and social exclusion (Marrone & Golowka, 2005; Russinova, Wewiorski, Lyass, Rogers, & Massaro, 2005). Growing research evidence supports that there are vast benefits of employment for persons with SMI. Above all, it is central to increased social inclusion, providing a sense of purpose in life and role in the greater world through which belonging and identity is attained (Krupa, 2004; Marrone & Golowka, 2005; Marwaha & Johnson, 2004). To date, limited research has investigated the importance of life course and present-time work experience, or its absence, to persons ageing with SMIs. However enough is known that for all people, lack of participation in a major life activity, such as work, can negatively impact later life identity.

From a narrative developmental viewpoint, later life is when interpretations of life experiences contribute to integrated personal narratives central to a coherent sense of self (Randall, 2011). Autobiographical material is understood through the lens of other life experiences, culture, and values that place importance on certain experiences, and the subsequent stories created are metaphors for self and meaning. While personal narratives tie together biography and meaning-making throughout the life course (Chase, 2011), their cohesive development is considered the primary later life task in narrative gerontology (Randall, 2011). As such, absent portions of culturally normative autobiographical material, such as an employment history, can lead to narrative foreclosure: narrative functioning breakdown, stemming from a sense that one's life story has lacked some significant, positive, or meaningful experiences that cannot be recovered (Freeman, 2011). For older persons with SMI, such missing pieces might impede recovery and decrease later life well-being.

Among participants in my study, narratives held shared themes that illuminated the importance and meaning of work across the lifespan into later life (Ogden, 2018). The importance of work was highlighted by the perseverance of participants towards vocational goals, even in the face of serious challenges such as psychiatric symptoms, homelessness, and addiction; and past the age when attaining new employment or reaching career goals was culturally normative. In addition to perseverance, their vocational narratives shared themes that purpose and identity were provided by work; having an income was important; and that psychiatric illness symptoms and psychiatric treatments had disrupted their work histories. I found that these participants' willingness to adapt and change vocational goals was not foreclosed by the presence of diagnosis, psychiatric or physical health symptoms, or ageing. Instead, participants expressed narrative hope. Increasing evidence suggests that engaging in competitive employment is possible even for those with active psychiatric symptoms and medication side effects, and might even decrease psychiatric symptoms (Anthony, 2008; Marrone & Golowka, 2005). Participants' narrative hope was thus not misplaced, but may not have been met with ample support, which is likely typical (Casper & Carloni, 2007). Although benefits of work in general, and in evidence-based supported employment programs in particular, is likely the same for older adults as for younger persons with SMI and for older adults in the general population, supported employment appears to be underutilised among older adults with SMI (Pratt, Van Citters, et al., 2008). This is despite research findings that older age does not negatively affect work attainment outcomes or the therapeutic value of work (Twamley, Narvaez, Becker, Bartels, & Jeste, 2008). Nonetheless, in a large-scale evaluation of supported employment effectiveness, Cook et al. (2012) found that younger age led to greater likelihood of employment placement through supported employment programs, suggesting possible age-related bias.

The need for improved vocational opportunities for older adults living with SMIs was apparent in my findings. It appeared in the stress described by one participant as he tried to make ends meet on his limited budget, while dreaming of a fast food hamburger. In another narrative, this need was apparent in the participant's sense she was not 'someone' because of her lack of income. In two other narratives, participants felt they could not say they had been 'successful' in life, because although they had worked, they had not worked in a way that pursued their goals and dreams. Due to the convergence of psychiatric illness and lack of opportunities, limited pay available in the vocational opportunities that they could engage in, and the limited financial support provided to disabled persons in the U.S. at this time all of my study's participants lived in poverty.

The Healing Potential of Social Relationships

SMIs are defined in part by their production of social disability – they interfere with one's ability to have and maintain close, healthy relationships. Therefore, recovering social relationships is an important aspect of recovery from SMIs and appears frequently throughout recovery-oriented material: social relationships are a central theme in first-person accounts of recovery from SMI diagnoses (i.e. Deegan, 1996; Gumber & Stein, 2013; Mead & Copeland, 2000) in qualitative findings of studies examining the subjective experience of, recovery from, and unmet needs of persons with SMIs (i.e. Boydell, Gladstone, & Crawford, 2002; Bradshaw et al., 2007; Davidson, 2003; Davidson et al., 2001; Gunnmo & Bergman, 2011; Ng et al., 2008, Ogden, 2014c); and in countless quantitative studies. Social support, including that from family, friends, and treatment providers, is associated with decreased self-stigma, while the converse is also true: lack of social support is associated with increased self-stigma (Chronister, Chou, & Liao, 2013). The combination of self-stigma and dissatisfaction with social relationships appear to be significant contributors to social isolation for persons with SMIs (Oliveira, Esteves, & Carvalho, 2015). Strong, positive social support promotes symptomatic recovery and improved outcomes (Ware, Hopper, Tugenberg, Dickey, & Fisher, 2008).

In my research, participants spent a good deal of time discussing interpersonal relationships and identified themes of relational losses and voids, relational adjustments and adaptations, and the need for solitude (Ogden, 2014c). Losses referred to relationships once held that were now lost. Voids were relationships participants had longed for but never came to fruition, such as having a spouse or children. But hope emerged through the stories of relational adjustments and adaptations. In relational adjustments, participants had been reunited with a previously lost relationship and the relationship had been adjusted to work better for them in the context of their current lives. In relational adaptations, participants established relationships that substituted for those absent because of relational losses and/ or voids. The new relationships were with either treatment providers or peers with mental illnesses: persons whom the participant would likely know only in a different capacity without the presence of a psychiatric diagnosis. The adapted relationships were characterised by centrality to the emotional well-being of the participants and took on significance beyond what might be expected in provider–client or even client–client relationships. One participant, for example, had lived with the same roommate for nearly 20 years, and considered him family. Although he had lost all contact with his wife and child early in his illness, his adaptations and adjustments in other relationships provided him with comfort and support. Social recovery was the rule, rather than the exception, and a priority, for the older adults in the study.

I also found that in client–provider relationships, continuity and reciprocity, without boundary violations, was central to the subjective, positive experience for the study participants (Ogden, 2014c).

Issues of relationship continuity challenged provider–client relationships, because the continuity and quality of such relationships over time might be even more important for older adults who have experienced decades of provider turnover. Participant concern that providers could terminate a relationship at any time by leaving his or her position added a sense of ill-ease to the relationships.

Across multiple studies of older adults with SMIs, participants construct the value of their treatment in terms of a strong, secure relationship with a treatment provider who was connected and caring, invested, reliable, and available (Green et al., 2008; Gunnmo & Bergman, 2011; Ogden, 2014c; Ware et al., 2008). Faced with social isolation and challenges establishing and developing emotionally intimate interpersonal relationships, these older adults may rely upon treatment providers who take on the importance of family and friends (Bradshaw et al., 2007; Ogden, 2014c). In terms of psychosocial treatment implications, when long-term engagement is an option in work with older adults with SMI, social workers and other mental health providers will do the greatest good by staying as long as possible in those positions. Agencies will do the greatest good by structuring themselves in a way to ensure that happens.

Peer support

My study's finding around of relational adaptations (Ogden, 2014c) supports recent findings about the importance of reciprocity in interpersonal relationships and the value of peer relationships, adding that time and a structured setting (such as a psychosocial clubhouse or work day treatment program) are important to development of peer relationships. Because true reciprocity is unavailable in ethical provider–client relationships, friendships, particularly with other persons with diagnoses of SMIs, become key to a sense of social connectedness for persons who face barriers to belonging elsewhere. In one clinical trial of peer-led recovery education, involved participants significantly improved on measures of recovery and hopefulness (Cook et al., 2012). In another study, peer-support was found to help individuals arm themselves against potential stigmatising experiences and was highly valued (Whitley & Campbell, 2014). Reciprocity in relationships, in which both parties are able to add to the others life and well-being, has been established as an important component of recovery for persons with SMIs (Davidson, 2003; Ware, Hopper, Tugenberg, Dickey, & Fisher, 2008). The growing momentum around peer support appears to be of special significance to older adults with SMIs. In one pilot study, peer specialists were able to help other older adults with SMIs to significantly improve their psychiatric self-management, and increased self-efficacy in other self-care areas, in a way that was perceived as feasible and acceptable to all (Fortuna et al., 2018). Supported socialisation programs for older adults with schizophrenia spectrum diagnoses, such as The Compeer Model (Davidson et al., 2001; Davidson et al., 2005) and the HOPE skills training program, which has age-specific adaptations (Pratt, Bartels, et al., 2008), need further development and dissemination.

Conclusion

Older adults with SMIs now constitute the fastest growing group of persons with SMIs (Meesters, 2014). For many organisations providing services to now ageing clients, their increasing needs provide multiple ethical and capacity dilemmas (i.e. Blady et al., n.d.). Available research on ageing with SMIs indicates later life is a time when multiple challenges that have built and interacted over a life course converge to create multiple pathologies and issues, but at the same time, many of these challenges are preventable and/or could be ameliorated with existing practices. Unfortunately, evidence-based, recovery-oriented services, such as peer-support, supported employment, and supported housing, are not routinely available to any populations of persons with SMI, including older adults (Drake & Whitley, 2014). Overall, first-person accounts from older adults with SMI finds their later life focus is on integrating a satisfying and whole sense of self and belonging in relation to housing, work, and to others, which is the developmental task of all older adults (Randall, 2011). Research, policy, and practices that serve the psychological and instrumental needs of these vulnerable and resilient older adults need development and dissemination.

References

Aldersey, H. M., & Whitley, R. (2015). Family influence in recovery from severe mental illness. *Community Mental Health Journal*, *51*(4), 467–476. https://doi.org/10.1007/s10597-014-9783-y

American Psychiatric Association. (2013). *Diagnostic and statistical manual of mental disorders (DSM-5)*. American Psychiatric Publications.

Andrews, A. O., Bartels, S. J., Xie, H., & Peacock, W. J. (2009). Increased risk of nursing home admission among middle aged and older adults with schizophrenia. *The American Journal of Geriatric Psychiatry: Official Journal of the American Association for Geriatric Psychiatry*, *17*(8), 697–705. https://doi.org/10.1097/JGP.0b013e3181aad59d

Anthony, W. A. (2008). Supported employment in the context of psychiatric rehabilitation. *Psychiatric Rehabilitation Journal*, *31*(4), 271–272. https://doi.org/10.2975/31.4.2008.271.272

Bankole, A., Cohen, C. I., Vahia, I., Diwan, S., Palekar, N., Reyes, P., ... Ramirez, P. M. (2008). Symptomatic remission in a multiracial urban population of older adults with schizophrenia. *The American Journal of Geriatric Psychiatry: Official Journal of the American Association for Geriatric Psychiatry*, *16*(12), 966–973. https://doi.org/10.1097/JGP.0b013e31818af801

Bartels, S. J., & Dums, A. R. (2003). Mental health policy and financing services for older adults with severe mental illness. In C. I. Cohen (Ed.), *Schizophrenia into later life: Treatment, research and policy* (pp. 177–194). American Psychiatric Publishing.

Bartels, S. J., & Pratt, S. I. (2009). Psychosocial rehabilitation and quality of life for older adults with serious mental illness: Recent findings and future research directions. *Current Opinion in Psychiatry*, *22*(4), 381–385. https://doi.org/10.1097/YCO.0b013e32832c9234

Bartels, S. J., Pratt, S. I., Mueser, K. T., Forester, B. P., Wolfe, R., Cather, C., ... Feldman, J. (2014). Long-term outcomes of a randomized trial of integrated skills training and preventive healthcare for older adults with serious mental illness. *The American Journal of Geriatric Psychiatry: Official Journal of the American Association for Geriatric Psychiatry*, *22*(11), 1251–1261. https://doi.org/10.1016/j.jagp.2013.04.013

Bellack, A. S. (2006). Scientific and consumer models of recovery in schizophrenia: Concordance, contrasts, and implications. *Schizophrenia Bulletin*, *32*(3), 432–442. https://doi.org/10.1093/schbul/sbj044

Blady, M., Officer, L. R. C. O., Welch, J., Wilson, S., Buckman, B., Glover, L., & Sandoval, L. (n.d.) *Aging in place in mental health housing. The bridge.* http://aclnys.org/wp-content/uploads/2017/05/02_Aging-in-Place.pdf

Blasi, G. L. (1990). Social policy and social science research on homelessness. *Journal of Social Issues*, *46*(4), 207–219. https://doi.org/10.1111/j.1540-4560.1990.tb01807.x

Bos, A. E. R., Pryor, J. B., Reeder, G. D., & Stutterheim, S. E. (2013). Stigma: Advances in theory and research. *Basic & Applied Social Psychology*, *35*(1), 1–9. https://doi.org/10.1080/01973533.2012.746147

Boydell, K. M., Gladstone, B. M., & Crawford, E. S. (2002). The dialectic of friendship for people with psychiatric disabilities. *Psychiatric Rehabilitation Journal*, *26*, 123–131. http://dx.doi.org/10.2975/26.2002.123.131

Bradshaw, W., Armour, M. P., & Roseborough, D. (2007). Finding a place in the world: The experience of recovery from severe mental illness. *Qualitative Social Work*, *6*(27), 27–47. https://doi.org/10.1177/1473325007074164

Bresnahan, M., Begg, M. D., Brown, A., Schaefer, C., Sohler, N., Insel, B., ... Susser, E. (2007). Race and risk of schizophrenia in a US birth cohort: Another example of health disparity?. *International Journal of Epidemiology*, *36*(4), 751–758. https://doi.org/10.1093/ije/dym041

Casper, E. S., & Carloni, C. (2007). Assessing the underutilization of supported employment services. *Psychiatric Rehabilitation Journal*, *30*(3), 182–188. https://doi.org/10.2975/30.3.2007.182.188

Castle, D. J., & Morgan, V. (2008). Epidemiology. In K. T. Mueser & D. V. Jeste (Eds.), *Clinical handbook of schizophrenia* (pp. 14–24). Guilford Press.

Chase, S. E. (2011). Narrative inquiry: Still a field in the making. In N. K. Denzin & Y. S. Lincoln (Eds.), *The Sage handbook of qualitative research* (4th ed., pp. 421–434). Sage Publications.

Chasteen, A. L., & Cary, L. A. (2015). Age stereotypes and age stigma: Connections to research on subjective aging. *Annual Review of Gerontology and Geriatrics*, *35*(1), 99–119. https://doi.org/10.1891/0198-8794.35.99

Chronister, J., Chou, C. C., & Liao, H. Y. (2013). The role of stigma coping and social support in mediating the effect of societal stigma on internalized stigma, mental health recovery, and quality of life among people with serious mental illness. *Journal of Community Psychology*, *41*(5), 582–600. https://doi.org/10.1002/jcop.21558

Clement, S., Schauman, O., Graham, T., Maggioni, F., Evans-Lacko, S., Bezborodovs, N., ... Thornicroft, G. (2015). What is the impact of mental health-related stigma on help-seeking? A systematic review of quantitative and qualitative studies. *Psychological Medicine*, *45*(1), 11–27. https://doi.org/10.1017/S0033291714000129

Cohen, C. I., Cohen, G. D., Blank, K., Gaitz, C., Katz, I. R., Leuchter, A., ... Shamoian, C. (2000). Schizophrenia and older adults. An overview: Directions for research and policy. *The American Journal of Geriatric Psychiatry: Official Journal of the American Association for Geriatric Psychiatry*, *8*(1), 19–28. https://doi.org/10.1097/00019442-200002000-00003

Cohen, C. I., Pathak, R., Ramirez, P. M., & Vahia, I. (2009). Outcome among community dwelling older adults with schizophrenia: Results using five conceptual models. *Community Mental Health Journal*, *45*(2), 151–156. https://doi.org/10.1007/s10597-008-9161-8

Cook, J. A., Steigman, P., Pickett, S., Diehl, S., Fox, A., Shipley, P., ... Burke-Miller, J. K. (2012). Randomized controlled trial of peer-led recovery education using building recovery of individual dreams and goals through education and support (BRIDGES). *Schizophrenia Research*, *136*(1–3), 36–42. https://doi.org/10.1016/j.schres.2011.10.016

Corrigan, P. W. (2016) *Principles and practices of psychiatric rehabilitation: An empirical approach* (2nd ed.). Guilford Press.

Coryell, W., Fiedorowicz, J., Solomon, D., & Endicott, J. (2009). Age transitions in the course of bipolar I disorder. *Psychological Medicine*, *39*(8), 1247–1252. https://doi.org/10.1017/S0033291709005534

da Silva, J., Gonçalves-Pereira, M., Xavier, M., & Mukaetova-Ladinska, E. B. (2013). Affective disorders and risk of developing dementia: Systematic review. *The British Journal of Psychiatry: The Journal of Mental Science*, *202*(3), 177–186. https://doi.org/10.1192/bjp.bp.111.101931

Davidson, L. (2003). *Living outside mental illness: Qualitative studies of recovery in schizophrenia*. New York University Press.

Davidson, L., O'Connell, M. J., Tondora, J., Staeheli, M., & Evans, A. C. (2005). Recovery in serious mental illness: Paradigm shift or shibboleth? In L. Davidson, C., Harding & L. Spaniol (Eds.), *Recovery from severe mental illnesses: Research evidence and implications for practice* (Vol. I, pp. 5–26). Center for Psychiatric Rehabilitation, Boston University.

Davidson, L., Stayner, D. A., Nickou, C., Styron, T. H., Rowe, M., & Chinman, M. L. (2001). "Simply to be let in": Inclusion as a basis for recovery. *Psychiatric Rehabilitation Journal*, *24*(4), 375–388. https://doi.org/10.1037/h0095067

Deegan, P. (1996). Recovery as a journey of the heart. *Psychiatric Rehabilitation Journal*, *19*(3), 91. https://doi.org/10.1037/h0101301

Deegan, P. E., & Drake, R. E. (2006). Shared decision making and medication management in the recovery process. *Psychiatric Services*, *57*(11), 1636–1639. https://doi.org/10.1176/ps.2006.57.11.1636

Dols, A., & Beekman, A. (2018). Older age bipolar disorder. *The Psychiatric clinics of North America*, *41*(1), 95–110. https://doi.org/10.1016/j.psc.2017.10.008

Drake, R. E., & Whitley, R. (2014). Recovery and severe mental illness: Description and analysis. *Canadian Journal of Psychiatry. Revue Canadienne de Psychiatrie*, *59*(5), 236–242. https://doi.org/10.1177/070674371405900502

Dupuis, A., & Thorns, D. C. (1998). Home, home ownership and the search for ontological security. *Sociological Review*, *46*(1), 25–47. http://dx.doi.org/10.1111/1467-954X.00088

Fazel, S., Khosla, V., Doll, H., & Geddes, J. (2008). The prevalence of mental disorders among the homeless in western countries: Systematic review and meta-regression analysis. *PLoS Medicine*, *5*(12), e225. https://doi.org/10.1371/journal.pmed.0050225

Flanagan, E. H., Davidson, L., & Strauss, J. S. (2007). Issues for DSM-v: Incorporating patients' subjective experiences. *The American Journal of Psychiatry*, *164*(3), 391–392. https://doi.org/10.1176/ajp.2007.164.3.391

Fortuna, K. L., DiMilia, P. R., Lohman, M. C., Bruce, M. L., Zubritsky, C. D., Halaby, M. R., ... Bartels, S. J. (2018). Feasibility, acceptability, and preliminary effectiveness of a peer-delivered and technology supported self-management intervention for older adults with serious mental illness. *The Psychiatric Quarterly*, *89*(2), 293–305. https://doi.org/10.1007/s11126-017-9534-7

Fortuna, K. L., Naslund, J. A., Aschbrenner, K. A., Lohman, M. C., Storm, M., Batsis, J. A., & Bartels, S. J. (2019). Text message exchanges between older adults with serious mental illness and older certified peer specialists in a smartphone-supported self-management intervention. *Psychiatric Rehabilitation Journal*, *42*(1), 57–63. https://doi.org/10.1037/prj0000305

Freeman, M. (2011). Narrative foreclosure in later life: Possibilities and limits. In G.M. Kenyon, E. Bohlmeijer & W.L. Randall (Eds.), *Storying later life: Issues, investigations, and interventions in narrative gerontology* (pp. 1–18). Oxford University Press.

Goffman, E. (1963). *Stigma: Notes on a spoiled identity*. Prentice Hall.

Green, C. A., Polen, M. R., Janoff, S. L., Castleton, D. K., Wisdom, J. P., Vuckovic, N., ... Oken, S. L. (2008). Understanding how clinician–patient relationships and relational continuity of care affect recovery from serious mental illness: STARS study results. *Psychiatric Rehabilitation Journal*, *32*(1), 9–22. https://doi.org/10.2975/32.1.2008.9.22

Gumber, S., & Stein, C. H. (2013). Consumer perspectives and mental health reform movements in the United States: 30 years of first-person accounts. *Psychiatric Rehabilitation Journal*, *36*, 187–194. http://dx.doi.org/10.1037/prj0000003

Gunnmo, P., & Bergman, H. F. (2011). What do individuals with schizophrenia need to increase their well-being? *International Journal of Qualitative Studies of Health and Well-Being*, *6*, 542–552. http://dx.doi.org/10.3402/qhw.v6i1.5412

Hafner, H., & Heiden, W. (2008). Course and outcomes. In K.T. Mueser & D.V. Jeste (Eds.), *Clinical handbook of schizophrenia* (pp. 100–116). Guilford Press.

Hanesworth, C., & Herman, D. (2019). Critical time intervention. In H. Larkin, A. Aykanian, & C. Streeter (Eds.), *Homelessness prevention and intervention in social work* (pp. 225–238). Springer.

Harvey, P. (2005). *Schizophrenia in late life*. American Psychological Association.

Hopper, K., Jost, J., Hay, T., Welber, S., & Haugland, G. (1997). Homelessness, severe mental illness, and the institutional circuit. *Psychiatric Services (Washington, D.C.)*, *48*(5), 659–665. https://doi.org/10.1176/ps.48.5.659

Jeste, D. V., & Nasrallah, H. A. (2003). Schizophrenia and Aging No More Dearth of Data?. *The American Journal of Geriatric Psychiatry*, *11*(6), 584–587. https://doi.org/10.1176/appi.ajgp.11.6.584

Jin, H., Folsom, D. P., Lindamer, L., Bailey, A., Hawthorne, W., Piedad, G., & Jeste, D. V. (2003). Patterns of public mental health service use by age in patients with schizophrenia. *American Journal of Geriatric Psychiatry*, *11*(5), 525–533. https://doi.org/10.1097/00019442-200309000-00007

Krupa, T. (2004). Employment, recovery, and schizophrenia: Integrating health and disorder at work. *Psychiatric Rehabilitation Journal*, *28*(1), 8–15. https://doi.org/10.2975/28.2004.8.15

Lamb, H. R., & Bachrach, L. L. (2001). Some perspectives on deinstitutionalization. *Psychiatric Services*, *52*(8), 1039–1045. https://doi.org/10.1176/appi.ps.52.8.1039

Link, B. G., & Phelan, J. C. (2001). Conceptualizing stigma. *Annual Review of Sociology*, *27*(1), 363–385. https://doi.org/10.1146/annurev.soc.27.1.363

Livingston, J. D., & Boyd, J. E. (2010). Correlates and consequences of internalized stigma for people living with mental illness: A systematic review and meta-analysis. *Social Science & Medicine (1982)*, *71*(12), 2150–2161. https://doi.org/10.1016/j.socscimed.2010.09.030

Lysaker, P. H., Roe, D., & Yanos, P. T. (2007). Toward understanding the insight paradox: Internalized stigma moderates the association between insight and social functioning, hope, and self-esteem among people with schizophrenia spectrum disorders. *Schizophrenia Bulletin*, *33*(1), 192–199. https://doi.org/10.1093/schbul/sbl016

Lubben, J.E. and Gironda, M.E. (2003) Centrality of Social Ties to the Health and Well-Being of Older Adults. In: Berkman, L. and Harooytan, L., Eds., *Social Work and Health Care in an Aging Society*, Springer Press, New York, 319–350.

Marrone, J., & Golowka, E. (2005) If work makes people with mental illness sick, what do unemployment, poverty and social isolation cause? In L. Davidson, C., Harding & L. Spaniol (Eds.), *Recovery from severe mental illnesses: Research evidence and implications for practice* (Vol. I, pp. 451–463). Center for Psychiatric Rehabilitation, Boston University.

Marwaha, S., & Johnson, S. (2004). Schizophrenia and employment – A review. *Social Psychiatry and Psychiatric Epidemiology*, *39*(5), 337–349. https://doi.org/10.1007/s00127-004-0762-4

Mead, S., & Copeland, M. E. (2000). What recovery means to us: Consumers' perspectives. *Community Mental Health Journal*, *36*, 313–328. http://dx.doi.org/10.1023/A:1001917516869

Mechanic, D. (2008). *Mental health and social policy: Beyond managed care* (5th ed.). Pearson Education.

Meeks, T. W., & Jeste, D. V. (2008). Older individuals. In K. T. Mueser & D. V. Jeste (Eds.), *Clinical handbook of schizophrenia* (pp. 390–397). Guilford Press.

Meesters, P. D. (2014). Late-life schizophrenia: Remission, recovery, resilience. *The American Journal of Geriatric Psychiatry: Official Journal of the American Association for Geriatric Psychiatry*, *22*(5), 423–426. https://doi.org/10.1016/j.jagp.2014.01.009

Ng, R. M., Pearson, V., Lam, M., Law, C. W., Chiu, C. P., & Chen, E. Y. (2008). What does recovery from schizophrenia mean? Perceptions of long-term patients. *The International Journal of Social Psychiatry, 54*, 118–130. http://dx.doi.org/10.1177/0020764007084600

Ogden, L. (2012, November). *Understanding pathways to wellness among older adults with schizophrenia: A case comparison.* [presentation]. The 58th Annual Program Meeting of the Council on Social Work Education. Washington, DC.

Ogden, L. P. (2014a). "My life as it is has value": Narrating schizophrenia in later years. *Qualitative Health Research, 24*(10), 1342–1355. https://doi.org/10.1177/1049732314546752

Ogden, L. P. (2014b). "Waiting to go home": Narratives of homelessness, housing and home among older adults with schizophrenia. *Journal of Aging Studies, 29*, 53–65. https://doi.org/10.1016/j.jaging.2014.01.002

Ogden, L. P. (2014c). Interpersonal relationship narratives of older adults with schizophrenia-spectrum diagnoses. *American Journal of Orthopsychiatry, 84*(6), 674–684. https://doi.org/10.1037/ort0000035

Ogden, L. P. (2018). "To fill the emptiness": Work in life history narratives of older adults with schizophrenia-spectrum diagnoses. *Qualitative Social Work, 17*(4), 556–576. https://doi.org/10.1177/1473325016688368

Olfson, M. (2016). Building the mental health workforce capacity needed to treat adults with serious mental illnesses. *Health Affairs, 35*(6), 983–990. https://doi.org/10.1377/hlthaff.2015.1619

Oliveira, S. E., Esteves, F., & Carvalho, H. (2015). Clinical profiles of stigma experiences, self-esteem and social relationships among people with schizophrenia, depressive, and bipolar disorders. *Psychiatry Research, 229*(1–2), 167–173. https://doi.org/10.1016/j.psychres.2015.07.047Get

Padgett, D. K. (2007). There's no place like (a) home: Ontological security among persons with serious mental illness in the United States. *Social Science & Medicine, 64*(9), 1925–1936. https://doi.org/10.1016/j.socscimed.2007.02.011

Padgett, D. K., & Henwood, B. F. (2012). Qualitative research for and in practice: Findings from studies with homeless adults who have serious mental illness and co-occurring substance abuse. *Clinical Social Work Journal, 40*, 187–193. http://dx.doi.org/10.1007/s10615-011-0354-1

Padgett, D., Henwood, B. F., & Tsemberis, S. J. (2016). *Housing first: Ending homelessness, transforming systems, and changing lives.* Oxford University Press.

Parks, J., Svendsen, D., Singer, P., & Foti, M. (2006). *Morbidity and mortality in people with serious mental illness.* National Association of State Mental Health Program Directors (NASMHPD) Medical Directors Council, Alexandria, VA. Available at: http://www.nasmhpd.org/general_files/publications/med_directors_pubs/Mortality%20and%20Morbidity%20Final%20Report%208.18.08.pdf

Pratt, S. I., Bartels, S. J., Mueser, K. T., & Forester, B. (2008). Helping older people experience success: An integrated model of psychosocial rehabilitation and health care management for older adults with serious mental illness. *American Journal of Psychiatric Rehabilitation, 11*, 41–60. https://doi.org/10.1080/15487760701853193

Pratt, S. I., Van Citters, A. D., Mueser, K. T., & Bartels, S. J. (2008). Psychosocial rehabilitation in older adults with serious mental illness: A review of the research literature and recommendations for development of rehabilitative approaches. *American Journal of Psychiatric Rehabilitation, 11*, 7–40. http://dx.doi.org/10.1080/15487760701853276

Randall, W. L. (2011). Memory, metaphor and meaning: Reading for wisdom in the stories of our lives. In G.M. Kenyon, E. Bohlmeijer & W.L. Randall (Eds.), *Storying later life: Issues, investigations, and interventions in narrative gerontology* (pp. 18–36). Oxford University Press.

Ribe, A. R., Laursen, T. M., Charles, M., Katon, W., Fenger-Grøn, M., Davydow, D., ... Vestergaard, M. (2015). Long-term risk of dementia in persons with schizophrenia: A Danish population-based cohort study. *JAMA Psychiatry, 72*(11), 1095–1101. https://doi.org/10.1001/jamapsychiatry.2015.1546

Russinova, Z., Wewiorski, N. J., Lyass, A., Rogers, E. S., & Massaro, J. M. (2005). Correlates of vocational recovery for persons with schizophrenia. In L. Davidson, C., Harding & L. Spaniol (Eds.), *Recovery from severe mental illnesses: Research evidence and implications for practice* (Vol. I, pp. 464–478). Center for Psychiatric Rehabilitation, Boston University.

Seng, J. S., Kohn-Wood, L. P., & Odera, L. A. (2005). Exploring racial disparity in posttraumatic stress disorder diagnosis: Implications for care of African American women. *Journal of Obstetric, Gynecologic and Neonatal Nursing, 34*(4), 521–530. https://doi.org/10.1177/0884217505278296

Shaw, M. (2004). Housing and public health. *Annual Review of Public Health, 25*, 397–418. http://dx.doi.org/10.1146/annurev.publhealth.25.101802.123036

Shibusawa, T., & Padgett, D. (2009). The experiences of "aging" among formerly homeless adults with chronic mental illness: A qualitative study. *Journal of Aging Studies, 23*, 188–196. https://doi.org/10.1016/j.jaging.2007.12.019

Substance Abuse and Mental Health Services Administration. (2012). *Results from the 2010 National Survey on Drug Use and Health: Mental Health Findings*, NSDUH Series H-42, HHS Publication No. (SMA) 11-4667. Substance Abuse and Mental Health Services Administration. https://www.samhsa.gov/data/sites/default/files/NSDUHNationalFindingsResults2010-web/2k10ResultsRev/NSDUHresultsRev2010.pdf

Susman, J. (1994). Disability, stigma and deviance. *Social Science & Medicine, 38*(1), 15–22. https://doi.org/10.1016/0277-9536(94)90295-X

Tomita, A., Lukens, E. P., & Herman, D. B. (2014). Mediation analysis of critical time intervention for persons living with serious mental illnesses: Assessing the role of family relations in reducing psychiatric rehospitalization. *Psychiatric Rehabilitation Journal, 37*(1), 4. https://doi.org/10.1037/prj0000015

Twamley, E. W., Narvaez, J. M., Becker, D. R., Bartels, S. J., & Jeste, D. V. (2008). Supported employment for middle-aged and older people with schizophrenia. *American Journal of Psychiatric Rehabilitation, 11*(1), 76–89. https://doi.org/10.1080/15487760701853326

Wardaugh, J. (1999). The unaccommodated woman: Home, homelessness and identity. *The Sociological Review, 47*(1), 91–109. https://doi.org/10.1111/1467-954X.00164

Ware, N. C., Hopper, K., Tugenberg, T., Dickey, B., & Fisher, D. (2008). A theory of social integration as quality of life. *Psychiatric Services, 59*(1), 27–33. https://doi.org/10.1176/ps.2008.59.1.27

Wartelsteiner, F., Mizuno, Y., Frajo-Apor, B., Kemmler, G., Pardeller, S., Sondermann, C., ... Hofer, A. (2016). Quality of life in stabilized patients with schizophrenia is mainly associated with resilience and self-esteem. *Acta Psychiatrica Scandinavica, 134*(4), 360–367. https://doi.org/10.1111/acps.12628

West, J. C., Wilk, J. E., Olfson, M., Rae, D. S., Marcus, S., Narrow, W. E., ... Regier, D. A. (2005). Patterns and quality of treatment for patients with schizophrenia in routine psychiatric practice. *Psychiatric Services, 56*(3), 283–291. https://doi.org/10.1176/appi.ps.56.3.283

Whitley, R., & Campbell, R. D. (2014). Stigma, agency and recovery amongst people with severe mental illness. *Social Science & Medicine (1982), 107*, 1–8. https://doi.org/10.1016/j.socscimed.2014.02.010

Wilk, J. E., West, J. C., Narrow, W. E., Rae, D. S., & Regier, D. A. (2005). Access to psychiatrists in the public sector and in managed health plans. *Psychiatric Services, 56*(4), 408–410. https://doi.org/10.1176/appi.ps.56.4.408

Wu, K. Y., Chang, C. M., Liang, H. Y., Wu, C. S., Chia-Hsuan Wu, E., Chen, C. H., ... Tsai, H. J. (2013). Increased risk of developing dementia in patients with bipolar disorder: A nested matched case-control study. *Bipolar Disorders, 15*(7), 787–794. https://doi.org/10.1111/bdi.12116

Suggested Readings

Davidson, L., Stayner, D. A., Nickou, C., Styron, T. H., Rowe, M., & Chinman, M. L. (2001). "Simply to be let in": Inclusion as a basis for recovery. *Psychiatric Rehabilitation Journal, 24*(4), 375–388. https://doi.org/10.1037/h0095067

Deegan, P. (1996). Recovery as a journey of the heart. *Psychiatric Rehabilitation Journal, 19*(3), 91. https://doi.org/10.1037/h0101301

Marrone, J., & Golowka, E. (2005) If work makes people with mental illness sick, what do unemployment, poverty and social isolation cause? In L. Davidson, C., Harding & L. Spaniol (Eds.), *Recovery from severe mental illnesses: Research evidence and implications for practice* (Vol. I, pp. 451–463). Center for Psychiatric Rehabilitation, Boston University.

Ogden, L. P. (2014c). Interpersonal relationship narratives of older adults with schizophrenia-spectrum diagnoses. *American Journal of Orthopsychiatry, 84*(6), 674–684. https://doi.org/10.1037/ort0000035

Ogden, L. P. (2018). "To fill the emptiness": Work in life history narratives of older adults with schizophrenia-spectrum diagnoses. *Qualitative Social Work, 17*(4), 556–576. https://doi.org/10.1177/1473325016688368

11
AGEING AND BRAIN INJURY LONG-TERM OUTCOMES IN ADULTS

Angela Colantonio and Melissa Biscardi

Introduction

Traumatic brain injury (TBI) is a leading cause of death and disability worldwide. It is estimated that 50–60 million people are affected by brain injury annually (Maas et al., 2017). According to the World Health Organization (WHO), the burden of TBI is expected to grow and surpass many diseases as the major cause of death and disability by the year 2020 (Humphreys, Wood, Phillips, & Macey, 2013; Hyder, Wunderlich, Puvanachandra, Gururaj, & Kobusingye, 2007; Lopez, Mathers, Ezzati, Jamison, & Murray, 2006; Mathers & Loncar, 2006; Roozenbeek, Maas, & Menon, 2013; Tabish & Syed, 2015). Although occurring more often in men, the number of women who sustain a TBI still represents a significant portion of the population and have the fastest growing incidence (Covassin, Savage, Bretzin, & Fox, 2018; Zemek et al., 2016). Many of these injuries are considered mild with the vast majority expected to recover and return to previous levels of functioning within three months (Cancelliere et al., 2016; Fadyl & McPherson, 2009). However, for a subset of individuals who have mild, moderate and more severe injuries there are longer term effects. Due to advances in medical technology, persons are surviving brain injury at an accelerated rate. Furthermore, because survival after TBI has increased, it is essential to know how people age with TBI. A disproportionate number of individuals are affected early in life, with critical consequences: an insult to the brain can be a significant factor in decreasing physiological reserve and as such the full impact of this injury may not be fully appreciated until later in life (Fuller, Ransom, Mandrekar, & Brown, 2016; Mosqueda, Burnight, Liao, & Kemp, 2004). As such, it is imperative that we strive towards strong understanding of how to maximise long-term outcomes for these individuals to ensure the best quality of life.

Recently there has been a call to view TBI as a chronic disease process and not an isolated event (Masel & DeWitt, 2010). Historically, when considering mild and moderate TBI there has been the perception that after a brief period of rehabilitation, little lasting effect will be faced. In fact, while many patients survive a TBI, a chronic disease process is often initiated and persists for many years and even decades. Following a TBI, individuals may experience impacts on multiple organ systems, some that are distant from the site of injury. These impacts include neuroendocrine disorders, neurological disorders, neurodegenerative diseases, psychiatric diseases, metabolic dysfunction and musculoskeletal complaints (Barton et al., 2016; Colantonio, Harris, Ratcliff, Chase, & Ellis, 2010; Daniel, Bonneville, Beckers, & Valdes-Socin, 2019; Mollayeva, Hurst, Escobar, & Colantonio, 2019; Toglia & Golisz, 2017; Sav, Rotondo, Syro, Serna & Kovacs, 2019). For this reason, TBI should be viewed and managed as a chronic disease. Consistent with the lens of TBI as a chronic condition, ageing with TBI in this chapter will be reviewed in the context of long-term outcomes and as such the long-term outcome literature

Table 11.1 Criteria used in diagnosing TBI (Orman et al., 2011; Brasure, et al., 2012; Menon et al., 2010)

TBI classification	Findings must not exceed
Mild	• Loss of consciousness of 30 minutes or less • An initial Glasgow Coma Scale of 13–15 • Posttraumatic amnesia not greater than 24 hours • Structural imaging normal
Moderate	• Loss of consciousness of 30 minutes to 24 hours • An initial Glasgow Coma Scale of 9–12 • Posttraumatic amnesia of 24 hours to seven days • Structural imaging normal or abnormal
Severe	• Loss of consciousness of greater than 24 hours • An initial Glasgow Coma Scale of 3–8 • Posttraumatic amnesia persists for greater than seven days • Structural imaging abnormal

will be reviewed. Further, we will address the literature with a sex and gender lens as this is considered a requisite for good science and is considered a central theme to this handbook.

TBI What Is It?

TBI is a complex pathophysiologic response to biomechanical forces imparted to the brain (Kutcher et al., 2016). It is an insult to the brain that is not congenital or degenerative in nature but results from a direct or indirect external biomechanical force that may include a diminished or altered state of consciousness (Menon et al., 2010). TBI may lead to temporary or permanent impairments in cognition, physical functioning and psychological well-being (Table 11.1). The common mechanism of TBI is a physical insult to the head resulting in focal damage, compression and shearing of tissues (Reifschneider, Auble, & Rose, 2015). TBI may also be caused by rotational and acceleration forces-deceleration forces, such as injuries frequently seen in whiplash and motor vehicle crashes.

Long-term Effects of TBI

Following a TBI individual may experience a broad range of impairments or negative health sequela. Impairments not present in the acute phase following injury may develop over time further complicating planning for the years that follow injury. This is further complicated by the fact that TBI results in a condition that may cause new health conditions to develop and that may cause existing health issues to progress in severity. There is clearly a need for clinicians and researchers to understand how health conditions persist – or indeed develop – over the long-term as individuals age following brain injury.

Neuroendocrine Disturbances

The neuroendocrine system is a complex regulatory mechanism that includes the hypothalamus, the pituitary and their connections to the brain, and extrahypothalamic regions. The development of neuroendocrine disturbances following TBI was first documented over 100 years ago in 1918 (Cyran, 1918). Since then, a significant number of studies in neurology, endocrine, and physiatry literature have shown the consequences of TBI on the neuroendocrine system (Gray, Bilski, Dieudonne, & Saeed, 2019) resulting from even mild TBIs such as sport-related concussions (Jordan, 2013; Snook,

Henry, Sanfilippo, Zeleznik, & Kontos, 2017), and blast-related mild TBIs in veterans (Ioachimescu, Hampstead, Moore, Burgess, & Phillips, 2015; Wilkinson et al., 2012). Longitudinal prospective studies have shown that some of the early abnormalities are transient, whereas new endocrine dysfunctions become apparent in the post-acute phase. While it is well accepted that disturbances to the neuroendocrine system can exist in the long-term, there continues to be much debate regarding the prevalence. Further to this, long-term survivors may exhibit varying degrees of disturbances over time (Giuliano et al., 2016; Izzo et al., 2016; Yang, Chen, Wang, Kuo, Cheng & Yang, 2016). Recent research has shown that in mild, moderate, or severe TBI, up to 60% of individuals will present with subnormal responses in at least one hormonal axis (Molaie & Maguire, 2018), however findings of disruption depend on timing post injury, the diagnostic test and threshold employed (Glyn & Agha, 2019; Klose & Feldt-Rasmussen, 2018; Kokshoorn et al., 2010). While the most frequently reported hormonal deficits include decreased growth hormone secretion and hypogonadism, followed by hypothyroidism, hypocortisolism, and diabetes insipidus (Aimaretti et al., 2005; Emelifeonwu, Flower, Loan, McGivern, & Andrews, 2020; Ranganathan et al., 2016; Schneider, Kreitschmann-Andermahr, Ghigo, Stalla, & Agha, 2007), undiagnosed hormone abnormalities not only go undetected but also untreated.

Reproductive Hormones and Health

One of the most common disturbances for both sexes involves disruptions to gonadotropins also known as reproductive hormones. It is well established in the literature that both men and women may experience disruptions in reproductive hormones and these disruptions may last many years after the initial injury. Long-term menstrual cycle function has been studied in women ageing with TBI after moderate to severe brain injury. In a sample of 104 women matched up to 12 years post injury, 46% reported experiencing amenorrhea with a duration of up to 60 months. Irregular cycles were reported among 68% of women post injury. These findings were significantly different from those of women who were matched on age, education and geographic location. There were no reported differences with respect to fertility, however, women with TBI had fewer live births. Menstrual difficulties post-TBI could be an indicator of neuroendocrine abnormalities which may affect areas of health such as cognition and mood (Colantonio et al., 2010). With more recent focus on concussion, menstrual cycle disruption has been documented even with this milder injury (Biscardi & Colantonio, 2018; Snook et al., 2017). There is a need for more extensive investigation of reproductive health outcomes among women long-term including how women experience menopause. There is virtually no exploration on this topic.

In men, lowered gonadotropins such as testosterone levels are found in both the acute phase and over time (Barton et al., 2016; Daniel et al., 2019; Kopczak et al., 2015). This may manifest as low energy, low libido, impaired cognition and poor everyday functioning (Wagner et al., 2012). Some research has suggested up to 44% of men experience decreased levels of testosterone. While in most cases the reproductive axis returns to normal some research has suggested persistent cases, in particular in the most severe TBI cases (Barton et al., 2016; Schneider et al., 2007). In one recent study of 126 individuals, testosterone deficiency was the most common neuroendocrine disturbance experienced between 1- and 2-years post injury (Kopczak et al., 2015). Further to this finding, in individuals who were followed for more than 5 years post injury, hormone disturbances increased in 25% of cases supporting the fact that neuroendocrine disturbances are in fact frequently experienced even in years post injury.

Given the frequency and persistence of hormone disturbances and their association with decreased cognition, increased functional dependence and global neurological impairments (Bondanelli et al., 2007; Wagner et al., 2012) screening of individuals for hormone disturbances following TBI according to the most recent Endocrine Society Clinical Practice Guideline (Fleseriu et al., 2016) is needed in order to allow for timely intervention and future planning.

Neurological Outcomes

The relationship between brain injury long-term cognitive decline has been subject of much media attention and investigation in recent years. TBI triggers progressive neurodegeneration and is a risk factor for various types of dementia. This is an important area of inquiry as the population continues to age in general and decreasing the risk for accelerated cognitive decline and dementias such as Alzheimer's disease has become a nationwide concern. Research on the structural ageing of brains following TBI versus individuals without a history of TBI examined 99 individuals with a history of TBI versus 113 control subjects and used neuroimaging to estimate the age of their brains. Results of this study found that TBI patients' brains were estimated to be older than their chronological age. This discrepancy increased with time since injury, suggesting that TBI accelerates the rate of brain atrophy (Cole et al., 2015). A more recent study examined 31 bilateral cortical regions for 66 active duty members and veterans with a history of TBI. Compared to the general population, those with a history of TBI showed that even after mild TBI accelerated age related cortical thinning was found (Santhanam et al., 2019). This may be an important factor in the increased susceptibility in TBI patients for dementia and other age-associated conditions such as memory loss. In fact, memory is one of the most commonly affected cognitive abilities after TBI and can be a source of its most disabling long-term effects (Sharp & Jenkins, 2015; Toglia & Golisz, 2017). While more research is needed in general, there is a specific need to examine sex related differences in risk for neurodegenerative outcomes.

A recently published study on 712,708 patients with both brain and spinal cord injury found that 4.5% of a population-based sample were identified with dementia over a median time of 53 months. Using sex stratified analyses, this study found that women were at greater risk of developing dementia earlier than men, all factors being equal. The risk was higher for persons with both brain and spinal cord injury. Socioeconomic status, disorders of the circulatory system, sleep disorders and vascular risk factors were associated with dementia as well. The study highlights the potential role for prevention by addressing sleep disorders. Sleep has been associated with protecting against toxic protein accumulation associated with dementia (Mollayeva et al., 2019).

Another important neurological outcome to consider as individuals age with TBI is the area of mental health. Mental health conditions are both a risk factor and consequence of a TBI. While an in-depth exploration is beyond the scope of this chapter, readers are encouraged to consider the development of anxiety, depression and suicide risk in this population. Some of the seminal work on long-term outcomes was documented by Draper and colleagues (2007) at ten or more years post mild to severe injury. They found that individuals with longer posttraumatic amnesia duration showed higher levels of anxiety, depression, and aggression as well as performing more poorly on cognitive measures. A follow up study from the same team supported these initial findings. Recent literature suggests that up to 25% of individuals sustaining a TBI have pre-injury mental health conditions that could affect clinical outcome and long-term recovery. This highlights the need for robust clinical case histories to inform prognosis and treatment options.

Depression is associated with poorer recovery following TBI yet awareness of the risk of depression post-TBI among providers and patients is low. A recent study using a large administrative dataset found the incidence of depression following TBI to be 79.5 (95% confidence interval (CI) 78.5, 80.5) per 1,000 person-years compared to 33.5 (95% CI 33.1, 34.0) per 1,000 person-years for those without TBI. The adjusted hazard ratio for depression following TBI was 1.83 (95% CI 1.79, 1.86) (Albrecht, Barbour, Abariga, Rao, & Perfetto, 2019). This supports earlier research showing that rates of psychiatric disturbances were high (65%) including depression, anxiety and substance use (Whelan-Goodinson, Ponsford, Johnston, & Grant, 2009). In addition to this increased risk overall, sex and age were predictors of depression with males and older adults at increased risk. The identification of depression in patients following TBI is of critical importance as these individuals may be at increased risk of suicide. One registry-based study of 34,529 deaths by suicide found that those with a history of TBI had an incident rate of 1.9 compared to those without a history of TBI (Madsen et al., 2018). A longitudinal study of over 200,000 patients in Ontario Canada found that patients with a history of concussion or mild TBI had a long-term increased risk of suicide (Fralick, Thiruchelvam, Tien, & Redelmeier, 2016). Greater attention to the long-term care of patients living in the community has the potential to identify those at risk and engage in prevention strategies.

Musculoskeletal Changes

Although literature on long-term musculoskeletal outcomes following TBI is limited, a small number of studies suggests that musculoskeletal complaints, including joint pain, spasticity, and arthritis, are more common in this population than in individuals who have not sustained a TBI (Brown, Hawker, Beaton, & Colantonio, 2011; Colantonio, Ratcliff, Chase, & Vernich, 2004; Hibbard, Uysal, Sliwinski, & Gordon, 1998; Jourdan et al., 2016; Ocampo-Chan, Badley, Dawson, Ratcliff, & Colantonio, 2014). Spasticity, the uncontrolled tightening of the muscles caused by disrupted signals from the brain, is a common problem experienced after moderate to severe TBI (Bell et al., 2016). Arthritis has been reported in individuals up to 24 years post injury. Research based on a large sample in the United States (US), found a high rate of self-reported arthritis - 30% - which is approximately twice the rate of self-reported arthritis among the US adult general population (Colantonio et al., 2004). Particularly noteworthy is that the biggest difference in reporting arthritis, compared to the general population, is within the 24–44 year age group (odd ratio 2.7) and not in the oldest age groupings. Potentially, this is a sign that individuals with TBI may be at risk for chronic health conditions usually experienced at a significantly older age and as such may be a sign of accelerated ageing.

Many possible mechanisms have been postulated for the high rate of musculoskeletal complaints. Recent literature has suggested that an injury to the brain may have a more systemic effect, developing in the weeks and months following the initial impact that affects the immune system (Balu, 2014). An increased immune response has implications for global inflammation, as well as more specific conditions affecting the joints, such as arthritis and gout. In addition, many TBI survivors sustain other injuries at the time of the initial injury. These injuries may have different patterns when considering sex and gender. Participants injured in motor vehicle crashes may have multiple injuries, particularly in the joints, that could lead to arthritic changes. Heterotopic ossification is known to occur after severe TBI (Cipriano, Pill, & Keenan, 2009), and could possibly lead to long-term musculoskeletal pain and abnormal pressure on joints. Altered postural alignment and asymmetry in motor control may predispose persons to arthritic changes. In addition, prolonged gait deviation, including changes in speed, cadence, width-of-base and stance-time on each leg, have been found to occur in individuals post-TBI (Williams, Morris, Schache, & McCrory, 2009). This may contribute to painful joints and degeneration of cartilage. It is important to document the extent to which these initial injuries may evolve into long-term musculoskeletal issues.

Musculoskeletal complaints in individuals with TBI are associated with limitations in activity and participation. Specifically, they report poorer self-rated health, poorer cognitive function, decreased physical function, and are less likely to be involved in age-appropriate productive activities (i.e. work and/or home-making). In addition, there appears to be significant association between self-reported arthritis and sleep disturbances in the TBI population (Ocampo-Chan et al., 2014) Female gender has also been associated with self-reported arthritis in women ageing with brain injury (Hibbard et al., 1998).

Mild TBI

Mild TBI also referred to as a concussion has gained increasing attention over the last 10 years, as the most common form of TBI (Cancelliere et al., 2016). Although termed mild, some individuals continue to have symptoms that persist over the long-term. In these individuals, while the transient physiological processes of the acute phase may have resolved, a chronic post-concussion syndrome persists. The extent of these effects may be magnified by multiple TBIs or comorbidities (Brush, Ehmann, Olson, Bixby, & Alderman, 2018).

Sex has been studied as an indicator of prognosis after mild traumatic brain injury (MTBI) and the subject of a systematic review. A study of over 200 studies revealed that only 7% of studies provided sex stratified data. In this review, MTBI was associated with a higher risk of epilepsy in large cohorts of people more than ten years post injury with the risk being higher among females. Females were also found to be at higher risk of suicide and use more health care services. No sex difference was found for risks of dementia and primary brain tumour, or post-traumatic stress syndrome (Cancelliere et al., 2016).

Chronic Traumatic Encephalopathy

A form of dementia that has received increasing attention is chronic traumatic encephalopathy. This is a condition that has historically been termed as 'dementia pugilistica' as it has been found in brains of deceased boxers. This neurodegenerative condition, is believed to be caused by multiple subconcussive hits to the head. Although this condition was described at least 100 years ago, there has been revived interest in it, particularly in relation to professional athletes. The studies which have received widespread attention tend to be focused on pathological samples of retired football players. At this point, there is no definition for chronic traumatic encephalopathy among persons who are living, and this is a work in progress. What is distinctly absent from the literature are samples that include women. One of the first published case studies of dementia pugilistica that involves a woman was described as a 'punch drunk wife' (Roberts, Whitwell, Acland, & Burton, 1990). The case study was about a female who was repeatedly abused by her husband to the point where she was diagnosed with cauliflower ears that are found in professional boxers due to repeated trauma to this area. Brain injury in the context of intimate partner violence (IPV) has been largely ignored in the literature despite the fact that internationally 1 in 3 women are affected by IPV and the majority of the hits are to the head face and neck (Haag, Jones, Joseph, & Colantonio, 2019; Haag, Sokoloff, et al., 2019). While IPV occurs across genders, it disproportionately affects women. A study found that spousal abuse was more common among dementia patients than a control group (Leung, Thompson, & Weaver, 2006). There is increasing realisation that future research on chronic traumatic encephalopathy has to be on diverse samples and must include women. A broad range of interventions need to be further studied to address the long-term effects of TBI in this context. A research team led by the University of Toronto has now developed a toolkit for front line service providers to address a very significant identified knowledge gap among providers working with abused women (www.abitoolkit.ca).

Key Issues

- Sex and Gender Considerations
- TBI as a chronic condition
- Community Integration

Sex Differences

It is well established that illnesses that affect adults as they age manifest differently in men and women. These include, but are not limited to, depression, arthritis, osteoporosis, brain injury and Alzheimer's disease (Alswat, 2017; Munivenkatappa, Agrawal, Shukla, Kumaraswamy, & Devi, 2016; van Vollenhoven, 2009). While researchers are increasingly recognising that sex has a significant effect on the psychological and physiological sequela following TBI, there has been a paucity of research on long-term outcomes after TBI that are sex specific. Little is known about the extent to which the long-term impact of brain injury specifically affects a woman's body.

One of the first systematic reviews on outcomes found that women reported worse outcomes and fared worse on up to 85% of measured outcomes when compared to males (Farace & Alves, 2000) however, issues of age as a confounder may not have been adequately considered. Also, recent work has shown that when compared to males, women self-report more frequent musculoskeletal pain and worse somatic and psychiatric outcomes (Styrke, Sojka, Björnstig, Bylund, & Stålnacke, 2013). There is some evidence that points towards structural vulnerability. Specifically, sex differences may be attributed to neck muscular strength. Researchers have reported that females have 50% less neck strength, 23% less neck girth and 43% less head–neck segment (Tierney et al., 2005). However, researchers have also reported that females have 50% greater head neck peak angular acceleration compared to males. It is possible that this increase in angular acceleration may lead to these aforementioned sex differences. There are neuroendocrine vulnerabilities that must also be considered. In particular, some research suggests that phase of the menstrual cycle at the time of injury may affect outcomes in women of reproductive age (Wunderle, Hoeger, Wasserman, & Bazarian, 2014).

In a 2010 study of 306 individuals post-injury, women reported more headaches and dizziness as well as increased loss of confidence compared with men (Colantonio et al., 2010). The symptoms more likely to affect daily functioning among women were the ability to initiate daily activities, high sex drive, and a need for supervision and assistance. These identified problem areas reflect gendered roles indicating that being cared for was more problematic for women likely due to reversed major caregiving roles. Although men were twice as likely to report high sex drive, women found it more problematic. Subsequent work from focus groups of survivors and caregivers revealed the increased potential for sexual abuse among women after brain injury (Colantonio et al., 2010; Haag et al., 2016).

Sex and gender are key factors to include when considering how individuals age with brain injury, but the intersection of other factors is also clearly important. Mollayeva, Mollayeva, and Colantonio (2018) provide a valuable guide regarding a framework that can be used to study sex and gender differences which are invariably intertwined.

TBI as a Chronic Condition

TBI can have lifelong and dynamic effects on health and wellbeing making its conceptualisation as a chronic condition appropriate (Masel & DeWitt, 2010). Evidence suggests that functional outcomes after TBI can show improvement or deterioration up to two decades after injury, and rates of all-cause mortality remain elevated for many years. Numerous studies have documented the longer-term mortality risk of persons ageing with TBI. These studies vary according the nature of the sample studied. For instance, predictors of post-acute mortality include younger age, comorbidity, level of disability through measurement of activity limitations. Generally, studies based on acute care and inpatient rehabilitation samples also vary in terms of their outcomes.

Deterioration, whether directly or indirectly associated with the original brain injury, necessitates a clinical approach as a chronic health condition, including identification of risk and protective factors, protocols for early identification, evidence-based preventive and ameliorative treatment, and training in self-management. Despite in and outpatient rehabilitation services, 50% of individuals suffering a moderate or severe TBI will experience gradual decline within the first 5 years following injury (Center for Disease Control, 2015).

Community Integration

One of the most important rehabilitation goals and outcomes after TBI is community integration. This construct has been operationalised in a multitude of ways but most commonly measured by the Community Integration Index that considers home, social and occupational integration. Devitt and colleagues (2006) proposed a framework to study this outcome which considers pre injury factors such as demographic and functioning, injury related factors such as injury severity and post injury factors such as post injury health and function as well as the environment (types of support, rehabilitation, finances and transportation). This study based on over 300 adults up to 24 years post moderate to severe TBI found that pre-injury behavioural problems, male gender, post injury cognitive and physical deficits, and lack of access to transportation were significant independent predictors of worse community integration outcomes (Devitt et al., 2006).

With respect to social integration, social failure is one of the most negative consequences associated with brain injury. TBI compromises important neurological functions for self-regulation and social behaviour and increases risk of behavioural disorder and psychiatric morbidity potentially compromising social integration. While multiple factors play a role in contact with the justice system, TBI is a risk factor for earlier, more violent, offending. Large longitudinal studies following cohorts of younger persons over time. One such study in Ontario have found a 2.5 increased risk of incarceration after a TBI in a sample of over 2.5 million young adults (McIsaac et al., 2016). Of importance to clinicians working with offenders; TBI is linked to poor engagement in treatment, in-custody infractions, and reconviction (Sariaslan, Sharp, D'Onofrio, Larsson, & Fazel, 2016; Williams et al., 2018). Incarceration has been associated with high levels of adverse early life experience particularly among women. TBI often occurs prior to first incidence of contact with the justice system (Colantonio et al., 2014). The role of intervention and support to prevent incarceration and recidivism needs further exploration.

Employment is an important community integration outcome that provides health, social, and economic benefit which is particularly relevant to persons who experience TBI early in their life. A broad range of long-term employment rates after TBI have been published and range by injury severity. Systematic reviews have identified that on average 41% of individuals are employed by 2 years post a moderate to severe injury (van Velzen, van Bennekom, Edelaar, Sluiter, & Frings-Dresen, 2009). Predictors of employment include male sex, lower severity and higher levels of social support. Vocational interventions that have been shown to be effective in return to work which include a range of supports which include job coaching and facilitating workplace accommodations (Trexler, Parrott, & Malec, 2016; van Dongen et al., 2018).

Traumatic Brain Injury Guidelines and Rehabilitation

Currently numerous guidelines exist with respect to the treatment of persons with TBI. For instance, the Ontario Neurotrauma Foundation has launched guidelines for adults with moderate to severe injuries in partnership with the Institut National d'excellence en Sante et en Services Sociaux (INESSS) (Ontario Neurotrauma Foundation, 2018). Further, there are guidelines for Concussion/Mild Traumatic Brain Injury and Persistent Symptoms (3rd edition) for adults which are also now available in lay format. These guidelines and those of others however are largely based on studies relevant to the condition in the early stages of recovery (Bayley et al., 2016; Marshall et al., 2020). While there are distinct guidelines for Diagnosing and Managing Pediatric Concussion, there are none devoted to persons who are ageing with TBI (National Institute of Neurological Disorders and Stroke, 2017). Given that this is the fastest growing segment of the population, this is an area that needs more research and knowledge transfer. Further, none of these guidelines are based on literature that gives explicit consideration to sex and gender.

The reality for TBI survivors is that longer term supports are needed which contrast with the fact that most services are offered in the earlier stages post injury. Much needs to be done to develop programming and policies that promote optimal ageing with TBI. For instance, in one study of moderate to severely injured women up to 12 years post injury, 40% reported that they did not receive care when needed despite using more family physician and community health services. The area with the greatest gap was for emotional/mental health problems. Further, women with TBI report more financial and structural barriers than matched control populations (Toor et al., 2016). Particular challenges have been identified with persons who have comorbid conditions. A particular care gap has been found among persons who experience both mental health, addictions and TBI, which are often used as exclusion criteria for mental health and brain injury services respectively. Given the heterogeneity of the TBI population flexible interdisciplinary models to provide care are needed. These priorities are consistent with gaps in care found in other studies (Colantonio et al., 2010).

Also important to realise is that many studies are not based on widely diverse populations or consider needs of particular target populations such as homeless and/or indigenous populations which require more tailored and culturally sensitive approaches (Keightley, King, et al., 2011; Keightley, Kendall, Jang et al., 2011).

Caregivers and TBI

The long-term impact of a TBI on caregivers can be significant. Caregiver burden has been associated with negative health and well-being outcomes, financial strain, mental health challenges, decreased life satisfaction and loneliness as well as social isolation that can exacerbate other problems (Manskow et al., 2017). A scoping review addressed interventions to reduce burden among family caregivers of persons ageing with TBI and concluded that the research is still in an early phase of development. However, the authors concluded that future research should emphasise the development an evaluation of interventions that aim to reduce objective burdens such as care coordination, financial responsibilities and challenging behaviours (Marshall et al., 2019).

Conclusion

Despite an increase in research focused on TBI, much still needs to be explored in terms of prognostic factors for recovery and opportunities to influence outcomes over time. The overall literature on ageing with brain injury particularly after moderate to severe injury points to accelerated ageing. This includes cognitive outcomes but also extends to other area of impairment such as musculoskeletal. An important area for practitioners is to maximise recovery over the long-term in an effort to prevent further decline. These interventions should be targeted at all levels of health and function.

Further, in this chapter we have made the case that ageing should be examined with sex and gender considerations in mind. We see similarities as well as some differences by sex. This could inform patient preferences and approaches to care. There has been little focus on women overall because historically most of the samples reflect incidence rates and are comprised of men. Overall there is still a great deal to examine as individuals age following TBI. Clinicians and researchers need to consider the specific impact of TBI on the development of health conditions is an important area of study particularly as this population ages. A better understanding of specific brain injury-related, physiological, modifiable and genetic factors that best predict either recovery or adverse cognitive outcomes as time since injury progresses will help to advance future developments in clinical care.

Finally, proposed priorities for improving long-term community integration of individuals with TBI and their caregivers was to development of interventions to optimise their functioning and participation, reducing caregiver burden and evaluating how emerging technology can facilitate delivery of care (Nalder et al., 2018).

References

Aimaretti, G., Ambrosio, M. R., Di Somma, C., Gasperi, M., Cannavò, S., Scaroni, C., ... Ghigo, E. (2005). Residual pituitary function after brain injury-induced hypopituitarism: A prospective 12-month study. *The Journal of Clinical Endocrinology and Metabolism*, *90*(11), 6085–6092. https://doi.org/10.1210/jc.2005-0504

Albrecht, J. S., Barbour, L., Abariga, S. A., Rao, V., & Perfetto, E. M. (2019). Risk of depression after traumatic brain injury in a large national sample. *Journal of Neurotrauma*, *36*(2), 300–307. https://doi.org/10.1089/neu.2017.5608

Alswat, A., K. (2017). Gender disparities in osteoporosis. *Journal of Clinical Medicine Research*, *9*(5), 382–387. https://doi.org/10.14740/jocmr2970w

Balu, R. (2014). Inflammation and immune system activation after traumatic brain injury. *Current Neurology and Neuroscience Reports*, *14*(10), 484. https://doi.org/10.1007/s11910-014-0484-2

Barton, D. J., Kumar, R. G., McCullough, E. H., Galang, G., Arenth, P. M., Berga, S. L., & Wagner, A. K. (2016). Persistent hypogonadotropic hypogonadism in men after severe traumatic brain injury: Temporal hormone profiles and outcome prediction. *The Journal of Head Trauma Rehabilitation*, *31*(4), 277–287. https://doi.org/10.1097/HTR.0000000000000188

Bayley, M., Swaine, B., Lamontagne, M. E., Marshall, S., Allaire, A. S., Kua, A., & Marier-Deschênes, P. (2016). *INESSS-ONF Clinical Practice Guideline for the Rehabilitation of Adults with Moderate to Severe Traumatic Brain Injury*. Ontario Neurotrauma Foundation. https://braininjuryguidelines.org/modtosevere/

Bell, K., & DiTommaso, C., & Model Systems Knowledge Translation Center. (2016). Information/Education page, spasticity and traumatic brain injury. *Archives of Physical Medicine and Rehabilitation*, *97*(1), 179–180. https://doi.org/10.1016/j.apmr.2015.05.010

Biscardi, M., & Colantonio, A. (2018). Sex, gender, and cultural considerations for rehabilitation research with older adults. In R. J. Gatchel, I. Z. Schultz, & C. T. Ray (Eds.), *Handbook of rehabilitation of older adults* (pp. 519–537). Springer. https://doi.org/10.1007/978-3-030-03916-5_28

Bondanelli, M., Ambrosio, M. R., Cavazzini, L., Bertocchi, A., Zatelli, M. C., Carli, A., ... Uberti, E. C. (2007). Anterior pituitary function may predict functional and cognitive outcome in patients with traumatic brain injury undergoing rehabilitation. *Journal of Neurotrauma*, *24*(11), 1687–1697. https://doi.org/10.1089/neu.2007.0343

Brasure, M., Lamberty, G. J., Sayer, N. A., Nelson, N. W., MacDonald, R., Ouellette, J., ... Wilt, T. J. (2012). *Multidisciplinary Postacute Rehabilitation for Moderate to Severe Traumatic Brain Injury in Adults*. Agency for Healthcare Research and Quality (US). (Comparative Effectiveness Reviews, No. 72.) Table 1, Criteria used to classify TBI severity. Retrieved from https://www.ncbi.nlm.nih.gov/books/NBK98986/table/introduction.t1/

Brown, S., Hawker, G., Beaton, D., & Colantonio, A. (2011). Long-term musculoskeletal complaints after traumatic brain injury. *Brain Injury*, *25*(5), 453–461. https://doi.org/10.3109/02699052.2011.556581

Brush, C. J., Ehmann, P. J., Olson, R. L., Bixby, W. R., & Alderman, B. L. (2018). Do sport-related concussions result in long-term cognitive impairment? A review of event-related potential research. *International Journal of Psychophysiology: Official Journal of the International Organization of Psychophysiology*, *132*(Pt A), 124–134. https://doi.org/10.1016/j.ijpsycho.2017.10.006

Cancelliere, C., Donovan, J., Stochkendahl, M. J., Biscardi, M., Ammendolia, C., Myburgh, C., & Cassidy, J. D. (2016). Factors affecting return to work after injury or illness: Best evidence synthesis of systematic reviews. *Chiropractic & Manual Therapies*, *24*(1), 32. https://doi.org/10.1186/s12998-016-0113-z

Center for Disease Control. (2015). Traumatic brain injury in the United States: Epidemiology and rehabilitation: Report to Congress. *U.S. Department of Health and Human Services*. Retrieved from https://www.cdc.gov/traumaticbraininjury/pdf/TBI_Report_to_Congress_Epi_and_Rehab-a.pdf

Cipriano, C. A., Pill, S. G., & Keenan, M. A. (2009). Heterotopic ossification following traumatic brain injury and spinal cord injury. *The Journal of the American Academy of Orthopaedic Surgeons*, *17*(11), 689–697. https://doi.org/10.5435/00124635-200911000-00003

Colantonio, A., Harris, J. E., Ratcliff, G., Chase, S., & Ellis, K. (2010). Gender differences in self reported long term outcomes following moderate to severe traumatic brain injury. *BMC Neurology*, *10*, 102. https://doi.org/10.1186/1471-2377-10-102

Colantonio, A., Howse, D., Kirsh, B., Chiu, T., Zulla, R., & Levy, C. (2010). Living environments for people with moderate to severe acquired brain injury. *Healthcare Policy/Politiques de Santé*, *5*(4), e120–e138. https://www.ncbi.nlm.nih.gov/pmc/articles/PMC2875897/pdf/policy-05-e120.pdf

Colantonio, A., Kim, H., Asbridge, M., Allen, S., Petgrave, J., & Brochu, S. (2014). Traumatic brain injury and early life experiences among men and women in a prison population. *Journal of Correctional Health Care*, *20*(4), 271–279. https://doi.org/10.1177/1078345814541529

Colantonio, A., Mar, W., Escobar, M., Yoshida, K., Velikonja, D., Rizoli, S., ... Cullen, N. (2010). Women's health outcomes after traumatic brain injury. *Journal of Women's Health*, *19*(6), 1109–1116. https://doi.org/10.1089=jwh.2009.1740

Colantonio, A., Ratcliff, G., Chase, S., & Vernich, L. (2004). Aging with traumatic brain injury: Long term health conditions. *International Journal of Rehabilitation Research*, *27*(3), 209–214. https://doi.org/10.1097/00004356-200409000-00006

Cole, J. H., Leech, R., & Sharp, D. J., & Alzheimer's Disease Neuroimaging Initiative. (2015). Prediction of brain age suggests accelerated atrophy after traumatic brain injury. *Annals of Neurology*, *77*(4), 571–581. https://doi.org/10.1002/ana.24367

Covassin, T., Savage, J. L., Bretzin, A. C., & Fox, M. E. (2018). Sex differences in sport-related concussion long-term outcomes. *International Journal of Psychophysiology: Official Journal of the International Organization of Psychophysiology*, *132*(Pt A), 9–13. https://doi.org/10.1016/j.ijpsycho.2017.09.010

Cyran, E. (1918). Hypophysenschädigung durch schädelbasisfraktur [Pituitary damage due to skull base fracture]. *Dtsch. Med.* Wochenschr [German Medical Weekly]. 44, 1261

Daniel, S., Bonneville, J.-F., Beckers, A., & Valdes-Socin, H. (2019). Prevalence and study of neuroendocrine deficits in a series of 75 patients following traumatic brain injury. *Endocrine Abstracts, 63*, P1104. https://doi.org/10.1530/endoabs.63.P1104

Devitt, R., Colantonio, A., Ratcliff, G., Chase, S., Dawson, D., & Teare, G. (2006). Prediction of long-term occupational performance outcomes for adults after moderate to severe traumatic brain injury. *Disability and Rehabilitation, 28*(9), 547–559. https://doi.org/10.1080/00222930500219258

Draper, K., Ponsford, J., & Schönberger, M. (2007). Psychosocial and emotional outcomes 10 years following traumatic brain injury. *The Journal of Head Trauma Rehabilitation, 22*(5), 278–287. https://doi.org/10.1097/01.HTR.0000290972.63753.a7

Emelifeonwu, J.A., Flower, H., Loan, J. J., McGivern, K., & Andrews, P. J. D. (2020). *Journal of Neurotrauma, 37*(2), 217–226. http://doi.org/10.1089/neu.2018.6349

Fadyl, J. K., & McPherson, K. M. (2009). Approaches to vocational rehabilitation after traumatic brain injury: A review of the evidence. *The Journal of Head Trauma Rehabilitation, 24*(3), 195–212. https://doi.org/10.1097/HTR.0b013e3181a0d458

Farace, E., & Alves, W. M. (2000). Do women fare worse? A metaanalysis of gender differences in outcome after traumatic brain injury. *Neurosurgical Focus, 8*(1), e6. https://doi.org/10.3171/foc.2000.8.1.152

Fleseriu, M., Hashim, I. A., Karavitaki, N., Melmed, S., Murad, M. H., Salvatori, R., & Samuels, M. H. (2016). Hormonal replacement in hypopituitarism in adults: An endocrine society clinical practice guideline. *The Journal of Clinical Endocrinology and Metabolism, 101*(11), 3888–3921. https://doi.org/10.1210/jc.2016-2118

Fralick, M., Thiruchelvam, D., Tien, H. C., & Redelmeier, D. A. (2016). Risk of suicide after a concussion. *CMAJ: Canadian Medical Association Journal/Journal de l'Association Medicale Canadienne, 188*(7), 497–504. https://doi.org/10.1503/cmaj.150790

Fuller, G. W., Ransom, J., Mandrekar, J., & Brown, A. W. (2016). Long-term survival following traumatic brain injury: A population-based parametric survival analysis. *Neuroepidemiology, 47*(1), 1–10. https://doi.org/10.1159/000445997

Giuliano, S., Talarico, S., Bruno, L., Nicoletti, F. B., Ceccotti, C., & Belfiore, A. (2016). Growth hormone deficiency and hypopituitarism in adults after complicated mild traumatic brain injury. *Endocrine, 58*(1), 115–123. https://doi.org/10.1007/s12020-016-1183-3

Gray, S., Bilski, T., Dieudonne, B., & Saeed, S. (2019). Hypopituitarism after traumatic brain injury. *Cureus, 11*(3), e4163. https://doi.org/10.7759/cureus.4163

Glyn, N., & Agha, A. (2019). The frequency and the diagnosis of pituitary dysfunction after traumatic brain injury. *Pituitary,* (22), 249–260.

Haag, H. L., Caringal, M., Sokoloff, S., Kontos, P., Yoshida, K., & Colantonio, A. (2016). Being a woman with acquired brain injury: Challenges and implications for practice. *Archives of Physical Medicine and Rehabilitation, 97*(2), S64–S70. https://doi.org/10.1016/j.apmr.2014.12.018

Haag, H. L., Jones, D., Joseph, T., & Colantonio, A. (2019). Battered and brain injured: Traumatic brain injury among women survivors of intimate partner violence. A scoping review. *Trauma Violence Abuse.* https://doi.org/10.1177/1524838019850623.

Haag, H. L., Sokoloff, S., MacGregor, N., Broekstra, S., Cullen, N., & Colantonio, A. (2019). Battered and brain injured: Assessing knowledge of traumatic brain injury among intimate partner violence service providers. *Journal of Women's Health, 28*(7), 990–996. https://doi.org/10.1089/jwh.2018.7299

Hibbard, M. R., Uysal, S., Sliwinski, M., & Gordon, W. A. (1998). Undiagnosed health issues in individuals with traumatic brain injury living in the community. *Journal of Head Trauma Rehabilitation, 13*(4), 47–57. https://doi.org/10.1097/00001199-199808000-00005

Humphreys, I., Wood, R. L., Phillips, C. J., & Macey, S. (2013). The costs of traumatic brain injury: A literature review. *ClinicoEconomics and Outcomes Research: CEOR, 5*, 281–287. https://doi.org/10.2147/CEOR.S44625

Hyder, A. A., Wunderlich, C. A., Puvanachandra, P., Gururaj, G., & Kobusingye, O. C. (2007). The impact of traumatic brain injuries: A global perspective. *NeuroRehabilitation, 22*(5), 341–353. https://doi.org/10.3233/NRE-2007-22502

Ioachimescu, A. G., Hampstead, B. M., Moore, A., Burgess, E., & Phillips, L. S. (2015). Growth hormone deficiency after mild combat-related traumatic brain injury. *Pituitary, 18*(4), 535–541. https://doi.org/10.1007/s11102-014-0606-5

Izzo, G., Tirelli, A., Angrisani, E., Cannaviello, G., Cannaviello, L., Puzziello, A., … Vitale, M. (2016). Pituitary dysfunction and its association with quality of life in traumatic brain injury. *International Journal of Surgery, 28*(Suppl 1), S103–S108. https://doi.org/10.1016/j.ijsu.2015.05.056

Jordan, B. D. (2013). The clinical spectrum of sport-related traumatic brain injury. *Nature Reviews Neurology, 9*(4), 222–230. https://doi.org/10.1038/nrneurol.2013.33

Jourdan, C., Bayen, E., Pradat-Diehl, P., Ghout, I., Darnoux, E., Azerad, S., ... Azouvi, P. (2016). A comprehensive picture of 4-year outcome of severe brain injuries. Results from the PariS-TBI study. *Annals of Physical and Rehabilitation Medicine, 59*(2), 100–106. https://doi.org/10.1016/j.rehab.2015.10.009

Keightley, M. L., King, G. E., Jang, S. H., White, R. J., Colantonio, A., Minore, J. B., ... Longboat-White, C. H. (2011). Brain injury from a first nations' perspective: Teachings from elders and traditional healers. *Canadian Journal of Occupational Therapy. Revue Canadienne d'Ergotherapie, 78*(4), 237–245. https://doi.org/10.2182/cjot.2011.78.4.5

Keightley, M., Kendall, V., Jang, S. H., Parker, C., Agnihotri, S., Colantonio, A., ... Bellavance, A. (2011). From health care to home community: An aboriginal community-based ABI transition strategy. *Brain Injury, 25*(2), 142–152. https://doi.org/10.3109/02699052.2010.541898

Klose, M., & Feldt-Rasmussen, U. (2018). Chronic endocrine consequences of traumatic brain injury – What is the evidence? *Nature Reviews Endocrinology, 14*(1), 57–62. https://doi.org/10.1038/nrendo.2017.103

Kokshoorn, N. E., Wassenaar, M. J., Biermasz, N. R., Roelfsema, F., Smit, J. W., Romijn, J. A., & Pereira, A. M. (2010). Hypopituitarism following traumatic brain injury: Prevalence is affected by the use of different dynamic tests and different normal values. *European Journal of Endocrinology, 162*(1), 11–18. https://doi.org/10.1530/EJE-09-0601

Kopczak, A., Krewer, C., Schneider, M., Kreitschmann-Andermahr, I., Schneider, H. J., & Stalla, G. K. (2015). The development of neuroendocrine disturbances over time: Longitudinal findings in patients after traumatic brain injury and subarachnoid hemorrhage. *International Journal of Molecular Sciences, 17*(1), 2. https://doi.org/10.3390/ijms17010002

Kutcher, S., Wei, Y., Costa, S., Gusmão, R., Skokauskas, N., & Sourander, A. (2016). Enhancing mental health literacy in young people. *European Child & Adolescent Psychiatry, 25*(6), 567–569. https://doi.org/10.1007/s00787-016-0867-9

Leung, F. H., Thompson, K., & Weaver, D. F. (2006). Evaluating spousal abuse as a potential risk factor for Alzheimer's disease: Rationale, needs and challenges. *Neuroepidemiology, 27*(1),13–16. https://doi.org/10.1159/000093894

Lopez, A. D., Mathers, C. D., Ezzati, M., Jamison, D. T., & Murray, C. J. (2006). Global and regional burden of disease and risk factors, 2001: Systematic analysis of population health data. *Lancet, 367*(9524), 1747–1757. https://doi.org/10.1016/S0140-6736(06)68770-9

Maas, A., Menon, D. K., Adelson, P. D., Andelic, N., Bell, M. J., Belli, A., ... InTBIR Participants and Investigators. (2017). Traumatic brain injury: Integrated approaches to improve prevention, clinical care, and research. *The Lancet. Neurology, 16*(12), 987–1048. https://doi.org/10.1016/S1474-4422(17)30371-X

Madsen, T., Erlangsen, A., Orlovska, S., Mofaddy, R., Nordentoft, M., & Benros, M., E. (2018). Association between traumatic brain injury and risk of suicide. *Journal of American Medical Association, 320*(6), 580–588. https://doi.org/10.1001/jama.2018.10211

Manskow, U. S., Friborg, O., Røe, C., Braine, M., Damsgard, E., & Anke, A. (2017). Patterns of change and stability in caregiver burden and life satisfaction from 1 to 2 years after severe traumatic brain injury: A Norwegian longitudinal study. *NeuroRehabilitation, 40*(2), 211–222. https://doi.org/10.3233/NRE-161406

Marshall, C. A., Nalder, E., Colquhoun, H., Lenton, E., Hansen, M., Dawson, D. R., ... Bottari, C. (2019). Interventions to address burden among family caregivers of persons aging with TBI: A scoping review. *Brain Injury, 33*(3), 255–265. https://doi.org/10.1080/02699052.2018.1553308

Marshall, S., Bayley, M., McCullagh, S., Berrigan, L., Fischer, L., Ouchterlony, D., Rockwell, C., Velikonja, D. (2018). *Guideline for concussion/mild traumatic brain injury and prolonged symptoms: 3nd edition (for adults 18+ years of age).* Ontario Neurotrauma Foundation. https://onf.org/knowledge-mobilization/acquired-brain-injury/guidelines-for-concussion-and-moderate-to-severe-traumatic-brain-injury/

Masel, B. C., & DeWitt, D. S. (2010). Traumatic brain injury: A disease process, not an event. *Journal of Neurotrauma, 27*(8), 1529–1540. https://doi.org/10.1089/neu.2010.1358

Mathers, C. D., & Loncar, D. (2006). Projections of global mortality and burden of disease from 2002 to 2030. *PLoS Medicine, 3*(11), e442. https://doi.org/10.1371/journal.pmed.0030442

McIsaac, K. E., Moser, A., Moineddin, R., Keown, L. A., Wilton, G., Stewart, L. A., ... Matheson, F. I. (2016). Association between traumatic brain injury and incarceration: A population-based cohort study *CMAJ Open, 4*(4), E746-E753. https://doi.org/10.9778/cmajo.20160072

Menon, D. K., Schwab, K., Wright, D. W., & Maas, A. I., & Demographics and Clinical Assessment Working Group of the International and Interagency Initiative toward Common Data Elements for Research on Traumatic Brain Injury and Psychological Health. (2010). Position statement: Definition of traumatic brain injury. *Archives of Physical Medicine and Rehabilitation, 91*(11), 1637–1640. https://doi.org/10.1016/j.apmr.2010.05.017

Molaie, A. M., & Maguire, J. (2018). Neuroendocrine abnormalities following traumatic brain injury: An important contributor to neuropsychiatric sequelae. *Frontiers in Endocrinology, 9*, 176. https://doi.org/10.3389/fendo.2018.00176

Mollayeva, T., Hurst, M., Escobar, M., & Colantonio, A. (2019). Sex-specific incident dementia in patients with central nervous system trauma. *Alzheimer's & Dementia*, *11*, 355–367. https://doi.org/10.1016/j.dadm.2019.03.003

Mollayeva, T., Mollayeva, S., & Colantonio, A. (2018). Traumatic brain injury: Sex, gender and intersecting vulnerabilities. *Nature Reviews. Neurology*, *14*(12), 711–722. https://doi.org/10.1038/s41582-018-0091-y

Mosqueda, L., Burnight, K., Liao, S., & Kemp, B. (2004). Advancing the field of elder mistreatment: A new model for integration of social and medical services. *The Gerontologist*, *44*(5), 703–708. https://doi.org/10.1093/geront/44.5.703

Munivenkatappa, A., Agrawal, A., Shukla, D., Kumaraswamy, D., & Devi, B. (2016). Traumatic brain injury: Does gender influence outcomes? *International Journal of Critical Illness and Injury Science*, *6*(2), 70–73. https://doi.org/10.4103/2229-5151.183024

Nalder, E. J., Zabjek, K., Dawson, D. R., Bottari, C. L., Gagnon, I., McFadyen, B. J., ... Niechwiej-Szwedo, E., & ONF-REPAR ABI Team. (2018). Research priorities for optimizing Long-term Community integration after brain injury. *The Canadian Journal of Neurological Sciences. Le Journal Canadien des Sciences Neurologiques*, *45*(6), 643–651. https://doi.org/10.1017/cjn.2018.334

National Institute of Neurological Disorders and Stroke. (2017). *Workshop Summary: Understanding traumatic brain injury in women*. National Institutes of Health. https://videocast.nih.gov/summary.asp?Live=26249&bhcp=1

Ocampo-Chan, S., Badley, E., Dawson, D. R., Ratcliff, G., & Colantonio, A. (2014). Factors associated with self-reported arthritis 7 to 24 years after a traumatic brain injury. *Perceptual and Motor Skills*, *118*(1), 274–292. https://doi.org/10.2466/15.PMS.118k12w2

Ontario Neurotrauma Foundation. (2018). *Guidelines for Concussion and Moderate to Severe Traumatic Brain Injury*. https://braininjuryguidelines.org/concussion/fileadmin/user_upload/Concussion_guideline_3rd_edition_final2019.pdf

Orman, J. A., Kraus, J. F., Zaloshnja, E., & Miller, T. (2011). Epidemiology. In J. M. Silver, T. W. McAllister, & S. C. Yudofsky (Eds.), *Textbook of traumatic brain injury* (2nd ed., pp. 3–22). American Psychiatric Publishing. https://www.appi.org/Textbook_of_Traumatic_Brain_Injury_Third_Edition

Ranganathan, P., Kumar, R. G., Davis, K., Mccullough, E. H., Berga, S. L., & Wagner, A. K. (2016). Longitudinal sex and stress hormone profiles among reproductive age and post-menopausal women after severe TBI: A case series analysis. *Brain Injury*, *30*(4), 452–461. https://doi.org/10.3109/02699052.2016.1

Reifschneider, K., Auble, B. A., & Rose, S. R. (2015). Update of endocrine dysfunction following pediatric traumatic brain injury. *Journal of Clinical Medicine*, *4*(8), 1536–1560. https://doi.org/10.3390/jcm4081536

Roberts, G. W., Whitwell, H. L., Acland, P. R., & Burton, C. J. (1990). Dementia in a punch-drunk wife. *Lancet*, *335*(8694), 918–919. https://doi.org/10.1016/0140-6736(90)90520-f

Roozenbeek, B., Maas, A. I., & Menon, D. K. (2013). Changing patterns in the epidemiology of traumatic brain injury. *Nature Reviews. Neurology*, *9*(4), 231–236. https://doi.org/10.1038/nrneurol.2013.22

Santhanam, P., Teslovich, T., Wilson, S. H., Yeh, P., Oakes, T. R., & Weaver, L. K. (2019). Decreases in white matter integrity of ventro-limbic pathway linked to post-traumatic stress disorder in mild traumatic brain injury. *Journal of Neurotrauma*, *36*(7), 1093–1098. https://doi.org/10.1089/neu.2017.5541

Sariaslan, A., Sharp, D. J., D'Onofrio, B. M., Larsson, H., & Fazel, S. (2016). Long-term outcomes associated with traumatic brain injury in childhood and adolescence: A nationwide Swedish cohort study of a wide range of medical and social outcomes. *PLoS Medicine*, *13*(8), e1002103. https://doi.org/10.1371/journal.pmed.1002103

Sav, A., Rotondo, F., Syro, L. V., Serna, C. A., & Kovacs, K. (2019). Pituitary pathology in traumatic brain injury: A review. *Pituitary*, *22*(3), 201–211. https://doi.org/10.1007/s11102-019-00958-8

Schneider, H. J., Kreitschmann-Andermahr, I., Ghigo, E., Stalla, G. K., & Agha, A. (2007). Hypothalamopituitary dysfunction following traumatic brain injury and aneurysmal subarachnoid hemorrhage: A systematic review. *JAMA*, *298*(12), 1429–1438. https://doi.org/10.1001/jama.298.12.1429

Sharp, D. J., & Jenkins, P. O. (2015). Concussion is confusing us all. *Practical Neurology*, *15*(3):172–186. https://doi.org/10.1136/practneurol-2015-001087

Snook, M. L., Henry, L. C., Sanfilippo, J. S., Zeleznik, A. J., & Kontos, A. P. (2017). Association of concussion with abnormal menstrual patterns in adolescent and young women. *JAMA Pediatrics*, *171*(9), 879. https://doi.org/10.1001/jamapediatrics.2017.1140

Steadman-Pare, D., Colantonio, A., Ratcliff, G., Chase, S., & Vernich, L. (2001). Factors associated with perceived quality of life many years after traumatic brain injury. *The Journal of Head Trauma Rehabilitation*, *16*(4), 330–342. https://doi.org/10.1097/00001199-200108000-00004

Styrke, J., Sojka, P., Björnstig, U., Bylund, P. O., & Stålnacke, B. M. (2013). Sex-differences in symptoms, disability, and life satisfaction three years after mild traumatic brain injury: A population-based cohort study. *Journal of Rehabilitation Medicine*, *45*(8), 749–757. https://doi.org/10.2340/16501977-1215

Taylor, C. A., Bell, J. M., Breiding, M. J., & Xu, L. (2017). Traumatic brain injury-related emergency department visits, hospitalizations, and deaths – United States, 2007 and 2013. *Morbidity and Mortality Weekly Report. Surveillance Summaries*, 66(9), 1–16. https://doi.org/10.15585/mmwr.ss6609a1

Tierney, R. T., Sitler, M. R., Swanik, C. B., Swanik, K. A., Higgins, M., & Torg, J. (2005). Gender differences in head-neck segment dynamic stabilization during head acceleration. *Medicine and Science in Sports and Exercise*, 37(2), 272–279. https://doi.org/10.1249/01.mss.0000152734.47516.aa

Toglia, J., & Golisz, K. (2017). Traumatic brain injury (TBI) and the impact on daily life. In N. D. Chiaravalloti & Y. Goverover (Eds.), *Changes in the brain: Impact on daily life* (pp. 117–143). Springer-Verlag Publishing. http://dx.doi.org/10.1007/978-0-387-98188-8_6

Toor, G. K., Harris, J. E., Escobar, M., Yoshida, K., Velikonja, D., Rizoli, S., ... Colantonio, A. (2016). Long-term health service outcomes among women with traumatic brain injury. *Archives of Physical Medicine and Rehabilitation*, 97(2 Suppl), S54–S63. https://doi.org/10.1016/j.apmr.2015.02.010

Trexler, L. E., Parrott, D. R., & Malec, J. F. (2016). Replication of a prospective randomized controlled trial of resource facilitation to improve return to work and school after brain injury. *Archives of Physical Medicine and Rehabilitation*, 97(2), 204–210. https://doi.org/10.1016/j.apmr.2015.09.016

van Dongen, C. H., Goossens, P. H., van Zee, I. E., Verpoort, K. N., Vliet Vlieland, T., & van Velzen, J. M. (2018). Short-term and long-term outcomes of a vocational rehabilitation program for patients with acquired brain injury in the Netherlands. *Journal of Occupational Rehabilitation*, 28(3), 523–530. https://doi.org/10.1007/s10926-017-9738-6

van Velzen, J. M., van Bennekom, C. V., Edelaar, M. J., Sluiter, J. K., & Frings-Dresen, M. H. (2009). How many people return to work after acquired brain injury: A systematic review. *Brain Injury*, 23(6) 473–488, https://doi.org/10.1080/02699050902970737

van Vollenhoven, R. F. (2009). Treatment of rheumatoid arthritis: State of the art 2009. *Nature Reviews Rheumatology*, 5(10), 531–541. https://doi.org/10.1038/nrrheum.2009.182

Wagner, A. K., Brett, C. A., McCullough, E. H., Niyonkuru, C., Loucks, T. L., Dixon, C. E., ... Berga, S. L. (2012). Persistent hypogonadism influences estradiol synthesis, cognition and outcome in males after severe TBI. *Brain Injury*, 26(10), 1226–1242. https://doi.org/10.3109/02699052.2012.667594

Whelan-Goodinson, R., Ponsford, J., Johnston, L., & Grant, F. (2009). Psychiatric disorders following traumatic brain injury: Their nature and frequency. *The Journal of Head Trauma Rehabilitation*, 24(5), 324–332. https://doi.org/10.1097/HTR.0b013e3181a712aa

Wilkinson, C. W., Pagulayan, K. F., Petrie, E. C., Mayer, C. L., Colasurdo, E. A., Shofer, J. B., ... Peskind, E. R. (2012). High prevalence of chronic pituitary and target-organ hormone abnormalities after blast-related mild traumatic brain injury. *Frontiers in Neurology*, 3, 11. https://doi.org/10.3389/fneur.2012.00011

Williams, G., Morris, M. E., Schache, A., & McCrory, P. R. (2009). Incidence of gait abnormalities after traumatic brain injury. *Archives of Physical Medicine and Rehabilitation*, 90(4), 587–593. https://doi.org/10.1016/j.apmr.2008.10.013

Williams, W. H., Chitsabesan, P., Fazel, S., McMillan, T., Hughes, N., Parsonage, M., & Tonks, J. (2018). Traumatic brain injury: Z potential cause of violent crime? *Lancet Psychiatry*, 5(10), 836–844. https://doi.org/10.1016/S2215-0366(18)30062-2

Wunderle, K., Hoeger, K. M., Wasserman, E., & Bazarian, J. J. (2014). Menstrual phase as predictor of outcome after mild traumatic brain injury in women. *The Journal of Head Trauma Rehabilitation*, 29(5), E1–E8. https://doi.org/10.1097/HTR.0000000000000006

Yang, W., Chen, P., Wang, T., Kuo, T. Y., Cheng, C. Y., & Yang, Y. H. (2016). Endocrine dysfunction following traumatic brain injury: a 5-year follow-up nationwide-based study. *Scientific Reports*, 6 (32987) (2016). https://doi.org/10.1038/srep32987

Zemek, R., Barrowman, N., Freedman, S. B., Gravel, J., Gagnon, I., McGahern, C., ... Pediatric Emergency Research Canada (PERC) Concussion Team. (2016). Clinical risk score for persistent postconcussion symptoms among children with acute concussion in the ED. *JAMA*, 315(10), 1014–1025. https://doi.org/10.1001/jama.2016.1203

Suggested Readings

Colantonio, A., Harris, J. E., Ratcliff, G., Chase, S., & Ellis, K. (2010). Gender differences in self reported long term outcomes following moderate to severe traumatic brain injury. *BMC Neurology, 10*, 102. https://doi.org/10.1186/1471-2377-10-102

Colantonio, A., Ratcliff, G., Chase, S., & Vernich, L. (2004). Aging with traumatic brain injury: Long term health conditions. *International Journal of Rehabilitation Research, 27*(3), 209–214. https://doi.org/10.1097/00004356-200409000-00006

Mollayeva, T., Hurst, M., Escobar, M., & Colantonio, A. (2019). Sex-specific incident dementia in patients with central nervous system trauma. *Alzheimer's & Dementia, 11*, 355–367. https://doi.org/10.1016/j.dadm.2019.03.003

Mollayeva, T., Mollayeva, S., & Colantonio, A. (2018). Traumatic brain injury: Sex, gender and intersecting vulnerabilities. *Nature Reviews. Neurology, 14*(12), 711–722. https://doi.org/10.1038/s41582-018-0091-y

12
AGEING WITH MULTIPLE SCLEROSIS

Marcia Finlayson, Michelle Ploughman, Julie Pétrin, and Roshanth Rajachandrakumar

Introduction

Multiple Sclerosis (MS) is a chronic, degenerative disease of the central nervous system (CNS). Although typically diagnosed between the ages of 20 and 40, the literature includes case studies and reviews that report diagnosis before age 6 (Yeh et al., 2009) and over age 80 (Abe, Tsuchiya, Kurosa, Nakai, & Shinomiya, 2000). People diagnosed after 50 years of age are referred to as having late-onset MS. Overall, older adults with MS (65+) represent between 3% and 12% of the total MS population (Polliack, Barak, & Achiron, 2001), which is estimated to be 2.3 million people worldwide (Multiple Sclerosis International Federation, 2013). MS prevalence rates range from less than 5 cases per 100,000 people in parts of Asia, South America, and Africa to over 290 cases per 100,000 people in parts of Canada (Multiple Sclerosis International Federation, 2013).

The diagnostic age range of MS together with prevalence data suggest that there may be as many as 350,000 people with MS aged 65 and older worldwide (Awad & Stuve, 2010). While these numbers seem relatively small, the general and disability-specific trends towards increasing life expectancy suggest that the numbers will increase over time. Over the past two decades, there has been a shift in peak prevalence of MS towards older ages (Kingwell et al., 2015). As a result, greater attention to the experiences and needs of people ageing with MS is required to inform policy and practice and maximise the likelihood they will have a healthy and meaningful old age.

The purpose of this chapter is to highlight existing research findings on these issues. The specific objectives of the chapter are to:

- Provide a brief overview of MS to contextualize the remainder of the chapter
- Highlight the experiences and challenges of people ageing with MS
- Describe the supports and strategies used by people ageing with MS to facilitate ageing-in-place, and
- Propose that greater attention to preventive care and lifestyle factors may enable people to age well with MS

Brief Overview of MS

Despite years of research, the cause of MS remains unclear. Nevertheless, epidemiological evidence points to a complex interaction of genetic and environmental factors (Belbasis, Bellou, Evangelou, Ioannidis, & Tzoulaki, 2015; Leray, Moreau, Fromont, & Edan, 2016). Smoking, obesity, low vitamin

D, and exposure to the Epstein Barr virus all contribute to increased MS risk (Thompson, Baranzini, Geurts, Hemmer, & Ciccarelli, 2018).

There are three main types of MS (relapsing-remitting, primary progressive, secondary progressive). Across all types, the disease leads to inflammation, demyelination, and axonal loss. A critical threshold of axonal loss must occur before disability is apparent, which means that much of the disease may be clinically silent (Bjartmar & Trapp, 2003; Trapp, Ransohoff, Fisher, & Rudick, 1999). Axonal loss is widely accepted as the most responsible factor leading to disease progression and irreversible disability (Álvarez-Cermeño, Costa-Frossard, & Villar, 2010), which is typically defined as the point when the individual needs an aid to walk about 100 metres, with or without resting.

There are several recognised factors contributing to accelerated MS progression; some modifiable and some not. Non-modifiable factors include being male and being diagnosed after age 50 (Guillemin et al., 2017). Modifiable factors include smoking, cardiovascular comorbidities, and low levels of vitamin D (Coetzee & Thompson, 2017; Hempel et al., 2017a; Ramachandran et al., 2013). Whether intervening to treat or manage these factors alter the disease course is not clear (Hempel et al., 2017b; Marrie et al., 2010; McKay et al., 2018).

Across all types of MS, common symptoms include loss of balance and mobility, extreme fatigue, muscle weakness, pain, depression, cognitive changes, visual disturbances, and changes in bladder and bowel function. Many of these symptoms are also similar to normal-age related changes (Stern, Sorkin, Milton, & Sperber, 2010), which may partially explain the growing evidence that accumulation of disability in MS is age-accelerated and age-dependent (Confavreux & Vukusic, 2006a, Confavreux & Vukusic, 2006b). Supporting this evidence are data showing that the proportion of people aged 65 and over with MS report significantly greater levels of symptomatology related to mobility, bladder function, cognitive changes, and mental health compared to their younger MS peers (Minden, Frankel, Hadden, Srinath, & Perloff, 2004). The reduction in life expectancy for people with MS is estimated to be between 6 and 10 years, depending on sex, type of MS, level of disability, and presence of comorbidities and other complications (Kingwell et al., 2012; Leray et al., 2015; Manouchehrinia, Tanasescu, Tench, & Constantinescu, 2016). Together, disease progression and symptomatology contribute to the experiences and challenges that people ageing with MS have shared with researchers over the past 20 years.

Experiences and Challenges of Ageing with MS

Remaining autonomous and living in one's own home are common desires for people as they grow older. People ageing with MS are no different. Yet, the combination of normal age-related changes, accumulated neurological impairments, and related disability can make the experience of ageing with MS challenging and elicit fear of the future (Finlayson, 2004). Qualitative and observational studies have uncovered three broad factors that contribute to these fears and challenge the ability of people ageing with MS to maintain their autonomy and ability to age-in-place.

Mobility and Falls

The day-to-day variability of MS symptoms influences all aspects of mobility for people ageing with MS, both inside the home and in the broader community. Older adults with MS express concerns over on-going functional losses, particularly related to mobility (Finlayson, 2004; Finlayson & Van Denend, 2003; Ploughman, Deshpande, Latimer-Cheung, & Finlayson, 2014). Their concerns are supported by data showing that people aged 65 years and older with MS need significantly more help than those under 65 years of age for basic activities-of-daily-living such as bathing (58% versus 36%), dressing (35% versus 21%), toileting (48% versus 26%), and indoor mobility (67% versus 38%) (Minden, Frankel, Hadden, Srinath, & Perloff, 2004).

As mobility impairments accumulate, the prevalence of mobility device use and falls among people ageing with MS increases. In those aged 55+, only 13.6% report using no form of mobility device while 58.6% report owning and using multiple devices (e.g., cane, walker, wheelchair) (Finlayson, Peterson, & Asano, 2014). The choices about whether and which mobility device to use are linked to the variability of symptoms, the demands of the physical environment, the availability of social supports, and personal factors such as perceived stigma (Finlayson & Van Denend, 2003). Yet, research suggests that using a variety of different devices increases the likelihood of experiencing a fall among people ageing with MS, perhaps because use of different devices limits skill development with any particular device (Finlayson, Peterson, & Asano, 2014). People with MS themselves attribute falls to a complex interaction of factors, including activity demands, environmental factors (including the use of mobility devices), and symptomology (Carling, Forsberg, & Nilsagård, 2018; Peterson, Ben Ari, Asano, & Finlayson, 2013).

Falls are a serious problem for people with MS in general, but particularly older adults with MS. Among those aged 45+, 50% of people with MS have experienced a fall in the past year (Finlayson, Peterson, & Cho, 2006) and among those who fall, half of those experience an injury that requires medical attention (Peterson, Cho, von Koch, & Finlayson, 2008). Given that risk of falls among people with MS increases with age (Sosnoff et al., 2011) and those aged 55–64 are particularly vulnerable (Matsuda, Verrall, Finlayson, Molton, & Jensen, 2015), it is not surprising that middle aged and older adults with MS report fear of falling and curtailing activities as a result (Comber et al., 2017; Peterson, Cho, & Finlayson, 2007). Even among those who primarily use a wheelchair for mobility, falls, fear of falling, and activity curtailment due to fear of falling are reported at relatively high rates (Rice, Kalron, Berkowitz, Backus, & Sosnoff, 2017). For family caregivers, the falls experienced by people with MS contribute to their own activity curtailment and need to be constantly on-guard (Carling, Nilsagård, & Forsberg, 2018).

Need for Assistance

The impact of falls on caregivers is just one example of the way in which MS can contribute to the need for assistance for people ageing with this disease. Need for assistance, and specifically concern about becoming a burden on caregivers, contributes to fears about the future among people ageing with MS (Finlayson, 2004).

Caregivers of people with MS aged 45 years and older include spouses, children, other relatives, friends, and neighbours (Finlayson & Cho, 2008). Given that MS is more common among women, and spousal caregivers represent the largest proportion of caregivers, it is not surprising that many MS caregivers are men. The most common tasks performed by caregivers of people ageing with MS include meal preparation, transportation, assistance with indoor mobility, getting dressed, and coordinating medical appointments. The most challenging tasks are assisting with bowel management, indoor mobility, and transfers in and out of the bed (Finlayson & Cho, 2008).

There is evidence that over half of MS caregivers spend greater than 20 hours per week doing caregiving tasks (Buchanan & Huang, 2012; Finlayson & Cho, 2008) and as many as 70% of them find caregiving emotionally draining (Buchanan & Huang, 2012). Despite this, caregiving for someone with MS can also provide a sense of accomplishment, particularly when the care recipient is older and caregiving has been of longer duration (Buchanan & Huang, 2012). Among spousal caregivers, caregiving has been found to provide an opportunity for personal development, an appreciation of day-to-day life, and reinforce a sense of commitment to one's partner (Appleton, Robertson, Mitchell, & Lesley, 2018). Yet, MS caregivers often worry that their efforts will be inadequate to avoid nursing home entry for the person with MS (Boeije, Duijnstee, & Grypdonck, 2003) and this worry is shared by people with MS themselves (Finlayson, 2004).

Worries about Institutionalisation

If informal caregivers are unable to provide adequate assistance in the home, and if home care services are unavailable, inadequate or unaffordable, nursing home entry may be the only option for some people with MS, regardless of age (Ogg, 2011). Older adults with MS express significant concern about this possibility, believing that nursing home entry would result in a complete loss of autonomy, separation from family, social isolation and loneliness, boredom, and financial burden (Finlayson, 2004).

Research shows that these beliefs are well-grounded given that people with MS are disproportionally represented in continuing care hospitals and nursing homes (Turcotte, Marrie, Patten, & Hirdes, 2017). They are also younger and more likely to be female compared to other service-recipients (Turcotte, Marrie, Patten, & Hirdes, 2017). Typical nursing home residents are older, more cognitively impaired, less likely to still be married, and less physically disabled compared to residents with MS (Buchanan, Wang, & Ju, 2002). While 74% of typical nursing home residents are over age 71, only about 20% of residents with MS fall into this age group (Buchanan, Wang, & Ju, 2002). Over 65% of residents with MS have intact or near-intact cognitive status compared to only 43% of typical residents (Buchanan, Wang, & Ju, 2002). Not surprisingly perhaps, over half of nursing home residents with MS are legally responsible for themselves, rather than having a guardian of some type (Buchanan, Wang, Huang, & Graber, 2001).

Perhaps because of the sociodemographic differences between themselves and other nursing home residents, those with MS have relatively low levels of engagement in activities within the residence, and report a strong preference for engaging in activities in their own room or outside of the facility (Buchanan, Wang, Huang, & Graber, 2001). This may contribute to the higher rates of depression and feelings of social isolation seen among people with MS living in nursing homes (Buchanan, Wang, & Ju, 2002). Ultimately, the typical nursing home is not a good socio-environmental fit for most people with MS who need this level of support and care. Their desire to find ways to age-in-place and maintain their quality of life in their own home is strong (Ploughman, Austin, Murdoch, Kearney, Fisk, et al., 2012; Ploughman, Austin, Murdoch, Kearney, Godwin, et al., 2012).

Supports and Strategies for Ageing-in-place

People ageing with MS report mobilising a range of supports and strategies to increase their success at ageing-in-place, including (a) accessing tangible supports (including specialised healthcare providers), (b) maintaining purpose, participation, and quality of life, and (c) actively engaging in health promoting behaviours.

Tangible Supports

Older adults with MS have identified transportation, accessible housing, professional home care, social well-being programs, pharmaceutical services, nutrition programs, and physical wellness/exercise programs as the most important services they needed to maintain their health and well-being in the community (Finlayson, Van Denend, & Shevil, 2004). They also describe the importance of access to assistive technology and a variety of health care professionals as key to their ability to maintain independent living (Putnam & Tang, 2007).

Timely access to health professionals who provide a supportive and understanding environment enables people ageing with MS to meet their MS management needs (Ploughman, Austin, Murdoch, Kearney, Fisk, et al., 2012; Ploughman, Austin, Murdoch, Kearney, Godwin, et al., 2012). In particular, bidirectional communication, dedicated attention and collaborative relationships with healthcare providers who have expert knowledge of MS are valued by people ageing with MS as they try to age-in-place (Finlayson, Van Denend, & Shevil, 2004; Ploughman, Austin, Murdoch, Kearney, Fisk, et al., 2012; Ploughman, Austin, Murdoch, Kearney, Godwin, et al., 2012). While knowledgeable and caring providers may help ameliorate MS symptoms, and prevent their worsening, it appears that people with MS receive fewer specialist consultations as they age. Visits to neurologists decrease as people with MS grow older (Minden et al., 2008). In addition, the availability and provision of physical and occupational therapy services is an area of significant unmet need for people ageing with MS (Finlayson, Garcia, & Cho, 2008; Finlayson et al., 2010; Lonergan et al., 2015), as are the services of a social worker or psychologist (Garcia & Finlayson, 2009; Turcotte, Marrie, Patten, & Hirdes, 2017). Needs for specialised providers are particularly high outside of urban areas and when people want to access therapies in order to maintain health and functioning rather than simply address a recent deterioration (Finlayson et al., 2010).

Using home care is relatively common among older adults with MS (Minden, Frankel, Hadden, Srinath, & Perloff, 2004). Home care supports, particularly the relationship between the provider and recipient, has been reported as a key factor contributing to ageing-in-place for older adults with MS (Wallack, Wiseman, & Ploughman, 2016). This may be because use of home care enables regular monitoring of comorbidities, which is a concern of people with MS (Ploughman, Austin, Murdoch, Kearney, Fisk, et al., 2012; Ploughman, Austin, Murdoch, Kearney, Godwin, et al., 2012). High use of ambulatory physician services is associated with 40–60% lower risk of nursing home entry among people with MS (Finlayson, Ekuma, Finlayson, Jiang, and Marrie, 2019). Effective management of comorbidities supports ageing-in-place (Sanai et al., 2016) and, in particular, management of mental health comorbidities is a key determinant of self-perceived health among older people with MS (Ploughman et al., 2017). Unfortunately, people ageing with MS report low satisfaction with the availability of counselling and psychological assistance (McCabe, Ebacioni, Simmons, McDonald, & Melton, 2015).

Many of the tangible supports that enable people with MS to age-in-place can require substantial out-of-pocket expenses (Ploughman, Austin, Murdoch, Kearney, Fisk, et al., 2012; Ploughman, Austin, Murdoch, Kearney, Godwin, et al., 2012). Therefore, it is not surprising that having supplementary health insurance that covers the costs of these services is important to people ageing with MS (Putnam & Tang, 2007). Unfortunately, 75% of older adults with MS report that they stopped working or retired early due to their disease, which may explain why 22% of them describe not having enough money to meet their needs (Ploughman et al., 2017). The importance of financial flexibility to health-related quality of life among people ageing with MS is, therefore, not surprising (Cichy, Bishop, Roessler, Li, & Rumrill, 2016; Ploughman et al., 2017). Whether or not people ageing with MS receive counselling or advice from qualified individuals in order to make appropriate financial plans for ageing-in-place is unknown.

Overall, research findings point to the critical role of tangible supports, which includes a wide range of health and community services, for enabling people with MS to age-in-place. Which services are most essential to address healthy ageing, MS management, and concomitant age-related comorbidities is unknown. Current findings point to team-based primary prevention in order to preempt unnecessary complications and hospitalisations and maintain quality of life while ageing-in-place.

Maintaining Purpose, Participation, and Quality of Life

Ageing-in-place well not only requires staying in one's home but also to the maintenance of optimal quality of life as one ages. Several groups worldwide have examined factors predictive of successful ageing with MS. Consistent findings show that lower levels of neurological impairment or disability predict higher ratings of health-related quality of life among older people with MS (Buhse, Banker, & Clement, 2014; Ploughman et al., 2017; Zhang, Becker, Stuifbergen, & Brown, 2017).

It could be argued that some aspects of MS-related and age-related disability are not modifiable and therefore people with MS, caregivers and healthcare providers should focus their efforts on aspects of living with MS that are modifiable. For example, when older people with MS who live at home are asked to describe what factors contribute to 'healthy ageing' from their own point of view, they most often attribute their quality of life to maintenance of social connections, positive attitude and healthy lifestyle habits (Wallack, Wiseman, & Ploughman, 2016). Three aspects of social connections have been found to be particularly important to the well-being of people ageing with MS: reciprocal relationships with family and friends, social engagement, and a strong support provider network (Wallack, Wiseman, & Ploughman, 2016). Maintaining one's purpose and participating in valued activities and life roles are also important for ageing well with MS (Wallack, Wiseman, & Ploughman, 2016; Zhang, Becker, Stuifbergen, & Brown, 2017). Among older women with MS, participation in household activities is predictive of better perceived health, even more so than level of disability (Ploughman et al., 2017). Both social connectedness and participating in valued activities can be considered modifiable aspects of ageing with MS, and directly impact health-related quality of life. Such activities are therefore important targets of wellness interventions.

Quality of life of people ageing with MS is also influenced by psychological health, particularly depressive symptoms (Ploughman et al., 2017; Zhang, Becker, Stuifbergen, & Brown, 2017) and feelings of stress (Cichy, Bishop, Roessler, Li, & Rumrill, 2016), both of which are treatable. Resilience, which is the capacity to overcome stressors or adversity, is considered important in ageing with a neurodegenerative and uncertain disease like MS (Ploughman, Austin, Murdoch, Kearney, Fisk, et al., 2012; Ploughman, Austin, Murdoch, Kearney, Godwin, et al., 2012). Evidence suggests that becoming a competent self-manager and building resilience takes about 10 years of experience living with MS. In addition to experience, it is possible to build resilience through active intervention, and doing so improves satisfaction with life roles (Alschuler, Arewasikporn, Nelson, Molton, & Ehde, 2018). Overall, research to date suggests that people ageing with MS can improve their quality of life, and addressing modifiable factors such as depression, stress and resilience may be a good place to start.

Actively Engaging in Health Promoting Behaviours

Research suggests that promoting wellness is one of the top three priorities endorsed by older people with MS (Wallack, Wiseman, & Ploughman, 2016). Although specific wellness strategies adopted by persons ageing with MS are highly individualised, the four most frequently reported ones include: attention to a healthy diet, participating in exercise, ensuring adequate sleep, and maintaining hobbies. About 54% of older people with MS living at home report participating in moderate to vigorous exercise (Ploughman et al., 2015). In fact, despite being more disabled, older people with MS who remain at home exercise more and engage in healthier lifestyle behaviours to a greater extent than their age-matched peers (Ploughman, Beaulieu, et al., 2014; Ploughman et al., 2015). Level of disability is a strong predictor of exercise participation among people ageing with MS, with those who are ambulatory being 1.9 times more likely to participate in moderate to vigorous exercise than those who are non-ambulatory. Higher levels of perseverance, less fatigue, fewer years with MS and fewer cardiovascular comorbidities are also predictors of exercise participation, while age, sex, level of social support, and financial resources are not (Ploughman et al., 2015). There is evidence though that health promotion and wellness programs are difficult for people ageing with MS to access, and many do not know what services are available to them (Plow, Cho, & Finlayson, 2010). Overall, research supports the need to develop, implement and evaluate wellness programs for people ageing with MS, particularly those who are more disabled and have a more progressive form of the disease.

Conclusion

Prior to the mid-1990s, the process of MS diagnosis was prolonged and treatment options were limited. In more recent years, the use of magnetic resonance imaging has reduced the time to diagnosis. The development of disease-modifying pharmaceutical agents has provided many new options for treatment. As MS diagnosis and treatments continue to advance, future cohorts of older adults with this disease may have significantly different experiences and needs than older adults with MS today, and in the past. Exactly how things will change is unknown, but we can speculate that the future older adults with MS may have a more stable disease course and experience more compressed periods of significant disability much later in life (University of California, San Francisco MS-EPIC Team, et al., 2016).

Based on what we currently know, there is a strong need for continued research on the issue of ageing with MS. The existing literature has enabled us to robustly describe the needs of older adults with MS and we have good evidence about the risk factors for several important adverse outcomes such as falls, institutionalisation, and disability. The challenge is that we have few evidence-based interventions to address these needs. Current knowledge suggests that research and clinical interventions should focus on strategies, services and supports that will permit people with MS to successfully age-in-place. Although there is growing evidence about the benefits of healthy lifestyle habits and rehabilitation in MS in general, these trials have typically excluded people over the age of 65, people with significant disability, and/or people with comorbidities. We need to expand the eligibility of these trials as well as the range of interventions being tested. Preventative approaches need to be tested, with long-term follow-ups to determine their effectiveness for outcomes that matter to people ageing with MS and those who care for them. Future research also needs to comprehensively assess the benefits of system-level interventions such as different models of service delivery, including primary care management, interdisciplinary team-based care, and broader community based services that go beyond the health care system to address issues such as housing and income support. Economic evaluations of these different interventions are needed to determine benefits beyond the individual, to the broader society.

While researchers continue to build evidence to inform best practices in support of people ageing with MS, we must continue to advocate for options for care so they are available when needed. The consolidated evidence indicates that the supports currently provided to older people with MS are limited, are less available in rural areas, and often cost more than people ageing with MS can afford. The time is now to address these pressing issues so that people ageing with MS can do so well, in their own homes and communities.

References

Abe, M., Tsuchiya, K., Kurosa, Y., Nakai, O., & Shinomiya, K. (2000). Multiple sclerosis with very late onset: A report of a case with onset at age 82 years and review of the literature. *Journal of Spinal Disorders*, *13*(6), 545–549. https://doi.org/10.1097/00002517-200012000-00017

Alschuler, K. N., Arewasikporn, A., Nelson, I. K., Molton, I. R., & Ehde, D. M. (2018). Promoting resilience in individuals aging with multiple sclerosis: Results from a pilot randomized controlled trial. *Rehabilitation Psychology*, *63*(3), 338–348. https://doi.org/10.1037/rep0000223

Álvarez-Cermeño, J. C., Costa-Frossard, L., & Villar, L. M. (2010). Importance of age at diagnosis in multiple sclerosis. *Expert Review of Neurotherapeutics*, *10*(3), 341–342. https://doi.org/10.1586/ern.10.10

Appleton, D., Robertson, N., Mitchell, L., & Lesley, R. (2018). Our disease: A qualitative meta-synthesis of the experiences of spousal/partner caregivers of people with multiple sclerosis. *Scandinavian Journal of Caring Sciences*, *32*(4), 1262–1278. https://doi.org/10.1111/scs.12601

Awad, A., & Stuve, O. (2010). Multiple sclerosis in the elderly patient. *Drugs & Aging*, *27*(4), 283–294. https://doi.org/10.2165/11532120-000000000-00000

Belbasis, L., Bellou, V., Evangelou, E., Ioannidis, J. P. A., & Tzoulaki, I. (2015). Environmental risk factors and multiple sclerosis: An umbrella review of systematic reviews and meta-analyses. *The Lancet Neurology*, *14*(3), 263–273. https://doi.org/10.1016/S1474-4422(14)70267-4

Bjartmar, C., & Trapp, B. D. (2003). Axonal degeneration and progressive neurologic disability in multiple sclerosis. *Neurotoxicity Research*, *5*(1), 157–164. https://doi.org/10.1007/BF03033380

Boeije, H. R., Duijnstee, M. S. H., & Grypdonck, M. H. F. (2003). Continuation of caregiving among partners who give total care to spouses with multiple sclerosis. *Health & Social Care in the Community*, *11*(3), 242–252. https://doi.org/10.1046/j.1365-2524.2003.00422.x

Buchanan, R. J., & Huang, C. (2012). Caregiver perceptions of accomplishment from assisting people with multiple sclerosis. *Disability and Rehabilitation*, *34*(1), 53–61. https://doi.org/10.3109/09638288.2011.587091

Buchanan, R., Wang, S., Huang, C., & Graber, D. (2001). Profiles of nursing home residents with multiple sclerosis using the minimum data set. *Multiple Sclerosis*, *7*(3), 189–200. https://doi.org/10.1177/135245850100700310

Buchanan, R., Wang, S., & Ju, H. (2002). Analyses of the minimum data set: Comparisons of nursing home residents with multiple sclerosis to other nursing home residents. *Multiple Sclerosis*, *8*(6), 512–522. https://doi.org/10.1191/1352458502ms823oa

Buhse, M., Banker, W. M., & Clement, L. M. (2014). Factors associated with health-related quality of life among older people with multiple sclerosis. *International Journal of MS Care, 16*(1), 10–19. https://doi.org/10.7224/1537-2073.2012-046

Carling, A., Forsberg, A., & Nilsagård, Y. (2018). Falls in people with multiple sclerosis: Experiences of 115 fall situations. *Clinical Rehabilitation, 32*(4), 526–535. https://doi.org/10.1177/0269215517730597

Carling, A., Nilsagård, Y., & Forsberg, A. (2018). Making it work: Experience of living with a person who falls due to multiple sclerosis. *Disability and Rehabilitation*, 1–8. https://doi.org/10.1080/09638288.2018.1514078

Cichy, K. E., Bishop, M., Roessler, R. T., Li, J., & Rumrill, P. D. Jr. (2016). Non-vocational health-related correlates of quality of life for older adults living with multiple sclerosis. *Journal of Rehabilitation, 82*(3).

Coetzee, T., & Thompson, A. (2017). When are we going to take modifiable risk factors more seriously in multiple sclerosis? *Multiple Sclerosis Journal, 23*(4), 494–495. https://doi.org/10.1177/1352458517694433

Comber, L., Coote, S., Finlayson, M., Galvin, R., Quinn, G., & Peterson, E. (2017). An exploration of fall-related, psychosocial variables in people with multiple sclerosis who have fallen. *British Journal of Occupational Therapy, 80*(10), 587–595. https//doi.org/10.1177/0308022617725492

Confavreux, C., & Vukusic, S. (2006a). Age at disability milestones in multiple sclerosis. *Brain: A Journal of Neurology, 129*(Pt 3), 595–605. https://doi.org/10.1093/brain/awh714

Confavreux, C., & Vukusic, S. (2006b). Natural history of multiple sclerosis: A unifying concept. *Brain: A Journal of Neurology, 129*(Pt 3), 606–616. https://doi.org/10.1093/brain/awl007

Finlayson, M. (2004). Concerns about the future among older adults with multiple sclerosis. *American Journal of Occupational Therapy, 58*(1), 54–63. https://doi.org/10.5014/ajot.58.1.54

Finlayson, M., & Cho, C. (2008). A descriptive profile of caregivers of older adults with MS and the assistance they provide. *Disability & Rehabilitation, 30*(24), 1848–1857. https://doi.org/10.1080/09638280701707324

Finlayson, M., Ekuma, O., Finlayson, G., Jiang, D., & Marrie, R. A. (2019). Ten-year trajectories of health care utilization by manitobans with MS predict nursing home entry. *Neurology. Clinical Practice, 9*(1), 16–23. https://doi.org/10.1212/CPJ.0000000000000553

Finlayson, M., Garcia, J. D., & Cho, C. (2008). Occupational therapy service use among people aging with multiple sclerosis. *American Journal of Occupational Therapy, 62*(3), 320–328. https://doi.org/10.5014/ajot.62.3.320

Finlayson, M. L., Peterson, E. W., & Asano, M. (2014). A cross-sectional study examining multiple mobility device use and fall status among middle-aged and older adults with multiple sclerosis. *Disability and Rehabilitation: Assistive Technology, 9*(1), 12–16. https://doi.org/10.3109/17483107.2013.782578

Finlayson, M. L., Peterson, E. W., & Cho, C. C. (2006). Risk factors for falling among people aged 45 to 90 years with multiple sclerosis. *Archives of Physical Medicine and Rehabilitation, 87*(9), 1274–1279. https://doi.org/10.1016/j.apmr.2006.06.002

Finlayson, M., Plow, M., & Cho, C. (2010). Use of physical therapy services among middle-aged and older adults with multiple sclerosis. *Physical Therapy, 90*(11), 1607–1618. https://doi.org/10.2522/ptj.20100072

Finlayson, M., & Van Denend, T. (2003). Experiencing the loss of mobility: Perspectives of older adults with MS. *Disability & Rehabilitation, 25*(20), 1168–1180. https://doi.org/10.1080/09638280310001596180

Finlayson, M., Van Denend, T., & Shevil, E. (2004). Multiple perspectives on the health service need, use, and variability among older adults with multiple sclerosis. *Occupational Therapy in Health Care, 17*(3–4), 5–25. https://doi.org/10.1080/J003v17n03_02

Garcia, J., & Finlayson, M. (2009). Mental health and mental health service use among people aged 45+ with multiple sclerosis. *Canadian Journal of Community Mental Health/Revue Canadienne de Sante Mentale Communautaire, 24*(2), 9–22. https://doi.org/10.7870/cjcmh-2005-0011

Guillemin, F., Baumann, C., Epstein, J., Kerschen, P., Garot, T., Mathey, G., Debouverie, M., & LORSEP Group (2017). Older Age at Multiple Sclerosis Onset Is an Independent Factor of Poor Prognosis: A Population-Based Cohort Study. *Neuroepidemiology, 48*(3-4), 179–187. https://doi.org/10.1159/000479516

Hempel, S., Graham, G. D., Fu, N., Estrada, E., Chen, A. Y., Miake-Lye, I., ... Wallin, M. T. (2017a). A systematic review of modifiable risk factors in the progression of multiple sclerosis. *Multiple Sclerosis, 23*(4), 525–533. https://doi.org/10.1177/1352458517690270

Hempel, S., Graham, G. D., Fu, N., Estrada, E., Chen, A. Y., Miake-Lye, I., ... Wallin, M. T. (2017b). A systematic review of the effects of modifiable risk factor interventions on the progression of multiple sclerosis. *Multiple Sclerosis, 23*(4), 513–524. https://doi.org/10.1177/1352458517690271

Kingwell, E., van der Kop, M., Zhao, Y., Shirani, A., Zhu, F., Oger, J., & Tremlett, H. (2012). Relative mortality and survival in multiple sclerosis: Findings from British Columbia, Canada. *Journal of Neurology, Neurosurgery, and Psychiatry, 83*(1), 61–66. https://doi.org/10.1136/jnnp-2011-300616

Kingwell, E., Zhu, F., Marrie, R. A., Fisk, J. D., Wolfson, C., Warren, S., ... Tremlett, H. (2015). High incidence and increasing prevalence of multiple sclerosis in British Columbia, Canada: Findings from over two decades (1991–2010). *Journal of Neurology, 262*(10), 2352–2363. https://doi.org/10.1007/s00415-015-7842-0

Leray, E., Moreau, T., Fromont, A., & Edan, G. (2016). Epidemiology of multiple sclerosis. *Revue Neurologique*, *172*(1), 3–13. https://doi.org/10.1016/j.neurol.2015.10.006

Leray, E., Vukusic, S., Debouverie, M., Clanet, M., Brochet, B., de Sèze, J., … Edan, G. (2015). Excess mortality in patients with multiple sclerosis starts at 20 years from clinical onset: Data from a large-scale French observational study. *PLoS ONE*, *10*(7), e0132033. https://doi.org/10.1371/journal.pone.0132033

Lonergan, R., Kinsella, K., Fitzpatrick, P., Duggan, M., Jordan, S., Bradley, D., … Tubridy, N. (2015). Unmet needs of multiple sclerosis patients in the community. *Multiple Sclerosis and Related Disorders*, *4*(2), 144–150. https://doi.org/10.1016/j.msard.2015.01.003

Manouchehrinia, A., Tanasescu, R., Tench, C. R., & Constantinescu, C. S. (2016). Mortality in multiple sclerosis: Meta-analysis of standardised mortality ratios. *Journal of Neurology, Neurosurgery, and Psychiatry*, *87*(3), 324–331. https://doi.org/10.1136/jnnp-2015-310361

Marrie, R. A., Rudick, R., Horwitz, R., Cutter, G., Tyry, T., Campagnolo, D., & Vollmer, T. (2010). Vascular comorbidity is associated with more rapid disability progression in multiple sclerosis. *Neurology*, *74*(13), 1041–1047. https://doi.org/10.1212/WNL.0b013e3181d6b125

Matsuda, P. N., Verrall, A. M., Finlayson, M. L., Molton, I. R., & Jensen, M. P. (2015). Falls among adults aging with disability. *Archives of Physical Medicine and Rehabilitation*, *96*(3), 464–471. https://doi.org/https://doi.org/10.1016/j.apmr.2014.09.034

McCabe, M. P., Ebacioni, K. J., Simmons, R., McDonald, E., & Melton, L. (2015). Unmet education, psychological and peer support needs of people with multiple sclerosis. *Journal of Psychosomatic Research*, *78*(1), 82–87. https://doi.org/10.1016/j.jpsychores.2014.05.010

McKay, K. A., Tremlett, H., Fisk, J. D., Zhang, T., Patten, S. B., Kastrukoff, L., … Marrie, R. A., & CIHR Team in the Epidemiology and Impact of Comorbidity on Multiple Sclerosis. (2018). Psychiatric comorbidity is associated with disability progression in multiple sclerosis. *Neurology*, *90*(15), e1316–e1323. https://doi.org/10.1212/WNL.0000000000005302

Minden, S. L., Frankel, D., Hadden, L. S., Srinath, K. P., & Perloff, J. N. (2004). Disability in elderly people with multiple sclerosis: An analysis of baseline data from the Sonya Slifka longitudinal multiple sclerosis study. *NeuroRehabilitation*, *19*(1), 55–67. https://doi.org/10.3233/NRE-2004-19107

Minden, S. L., Hoaglin, D. C., Hadden, L., Frankel, D., Robbins, T., & Perloff, J. (2008). Access to and utilization of neurologists by people with multiple sclerosis. *70*(13 Part 2), 1141–1149. https://doi.org/10.1212/01.wnl.0000306411.46934.ef%

Multiple Sclerosis International Federation. (2013). *Atlas of MS 2013*. Available at: https://www.msif.org/about-us/who-we-are-and-what-we-do/advocacy/atlas/

Ogg, M. (2011). Running out of time, money, and independence? *Health Affairs*, *30*(1), 173–176. https://doi.org/10.1377/HLTHAFF.2010.0857

Peterson, E. W., Ben Ari, E., Asano, M., & Finlayson, M. L. (2013). Fall attributions among middle-aged and older adults with multiple sclerosis. *Archives of Physical Medicine and Rehabilitation*, *94*(5), 890–895. https://doi.org/10.1016/j.apmr.2012.11.027

Peterson, E. W., Cho, C. C., & Finlayson, M. L. (2007). Fear of falling and associated activity curtailment among middle aged and older adults with multiple sclerosis. *Multiple Sclerosis*, *13*(9), 1168–1175. https://doi.org/10.1177/1352458507079260

Peterson, E. W., Cho, C. C., von Koch, L., & Finlayson, M. L. (2008). Injurious falls among middle aged and older adults with multiple sclerosis. *Archives of Physical Medicine and Rehabilitation*, *89*(6), 1031–1037. https://doi.org/10.1016/j.apmr.2007.10.043

Ploughman, M., Austin, M. W., Murdoch, M., Kearney, A., Fisk, J. D., Godwin, M., & Stefanelli, M. (2012). Factors influencing healthy aging with multiple sclerosis: A qualitative study. *Disability and Rehabilitation*, *34*(1), 26–33. https://doi.org/10.3109/09638288.2011.585212

Ploughman, M., Austin, M. W., Murdoch, M., Kearney, A., Godwin, M., & Stefanelli, M. (2012). The path to self-management: A qualitative study involving older people with multiple sclerosis. *Physiotherapy Canada*, *64*(1), 6–17. https://doi.org/10.3138/ptc.2010-42

Ploughman, M., Beaulieu, S., Harris, C., Hogan, S., Manning, O. J., Alderdice, P. W., … Godwin, M. (2014). The Canadian survey of health, lifestyle and ageing with multiple sclerosis: Methodology and initial results. *BMJ Open*, *4*(7), e005718. https://doi.org/10.1136/bmjopen-2014-005718

Ploughman, M., Collins, K., Wallack, E. M., Monks, M., & Mayo, N., & Health, Lifestyle, and Aging with MS Canadian Consortium. (2017). Women's and men's differing experiences of health, lifestyle, and aging with multiple sclerosis. *International Journal of MS Care*, *19*(4), 165–171. https://doi.org/10.7224/1537-2073.2016-014

Ploughman, M., Deshpande, N., Latimer-Cheung, A. E., & Finlayson, M. (2014). Drawing on related knowledge to advance multiple sclerosis falls-prevention research. *International Journal of MS Care*, *16*(4), 163–170. https://doi.org/10.7224/1537-2073.2014-052

Ploughman, M., Harris, C., Wallack, E. M., Drodge, O., Beaulieu, S., & Mayo, N., & Health Lifestyle and Aging with MS Canadian Consortium. (2015). Predictors of exercise participation in ambulatory and non-ambulatory older people with multiple sclerosis. *PeerJ, 3*, e1158. https://doi.org/10.7717/peerj.1158

Plow, M., Cho, C., & Finlayson, M. (2010). Utilization of health promotion and wellness services among middle-aged and older adults with multiple sclerosis in the mid-west US. *Health Promotion International, 25*(3), 318–330. https://doi.org/10.1093/heapro/daq023

Polliack, M. L., Barak, Y., & Achiron, A. (2001). Late-onset multiple sclerosis. *Journal of the American Geriatrics Society, 49*(2), 168–171. https://doi.org/10.1046/j.1532-5415.2001.49038.x

Putnam, M., & Tang, F. (2007). Multiple sclerosis, aging and support service utilization. *Journal of Rehabilitation, 73*(4), 3–-14.

Ramachandran, S., Strange, R. C., Kalra, S., Nayak, D., Zeegers, M. P., Gilford, J., & Hawkins, C. P. (2013). Progression of disability in multiple sclerosis: A study of factors influencing median time to reach an EDSS value. *Multiple Sclerosis and Related Disorders, 2*(2), 109–116. https://doi.org/10.1016/j.msard.2012.09.004

Rice, L., Kalron, A., Berkowitz, S., Backus, D., & Sosnoff, J. J. (2017). Fall prevalence in people with multiple sclerosis who use wheelchairs and scooters. *Medicine, 96*(35). https://doi.org/10.1097/MD.0000000000007860

Sanai, S. A., Saini, V., Benedict, R. H., Zivadinov, R., Teter, B. E., Ramanathan, M., & Weinstock-Guttman, B. (2016). Aging and multiple sclerosis. *Multiple Sclerosis Journal, 22*(6), 717–725. https://doi.org/10.1177/1352458516634871

Sosnoff, J. J., Socie, M. J., Boes, M. K., Sandroff, B. M., Pula, J. H., Suh, Y., … Motl, R. W. (2011). Mobility, balance and falls in persons with multiple sclerosis. *PLoS ONE, 6*(11), e28021. https://doi.org/10.1371/journal.pone.0028021

Stern, M., Sorkin, L., Milton, K., & Sperber, K. (2010). Aging with multiple sclerosis. *Physical Medicine & Rehabilitation Clinics of North America, 21*(2), 403–417. https://doi.org/10.1016/j.pmr.2009.12.008

Thompson, A. J., Baranzini, S. E., Geurts, J., Hemmer, B., & Ciccarelli, O. (2018). Multiple sclerosis. *The Lancet, 391*(10130), 1622–1636. https://doi.org/10.1016/S0140-6736(18)30481-1

Trapp, B., Ransohoff, R., Fisher, E., & Rudick, R. (1999). Neurodegeneration in multiple sclerosis: Relationship to neurological disability. *The Neuroscientist, 5*(1), 48–57. https://doi.org/10.1177/107385849900500107

Turcotte, L. A., Marrie, R. A., Patten, S. B., & Hirdes, J. P. (2017). Clinical profile of persons with multiple sclerosis across the continuum of care. *Canadian Journal of Neurological Sciences/Journal Canadien des Sciences Neurologiques, 45*(2), 188–198. https://doi.org/10.1017/cjn.2017.274

University of California, San Francisco MS-EPIC Team:, Cree, B. A., Gourraud, P. A., Oksenberg, J. R., Bevan, C., Crabtree-Hartman, E., Gelfand, J. M., Goodin, D. S., Graves, J., Green, A. J., Mowry, E., Okuda, D. T., Pelletier, D., von Büdingen, H. C., Zamvil, S. S., Agrawal, A., Caillier, S., Ciocca, C., Gomez, R., Kanner, R., ... Hauser, S. L. (2016). Long-term evolution of multiple sclerosis disability in the treatment era. *Annals of Neurology, 80*(4), 499–510. https://doi.org/10.1002/ana.24747

Wallack, E. M., Wiseman, H. D., & Ploughman, M. (2016). Healthy aging from the perspectives of 683 older people with multiple sclerosis. *Multiple Sclerosis International, 2016*. https://doi.org/10.1155/2016/1845720

Yeh, E. A., Chitnis, T., Krupp, L., Ness, J., Chabas, D., Kuntz, N., & Waubant, E., & US Network of Pediatric Multiple Sclerosis Centers of Excellence. (2009). Pediatric multiple sclerosis. *Nature Reviews. Neurology, 5*(11), 621–631. https://doi.org/10.1038/nrneurol.2009.158

Zhang, W., Becker, H., Stuifbergen, A. K., & Brown, A. (2017). Predicting health promotion and quality of life with symptom clusters and social supports among older adults with multiple sclerosis. *Journal of Gerontological Nursing, 43*(10), 27–36. https://doi.org/10.3928/00989134-20170406-04

Suggested Readings

Appleton, D., Robertson, N., Mitchell, L., & Lesley, R. (2018). Our disease: A qualitative meta-synthesis of the experiences of spousal/partner caregivers of people with multiple sclerosis. *Scandinavian Journal of Caring Sciences, 32*(4), 1262–1278. https://doi.org/10.1111/scs.12601

Finlayson, M. (2004). Concerns about the future among older adults with multiple sclerosis. *American Journal of Occupational Therapy, 58*(1), 54–63. https://doi.org/10.5014/ajot.58.1.54

Matsuda, P. N., Verrall, A. M., Finlayson, M. L., Molton, I. R., & Jensen, M. P. (2015). Falls among adults aging with disability. *Archives of Physical Medicine and Rehabilitation, 96*(3), 464–471. https://doi.org/https://doi.org/10.1016/j.apmr.2014.09.034

Wallack, E. M., Wiseman, H. D., & Ploughman, M. (2016). Healthy aging from the perspectives of 683 older people with multiple sclerosis. *Multiple Sclerosis International, 2016*. https://doi.org/10.1155/2016/1845720

13
AGEING WHEN BEING AUTISTIC

Hilde M. Geurts, Rebecca Charlton, and Lauren Bishop

The Case of a 73-Year-Old Autistic Woman

C. is a woman of 73 years of age and she is autistic. She received her diagnosis at the age of 67, right after she retired from her job in a specialised art book store. She has a partner (no children) of whom she takes care as he had a series of strokes. C. comes from a family of six children, and was always a loner. She loved to read and was as long as she can remember interested in the arts. Her favourite art period was, and is, the Dutch Golden Age, and she knows everything there is to be known about Rembrandt, Rubens, Vermeer et cetera. As a child, she did have one friend who was, like her, a fanatic art fan. At both middle and high school she was bullied a lot and it was a relief when she was allowed to study art history at the university. Here she was among like-minded people and met her husband. As an adult she lived a quiet life with her husband and her work in the art store was a perfect match. C. has a history of depressive periods and is rather anxious especially when expected to meet (new) people. After her retirement she became fully depressed and hardly left her house. In this period her husband had his first stroke. He could not talk or move anymore, but she realised this only after a couple of days. She thought he was fooling her. Only after consulting her neighbour she called the GP. Her days are now filled with reading, and taking care of her husband and the only other person she talks to are her neighbour and her psychologist. C. is worried what will happen when her husband dies. She does not feel it is good to live on her own much longer, but at the same time she is scared what will be waiting for her when she has to move to a home for older adults. She does not like to be touched, cannot deal with specific sounds, and unexpected changes in her daily schedule.

Ageing When Being Autistic

Changes in physical health, cognitive processes, daily routines, social environment, and future prospects are a normative part of the ageing process for all adults. However, differences among people in the timing and course of these changes are large. We are just beginning to learn how people with an autism spectrum condition (ASC)[1] diagnosis are affected by the normative ageing process and by ageing-related changes associated with ASCs.

An ASC is a lifelong developmental disability characterised by challenges in social interactions and communication, difficulties dealing with unpredictability, and sensory sensitivities (Lai & Baron-Cohen, 2015). In the DSM-5 (American Psychiatric Association, 2013) this is referred to as autism spectrum disorder. To meet this criteria people need to have persistent problems in two domains: (1) Social communication and social interaction across multiple contexts, as manifested currently or by history and (2) Restricted, repetitive patterns of behaviour, interests, or activities. Importantly, although these characteristics need to be present during early development, they may fully manifest when social demands exceed the limited capacities. Moreover, overt characteristics could be masked later in life by strategies learnt during development. This is of importance as in late adulthood there are roughly two groups of autistic adults: (1) Adults with a childhood diagnosis of ASC and (2) Adults who received their diagnosis (or self identify) during (late) adulthood.

In the earliest couple of decades after autism was described in the research literature the prevalence was estimated to be low (around 0.04%, Lotter, 1966). Nowadays, the estimated prevalence of ASC is approximately 1% (e.g. Brugha et al., 2011) irrespective of age, although some studies estimate prevalence to be as high as 3% (Fombonne, 2018). Moreover, where before it was thought that the male: female ratio was 4:1, currently it is believed to be 3:1 or even less skewed (Loomes, Hull, & Mandy, 2017). The percentage of individuals with a co-occurring intellectual disability has also changed; initial estimates were approximately 70%, but current estimates are 11–26% (Rydzewska et al., 2018). These three major changes in autism-related figures are likely to be caused by the broadening definition and improved recognition of autism. The change in the definition of autism is sometimes a crucial factor in understanding observed differences across studies and across age cohorts. However, the majority of autism research has focused on children, teens, and young adults (Mukaetova-Ladinska et al., 2012), but fortunately in the last decade autism in older people is gaining research attention.

The first descriptions of older autistic adults were case reports of late diagnoses (James, Mukaetova-Ladinska, Reichelt, Briel, & Scully, 2006, $n = 5$ [age range 67–84]; Naidu, James, Mukatoeva-Ladinska, & Briel, 2006, $n = 1$ [66 years]; van Niekerk et al., 2011, $n = 3$ [age range 72–83]). Since these case reports a few larger data-rich studies have been published, but the majority of papers on older autistic adults describe the need for research about this specific age group (Barber, 2015; Happé & Charlton, 2012; Michael, 2016; Perkins & Berkman, 2012; Roestorf et al., 2019). The dominant view (often implicitly) expressed in these articles is that autistic adults have an increased risk of accelerated ageing (i.e. steeper age-related physical and mental deterioration). A recent qualitative study (Hickey, Crabtree, & Stott, 2018) of 13 autistic adults diagnosed in adulthood, over 50 years of age (range 53–71), concluded that various challenges faced by older adults are similar among autistic adults independent of their age. Moreover, being autistic is seen as a vulnerability factor for early onset cognitive ageing or neurodegenerative diseases like dementia. People with an ASC diagnosis seem to have shortened lifespans and are more likely to be physically less healthy than those without ASC (e.g. Bishop-Fitzpatrick & Rubenstein, 2019; Croen et al., 2015; Hirvikoski et al., 2016). Additionally, well known age-related vulnerability for cognitive decline such as low social participation and physical activity, stress, and having more than one diagnosis (mental and/or physical) are prevalent among autistic adults. This demonstrates that autism is not just a transient developmental phase in childhood and that it is of relevance to focus on old-aged autistic adults. So, there is a need for more knowledge regarding ageing in autistic adults because (a) little is known and (b) what is known so far seems worrying. In the current chapter we will focus on the recent findings on late adulthood of autistic adults regarding ASC characteristics, well-being, mental and physical health, the ageing brain, and cognitive ageing.

General Well-being/Outcomes

There is an ongoing discussion about how to best measure well-being in autistic adults and account for the impact of the specific lived experiences (e.g. McConachie et al., 2018). In general well-being and quality of life can be measured in a number of different ways, either objectively (based on relationships with family members, neighbourhood resources, housing, and physical and mental health) (Bishop-Fitzpatrick et al., 2016) or subjectively reported by either parents (or other relatives/partners) and autistic adults.

A relatively large body of research finds that a small majority of autistic adults achieve 'good' objective well-being, as defined by normative outcomes in the domains of housing, work, and relationship status, but also many individuals' outcomes are less positive (for review, see Henninger & Taylor, 2013; Magiati, Tay, & Howlin, 2014). Objective well-being may be considered better when a broader range of objective outcomes, including relationships with family members, neighbourhood resources, and physical and mental health are taken into account (Bishop-Fitzpatrick et al., 2016). Subjective well-being is reported to be low according to either parents (or other relatives/partners) and autistic adults themselves (Hong, Bishop-Fitzpatrick, Smith, Greenberg, & Mailick, 2016; van Heijst & Geurts, 2015) on a broad range of life domains, such as psychological and physical health, access to care, living circumstances when compared to adults without ASC (e.g. Bishop-Fitzpatrick, Mazefsky, & Eack, 2018). However, findings of a few recent studies do suggest otherwise (Deserno et al., 2019; Hong et al., 2016; Moss, Mandy, & Howlin, 2017). For example the autistic adults' self-reported well-being seems to be similar to adults without an ASC diagnosis (Hong et al., 2016; Moss et al., 2017). The participants in these studies did often not have a co-occurring intellectual disability, while the prevalence of intellectual disabilities was often high in older studies. Hence, ASC itself might not be the relevant factor here, but the associated physical and mental problems as well as the person-environment fit might be much more important (Rubenstein & Bishop-Fitzpatrick, 2019). This is especially likely so for those that have an (above) average intellectual level.

Notably, much of the existing research on well-being and quality of life focuses on autistic people in early to middle adulthood. We know comparatively little about well-being and quality of life for autistic people near the end of life: a recent meta-regression of studies examining quality of life in autistic adults identified a mean age across studies of 35.64 years (Kim & Bottema-Beutel, 2019). Fortunately, studies of quality of life in the three largest cohorts (Bishop-Fitzpatrick, Mazefsky, & Eack, 2018; Deserno, Borsboom, Begeer, & Geurts, 2017; McConachie et al., 2018) studied to date include autistic adults up to the age of 91 years.

While not studied systematically yet, one worry for older autistic individuals and their loved ones is how well-being and quality of life might change in later-life. Notably, existing service systems designed to support the needs of older adults in the general population may not suit the specific needs of older autistic adults. For instance, housing for the elderly might not be suited for the needs of autistic people. Nursing care may also pose specific challenges because it is often provided in communal settings which could be problematic for older autistic adults with sensory sensitivities. Staff and clinicians in nursing facilities receive little to no training on the specific needs of autistic adults. Access to care and housing are both important themes for well-being, and differences across countries exist. For example the health care system in the United States, is rather different from the health care system in Scandinavia. Cross-cultural and cross-health-care system comparisons can help us examine and resolve potential disparities in care.

ASC Characteristics

The diagnostic status seems relatively stable from childhood to middle adulthood, and even when diagnostic criteria are no longer met both ASC symptomatology and associated challenges often persist (Bastiaansen et al., 2011; Magiati et al., 2014; Totsika, Felce, Kerr, & Hastings, 2010). However, apart from a few exceptions (e.g. Bastiaansen et al., 2011; Esbensen, Seltzer, Lam, & Bodfish, 2009; Totsika et al., 2010), the majority of the 'older' adults participating in adult ASC studies were in their (late) forties or early fifties. Interestingly two separate cross-sectional studies examining 18–55 year olds (Happé et al., 2016) and 19–79 year olds (Lever & Geurts, 2018) with an ASC diagnosis, both showed increasing autistic traits (using the Autism Quotient; AQ) with age up to the end of middle age after which these seemed to decrease in the 55+ group (Lever & Geurts, 2018). However a further study of those aged from 18 to over 60[2] also using the AQ, showed no evidence of age-differences in autistic traits (Siebes, Muntjewerff, & Staal, 2018). In studies examining autistic traits in those without an ASC diagnosis, no significant age-associations were observed in either those referred for possible, but not confirmed ASC diagnosis aged 18–55 (Happé et al., 2016) or in typical adults aged 61–88 years old (Wallace, Budgett,

& Charlton, 2016). Whether in senescence specific behaviours or ASC characteristics arise or disappear cannot be answered based on these cross-sectional studies. The qualitative study by Hickey, Crabtree and Stott (2017) suggests no crucial alterations in ASC traits with age. Late diagnosed autistic adults are often those with higher IQ. Moreover, a clinical observation is that older autistic adults are often (a) better at blending in due to camouflaging/masking; (b) better at coping with being different; and (c) more at ease with being different and, therefore, less reluctant to overtly showing so called autistic behaviour.

When working in old-age care, it would be beneficial when one is aware and accepting of specific (a) typicalities which are more often observed in autistic adults. For example, many autistic adults experience hypo- and hypersensitivities. Recognising that these sensitivities can co-exist, but can also suddenly change from hypo- to hypersensitivity or vice versa may lead to improved care. For example, sensitivity to fabrics can be the cause of sleeping problems. Also, not responding to others does not imply a lack of interest, but can be a way to deal with overwhelming sensory input. During their life, autistic adults have often disentangled how to deal with their sensitivities (e.g. wearing sunglasses indoors to protect from light sensitivity), so acceptance of their own chosen solutions is recommended. Moreover, many autistic adults have had negative experiences with health care workers and/or have been bullied in the past. It is, therefore, crucial to provide safety and recognition. Importantly, one needs to realise that autism might have not been recognised yet in older individuals. Typical instruments used in adulthood (like the AQ and Autism Observational Schedule [ADOS] module 4) can be used, but diagnosis primarily relies on an extensive interview with the person and someone who has known them for a long time. There is, unfortunately, no golden standard for assessing ASC in older individuals.

Physical and Mental Health

Autistic adults show a wide range of highly prevalent mental (Houghton, Ong, & Bolognani, 2017; Lever & Geurts, 2016b; Nylander, Axmon, Björne, Ahlström, & Gillberg, 2018) and physical health conditions (Bishop-Fitzpatrick & Rubenstein, 2019; Croen et al., 2015; Fortuna et al., 2016; Houghton et al., 2017). It is largely unclear whether these conditions have the same etiological origin as ASC or result from living with ASC (Rubenstein & Bishop-Fitzpatrick, 2019). Nonetheless, the association of a wide range of serious health conditions with ASC likely grows stronger with increasing age as many prevalent health conditions are common among older adults. The most commonly associated physical health conditions are immune conditions, sleep disorders, cardiovascular disease, and gastrointestinal conditions (e.g. Bishop-Fitzpatrick & Rubenstein, 2019; Croen et al., 2015; Fortuna et al., 2016; Houghton et al., 2017). Importantly, some physical health conditions such as cardiovascular risk factors and disease increase the risk of developing not only Vascular Dementia, but also Alzheimer's Disease or Mixed Dementias (Langa, Foster, & Larson, 2004). The most commonly associated mental health conditions are anxiety, mood, and psychotic disorders (Houghton, Ong, & Bolognani, 2017; Lever & Geurts, 2016b; Nylander, Axmon, Björne, Ahlström, & Gillberg, 2018). In old-age care, it is important to always assess potential associated health conditions as autistic adults might not experience or express their own health concerns in the same way as adults from the general population. Moreover, eating patterns might need extra attention as eating disorders are prevalent in people with ASC as people can experience difficulties with knowing when to eat, might not recognise the feeling of being hungry/thirsty, or have very specific requirements regarding food. Alertness regarding changes in health status is crucial to prevent serious outcomes. Standardised regular assessment of the aforementioned conditions is recommended, as is monitoring for health conditions that present with ASC at an earlier age than in the general population.

The assumption of accelerated ageing is, as previously discussed, partly based on the observed increased risk for neurodegenerative diseases in autistic adults (Bishop-Fitzpatrick & Rubenstein, 2019; Croen et al., 2015; Starkstein, Gellar, Parlier, Payne, & Piven, 2015). For example the prevalence of dementia (type unspecified) was much higher in autistic adults over 18 years of age (2.26%) as compared to controls (0.5%) (Croen et al., 2015). Also in a group of autistic adults aged 40–88 years dementia was highly prevalent (5%) (Bishop-Fitzpatrick & Rubenstein, 2019). Seemingly contrasting findings has been observed in a study by Oberman and Pascual-Leone (2014) as in their study only 3.8% of the autistic older adults had an additional dementia diagnosis (<3.8%), while the estimated prevalence of dementia in the total sample was 13%. This observation of dementia in the total sample is remarkably high, which calls into question the validity of the comparison group. Nonetheless, findings are not yet consistent and, unfortunately, no distinction regarding the type of dementia has been made.

Another known neurodegenerative disorder which seems to be more prevalent in autistic adults compared to individuals in the general population is Parkinson's disease. Croen and colleagues (2015) found a Parkinson's disease prevalence of 0.93% compared to 0.05% in adults without ASC in a study of adults aged 18+. In a much smaller study, Starkstein and colleagues (2015) reported a prevalence of Parkinsonism between 16% and 32% in autistic adults over 40 years of age. This is remarkably high as in the general population of adults over 65 years of age, the prevalence of Parkinson's disease is approximately 2.6% (de Rijk et al., 1997). Whether these preliminary observations of prevalent neurodegenerative disease in autistic people are evidence of *accelerated* or *early* ageing (i.e. a parallel ageing pattern) remains to be determined. Either way, it will be difficult to disentangle whether the observed behavioural and physical problems associated with neurodegenerative disease are an intrinsic part of ASC or not. Again it is recommended that there is extra alertness to the possibility of developing neurodegenerative disorders in older autistic adults, and that neurodegenerative disease may present at earlier ages or progress more quickly.

Brain and Cognition

Atypical brain development is considered to be at the start of the different developmental trajectories observed in autistic people. The idea is that early atypical brain development (Courchesne, Campbell, & Solso, 2011; Donovan & Basson, 2017) has cascading effects on cognitive development. The major hypothesis is that there is less connectivity (i.e. reduced white matter microstructure) across different brain areas. In old-age, increasing age is associated with a reduction in white matter microstructure (e.g. Damoiseaux, 2017; Westlye et al., 2010), which in turn relates to reduced cognitive performance (e.g. Jolly et al., 2016; Tomimoto, 2015). Developmental studies across the lifespan show that white matter microstructure development follows an inverted u-shape with white matter developing until the 30s and then declining after ±50 years of age (e.g. Damoiseaux, 2017; Westlye et al., 2010). Longitudinal studies of white matter microstructure in ageing show widespread age-related decline across the brain over even short time periods (i.e. 2 years, Barrick, Charlton, Clark, & Markus, 2010). Brain studies in old aged autistic adults are virtually non-existent. Only a few small imaging studies have focused specifically on middle and old aged autistic adults (e.g. Baxter et al., 2019; Braden et al., 2017; Koolschijn, Caan, Teeuw, Olabarriaga, & Geurts, 2017; Koolschijn & Geurts, 2016). Based on these findings, one can carefully conclude that no major differences are apparent with respect to brain volume and cortical thickness in autistic compared to non-autistic individuals. However, functional activation patterns still differ between autistic and non-autistic groups, and white matter microstructure may even show increased risk of decline in autistic adults compared to neurotypical controls (although note the small age-associations in neurotypical controls in this study). Given that these are all cross-sectional studies, longitudinal studies are crucial to determine whether this is indeed the case and how this relates to cognition.

Others suggested that the neurobiological make up (i.e. atypical brain development) of those with an ASC will actually protect against cognitive ageing (Oberman & Pascual-Leone, 2014). The hypothesis is that their brain is hyper plastic (quickly modulating synaptic connections in reaction to environmental changes) and, therefore, for a longer period protected against cognitive decline as age-related reductions in brain plasticity has been related to cognitive decline. The 'autistic' brain is, according to the authors, too plastic during development which is beneficial during ageing as older individuals with a lack of plasticity (hypo-plastic) are more prone to develop dementia. A way to learn about brain development is indeed to focus on the prevalence of neurodegenerative diseases (see previous section), but measuring cognition is yet another approach to address brain ageing.

The cognitive challenges autistic individuals often encounter as children (e.g. slower information processing, decreased cognitive flexibility) are the domains that are especially sensitive to cognitive ageing (Geurts & Vissers, 2012; Happé & Charlton, 2012). Additionally, aspects of the cognitive profile of autistic children and young adults shows striking resemblance with cognitive profiles of older adults without ASC (Bowler, Gaigg, & Gardiner, 2014). This ageing analogy implies that we can learn from the cognitive ageing literature to understand autistic information processing, as younger autistic adults cognitive profiles mimic those of older adults without ASC. However, the observation of an old-age cognitive profile in young or middle aged autistic adults has also led to the assumption of accelerated cognitive ageing in (old) autistic adults.

There are a handful of cognitive studies including middle and old aged autistic adults and findings are inconsistent. On a group level the majority of studies find hardly any differences in cognitive profile (Davids, Groen, Berg, Tucha, & van Balkom, 2016; Geurts & Vissers, 2012; Lever & Geurts, 2016a), whereas others did observe some subtle cognitive differences (Baxter et al., 2019; Braden et al., 2017; Powell, Klinger, & Klinger, 2017). Autistic older adults do consistently report more cognitive challenges (Davids et al., 2016; Lever & Geurts, 2016a; van Heijst & Geurts, 2015), but this is often not reflected in their performance on cognitive tasks.

Moreover, hardly any evidence in these cross-sectional studies has been observed for accelerated cognitive ageing although some findings do suggest that, if anything, executive control processes are at risk. So far findings across executive function tasks are rather inconsistent. In contrast, parallel cognitive ageing trajectories seem to be more likely at an older age. This implies that the observed cognitive profile of middle-aged autistic adults is similar to old aged non-autistic adults (i.e. the ageing analogy). Interestingly, there is also some early evidence that older autistic adults experience fewer cognitive challenges compared to older non-autistic adults, which would fit with an idea of (learned) beneficial cognitive strategies. A caveat of all aforementioned studies is that the majority of the autistic participants had an IQ within or above the normal range. So, ageing patterns might be different with conditions often present (see earlier section) in autistic adults. To this point, there seems to be most evidence for parallel cognitive ageing, but longitudinal studies are needed to determine the actual changes in cognition.

Based on one seminal, but small, longitudinal ASC study (Howlin, Savage, Moss, Tempier, & Rutter, 2014), one can argue that the developmental trajectories for adult outcomes for people who were diagnosed with ASC approximately 30 years ago, are too diverse to have a single overall conclusion. While, for example, some participants had a relatively good cognitive outcome (no change in intellectual level or a slight increase), other participants' aggressive behaviour was so severe that their intellectual ability could not be assessed (Howlin, Savage, Moss, Tempier, & Rutter, 2014). Actually, none of these individuals ever developed language above a 3-year level. Hence, it is likely that old-age cognitive-trajectories will be diverse among the group of older autistic adults.

The future challenge is to disentangle who is at risk for accelerated cognitive ageing and who is somehow protected. For now results imply that it is worthwhile to assess cognition regularly in order to ensure that someone's unique profile of cognitive strengths and weaknesses will be known and potential deterioration (or improvements) will be noticed. However, there is no typical 'autistic' cognitive profile in old-aged autistic adults.

Conclusion

Given the newness of the literature on ageing in autistic people, we must take care not to draw strong conclusions. However, both qualitative and quantitative data do suggest that older autistic adults encounter a wide range of physical and mental health challenges typically associated with ageing. We identified three key issues:

1. More research that fully and carefully characterises the social, physical, and cognitive ageing process for autistic people is warranted
2. It is likely that autism is associated with more physical and mental health conditions; this warrants extra care for older autistic people and autism-specific training for physicians and other clinicians who practice with older adults
3. Age-related neurodegenerative diseases are hard to distinguish from the well-established physical, mental, and cognitive challenges older autistic adults experience. Hence, in old-age care this warrants thorough assessment

We, therefore, argue that when being autistic or when working with autistic older adults one needs to be aware of the so called old-age profile which middle aged autistic adults can exhibit. Autistic adults may experience, perform, and impress as being older when considering their actual age. It is of importance that autism knowledge is used to adjust typical old-age solutions in order to meet the needs of middle-aged and older autistic individuals.

Notes

1 In this chapter we will refer to adults with an ASC diagnosis as 'autistic adults' because recent research indicates that identity-first language (as opposed to person-first language) is the terminology adults themselves prefer (Kenny et al., 2016). Moreover, this terminology fits well with the idea of both ASC as neurodiversity and being a disability. We do, however, acknowledge that preferences related to use of identity-first versus person-first language are heterogeneous and that some autistic adults, their loved ones, and their service providers may have differing preferences related to language use.
2 Although the sample sizes were smaller in those over 50 and the maximum age is not reported (18–30, $n = 175$; 30–40, $n = 125$; 40–50, $n = 135$; 50–60, $n = 87$; >60, $n = 40$).

References

American Psychiatric Association. (2013). *Diagnostic and statistical manual of mental disorders* (5th ed.). https://doi.org/10.1176/appi.books.9780890425596

Barber, C. (2015). Old age and people on the autism spectrum: A focus group perspective. *British Journal of Nursing*, 24(21), 1054–1057. https://doi.org/10.12968/bjon.2015.24.21.1054

Barrick, T. R., Charlton, R. A., Clark, C. A., & Markus, H. S. (2010). White matter structural decline in normal ageing: A prospective longitudinal study using tract-based spatial statistics. *NeuroImage*, 51(2), 565–577. https://doi.org/10.1016/j.neuroimage.2010.02.033

Bastiaansen, J. A., Thioux, M., Nanetti, L., van der Gaag, C., Ketelaars, C., Minderaa, R., & Keysers, C. (2011). Age-related increase in inferior frontal gyrus activity and social functioning in autism spectrum disorder. *Biological Psychiatry*, 69(9), 832–838. https://doi.org/10.1016/j.biopsych.2010.11.007

Baxter, L. C., Nespodzany, A., Walsh, M. J. M., Wood, E., Smith, C. J., & Braden, B. B. (2019). The influence of age and ASD on verbal fluency networks. *Research in Autism Spectrum Disorders*, 63, 52–62. https://doi.org/10.1016/j.rasd.2019.03.002

Bishop-Fitzpatrick, L., Hong, J., Smith, L. E., Makuch, R. A., Greenberg, J. S., & Mailick, M. R. (2016). Characterizing objective quality of life and normative outcomes in adults with autism spectrum disorder: An exploratory latent class analysis. *Journal of Autism and Developmental Disorders*, 46(8), 2707–2719. https://doi.org/10.1007/s10803-016-2816-3

Bishop-Fitzpatrick, L., Mazefsky, C. A., & Eack, S. M. (2018). The combined impact of social support and perceived stress on quality of life in adults with autism spectrum disorder and without intellectual disability. *Autism: The International Journal of Research and Practice*, 22(6), 703–711. https://doi.org/10.1177/1362361317703090

Bishop-Fitzpatrick, L., & Rubenstein, E. (2019). The physical and mental health of middle aged and older adults on the autism spectrum and the impact of intellectual disability. *Research in Autism Spectrum Disorders*, 63, 34–41. https://doi.org/10.1016/j.rasd.2019.01.001

Bowler, D. M., Gaigg, S. B., & Gardiner, J. M. (2014). Binding of multiple features in memory by high-functioning adults with autism spectrum disorder. *Journal of Autism and Developmental Disorders*, *44*(9), 2355–2362. https://doi.org/10.1007/s10803-014-2105-y

Braden, B. B., Smith, C. J., Thompson, A., Glaspy, T. K., Wood, E., Vatsa, D., ... Baxter, L. C. (2017). Executive function and functional and structural brain differences in middle-age adults with autism spectrum disorder. *Autism Research: Official Journal of the International Society for Autism Research*, *10*(12), 1945–1959. https://doi.org/10.1002/aur.1842

Brugha, T. S., McManus, S., Bankart, J., Scott, F., Purdon, S., Smith, J., Bebbington, P., Jenkins, R., & Meltzer, H. (2011). Epidemiology of autism spectrum disorders in adults in the community in England. *Archives of general psychiatry*, *68*(5), 459–465.

Courchesne, E., Campbell, K., & Solso, S. (2011). Brain growth across the life span in autism: Age-specific changes in anatomical pathology. *Brain Research*, *1380*, 138–145. https://doi.org/10.1016/j.brainres.2010.09.101

Croen, L. A., Zerbo, O., Qian, Y., Massolo, M. L., Rich, S., Sidney, S., & Kripke, C. (2015). The health status of adults on the autism spectrum. *Autism: The International Journal of Research and Practice*, *19*(7), 814–823. https://doi.org/10.1177/1362361315577517

Damoiseaux, J. S. (2017). Effects of aging on functional and structural brain connectivity. *NeuroImage*, *160*, 32–40. https://doi.org/10.1016/j.neuroimage.2017.01.077

Davids, R. C. D., Groen, Y., Berg, I. J., Tucha, O. M., & van Balkom, I. D. C. (2016). Executive functions in older adults with autism spectrum disorder: Objective performance and subjective complaints. *Journal of Autism and Developmental Disorders*, *46*(9), 2859–2873. https://doi.org/10.1007/s10803-016-2831-4

de Rijk, M. C., Tzourio, C., Breteler, M. M., Dartigues, J. F., Amaducci, L., Lopez-Pousa, S., ... Rocca, W. A. (1997). Prevalence of parkinsonism and Parkinson's disease in Europe: The EUROPARKINSON collaborative study. European Community concerted action on the epidemiology of Parkinson's disease. *Journal of Neurology, Neurosurgery, and Psychiatry*, *62*(1), 10–15. https://doi.org/10.1136/jnnp.62.1.10

Deserno, M. K., Borsboom, D., Begeer, S., Agelink van Rentergem, J. A., Mataw, K., & Geurts, H. M. (2019). Sleep determines quality of life in autistic adults: A longitudinal study. *Autism Research*, *12*(5), 794–801. https://doi.org/10.1002/aur.2103

Deserno, M. K., Borsboom, D., Begeer, S., & Geurts, H. M. (2017). Multicausal systems ask for multicausal approaches: A network perspective on subjective well-being in individuals with autism spectrum disorder. *Autism*, *21*(8), 960–971. https://doi.org/10.1177/1362361316660309

Donovan, A. P. A., & Basson, M. A. (2017). The neuroanatomy of autism – A developmental perspective. *Journal of Anatomy*, *230*(1), 4–15. https://doi.org/10.1111/joa.12542

Esbensen, A., Seltzer, M., Lam, K., & Bodfish, J. (2009). Age-related differences in restricted repetitive behaviors in autism spectrum disorders. *Journal of Autism and Developmental Disorders*, *39*(1), 57–66. https://doi.org/10.1007/s10803-008-0599-x

Fombonne, E. (2018). Editorial: The rising prevalence of autism. *Journal of Child Psychology and Psychiatry*, *59*(7), 717–720. https://doi.org/10.1111/jcpp.12941

Fortuna, R. J., Robinson, L., Smith, T. H., Meccarello, J., Bullen, B., Nobis, K., & Davidson, P. W. (2016). Health conditions and functional status in adults with autism: A cross-sectional evaluation. *Journal of General Internal Medicine*, *31*(1), 77–84. https://doi.org/10.1007/s11606-015-3509-x

Geurts, H. M., & Vissers, M. E. (2012). Elderly with autism: Executive functions and memory. *Journal of Autism and Developmental Disorders*, *42*(5), 665–675. https://doi.org/10.1007/s10803-011-1291-0

Happé, F., & Charlton, R. A. (2012). Aging in autism spectrum disorders: A mini-review. *Gerontology*, *58*(1), 70–78. https://doi.org/10.1159/000329720

Happé, F. G., Mansour, H., Barrett, P., Brown, T., Abbott, P., & Charlton, R. A. (2016). Demographic and cognitive profile of individuals seeking a diagnosis of autism spectrum disorder in adulthood. *Journal of Autism and Developmental Disorders*, *46*(11), 3469–3480. https://doi.org/10.1007/s10803-016-2886-2

Henninger, N. A., & Taylor, J. L. (2013). Outcomes in adults with autism spectrum disorders: A historical perspective. *Autism*, *17*(1), 103–116. https://doi.org/10.1177/1362361312441266

Hickey, A., Crabtree, J., & Stott, J. (2018). 'Suddenly the first fifty years of my life made sense': Experiences of older people with autism. *Autism*, *22*(3), 357–367. https://doi.org/10.1177/1362361316680914

Hirvikoski, T., Mittendorfer-Rutz, E., Boman, M., Larsson, H., Lichtenstein, P., & Bölte, S. (2016). Premature mortality in autism spectrum disorder. *British Journal of Psychiatry*, *208*(3), 232–238. https://doi.org/10.1192/bjp.bp.114.160192

Hong, J., Bishop-Fitzpatrick, L., Smith, L. E., Greenberg, J. S., & Mailick, M. R. (2016). Factors associated with subjective quality of life of adults with autism spectrum disorder: Self-report versus maternal reports. *Journal of Autism and Developmental Disorders*, *46*(4), 1368–1378. https://doi.org/10.1007/s10803-015-2678-0

Houghton, R., Ong, R. C., & Bolognani, F. (2017). Psychiatric comorbidities and use of psychotropic medications in people with autism spectrum disorder in the United States. *Autism Research: Official Journal of the International Society for Autism Research, 10*(12), 2037–2047. https://doi.org/10.1002/aur.1848

Howlin, P., Savage, S., Moss, P., Tempier, A., & Rutter, M. (2014). Cognitive and language skills in adults with autism: A 40-year follow-up. *Journal of Child Psychology and Psychiatry, 55*(1), 49–58. https://doi.org/10.1111/jcpp.12115

James, I. A., Mukaetova-Ladinska, E., Reichelt, F. K., Briel, R., & Scully, A. (2006). Diagnosing aspergers syndrome in the elderly: A series of case presentations. *International Journal of Geriatric Psychiatry, 21*(10), 951–960. https://doi.org/10.1002/gps.1588

Jolly, T. A., Cooper, P. S., Badwi, S. A., Phillips, N. A., Rennie, J. L., Levi, C. R., ... Karayanidis, F. (2016). Microstructural white matter changes mediate age-related cognitive decline on the Montreal Cognitive Assessment (MoCA). *Psychophysiology, 53*(2), 258–267. https://doi.org/10.1111/psyp.12565

Kenny, L., Hattersley, C., Molins, B., Buckley, C., Povey, C., & Pellicano, E. (2016). Which terms should be used to describe autism? Perspectives from the UK autism community. *Autism, 20*(4), 442–462. https://doi.org/10.1177/1362361315588200

Kim, S. Y., & Bottema-Beutel, K. (2019). A meta regression analysis of quality of life correlates in adults with ASD. *Research in Autism Spectrum Disorders, 63*, 23–33. https://doi.org/10.1016/j.rasd.2018.11.004

Koolschijn, P. C. M. P., Caan, M. W. A., Teeuw, J., Olabarriaga, S. D., & Geurts, H. M. (2017). Age-related differences in autism: The case of white matter microstructure. *Human Brain Mapping, 38*(1), 82–96. https://doi.org/10.1002/hbm.23345

Koolschijn, P. C. M. P., & Geurts, H. M. (2016). Gray matter characteristics in mid and old aged adults with ASD. *Journal of Autism and Developmental Disorders, 46*(8), 2666–2678. https://doi.org/10.1007/s10803-016-2810-9

Lai, M.-C., & Baron-Cohen, S. (2015). Identifying the lost generation of adults with autism spectrum conditions. *The Lancet Psychiatry, 2*(11), 1013–1027. https://doi.org/10.1016/S2215-0366(15)00277-1

Langa, K. M., Foster, N. L., & Larson, E. B. (2004). Mixed dementia: Emerging concepts and therapeutic implications. *JAMA, 292*(23), 2901. https://doi.org/10.1001/jama.292.23.2901

Lever, A. G., & Geurts, H. M. (2016a). Age-related differences in cognition across the adult lifespan in autism spectrum disorder. *Autism Research: Official Journal of the International Society for Autism Research, 9*(6), 666–676. https://doi.org/10.1002/aur.1545

Lever, A. G., & Geurts, H. M. (2016b). Psychiatric co-occurring symptoms and disorders in young, middle-aged, and older adults with autism spectrum disorder. *Journal of Autism and Developmental Disorders, 46*(6), 1916–1930. https://doi.org/10.1007/s10803-016-2722-8

Lever, A. G., & Geurts, H. M. (2018). Is older age associated with higher self- and other-rated ASD characteristics? *Journal of Autism and Developmental Disorders, 48*(6), 2038–2051. https://doi.org/10.1007/s10803-017-3444-2

Loomes, R., Hull, L., & Mandy, W. P. L. (2017). What is the male-to-female ratio in autism spectrum disorder? A systematic review and meta-analysis. *Journal of the American Academy of Child & Adolescent Psychiatry, 56*(6), 466–474. https://doi.org/10.1016/j.jaac.2017.03.013

Lotter, V. (1966). Epidemiology of autistic conditions in young children: 1. Prevalence. *Social Psychiatry, 1*(3), 124–135. https://doi.org/10.1007/BF00584048

Magiati, I., Tay, X. W., & Howlin, P. (2014). Cognitive, language, social and behavioural outcomes in adults with autism spectrum disorders: A systematic review of longitudinal follow-up studies in adulthood. *Clinical Psychology Review, 34*(1), 73–86. https://doi.org/10.1016/j.cpr.2013.11.002

McConachie, H., Mason, D., Parr, J. R., Garland, D., Wilson, C., & Rodgers, J. (2018). Enhancing the validity of a quality of life measure for autistic people. *Journal of Autism and Developmental Disorders, 48*(5), 1596–1611. https://doi.org/10.1007/s10803-017-3402-z

Michael, C. (2016). Why we need research about autism and ageing. *Autism, 20*(5), 515–516. https://doi.org/10.1177/1362361316647224

Moss, P., Mandy, W., & Howlin, P. (2017). Child and adult factors related to quality of life in adults with autism. *Journal of Autism and Developmental Disorders, 47*(6), 1830–1837. https://doi.org/10.1007/s10803-017-3105-5

Mukaetova-Ladinska, E. B., Perry, E., Baron, M., & Povey, C., & on behalf of the Autism Ageing Writing Group. (2012). Ageing in people with autistic spectrum disorder: Ageing in people with autistic spectrum disorder. *International Journal of Geriatric Psychiatry, 27*(2), 109–118. https://doi.org/10.1002/gps.2711

Naidu, A., James, I., Mukatoeva-Ladinska, E., & Briel, R. (2006). Diagnosis of asperger syndrome in a 66-year-old male presenting with depression. *International Psychogeriatrics, 18*(1), 171–173. https://doi.org/10.1017/S1041610206213474

Nylander, L., Axmon, A., Björne, P., Ahlström, G., & Gillberg, C. (2018). Older adults with autism spectrum disorders in Sweden: A register study of diagnoses, psychiatric care utilization and psychotropic medication of 601 individuals. *Journal of Autism and Developmental Disorders, 48*(9), 3076–3085. https://doi.org/10.1007/s10803-018-3567-0

Oberman, L. M., & Pascual-Leone, A. (2014). Hyperplasticity in autism spectrum disorder confers protection from Alzheimer's disease. *Medical Hypotheses*, *83*(3), 337–342. https://doi.org/10.1016/j.mehy.2014.06.008

Perkins, E. A., & Berkman, K. A. (2012). Into the unknown: Aging with autism spectrum disorders. *American Journal on Intellectual and Developmental Disabilities*, *117*(6), 478–496. https://doi.org/10.1352/1944-7558-117.6.478

Powell, P. S., Klinger, L. G., & Klinger, M. R. (2017). Patterns of age-related cognitive differences in adults with autism spectrum disorder. *Journal of Autism and Developmental Disorders*, *47*(10), 3204–3219. https://doi.org/10.1007/s10803-017-3238-6

Roestorf, A., Bowler, D. M., Deserno, M. K., Howlin, P., Klinger, L., McConachie, H., ... Geurts, H. M. (2019). "Older adults with ASD: The consequences of aging". Insights from a series of special interest group meetings held at the International society for autism research 2016–2017. *Research in Autism Spectrum Disorders*, *63*, 3–12. https://doi.org/10.1016/j.rasd.2018.08.007

Rubenstein, E., & Bishop-Fitzpatrick, L. (2019). A matter of time: The necessity of temporal language in research on health conditions that present with autism spectrum disorder. *Autism Research: Official Journal of the International Society for Autism Research*, *12*(1), 20–25. https://doi.org/10.1002/aur.2010

Rydzewska, E., Hughes-McCormack, L. A., Gillberg, C., Henderson, A., MacIntyre, C., Rintoul, J., & Cooper, S.-A. (2018). Prevalence of sensory impairments, physical and intellectual disabilities, and mental health in children and young people with self/proxy-reported autism: Observational study of a whole country population. *Autism: The International Journal of Research and Practice*, *23*(5), 1201–1209. https://doi.org/10.1177/1362361318791279

Siebes, R., Muntjewerff, J.-W., & Staal, W. (2018). Differences of symptom distribution across adult age in high functioning individuals on the autism spectrum using subscales of the autism spectrum quotient. *Journal of Autism and Developmental Disorders*, *48*(11), 3939–3944. https://doi.org/10.1007/s10803-018-3657-z

Starkstein, S., Gellar, S., Parlier, M., Payne, L., & Piven, J. (2015). High rates of parkinsonism in adults with autism. *Journal of Neurodevelopmental Disorders*, *7*(1), 29. https://doi.org/10.1186/s11689-015-9125-6

Tomimoto, H. (2015). White matter integrity and cognitive dysfunction: Radiological and neuropsychological correlations: White matter integrity and cognitive function. *Geriatrics & Gerontology International*, *15*, 3–9. https://doi.org/10.1111/ggi.12661

Totsika, V., Felce, D., Kerr, M., & Hastings, R. P. (2010). Behavior problems, psychiatric symptoms, and quality of life for older adults with intellectual disability with and without autism. *Journal of Autism and Developmental Disorders*, *40*(10), 1171–1178. https://doi.org/10.1007/s10803-010-0975-1

van Heijst, B. F., & Geurts, H. M. (2015). Quality of life in autism across the lifespan: A meta-analysis. *Autism*, *19*(2), 158–167. https://doi.org/10.1177/1362361313517053

van Niekerk, M. E. H., Groen, W., Vissers, C. T. W. M., van Driel-de Jong, D., Kan, C. C., & Oude Voshaar, R. C. (2011). Diagnosing autism spectrum disorders in elderly people. *International Psychogeriatrics*, *23*(05), 700–710. https://doi.org/doi:10.1017/S1041610210002152

Wallace, G. L., Budgett, J., & Charlton, R. A. (2016). Aging and autism spectrum disorder: Evidence from the broad autism phenotype: BAP and aging. *Autism Research*, *9*(12), 1294–1303. https://doi.org/10.1002/aur.1620

Westlye, L. T., Walhovd, K. B., Dale, A. M., Bjørnerud, A., Due-Tønnessen, P., Engvig, A., ... Fjell, A. M. (2010). Life-span changes of the human brain white matter: Diffusion tensor imaging (DTI) and volumetry. *Cerebral Cortex*, *20*(9), 2055–2068. https://doi.org/10.1093/cercor/bhp280

Suggested Readings

Hickey, A., Crabtree, J., & Stott, J. (2018). 'Suddenly the first fifty years of my life made sense': Experiences of older people with autism. *Autism*, *22*(3), 357–367. https://doi.org/10.1177/1362361316680914

Happé, F., & Charlton, R. A. (2012). Aging in autism spectrum disorders: A mini-review. *Gerontology*, *58*(1), 70–78. https://doi.org/10.1159/000329720

Lai, M.-C., & Baron-Cohen, S. (2015). Identifying the lost generation of adults with autism spectrum conditions. *The Lancet Psychiatry*, *2*(11), 1013–1027. https://doi.org/10.1016/S2215-0366(15)00277-1

van Niekerk, M. E. H., Groen, W., Vissers, C. T. W. M., van Driel-de Jong, D., Kan, C. C., & Oude Voshaar, R. C. (2011). Diagnosing autism spectrum disorders in elderly people. *International Psychogeriatrics*, *23*(05), 700–710. https://doi.org/doi:10.1017/S1041610210002152

PART III

Forwarding Social Inclusion

14
COMMUNITY PARTICIPATION AND ENGAGEMENT FOR PERSONS AGEING WITH PHYSICAL DISABILITY

Rachel Heeb, Courtney Weber, Jessica Dashner, and Kerri Morgan

Introduction

Globally, the age composition of most societies is skewing older as the proportion of adults over age 60 increases. One of the populations that is part of this demographic shift is people ageing with disabilities, particularly those living in nations with more advanced social and economic development, who have benefitted from medical advances and improvements in healthcare, resulting in increased life expectancies (Courtney-Long et al., 2015). The term *ageing with a disability* refers to persons with a lifelong disability, early onset of a disability, or who acquired a disability in mid-life, and are living into later life. People ageing with physical disability (PAwPD) tend to experience an acceleration of ageing-related conditions compared to the general population that often contributes to the onset of new, or increased severity of existing, functional limitations (Courtney-Long et al., 2015). Functional limitations, particularly when combined with limitations in supportive services and environmental accessibility, tend to reduce engagement in meaningful life activities by PAwPD including participation in their communities, which is noted to be important for successful ageing.

This chapter explores individual and environmental factors that influence community participation among PAwPD. Definitions of participation and community participation vary across the research literature depending on what aspect of participation is being explored. For example, the International Classification of Functioning, Disability, and Health (ICF) provides an all-encompassing definition of participation as an individual's involvement in a range of different life situations (World Health Organization, 2001). Other definitions of participation are broader, going beyond the individual to consider the complex interaction of the person, the activity and the environment as essential components (Gray, Hollingsworth, Stark, & Morgan, 2006; Mallinson & Hammel, 2010). For this chapter, we build on these definitions by including the overall involvement and nature of involvement of the individual – the quality and quantity of how someone lives and interacts with his or her community in a meaningful way – in our operationalisation of community participation.

Understanding Changes in Community Participation Among PAwPD

There is a growing body of research on participation among the general population of persons with disabilities (Hammel et al., 2008). Specific to PAwPD, however, research-based literature is fairly minimal. What evidence-based knowledge we do have indicates that people with disabilities often experience physical and cognitive difficulties related to the acceleration of ageing (Molton, Goetz, Jensen, & Verrall, 2012), with early onset of secondary and age-related chronic health conditions being common among PAwPD (LaPlante, 2014). We know that those secondary and age-related chronic conditions can undermine functional abilities, leading to poorer quality of life and well-being (Jette & Field, 2007; Verbrugge, Latham, & Clarke, 2017). What we need to know more about – and what warrants further investigation – is the relationship between ageing, health and declines in community participation for PAwPD.

Increasing knowledge in this area is particularly important because emerging evidence points to the importance of community participation for successful ageing with a disability (Molton & Yorkston, 2017). In a secondary analysis of a cohort study conducted by Gray, Hollingsworth, Stark, and Morgan (2008) of 604 people with long-term mobility impairments, PAwPD aged 50–65 years exhibited significantly lower participation rates than those aged 18–49 years, as measured by the Facilitators and Barriers Survey of environmental influences on community participation. Strikingly, participants in the 50–65 age cohort had participation patterns similar to adults aged ≥65 for all destinations except going to church or the pharmacy. Other findings indicated that changes in health and function were associated with ageing with disability, such as secondary conditions and accelerated ageing; and that these changes can negatively impact an individual's participation in everyday life activities, dining out, visiting friends, volunteering or working, shopping. Findings from this study suggest that community participation patterns (Gray et al., 2008) may be linked to trajectories of functional decline for people ageing with disability noted in larger population-level analysis (Verbrugge et al., 2017).

Declining participation is often a signal of reduced health (Chatteri et al., 2015). Findings from Gray et al. (2008) are consistent with other research that has suggested health declines related to ageing, increased morbidity, secondary conditions, and declining functional ability may influence the participation in everyday life activities for people ageing with long-term physical disability (Groah & Kehn, 2010; Kemp, Adkins, & Thompson, 2004; Tonack et al., 2008). The interaction of reduced health and declining participation can lead to social isolation (Wallace, Theou, Pena, Rockwood, & Andrew, 2015) or other negative quality of life outcomes. Studies investigating participation for individuals with a variety of long-term physical disabilities demonstrated significant social and health disadvantages for those with persistent (early-onset) disability as compared to late-onset disability (Verbrugge et al., 2017). Specifically, individuals who acquired disability early in life were found to experience greater difficulty with activities of daily living as compared to persons with late-onset disability. In deeper, qualitative analyses of persons with spinal cord injury, multiple sclerosis, and post-polio syndrome, PAwPD have voiced concerns about physical symptoms worsening over time, psychosocial adjustment, and what their futures hold (Yorkston, McMullan, Molton, & Jensen, 2010). Regardless of diagnosis, PAwPD often experience similar obstacles to ageing well.

Health declines and ageing-related changes in participation may be influenced not only by physical changes within the person (e.g. pain, secondary health conditions) but also factors in the environment (e.g. natural and architectural barriers in the home and community) (Jensen et al., 2013). For decades, researchers studying ageing have identified factors predictive of successful ageing, but most of this work has focused on avoiding disability. The vast majority literature on successful ageing focuses on the general older adult population, excluding the perspectives of PAwPD (Molton & Yorkston, 2017). However, there is an emerging call to expand models of successful ageing to include PAwPD (Molton & Yorkston, 2017), with critics arguing that omitting disability and chronic illness is an unrealistic goal of these models (Depp & Jeste, 2006). PAwPD have contributed concepts of autonomy, social connection, physical health, and adaptation as important elements of a broader model of successful ageing (Molton & Yorkston, 2017) and factors that are important to know more about. For example, a study by Dashner et al. (2019) examined the community participation of 692 community dwelling adults with physical, vision and hearing impairments and found differences in the participation at various community sites based on age. Specifically, individuals older than 50 more frequently visited sites that related to health (i.e. pharmacies) while individuals 50 or younger visited restaurants, movie theatres, and shopping malls more frequently. Understanding this variance in visitation, including identifying specific factors that influence changes in visitation patterns among PAwPD and the breadth of their community participation, will help inform both informal actions and formal interventions to facilitate participation.

We also need to understand more about how specific supports and services facilitate successful ageing and community participation of PAwPD. While traditional rehabilitation interventions target age-related changes through activities such as management of medication, exercise, and diet (Groah & Kehn, 2010; Jiang, Dai, & Jiang, 2006), they are often one-time interventions provided as acute rehabilitation services. People seldom return for additional services without having a new, or substantial change in an existing, secondary health condition (Jette & Field, 2007). In the United States, few ongoing services and supports are provided to PAwPD unless they qualify for them based on low-income status and eligibility for public health insurance (Medicaid) or other public programs for low-income or medically needy individuals. Eligibility varies across states, but generally the income eligibility is set at the federal poverty line for a one-person household or below – $12,760 USD in 2020 (ASPE, 2020). The lack of regular access to supports and service outside of low-income programs may lead to a reduction in participation by PAwPD, but research still needs to be done to clearly establish this relationship.

When services are available, they often are not provided from the disability perspective of independent living and participation, but rather a medical model of service delivery. Historically, ageing and disability service systems have been separate, this is increasingly being recognised as problematic and in need of change. Researchers have pointed to the need to bridge service networks, and organisations have addressed these concerns through the development of federal programs such as the Aging and Disability Resource Centers (ADRCs) that attempt to streamline access to long-term support services (LTSS) (Nalder et al., 2017; Putnam, 2014). At the local level, other approaches to create stronger partnerships across ageing and disability networks that are organic to a region or area, have been tried. One example of this is the Community Based Research Network (CBRN) started by researchers at Washington University in St. Louis, formally called the Missouri Aging and Disability Research Network. Its membership includes representation from Centers for Independent Living (CILs) serving people with disabilities and Area Agencies on Aging (AAA) serving the ageing population. The goals of the network are to: (1) Develop interventions for PAwPD (2) Help people learn about evidence-based practice delivered in the community (3) Understand the bridge between disability and ageing services (4) Be part of a coalition of providers that bridge across ageing and disability and (5) Link with researchers, agencies and participants to share knowledge (Minor et al., 2020). Given that the trajectories of physical functioning for PAwPD are extremely variable, creating partnerships across ageing and disability services is needed to facilitate better understand and meet LTSS needs and support community participation.

The Role of Personal Factors and Health in Community Participation

For PAwPD, community participation is influenced by multiple factors, including physical health, cognitive function, psychosocial health, and the environment. Typically occurring age-related risk factors and chronic conditions (e.g. falls, depression, heart disease, diabetes, hypertension, obesity, and arthritis) can negatively impact the overall health of PAwPD (Jette & Field, 2007; Kinne, Patrick, & Doyle, 2004). People with long-term disability are also more likely than the general population to experience sleep disturbances, anxiety, and depression (Battalio, Glette, Alschuler, & Jensen, 2018). PAwPD tend to have these conditions earlier, at greater rates and experience a great associated impact on their functional abilities and community participation compared to their age-matched counterparts without disabilities (Molton et al., 2014).

PAwPD may also experience additional secondary health conditions associated with their primary disability. These often include pain, fatigue, pressure ulcers, and bladder or bowel dysfunction. If these conditions are not adequately managed, they can impair participation in desired daily activities and may result in hospital visits that could have been prevented (Jensen et al., 2013; Molton et al., 2014; Molton

& Yorkston, 2017). Additionally, PAwPD who use mobility devices, such as manual wheelchairs, are at increased risk for the development of upper extremity injuries and joint problems associated with improper propulsion techniques and overuse. In some instances, ageing-related changes in ability and secondary health conditions can affect independence and community participation as much as, or sometimes more than, the primary disability itself among people with early and midlife-onset disability (Gray et al., 2008).

The combination of secondary disability-related conditions and conditions associated with ageing may also result in changes in cognitive function. For example, individuals ageing with multiple sclerosis or cerebral palsy may have certain cognitive traits associated with their primary diagnosis that differ from those a person with a spinal cord injury may acquire following their injury (Cohen et al., 2017; Watanabe, 2015). Secondary conditions accompanying a physical disability (e.g. chronic pain, fatigue) can impact attention, memory and social interaction (Craig, Guest, Tran, & Middleton, 2017) as well as community mobility (Cohen et al., 2017). Many PAwPD take medication to manage their symptoms, and medication side effects can include sleep problems and executive function impairment (Cohen et al., 2017). Furthermore, the general ageing process includes cognitive changes in areas such as memory, judgment, abstract thinking, and language (Di Carlo et al., 2000).

Regardless of the primary diagnosis, PAwPD often experience cognitive changes that result in changes in participation (Cohen et al., 2017; Di Carlo et al., 2000; Wanigatunga et al., 2018). Maintaining autonomy and providing choice for PAwPD is a key to successful ageing as health and function status changes (Ansello, 2014). So too is ensuring that the environment is supportive of their changing abilities and facilitates participation.

The Role of Environmental Factors in Community Participation

Disability is a result of complex interactions between an individual's capacities and the physical and social environments in which they live and act (World Health Organization, 2001). These interactions change over time. As personal abilities change with the ageing process, PAwPD may find that there is no longer a strong match between their capabilities and their environments – their person-environment fit may be out of balance.

There is a lack of specific evidence related to which environmental components contribute to decreasing participation for PAwPD. Literature on participation is mostly focused on either adults with physical disability in general or on individuals over age 65. However, given the presence of the above mentioned physical, cognitive and mental health conditions, understanding unique changes in the person-environment fit is critical for designing interventions that facilitate participation among PAwPD. For example, a recent study specifically examining the environmental influences on people ageing with spinal cord injury found that climatic conditions and inaccessibility of public and private spaces were the most frequently perceived barriers. The researchers also identified that participants with less physical independence and older participants were more likely to report accessibility issues (Reinhardt, Ballert, Brinkhof, & Post, 2016). More studies like this are needed. However, drawing from the currently available research, we know that physical barriers in the environment contribute to reduced participation for persons with disabilities regardless of age. Barriers such as stairs, uneven terrain, narrow and heavy doorways, and inaccessible restrooms limit access to community sites. Ramp location, doorway width, lighting, and floor finishes are also barriers which can cause significant restrictions in navigating public spaces. Encountering physical and sensory barriers (inadequate lighting, lack of contrast, background noise) in the community can decrease the frequency of participation as well as the overall enjoyment one receives from engagement in community activities. PAwPD may need access to additional environmental support to negotiate physical barriers and improve their community mobility. Despite the accessibility requirements outlined in the Americans with Disabilities Act (1990), it is not uncommon for persons with disabilities in the United States to encounter physical barriers or lack of accommodations in public spaces.

In addition to physical barriers, the social environment can significantly impact community participation for persons with disabilities in general, including PAwPD. Social environments include attitudes of others in the community as well as an individual's social network and resources. For example, stigmatisation may lead to negative self-perception, social isolation, and reduced community participation for PAwPD. Cultural beliefs surrounding disability may also directly influence opportunities for engagement and participation. Related to social resources, PAwPD may require assistance as they age and rely on family and friends to help them with daily activities. If this type of informal support is not readily available, the individual may be less able to, or less inclined to, engage in activities outside of their home and in the community. The result may be an increased risk of social isolation. Long-term isolation can have substantial consequences for health and mental health. Interventions to reduce isolation particularly for PAwPD, who may have limited social or economic resources to address isolation on their own, are needed. Personal income can also dramatically influence community participation. PAwPD have reported that engaging in recreational activities is often unfeasible due to cost of needed supports and accommodations (Hammel et al., 2015; Reinhardt et al., 2016). In sum, further research is needed to examine the environmental facilitators and barriers specifically for PAwPD in order to improve community participation, including how supports and services can support this aim.

The Role of Supports and Services in Community Participation

Community-based supports and services can help facilitate community participation for persons with disabilities. This includes a wide range of personal care and assistance services that support engagement in daily life activities (Reaves & Musumeci, 2015). In the United States, the Supreme Court decision Olmstead v. L.C., 527 U.S. 581 (1999) ruled that the Americans with Disabilities Act requires people with disabilities be provided the option of receiving community-based supports and services (rather than just institutionalisation), which ignited an increased demand for long-term services and support (LTSS). Provision of LTSS to PAwPD poses new challenges for service networks that have traditionally addressed either ageing or disability service needs but not both (Putnam, 2014). PAwPD who need a holistic service approach are placing new demands on LTSS providers (Reinhard, Kassner, Houser, & Mollica, 2011) and spotlighting serious gaps in service delivery to support ageing in place and community living in later life for PAwPD. Many PAwPD are not old enough to qualify for supports from ageing services, and certain aspects of their needs may not fit well within disability service frameworks, which place often more emphasis on employment-related supports and services rather than LTSS.

Literature surrounding evidence-based programs and practice within LTSS, specifically for PAwPD, is sparse. Evidence drawn from research on younger persons with disability and older adults suggests that effective coping strategies and the ability to navigate and adapt to major life transitions (LaPlante, 2014; Molton & Yorkston, 2017; Tesch-Römer & Wahl, 2017) are important for maintaining quality of life. Thus, supports that align with these personal skills including those that build self-efficacy, teach self-management, and encourage positive health behaviour and healthy lifestyles should be incorporated into programming related to community participation. Additionally, inclusion of PAwPD in fall prevention, nutrition education, and physical activity programs can support health and participation. For example, facilities such as adapted gyms that contain specialised equipment for people with physical disabilities can support community participation, acting as a place for both physical activity and positive social interaction.

Use of assistive technology (AT), which includes any product or system that is used to facilitate participation and improve functional capabilities of individuals with disabilities, is another means of supporting community participation and autonomy of PAwPD that includes developing individual self-efficacy. Categories of AT include seating and mobility, vision technology, augmentative and alternative communication, and pervasive computing technologies. While there are inequalities in access to AT in the U.S. related to costs and insurance coverage, there is progress by manufacturers towards making AT more affordable, user-friendly, and accessible.

While LTSS do not usually include health care services, health care professionals such as occupational therapists can help address environmental barriers at home that limit the effectiveness of LTSS. For example, interventions may include providing education on technology or assistive equipment and its use (e.g. grab bars or handrails), helping identify and make home modifications (such as widening doorways), and improving the navigability of home spaces (through moving or rearranging the contents of the home). Research demonstrates the effectiveness of home modifications for preventing falls, reducing caregiver stress, and improving occupational performance around the home (Stark, Sanford, & Keglovits, 2015). Being adequately supported in one's home environment helps facilitate the ability to participate in the community.

Availability of health services also supports community engagement by ensuring PAwPD have acute and long-term health needs met. The shift towards telemedicine, which for the general population can improve access to care and overcome barriers such as transportation, reduces barriers to care particularly for persons with disabilities. A systematic review of the effectiveness of telemedicine found its commonly cited benefits include shorter wait times, higher levels of patient satisfaction, positive impacts on the general use of health services, and more consistent monitoring for patients with chronic conditions (Ekeland, Bowes, & Flottorp, 2010). There is general agreement that telemedicine is promising, yet more research is needed to identify the most effective delivery and formatting.

Finally, supports and services play an important role in empowering PAwPD to participate in their communities. The combination of LTSS, disability and ageing-related programming, and health services help to balance the person-environment fit and support PAwPD to live in their communities and age successfully.

Conclusion

PAwPD experience a unique set of challenges related to community participation as members of both the disability and ageing communities, although we have much to learn still about what these are and how we can more effectively address them. Additional research is needed to further identify facilitators and barriers to community participation experienced by this population and to develop evidence-based interventions to improve their health and well-being. Understanding more about where to target interventions – towards the person or the environment or both, when, how, and by whom – is important for reducing the tendency for community participation to decline as people age with disability. Building a stronger knowledge base will also support more effective practice and policy development related to increasing community participation of persons with disabilities across the life course.

References

Americans with Disabilities Act. (1990). Americans with Disabilities Act of 1990, Pub. L. No. 101-336, § 2, 104 Stat. 328.

Ansello, E. F. (2014). Public policy writ small: Coalitions at the intersection of aging and lifelong disabilities. *Public Policy and Aging Report, 14*, 3–6. https://doi.org/10.1093/ppar/14.4.1

ASPE. (2020). *Poverty guidelines*. U.S. Department of Health and Human Services. https://aspe.hhs.gov/poverty-guidelines

Battalio, S. L., Glette, M., Alschuler, K. N., & Jensen, M. P. (2018). Anxiety, depression, and function in individuals with chronic physical conditions: A longitudinal analysis. *Rehabilitation Psychology, 63*(4), 532–541. https://doi.org/10.1037/rep0000231

Chatterji, S., Byles, J., Cutler, D., Seeman, T., & Verdes, E. (2015). Health, functioning, and disability in older adults--present status and future implications. *Lancet (London, England), 385*(9967), 563–575. https://doi.org/10.1016/S0140-6736(14)61462-8

Cohen, M. L., Tulsky, D. S., Holdnack, J. A., Carlozzi, N. E., Wong, A., Magasi, S., … Heinemann, A. W. (2017). Cognition among community-dwelling individuals with spinal cord injury. *Rehabilitation Psychology, 62*(4), 425–434. https://doi.org/10.1037/rep0000140

Courtney-Long, E. A., Carroll, D. D., Zhang, Q. C., Stevens, A. C., Griffin-Blake, S., Armour, B. S., & Campbell, V. A. (2015). Prevalence of disability and disability type among adults—United States, 2013. MMWR. *Morbidity and Mortality Weekly Report, 64*(29), 777. https://www.cdc.gov/mmwr/preview/mmwrhtml/mm6429a2.htm

Craig, A., Guest, R., Tran, Y., & Middleton, J. (2017). Cognitive impairment and mood States after spinal cord injury. *Journal of Neurotrauma, 34*(6), 1156–1163. https://doi.org/10.1089/neu.2016.4632

Dashner, J., Espin-Tello, S. M., Snyder, M., Hollingsworth, H., Keglovits, M., Campbell, M. L., ... Stark, S. (2019). Examination of community participation of adults with disabilities: Comparing age and disability onset. *Journal of Aging and Health, 31*(10 Suppl), 169S–194S. https://doi.org/10.1177/0898264318816794

Depp, C. A., & Jeste, D. V. (2006). Definitions and predictors of successful aging: A comprehensive review of larger quantitative studies. *The American Journal of Geriatric Psychiatry, 14*(1), 6–20. https://doi.org/10.1097/01.JGP.0000192501.03069.bc

Di Carlo, A., Baldereschi, M., Amaducci, L., Maggi, S., Grigoletto, F., Scarlato, G., & Inzitari, D. (2000). Cognitive impairment without dementia in older people: Prevalence, vascular risk factors, impact on disability. The Italian longitudinal study on aging. *Journal of the American Geriatrics Society, 48*(7), 775–782. https://doi.org/10.1111/j.1532-5415.2000.tb04752.x

Ekeland, A. G., Bowes, A., & Flottorp, S. (2010). Effectiveness of telemedicine: A systematic review of reviews. *International Journal of Medical Informatics, 79*(11), 736–771. https://doi.org/10.1016/j.ijmedinf.2010.08.006

Gray, D. B., Hollingsworth, H. H., Stark, S., & Morgan, K. A. (2008). A subjective measure of environmental facilitators and barriers to participation for people with mobility limitations. *Disability and Rehabilitation, 30*(6), 434–457. https://doi.org/10.1080/09638280701625377

Gray, D. B., Hollingsworth, H. H., Stark, S. L., & Morgan, K. A. (2006). Participation survey/mobility: Psychometric properties of a measure of participation for people with mobility impairments and limitations. *Archives of Physical Medicine and Rehabilitation, 87*(2), 189–197. https://doi.org/10.1016/j.apmr.2005.09.014

Groah, S., & Kehn, M. (2010). The state of aging and public health for people with spinal cord injury: Lost in transition?. *Topics in Spinal Cord Injury Rehabilitation, 15*(3), 1–10. https://doi.org/10.1310/sci1503-1

Hammel, J., Magasi, S., Heinemann, A., Gray, D. B., Stark, S., Kisala, P., ... Hahn, E. A. (2015). Environmental barriers and supports to everyday participation: A qualitative insider perspective from people with disabilities. *Archives of Physical Medicine and Rehabilitation, 96*(4), 578–588. https://doi.org/10.1016/j.apmr.2014.12.008

Hammel, J., Magasi, S., Heinemann, A., Whiteneck, G., Bogner, J., & Rodriguez, E. (2008). What does participation mean? An insider perspective from people with disabilities. *Disability and Rehabilitation, 30*(19), 1445–1460. https://doi.org/10.1080/09638280701625534

Jensen, M. P., Truitt, A. R., Schomer, K. G., Yorkston, K. M., Baylor, C., & Molton, I. R. (2013). Frequency and age effects of secondary health conditions in individuals with spinal cord injury: A scoping review. *Spinal Cord, 51*(12), 882–892. https://doi.org/10.1038/sc.2013.112

Jette, A. M., & Field, M. J. (Eds.). (2007). *The future of disability in America.* National Academies Press. https://doi.org/10.17226/11898

Jiang, S. D., Dai, L. Y., & Jiang, L. S. (2006). Osteoporosis after spinal cord injury. *Osteoporosis International, 17*(2), 180–192. https://doi.org/10.1007/s00198-005-2028-8

Kemp, B., Adkins, R., & Thompson, L. (2004). Aging with a spinal cord injury: What recent research shows. *Topics in Spinal Cord Injury Rehabilitation, 10*(2), 175–197. https://doi.org/10.1310/LN1A-CK97-33AC-QFF3

Kinne, S., Patrick, D. L., & Doyle, D. L. (2004). Prevalence of secondary conditions among people with disabilities. *American Journal of Public Health, 94*(3), 443–445. https://doi.org/10.2105/ajph.94.3.443

LaPlante, M. P. (2014). Key goals and indicators for successful aging of adults with early-onset disability. *Disability and Health Journal, 7*(1 Suppl), S44–S50. https://doi.org/10.1016/j.dhjo.2013.08.005

Mallinson, T., & Hammel, J. (2010). Measurement of participation: intersecting person, task, and environment. *Archives of physical medicine and rehabilitation, 91*(9 Suppl), S29–S33. https://doi.org/10.1016/j.apmr.2010.04.027

Minor, B., Dashner, J., Espin-Tello, S., Bollinger, R., Keglovits, M., Stowe, J., ... Stark, S. (2020). Development and implementation of a community–based research network. *Journal of Clinical and Translational Science,* 1–24. https://doi.org/10.1017/cts.2020.45

Molton, I., Goetz, M., Jensen, M., & Verrall, A. (2012). D156: Evidence for "accelerated aging" in older adults with disability? *Journal of the American Geriatrics Society, 60*(S4), S239. https://onlinelibrary.wiley.com/doi/abs/10.1111/j.1532-5415.2012.04000.x

Molton, I. R., Terrill, A. L., Smith, A. E., Yorkston, K. M., Alschuler, K. N., Ehde, D. M., & Jensen, M. P. (2014). Modeling secondary health conditions in adults aging with physical disability. *Journal of Aging and Health, 26*(3), 335–359. https://doi.org/10.1177/0898264313516166

Molton, I. R., & Yorkston, K. M. (2017). Growing older with a physical disability: A special application of the successful aging paradigm. *The Journals of Gerontology. Series B, Psychological Sciences and Social Sciences, 72*(2), 290–299. https://doi.org/10.1093/geronb/gbw122

Nalder, E. J., Putnam, M., Salvador-Carulla, L., Spindel, A., Batliwalla, Z., & Lenton, E. (2017). Bridging knowledge, policies and practices across the ageing and disability fields: A protocol for a scoping review to inform the development of a taxonomy. *BMJ Open*, *7*(10), e016741. https://doi.org/10.1136/bmjopen-2017-016741

OLMSTEAD v. L.C. (98-536) 527 U.S. 581. (1999).

Putnam, M. (2014). Bridging network divides: Building capacity to support aging with disability populations through research. *Disability and Health Journal*, *7*(1 Suppl), S51–S59. https://doi.org/10.1016/j.dhjo.2013.08.002

Reaves, E. L., & Musumeci, M. (2015). *Medicaid and long-term services and supports: A primer*. The Kaiser Family Foundation. https://www.kff.org/medicaid/report/medicaid-and-long-term-services-and-supports-a-primer/

Reinhard, S. C., Kassner, E., Houser, A., & Mollica, R. (2011). *Raising expectations: A state scorecard on long-term services and supports for older adults, people with physical disabilities, and family caregivers*. AARP. https://assets.aarp.org/rgcenter/ppi/ltc/ltss_scorecard.pdf

Reinhardt, J., Ballert, C., Brinkhof, M., & Post, M. (2016). Perceived impact of environmental barriers on participation among people living with spinal cord injury on Switzerland. *Journal of Rehabilitation Medicine*, *48*(2), 210–218. https://doi.org/10.2340/16501977-2048

Stark, S., Sanford, J., & Keglovits, M. (2015). Environment factors: Physical and natural environment. In C. H. Christiansen, C. M., Baum, & J. D. Bass. *Occupational therapy: Performance, participation, and well-being* (4th ed., 387–420). SLACK Incorporated.

Tesch-Römer, C., & Wahl, H. W. (2017). Toward a more comprehensive concept of successful aging: Disability and care needs. *The Journals of Gerontology. Series B, Psychological Sciences and Social Sciences*, *72*(2), 310–318. https://doi.org/10.1093/geronb/gbw162

Tonack, M., Hitzig, S. L., Craven, B. C., Campbell, K. A., Boschen, K. A., & McGillivray, C. F. (2008). Predicting life satisfaction after spinal cord injury in a Canadian sample. *Spinal Cord*, *46*(5), 380–385. https://doi.org/10.1038/sj.sc.3102088

Verbrugge, L. M., Latham, K., & Clarke, P. J. (2017). Aging with disability for midlife and older adults. *Research on Aging*, *39*(6), 741–777. https://doi.org/10.1177/0164027516681051

Wallace, L. M., Theou, O., Pena, F., Rockwood, K., & Andrew, M. K. (2015). Social vulnerability as a predictor of mortality and disability: Cross-country differences in the survey of health, aging, and retirement in Europe (SHARE). *Aging Clinical and Experimental Research*, *27*(3), 365–372. https://doi.org/10.1007/s40520-014-0271-6

Wanigatunga, A. A., Manini, T. M., Cook, D. R., Katula, J., Fielding, R. A., Kramer, A. F., ... Nocera, J. R. (2018). Community-based activity and sedentary patterns are associated with cognitive performance in mobility-limited older adults. *Frontiers in Aging Neuroscience*, *10*, 341. https://doi.org/10.3389/fnagi.2018.00341

Watanabe, L. (2015, April). *Cognitive Conundrum*. Mobility Management. https://mobilitymgmt.com/Home.aspx

World Health Organization. (2001). *International Classification of Functioning, Disability, and Health (ICF)*. World Health Organization. https://www.who.int/classifications/icf/en/

Yorkston, K. M., McMullan, K. A., Molton, I., & Jensen, M. P. (2010). Pathways of change experienced by people aging with disability: A focus group study. *Disability and Rehabilitation*, *32*(20), 1697–1704. https://doi.org/10.3109/09638281003678317

Suggested Readings

Dashner, J., Espin-Tello, S. M., Snyder, M., Hollingsworth, H., Keglovits, M., Campbell, M. L., ... Stark, S. (2019). Examination of community participation of adults with disabilities: Comparing age and disability onset. *Journal of Aging and Health*, *31*(10 Suppl), 169S–194S. https://doi.org/10.1177/0898264318816794

LaPlante, M. P. (2014). Key goals and indicators for successful aging of adults with early-onset disability. *Disability and Health Journal*, *7*(1 Suppl), S44–S50. https://doi.org/10.1016/j.dhjo.2013.08.005

Molton, I. R., & Yorkston, K. M. (2017). Growing older with a physical disability: A special application of the successful aging paradigm. *The Journals of Gerontology. Series B, Psychological Sciences and Social Sciences*, *72*(2), 290–299. https://doi.org/10.1093/geronb/gbw122

Putnam, M. (2014). Bridging network divides: Building capacity to support aging with disability populations through research. *Disability and Health Journal*, *7*(1 Suppl), S51–S59. https://doi.org/10.1016/j.dhjo.2013.08.002

15
DESIGN FOR ONE IS DESIGN FOR ALL

The Past, Present, and Future of Universal Design as a Strategy for Ageing-in-Place with Disability

Jon A. Sanford and Elena T. Remillard

Introduction: Environment, Ageing, and Disability

The interactions among environment, ageing, and disability have long been described through a variety of ecological models. In contrast to medical models that define disability as an impairment in body function and structure, suggesting that disability is internal to an individual, social ecological models are grounded in the idea that disability is not an inevitable outcome of having an impairment. Rather, ecological models propose that limitation in functional ability is a predisposition to, not a determinant of disability, and that disability is an interaction between an individual's impairment and contextual factors.

One of the first social ecological models, the Environmental Press Model introduced in 1973 (Lawton & Nahemow, 1973), began a movement towards looking at the fit, or lack thereof, between the person and his/her environment to explain levels of disability that are beyond what would be expected from age-related deficits alone. Lawton and Nahemow's initial model, which arose from the fields of gerontology and environmental psychology, describes maladapted behaviour (e.g. disability) as the result of the demands of the environment (press) exceeding an individual's abilities (i.e. competence). Conversely, it argues that environments that are supportive of, or fit an individual's abilities, have lower environmental press, resulting in adaptive behaviour.

Despite its seminal theoretical contribution in describing the role of the environment as a contributor to disability, the person-environment fit model neither defined the pathways of environmental intervention nor accounted for the breadth and complexity of rehabilitation interventions beyond the environment, such as changes to the person and the activities in which he/she performed. By the mid-1990s a number of more nuanced ecological models emerged in occupational therapy (OT) and rehabilitation medicine addressing these dynamics. The OT models that emerged vary in the ways they portray the interactions among person, environment, and occupation factors, but their overall theoretical contribution is the addition of activity demands – or what it takes to do an activity – as a risk factor for disability (e.g. Law et al., 1996). Rehabilitation medicine models (Brandt & Pope, 1997) took another approach and pushed the ecological model beyond a descriptive framework into an intervention model where the environment is identified as viable pathway to reducing disability.

These additions to the ecological model contributed to a broader, psycho-social approach to rehabilitation and public health that was codified in the International Classification of Functioning, Disability, and Health (ICF) (World Health Organization, 2001). In contrast to earlier models, the ICF describes disability as a continuum on which individuals function at different levels due to the complex interaction of body functions and structures, activities, and participation with personal and environmental contextual factors (World Health Organization, 2001; World Health Organization, 2015). The ICF model differentiates between what individuals with a health condition can do (capacity to engage in activities and participate based on their body functions and structures) and what they actually do (activity and participation performance) as an outcome of their interactions with the context in which performance occurs. Context can act as either a barrier or facilitator. For individuals with multiple health conditions, such as those who acquired impairments in early to mid-life and are *ageing with disability* (Figure 15.1), this relationship between the person, environment, and activity limitation and participation restriction becomes even more complex (Field & Jette, 2007; Verbrugge & Yang, 2002).

Integrating models from ageing, disability and public health, the TechSAge Model of Ageing and Disability (Figure 15.2) was developed to illustrate the effects of environmental factors on activity and

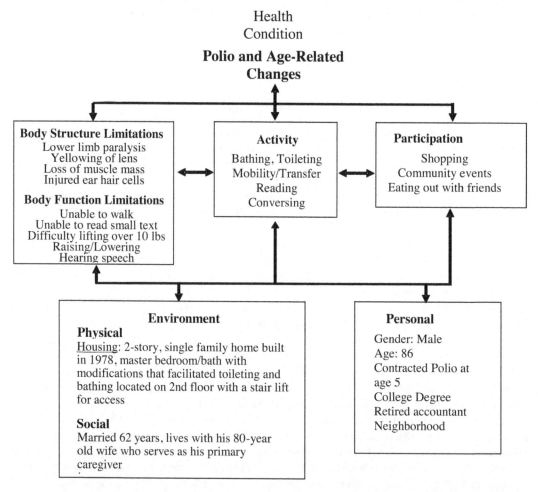

Figure 15.1 ICF model illustrating ageing with disability through the persona of Ralph, an 86-year-old male with Polio, a long-term health condition, who is also experiencing age-related changes in vision and hearing. Although Ralph had environmental modifications that accommodated his lower limb paralysis in middle age, his age-related loss of muscle mass made transfer difficult, impacting his use of the stair lift, as well as the toilet and bathtub modifications. In addition, without intervention, his hearing and vision limitations restrict his participation in life activities.

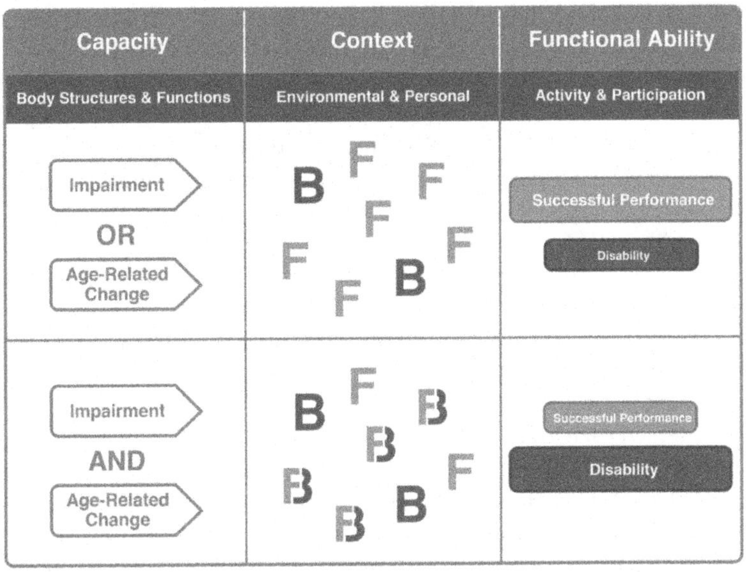

Figure 15.2 TechSAge Model of Ageing and Disability. The second row represents individuals who have a pre-existing impairment OR age-related changes. Environmental factors act either as Facilitators (F's) or Barriers (B's), creating demands on a person's abilities (i.e. Capacity) that result in either successful performance or disability (i.e. Limitations and restrictions in activity and participation, respectively). The bottom row represents individuals have a long-term impairment AND who are ageing, which can significantly reduce one's abilities. As a result, environmental factors that previously acted as facilitators now act as barriers creating increased disability. (As described in Mitzner et al., 2017).

participation of people who are ageing with long-term impairments. The model conceptualises the relationship between capacity (body structures and function), context (personal and environmental facilitators and barriers), and functional ability (activity and performance outcomes) for people who have either an impairment *or* age-related changes compared to those who have an impairment *and* age-related changes. Thus, even when one's environment is held constant, as an individual grows older with a long-term impairment, facilitators that previously resulted in successful activity and participation can become barriers with disability outcomes (Mitzner, Sanford, & Rogers, 2018).

The change from facilitator to barrier occurs because individuals ageing with disability, not only have long-term impairments, but also experience the effects of normative age-related changes. In contrast to people who only experience normative age-related changes in later life (known as *ageing into disability*), the cumulative effects of an impairment over a sustained period of time interacting with changes or conditions in later life create complex and compounding challenges. As a result, individuals ageing with disability may experience a multitude of barriers in the physical and digital words, above and beyond persons ageing into disability. As this happens, compensatory environmental interventions, such as assistive technologies and accessible designs, that successfully reduced disability when individuals with impairments were younger, as illustrated by Ralph in Figure 15.1, often turn into barriers to activity and participation in later life due to the additive effects of age-related changes.

Design and technology interventions that reduce environmental press by providing appropriate contextual support can, theoretically, facilitate successful performance of activities and participation at any age. To date, most design and technology interventions have focused on specialised assistive technologies and accessible designs that compensate for the particular functional (e.g. eyeglasses, wheelchairs) or activity limitations (e.g. toileting, bathing) experienced by people ageing into disability (typical older adults) or those with specific impairments in body function or structure (often younger and middle-aged persons with disabilities).

These interventions strategies are limited in two ways. First, they do not specifically address the needs of the crossover population of individuals ageing with disability (Beer, Mitzner, Stuck, & Rogers, 2015; Campbell & Putnam, 2017; Harrington, Mitzner, & Rogers, 2015). Second, they do not directly compensate for participation restrictions experienced by either this population, those who are ageing into disability or younger individuals with disabilities. One way to address the compound and complex environmental barriers to activity limitations and participation restrictions for people ageing with disability these limitations is through a Universal Design (UD) approach that promotes design that is usable by all people, to the greatest extent possible, without the need for adaptation or specialised design (Mace, Hardie, & Plaice, 1991).

Most importantly, because UD is a strategy that focuses on design for all, rather than just older adults or individuals who have a disability, UD is the same for everyone. As mainstream everyday design, UD is both usable and inclusive, which suggests that it is a promising approach for addressing the variety of activity limitations and participation restrictions experienced by people ageing with disability, as well as the general population as a whole.

Despite its strengths, UD has often been criticised and dismissed as an unrealistic utopian ideal. Whereas we recognise that UD is unattainable as it was originally conceived in the physical world, this chapter will propose that a UD approach is not only a viable and enviable design strategy to promote ageing-in-place with disability compared to specialised design, but also an achievable and realistic approach when recast as a merger between the physical and digital worlds. To present that case, this chapter traces the evolution of UD from its origins in specialised design to its future as the integration of digital technology with physical design.

From Design for One to Design for All and Back Again: The Evolution of Universal Design to Support Ageing-in-Place with Disability

Design for One: Specialised Design for Ageing OR Disability

Typically, products, devices, buildings, and systems are designed for the 'average' user with normative abilities and without impairments. Not surprisingly, most of these everyday designs present barriers to use by people who have limitations in their functional abilities. To overcome barriers with everyday designs, compensatory specialised designs, including assistive technologies (AT) and accessible designs (AD), act as interventions to facilitate activity performance by people with disabilities.

Assistive Technology

In the U.S., an AT device is defined in the Technology-Related Assistance for Individuals with Disabilities Act of 1988 (1988), as 'any item, piece of equipment, or product system, whether acquired commercially, modified, or customised, that is used to increase, maintain, or improve functional capabilities of individuals with disabilities' (Technology-Related Assistance for Individuals with Disabilities Act of 1988, 1988). AT typically includes adaptive equipment, devices and products that compensate for either reduced capacity due to impairment in body function and/or structure or specific activity limitations. These can be considered within the ICF model. In general, AT that can be used for multiple activities, such as a wheelchair, reacher, or magnifier, can directly improve an individual's capacity by mitigating the effects of impairment. In this way, the AT acts on the capacity domain and can indirectly reduce activity limitations. For example, a magnifier can minimise the effects of vision loss by increasing the size of text, which can enable individuals to engage in any activity that requires reading (Figure 15.3).

In contrast, AT designed for a single, specific activity, such as a bath tub bench or toilet safety frame, act directly on the activity domain by mitigating the effects of environmental barriers that create restrictions in a given activity (National Academies of Sciences, Engineering and Medicine, 2017). For example, toilet grab bars compensate for the loss of ability to raise and lower oneself by overcoming environmental barriers created by a toilet that requires sit-to-stand abilities.

Design for One is Design for All

Figure 15.3 Magnification.

Accessible Design

In the United States, AD in public facilities is primarily guided by the Americans with Disabilities Act (ADA) and its amendments (1990, 2008) and the ADA Accessibility Standards (Department of Justice, 2010). The accessibility standards set minimum requirements necessary for people with disabilities to access public facilities in order to engage in the types of activities that will enable them participate in societal roles, such as employment, education, shopping, culture, and community service. It is important to note that although residential and work environments are not specifically subject to the ADA Accessibility Standards and often have their own practice guidelines, these guidelines are often influenced by the ADA requirements.

As promulgated and practiced, AD, like AT, is a prosthetic, specialised design that compensates for limitations with specific types and levels of abilities by reducing or eliminating environmental barriers to activity. For example, curb ramps at street crossings enable people who use wheeled mobility aids to cross the street, whereas tactile warnings on those curb ramps are needed to warn people with vision limitations that they are about to enter a street crossing. Unlike AT, which mitigates barriers to activity either directly by facilitating performance of specific tasks, or indirectly by enhancing capacity, AD, only acts on directly on barriers associated with activity limitations. As a result, activity-focused AD and AT interventions are often used interchangeably. For example, grab bars may be considered AT or AD.

Benefits of Specialised Design

Specialised Designs can offer many benefits to individuals with specific impairments, including improved performance of, and increased confidence in, a range of activities in the home, work, and community. Effective specialised designs can reduce risk of injury (i.e. falls) as well as functional decline and disability. Such improvements can ultimately reduce caregiving needs and increase one's ability to live independently and age-in-place. For many individuals, this means continuing to live in the home of their choice and avoiding re-location to senior housing or long-term care facilities.

Limitations of Specialised Design

Despite the technical success of traditional specialised design strategies in increasing function for individuals with disabilities, specialised design is, at its very core, design for one. Whether it is a one-off design for *one individual* or a generic design intended for *one group of individuals* that share similar functional limitations, specialised design is not intended for the mainstream market. Therefore, despite its goal of promoting participation by facilitating activity, specialised design suffers from a variety of practical, aesthetic and social obstacles, that have resulted in stigmatising, segregating, and signalising environments described below.

First, implementing different design solutions for each individual or type of functional limitation only works when it is accommodating a specific impairment, and not so well when an individual has multiple and competing limitations. For example, a screen reader, which reads the text out loud is a typical AT solution to make a computer screen accessible to someone who is blind. This may work pretty well until that individual begins to lose hearing function as a result of age-related hearing loss.

Second, specialised designs are rarely useful to anyone other than the one individual or group of individuals who need them. As a result, specialised designs that remove barriers to activity for one individual may result in new barriers for another, whether the latter previously had a limitation with that particular activity or not. Take the case of the curb ramp and tactile warning. Removing the curb, which is a barrier to a wheeled mobility device, created a barrier to blind individuals who use long canes because they used the curb to detect the transition between sidewalk and street. The solution was the requirement for raised truncated domes (i.e. bumps) to provide tactile warnings at curb ramps. Whereas the resulting may have solved the safety issue for blind pedestrians, they often create a mobility barrier for the same wheelchair users for whom the curb ramps were intended.

The same type of problem can be attributed to home modifications when more than one person needs to use a particular design. For example, Ralph who was described in the ICF persona in Figure 15.1, uses a tub bench to be able to transfer to the tub for a seated shower. His wife, on the other hand, likes to take hot baths. She would have no difficulty getting in and out of the tub, but for the 30″ long, 17 pound tub bench that is in the way. Even if she could manage to lift it up, where could she put it in the small confines of a bathroom where it would not be a tripping hazard (Figure 15.4)?

Third, specialised designs typically draw unwanted attention to individuals who need them. By virtue of their emphasis on function over form, specialised designs are typically utilitarian, band-aid solutions. They are often a-contextual solutions that stand out and are not integrated with everyday designs that define the context. For example, being the only one in a neighbourhood with a ramp to the front door clearly identifies the resident as a person with a disability. By drawing unwanted attention to differences in ability, specialised designs often become unintended symbols of the disability, itself (Sanford, 2012). As a result, it is often preferable to go without or give up using a specialised design, such as only using a walker in one's own home, rather than suffer the stigma of being less able, sick or different.

Finally, specialised design is driven entirely by facilitating activity (see Figure 15.5), either indirectly by mitigating the effects of impairment (AT) or directly by removing environmental barriers to that activity (AT and AD). Without a direct pathway to reducing participation restrictions, specialised design presumes that there is a linear relationship between activity limitation and participation restriction whereby facilitating activity will result in increased participation. Such experiments in the 'activity-begets-participation' paradigm have demonstrated that even if we build it, not everyone will come (Sanford, 2012). For example, the increased accessibility of public streets and transportation to promote mobility (i.e. activity) since the advent of the ADA has not significantly increased employment (i.e. participation) rates of people with disabilities. These data are not surprising as the ICF presents a more complex, non-linear model which predicts that participation is the result of multiple interactions among the various constructs, not just activity.

Design for All: Universal Design for Ageing and Disability

UD is a term that was coined by Ron Mace, an architect with a disability, leading advocate of accessibility legislation, designer of assistive devices and founding director of the Center for Universal Design at NC State University (Sanford, 2012). Despite his staunch support for traditional AT and AD strategies, Mace developed the concept of UD to describe design of everyday products, buildings and spaces

Figure 15.4 Storage of technology.

in order to overcome the limitations inherent in the design-for-one paradigm of specialised design described above. There are four main reasons for using UD.

First, as the 'design of products and environments to be usable by all people, to the greatest extent possible, without the need for adaptation or specialized design' (Mace et al., 1991), UD, by its very definition, does not seek different design solutions for each individual or type of functional limitation. Rather, it seeks to achieve mainstream, everyday design that makes usability and inclusivity the design norm rather than the exception. By integrating the objectives of specialised design into everyday design, UD is not just hard to see, it is invisible (Sanford, 2012).

Second, UD is a performance-based approach that is founded on the understanding that disability is not a single point requiring specialised intervention, but is a part of a spectrum of human cognitive, motor, sensory and communication abilities that range in function from no ability to maximum ability (Sanford, 2012). By simultaneously accommodating the spectrum of abilities in every design, usability by all obviates the need for accessibility by one and there is no distinction between someone who needs an accommodation and who does not who do not.

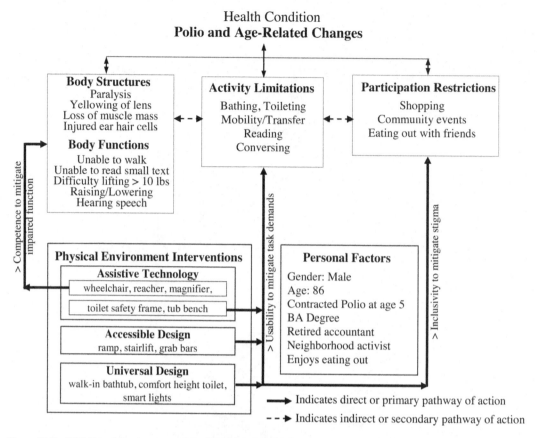

Figure 15.5 ICF-Based Environmental Intervention Model for Ralph, an 86-year-old male ageing with a long-term mobility disability illustrating how examples of appropriate physical environmental interventions impact body functions and structures, activity limitations, and participation restrictions. (Adapted from National Academies of Sciences, Engineering, and Medicine, 2017).

Third, UD addresses both function and form as integral parts of the design process. As a result, UD not only addresses barriers pragmatically, but also aesthetically through contextual scale and character. The result is everyday design that is intended to achieve broad appeal in order to avoid the stigma of disability (Steinfeld & Maisel, 2012).

Finally, UD is intended to address the stigma, segregation, and social shortcomings of specialised design by directly enhancing participation as well as activity performance (Figure 15.5). It is rooted in ideas of equitability and inclusivity, which are the design goals for participation. Unlike specialised design, UD is not restricted to a linear process that relies on an intervention pathway that directly facilitates activity performance and as a result, secondarily and indirectly promotes participation. Rather, UD considers the activity and participation equally, with activity performance the direct outcome of design usability, and participation the direct outcome of socially-focused design inclusivity in addition to the indirect outcome of successful engagement in life's activities.

Principles of Universal Design

UD does not prescribe a set of design attributes and rules of what must be done, but rather principles that describe why and how to do it. The seven principles of UD[1] were developed by an inter-disciplinary group of experts to provide performance-based goals and guidelines for UD (Connell et al., 1997). The principles capture the constructs of both activity and participation. The first principle, equitable use, emphasises participation through inclusivity, whereas activity through usability is the basis of the following six principles: flexibility in use, simple, and intuitive use, perceptible information, tolerance for error, low physical effort, and size and space for approach and use (Table 15.1).

Table 15.1 The Principles of Universal Design © 1997 NC State University, The Center for Universal Design

1. **Equitable Use:** The design is useful and marketable to people with diverse abilities
    1a. Provide the same means of use for all users: identical whenever possible; equivalent when not
    1b. Avoid segregating or stigmatising any users
    1c. Provisions for privacy, security, and safety should be equally available to all users
    1d. Make the design appealing to all users
2. **Flexibility in Use:** The design accommodates a wide range of individual preferences and abilities
    2a. Provide choice in methods of use
    2b. Accommodate right- or left-handed access and use
    2c. Facilitate the user's accuracy and precision
    2d. Provide adaptability to the user's pace
3. **Simple and Intuitive Use:** Use of the design is easy to understand, regardless of the user's experience, knowledge, language skills, or current concentration level
    3a. Eliminate unnecessary complexity
    3b. Be consistent with user expectations and intuition
    3c. Accommodate a wide range of literacy and language skills
    3d. Arrange information consistent with its importance
    3e. Provide effective prompting and feedback during and after task completion
4. **Perceptible Information:** The design communicates necessary information effectively to the user, regardless of ambient conditions or the user's sensory abilities
    4a. Use different modes (pictorial, verbal, tactile) for redundant presentation of essential information
    4b. Provide adequate contrast between essential information and its surroundings
    4c. Maximise 'legibility' of essential information
    4d. Differentiate elements in ways that can be described
    4e. Provide compatibility with a variety of techniques or devices used by people with sensory limitations
5. **Tolerance for Error:** The design minimises hazards and the adverse consequences of accidental or unintended actions
    5a. Arrange elements to minimise hazards and errors: most used elements, most accessible; hazardous elements eliminated, isolated, or shielded
    5b. Provide warnings of hazards and errors
    5c. Provide fail-safe features
    5d. Discourage unconscious action in tasks that require vigilance
6. **Low Physical Effort:** The design can be used efficiently and comfortably and with a minimum of fatigue
    6a. Allow user to maintain a neutral body position
    6b. Use reasonable operating forces
    6c. Minimise repetitive actions
    6d. Minimise sustained physical effort
7. **Size and Space for Approach and Use:** Appropriate size and space is provided for approach, reach, manipulation, and use regardless of user's body size, posture, or mobility
    7a. Provide a clear line of sight to important elements for any seated or standing user
    7b. Make reach to all components comfortable for any seated or standing user
    7c. Accommodate variations in hand and grip size
    7d. Provide adequate space for the use of assistive devices or personal assistance

Benefits of UD

UD is intended to engender both positive activity and participation outcomes by focusing on all abilities of all individuals rather than on people with disabilities alone. As a result, UD is not just about access for some, it is about usability and inclusion for all.

In addition to being usable and inclusive, UD is useful, contextual, and sustainable. First, because UD considers the range of human abilities it sets a baseline for usability that will reduce or eliminate need for specialised designs. As a result, any particular design has the potential to be useful to anyone regardless of ability. Second, as everyday design UD is contextual, seamlessly integrating into its context of application, making it, for all intents and purposes, invisible. Finally, UD is sustainable design. By being useable across the lifespan of an individual as well as the lifespan of our environments, UD not only works in the present, but can continue to support others in the future.

Limitations of UD

In Greek mythology, Panacea is the goddess of universal remedy. So too, UD is championed as the remedy that will ensure usability and inclusivity for all. While conceptually appealing, being a universal cure-all would require widespread adoption and implementation. In the three decades since UD's beginnings, this has not been the case (Sanford, 2017). UD has not only failed to achieve widespread adoption as an approach to mainstream design, it has failed to replace AT and AD as an approach to design for people with disabilities. These failures can be attributed to four factors:

First, UD is a cliché on one hand, and an enigma on the other. Most often, the design and marketing of UD-branded products, environments, and technologies are targeted to audiences of people with disabilities or older adults, which suggests that UD is nothing more than a cliché – specialised design in a UD wrapper. This misrepresentation of UD is completely incompatible with Principle 1, which promotes everyday designs targeted to all users. Further, while this strategy might give the appearance of increasing the availability of UD overall, the result is that there are more examples of accessible design and relatively few good examples of UD.

UD is also an enigma. The 'design for all individuals of all abilities to the greatest extent possible' is often interpreted as a one-size-fits-all approach to design for which there is only one ideal solution to any problem. The performance nature, flexibility and sometimes conflicting interests represented in 29 guidelines spread over the seven principles, suggests that there are many possible solutions, depending on the design approach and to what extent each of the guidelines are applied. This interpretation also fails to consider that the seven UD principles and their respective guidelines are not black and white, but shades of grey that, like any other design goals, generally require trade-offs in design that might favour one principle over another, depending on other design goals (e.g. cost) and target populations.

Second, public policy favours specialised designs over mainstream interventions, providing disincentives for UD as a design approach to ageing-in-place with disability. The ADA requires implementation of accessibility standards in public facilities. Standards are promulgated as prescriptive requirements (e.g. the size and location of a toilet grab bar) that mandate specific designs to remove barriers to activity (e.g. get on and off a toilet). While ADA standards define a set of prescriptive rules of what to do, UD, as articulated by a set of performance guidelines (i.e. Principles of UD), defines why it should be done. Unfortunately, most requirements in the ADA accessibility standards are a throwback to guidelines developed in the mid 20th century to accommodate young, male veterans who used manual wheelchairs, but had good upper body strength. As a result, although the standards were not intended to meet the needs of people ageing with disability, they are nonetheless mandated by law with quantifiable requirements (e.g. a ramp is 1:12 or slopes 1 vertical inch every 12 inches in length; Sanford, Echt, & Malassigné, 1999). UD solutions that are open to interpretation and/or do not meet these requirements, are not permitted, even if evidence suggests that they would better meet the needs of older adults ageing with disability (Lee et al., 2017; Sanford & Bosch, 2013).

Health reimbursement policies in the Centers for Medicare/Medicaid Services (CMS) related to Medicaid and Medicare, the two major public insurance systems in the U.S., are also a major disincentive to implementing UD interventions. Although policies are slowly changing to allow individuals to make decisions, under certain circumstances, about what interventions best meet their own needs, they are traditionally based on a person-centric medical model that focuses on health and activity outcomes of individual clients. As such, reimbursement typically covers interventions that have direct benefit to the health and activity of individual clients. These include personal assistance and assistive and medical technologies, and, depending on the state, some limited home modifications. It does not cover interventions that provide additional benefits to the client, such as participation in social roles. Similarly, CMS does not typically cover design solutions that have the potential to benefit others in addition to the individual in need such as mainstream UD solutions that might be usable and useful to other family members living at home.

Finally, adoption of UD is hampered by the perception that it is a utopian concept that has an absolute idealist agenda, an exclusionary structure and unrealistic goals (Steinfeld & Tauke, 2002). The result is that designers consider it impractical and a waste of time and resources because it is not achievable. Nonetheless, it imagines what the world should be, not necessarily what the world will be. And if not for all, then for whom? On the one hand, virtually every design falls short of its target criteria and goals (think, v. 2.0, 3.0…). Therefore, if we don't set our design goal unrealistically high, we are likely to fall far shorter from the ideal than we will if we set the ideal as the design goal. More importantly, this will require even more iterations to reach the ideal (think versions 1.2, 1.3, 1.4…). On the other hand, if we set our goals unrealistically high then we might just come a lot closer to the goal in a much shorter time (think v 2, period). Admittedly, physical designs that are usable and inclusive of everyone are probably not technically achievable, but everything changes when digital technologies are integrated into the physical.

Design for One: Ability-Based Design for People Ageing with Disability

As we have seen, traditional design approaches for ageing and disability are compensatory. They can be reactive, prosthetic designs to offset the loss of a specific ability by enhancing or supporting that ability to (i.e. AT or AD), or proactive pre-emptive designs that anticipate low levels or loss of all ability(ies) and provide alternative means of use to support and make use of one's highly functioning abilities (UD). While UD shifts the focus from what cannot be done to what can be done, it is still built around a population-based approach to ability that assumes fairly homogenous abilities across ability types (e.g. people with loss of upper body motor function, people with vision loss, people with cognitive limitations, etc.).

In recent years, a new approach has emerged that has shifted away from design based on assumptions of what a group of people can do to a focus on designing for what one individual can do. Centred primarily in interactive technology systems, Ability-Based Design (ABD) has been applied to overcome biases and general assumptions of ability among designers (Wobbrock, Gajos, Kane, & Vanderheiden, 2018). To overcome designer expectations of broad categories of sensory, motor, cognitive, and communication abilities-based perceptions of an 'average user' (e.g. blind, deaf, wheelchair user, memory impaired, or speech disorder), ABD attempts to accommodate each specific type of ability when developing a design. For example, accommodating visual abilities could include: near vision, far vision, light sensitivity, colour discrimination, and contrast sensitivity.

By accommodating all known abilities, ABD is capable of adapting and customising interfaces and functions to the abilities and preferences of any individual user through user adaptation, auto-adaptation, and auto-personalisation. User adaptation strategies enable individual users to manually configure a system to match their own abilities or preferences. For example, smart phones and tablets (see Figure 15.6) typically provide users with the capability to adjust interface settings such as those for

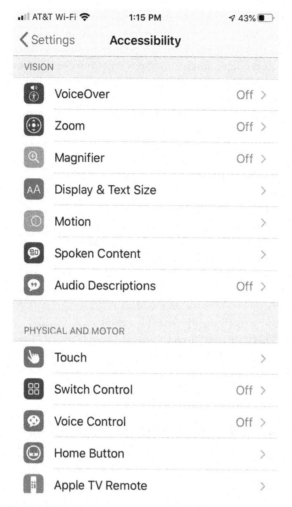

Figure 15.6 iPhone user adaption of interfaces.

display (e.g. zoom, font size colour contrast, zoom), output (e.g. captioning, audio), and navigation (e.g. keystroke shortcuts).

In addition, user responsive adaptation of interfaces and functions can be automated to enable users to have streamlined ways to access the input and output methods they need on any system. Using machine learning and artificial intelligence, auto-adaption systems are able to detect, observe, model and automatically adapt to a user's behaviour or ability. For example, the Nest Learning Thermostat automatically adjusts home temperature based on past history or uses proximity sensors to go into vacation mode when no movement is detected. Similarly, products can use auto contextual adaptation, which responds to changes in the environment to support user abilities. For example, the iPhone changes the visual interface and device functions in response to changes in environmental lighting conditions.

Finally, auto-personalisation is a strategy that transcends adapting various interface characteristics and functions by customising entire interfaces to help each individual have the best possible interface fit. This strategy is being applied on a large scale with the development of the Global Public Inclusive Infrastructure (GPII) initiative (Vanderheiden & Treviranus, 2011; Vanderheiden et al., 2012). Based on a 'one-size-fits-one' approach (Wobbrock et al., 2018; Vanderheiden et al., 2012), GPII is a cloud-based system of stored interface applications (Figure 15.7) built to support each users' abilities and preferences (e.g. large type,

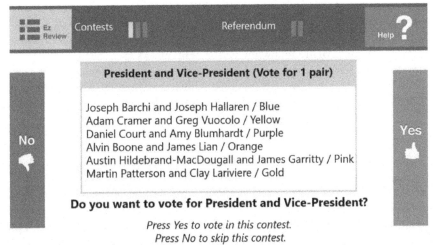
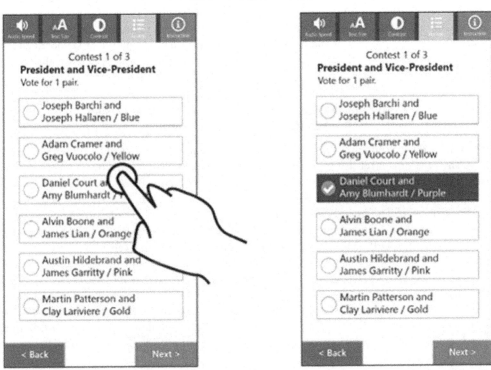

Figure 15.7 Electronic election ballots. Two election ballots (left, EZ Ballot; right, Quick Ballot) which were designed according to UD Principles, have a different look and feel, but the hardware remains the same.

audio aids, captions, high-contrast screens, on-screen keyboard). Ultimately, auto-personalisation would enable users to have their own customised and familiar interface for any software application.

Benefits of ABD

Regardless of which ABD strategy is employed, ability-based systems work to match users' individual abilities as opposed to interface designs based on general population-based assumptions of ability

(Wobbrock, Gajos, Kane, & Vanderheiden, 2018). ABD's greatest strength is its use of cloud-based storage of personalised information. Whether it be the capability of downloading an entire customised interface, such as GPII, or individual adaptations for various interface features, such as font size or contrast, cloud storage enables ABD to follow the person. This allows user-specific interfaces or interface characteristics that are already adapted to a user's needs to be accessed from any computer, anywhere. As a result, interfaces do not have to be customised, which may require assistance from another (e.g. caregiver or IT professional) every time new machine or new version of an application is used.

Limitations of ABD

Although ABD cloud-based systems open up a new world of possibilities beyond the constant customisation of application interfaces to match the abilities of any user, it is not without its limitations. The most obvious challenge in enabling the design to fit the abilities of any user, is to first identify the potential set of abilities that are needed to interact with a design and then to create a design capable of accommodating any of those abilities interchangeably and equally. For example, while the motor ability of dexterity is necessary to use a smartphone interface, the motor ability to ambulate is not.

In addition, ABD has been limited to the context of interactive computing, where sensing, adapting, and configuring are technological possibilities. While it works well in the digital world for customising interfaces for software applications and hardware input devices, such as a mouse or keyboard, applying the same ABD strategies to the physical world is more challenging. However, as we shall see, not beyond the realm of possibility.

Design for One is Design for all: The Future of Design for Ageing-in-Place with Disability

The physical world is changing. Digital interfaces are commonly used on virtually all physical artefacts that have any type of control that is or can be electrically-, battery- or solar-powered, including electronics, communication devices, window shades, water faucets, lights, thermostats, door locks, and an array of other devices. Further, more and more of these digital interfaces are 'connected'. The proliferation of so-called Internet of Things (IoT) devices has created the opportunity not only to take ABD from the digital world and into the physical, but at the same time, to conceptualise ABD in a UD framework.

First and foremost, UD Principles can guide the design of interfaces that can accommodate any of the interchangeable abilities identified as being able to equally operate a specific device. However, we need to turn UD, on its head. Rather than try and develop unique UD interfaces for each IoT device, which is likely unachievable, a better goal would be to develop universal IoT devices that would enable user-adapted ABD interfaces to be used across different devices. Enabling each user to apply one interface across devices will ensure usability of any device, without specialised design or the need to continually adapt and set up interfaces as devices are changed/added to a system. This approach to UD also ensures inclusivity for all. Only the software interfaces differ among users. The hardware is the same, regardless of ABD interface. As a result, all users, regardless of ability, would be able to obtain and operate any device.

As a first step towards demonstrating the feasibility of a 'Design for One is Design for All' approach, two general government election ballots were designed and evaluated to validate the premise that multiple interfaces on the same Microsoft Tablet hardware platform could be used by people with different visual abilities to achieve the same outcomes. Although the ballot interfaces were designed using a UD approach, each interface was designed specifically to address different visual abilities of users.

The primary difference between the two ballots (see Figure 15.7) was the selection and navigation process. The first interface, EZ Ballot, was designed with a linear, binary yes/no input system for all selections that fundamentally re-conceptualises ballot design to provide the same simple and intuitive voting experience for all voters, regardless of ability or I/O interface used. The second interface,

QUICK Ballot was designed to minimise voting effort by using a random or nonlinear input selection that is similar to the current electronic voting systems.

In a comparative study of individuals with and without vision loss, participants who were blind or partially sighted made fewer errors and preferred EZ Ballot; while users without vision loss made fewer errors and preferred QUICK Ballot. However, all participants were able to use both ballots independently to complete voting tasks similar to what they would encounter on a real ballot. Although the degree of usability varied according to a user's abilities and preferences, both software ballot interfaces were usable.

Let's assume that nothing is perfect. If we go back to the definition of UD, it is stated as 'the design of all products and environments to be usable by all people to the greatest extent possible without the need for specialised design or adaptation' (Mace et al., 1991). Let's focus on the phrase *usable by all people*. Usable by all people does not explicitly state that any design has to be the ideal best fit for every person on the planet. It merely states that it has to be useable, that is, able to be used or capable of being used. This suggests, that UD could be the ideal best fit for one individual and be difficult, yet still usable by another. Alternatively, it might be usable by all, but not an ideal fit for any one individual. This understanding of UD allows the designer to make reasonable trade-offs to ensure usability and inclusivity for all even if it is not a perfect fit for everyone.

Like the tale of two ballots, this suggests that universal usability can be achieved through the design of digital software interfaces while implementing those interfaces on hardware that is universal designed can achieve equitable use and inclusivity. As a result, design does not necessarily have to be built to achieve an absolute ideal level of usability by all. Rather, it must achieve functional usability with absolute inclusivity for all.

Post-Script: The Past, Present and Future of Universal Design for Ageing-in-Place with Disability

The past history of design for ageing with disability is captive to the perpetual barriers of cost, complexity, configuration, maintenance, and stigma of specialised designs. The present is paralyzed by the inability to achieve, in the physical world, the ideal that UD purports to be. The future, holds great promise for the integration of physical and digital technologies.

Clearly, the design of physical artefacts and their interfaces is fixed, with limited flexibility to achieve a high level of usability for all individuals in one design, and at great cost to develop many designs that would enable a high level of overall usability. In contrast, digital interfaces are dynamic and easily adapted for use in a single piece of hardware. In addition, they are relatively easy and quick to produce and, as such, it is comparatively inexpensive to produce multiple or adaptable interfaces to achieve high levels of overall usability. Therefore, digital technologies offer the possibility of seamless integration of multiple or customisable software interfaces into the same physical artefact. In the end, digital technologies are future of UD, while at the same time, UD is the future of digital technologies as it creates the framework for ABD to be captured and proliferated in the physical world.

Note

1 ©The Center for Universal Design, NC State University, 1997.

References

Americans with Disabilities Act. (1990). Americans with Disabilities Act of 1990, Pub. L. No. 101-336, § 2, 104 Stat. 328.
Americans with Disabilities Act Amendments Act. (2008). Americans with Disabilities Act Amendments Act of 2008. Pub. L. No. 110-325, 122 Stat. 3553.

Beer, J. M., Mitzner, T. L., Stuck, R. E., & Rogers, W. A. (2015). Design considerations for technology interventions to support social and physical wellness for older adults with disability. *International Journal of Automation and Smart Technology (AUSMT)*, 5(4), 249–264. https://doi.org/10.4017/gt.2015.14.1.004.00

Brandt, J., & Pope, A. M. (1997). *Enabling America: Assessing the role of rehabilitation science and engineering*. National Academies Press. https://doi.org/10.17226/5799

Campbell, M. L., & Putnam, M. (2017). Reducing the shared burden of chronic conditions among persons aging with disability and older adults in the United States through bridging aging and disability. *Healthcare*, 5(3), 56. https://doi.org/10.3390/healthcare5030056

Connell, B. R., Jones, M., Mace, R., Mueller, J., Mullick, A., Ostroff, E., … Vanderheiden, G. (1997). *The principles of universal design*. NC State University, The Center for Universal Design. https://projects.ncsu.edu/ncsu/design/cud/pubs_p/docs/poster.pdf

Department of Justice. (2010). *2010 ADA Standards for Accessible Design*. U.S. Government. https://www.ada.gov/regs2010/2010ADAStandards/2010ADAStandards.pdf

Field, M., & Jette, A. (2007). *The future of disability in America*. The National Academies Press. https://doi.org/10.17226/11898

Harrington, C. N., Mitzner, T. L., & Rogers, W. A. (2015). Understanding the role of technology for meeting the support needs of older adults in the USA with functional limitations. *Gerontechnology*, 14, 21–31. https://doi.org/10.4017/gt.2015.14.1.004.00

Law, M., Cooper, B., Strong, S., Stewart, D., Rigby, P., & Letts, L. (1996). The person-environment-occupation model: A transactive approach to occupational performance. *Canadian Journal of Occupational Therapy*, 63(1), 9–23. https://doi.org/10.1177/000841749606300103

Lawton, M. P., & Nahemow, L. (1973). Ecology and the ageing process. In C. Eisdorfer & M. P. Lawton (Eds.), *Psychology of adult development and ageing* (pp. 619–674). American Psychological Association. https://doi.org/10.1037/10044-020

Lee, S. J., Sanford, J., Calkins, M., Melgen, S., Endicott, S., & Phillips, A. (2017). Beyond ADA accessibility requirements: Meeting seniors' needs for toilet transfers, *Health Environments Research and Design Journal*, 1–13. https://doi.org/10.1177/1937586717730338

Mace, R., Hardie, G., & Plaice, J. (1991). Accessible environments: Toward universal design. In: White, E.T. (Ed.) *Innovation by design* (pp. 155–175). Van Nostrand Reinhold Publishers. Retrieved from https://projects.ncsu.edu/ncsu/design/cud/pubs_p/docs/ACC%20Environments.pdf

Mitzner, T. L., Sanford, J. A., & Rogers, W. A. (2018). Closing the capacity-ability gap: Using technology to support aging with disability. *Innovation in Aging*, 2(1), 1–8. https://doi.org/10.1093/geroni/igy008

National Academies of Sciences, Engineering and Medicine. (2017). *The promise of assistive technology to enhance activity and work participation*. The National Academies Press. https://doi.org/10.17226/24740.

Sanford, J. A. (2012). *Universal design as a rehabilitation strategy: Design for the ages*. Springer.

Sanford, J. A. (2017). Achieving universal design: One if by product, two if by process, three if by panacea. In: M. Antona & C. Stephanidis (Eds.), *Universal access in human–computer interaction. Design and development approaches and methods*. UAHCI 2017. Lecture Notes in Computer Science (Vol. 10277). Springer. https://doi.org/10.1007/978-3-319-58706-6

Sanford, J. A., & Bosch, S. J. (2013). An investigation of non-compliant toilet room design for assisting persons on to and off of the toilet, *Health Environments Research and Design*, 6(2), 43–57. https://doi.org/10.1177/193758671300600205

Sanford, J. A., Echt, K., & Malassigné, P. (1999). An E for ADAAG: The case for accessibility guidelines for the elderly based on three studies of toilet transfer. *Journal of Physical and Occupational Therapy in Geriatrics*, 16(3/4), 39–58. https://doi.org/10.1080/J148v16n03_03

Steinfeld, E., & Maisel, J. L. (2012). *Universal design: Creating inclusive environments*. John Wiley & Sons, Inc.

Steinfeld, E., & Tauke, B. (2002). Universal designing. *Universal design* (17), 165–190.

Technology-Related Assistance for Individuals with Disabilities Act of 1988. (1988). P.L. 100-407, 102 Stat. 1044.

Vanderheiden, G., & Treviranus, J. (2011). Creating a global public inclusive infrastructure. In Stephanidis, C. (Ed.) *Universal access in human-computer interaction. Design for all and inclusion*. UAHCI 2011. Lecture Notes in Computer Science (Vol. 6765). Springer. https://doi.org/10.1007/978-3-642-21672-5_57

Vanderheiden, G. C., Treviranus, J., Martinez Usero, J. A., Bekiaris, E., Gemou, M., & Chourasia, A. O. (2012). Auto-personalization: Theory, practice and cross-platform implementation. *Proceedings of the Human Factors and Ergonomics Society Annual Meeting*, 56(1), 926–930. https://doi.org/10.1177/1071181312561193

Verbrugge, L. M., & Yang, L. (2002). Aging with disability and disability with aging. *Journal of Disability Policy Studies*, 12(4), 253–267. https://doi.org/10.1177/104420730201200405

Wobbrock, J., Gajos, K., Kane, S., & Vanderheiden, G. (2018). Ability-based design. *Communications of the ACM*, 61(6), 62–71. https://doi.org/10.1145/3148051

World Health Organization. (2001). *International classification of functioning, disability and health.* World Health Organization. https://www.who.int/classifications/icf/en/

World Health Organization. (2015). *Implemented ICF update proposals 2015.* World Health Organization. https://www.who.int/classifications/2015icfupdates.pdf?ua=1

Suggested Readings

Beer, J. M., Mitzner, T. L., Stuck, R. E., & Rogers, W. A. (2015). Design considerations for technology interventions to support social and physical wellness for older adults with disability. *International Journal of Automation and Smart Technology (AUSMT), 5*(4), 249–264. https://doi.org/10.4017/gt.2015.14.1.004.00

Harrington, C. N., Mitzner, T. L., & Rogers, W. A. (2015). Understanding the role of technology for meeting the support needs of older adults in the USA with functional limitations. *Gerontechnology, 14,* 21–31. https://doi.org/10.4017/gt.2015.14.1.004.00

Sanford, J. A. (2012). *Universal design as a rehabilitation strategy: Design for the ages.* Springer.

Wobbrock, J., Gajos, K., Kane, S., & Vanderheiden, G. (2018). Ability-based design. *Communications of the ACM, 61*(6), 62–71. https://doi.org/10.1145/3148051

16
SUPPORT FOR DECISION-MAKING AS PEOPLE AGE WITH A COGNITIVE IMPAIRMENT

Terry Carney and Shih-Ning Then

Introduction

Law and human rights treaties set norms, rules and standards. Citizens actual lived experience of the law is another matter entirely. This is particularly so for people with a cognitive disability. Laws originally designed to be benignly protective can crush individual agency and choice when paternalistic best interest thinking runs riot. This denial of human agency is the nub of criticism of adult guardianship laws which appoint someone else as a 'substitute' decision-maker for a cognitively impaired person. It led the international community to adopt a new treaty, the UN *Convention of the Rights of Persons with Disabilities* (CRPD), under which substitute decision-making is supposed to be replaced by the idea of support for decision-making. But it is one thing to lay down a new principle and quite another to bring it to reality across the diverse circumstances of lived lives of people experiencing a cognitive impairment. Ageing adds a further layer of complexity to this task and brings its own age-related risk of cognitive impairment in the form of acquiring a dementia.

This chapter explores some ideas about the compounding effect (or 'intersectionality') when two already complex fields of practice and research come together in the lives of the same individual. For example, ageing with a cognitive disability not only raises disability-specific issues such as loss of close family or other previously relied on social supports, but also ageing-specific complications such as discrimination in the form of ageism, risks of elder abuse and navigating residential aged care systems. The argument we make here rejects simple legal or social panaceas which adopt a 'one-size-fits-all' approach. Instead we favour the more complex recipe of genuinely personalised and flexibly adaptive forms of social supports as cognitively impaired people enter and traverse this life stage.

The argument opens with a review of basic research, including taxonomies which may assist in understanding the diversity of different needs and circumstances of ageing with a cognitive impairment. It then turns to three key issues. We start by asking about the role of law reform to accommodate support for decision-making, concluding that it makes an essential but probably minor contribution to progress overall. The chapter then reviews some of the experience with development of programs or services geared towards capacity-building development or facilitation of support for decision-making. Here we conclude that, while still at very early stages, capacity-building for supporters faces many difficulties accommodating varying individual circumstances and social contexts, and its effectiveness and cost benefit remains a work in progress. The final issue considers supported decision-making for people with a dementia. It is shown that this group present very diverse and somewhat different needs to those of others with a cognitive impairment, posing perhaps the largest test for the new paradigm of support as a substitute for guardianship. The conclusion points both to the large agenda for future research into support for decision-making and the largely unknown needs of aged cohorts of people with a pre-existing cognitive impairment due to intellectual disability, acquired brain injury (ABI) or chronic and severe mental illness.

Prior Research

Background Literature and Inquiries

Support for decision-making for people with a cognitive impairment received a major fillip with the coming into force of the CRPD. The so-called 'equality principle' of article 12 of that international treaty ushered in a new paradigm where incapacity was no longer to be the basis for intervention in the lives of a person with impaired cognition, their legal and social agency was to be presumed, and the responsibility of the state (and civil society) was to enable people to realise their will, preferences and rights. While disability organisations were instrumental in the development of the CRPD, and in particular article 12 in its final iteration, there was a notable absence of dementia representatives and organisations (Donnelly, 2019). It is perhaps only more recently that there have been calls for dementia as a form of cognitive disability to be embraced within supported decision-making's developing discourse (Shakespeare, Zeilig, & Mittler, 2019).

In Australia, major reports by Australian Victorian Law Reform Commission (2012), the federal commission (ALRC, 2014) and NSW (2018), soon put flesh on the bones of these principles (Alston, 2017). Ageing has also been a focus for the federal Commission. The ALRC has provided an extensive blueprint addressing elder abuse (ALRC, 2017), and aged care currently is the subject of a wider Royal Commission Inquiry (Australia, 2019a). Yet another Royal Commission is examining violence, abuse, neglect and exploitation of people with disability (Australia, 2019b). As is the case internationally, however, little legislative action has yet been taken on either issue.

While there is literature on support for decision-making for each of the four main groups of people with cognitive impairment, including older people with a dementia, there is little direct research on decision support implications of *ageing* with a pre-existing cognitive impairment due to an intellectual disability, ABI or mental illness. Kohn and Blumenthal (2014) critically analyse the contribution of supported decision-making as people age with an intellectual disability (also Bigby, 1997; Bigby, Bowers, & Webber, 2011), while Shogren and colleagues reviewed the literature on supported decision-making across ageing, intellectual disability and mental illness (Shogren, Wehmeyer, Lassmann, & Forber-Pratt, 2017). There is also more general literature, such as on quality of life issues associated with being an older person with a cognitive impairment due to intellectual disability (Schepens, Puyenbroeck, & Maes, 2019). Even so, the cupboard is fairly bare.

Some Taxonomies

Taxonomies are necessarily crude heuristic approximations, but such models can help to scope the nature of the matters to be engaged. They can constitute something of a halfway house between the often generalised character of the legal norm and the lived experience of its operation. Time and again socio-legal research reveals that the law on the books has little effect, has unintended outcomes, or operates in an unexpected fashion. But taxonomies can help clear away some misunderstandings.

First, cognitive disability is not 'all of a piece': it is not a single constant but differs on many dimensions across a wide spectrum. There are quite major differences even as between its main origins. A person born with an intellectual disability may develop many social assets and capabilities (life skills) but unlike most adults with an ABI, they and those around them cannot turn for guidance to deep values and reflections laid down during a pre-impairment stage of life. Someone experiencing cognitive impairment during recurrent episodes of serious mental illness, when well can make an advance directive anticipating how they want decisions to be made, and can even review and remake it in light of experience after any subsequent episode of loss of capacity (Carney, 2019). Cognitive decline due to a dementia such as Alzheimer's disease can also be planned for (due to its escalating risk in later years of the ageing), but it has a downward trajectory rather than the more stable cognitive abilities for intellectual disability and ABI, or the recurrent dips and recovery more characteristic of chronic mental illness (Carney, 2020).

Second, law itself also is not 'all of a piece'. While admittedly a crude taxonomy, laws in the domains of ageing and disability can variously be classified as protective (guardianship and elder abuse), supportive (aged care or disability funding), preventive (regulation of residential care quality) or empowering (as support for decision-making or an advance directive seeks to be) (Carney, 2012; Doron, 2003). Each of these basic types has different strengths and limitations. Even the common regulatory form of law designed to promote and enforce standards, such as the quality and safety of disability services or residential aged care, demonstrably struggle to achieve their purpose, as evidenced in the Royal Commissions of Inquiry in both fields at the time of writing (Australia, 2019a, 2019b). Another of the ways typologies become important is when underlying rationales of models conflict or are underdeveloped. This has proved to be the case with the design of Australia's laudable but flawed scheme of funding and personalised support packages for people with substantial disabilities, under the National Disability Insurance Scheme (NDIS) (Bigby, 2020; Carney, Then, Bigby, Wiesel, & Douglas, 2019), in part because of the unusual actuarial foundation of its 'insurance' rationale.

Third, nor is the lived experience of law by people with cognitive impairments anything like 'all of a piece' either. This is true at the high level of design as well as individual lived lives. For example, the new guiding lodestar principle for the CRPD – support for decision-making – commendably sought to improve on criticism of the long-standing 'best interests of the person' test as being unduly vague or patronising, by replacing it with the superficially very appealing concentration on advancing the 'will, preferences and rights' of the person supported. But when more deeply interrogated, the phrase was found to contain two rather antagonistic notions (present 'wishes' vs. past deep 'preferences'), risked smuggling back paternalist best interests disguised as deep preferences, and proved to call for quite nuanced and diverse applications in practice (Carney, Then, Bigby, Wiesel, Douglas, et al., 2019; Szmukler, 2019). That sophisticated, individualised and context sensitive practice required to implement support for decision-making has now been documented across all domains of cognitive impairment, most recently for Australia for people with a dementia (Sinclair, Bajic-Smith, et al., 2019).

Finally, it is helpful to consider the taxonomy of the various kinds of support (none of which, by definition, takes away any part of the decision-making authority of the person being supported). Mary Donnelly adopts but supplements six dimensions of support first advanced by Bach and Kerzner (2010) in their original paradigm, writing that these are:

> life planning (choosing priorities in the context of values); independent advocacy (helping the person express his or her will and preferences); communicational and interpretative supports (representing the person's often unique forms of communication); representational supports (representing the person's will and preferences on the basis of long-standing relationships and/ or shared life experiences); relationship building supports (assisting the person in building personal support relationships); and, administrative supports (completing formal and procedural requirements)
>
> Donnelly, 2019, p. 3

For dementia in particular, Donnelly adds the importance of taking account of the person's 'range and complexity of life experiences' that elevate risks of abuse and neglect, and of accounting for the normative assumptions about how 'past' and 'present' will and preferences either are resolved (if one is favoured over the other) or are reconciled by locating a middle-ground. These two are of course equally pertinent to the design and assessment of support for decision-making across all forms of cognitive impairment.

In short, what these taxonomies reveal is that there is much complexity and many moving parts to be considered when thinking about support for decision-making as a replacement for or adjunct to substitute decision-making such as adult guardianship.

Individual Rights and Relational Autonomy

While one of the aims of the CRPD was to clearly articulate the *individual* rights owed to those with disabilities by member states, the *relational* nature of support for decision-making required under the CRPD can hardly be ignored (Harding, 2016). Little empirical evidence yet exists of how 'good' support is provided, but what little evidence there is points to the need for a trusting relationship between the supporter and the decision-maker, often as a result of a long standing relationship (Douglas & Bigby, 2018). In addition, unsurprisingly, those closest to those with cognitive disabilities, seem better placed to communicate with and determine the 'will and preference' of the person with a disability when compared with a stranger (Sinclair, Gersbach, et al., 2019). For older people with disabilities, and in particular dementia, long held beliefs or practices of people can 'shine a light' on determinations of what the decision-maker wants. While these findings may seem self-evident, the tension between individual rights and relational support may result in different interpretations of what supported decision-making actually entails for those in different professions – such as health care professionals or lawyers – when dealing with different decisions (Sinclair, Bajic-Smith, et al., 2019).

Key Issues

1. Supported Decision-making Law Reform Is Just a Start?

Substitute decision-making under adult guardianship appointments or delegation of decision-making under a power of attorney that operates when capacity is lost (an enduring power) depends on law. So, its full or partial replacement by CRPD compliant supported decision-making is also assumed to be the province of law reform. But this is only partially true, and then mainly for some groups of cognitively impaired in particular.

Unlike substitute decision-making that takes away a person's authority to choose and execute a decision, supported decision-making, as the name implies, involves supporting a person to better *realise* their decisional agency. A supporter acquires no portion of the decision-making authority of the person being supported. Support can readily be provided informally without any new laws, as already occurs socially through normal conversations and advice in our daily lives. Genuinely facilitative *support* of another person's decision-making is less likely to miscarry (by degenerating into coercion) and the harm done is less than is the case when informal arrangements involve a de facto assumption of substitute decision-making (such as when a younger relative 'takes over' an older person's electronic banking). But in both cases legislative authority is needed whenever the informal arrangement is challenged, whether by someone viewing a supporter as engaging in 'undue influence' of the supposed decisions of the person supported, or by a bank querying the basis for someone using another's log-ins to effectively make their banking decisions.

In the case of legally recognised supported decision-making, the two main authorisations conferred on the supporter are to access information on behalf of the person supported (not otherwise possible due to privacy protections) and to communicate or assist giving effect to the decision of the person being supported. As now is the case in the Australian state of Victoria, legislative reforms among other things authorise appointment of a supporter either by the person themselves or by an independent tribunal, granting such supporters both sets of powers. Although the CRPD is interpreted to not permit retention of tests of capacity and to require repeal of adult guardianship altogether, these reforms tend to ease rather than eliminate the threshold of understanding for a person to make their own appointment, and provide for support to be the first consideration before turning to guardianship.

Despite very strong endorsement in the literature for the CRPD and its widespread ratification, not all countries have accepted its obligations in full (Australia and Canada being just two of 12 countries to have entered formal reservations to preserve some substitute decision-making see Donnelly, 2019, p. 2). Parliaments have also been slow to act to introduce law reforms even along the modest lines of those described for Victoria, despite the impressive blueprints drawn up by law reform commissions (Then, Carney, Bigby, & Douglas, 2018). International progress also has been glacial (Kanter & Tolub, 2017), perhaps due to the abstract character of the norm and its framing as a civil (individual) rather than as a socio-economic right (Carney, 2017b). Thus in the US as at mid-2019, just nine states had enacted provision for appointing a supporter by way of a standard form or ordinary agreement, with proposals pending in six other states (Whitlatch, 2019).

In any event, law reform arguably is only one part of the picture. The opportunity to choose and appoint a supporter is more meaningful for a person with an early diagnosis of a dementia or in anticipation of episodes of cognitive impairment due to mental illness, than it is for members of other groups. For older people developing a dementia, the medical and in particular the *social* trajectory of the condition means that what starts out as genuine support fully directed and engaged by the person, eventually transitions to at best heavy external interpretation of preferences, if not outright paternalism (Carney, 2020; Sinclair, Bajic-Smith, et al., 2019; Sinclair et al., 2018). The decisions over which support and autonomy is retained also shrink in scope and significance as a dementia progresses.

The lower thresholds of understanding often required to make a formal appointment of a supporter when the law allows it, means that this avenue is not closed to someone already experiencing cognitive impairment due to intellectual disability or an ABI. But any such appointment would track quite closely to what would have occurred informally in any event; thus, making such an appointment less appealing. Likewise, the current lack of meaningful safeguards to keep official supporter appointments on track, means that the risk of things going wrong may not be very different to outcomes of purely *informal* support (Carney, 2017a, 2017c). Similar complexity is found in the use or otherwise of advance directives by someone with a dementia (Blake, Doray, & Sinclair, 2018).

A challenge for everyone ageing with a pre-existing cognitive impairment due to intellectual disability, an ABI or even mental health, is that the pool of suitable supporters continues to be depleted as family networks age; an issue also for later stage dementia care.

2. Delivering Meaningful Support for Decision-making Is Challenging

Australia has been at the forefront of small-scale experiments in design and delivery of support for decision-making. But, while valuable lessons have been learned, these pilots lack the rigor needed to draw more definitive conclusions and are very patchy in their coverage of groups with cognitive impairments (Bigby et al., 2017). As one of us has written of the Australian pilots:

> A host of design deficiencies were identified, including inadequate attention to actual decisional support (measuring too many *other* factors), a focus on the *room* for choice rather than on the actual *processes* of support for decision making, lack of agreement around how to measure the *scale* of decisions, and general conceptual sloppiness, in that: '[a]cross the literature, choice and decision making were not clearly defined or distinguished from each other'
> Carney, 2017c, p. 52 [quoting Bigby et al., 2017, p. 11]

While lack of an evidence base is no reason not to continue to encourage proceeding apace with these new social policy initiatives (Gooding, 2015, p. 69), there is a need for evaluation. Internationally research however is no further advanced than in 2013, when Kohn and colleagues concluded that it was 'impossible to know' if supported decision-making 'actually empowers' and there was 'reason to be concerned' that it 'might actually have the opposite effect, disempowering such individuals or making them more vulnerable to manipulation, coercion, or abuse' (Kohn, Blumenthal, & Campbell, 2013, p. 1114).

As is the case in Australia and overseas, intellectual disability is the most popular site for establishment of individual relationships of support or supporter networks (Glen, 2020; Nunnelley, 2015, p. 10). Support arrangements are less prevalent and are less easily marshaled for other forms of cognitive impairment. The pioneering Canadian 'agreements' machinery for supported decision-making in the province of British Columbia in 2000, for instance, is little used by people with a dementia or those with an ABI (Donnelly, 2019, p. 5).

Social isolation is problematic for organising support for individuals with a cognitive impairment in a number of ways. First because it is costly to recruit and develop the capacity of a stranger to volunteer to serve as a supporter when close family are non-existent. Second because these relationships of support prove to be less durable than naturally evolving ones. And finally, because the supporter is less likely to be capable of reading and acting to realise the will and preferences of the person being supported.

This last is a largely unresolved conundrum in the way all programs of support operate, not just those reliant on support from a stranger to the person. Knowing whether on balance the program genuinely facilitates the expression of the will, preferences and rights of the person assisted, or instead reverts to a disguised (i.e. unintended) paternalism, involves subtle qualitative assessments. This proved almost impossible to reach a conclusion about in a qualitative fieldwork study, commissioned for the Ontario Law Commission, to assess support networks (such as micro boards and circles of support) in the provinces of British Columbia and Ontario (Nunnelley, 2015, p. 67, 75). Australian fieldwork found similar difficulties in evaluating supporter-supported person dyads (Carney, Then, Bigby, Wiesel, Douglas, et al., 2019).

3. Support for Decision-making in Dementia Care is Especially Challenging

Support for decision-making is always characterised by considerable diversity of factors in play in the domains of the person's context, environmental factors and the types of supports needed, as the literature review by Shogren and colleagues reveals (Shogren et al., 2017). The role of support for decision-making over the course of cognitive decline due to a dementia is, if anything, more complex than for other groups, for several reasons.

First, in the early stages following diagnosis of early stage dementia there will often be a partner or close family member who will assume responsibility for providing assistance, and who likely will do a good job of facilitating realisation of will, preferences and rights at this time. Only later will they transition to the more burdensome care management and de facto surrogate decision-making role largely unimaginable to either of them originally (Lord, Livingston, & Cooper, 2015). Over half of aged care residents in Australia have dementia (AIHW, 2017, pp. 182–183), and well over a third of people with dementia in England reside in a care home (Wittenberg et al., 2019). Given these proportions of dementia residents, the necessity for the 'system' as well as individuals working within the residential aged care sector to be aware of what good supported decision-making is and how it operates, is essential to its realisation.

Second, at that early stage and on the evidence to date, enduring power of attorney (or even guardianship) appointments may prove to be the most appealing options should any formal preparations be made while the person still is able to do so. There are a variety of reasons for this. People of this age will culturally be more familiar with and trusting of powers of attorney, assuming they even have someone available to appoint (Nunnelley, 2015, p. 59). They and their circle of close others are less likely to appreciate CRPD Committee aversion to instruments which come into operation in the future on loss of capacity. For an ordinary person of retirement age, there is a fine and hard to appreciate distinction between the acceptability of delegation of power of decision-making by a person retaining full cognition (because it can still be terminated at will) and criticism of such delegation under an enduring power which then is unable to be recalled. Changing the climate of opinion to favour electing to use any newly introduced formal or informal 'supporter' role in place of these more established or commonplace instruments may not prove to be easy. In addition, at least some people with dementia are more likely to have built up financial assets over their lifetime. Those individuals and their legal or financial advisors may seek legally recognised mechanisms that offer more 'protection' for those assets to be used in a way the individual wishes, and also guard against exploitation of those assets (Donnelly, 2019).

Third, using advance planning instruments to lock-in continuation of an individual's *own* past preferences and values often is not the way people choose to organise things. Rather than subscribe to notions of *individual* agency and autonomy, the focus is on relational understandings of their lived lives within their family or other networks (for a brief summary of relational agency see Donnelly, 2019, p. 2). In a form of 'muddling along' they instead favour consensual discussion to find the 'most agreeable outcome' in a given situation (Blake, Doray, & Sinclair, 2018, pp. 209–210, 214). Any consideration of legal advance planning tools then tends to be late and of limited utility (Carney, 2020, p. 8; Dening, Jones, & Sampson, 2011).

Fourth, research demonstrates how diverse and changing are the circumstances and needs for support for decision-making on the part of someone with a dementia over the course of the disease. Others have identified the acute dilemmas that can result when those with dementia start making choices apparently at odds with their long-held views, practices and beliefs (Donnelly, 2019; O'Connor, 2019). As a consequence, a very wide and rich spectrum of different forms of support for (or ultimately proxy) decision-making requires to be made available. And for this older cohort of people with cognitive impairments, retention of the 'trust' (or confidence) of the person with the dementia is especially critical (Sinclair, Bajic-Smith, et al., 2019, pp. 601–602). Consequently, it appears likely that supported decision-making alternatives in this group will have lower take-up than for other groups, with corresponding higher incidence of formal substitute decision-making (enduring powers or adult guardianship) or continued reliance on de facto substitute decision-making under informal arrangements.

Conclusion

The future holds some promise for decision-making by people ageing with an existing cognitive impairment or one recently acquired in the form of a dementia. An evidence base on how best to craft and deliver support for decision-making is beginning to accumulate, along with assessments of its robustness and durability over time (Douglas & Bigby, 2018). More nuanced assessments are emerging on how to frame the CRPD right to support for decision-making (Arstein-Kerslake, Watson, Browning, Martinis, & Blanck, 2017). Qualitative studies are shedding light on decision-making support in the particular circumstances of people living with a dementia (Sinclair, Bajic-Smith, et al., 2019) including how couples work things out (Sinclair et al., 2018).

There is certainly much more to be done to understand the needs of people with a dementia. However, the research cupboard is virtually completely bare when it comes to understanding how support needs may change for someone as they age with an *existing* cognitive impairment due to intellectual impairment, ABI or mental illness. The situation for people with a dementia may hint that they too will encounter added difficulties as social networks deplete over time, as needs become more acute due to compounding effects of illness or ageing, and as greater reliance is placed on services rather than informal family or civil society support.

Only ongoing research will tell whether such simple hypotheses of what might extrapolate from one group to another are actually borne out. Experience suggests that it is wise to instead expect the unexpected once the research is in.

References

AIHW. (2017). *Australia's welfare 2017*. Australian Institute of Health and Welfare. https://www.aihw.gov.au/getmedia/088848dc-906d-4a8b-aa09-79df0f943984/aihw-aus-214-aw17.pdf.aspx?inline=true

ALRC. (2014). *Equality, capacity and disability in commonwealth laws: Final report*. Australian Law Reform Commission. https://www.alrc.gov.au/publication/equality-capacity-and-disability-in-commonwealth-laws-alrc-report-124/

ALRC. (2017). *Elder abuse: A national legal response*. Australian Law Reform Commission. https://www.alrc.gov.au/publications/elder-abuse-report

Alston, B. (2017). Towards supported decision-making: Article 12 of the Convention on the Rights of Persons with Disabilities and guardianship law reform. *Law in Context, 35*(2), 21–43. https://journals.latrobe.edu.au/index.php/law-in-context/article/view/10

Arstein-Kerslake, A., Watson, J., Browning, M., Martinis, J., & Blanck, P. (2017). Future directions in supported decision-making. *Disability Studies Quarterly, 37*(1). http://dsq-sds.org/article/view/5070/4549

Australia. (2019a). *Interim report: Neglect*. Royal Commission into Aged Care Quality and Safety. https://agedcare.royalcommission.gov.au/publications/Pages/interim-report.aspx

Australia. (2019b). *Royal Commission into Violence, Abuse, Neglect and Exploitation of People with Disability*. https://disability.royalcommission.gov.au/Pages/default.aspx

Bach, M., & Kerzner, L. (2010). *A new paradigm for protecting autonomy and the right to legal capacity*. Law Commission of Ontario. https://www.lco-cdo.org/wp-content/uploads/2010/11/disabilities-commissioned-paper-bach-kerzner.pdf

Bigby, C. (1997). When parents relinquish care: Informal support networks of older people with intellectual disability. *Journal of Applied Research in Intellectual Disabilities, 10*(4), 333–344. https://doi.org/10.1111/j.1468-3148.1997.tb00028.x

Bigby, C. (2020) Dedifferentiation and people with intellectual disabilities in the Australian National Disability Insurance Scheme: Bringing research, politics and policy together. *Journal of Intellectual and Developmental Disabilities*. https://doi.org/10.3109/13668250.2020.1776852

Bigby, C., Bowers, B., & Webber, R. (2011). Planning and decision making about the future care of older group home residents and transition to residential aged care. *Journal of Intellectual Disability Research, 55*(8), 777–789. https://doi.org/10.1111/j.1365-2788.2010.01297.x

Bigby, C., Douglas, J., Carney, T., Then, S.-N., Weisel, I., & Smith, L. (2017). Delivering decision-making support to people with cognitive disability – What has been learned from pilot programs in Australia from 2010–2015. *Australian Journal of Social Issues, 52*, 222–240. https://doi.org/10.1002/ajs4.19

Blake, M., Doray, O., & Sinclair, C. (2018). Advance care planning for people with dementia in Western Australia: An examination of the fit between the law and practice. *Psychiatry, Psychology and Law, 25*(2), 197–218. https://doi.org/10.1080/13218719.2017.1351904

Carney, T. (2012). Guardianship, citizenship, & theorizing substitute-decision making law. In I. Doron & A. Soden (Eds.), *Beyond elder law: New directions in law and ageing* (pp. 1–17). Springer. https://doi.org/10.1007/978-3-642-25972-2_1

Carney, T. (2017a). Australian guardianship tribunals: An adequate response to CRPD disability rights recognition and protection of the vulnerable over the lifecourse? *Journal of Ethics in Mental Health, 10*(Sp). http://www.jemh.ca/issues/v9/theme3.html

Carney, T. (2017b). Prioritising supported decision-making: Running on empty or a basis for glacial-to-steady progress? *Laws, 6*(18), 1–14. https://ssrn.com/abstract=3058502

Carney, T. (2017c). Supported decision-making in Australia: Meeting the challenge of moving from capacity to capacity-building? *Law in Context, 35*(2), 44–63. https://journals.latrobe.edu.au/index.php/law-in-context/article/view/12

Carney, T. (2019). Adult guardianship and other financial planning mechanisms for people with cognitive impairment in Australia. In L. Ho & R. Lee (Eds.), *Special needs financial planning: A comparative perspective* (pp. 3–29). Cambridge University Press. https://doi.org/10.1017/9781108646925.001

Carney, T. (2020). People with dementia and other cognitive disabilities: Relationally vulnerable or a source of agency and care? *Elder Law Review, 12*(1), pp. 1–21; *Sydney Law School* Research Paper No. 20/17. Available at SSRN: https://ssrn.com/abstract=3561294

Carney, T., Then, S.-N., Bigby, C., Wiesel, I., & Douglas, J. (2019). National Disability Insurance Scheme decision-making: Or when tailor-made caseplanning met Taylorism and the algorithms? *Melbourne University Law Review, 42*(3), 780–812.

Carney, T., Then, S.-N., Bigby, C., Wiesel, I., Douglas, J., & Smith, E. (2019). Realising 'Will Preferences and Rights': Reconciling differences on best practice support for decision-making? *Griffith Law Review, 28*(4). Ahead of print online. https://www.tandfonline.com/doi/full/10.1080/10383441.10382019.11690741.

Dening, K., Jones, L., & Sampson, E. (2011). Advance care planning for people with dementia: A review. *International Psychogeriatrics, 23*(10), 1535–1551. https://doi.org/10.1017/S1041610211001608

Donnelly, M. (2019). Deciding in dementia: The possibilities and limits of supported decision-making. *International Journal of Law and Psychiatry, 66*, 101466. https://doi.org/10.1016/j.ijlp.2019.101466

Doron, I. (2003). A multi-dimensional model of elder law: An Israel example. *Ageing International, 28*(3), 242–259. https://doi.org/10.1007/s12126-002-1006-0

Douglas, J., & Bigby, C. (2018). Development of an evidence-based practice framework to guide decision making support for people with cognitive impairment. *Disability & Rehabilitation, 42*(3), 434–441. https://doi.org/10.1080/09638288.2018.1498546

Glen, K. B. (2020). *Supported decision-making from theory to practice: Further reflections on an intentional pilot project*. City University New York. https://sdmny.hunter.cuny.edu/download/glen-piloting-personhood/

Gooding, P. (2015). Navigating the 'flashing amber lights' of the right to legal capacity in the United Nations Convention on the Rights of Persons with Disabilities: Responding to major concerns. *Human Rights Law Review, 15*(1), 45–71. https://doi.org/10.1093/hrlr/ngu045

Harding, R. (2016). Care and relationality: Supported decision making under the UN CRPD. In R. Harding, R. Fletcher, & C. Beasley (Eds.), *ReValuing care in theory, law and policy* (pp. 114–130). Routledge.

Kanter, A., & Tolub, Y. (2017). The fight for personhood, legal capacity, and equal recognition under law for people with disabilities in Israel and beyond. *Cardozo Law Review, 39*(2), 557–610. http://cardozolawreview.com/wp-content/uploads/2018/08/KANTER.TOLUB_.39.2.pdf

Kohn, N. A., & Blumenthal, J. A. (2014). A critical assessment of supported decision-making for persons aging with intellectual disabilities. *Disability and Health Journal, 7*(1), S40-S43. https://doi.org/10.1016/j.dhjo.2013.03.005

Kohn, N. A., Blumenthal, J. A., & Campbell, A. T. (2013). Supported decision-making: A viable alternative to guardianship? *Penn State Law Review, 117*(4), 1111–1157. http://www.pennstatelawreview.org/117/4%20Final/4-Kohn%20et%20al.%20(final)%20(rev2).pdf

Lord, K., Livingston, G., & Cooper, C. (2015). A systematic review of barriers and facilitators to and interventions for proxy decision-making by family carers of people with dementia. *International Psychogeriatrics, 27*(8), 1301–1312. https://doi.org/10.1017/S1041610215000411

NSW. (2018, May). *Review of the Guardianship Act 1987*. New South Wales Law Reform Commission. http://www.lawreform.justice.nsw.gov.au/Documents/Current-projects/Guardianship/Report/Report%20145.pdf

Nunnelley, S. (2015). *Personal support networks in practice and theory: Assessing the implications for supported decision-making law*. Law Commission of Ontario. https://www.lco-cdo.org/wp-content/uploads/2015/04/capacity-guardianship-commissioned-paper-nunnelley.pdf

O'Connor, D. (2019). Practising social citizenship in a context of compromised decision-making capacity: Realizing and protecting human rights. *Elder Law Review, 12*(lvi). https://www.westernsydney.edu.au/__data/assets/pdf_file/0017/1633040/JANUARY_2020_D_OCONNOR_Citizenship_and_assessing_incapacity.pdf

Schepens, H. R. M. M., Puyenbroeck, J. V., & Maes, B. (2019). How to improve the quality of life of elderly people with intellectual disability: A systematic literature review of support strategies. *Journal of Applied Research in Intellectual Disabilities, 32*(3), 483–521. https://doi.org/10.1111/jar.12559

Shakespeare, T., Zeilig, H., & Mittler, P. (2019). Rights in mind: Thinking differently about dementia and disability. *Dementia, 18*(3), 1075–1088. https://doi.org/10.1177/1471301217701506

Shogren, K. A., Wehmeyer, M. L., Lassmann, H., & Forber-Pratt, A. (2017). Supported decision making: A synthesis of the literature across intellectual disability, mental health, and aging. *Education and Training in Autism and Developmental Disabilities, 52*(2), 144–157. https://www.jstor.com/stable/26420386

Sinclair, C., Bajic-Smith, J., Gresham, M., Blake, M., Bucks, R. S., Field, S., ... Kurrle, S. (2019). Professionals' views and experiences in supporting decision-making involvement for people living with dementia. *Dementia*. Advance online publication. https://doi.org/10.1177/1471301219864849

Sinclair, C., Gersbach, K., Hogan, M., Blake, M., Bucks, R., Auret, K., ... Kurrle, S. (2019). "A real bucket of worms": Views of people living with dementia and family members on supported decision-making. *Journal of Bioethical Inquiry, 16*(4), 587–608. https://doi.org/10.1007/s11673-019-09945-x

Sinclair, C., Gersbach, K., Hogan, M., Bucks, R. S., Auret, K. A., Clayton, J. M., ... Kurrle, S. (2018). How couples with dementia experience healthcare, lifestyle, and everyday decision-making. *International Psychogeriatrics, 30*(11), 1639–1647. https://doi.org/10.1017/S1041610218000741

Szmukler, G. (2019). "Capacity", "best interests", "will and preferences" and the UN Convention on the Rights of Persons with Disabilities. *World Psychiatry, 18*(1), 34–41. https://doi.org/10.1002/wps.20584

Then, S.-N., Carney, T., Bigby, C., & Douglas, J. (2018). Supporting decision-making of adults with cognitive disabilities: The role of law reform agencies – Recommendations, rationales and influence. *International Journal of Law & Psychiatry, 61*(Nov/Dec), 64–75. https://doi.org/https://doi.org/10.1016/j.ijlp.2018.09.001

Victorian Law Reform Commission. (2012). *Guardianship: Final Report*. Victorian Law Reform Commission. https://www.lawreform.vic.gov.au/projects/guardianship/guardianship-final-report

Whitlatch, M. (2019). *Supported Decision-Making: Update on US Trends*. National Resource Center on Supported Decision Making. http://www.supporteddecisionmaking.org/sites/default/files/NRC-SDM-Presentation-US-Trends-190517.pdf

Wittenberg, R., Knapp, M., Hu, B., Comas-Herrera, A., King, D., Rehill, A., ... Kingston, A. (2019). The costs of dementia in England. *International Journal of Geriatric Psychiatry, 34*(7), 1095–1103. https://doi.org/10.1002/gps.5113

Suggested Readings

ALRC. (2014). *Equality, capacity and disability in commonwealth laws: Final report*. Australian Law Reform Commission. https://www.alrc.gov.au/publication/equality-capacity-and-disability-in-commonwealth-laws-alrc-report-124/

Bigby, C., Douglas, J., Carney, T., Then, S.-N., Weisel, I., & Smith, L. (2017). Delivering decision-making support to people with cognitive disability – What has been learned from pilot programs in Australia from 2010-2015. *Australian Journal of Social Issues, 52*, 222–240. https://doi.org/10.1002/ajs4.19

Douglas, J., & Bigby, C. (2018). Development of an evidence-based practice framework to guide decision making support for people with cognitive impairment. *Disability & Rehabilitation, 42*(3), 434–441. https://doi.org/10.1080/09638288.2018.1498546

Then, S.-N., Carney, T., Bigby, C., & Douglas, J. (2018). Supporting decision-making of adults with cognitive disabilities: The role of law reform agencies – Recommendations, rationales and influence. *International Journal of Law & Psychiatry, 61*(Nov/Dec), 64–75. https://doi.org/https://doi.org/10.1016/j.ijlp.2018.09.001

Sinclair, C., Gersbach, K., Hogan, M., Blake, M., Bucks, R., Auret, K., ... Kurrle, S. (2019). "A real bucket of worms": Views of people living with dementia and family members on supported decision-making. *Journal of Bioethical Inquiry, 16*(4), 587–608. https://doi.org/10.1007/s11673-019-09945-x

17
INTERNALISED AGEISM AND THE USER GAZE IN ELDERCARE

Identifying New Horizons of Possibilities Through the use of a Disability Lens

Håkan Jönson, Annika Taghizadeh Larsson, and Tove Harnett

Introduction

National surveys show that most users of eldercare in Sweden are content with the help they get. In this chapter we will argue that views and expectations among people who receive eldercare are constrained by a narrowed user gaze that becomes visible when concepts and models that are used in disability policies and services are introduced.

The disability rights movement became influential in many countries from 1950s to 1960s onwards (Jeppsson Grassman and Whitaker, 2013). In the Anglo-Saxon countries, the *social model* of disability was launched in order to move the responsibility of problems encountered by people with impairments from their bodies, to a disabling society. The adjacent 'Nordic relational model of disability' (Shakespeare, 2006) was proposed in the 1980s, framing disability as 'environmentally relative'.

In line with these ideologies, services have been designed with the aim of enabling people with disabilities to participate and become active members of society (Erlandsson, 2014; Jönson & Taghizadeh Larsson, 2009). One example of this was the introduction of the Disability Act (The Act Concerning Support and Service for Persons with Certain Functional Impairments – LSS – see http://rkrattsbaser.gov.se/sfst?bet=1993, p. 387) and the highly individualised support system of personal assistance in Sweden in 1994, which has significantly improved opportunities for persons with disabilities and extensive support needs to take control over their own living conditions. What is of particular interest for this chapter is that personal assistance under this system can only be granted to people before they reach 65, but those who were granted assistance before the age of 65 are entitled to keep this support for the rest of their lives. This has created a situation where there are persons of the same age with similar support needs that receive very different kinds of support depending upon if they first received personal assistance before or after they turned 65. Most older people with care needs receive help within the system of *eldercare*, mainly in the form of home care or nursing home care, but a small number of people receive support in the form of personal assistance within the system of *disability services*.

From an international perspective, the standard of Swedish eldercare is considered to be high and nursing homes are unique in the sense that residents have their own apartments with private bathrooms and a kitchenette and even if the 'apartment' is a room off a corridor, residents have formal status as legal tenants. Alongside the overall goal to provide 'a reasonable standard of living', dignity and wellbeing are the two leading concepts in the Social Service Act that regulate eldercare (see http://rkrattsbaser.gov.se/sfst?bet=2001:453). Every year, The National Board of Health and Welfare (NBHW) conducts a full-scale user-survey that solicits the opinions of people receiving eldercare and despite some methodological limitations, the overall results are usually quite positive. Results from single municipalities differ, but on a national level 88% of those who receive home care and 81% who received residential care reported being content with the services they received in 2018 (Socialstyrelsen, 2018). When the data is broken down into specific areas, there are aspects that evoke more or less criticism but in general, users of eldercare are content. Could it be that this self-reported user satisfaction mirrors more than the actual quality of care and life of those receiving support within Swedish eldercare? Is something else going on?

As compared to their younger peers, older persons with support needs have 'a propensity to accept less, and hence to demand less' according to Kane and Kane (2005, p. 52) who suggest that this difference in expectations is a reflection of societal ageism. In this chapter we show how ageism is rationalised and justified through the organisation of the support system of elder care, where comparisons for older persons with support needs point in a particular direction – towards the context of care, towards other care users, and towards the failing bodies of ageing people (Jönson & Harnett, 2016). The ageing experience, as it is typically constructed in our society and in eldercare, provides older people and their relatives with a particular 'user gaze'. This is in contrast to disability ideology, that has provided people with impairments and support needs with other types of references and expectations. Our suggestion is that learning from older people who receive support from disability services in the form of personal assistance could provide an important basis for improvements in elder care. People who acquired impairments as younger adults and live their (later) lives supported by disability services may introduce ways of evaluating services that challenge taken for granted understandings within the system of eldercare. These ways of evaluating services could be used to imagine horizons of possibilities that seem to be beyond imagination within the present system of eldercare. To explore this, we use Sweden as a case example and investigate and compare accounts of service users dealing with experiences and expectations of support services – and of life – among, on the one hand, older people who only receive eldercare and, on the other hand, older people who have experiences from disability services.

A Framework for Analysing Support for Older People

A review reveals that policies, practice, activism, and knowledge production on disability and ageing are perceived to be very different and this has evoked questions on how differences can be reworked into a common framework (Bickenbach et al., 2012; Erlandsson, 2014; Putnam, 2002; Weber & Wolfmayr, 2006). Researchers have suggested that the active consumers and activists of the disability movement could be a role model for older people in need of care. Similar ideas were the starting point for our research project titled 'Improving eldercare through the use of a disability lens' funded by the Swedish Research Council for Health, Working Life and Welfare. In this project, we used models from disability research and policies, in order to introduce new ways of thinking about eldercare.

Merton (1968) suggests that individuals use selected reference groups as standards for different types of personal comparisons. The normative function refers to norms that individuals are measured by or strive to live up to, for instance when identifying with a particular group. The comparative function refers to standards or points of departure for comparisons among individuals, groups, or categories. Comparative reference groups are used as a basis for claims that individuals or groups are deprived or treated unjustly. In this chapter, we will use this latter type of reference to discuss the presence and absence of 'others' to refer to when evaluating the care and assistance support that is provided to older adults.

Using reference group theory, we have developed a framework for the analysis of concepts like rights, justice, and equity for people receiving eldercare. The framework, called the 'Equal Rights Framework' (Jönson & Harnett, 2016), is based on the Scandinavian normalisation principle (Nirje, 1992) and its claim that (younger) persons with impairments should be provided with living conditions that are as similar as possible as those of other members of society. The Equal Rights Framework differs between references that are internally oriented to care and impairment or externally oriented to comparisons outside care and impairment. For a detailed description see Jönson and Harnett (2016). For example, a resident in a nursing home who wants to have a daily shower based on the fact that 'I used to have a daily shower before moving here' uses an external reference to personhood. A care worker who states that 'you are in a nursing home now and other residents shower once a week, so you will have to adapt to the way we do it here' uses internal references to the context of care and the category of nursing home residents. The argument 'it's normal for any person to have a daily shower so that should apply to me' is an externally oriented reference to the category 'people in general'. We propose that the use and acceptance of different references results in differing views on the quality of care and life among users of eldercare and disability services.

Data

Data analysis presented in this chapter comes from two studies within the project which are detailed elsewhere (Harnett & Jönson, 2014, 2017). The first study by Harnett and Jönson (2014) aimed to investigate what residents, relatives, managers, and staff defined as normality, individualisation/personalisation, justice, and equity for persons receiving help in the form of nursing home care. Data consisted of a total of 20 interviews with groups and individuals at four nursing homes. In total we interviewed 46 persons: 19 residents, 6 family members, 4 managers, and 17 staff members (The project was approved by the regional ethics review board in Lund (Dnr 2013/349)). The facilities were located in or on the outskirts of two medium sized Swedish municipalities. The interviews featured themed questions and five vignettes, where the interviewees were asked to elaborate on what they regarded as personalised, just and equal care (Harnett & Jönson, 2014). The second study aimed at identifying similar aspects in care/help for persons living in ordinary housing (Johansson & Taghizadeh Larsson, 2017). In total, 20 persons aged 65 and above participated in the studies. Among the persons were both those who had eldercare in the form of home care and those who had disability services in the form of personal assistance. Several had a combination of support services, such as home care combined with disability services and personal assistance combined with home care or regular short-term stays in residential care. Interviewees were residents in ten municipalities of varying size. The interviews were relatively free in their structure and focused on how the people experienced the help they received; what a normal day looked like; what they thought was especially good or bad and if they felt they could live a normal life. A spouse/partner participated in four of the interviews.

Experiences of Nursing Homes: Internal Comparisons

When we interviewed people who lived in nursing homes they could easily relate to goals that care should be personalised, but found it difficult to relate to the meaning of concepts like 'a normal life', 'equity', and 'rights'. The term 'equity' was in some of the interviews interpreted as a suggestion that everyone should get the same treatment and then rejected with reference to the goal of personalisation: 'There can never be equal treatment, because each one has their needs' (Elsa, resident). In other instances, residents argued that different treatment should only occur when needs were different: 'It should be equal, there should be no difference between people there. They have different needs, but if care is different, then it should be because there are different needs' (Alfred, relative).

In addition to this position, injustices at the facility were also mentioned. An interview with two residents who discussed the possibility of having needs attended to, provides an example. Initially, resident Elsa claimed that 'there were more staff when I came here than there is now'. Elsa was frustrated from having to wait for help. Resident Ruth argued that 'they can't just let go of what they are doing and go to another, so you must accept that it may take a while'. Following this she added:

RUTH: And it should be the same for all, that everyone should have to wait. But it is not.
INTERVIEWER: What do you mean Ruth?
RUTH: Well, that there are some that are attended to immediately. And others who have to wait until it's fairly calm or how to put it, there is a difference between people and people. Yes, I do not know how to express it, but I feel that there is a difference between people and people.

This type of dissatisfaction occurred in several interviews, and involved the experience among residents of having to wait for help for a longer time than others, not being brought to as many excursions as others, being served after others since the facility tended to serve food in a particular order, or having a designated contact person among the staff who was less attentive compared to other staff members. Care and the entire stay at the facilities should focus on individual needs, but there should, according to residents, not be a difference between people and people. In a previous article, we have described this as a position in Swedish eldercare that speaks against signs of favouritism or social inequality (Harnett & Jönson, 2014).

What our interviews with residents showed was an interplay between two positions. The first was based on the experience among residents of having a relatively good situation and confidence in the organisation's intention to provide equal care. Residents and relatives accepted differences, because these were assumed to be based on different needs of residents. This trust-based position included suggestions that the staff did the best they could.

The second position expressed discontent that referred to experienced or suspected differences that were interpreted as unjust inequalities. This position was very easy to evoke in examples that concerned differences among residents in the same nursing home. During interviews, one vignette that was presented to interviewees concerned two female friends in a nursing home visiting a museum in the company of their designated contact persons, and another resident complaining that she also wants to visit a museum. This was perceived, and in particular by the residents, as a grave injustice, and it was generally suggested that the third woman should be brought along to the museum, despite the fact that the activity was presented as a visit by two *friends*. Outside of a care context it would hardly been considered unfair if two friends went to a museum without bringing a neighbour along. At the care facility, this reference to friends and neighbours was not regarded as valid.

There were cases where the second position was criticised, for instance in statements on complaints of residents being served before others: 'One needs to be very careful with such comparisons' (Arthur, resident). During an interview with relatives, an adult daughter was disappointed with the inability of staff to help develop the interests of the residents, as this would counteract the tendency to perceive minor and insignificant events at the facility as major concerns: 'Because it's this corridor, it's these people, that's what they do, say or don't that becomes their world' (Britt-Marie, relative). The facility, or rather the unit, became a small world where people compared themselves to each other – a psychological phenomenon according to the daughter.

In a few instances residents and relatives mentioned difference *between* care facilities as a problem, for instance when comparing the food at their own facility, with another facility that had its own chef. Most notably, however, was the absence of comparisons between residents of nursing homes and the general population of older people, or members of society. Whereas people with disability services have been 'educated' to use external comparisons and that their support should enable them to live as other members of society, the interviewees in nursing homes used internal comparisons and talked about being able to live like others in the same ward.

To summarise, justice/injustice and equality/inequality for persons in nursing homes tend to take as a point of departure the situation of others in the same nursing home. The user gaze was based on comparisons internal to the context of care and the category of care users (Jönson & Harnett, 2016). 'It should be the same for all', Ruth declared in the quotation above, 'everyone should have to wait'. Other residents became the comparison group. Justice was a matter of residents having it equally good or bad.

Living at Home

We also conducted interviews with 20 home-dwelling older people, aged 65 years and older, who received elder care in the form of home care, disability services in the form of personal assistance or both. As previously mentioned, personal assistance can only be granted to people before they reach 65. However, persons who have been granted assistance at earlier ages can retain this the rest of their lives, although the number of personal assistance hours allotted cannot increase. Those who age with personal assistance and need support beyond the hours they were granted before age 65, can apply for elder care as a compliment. This means that some home-dwelling older people have support from both eldercare services, according to the Social Service Act and personal assistance according to the Disability Act. The interviews conducted for this study concerned older people's views about their everyday lives and the help they received. We found that those who received disability services invoked different comparisons than those who only had eldercare services.

Home Care Recipients: Frustrated, but not Dissatisfied

Six of the interviewees only received home care from eldercare services. Although they did not express any harsh complaints, they described a constant uncertainty about *when* the home care staff was going to turn up and *what* kind of help they could expect. According to the interviewees there were a number of rules to abide by: for instance, the home care staff were not allowed to change light bulbs, empty cat litter boxes or carry any groceries in case they did some shopping during their weekly accompanied walk. Some interviewees were also a bit annoyed by having to be active and participate in the help they received, such as to wipe the table when the care staff did the cleaning. In the Swedish home care system this is referred to as a help to self-help approach; help is provided with a pedagogical undertone that aims at strengthening or keeping abilities of care users (Elmersjö, 2014, 2018). This approach is very different from the ideology behind personal assistance, where the ideal type role of staff is to act as the arms and legs of the service user (Erlandsson, 2014). The interviewees who only had support from home care were frustrated and highlighted problems in the way home help was organised, but at the same time they were careful to point out that they were *not* dissatisfied. Instead they expressed loyalty towards the staff who were portrayed as victims of poor working conditions:

JILL: But I can see that they are stressed and then I don't bother to… [say anything]. If it is something that can wait, then I let it be.
INTERVIEWER: Yes.
JILL: Because they do the best they can.

Since the staff did 'the best they can' it appeared logical not to complain, particularly not if complaints could have negative repercussions on the already over-burdened workers. Another way that interviewees played down their critique was by developing it into self-blame. One person described herself as 'overly petty', another as 'grumpy' and by doing so they directed attention to their own shortcomings, rather than to the care itself. Carina, for instance, described problems in the home care, but finished by saying:

CARINA: So, I should not complain. Everyone is not petty like me. I think it is me being the bad one.
INTERVIEWER: The bad one?
CARINA: Yes, saying that they are not always that good.

The dissatisfaction about the help Carina received was reframed into an issue about her own personality.

Personal Assistance in Comparison with Eldercare

Among our interviewees, five had both disability services in the form of personal assistance and eldercare services (home care or short-term nursing home care). These people perceived home care and nursing home care in a completely different way compared to those who based their experiences on having home care only. Interviewees who also had experiences of personal assistance, had another kind of user gaze and a much more critical view of eldercare services. They talked about eldercare in terms of structural problems relating to staffing and the organisation of care.

Personal assistance is by definition an individually designed support provided by a limited number of persons. Apart from the fact that the interviewed assistant users only had a few people who helped them, they had also been involved in selecting these people. It was this type of personalisation they were used to and it was also based on these experiences that they assessed eldercare services. Gunnel, an interviewee with both personal assistance and home care services described her situation as:

INTERVIEWER: You have done job interviews with your assistants and selected them, or what did you do?
GUNNEL: They pay a visit and I try them out. A lot is about personality and how we work together. You can never get along with all the others, with the home care people. I like some of them and I think it works between us... if they are a little calmer you know. But some of them almost give me the shivers. It's terrible. It is good that there is home care, but it is organised completely the wrong way.
INTERVIEWER: And what do you think is the biggest problem?
GUNNEL: The biggest problem is that ... there are a lot of different people, it can be 25-30 different in two weeks. And there is not enough time. They are so stressed.

Gunnel's experience of personal assistance provided a frame of reference for her assessment of home care services. The home care was perceived as problematic and organised the wrong way so that users had to meet lots of different people. One resident who had moved to an eldercare facility with his wife described the home care arrangement as a 'bicycle race' and argued that life at the care facility was better since relatively fewer persons provided help. Even if interviewees who only received home care were frustrated about the large number of staff coming to their homes, they could not see how help could be organised any other way. A different user gaze was not possible to apply without the experience of personal assistance.

Having disability services in the form of personal assistance made users more critical of arrangements within the system of eldercare. The interview with Robert and his wife provides an example. Robert, who lived at home, had a shower every day with the help of his personal assistant. He stayed every fourth weekend at a short-term respite elder care facility, where he did not shower since he felt that being showered by unfamiliar women – 'new girls' as he put it – threatened his integrity. Had Robert lived in the care facility or received home care, it would have been natural for him to compare with the situation of other care users, who frequently encounter 'new girls'. It is not possible to know if persons like Gunnel and Robert would state that they are content or not if they filled in the national Swedish user survey on eldercare. Their comments are however similar to previous studies (Forsell, 2004) where assistance users were critical of eldercare and unhappy with its lack of flexibility and continuity and the 'pedagogical undertone' that is perceived as limiting and belittling.

Discussion: Challenging the Internalised Ageism among Care Users

Our suggestion, based on the analyses within the project, is that the societal organisation of eldercare, and probably of the entire ageing experience, prompts older persons with help needs to apply a particular user gaze. Evaluation from this gaze is based on comparisons that are primarily internal to care and impairment. The internalisation of this gaze constitutes a form of self-ageism that is difficult to challenge unless other forms of help are invoked.

Interviewees who only received home care displayed a user gaze that was based on expectations of the kind of help home care could provide. Their demands were shaped by what they knew was possible to get and knowing that they could only receive help to go out once or twice per week, nobody demanded to get out once a day. We asked persons with home care if they could live a normal life and what their life and would look like if they could wish freely. But these questions were difficult to answer and it seemed as if they had never really thought about their situation in that way:

INTERVIEWER: Do you think you can live a normal life with home care?
ANITA: (Laughter). Yes, I guess so. How else would it be?
INTERVIEWER: What do you think is most important to say? What do you think, now, when you went to this interview, that this is what I want to say?
ANITA: No, it is… Nothing really. Just this with the times that I think is a bit of a shame. But it is what it is.
INTERVIEWER: And as I have understood you, there are many different people?
ANITA: Sure. But what can they do? They can't do it any other way?

In many cases, the care users' expectations were limited by rules that had never been challenged or questioned. There were no references available that could help eldercare users to advance their discontent beyond a type of complaints about arrangement that they did not challenge.

One type of reference that has been emphasised in official eldercare policies refers to the personhood and the protection of identity of the person; policies state that particular attention should be payed to the established interests and habits of the individual (Socialutskottets betänkande, 2009). When applying the equal rights framework (Jönson & Harnett, 2016), references to habits of the individual could be regarded as an attempt to focus on person-centred comparisons that are external to care. A person who has always gone for walks or taken a shower everyday could use this as a point of reference for claiming the right to support for continuing with these daily routines.

What our interviews reveal is that these type of comparisons are often constrained by the idea that older care users have become 'different' due to illnesses and disabilities that are almost regarded as part of the ageing process (Harnett & Jönson, 2017). These ideas were also present among the elder care users that we interviewed. Illness or impairment were regarded as the causes for having limited possibilities of living a normal life and since this made care users different from before it appears logical not to demand support to continue with previous habits. Residents at the nursing homes that we visited described how age and frailty made them incomparable to their previous selves which is illustrated by an extract from an interview with two residents called Betty and Denise:

INTERVIEWER: But if you were to compare with something, to say what is normal when living in a nursing home, what would you compare with then?
BETTY: No, with what you manage.
INTERVIEWER: What you manage?
BETTY: It's not like before, when you lived at home and could walk.
INTERVIEWER: No.
BETTY: Now you sit, you almost don't get out or do anything.
INTERVIEWER: You sit and almost don't get out.
DENISE: No, no, so it's quite boring I think.
BETTY: Since you end up in this wheelchair.
INTERVIEWER: No.
BETTY: So there is not much you can do, there is really not.
DENISE: But it's the disease that causes… that you can't live a normal life.

The residents were dissatisfied with not getting out but did not see the previous life as a relevant comparison. Instead of talking about what kind of support they would need to get out more often, they adjusted their expectations according to the standard of living that they knew they could get at the nursing home. It was not the organisation of care, but their bodies that were the reasons for not being able to do things.

Reasoning about similar matters, interviewees with disability services in the form of personal assistance displayed a different user gaze that was based on other types of references, and interviewee Barbro provides an example:

BARBRO: I mean ... It's not that I have a disability because I think its great fun. No, but now that I have a disability, I think somehow that you should have the opportunity to live like other people/.../
INTERVIEWER: What is this to live like others do you think?
BARBRO: Yes ... to live like others mean to be able to do things when it suits me. Not when it suits the home care or someone else... Some mornings I just get into my head 'Today I have to go there!' And then we do it. I have the assistance all the time so it works very well. I think that is to live like others. To have full right over my own life.

Barbro made comparison to 'others' and argued that a normal life for her was to be able to 'live like others'. According to the equal rights framework, this constitutes an external reference, that is, a comparison that does not depend on the actual care context or from the functional impairments (Jönson & Harnett, 2016). Barbro had lived with disability for many years and her frame of reference had been shaped by the disability movement that she was a part of. The disability movement has strived to 'educate' its members to understand disability as something caused by society and that society is responsible for enabling people with disability to live like others (Ratzka, 2013). This view is entirely different from that of Betty and Denise in the previous quote, who perceived their frail bodies as legitimate reasons for not being able to get outdoors. The view that they expressed could be regarded as a form of internalised ageism, where the ageing process rather than the organisation of the society is seen as the main problem of older persons with support needs (Harnett & Jönson, 2017).

In addition, interviewees who only had experience of eldercare services expressed trust and loyalty to the staff and the care system, and while such trust is a necessary part of care, it may also hide shortcomings related to the organisation of support to older people. Our study shows that the user gaze in eldercare focuses on internal comparisons. Demands and expectations are shaped by what is possible to get in the current elder care system, so that no one will ask to go for more than one walk per week if that is the expected scenario in nursing homes. The body and impairments are seen as obstacles and focus is on the ageing body rather than society's support system.

Demands and expectations among people with eldercare is limited to what is possible for other people who also have eldercare. As long as the living conditions for other people with eldercare is equally good, but also equally bad, it is considered as fair. This makes eldercare its own world with its own logic where the current organisation appears as given.

In order to improve elder care, surveys on self-reported user satisfaction may not be the best or most efficient tool. As we have shown in this chapter, views and expectations among older people who receive support services may be constrained by a narrowed user gaze shaped by what is possible to get in the current elder care system and based on comparisons internal to the context of care and the category of care users. The accounts of older people who have disability services show that this gaze is not given but could be opened up through conscious efforts. By introducing references external to the category of people with disabilities, the disability movement has successfully educated not only its members, but also policymakers and researchers, that people with disabilities have the right to live like others and that society is responsible to make this possible also for people with extensive support needs by introducing more flexible and individualised support services. Likewise, external references oriented to comparisons outside care and impairment could be taught and applied by older people with impairments as well as by researchers and activists aiming to improve elder care – and the living conditions of older people with support needs.

References

Bickenbach, J. E., Bigby, C., Salvador-Carulla, L., Heller, T., Leonardi, M., LeRoy, B., ... Spindel, A. (2012). The Toronto declaration on bridging knowledge, policy and practice in aging and disability: Toronto, Canada, March 30, 2012. *International Journal of Integrated Care, 12.* https://doi.org/10.5334/ijic.1086

Elmersjö, M. (2014). *Kompetensfrågan inom äldreomsorgen. Hur uppfattningar om kompetens formar omsorgsarbetet, omsorgsbehoven och omsorgsrelationen* [Competence issues in elderly care: How perceptions of competence shape the care work, the care needs and the care relationship]. Linnéuniversitetet.

Elmersjö, M. (2018). The principle of help to self-help in Sweden: A study of representations and norms regarding old age and care needs and their moral and ethical implications for care work. *Nordic Social Work Research*, 1–13. https://doi.org/10.1080/2156857X.2018.1551240

Erlandsson, S. (2014). *Hjälp att bevara eller förändra? Åldersrelaterade diskurser om omsorg, stöd och service* [Help preserve or change? Age-related discourse on care, support and service]. Stockholms universitet.

Forsell, E. (2004). *Assistansersättning efter 65 – Utvärdering av de nya reglerna*. RFV analyserar [Assistance compensation after 65: Evaluation of the new rule]. Riksförsäkringsverket.

Harnett, T., & Jönson, H. (2014). Sill och potatis till den ena och entrecote till den andra? Individanpassning och likvärdighet på särskilda boenden för äldre [Herring and potatoes to one and entrecote to the other? Individual customization and equivalence on special housing for the elderly]. *Socialvetenskaplig Tidskrift*, *21*(3/4), 246–265.

Harnett, T., & Jönson, H. (2017). "They are different now" – Biographical continuity and disruption in nursing home settings. *Journal of Aging Studies*, *42*, 1–8. https://doi.org/10.1016/j.jaging.2017.05.003

Jeppsson Grassman, E., & Whitaker, A. (Eds.). (2013). *Ageing with disability: A lifecourse perspective*. Policy Press.

Johansson, S. & Taghizadeh Larsson, A. (2017). Omsorg och personlig assistans [Care and personal assistance]. In: S. Johansson (Ed.), *Social omsorg i socialt arbete: grunder och fördjupningar [Social care in social work: Foundations and specializations]*. Gleerups.

Jönson, H., & Harnett, T. (2016). Introducing an equal rights framework for older persons in residential care. *The Gerontologist*, *56*(5), 800–806. https://doi.org/10.1093/geront/gnv039

Jönson, H., & Taghizadeh Larsson, A. (2009). The exclusion of older people in disability activism and policies – A case of inadvertent ageism? *Journal of Aging Studies*, *23*(1), 69–77. https://doi.org/10.1016/j.jaging.2007.09.001

Kane, R. L., & Kane, R. A. (2005). Ageism in healthcare and long-term care. *Generations*, *29*(3), 49–54.

Merton, R. K. (1968). *Social theory and social structure*. Free Press.

Nirje, B. (1992). *The normalization principle papers*. Uppsala universitet reprocentralen HSC.

Putnam, M. (2002). Linking aging theory and disability models: Increasing the potential to explore aging with physical impairment. *The Gerontologist*, *42*(6), 799–806. https://doi.org/10.1093/geront/42.6.799

Ratzka, A. (2013). Independent living-rörelsen banade vägen [The independent living movement paved the way]. In: P. Brusén & K. Flyckt (Eds.), *Perspektiv på personlig assistans [Perspective on personal assistance]*. Gothia.

Shakespeare, T. (2006). The social model of disability. In L. J. Davis (Ed.), *The disability studies reader* (2nd ed., pp. 197–204). Routledge.

Socialstyrelsen. (2018). *Så tycker de äldre om äldreomsorgen 2016* [What do the elderly think about the elderly? 2016]. *En rikstäckande undersökning av äldres uppfattning om kvaliteten i hemtjänst och särskilt boende* [A nationwide survey of the elderly's perception of the quality of home care and special housing]. Socialstyrelsen.

Socialutskottets betänkande. (2009). *Värdigt liv i äldreomsorgen* [Worthy life in the elderly]. 2009/10:SoU18.

Weber, G., & Wolfmayr, F. (2006). The Graz declaration on disability and ageing. *Journal of Policy and Practice in Intellectual Disabilities*, *3*(4), 271–276. https://doi.org/10.1111/j.1741-1130.2006.00090.x

Suggested Readings

Jönson, H., & Harnett, T. (2016). Introducing an equal rights framework for older persons in residential care. *The Gerontologist*, *56*(5), 800–806. https://doi.org/10.1093/geront/gnv039

Jönson, H., & Taghizadeh Larsson, A. (2009). The exclusion of older people in disability activism and policies – a case of inadvertent ageism? *Journal of Aging Studies*, *23*(1), 69–77. https://doi.org/10.1016/j.jaging.2007.09.001

Kane, R. L., & Kane, R. A. (2005). "Ageism in healthcare and long-term care". *Generations*, *29*, 49–54.

Putnam, M. (2002). Linking aging theory and disability models: Increasing the potential to explore aging with physical impairment. *The Gerontologist*, *42*(6), 799–806. https://doi.org/10.1093/geront/42.6.799

18
CREATING AGE AND DISABILITY FRIENDLY COMMUNITIES TO SUPPORT HEALTHY AND MEANINGFUL AGEING

Friedrich Dieckmann and Christiane Rohleder

Growing Importance of an Inclusive Social Planning for Older People with a Lifelong Disability

The growing number of older people and the increasing life expectancy require new solutions worldwide with regard to quality of life, social participation and health in old age (World Health Organization, 2017). These developments also apply to people with lifelong disabilities, especially for people with an intellectual disability. Their life expectancy has increased enormously due to better medical care as well as improvements in socio-economic circumstances and social support structures (Bittles & Glasson, 2004; Chang et al., 2011; Dieckmann, Giovis, & Offergeld, 2015; Naue et al., 2013). An increasing number has the opportunity to reach the age of retirement. The previous chapters have clearly shown that this development requires adaptation of existing support systems to the needs of elderly citizens with lifelong disabilities. Since most physical and cognitive disabilities are age-related, the scientific discourse as well as worldwide initiatives focus mainly on the discussion, development and evaluation of age- and dementia-friendly communities (e.g. Beard & Petitot, 2010; Buckner et al., 2018; Lin & Lewis, 2015; Mitchell, 2014; Scharlach, 2017; World Health Organization, 2007). However, it is becoming increasingly clear that in the course of demographic change, addressing the common needs of adults with lifelong disabilities and older people can have many positive effects on the quality of life of both groups (e.g. Bickenbach et al., 2012; National Council on Disability, 2004).

According to the ICF model of disability (World Health Organization, 2002), a meaningful and healthy life in old age is dependent on both personal and environmental factors. Environments, and the way older people interact with them, are major determinants of their activities. The environment provides the resources or barriers that ultimately decide whether older people can engage in activities that matter to them (World Health Organization, 2017, p. 5). In old age higher risks of reduced mobility and decreases in cognitive performance can lead to a stronger focus on the immediate socio-spatial environment, the neighbourhood. In order to maintain an independent and self-determined life as long as possible, there is a need for barrier-free and age-appropriate living environments including opportunities for health supporting social and physical activities as well as appropriate medical support.

Although the financial and social resources for ageing differ and some groups of persons with disabilities age prematurely, people with a lifelong disability as well as those who acquire an impairment in old age have some similar experiences and common interests. First of all, the vast majority of both groups want to age in place, to stay as long as possible in their familiar environments. Furthermore, they are likely to want to continue learning, to build and maintain meaningful social relationships and activities, and to engage in civic and social life as long as possible (Bigby & Wiesel, 2019). But there are also differences in lifestyles, particularly the greater dependence of people with intellectual disabilities on professional help, their smaller social networks and their socio-economic disadvantages. Thus, their concerns are not automatically addressed by the concepts of age- or dementia-friendly cities. There is a need for integrated social planning of the different sectors that support older and disabled persons, for 'bridging knowledge, policy and practice in ageing and disability' (Bickenbach et al., 2012, p. 1) to improve living conditions and social services in the immediate social environment of older people.

This chapter outlines an approach to the design of age friendly communities for older people with a disability, based on a model for an integrated community planning process (Schäper et al., 2019). The approach combines top-down and bottom-up approaches to ensure the responsibilities of local politics and authorities, the cooperation of various professional stakeholders and the participation of older people with and without disabilities as well as their relatives in the planning process. It was developed in the context of the German welfare-system. To transfer the model would require tailoring planning processes to the respective societal and political contexts.

Prerequisites for an Integrated Inclusive Social Planning for Old Age: Guidelines to Assure the Cooperation of Funding Authorities and Service Providers

In Germany as in many other countries, support for elderly persons, long-term care and assistance for people with lifelong disabilities are located in different areas of the social security system and financed by different funding authorities. The local authorities are responsible for providing counselling services, activity programs, and senior centres as well as opportunities for voluntary work for senior citizens. In addition, the municipalities have the task of improving the outpatient care of elderly people in need of support from low-threshold, complementary care services, such as driving or voluntary visiting services. The long-term care insurance covers part of the costs in case of a need for nursing care. It finances, for example, outpatient nursing services, day, night, and short-term care as well as inpatient care in nursing homes and residential group homes for elderly persons. This service area is regulated according to market-principles with profit-oriented providers. Hence there are restrictions for care planning on the local level.

In order to improve the care situation for senior citizens, neighbourhood-oriented approaches in the sense of closer cooperation in the district between institutions, specialist services, and voluntary initiatives have gained importance in recent years (Mehnert & Kremer-Preiß, 2017; Michell-Auli & Kremer-Preiß, 2013). The aim of a neighbourhood orientation is to enable elderly people to remain in their homes as long as possible, to support informal care givers and thus to avoid institutionalisation. This neighbourhood orientation to old-age policy initially appears positive. But Bigby (2004, p. 244f.) points out that compared to policy for disabled people, participation, inclusion, and autonomy play only a subordinate role.

The needs of citizens with a lifelong disability are met by social support for integration. In recent decades a system of services and facilities to support housing and living, work, family life, and leisure time activities has been set up. There are special offers and services for persons with intellectual disabilities and persons with a mental illness. The majority of people with an intellectual disability still live in facilities or residential groups that are only partially community-based. The support is mostly provider-oriented. There are only a few cross-sector collaborations. As a consequence, although person-centred planning may be legally required, the number of people with an intellectual disability receiving support in their own homes is increasing slowly.

Persons with a severe mental illness are much more likely to live in community care and have access to a system of community-based social psychiatric services and meeting facilities. However, although the care structure is community-based, people with a severe mental illness mostly remain segregated. They are included into the psychiatric community, but poorly integrated into mainstream activities. Therefore, it is not surprising that, as in various other Western countries (e.g. Netherlands: Meesters, 2019, p. 137), the social needs of older citizens with severe mental illness are often not met.

For those persons with lifelong disabilities who reach the age of retirement new services have been created, e.g. specialised day programs that 'replace' sheltered workshops. But such services poorly meet the requirements of the Convention on the Rights of Persons with Disabilities (CRPD) because they limit the possibilities of a self-determined life style in old age.[1] The CRPD stresses that there are no age limits for the full integration of people with disabilities into the community. On the contrary, various articles of the Convention, in particular Articles 8, 16, 25b, stress the special need for protection of elderly disabled people. Of particular importance for local planning processes are the possibilities of choice of place of residence and access to community support services (Art. 19), facilitation of low-cost mobility (Art. 20), and access to leisure, recreation, and sports activities (Art. 30). Until now, however, the various institutions and service providers in the field of old age, community care, and disability have worked separately with their own agendas, logic, and own planning bodies and mechanisms.

It is obvious that an integrated social planning approach at community level is needed to support healthy and meaningful ageing for senior citizens with lifelong disabilities. It should not only focus on the provision and coordination of facilities and services, but necessarily also include measures to raise awareness among the population. But changing previously separate social planning practices is a complex process. It affects the financial interests of the various funding agencies and requires a willingness to abandon separate responsibilities in favour of joint decisions. It is therefore useful in this process to follow some guidelines.

Responsible Lead Management Role of the Municipality

A prerequisite for inclusive municipal social planning is the willingness of all stake holders – political decision-makers, funding authorities, social planners as well as service providers – to critically review previous planning procedures and service delivery routines and to cooperate for the benefit of the growing number of older disabled persons. Given their different interests, there is a need for a management lead to take responsibility for the process, not for the decisions. The leading role should lie with the local government since social inclusion and participation mainly take place in the realm of the local community. Thus, local authorities have a key role in managing the challenges of demographic change. National and international agendas stress the important role, local governments play in defining the mechanisms by which services can be coordinated and regulated across sectors and providers (BMFSFJ, 2016; World Health Organization, 2015).

Shared Principles of an Inclusive Planning

Since different local departments and services as well as funding authorities have their own planning traditions it is crucial, to base the planning process on common guiding principles. They allow assessment of whether the planning steps and all decisions taken contribute to the overall objectives of inclusive planning. We recommend focusing on a small number of principles: social inclusion, neighbourhood orientation, user involvement, and person-centred approach.

Social inclusion: According to Novak Amado, Stancliffe, McCarron, and McCallion (2013), there are five levels of inclusion, ranging from physical presence in the neighbourhood, joint activities in community facilities, to intimate partnerships between people with and without disabilities. The first two stages can be positively influenced by an integrated social planning process. On the one hand, in the form of specialised community-based services and activities for persons with lifelong disabilities and, on the other hand, by cooperating with and opening up regular services to elderly people with lifelong disabilities. A key objective of municipal inclusive planning for old age is to ensure that policies and measures enable older people with a lifelong disability to have self-determined access to specialised and general services and activities so that they can make choices.

Neighbourhood orientation: Neighbourhood orientation means the concentration of planning processes on social spaces in which older people spend their daily lives and 'therefore interact and share bonds, common social institutions and patterns of social practice' (Carey, 2011, p. 191). Due to more limited mobility, the formal and informal resources in the neighbourhood become increasingly important in old age. Age- and disability-friendly communities allow people to remain in their familiar local surroundings for as long as possible. The local neighbourhood can offer orientation, social encounters and informal resources of support. In connection with dementia, Mitchell (2014, p. 185) points out that an active and meaningful life in old age requires opportunities for outside activities. Findings from international longitudinal studies suggest, that the physical, social, and economic structure of the neighbourhood can support a healthy ageing (Beard & Petitot, 2010, p. 443). Thus, neighbourhood orientation can enhance individual autonomy in old age. Planning processes need to focus on small scale perspectives and support a welfare-mix that enables and extends an active and independent life in old age. Disadvantages in neighbourhoods with low socioeconomic status have to be taken into account.

Citizen participation: Integrated social planning for old age requires citizen participation to allow older citizens a political say in the development of the neighbourhood. Furthermore, as neighbourhoods differ very much in size, function, and especially socioeconomic status it is important to involve older people with and without disability and their informal and professional supporters in the planning process, since older residents know best what is necessary. This applies to the discussion of necessary services as well as the priorities in neighbourhood development.

Person centred approach: If separate help systems and planning traditions are to work together, there is always the danger of concentrating in a supply-oriented manner on already existing structures and services. A person-centred approach can help to evaluate all the steps taken in order to determine whether the measures are geared to the needs of those affected. Person-centred inclusive planning for old age respects the resources and abilities of older people and acknowledges the need to adapt services to individual needs.

Areas of Integrated Social Planning for Older People with and without a Disability

Scope of Planning

Social planning for senior citizens as well as for citizens with disabilities can no longer be limited to specialised institutions and services for these groups of people. Rather, it extends to all areas that promote or hinder individual life and social participation in the community. The target areas formulated for age-friendly and inclusive communities have considerable overlap. For example, Michell-Auli and Kremer-Preiß (2013, p. 15ff) identify six thematic areas for the development of age-friendly neighbourhoods: sensitivity for the needs of old age and awareness of discrimination; supportive social infrastructure (contact and opportunities for encounter, neighbourhood help, civic involvement); a barrier-free environment and accessible local supply; needs-oriented, low-barrier housing using new technologies; services that guarantee a mix of informal and professional support; counselling close to the place of residence and from a single counselling centre. In comparison: A Livable Community for Adults with Disabilities is defined by the National Council on Disability (2004, p. 9) in the US as one that:

- Provides affordable, appropriate, accessible housing
- Ensures accessible, affordable, reliable, safe transportation
- Adjusts the physical environment for inclusiveness and accessibility
- Provides work, volunteer, and education opportunities
- Ensures access to key health and support services
- Encourages participation in civic, cultural, social, and recreational activities.

Social planning for old age focuses on one or more of the following topics:

Raising awareness in neighbourhoods: To be appreciative and mindful with each other, especially in relationships among neighbours, protects against exclusion and identifies needs for help. However, attitudes and help among neighbours cannot be prescribed. But the awareness of their value can be increased and barriers to making contact can be reduced.

Volunteering: Especially in old age many people want to do voluntary work, others are looking for volunteers for joint activities or for help in everyday life.

Accessibility: Socio-spatial environments and services in the community are barrier-free if they can be found, accessed, and used by potential users. When designing a barrier-free environment, potential movement, perception, communication, and cognitive impairments as well as the use of aids by the persons concerned have to be considered.

Mobility: To what extent can people with mobility impairments safely reach the destinations relevant to them at the desired points in time and within a reasonable length of time? All types of transport and the fact that many people with disabilities need personal assistance to move in traffic must be taken into account.

Housing: In addition to housing adaptation and the provision of affordable, appropriate, and barrier-free housing, this also includes the planning of alternative forms of dwelling, such as shared housing and shared flats with assistance and care, as well as group homes and care facilities.

Support services: This includes above all assistance and care services, household-related services, and family support services in the disability sector. These services should be combined and work together with informal supporters to form a person-centred mix of support. The professional services also aim to relieve the burden on supporting relatives.

Social encounters and activities: Are there opportunities for meeting and contact in the neighbourhood? Are activities offered by associations, sports clubs, educational institutions, libraries, churches, and other community organisations attractive, accessible, and usable for older people as well? To what extent are meeting places and activities open to people with disabilities? How can elderly people with and without disabilities easily and comprehensively inform themselves about activities for organising free time? To what extent are specific facilities necessary, such as day care, daytime options for people with disabilities or chronic mental illness, lunch, or dinner opportunities? Is it possible to open such facilities to other target groups?

Local supply and everyday services in the vicinity: It should be possible to buy goods and services for daily or regular needs in accessible spatial proximity. Food shops, bakeries, restaurants, hairdressers, pharmacies, banks, and post offices are important meeting points in the neighbourhood.

Work and employment: Job opportunities in retirement are of interest to many senior citizens for financial reasons and partly because they wish to remain active.

Health and medical care: Are the medical care structures of local medical practices, therapeutic services, and regional acute and rehabilitation clinics sufficiently available? Are these appropriate for people with various types of disabilities? Are therapeutic services such as physiotherapy, occupational therapy, speech therapy available? Are there any local health promotion programs? What are the possibilities in the community to develop a health-promoting lifestyle?

End of life care: Supporting elderly people and their relatives at the end of life is the task of palliative care. In addition to palliative medical and nursing care, it also includes psychosocial and spiritual support in the last phase of life. Out-patient and in-patient hospice services and support for mourners assume important functions in communities. But often these services are not prepared to work with persons with intellectual disabilities.

Counselling and information: Counselling services for support in old age or disability need to be coordinated. A counselling centre or information point should address all kinds of people in old age and their relatives. It should be easy to find, spatially accessible and have long opening hours. Counselling should not be distorted by specific interests of service providers, but it requires their cooperation as well as knowledge about the variety of potential social and health benefits available.

Political participation: The participation of older people in the diversity of political decision-making processes in the community is an important goal of participation-oriented social planning.

Planning Areas

Planning projects cover planning areas of different sizes. Social planning is the responsibility of cities and rural districts with their municipalities. This is the level at which the local political bodies make decisions and this is where the administrative responsibilities are usually located. The focus on neighbourhoods, by which we mean urban districts/quarters or rural communities, aims to ensure that the measures fit more precisely into the socio-spatial environment of the citizens and are generated from there. In addition, social planning has also to consider the locations and catchment areas of services and supply areas that extend beyond the boundaries of a neighbourhood.

Strategic Elements and a Process Model for Integrated Social Planning

Various process models have been proposed for social planning with regard to persons with disabilities (e.g. Rohrmann, Schädler, Kempf, Konieczny, & Windisch, 2014). As an example, the model of Schäper et al. (2019) for integrated municipal social planning, which targets older citizens with and without disabilities, is presented here. The model was developed on the basis of an ongoing evaluation of two planning projects in an urban district with 25,500 inhabitants (Münster-Hiltrup) and in a rural community with 8,000 inhabitants (Wettringen in the district of Steinfurt) in north-western Germany. Schäper et al. (2019) describe strategic and structural elements as well as a process model for integrated social planning.

Strategic Planning Elements

Political mandate: Social planning needs political legitimation. To legitimate their actions, social planners need a political mandate from the municipal bodies. Social planers can do much to place issues on the political agenda by means of regular social reporting, communication with relevant actors, and cooperation in municipal boards.

Work structures: Which structures are used for integrated social planning and which should be further developed? Four types of structures can be distinguished: municipal administration, municipal political boards, cooperation structures, and participation structures. Neighbourhood-oriented social planning will integrate or create work structures at the neighbourhood level, alongside those at the city and district level. In the administration, it is important to structurally promote cooperation between the various specialist planning departments for senior citizens, for persons with disabilities and for chronically mentally ill persons, e.g. by integrating them into a joint department. When forming project teams, contact persons in the neighbourhood (municipal administration, neighbourhood managers, or similar) should become team members. Political bodies at neighbourhood level are to be involved in the process.

Integrated social planning requires both participation and cooperation structures. In planning, participation and cooperation are two different processes. Each has a different objective. Roles are distributed differently, distinguished methods are used. Participation assumes a central decision-making process within the political-administrative system in which third parties participate (Bischoff, Selle, & Sinning, 2005, p. 49). Citizens and other actors can be involved in the planning process, but without the decision-making sovereignty of politics and administration being removed. In many countries, issues such as the planning of services for people with disabilities or the local transport plan are decided at local level. In the model, participation structures are understood as temporary forms of citizen participation in concrete planning projects.

The situation is different when planning tasks can only be solved through cooperation. Cooperation is a negotiation and decision-making process between numerous actors in the community. 'There is no longer the individual actor who lets others participate in his decisions. Rather, all are co-operators who can contribute something to the solution of a task may also bring in their own decision-making competences' (Bischoff et al., 2005, p. 50 [translation FD]). For example, the various providers must be won over for the inclusive organisation of leisure time activities in the community. Local supply through retail cannot be easily created by planning either. Often the municipality is only a coordinating partner here, which pays attention to the fit of solutions to municipal goals. Cooperation in planning projects only works if a culture of cooperation with structures and agreements that are binding in character is created. Cooperation structures are, for example, associations of self-advocate groups, local conferences of stakeholders in community psychiatry or working groups on ageing in a neighbourhood.

Person-oriented key objectives: Person-oriented key objectives are formulated from the perspective of a citizen (person-oriented) and with reference to the neighbourhood. To give an example: the planning team in Münster-Hiltrup formulated the following person-oriented goals for housing after a future conference with citizens: 'Persons with and without disabilities should be able to stay in their neighbourhood, even if their support needs change in old age. They should be able to stay in their own homes, as long as the need for support does not exceed certain qualitative and quantitative limits. In the neighbourhood, inclusion-oriented support and residential services are available that fit to the citizens' specific needs'.

Person-oriented key objectives are supposed to have a steering function with regard to the diverse and concurrent interests involved in the planning process. They provide criteria for the assessment of proposals. In the concrete projects, social planners found it difficult to phrase person-oriented objectives. Once formulated, however, the key objectives were very understandable for all population groups, including people with intellectual disabilities.

Neighbourhood-oriented, GIS-based social reporting: For a neighbourhood-oriented prospective social planning, a regular socio-spatial analysis of data on the distribution of target groups, facilities, services and offerings in the neighbourhoods and in the entire city or district area is of great importance. A geographical information system (GIS) is characterised by the fact that the spatial component of data is included in the analysis and that extended evaluation possibilities are available. It is suitable for delimiting neighbourhoods, merging, analysing, and visualising data within neighbourhoods. For example, smaller-scale analyses are able to identify imbalances of age structures and the distribution of people with disabilities among different neighbourhoods. GIS-analysis shows where services or facilities are missing or in surplus. The spatial proximity of facilities or services reveals potentials for the networking of service providers. GIS are used by other planning units (e.g. in urban planning) and make the cooperation with them easier.

Planning Process

Integrated social planning according to Schäper et al. (2019) divides the planning process into four phases: planning phase, execution of the planning, implementation of the planning results and evaluation (see Figure 18.1).

Planning assignments can result from the general and specific objectives of municipal development planning, from the analyses of social reporting or from problems raised by other stakeholders. In the planning phase and during the execution of the planning, the social planners have to keep five tasks in mind simultaneously, which are interwoven with each other:

- The processing of the content-related problem includes defining objectives and tasks, determining needs, developing and evaluating solutions, and deriving measures.
- For the early detection of problems, the development of solutions and the implementation of measures, it is necessary to cooperate with other actors. For this purpose, existing cooperation structures should be used or missing ones, e.g. in the neighbourhood, should be created. The cooperation has to be shaped in the planning process and beyond.

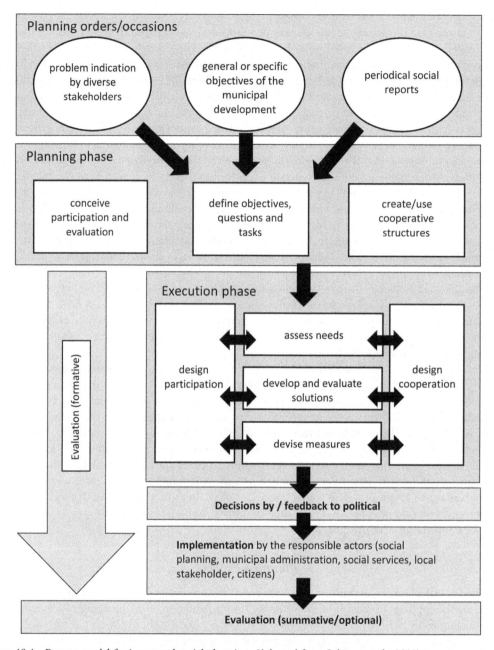

Figure 18.1 Process model for integrated social planning. (Adapted from Schäper et al., 2019).

- The participation of citizens in the context of a concrete planning project has also to be designed and continuously shaped.
- In order to improve social planning, the execution phase and the implementation of the planning results should be continuously evaluated (formative evaluation). A summative evaluation can follow, in which the effects of measures are tested.
- Social planning also includes close cooperation with political bodies, e.g. formulating planning assignments, reporting, preparing draft resolutions.

Designing Participation

In the context of a concrete planning process, the question arises as to who is involved, when and to what extent. Who represents the interests of people in old age, persons with disabilities and their informal supporters? Citizens with and without disabilities can be involved in formal political bodies (e.g. commissions for inclusion), in permanent cooperation structures as well as in the temporary planning projects.

In addition to members of the target groups themselves, representatives of self-advocate groups and other actors who claim to advocate for these target groups should be considered. Often these are, for instance, welfare organisations that pursue their own interests as providers, but also have valuable local information about target groups.

The level of participation in individual process steps should be determined, whereby one can orientate oneself on a stage model, as described by Straßburger and Rieger (2014) following Arnstein (1969). Here, a distinction is made between non-participation, preliminary stages of participation (such as informing, asking for opinions and assessments, obtaining lifeworld expertise) and three stages of participation: enabling co-determination, partial transfer of decision-making competences, and complete transfer of decision-making powers.

People with a high need for support in old age and people with mental or intellectual impairments are among the population groups that seldom participate in the public citizens' meetings or bring their interests to bear there. How can these 'weak interests' (Young, 2000) be included and made visible in the planning process? Both the formal participation formats anchored in law (e.g. hearings, committees) and commonly used informal methods of participation (e.g. Future Workshop, Jungk & Müllert, 1987), Future Search Conference (Weisbord & Janoff, 1995), Planning for Real (Gibson, 1979) can be made more accessible and supplemented by outreach methods. For example, Schäper et al. (2019) started citizen participation in the neighbourhoods with a two-hour kick-off meeting in which interest-specific work groups were formed. Over the course of a year, five work groups held 3–5 meetings. Each work group covered a specific topic such as accessibility in public spaces, opportunities for encounters and activities, and assisted living. The citizen participation concluded with a public meeting after one year, where first results and further planning steps were presented. Addressing target groups directly, the cooperation with professional and informal supporters, the continuous use of a simple language, a sensitive moderation, presentations by representatives of different target groups, an appropriate time frame, and accessibility contributed to the fact that participants felt socially acknowledged and taken seriously. People with disabilities appreciated the contact to other non-disabled citizens.

The outreach methods used by Schäper et al. (2019) included focus group interviews with older chronically mentally ill people at their meeting points. A neighbourhood inspection with simultaneous interviews (walk–through interviews, Zimring, 1987) was conducted with six citizens with different impairments (including a severely visually impaired woman and a man suffering from dementia). A different approach was used to work with service providers and funding authorities. Case vignettes were created and introduced to them. Alternative and cross-sectional solutions were discussed in scenario workshops. Sok, Kok, Royers, and Panhuizen (2009) give further advice on how participation methods can be adapted to include persons with intellectual disabilities. However, as Rohleder (2017) points out for the development of evaluation instruments, the interests of the diversity of groups have to be respected when adapting participation processes. Inclusive formats that are exclusively geared towards persons with intellectual disabilities will not succeed.

Key Issues

The integrated social planning model presented is complex. Its complete implementation at the municipal level will take several years. But it is worthwhile in the long run. The following key issues should be considered.

- Since, in the course of demographic change, more and more cities and municipalities want and have to implement age-friendly structures in social planning processes, it is imperative that the needs of older people with lifelong disabilities are considered in these processes from the very beginning.
- This requires the willingness of political decision-makers, funding agencies, and service providers to see the necessity, but above all the opportunities, of cross-sectoral cooperation for senior citizens with and without lifelong disabilities for a healthy and meaningful life in old age.
- There are numerous areas that need to be addressed in the planning process. It is therefore advisable to start with one or two selected fields of action. This will make successes visible for all those involved, especially for senior citizens. Other relevant planning areas can then be worked on step by step.
- The social planners' tasks include cooperation with the municipal administration and municipal boards and the design of long-term cooperation structures and project-related, temporary participation structures.
- Citizen participation is of particular importance. Participation methods are to be selected and adapted in such a way that the diversity of population groups is addressed. Beside methods for larger groups, workshops, and working groups, outreach methods should be used to incorporate the views of population groups that for various reasons are underrepresented in public meetings.

Conclusion

The need to develop age-friendly communities is a global issue in the face of demographic change. In this context, there is an increasing demand for age and disability to be taken into account together in the development of person-centred support structures. There are already programmatic considerations. But so far there are hardly any studies that examine the implementation of integrated social planning for old age. Furthermore, there remains the question of the transferability of planning models to other societies and welfare-systems. For the future there is a need for international comparative studies that compare planning practices and their country-specific social and cultural contexts.

Note

1 See Convention on the Rights of Persons with Disabilities (CRPD) https://www.un.org/development/desa/disabilities/convention-on-the-rights-of-persons-with-disabilities.html

References

Amado, A. N., Stancliffe, R. J., McCarron, M., & McCallion, P. (2013). Social inclusion and community participation of individuals with intellectual/developmental disabilities. *Intellectual and Developmental Disabilities*, 51(5), 360–375. https://doi.org/10.1352/1934-9556-51.5.360

Arnstein, S. (1969). A ladder of citizen participation. *Journal of the American Planning Association*, 35(4), 216–224. https://doi.org/10.1080/01944366908977225

Beard, J. R., & Petitot, C. (2010). Ageing and urbanization: Can cities be designed to foster active ageing? *Public Health Reviews*, 32(2), 427–450. https://doi.org/10.1007/BF03391610

Bickenbach, J., Bigby, C., Salvador-Carulla, L., Heller, T., Leonardi, M., LeRoy, B., … Spindel, A. (2012). The Toronto declaration on bridging knowledge, policy and practice in aging and disability: Toronto, Canada, March 30, 2012. *International Journal of Integrated Care*, 12. https://doi.org/10.5334/ijic.1086

Bigby, C. (2004). *Ageing with a lifelong disability*. Kingsley. https://doi.org/10.1002/gps.1250

Bigby, C., & Wiesel, I. (2019). Using the concept of encounter to further the social inclusion of people with intellectual disabilities: What has been learned? *Research and Practice in Intellectual and Developmental Disabilities*, 6(1), 39–51. https://doi.org/10.1080/23297018.2018.1528174

Bischoff, A., Selle, K., & Sinning, H. (2005). *Informieren, Beteiligen, Kooperieren. Kommunikation in Planungsprozessen. Eine Übersicht zu Formen, Verfahren und Methoden* [Inform, participate, cooperate: Communication in planning processes: An overview of forms, procedures, and methods]. Dortmunder Vertrieb für Bau- und Planungsliteratur. https://lib.ugent.be/catalog/rug01:001028166

Bittles, A., & Glasson, E. (2004). Clinical, social, and ethical implications of changing life expectancy in Down syndrome. *Developmental Medicine & Child Neurology, 46*(4), 282–286. https://doi.org/10.1017/s0012162204000441

BMFSFJ – Bundesministerium für Familie, Senioren, Frauen und Jugend [Federal Ministry of Family Affairs]. (2016). *Siebter Bericht zur Lage der älteren Generation in der Bundesrepublik Deutschland. Sorge und Mitverantwortung in der Kommune* [Seventh report on the situation of the older generation in the Federal Republic of Germany. Concern and responsibility in the community]. *Aufbau und Sicherung zukunftsfähiger Gemeinschaften* [Building and securing sustainable communities]. Berlin. https://www.siebter-altenbericht.de/fileadmin/altenbericht/pdf/Der_Siebte_Altenbericht.pdf

Buckner, S., Mattocks, C., Rimmer, M., & Lafortune, L. (2018). "An evaluation tool for age-friendly and dementia friendly communities", *Working with Older People, 22*(1), 48–58. https://doi.org/10.1108/WWOP-11-2017-0032

Carey, A. C. (2011). The quest for community: Intellectual disability and the shifting meaning of community in activism. In A. Carey & R. Scotch (Eds.), *Disability and community (research in social science and disability* (Vol. 6, pp. 189–213). Emerald Group Publishing Limited. https://doi.org/10.1108/S1479-3547(2011)0000006011

Chang, C. K., Hayes, R. D., Perera, G., Broadbent, M. T., Fernandes, A. C., Lee, W. E., ... Stewart, R. (2011). Life expectancy at birth for people with serious mental illness and other major disorders from a secondary mental health care case register in London. *PLoS ONE, 6*(5), e19590. https://doi.org/10.1371/journal.pone.0019590

Dieckmann, F., Giovis, C., & Offergeld, J. (2015). The life expectancy of people with intellectual disability in Germany. *Journal of Applied Research in Intellectual Disabilities, 28*(5), 373–382. https//doi.org/10.1111/jar.12193

Gibson, T. (1979). *Planning for real. A user guide*. Neighbourhood Initiatives Foundation.

Jungk, R., & Müllert, N. (1987). *Future workshops: How to create desirable futures*. Institute for Social Inventions.

Lin, S., & Lewis, F. M. (2015). Dementia friendly, dementia capable, and dementia positive: Concepts to prepare for the future. *The Gerontologist, 55*(2), 237–244. https://doi.org/10.1093/geront/gnu122

Meesters, P. D. (2019). Community treatment needs. In C. I. Cohen & P. D. Meesters (Eds.), *Schizophrenia and psychoses in later life. New perspectives on treatment, research, and policy* (pp. 135–145). Cambridge University Press. https://doi.org/10.1017/9781108539593

Mehnert, T., & Kremer-Preiß, U. (2017). *Handreichung Quartiersentwicklung. Praktische Umsetzung sozialraumorientierter Ansätze in der Altenhilfe* [Guideline for district development: Practical implementation of social space-oriented approaches in elderly care]. KDA-Verlag. Retrieved from https://www.baulinks.de/webplugin/2016/0858.php4

Michell-Auli, P., & Kremer-Preiß, U. (2013). *Quartiersentwicklung. KDA-Ansatz und kommunale Praxis* [District development: KDA approach and community practice]. KDA-Verlag.

Mitchell, L. (2014). A step too far? Designing dementia-friendly neighbourhoods. In R. Cooper, E. Burton & C. L. Cooper (Eds.), *Wellbeing: A complete reference guide, volume II, wellbeing and the environment* (pp. 185–218). Wiley.

National Council on Disability. (2004). *Livable communities for adults with disabilities*. Washington. https://ncd.gov/rawmedia_repository/27da565e_a048_4844_ad82_0b37ba47af7d.pdf

Naue, U., Nordentoft, M., Wahlbeck, K., Hällgren, J., Westman, J., Ösby, U., ... Laursen, T. M. (2013). Excess mortality, causes of death and life expectancy in 270,770 patients with recent onset of mental disorders in Denmark, Finland and Sweden. *PLoS ONE* 8(1): e55176. http://doi.org/10.1371/journal.pone.0055176

Rohleder, C. (2017). Inklusive Veranstaltungen evaluieren – (K)ein Thema für die empirische Sozialforschung (?) [Evaluate inclusive events – A topic for empirical social research]. *Teilhabe [Participation], 56*(4), 156–162.

Rohrmann, A., Schädler, J., Kempf, M., Konieczny, E., & Windisch, M. (Eds.). (2014). *Inklusive Gemeinwesen Planen* [Integrated community planning]. Ministerium für Arbeit, Integration und Soziales des Landes NRW [Ministry of Labor, Integration and Social Affairs of the State of North Rhine-Westphalia]. https://inklusionskataster-nrw.de/infothek/planung

Schäper, S., Dieckmann, F., Rohleder, C., Rodekohr, B., Katzer, M., & Frewer-Graumann, S. (2019). *Inklusive Sozialplanung für Menschen im Alter* [Integrated social planning for people of old age]. Kohlhammer.

Scharlach, A. E. (2017). Aging in context: Individual and environmental pathways to aging-friendly communities – The 2015 Matthew A. Pollack award lecture. *The Gerontologist, 57*(4), 606–618. https://doi.org/10.1093/geront/gnx017

Sok, K., Kok, E., Royers, T., & Panhuizen, B. (2009). *Clientenparticipatie in beeld. Inventarisatie praktijkvoorbeelden van clientenparticipatie* [Client participation in the picture. Inventory of practical examples of client participation]. MOVISIE. https://www.kindengezin.be/img/RapportClientenparticipatie.pdf

Straßbuger, G., & Rieger, J. (Eds.) (2014). *Partizipation kompakt. Für Studium, Lehre und Praxis sozialer Berufe* [Participation compact: For studying, teaching, and practicing social professions]. Juventa.

Weisbord, M., & Janoff, S. (1995). *Future search. An action guide to finding common ground in organisations and communities.* Berrett Kohler Publishers.

World Health Organization. (2002). *Towards a common language for functioning, disability and health.* ICF. World Health Organization. https://www.who.int/classifications/icf/icfbeginnersguide.pdf [01.05.2010]

World Health Organization. (2007). *Global age-friendly cities. A guide.* World Health Organization. https://www.who.int/ageing/publications/Global_age_friendly_cities_Guide_English.pdf

World Health Organization. (2015). *WHO global disability action plan 2014–2021. Better health for all people with disability.* World Health Organization. https://apps.who.int/iris/bitstream/handle/10665/199544/9789241509619_eng.pdf;jsessionid=EB41A9A1453D6A8A288A2469E26C4F23?sequence=1

World Health Organization. (2017). *Global strategy and action plan on ageing and health.* World Health Organization. https://www.who.int/ageing/WHO-GSAP-2017.pdf?ua=1

Young, I. (2000). *Inclusion and democracy.* Oxford University Press. https://doi.org/10.1093/0198297556.001.0001

Zimring, C. (1987). Evaluation of designed environments. In R. Bechtel, R. Marans & W. Michelson (Eds.), *Methods in environmental and behavioral research* (pp. 270–300). van Nostrand Reinhold.

Suggested Readings

Amado, A. N., Stancliffe, R. J., McCarron, M., & McCallion, P. (2013). Social inclusion and community participation of individuals with intellectual/developmental disabilities. *Intellectual and Developmental Disabilities, 51*(5), 360–375. https://doi.org/10.1352/1934-9556-51.5.360

Bigby, C., & Wiesel, I. (2019). Using the concept of encounter to further the social inclusion of people with intellectual disabilities: What has been learned? *Research and Practice in Intellectual and Developmental Disabilities, 6*(1), 39–51.

Scharlach, A. E. (2017). Aging in context: Individual and environmental pathways to aging-friendly communities – The 2015 Matthew A. Pollack award lecture. *The Gerontologist, 57*(4), 606–618. https://doi.org/10.1093/geront/gnx017

World Health Organization. (2015). *WHO global disability action plan 2014–2021. Better health for all people with disability.* World Health Organization. https://apps.who.int/iris/bitstream/handle/10665/199544/9789241509619_eng.pdf;jsessionid=EB41A9A1453D6A8A288A2469E26C4F23?sequence=1

PART IV

Intellectual Disability as a Case Example

19
THE EMERGENCE OF AGEING WITH LONG-TERM DISABILITY POPULATIONS

Philip McCallion, Lisa Ferretti, and Mary McCarron

Introduction

The history of our understanding of long-term disability populations, of people with intellectual disabilities, developmental disabilities, learning disabilities, mental retardation, and so many other labels for people is rooted in the educational, quality of life, need for protection, normalisation, and even eugenic ideas of professionals and philosophical movements over the last century and a half. For the purposes of this chapter the term people with intellectual and developmental disabilities (I/DD) will be used. Much of professional thought focused upon relatively small groups, those admitted to schools and institutions, and lives were often reduced to professional interests such as understanding genetics, advancing educational processes, developing function and self-sufficiency, and reducing burden on families and society. As Schreenberger noted (1983), historically, such partialised perspectives meant there was little attention to the lifespan of individuals. Those lifespans were often short.

Life expectancy for persons with intellectual disability (ID) was an average 18.5 years in 1930 but by the 1970s in the U.S. had risen to 59.1 years (Braddock, 1999). There are reports of similar growth during this period in the UK, other European countries and Australia (Bigby, McCallion, & McCarron, 2014). The increase is attributed to major changes in access to medical care, medical and pharmacological interventions addressing syndromes causing I/DD, and better management of infections and chronic conditions (Bittles et al., 2002). There are also beliefs that the dramatic increase in longevity resulted from a fundamental change in approaches to care because of the deinstitutionalisation movement in many countries and the beginning of normalisation and person-centred philosophies to better manage care (McCallion, Jokinen, & Janicki, 2017).

The adoption of a professional emphasis on community placement of individuals was also initially a partialising perspective. The emphasis was on serving children in community schools albeit initially in segregated classrooms, and creating group homes for young and sometimes middle-aged adults where they would experience employment and being part of a neighbourhood and ideally, accessing community health resources. What would happen when that 10 year old student or the 35 year old adult later turned 50 or 60 years was not actively considered, perhaps because popular conceptions were still that people with I/DD were not and would not be living to older age.

Two seminal books, *Aging and Developmental Disabilities: Issues and Approaches* written by Matthew Janicki and Henryk Wisniewski and published in 1985, and *Aging and Mental Retardation: Extending the Continuum* written by Martin Krauss and Marsha Seltzer published in 1987, disrupted the view of lives of people with I/DD as the age by: (1) Advancing a lifespan approach that included families, and identified that large numbers of people with I/DD had lived and were continuing to live with families (2) Documenting people with I/DD were getting older and (3) Raising the concern that service systems and professional perspectives were unprepared to support ageing persons with I/DD and their more aged family caregivers (Janicki & Wisniewski, 1985; Krauss & Seltzer, 1987). These changes also occurred within a historical timeline of services for people with I/DD.

The Health and Ageing Era

History is often understood and explained in terms of eras. For people with I/DD there have been three somewhat distinct eras, although history is never tidy, so there has also been a lot of overlap and reaffirmation/exploration of the transitions of each era. The three eras have been an institutionalisation era (late 19th century through 1970), a deinstitutionalisation era (principally 1970 through 2000) and, the most recent, a health and ageing era (1985 to present). There is some overlap between the eras and beginning and ending dates vary somewhat by jurisdiction. The first two eras were also marked with efforts around advancement of education, day programming, and employment with segregation versus desegregation and gradations of integration and self-determination underpinning each era and providing measures of progress. In the current era, people with I/DD have benefited from the successes particularly of de-institutionalisation, which includes both ageing successfully and greater opportunities for community involvement, acceptance, and integration. They are also experiencing some consequences of prior era successes in terms of improved health and longevity as well as a greater range of personal growth and fulfilment opportunities. However, there is also greater onset of age associated health concerns, and difficulties in finding meaningful employment in adulthood and transitioning to retirement in older age. The health and ageing era includes further challenges of:

- Less than optimal community involvement, acceptance, and integration
- Ambivalence in advocacy and I/DD service delivery about full integration into general population services and options
- The re-opening of debates because increased longevity and associated greater health concerns combined with the dismantling of segregated services means that general population services may be a source of less than optimal care and a pathway to segregated services such as nursing homes for all persons ageing

Nevertheless, work over the most recent decades does mean that the interests of those who are ageing with I/DD are now better known and are actively being considered within I/DD, ageing, and healthcare systems. Finally, the growing recognition and acceptance that people with I/DD will and do age may also mean greater early attention to health promotion and the strategies for healthy and successful ageing and for ageing in place where desired that mirror efforts for the general population.

Caregiving

Attention to the ageing of people with I/DD first occurred in the 1980s and 1990s and was part of a growing attention to the numbers of family caregivers supporting persons with I/DD who were themselves ageing. There was deserved priority given to addressing the abuse histories of institutions and the inappropriateness of segregation but there was beginning realisation that the majority of people with ID were cared for at home, often without government-supported resources. Large numbers of persons with I/DD were being discovered living at home and cared for by individuals often in their 40s and 50s who would rapidly become caregivers in their 60s and 70s, even 80s and 90s: caregiving for the person with I/DD was, therefore, expected to move from parents to siblings, but siblings were reported to be unprepared. Also, the numbers of family members available to care was declining with changing birth rates in both developed and developing countries and with increased employment of women, the primary group of current caregivers was further reducing.

A book of the period *The elderly caregiver: Caring for adults with developmental disabilities*, edited by Karen Roberto and published in 1993, captured that there was an expectation of an imminent caregiving crisis with (1) The number of persons with I/DD at home largely unknown (2) A generation of caregivers shielding their family members from government supported services systems they did not trust and (3) Not enough public resources budgeted to address an onslaught of persons in need of services (Lightfoot & McCallion, 2016; Smith, Fullmer, & Tobin, 1994). Despite these differing perspectives, all agreed that new resources were needed to better support current and future planning for these families, including thoughtful provision of respite and other supportive services and the development of alternative living situation resources (Heller & Factor, 1991). There was also encouragement for health promotion for both caregiver and care recipient, counterbalanced by concerns for the potential of financial and other exploitation of people with I/DD whose resources might instead be used to support the whole household, rather than targeted at the individual with I/DD as intended.

These changes were advocated for within the shadow of the institutionalisation era when the relationship between families and services were often conflictual, leading to families rejecting the service system and its 'discarding' of people with I/DD (McCallion & Toseland, 1993). The remade service system that emphasised deinstitutionalisation and community integration, again with stated good intentions, for some families risked conflict again by having an appearance of 'discarding' caregivers and a focus solely on the person with I/DD and a disregard for the family in which the person with I/DD lived and its values. The discovery of families who were not middle class in education and income, were families of colour, and where caregivers were relatives other than parents or siblings raised concerns that there was cultural, economic and generational insensitivities in supposedly benefitting perspectives of service systems (McCallion & Grant-Griffin, 2000; McCallion, Janicki, & Grant-Griffin, 1997). Interestingly, 30 years after the projections of the late 1980s and early 1990s, there has been a realisation of the projected decline in available family caregivers, further increases in sibling-provided care and female employment outside the home, yet, (1) The majority of people with I/DD continue to be cared for by family members (2) Economic realities and changing service philosophy approaches – self-determination, home and community-based services, participant direction and self-managed budgets – encourage maintenance in current care settings, or ageing in place, rather than wholesale movement to out of home community settings and (3) There is growing interest in the value of mutual aid in family caregiving situations (Brennan, McCausland, McCallion, & McCarron, 2020; Lightfoot & McCallion, 2016).

When persons with I/DD were not expected to live into old age, parents would often outlive their offspring with few services developed or provided (McCallion & Kolomer, 2003). With sizeable groups of individuals with I/DD now ageing and living at home, the demand for formal services is heightened to levels greater than for the general population (Bigby, Wilson, et al., 2014; Jackson, Howe, & Nakashima, 2010). People with I/DD and their caregivers are also reported to have lower rates of employment than the general population with incomes close to, or below poverty lines (Bigby, McCallion, et al., 2014; McCallion & McCarron, 2015). Equally, there is little respite from such caregiving for the caregiver (Brennan, McCausland, McCallion, & McCarron, 2020; Lightfoot & McCallion, 2016) further straining the available informal resources. There remain families where caregivers feel overwhelmed, and persons with I/DD feel life desires are stifled. Continuing demographic shifts may lead to catastrophic situations for families rather than challenging situations as envisioned in the 1980s and 1990s (Brennan et al., 2020; Hahn et al., 2016). Creating an environment of respect and inclusion where the strengths of the family and the ageing person with I/DD are clearly included and appreciated was both the initial and the continuing challenge both for service delivery and the training of new professionals (Lightfoot & McCallion, 2016).

Dementia

There was also early recognition that longer lives for persons with I/DD may mean increases across the lifespan in chronic health conditions including dementia and late onset disabilities as is seen in the general population. There was growing awareness that dementia in persons with Down syndrome (DS), in particular, exceeded that of the general population. An early study reported a prevalence of 2% in persons with DS aged 30–39 years, 9.4% in persons aged 40–49 years, 36.1% in persons aged 50–59 years, and 54.5% in persons aged 60–69 years (Prasher, 1995) as compared to general population rates of between 4.3% and 10% in persons aged 65 years and over (McCallion, Swinburne, Burke, McGlinchey, & McCarron, 2013). Reports of the prevalence of dementia for other persons with ID (who do not have DS) proved more equivocal, with both findings of rates similar to the general population (Janicki & Dalton, 2000) and of higher rates (Cooper, 1997).

Later studies have confirmed what was suspected in the 1980s, that as well as being influential in the onset of DS, amyloid precursor protein (APP) is also produced by chromosome 21 and because people with DS overexpress APP (Jennings et al., 2015), the over-expression leads to the development of amyloid plaques – the hallmark of Alzheimer's disease, a primary form of dementia. The early and greater onset of dementia in people with DS and the ability to isolate a key process to chromosome 21 initially created great interest in the disease and its progress in people with DS. It was believed that discoveries here would lead to breakthroughs for the general population. As is often the case, particularly in Alzheimer's disease research early promise was disappointed and general population researchers largely lost interest in this group (Janicki & Dalton, 2000). Recent funding initiatives and the formation of international research groups, meaning the availability of larger samples, have re-created this interest in dementia in people with DS and greater advocacy for their inclusion in clinical trials (McCarron, Carroll, & McCallion, 2017).

Later studies continue to confirm that people with DS and dementia experience co-occurring late onset epilepsy, an early and precipitous but then extended decline, and significant added care concerns (McCarron, McCallion, Reilly, & Mulryan, 2014). I/DD service systems and out of home placement options were identified as ill-prepared (Janicki, McCallion, & Dalton, 2002). Similarly, general sector dementia assessment and treatment programs proved unwilling to include people with DS and were challenged by the age earlier onset of symptoms and the inappropriateness of widely used assessment instruments which were not sufficiently sensitive to detect differences between the symptoms and manifestations of life-long I/DD and newly onset symptoms of dementia (McCarron et al., 2017). Most concerning was the widespread development of dementia options and education that adopted age related descriptions, recommendations for assessment and post diagnostic care ill-suited for many people with DS and encouraged research that usually excluded people with DS and dementia (Janicki & Dalton, 2000; McCallion et al., 2017).

In response both to increasing awareness of dementia in people with DS and other I/DD and to address the concerns being identified, a series of documents and related trainings were developed by an international group of researchers to correct misconceptions about dementia in people with I/DD and to offer guidance on assessment and post diagnosis care (Aylward, Burt, Thorpe, & Lai, 1997; Burt & Aylward, 2000). This guidance is regularly updated (Jokinen, Janicki, Keller, McCallion, & Force, 2013; Moran et al., 2013) but the initial guidance documents continue to be influential. Subsequent work also addressed the need for services re-design and for physical improvements in living situations and other program provision such as day services (Janicki et al., 2002; Nickle & McCallion, 2005).

This was also a challenging moment for I/DD services. Patterns for the general population were to place persons with dementia in nursing homes and then to develop within such homes specialised dementia units. On the one hand, there were arguments that 'living in the community just like everyone else' meant that advocates and services providers needed to be open to the nursing home option for people with I/DD. On the other hand, there were concerns not to return to discredited institutional models for care of people with I/DD. The differences in the onset of the disease in people, particularly with DS also argued for differences with general accepted models for I/DD care, but did not justify a segregated response. Instead work on the development of dementia care for people with I/DD has been designed since then to be responsive to their specific needs and to serve as an exemplar for care for everyone with dementia (Janicki et al., 2002). The adoption in some countries of I/DD models for dementia care for everyone is a testament to the value of this approach (Traphagan & Nagasawa, 2008).

Work and Retirement

People with I/DD have not traditionally had access to regular paid employment with most vocational services provided in segregated workplaces such as sheltered workshops, and many there receiving less than minimum wages and working on a very part time basis. The majority of people with I/DD have been unemployed with a number attending day programs and other gainful employment-substitution activities (McGlinchey, McCallion, Burke, Carrol, & McCarron, 2013; Unger, Campbell, & McMahon, 2004). Yet, there is also evidence of people with I/DD placing value on these work and other opportunities. For example, in Ireland, in a national study, the majority of individuals with I/DD participating in day programming described themselves as going to work and reported high satisfaction levels with their 'employment' (McGlinchey et al., 2013). The same study found among participants with I/DD developed ideas around ageing and retirement (Burke, McCallion, & McCarron, 2014). As well as being concerned if such aspirations may be fulfilled it is also important to consider how ideas around retirement for people with I/DD have evolved.

Thinking in the 1980s and 1990s was that there would be a growing group of older, retired persons with I/DD, who, similar to what was being discussed then about the rest of the population, would be both living longer and retiring younger (Sutton, Factor, Hawkins, Heller, & Seltzer, 1993). That aspirational picture has not weathered the last couple of decades well for most people as recessions, changes in pension entitlements, and healthcare costs have increased the likelihood for many of working longer and not necessarily having their aspirations met. People with I/DD always had more limited opportunities in older age with almost minimal likelihood of retiring with a pension, sharing those years with a spouse/partner and finding meaningful experiences. There were also concerns in the 1990s about limited choices regarding retirement (Ashman & Suttie, 1996), unprepared services providers and staff (Bigby, 1992, 1998), few personal and financial resources for retirement, and little preparatory education (Sutton, Factor, Hawkins, Heller, & Seltzer, 1993). Early findings (Bigby, 1998; Buys & Rushworth, 1997) were of retired persons with I/DD being unhappy with their retirement activities. There were some efforts to develop alternatives. Heller, Miller, Hsieh, and Sterns (2000) designed and successfully taught a training program about later life planning issues including making choices about current and potential residence, work options, health and well-being, use of leisure time and recreation, use of formal and informal supports, and how to set goals and make action plans. As well as choices around housing, futures planning activities, an increasing emphasis on life-style changes and improved leisure and life satisfaction (Mahon & Goatcher, 1999) also helped in developing retirement plans for some. This was also a time when there were efforts to integrate people with I/DD into senior centres and into other day programming targeted at the general retired population to increase retirement alternatives (LePore & Janicki, 1991, 1997).

The options for retirement have been heavily influenced in the period since by a continuing failure to dramatically increase the numbers of persons with I/DD who are employed (Lysaght, Cobigo, & Hamilton, 2012) and therefore able to accumulate the resources, experiences and relationships that will support retirement. Lack of pensions and opportunities to choose a retirement lifestyle remains a concern. More recent efforts have targeted the building of older adult relationships, the opportunity to participate in the same activities as other retirees enjoy and individual confidence in people with I/DD, families and staff that retirement is possible (Bigby, Wilson, Balandin, & Stancliffe, 2011; Stancliffe, Wilson, Gambin, Bigby, & Balandin, 2013).

End of Life

Increasing chronic illness associated with getting older among people with I/DD highlights the challenges for general health services in providing care but also means that similar to the general population death is more likely to be a result of prolonged illness rather than abrupt events. End of life therefore poses its own challenges for general health care, specialised palliative and hospice care, and ongoing care from I/DD services systems. The situation for people with I/DD is further complicated by consent and legal status issues. Although the period of the 1980s and 1990s was marked by initiatives to recognise and advance self-determination by people with I/DD, issues of death and dying were largely absent from that debate. Interestingly this was perhaps because this is one area of people with I/DD's lives where multiple systems are involved and it is unclear who is 'in charge' or who wants to be. As persons with I/DD experience terminal illness and approach their end of life, this is challenging for the staff in I/DD settings and hospice and other palliative care staff are also not well equipped to understand the care of persons with ID (Tuffrey-Wijne, 1997; McCallion & McCarron, 2004). Tuffrey-Wijne (2002) suggested that collaborative working relationships between ID staff and palliative care staff may improve care and encourage greater exchange of expertise.

Tuffrey-Wijne (2002) and Todd (2004) noted in early studies that when staff working in ID care are equipped to report important changes to palliative care staff, this has proven critical to good symptom management in terminal care. Fahey-McCarthy, McCarron, Connaire, and McCallion (2010) go further and recommended (a) raising awareness among staff in both systems of the philosophies underpinning care and the expertise inherent in both I/DD and specialist palliative care services, (b) having I/DD staff understand that staff in specialist palliative care offer skills around symptom management and are an external source of support that may be vital to navigating final days, (c) having hospice and palliative care services staff better understand their role given that staff in I/DD services are first highly dedicated and committed to providing optimal care making them an important resource but second, sometimes lack knowledge and skills in assessing and managing pain, constipation, dyspnea, fevers, nutrition, and hydration, and (d) equipping specialist palliative care staff to address their communication difficulties with persons with I/DD, and with better understanding of care needs of people with I/DD, I/DD service structures and where specialist palliative care fits and bests addresses the gaps in current service provision.

The accumulating work and experience with palliative care and end of life is pointing out other needs to include re-evaluating the skill mix among staff in care settings as more persons present with advanced disease and additional education and palliative care intervention guidelines are also needed. Particularly if I/DD services staff are to develop the ability to care for dying persons in their chosen place or home (McCallion, McCarron, Fahey-McCarthy, & Connaire, 2012). The consensus emerging is that approaches that draw upon the perspectives of staff within I/DD services and specialist palliative care including core philosophies, common strengths and contributions to care offered by each service system will encourage greater creativity in determining the roles and timing of palliative care for persons with intellectual disabilities and advanced disease (McCallion et al., 2012; McCarron, McCallion, Fahey-McCarthy, Connaire, & Lane, 2010).

Crossing Systems

As awareness of the ageing of people with I/DD and dementia was building important questions were asked about the potential to have needs related to ageing, poorly resourced and prepared for in the I/DD service system, addressed through services systems for the general ageing population (Hawkins & Eklund, 1989). In the U.S., Wu (1987), Ansello and Rose (1989), and McCallion and Janicki (1997) outlined important hurdles in collaborative work between general population ageing and I/DD services agencies: (a) Differences in language, philosophy, and priorities with the same words often meaning different things (b) Uncertainty about who meets criteria for I/DD; and the numbers of people involved;

(c) Lack of knowledge about needs of older life-long caring families makes it difficult to plan for their inclusion in services (d) Major differences in systems in how services are funded and organised (e) An absence of clear-cut goals in either system for ageing persons with I/DD and their families makes joint planning difficult (f) Meetings, trainings, and consultations to create a unified approach being perceived by workers in both service systems as themselves a hindrance to efforts to meet needs they poorly understand (g) Resistance from other ageing constituencies to including persons with I/DD in ageing services – who are seen as having their own system that is better resourced than ageing services (h) Suspicions that cooperative efforts to serve persons with I/DD and their ageing families are more likely to take resources from already served populations rather than add to service options (i) Difficulty in brokering cooperative efforts in an impartial and nonthreatening manner and (j) The need to address a lack of personnel trained in both service systems.

Much of the work since has been targeted at addressing these hurdles. There was an early demonstration program in the United States in the late 1990s that showed it was possible to reach older caring families through outreach by ageing services (Janicki, McCallion, Force, Bishop, & LePore, 1998). Case studies and manuals supporting exemplary practices also emerged (Janicki, 1993, 1996; LePore & Janicki, 1991, 1997). A particular challenge in many countries was the age at which persons with I/DD would be considered 'ageing' and therefore eligible for services. Here too, there were examples of creative thinking and examples of persons younger than traditional age cut-offs such as 60 or 65 years old being able to access some ageing services given that their caregiver met the cut-offs (Janicki, McCallion, Force, Bishop, & LePore, 1998). Throughout the 1990s there were also jointly funded demonstration projects where adults with I/DD in their fifties attended the same day programs as general population older adults in their 60s and 70s (LePore & Janicki, 1991, 1997).

Greater advancement of joint or similar if parallel initiatives have awaited more recent times. Ideas of ageing in place, consumer directed/participant directed services, personal budgets, and person-centred planning have driven much of this innovation (Mahoney, Meiners, Shoop, & Squillace, 2003; McCallion et al., 2017). The recent merging of the Administration on Ageing and the Administration on Developmental Disability under an Administration on Community Living in the United States and the implementation of the National Disability Insurance Scheme in Australia (Olney & Dickinson, 2019) are examples both that challenges to joint working across systems remain, but also that significant progress is being made.

Conclusion

The crises in care for people with I/DD in the period 1960–90 produced a revolution in care that is continuing in many countries and is realised first through movement away institutional to community-based delivery of services. The revolution has also very imperfectly worked again since the 1990s to address the needs of families continuing to care at home. Perhaps most importantly the public presence of people with I/DD has grown, ideas like ageing in place, self-determination, person-centred and most recently relationship-centred care, and normalisation have been considered and implemented, and the value of participation in society, the forming and maintenance of relationships, enjoying retirement and choice in how one lives and dies are part of the lives of many. There is more to be done. Addressing and managing health concerns while advancing continued participation and ensuring that community gains are not lost are the new era's challenges for people with I/DD.

References

Ansello, E. F., & Rose, T. R. (1989). *Aging and lifelong disabilities: Partnership for the twenty-first century*. University of Maryland Center on Aging.

Ashman, A. F., & Suttie, J. N. (1996). The social and community involvement of older Australians with intellectual disabilities. *Journal of Intellectual Disability Research 40*(2), 120–129. https://doi.org/10.1111/j.1365-2788.1996.tb00613.x.

Aylward, E., Burt, D. B., Thorpe, L. U., & Lai, F. (1997). Diagnosis of dementia in individuals with intellectual disability. *Journal of Intellectual Disability Research, 41*(2), 152–164. https://doi.org/10.1111/j.1365-2788.1997.tb00692.x

Bigby C. (1992). Access and linkage: Two critical issues for older people with an Intellectual Disability in utilizing day activities and leisure services. Australia & New Zealand *Journal of Intellectual Disabilities, 18*(2), 95–109.

Bigby, C. (1998). Shifting responsibilities: Patterns of formal service use by older people with intellectual disability in Victoria. *Journal of Intellectual &Developmental Disability, 23*(3), 229–243. https://doi.org/10.1080/13668259800033721

Bigby, C., McCallion, P., & McCarron, M. (2014). Serving an elderly population. In M. Agran, F. Brown, C. Hughes, C. Quirk, & D. Ryndak (Eds.), *Equality & full participation for individuals with severe disabilities: A vision for the future* (pp. 319–348). Paul H. Brookes.

Bigby, C., Wilson, N. J., Balandin, S., & Stancliffe, R. J. (2011). Disconnected expectations: Staff, family and supported employee perspectives about retirement. *Journal of Intellectual & Developmental Disability, 36*(3), 167–174. https://doi.org/10.3109/13668250.2011.598852

Bigby, C., Wilson, N. J., Stancliffe, R. J., Balandin, S., Craig, D., & Gambin, N. (2014). An effective program design to support older workers with intellectual disability to participate individually in community groups. *Journal of Policy and Practice in Intellectual Disabilities, 11*(2), 117–127. https://doi.org/10.1111/jppi.12080

Bittles, A., Petterson, B., Sullivan, S., Hussain, R., Glasson, E., & Montgomery, P. (2002). The influence of intellectual disability on life expectancy. *Journal of Gerontology: Medical Sciences, 57A*(7), M470–M472. https://doi.org/10.1093/gerona/57.7.m470

Braddock, D. (1999). Aging and developmental disabilities: Demographic and policy issues affecting American families. *Mental Retardation, 37*(2), 155–161. https://doi.org/10.1352/0047-6765(1999)037<0155:AADDDA>2.0.CO;2

Brennan, D., McCausland, D., McCallion, P., & McCarron, M. (2020). Approaches to and outcomes of future planning for family carers of adults with an intellectual disability: A systematic review. *Journal of Applied Research in Intellectual Disabilities.* Advanced online publication. https://doi.org/10.1111/jar.12742

Burke, E., McCallion, P., & McCarron, M. (2014). What it's like to grow older: The ageing perceptions of people with intellectual disability in Ireland. *Intellectual & Developmental Disabilities, 52*(3), 205–219. https://doi.org/10.1352/1934-9556-52.3.205

Burt, D. B., & Aylward, E. H. (2000). Test battery for the diagnosis of dementia in individuals with intellectual disability. *Journal of Intellectual Disability Research, 44*(2), 175–180. https://doi.org/10.1046/j.1365-2788.2000.00264.x

Buys, L., & Rushworth, J. (1997). Community services available to older adults with intellectual disabilities. *Journal of Intellectual and Developmental Disabilities, 22*(1), 29–38. https://doi.org/10.1080/13668259700033271

Cooper, S.-A. (1997). Epidemiology of psychiatric disorders in elderly compared to younger people with learning disabilities. *British Journal of Psychiatry, 170,* 375–380. https://doi.org/10.1192/bjp.170.4.375

Fahey-McCarthy, E., McCarron, M., Connaire, K., & McCallion, P. (2010). Developing an education intervention for staff supporting persons with intellectual disability and advanced dementia. *Journal of Policy and Practice in Intellectual Disabilities, 6*(4), 267–275. https://doi.org/10.1111/j.1741-1130.2009.00231.x

Hahn, J. E., Gray, J., McCallion, P., Ronneberg, C., Stancliffe, R., Heller, T., ... Janicki, M. P. (2016). Transitions in aging: Health, retirement, and later life: Review of research, practice and policy. In AAIDD (Ed.), *Critical issues in intellectual and developmental disabilities* (pp. 49–74). American Association on Intellectual and Developmental Disabilities.

Hawkins, B. A., & Eklund, S. J. (1989). Aging and developmental disabilities: Interagency planning for an emerging population. *Journal of Applied Gerontology, 8*(2), 168–174.

Heller, T., & Factor, A. (1991). Permanency planning for adults with mental retardation living with family caregivers. *American Journal on Mental Retardation, 96,* 163–176. https://doi.org/10.1177/073346488900800203

Heller, T., Miller, A., Hsieh, K., & Sterns, H. (2000). Later-life planning: Promoting knowledge of options and choice-making. *Mental retardation, 38*(5), 395–406. http://doi.org/10.1352/0047-6765(2000)038<0395:LPPKOO>2.0.CO;2

Jackson, R., Howe, N., & Nakashima, K. (2010). *Global aging preparedness index.* Center for Strategic and International Studies. https://csis-prod.s3.amazonaws.com/s3fs-public/legacy_files/files/publication/101014_GlobalAgingIndex_DL_Jackson_LR.pdf

Janicki, M. P. (1993). *Building the future: Planning and community development in aging and developmental disabilities.* New York State Office of Mental Retardation and Developmental Disabilities.

Janicki, M. P. (1996). *Help for older people caring for an adult with a developmental disability.* New York State Developmental Disabilities Planning Council.

Janicki, M. P., & Dalton, A. J. (2000). Prevalence of dementia and impact on intellectual disability services. *Mental Retardation, 38*(3), 277–289.

Janicki, M. P., McCallion, P., & Dalton, A. J. (2002). Dementia-related care decision-making in group homes for persons with intellectual disabilities. *Journal of Gerontological Social Work, 38*(1/2), 179–196. https://doi.org/10.1352/00476765(2000)038<0276:PODAIO>2.0.CO;2

Janicki, M., McCallion, P., Force, L., Bishop, K., & LePore, P. (1998). Area agency on aging outreach and assistance models for households with older carers of an adult with a disability. *Journal of Aging and Social Policy, 10*(1), 13–36. https://doi.org/10.1300/j031v10n01_02

Janicki, M. P., & Wisniewski, H. M. (Eds.). (1985). *Aging and developmental disabilities: Issues and approaches*. Paul H. Brooks Publishing

Jennings, D., Seibyl, J., Sabbagh, M., Lai, F., Hopkins, W., Bullich, S. … Marek, K. (2015). Age dependence of brain β-amyloid deposition in down syndrome: An [^{18}F]florbetaben PET study. *Neurology 84*(5), 500–507. https://doi.org/10.1212/WNL.0000000000001212

Jokinen, N., Janicki, M. P., Keller, S., McCallion, P., & Force, L. T. (2013). Guidelines for structuring community care and supports for people with intellectual disabilities affected by dementia. *Journal of Policy & Practice in Intellectual disabilities, 10*(1), 1–24. https://doi.org/10.1111/jppi.12016

Krauss, M. W., & Seltzer, M. M. (1987). *Aging and mental retardation: Extending the continuum*. The American Association on Mental Retardation.

LePore, P., & Janicki, M. P. (1991). *The wit to wit – How to integrate older adults with a developmental disability into community aging programs* (2nd ed.). New York State Office for the Aging.

LePore, P., & Janicki, M. P. (1997). *The wit to wit – How to integrate older adults with a developmental disability into community aging programs* (3rd ed.). New York State Office for the Aging.

Lightfoot, E., & McCallion, P. (2016). Older adults and developmental disabilities. In B. Berkman & D. Kaplan (Eds.), *Handbook of social work in health & aging* (2nd ed., pp. 489–499). Oxford University Press

Lysaght, R., Cobigo, V., & Hamilton, K. (2012). Inclusion as a focus of employment-related research in intellectual disability from 2000 to 2010: A scoping review. *Disability and Rehabilitation, 34*(16), 1339–1350.

Mahon, M. J., & Goatcher, S. (1999). Later-life planning for older adults with mental retardation: A field experiment. *Mental Retardation, 37*(5), 371–382. https://doi.org/10.3109/09638288.2011.644023

Mahoney, K. J., Meiners, M. R., Shoop, D. M., & Squillace, M. R. (2003). Cash and Counseling and managed long-term care? *Care Management Journals, 4*(1), 18–22.

McCallion, P., & Grant-Griffin, L. (2000). Redesigning services to meet the needs of multi-cultural families. In M.P. Janicki, & E. Ansello (Eds.), *Aging and developmental disabilities* (pp. 97–108). Paul Brookes Publishing Company.

McCallion, P., & Janicki, M. P. (1997). Area agencies on aging: Meeting the needs of persons with developmental disabilities and their aging families. *Journal of Applied Gerontology, 16*(3), 270–284. https://doi.org/10.1177/073346489701600304

McCallion, P., Janicki, M. P., & Grant-Griffin, L. (1997). Exploring the impact of culture and acculturation on older families caregiving for persons with developmental disabilities. *Family Relations, 46*, 347–357. https://doi.org/10.2307/585095

McCallion, P., Jokinen, N., & Janicki, M. P. (2017). Aging. In M.L. Wehmeyer, I. Brown, M. Percey, K.A. Shogren, & M. Fung (Eds.), *A comprehensive guide to intellectual and developmental disabilities* (pp. 639–654). Paul Brookes Press.

McCallion, P., & Kolomer, S. R. (2003). Understanding and addressing psychosocial concerns among aging family caregivers of persons with intellectual disabilities. In P. W. Davidson, V. P. Prasher, & M. P. Janicki (Eds.), *Mental health, intellectual disabilities and the ageing process* (pp. 179–195). Blackwell Publishing Ltd.

McCallion, P., & McCarron, M. (2004). Ageing and intellectual disabilities: A review of recent literature. *Current Opinion in Psychiatry, 17*(5), 349–352.

McCallion, P., & McCarron, M. (2015). People with disabilities entering the Third age. In E.G. Iriarte, R. McConkey, & R. Gilligan (Eds.), *Disability and human rights: Global perspectives* (pp. 217–230). Palgrave McMillan.

McCallion, P., McCarron, M., Fahey-McCarthy, E., & Connaire, K. (2012). Meeting the end of life needs of older adults with intellectual disabilities. In E. Chang & A. Johnson (Eds.), *Contemporary and innovative practice in palliative care* (pp. 255–267). Intech.

McCallion, P., Swinburne, J., Burke, E., McGlinchey, E., & McCarron, M. (2013). Understanding the similarities and differences in aging with an intellectual disability: Linking Irish general population and intellectual disability datasets. In R. Urbano (Ed.), *Using secondary datasets to understand persons with developmental disabilities and their families (IRRDD-45)*. Academic Press.

McCallion, P., & Toseland, R. W. (1993). Empowering families of adolescents and adults with developmental disabilities. *Families in Society, 74*(10), 579–589. https://doi.org/10.1177/104438949307401001

McCarron, M., Carroll, R., & McCallion, P. (2017). A prospective 20 year longitudinal follow-up of dementia in persons with down syndrome. *Journal of Intellectual Disability Research, 61*(9), 843–852. https://doi.org/10.1111/jir.12390

McCarron, M., McCallion, P., Fahey-McCarthy, E., Connaire, K., & Lane, J. (2010). Supporting persons with down syndrome and advanced dementia: Challenges & care concerns, *Dementia, 9*(2), 285–298. https://doi.org/10.1177/1471301209354025

McCarron, M., McCallion, P., Reilly, E., & Mulryan, N. (2014). A prospective 14 year longitudinal follow-up of dementia in persons with down syndrome. *Journal of Intellectual Disability Research, 58*(1), 61–70. https:/doi.org/10.1111/jir.12074

McGlinchey, E., McCallion, P., Burke, E., Carrol, R., & McCarron, M. (2013). Examining the area of employment in older adults with an intellectual disability in Ireland. *Journal of Applied Research in Intellectual Disabilities, 26*(4), 335–343. https:/doi.org/10.1111/jar.12046

Moran, J., Keller, S. M., Janicki, M. P., Singh, B., Rafii, M., & Kripke, C., & National Task Group Section on Health Care Practices, Evaluation, Diagnosis, and Management. (2013). Position paper on evaluation and assessment for medical care of adults with intellectual disabilities with dementia. *Mayo Clinic Proceedings, 88*(8), 831–840. http://dx.doi.org/10.1016/j.mayocp.2013.04.024

Nickle, T., & McCallion, P. (2005). Redesigning day programmes. *The Frontline of Learning Disability, 64,* 27–28.

Olney, S., & Dickinson, H. (2019). Australia's new National Disability Insurance Scheme: Implications for policy and practice. *Policy Design & Practice 2*(3), 275–290. https://doi.org/10.1080/25741292.2019.1586083

Prasher, V. P. (1995). End-stage dementia in adults with down syndrome. *International Journal of Geriatric Psychiatry 10*(12), 1067–1069. https://doi.org/10.1002/gps.930101213

Roberto, K. A. (Ed.). (1993). *The elderly caregiver: Caring for adults with developmental disabilities.* Sage Publications, Inc.

Scheerenberger, R.C. (1983). *A history of mental retardation.* Baltimore: Brookes.

Smith, G. C., Fullmer, E. M., & Tobin, S. S. (1994). Living outside the system: An exploration of older families who do not use day programs. In M. M. Seltzer, M. W. Krauss, & M. P. Janicki (Eds.), *Life course perspectives on adulthood and old age* (pp. 19–37). American Association on Mental Retardation.

Stancliffe, R. J., Wilson, N. J., Gambin, N., Bigby, C., & Balandin, S. (2013). *Transition to retirement: A guide to inclusive practice.* Sydney University Press

Sutton, E., Factor, A., Hawkins, B., Heller, T., & Seltzer, G. (Eds.). (1993). *Older adults with developmental disabilities: Optimizing choice and change.* Brookes Publishing.

Todd, S. (2004). Death counts; The challenge of death and dying in learning disability services, *Learning Disability Practice, 7*(10), 12–15. https://doi.org/10.7748/ldp2004.12.7.10.12.c1551

Traphagan, J. W., & Nagasawa, T. (2008). Group homes for elders with dementia in Japan. *Care Management Journal, 9*(2), 89–96. https://doi.org/10.1891/1521-0987.9.2.89

Tuffrey-Wijne, I. (1997). Bereavement in people with learning disabilities. *European Journal of Palliative Care, 4*(5), 170–173.

Tuffrey-Wijne, I. (2002). The palliative care needs of people with intellectual disabilities: A case study. *International Journal of Palliative Nursing, 8*(5), 222–232. https://doi.org/10.12968/ijpn.2002.8.5.10369

Unger, D. D., Campbell, L., & McMahon, B. T. (2004). Workplace discrimination and mental retardation: The national EEOC ADA research project. *Journal of Vocational Rehabilitation, 23*(3), 145–154.

Wu, I. (1987). *Barriers and strategies: Barriers to and strategies for the integration of older persons with developmental disabilities within aging network services.* New York State Office for the Aging.

Suggested Readings

Bigby, C., McCallion, P., & McCarron, M. (2014). Serving an elderly population. In M. Agran, F. Brown, C. Hughes, C. Quirk, & D. Ryndak (Eds.), *Equality & full participation for individuals with severe disabilities: A vision for the future* (pp. 319–348). Paul H. Brookes.

Hahn, J. E., Gray, J., McCallion, P., Ronneberg, C., Stancliffe, R., Heller, T., … Janicki, M. P. (2016). Transitions in aging: Health, retirement, and later life: Review of research, practice and policy. In AAIDD (Ed.), *Critical issues in intellectual and developmental disabilities* (pp. 49–74). American Association on Intellectual and Developmental Disabilities.

Janicki, M. P., Henderson, C. M., Davidson, P. W., McCallion, P., Taets, J. D., Force, L. T., … Ladrigan, P. M. (2002). Health characteristics and health services utilization in older adults with intellectual disabilities living in community residences. *Journal of Intellectual Disability Research, 46*(4), 287–298. https://doi.org/10.1046/j.1365-2788.2002.00385.x

Janicki, M. P., & Wisniewski, H. M. (Eds.). (1985). *Aging and developmental disabilities: Issues and approaches.* Paul H. Brooks Publishing.

Krauss, M. W., & Seltzer, M. M. (1987). *Aging and mental retardation: Extending the continuum.* The American Association on Mental Retardation.

20
HEALTH AND WELLNESS AMONG PERSONS AGEING WITH INTELLECTUAL DISABILITY

Darren McCausland, Philip McCallion, and Mary McCarron

Introduction

This chapter discusses the health and well-being of people ageing with an intellectual disability using a social determinants of health lens, taking into account various personal and environmental factors that influence health. Use of this approach may help to stimulate debate both of the social determinants framework itself, and of ways to contextualise and assess health and well-being for this population. We argue that the social determinants model facilitates a broader understanding of contributors to health for adults ageing with an intellectual disability, highlighting structural and intermediary factors shaping health outcomes and inequalities.

Ageing and Health

McMunn, Breeze, Goodman, Nazroo, and Oldfield (2006) noted that a shift in the perception of ageing – from being a time of illness, poverty, and decline, to one free from previous constraints of childcare and employment – was supported by concepts of successful ageing in the USA (Rowe & Kahn, 1997) and the third age in the UK (Laslett, 1991). These perspectives were consistent with positive concepts of ageing, including Activity Theory (Havighurst, 1963), Continuity Theory (Atchley, 1989), and Selective Optimization with Compensation (Baltes & Baltes, 1990), which view ageing in terms of striving to maintain well-being through activity, continuity and prioritisation. Research has also shown that older people with positive attitudes towards ageing have better physical and cognitive health outcomes (Robertson, King-Kallimanis, & Kenny, 2016; Robertson, Savva, King-Kallimanis, & Kenny, 2015). However, the image of active, healthy ageing is far from a universal experience in practice, with variance associated with socio-economic factors (McMunn et al., 2006).

Health conditions common to the ageing experience include hearing and sight conditions, osteoarthritis, back and neck pain, chronic obstructive pulmonary disease, diabetes, depression, and dementia; with several of these conditions more likely to be experienced at the same time as people age (World Health Organization, 2018). The most prevalent conditions identified in a longitudinal study of older Irish adults included hypertension (38%), arthritis (39%), and pain (35%) (McNicholas & Laird, 2018). Older age may also present complex health states commonly called 'geriatric syndromes', including frailty, urinary incontinence, falls, delirium, and pressure ulcers (World Health Organization, 2018). Many health conditions increase with age, but may be modified by health behaviours (Kenny, Turner, & Donoghue, 2018). Frailty, for example is a dynamic process and people may move into but also out of frailty, as it is associated with personal circumstances and social conditions including marital status, co-habitation, educational attainment, and social engagement (Kenny et al., 2018).

The WHO World Report on Ageing and Health stated that, while there is strong evidence that people today are living longer, there is little consistent evidence to support the suggestion that older people today are experiencing these added years in good health (World Health Organization, 2015). Inequalities in health outcomes for older people may be explained by genetic inheritance or by individual choices; much is also shaped by the physical and social environment beyond the control of individuals. Outcomes are also shaped by personal characteristics including sex, ethnicity, and family circumstances (World Health Organization, 2015). Financial security, or lack thereof, is another major obstacle to healthy ageing and equity (Commission on Social Determinants of Health, 2008). Older people in Europe are at greater risk of financial insecurity but variation in policy means that those in some countries are better protected than others (OECD, 2008). Generally, individual financial security changes little across the life course in higher income countries (Middleton et al., 2007; OECD, 2008), meaning those born poor remain poor (World Health Organization, 2015). In lower income countries, such as sub-Saharan Africa, households comprised of older people are less financially secure than younger or mixed households (Zimmer & Das, 2014). Particular groups are also more at risk of financial insecurity, including women and older people living alone, who are often widowed older women (OECD, 2008; Rodrigues, Huber, & Lamura, 2012).

The risk of poverty to health in ageing is particularly felt with regard to meeting adequate housing requirements including heating during cold weather (United Nations, 2014). McLoughlin and Scarlett (2018) found that over half (57.6%) of older Irish people had inadequate housing. Living in deprived neighbourhoods which are less safe and have less access to resources including healthcare and healthy food present further health risks (Gibson et al., 2011; Swedish National Institute of Public Health, 2007). Low neighbourhood social cohesion is associated with poorer self-rated health and lower quality of life scores (McLoughlin & Scarlett, 2018). Such housing and neighbourhood factors may combine to pose an additional risk to mental health (Beard et al., 2009; McLoughlin & Scarlett, 2018).

Poverty and poor health outcomes including disability tend to mutually reinforce and disadvantages accumulate (Dannefer, 2003). Furthermore, there are suggestions that socio-economic inequalities decline in the oldest age groups and may reflect selective mortality and occupational differences and histories (McMunn et al., 2006).

Tackling the impact of socio-economic inequalities on health requires an understanding of their mechanisms and causal pathways (Shokouh et al., 2017). Further, different types of social or environmental factors operate at different levels and in different ways, some of which may be beyond an individual's capacity to influence, and others which may be more modifiable. An appreciation of the social determinants of health model, largely absent in most studies of ageing with intellectual disability to date may help in examining the health status of this group, and ultimately shape policy responses.

Social Determinants of Health

The social determinants model 'offers a window into the microlevel processes by which social structures lead to individual health or illness, and offers the opportunity to consider the macrolevel processes by which power, relationships and political ideology shape the quality of these social structures' (Raphael, 2006, p. 668). However, the very fact that social processes may impact on biological systems in the human body, and that this differs depending on social class, education, and a whole range of factors throughout the life course, must also be explained (Kelly, Bonnefoy, Morgan, & Florenzano, 2006). For example the psychobiological stress response explains how different health outcomes may arise when stressors (e.g. daily hassles, life events) and resistance and vulnerability factors (e.g. social support, coping response) differ between individuals (Brunner & Marmot, 2006). Regardless of mediating and biological causal factors such as genetic structure, nutritional status or resilience, ultimately 'there is a plausible causal pathway from a number of social factors or social determinants to biological structures in the individual human body' (Kelly, Bonnefoy, Morgan, & Florenzano, 2006, p. 12).

A Social Determinants of Health Framework

In the USA, the social determinants of health have been described as 'conditions in the environments in which people are born, live, learn, work, play, worship, and age that affect a wide range of health, functioning, and quality-of-life outcomes and risks' (Office of Disease Prevention and Health Promotion, 2014). This 'place based' framework developed by the Federal Healthy People 2020 includes five key areas circling around a social determinants core: economic stability; education; social and community context; health and health care; and neighbourhood and built environment.[1]

Other frameworks have attempted to explain different levels of social determinants and the dynamic within an overall construct. For example the Dahlgren and Whitehead (1991) framework[2] portrays main determinants operating at different levels, emanating out from:

1. The 'fixed' individual characteristics including age, sex, and genetics at the centre
2. Individual lifestyle factors and behaviours surrounding that
3. Social and community supports as a layer between the two prior elements
4. Living and working conditions, which include work, education, agriculture, and food production as well as unemployment, water and sanitation, health care services, and housing
5. At the macrolevel, the overarching societal-level factors including socio-economic, cultural, and environmental conditions

The World Health Organisation (WHO) framework by Solar and Irwin (2010) distinguished further between 'structural' and 'intermediary' social determinants.[3] It illustrates the relationships between different types of determinants, including the health system itself as a determinant, and the overall dynamic that shapes health outcomes for individuals. In the WHO framework, social, economic, and political mechanisms give rise socio-economic positions in which people are grouped according to certain factors including education, occupation, and income with people's socio-economic positions shaping specific determinants of health status or 'intermediary determinants'. Driven by their respective social status, individuals experience different exposure and vulnerability to health conditions.

Poor health outcomes can then 'feed back' on socio-economic position, for example impacting on employment and income, with inequalities and health outcomes reinforcing each other, as noted above (Dannefer, 2003). The WHO framework defines 'context' as 'all social and political mechanisms that generate, configure and maintain social hierarchies' (Solar & Irwin, 2010, p. 5), and includes the educational system, labour market, political institutions as well cultural and societal values. Structural mechanisms 'generate stratification and social class divisions in the society and define individual socio-economic position within hierarchies of power, prestige and access to resources' (Solar & Irwin, 2010, p. 5). These mechanisms are rooted in the social, economic, and political processes and institutions. Taken together, the context, structural mechanisms and socio-economic outcome for individuals constitute structural determinants, referred to as the 'social determinants of health inequities'. These function through a set of intermediary determinants to shape particular health outcomes for individuals, including material circumstances, behaviours, and biological factors; and psychosocial factors which includes living circumstances, relationships, and social support (Solar & Irwin, 2010).

In all of these frameworks, social determinants influence health across the lifespan at both the individual and the societal level. Despite many of the same social factors impacting greatly on the health of people with disabilities, as a group they are far less visible than other groups within the social determinants discourse (Wolbring, 2011). This chapter attempts to address this by situating our analysis of health and wellbeing for older people with intellectual disabilities within a social determinants framework. Given restrictions of space, we will focus primarily on intermediary determinants within a social and community context.

Social Determinants of Health for Older Adults with an Intellectual Disability

People with disabilities experience poorer health than people without disabilities often due to secondary risks associated with some health conditions or impairments they experience (Emerson et al., 2015). However, people with disabilities as a group with generally low incomes and who experience discrimination also experience higher rates of common health conditions; poorer health outcomes; and restricted access to timely effective health care (Emerson et al., 2011; Emerson et al., 2015). In a life course perspective, there are also cumulative effects of health inequalities that compound over time (Raphael, 2006). For people with intellectual disabilities such health inequalities begin early in their lives, and their cumulative effect and adverse health outcomes inevitably impact most heavily as they get older (Emerson, Baines, Allerton, & Welch, 2012).

Ireland: A Case Study

To illustrate the value of social determinants of health as a framework to better understand the contributors to the health inequalities experienced by people ageing with an intellectual disability, we will focus on Ireland as a case study, using data from the Intellectual Disability Supplement to the Irish Longitudinal Study on Ageing (IDS-TILDA). Poorer health outcomes have been identified for older people with intellectual disabilities. For example 71% people with intellectual disabilities aged 40 years and above were found to be multimorbid (i.e. having two or more chronic conditions), and this increased to 86% for those aged 65 plus. This compares with a rate of 73% for the general Irish population of older adults (Hernández, Reilly, & Kenny, 2019) and reports from a systematic review of prevalence studies of older adult community samples which found a median prevalence of 63% and a mode of 67% (Salive, 2013). Such data have limitations, as studies did not use the same list of chronic conditions. Nevertheless, rates are higher for people with intellectual disabilities and often at earlier ages (McCallion, Burke, et al., 2013; McCallion, Swinburne, et al., 2013; McCarron et al., 2013). For people with intellectual disabilities there is the additional challenge that as a group their relationships (unlikely to have spouses and or children), financial resources (unlikely to have jobs and savings), educational levels (most have not completed elementary education), health behaviours (physical activity and healthy eating), and access to healthcare are more likely to be impoverished (McCarron, Haigh, & McCallion, 2017). Using this model, these outcomes can be traced to structural and intermediary social determinants (within the WHO model).

At a structural level, the socio-economic positions of this population demonstrate a societal disadvantage compared to the general population. For example one-third (33%) of older people with intellectual disabilities had no formal education at all, almost three-quarters (74%) had not completed primary level schooling, and less than 2% had achieve a second-level qualification (McCarron et al., 2011; McCausland, 2016). In terms of employment, just 6.6% of older adults with intellectual disabilities were in employment and 70% had never done paid work in their lives (McCausland, Carroll, McCallion, & McCarron, 2020; McCausland, McCallion, Brennan, & McCarron, 2020). And with regard to housing, just 16% were living independently or with family (McCarron, Haigh, & McCallion, 2017), while 75% had no choice in where they lived and 86% had no choice in who they lived with (McCarron et al., 2011). For people with intellectual disabilities, socio-economic positions such as these stem from social, economic, and political processes and the prevailing cultural and societal values of Irish society over many years. This has, for example resulted in an older generation living with the historical legacy of institutional living (Health Service Executive, 2011).

With regard to the intermediary determinants of the WHO model, findings from IDS-TILDA illustrate the context in which particular health outcomes are shaped for individuals ageing with an intellectual disability including living circumstances, relationships, and social support that comprise 'psychosocial factors' within the framework. Statistical analysis (hierarchical ordinary least squares regression) examining the contribution of environmental, enabling, predisposing, need and all combinations of the sets of variables conducted using the IDS-TILDA data confirmed the importance of family contact, transportation and health care access to personal health choices for older people with intellectual disabilities (McCallion, Burke, et al., 2013; McCallion, Swinburne, et al., 2013).

Living Circumstances

As noted above, the majority of older people with an intellectual disability in Ireland had no choice about where they lived or who they lived with, and a majority lived in either congregated settings (44%) or shared group homes with other people with intellectual disabilities located in the general community (40%) (McCarron, Haigh, & McCallion, 2017). IDS-TILDA has found that living circumstance is directly linked to health outcomes, and is also associated with many social determinants. For example people living in a congregated setting were significantly more likely to report multiple falls than those living in family or independent settings (Foran, McCallion, & McCarron, 2016). Institutional living was also strongly associated with polypharmacy (taking 5–9 medicines) and excessive polypharmacy (10 or more medicines) after adjusting for other factors (O'Dwyer, Peklar, McCallion, McCarron, & Henman, 2016). With regard to mental health, degree of urbanicity was associated with treatment by a psychiatrist (Ramsay, Mulryan, McCallion, & McCarron, 2016). People living in family or independent settings were more likely to report positive mental health than those in congregated settings or community group homes, while the rate of depressive symptoms for those in congregated and group home settings was almost double that of people in independent and family homes (Sheerin, Carroll, Mulryan, McCallion, & McCarron, 2017).

Living circumstance was a factor in a broad range of social indicators. For example older adults with intellectual disabilities living in community group homes were more likely to be engaged in occupational activity than those living in congregated settings (McCausland, McCallion, et al., 2020). People living in any disability service accommodation were more likely to depend on staff-driven transport, and people living in congregated settings were less likely to use public transport than those living in community settings (McCausland, Stancliffe, McCallion, & McCarron, 2019). Residence was the strongest predictor of choice-making for key life decisions for older people with intellectual disabilities, with those in independent and family settings more likely to exercise choice than those in congregated residences (McCausland, McCallion, Brennan, & McCarron, 2018a). People living in community based residences were more likely to vote than those in congregated settings (McCausland et al., 2018a). And having non-resident friends was most strongly predicted by residence type, with those in independent/family homes more likely to have such friends (McCausland, McCallion, Brennan, & McCarron, 2018b).

Relationships and Social Support

Social support including our relationships with family, friends, and others constitutes another important social determinant of health. IDS-TILDA has identified that the social networks of older people with intellectual disabilities differ greatly to the general population. Practically none of this population married or had children, compared to 92% of the older general Irish population who were married or were previously married (Nolan et al., 2014) and nine in ten of those who had married had children (Kamiya & Sofroniou, 2011). This means that people ageing with an intellectual disability lose out on the quality of life benefit associated with being married and having children and grandchildren (McCrory, Leahy, & McGarrigle, 2014). In place of intimate family supports of their own, this population depend on siblings, nephews, and nieces for family contact, particularly as they age and lose parents; or on paid support staff, who often provide social and emotional support (McCausland et al., 2018b). With regards to friendship, the vast majority of people ageing with an intellectual disability (92%) reported having friends, and just over half had a best friend (McCausland, Carroll, et al., 2020; McCausland, McCallion, et al., 2020). People with intellectual disabilities also had fewer friends and depend heavily

Table 20.1 Logistic regression for self/proxy-reported physical health ($n = 447$)

Independent variables	Good-excellent physical health	
	Odds Ratio (95% CI)	p-value
Helped friends or neighbours		
No	1.0	
Yes	8.38 (1.77–39.74)	<0.01
Feel part of local community		
No	1.0	
Yes	2.07 (1.10–3.88)	<0.05

Nagelkerke $R^2 = 0.10$.

Variables used as the reference category have an OR = 1.0.

on co-residents and staff for friendship due to restricted social opportunities (McCausland, Carroll, et al., 2020; McCausland, McCallion, et al., 2020).

Community Engagement

As reported above, a significant proportion of this cohort remains resident in accommodation that is segregated from the general population. Just one in four participants (24%) were members of a community group, and membership of such groups was associated with community residence (McCausland, 2016). Family contact was the strongest predictor of engagement in community activities (McCausland, 2016) and family proximity the strongest predictor of family contact (McCausland et al., 2018b). As noted above, older adults with an intellectual disability had fewer close family members than the general older population. It was also identified that fewer lived in close proximity to family compared to the general population (Kamiya & Sofroniou, 2011; McCausland et al., 2018b). As such, low levels of community engagement place adults ageing with an intellectual disability are at greater risk of adverse outcomes.

Social Determinants Associated with Self/Proxy Rated Health

Two logistic regression models using Wave 3 IDS-TILDA data for (1) Self/proxy rated physical health and (2) Self/proxy rated mental health offer additional insights on intermediary social determinants.

Table 20.1 shows that, when controlling for other variables, respondents who had given help to friends or neighbours were more likely to report better physical health (OR = 8.38, $p < 0.01$); as was the case with respondents who said that they felt part of their local community (OR = 2.07, $p < 0.05$). All other independent variables were not significant in a model predicting 10% of variance in self/proxy-rated physical health (Nagelkerke R^2).

With regard to mental health, Table 20.2 shows that residence was the strongest predictor of mental health, wherein people living in independent or family residences were more likely to report better mental health than those living in congregated settings (OR = 5.15, $n < 0.05$). Community belonging again predicted a better mental health outcomes, (OR = 1.87, $p < 0.05$).

These analyses demonstrate again how social determinants within a social and community context may influence health outcomes.

Key Issues

Key findings emerging from our analysis in this chapter include:

- The social determinants of health provide a framework for a broader examination of health for older people with an intellectual disability, by considering social inclusion and community participation.

Table 20.2 Logistic regression for self/proxy-reported mental health ($n = 444$)

Independent variables	Good-excellent mental health	
	Odds Ratio (95% CI)	p-value
Residence type		
Congregated	1.0	
Independent/family	5.15 (1.46–18.12)	<0.05
Feel part of local community		
No	1.0	
Yes	1.87 (1.07–3.27)	<0.05

Nagelkerke $R^2 = 0.10$.
Variables used as the reference category have an OR = 1.0.

- The comparative disadvantage of older people with an intellectual disability is apparent at a structural level, where the historical legacy of government policies and prevailing social and cultural values excluded this population in areas such as education, employment, and housing.
- Through the lens of intermediary social determinants that shape health outcomes, older people with an intellectual disability are further disadvantaged with regard to living circumstances, social support and community engagement.

Discussion

New concepts of ageing that emerged in the later 20th century signalled a shift in thinking about growing older, from being a time of illness, poverty, and decline, to a time of activity unburdened by constraints of childcare and employment. However, in practice, increased prevalence of a range of chronic conditions and multi-morbidity remains for a majority of people. Findings of a range of inequalities in health outcomes for different cohorts in society resulting from their socio-economic positions are compounded for people ageing with an intellectual disability, who also face increasing age-related conditions and other risks, including secondary risks associated with some conditions or impairments, and disability discrimination. Given the evident importance of socio-economic and other personal and environmental factors, health outcomes are not explained using a solely biomedical approach. A broader contextual consideration is required to assess and address health and health outcomes for people with intellectual disability as they age. The social determinants of health model provides an opportunity for such an assessment.

In distinguishing between *structural* and *intermediary* social determinants, and identifying the dynamic relationship between different types and levels of determinants, the WHO framework facilitates a more complex consideration of health outcomes and of the personal and environmental factors that shape such outcomes. This lens confirmed that the socio-economic, political and cultural context in Ireland, for example has resulted in disadvantaged socio-economic positions and access for this population, evident in the education, employment, and housing findings presented; supporting a view of greater exposure to the social gradient of health outcomes (Emerson et al., 2015).

Our analysis of determinants at the intermediary level also demonstrated increased risk of poorer health outcomes related to social support and community participation with living circumstances, most notably differences between congregated versus community-based living, and levels of occupational engagement, transportation usage, choice-making, voting, and having friends outside one's own home making a difference. We also demonstrated how adults ageing with an intellectual disability are relatively disadvantaged compared to peers in the general population with regard to family, friends, and wider social networks. As such, they often miss out on the quality of life benefits associated with, for example marriage and supporting/supportive children and grandchildren (McCrory, Leahy, & McGarrigle, 2014). Similarly, relative exclusion from community engagement activities may further impact on health outcomes. In a social determinants model, these findings support suggestions in the literature that people ageing with an intellectual disability may be at increased risk of poor health outcomes and inequalities which further compound over their life course (Emerson et al., 2012; Raphael, 2006).

Our additional analysis of self/proxy-rated health and mental health further supported the case for a broader-based analysis of health outcomes for adults ageing with an intellectual disability. A range of social factors including independent or family residence, community belonging, and giving help to friends and neighbours, were associated with differences in physical and mental health outcomes and may potentially be more influential to health outcomes than age or degree of intellectual disability. Additional research utilising a social determinants perspective is needed to further explore and support these initial findings.

The findings also suggest an opportunity to improve poor health outcomes of older adults with an intellectual disability by addressing modifiable social determinants of their health. The challenge is these modifiable factors have deep roots within the economic, political, social, and cultural fabric of society. As such, a 'root and branch' approach starting at policy level is probably required. Political commitment worldwide to implementing the United Nations *Convention on the Rights of Persons with Disabilities* would likely go a long way towards achieving this aim (United Nations, 2006).

Nonetheless, change may be possible more immediately. For example Kenny et al. (2018) suggested for the general older population that, while chronic conditions associated with ageing impact negatively on quality of life, social integration, and supportive friendships may have a moderating effect for long-term health and well-being (Kenny et al., 2018). Positive attitudes amongst older people towards ageing may also support better health outcomes (Robertson et al., 2016; Robertson et al., 2015). IDS-TILDA findings among participants of negative perceptions of ageing (Burke, McCarron, Carroll, McGlinchey, & McCallion, 2014) may be a starting point for intervention.

Conclusion

This chapter has made the case for broader-based examination of health and health outcomes for adults ageing with an intellectual disability, and recommends the social determinants of health model. Additional research is needed to further examine and support these initial explorations, and offer comparative analyses across a range of different countries. Further exploration is also required on the influence of structural-level determinants, and of how policy and societal-level responses may affect change in the socio-economic positions of older adults with intellectual disabilities and create a more supportive context that supports improved intermediary social determinants of health and ultimately better health outcomes and quality of life.

Notes

1 See Healthy People 2020: https://www.healthypeople.gov/2020/topics-objectives/topic/social-determinants-of-health
2 See European strategies for tackling social inequities in health: Leveling up Part 2: https://www.euro.who.int/__data/assets/pdf_file/0018/103824/E89384.pdf
3 See Solar O, Irwin A. A conceptual framework for action on the social determinants of health. Social Determinants of Health Discussion Paper 2 (Policy and Practice). https://www.who.int/sdhconference/resources/ConceptualframeworkforactiononSDH_eng.pdf?ua=1

References

Atchley, R. C. (1989). A continuity theory of normal aging. *The Gerontologist, 29*(2), 183–190. https://doi.org/10.1093/geront/29.2.183

Baltes, P. B., & Baltes, M. M. (1990). Psychological perspectives on successful aging: The model of selective optimization with compensation. *Successful Aging: Perspectives from the Behavioral Sciences, 1*(1), 1–34. https://doi.org/10.1017/CBO9780511665684.003

Beard, J. R., Cerdá, M., Blaney, S., Ahern, J., Vlahov, D., & Galea, S. (2009). Neighborhood characteristics and change in depressive symptoms among older residents of New York City. *American Journal of Public Health, 99*(7), 1308–1314. https://doi.org/10.2105/AJPH.2007.125104

Brunner, E., & Marmot, M. (2006). Social organization, stress, and health. In M. Marmot & R. G. Wilkinson (Eds.), *Social determinants of health* (2nd ed., pp. 6–30). Oxford University Press.

Burke, E., McCarron, M., Carroll, R., McGlinchey, E., & McCallion, P. (2014). What it's like to grow older: The aging perceptions of people with an intellectual disability in Ireland. *Intellectual and Developmental Disabilities, 52*(3), 205–219. https://doi.org/10.1352/1934-9556-52.3.205

Commission on Social Determinants of Health. (2008). *Closing the gap in a generation: Health equity through action on the social determinants of health*. World Health Organization. https://apps.who.int/iris/bitstream/handle/10665/43943/9789241563703_eng.pdf;jsess

Dahlgren, G., & Whitehead, M. (1991). *Policies and strategies to promote social equity in health*. Institute for Future Studies. https://core.ac.uk/download/pdf/6472456.pdf

Dannefer, D. (2003). Cumulative advantage/disadvantage and the life course: Cross-fertilizing age and social science theory. *The Journals of Gerontology Series B: Psychological Sciences and Social Sciences, 58*(6), S327–S337. https://doi.org/10.1093/geronb/58.6.S327

Emerson, E., Baines, S., Allerton, L., & Welch, V. (2012). *Health inequalities & people with learning disabilities in the UK: 2012*. Learning Disabilities Observatory. http://complexneeds.org.uk/modules/Module-4.1-Working-with-other-professionals/All/downloads/m13p020c/emerson_baines_health_inequalities.pdf

Emerson, E., Madden, R., Graham, H., Llewellyn, G., Hatton, C., & Robertson, J. (2011). The health of disabled people and the social determinants of health. *Public Health, 125*(3), 145–147. https://doi.org/10.1016/j.puhe.2010.11.003

Emerson, E., Vick, B., Rechel, B., Muñoz-Baell, I., Sørensen, J., & Färm, I. (2015). *Health Inequalities and People with Disabilities in Europe* (Vol. Background Paper 5): Social Exclusion, Disadvantage, Vulnerability and Health Inequalities task group supporting the Marmot region review of social determinants of health and the health divide in the EURO region. https://www.researchgate.net/publication/277078091_Health_Inequalities_and_People_with_Disabilities_in_Europe_Background_Paper_5_for_the_Social_Exclusion_Disadvantage_Vulnerability_and_Health_Inequalities_task_group_supporting_the_Marmot_region_review

Foran, S., McCallion, P., & McCarron, M. (2016). 296 The prevalence of falls among older adults with intellectual disability in Ireland. *Age and Ageing, 45*(suppl_2), ii13–ii56. https://doi.org/10.1093/ageing/afw159.253

Gibson, M., Petticrew, M., Bambra, C., Sowden, A. J., Wright, K. E., & Whitehead, M. (2011). Housing and health inequalities: A synthesis of systematic reviews of interventions aimed at different pathways linking housing and health. *Health & Place, 17*(1), 175–184. https://doi.org/10.1016/j.healthplace.2010.09.011

Havighurst, R. J. (1963). Successful aging. *Processes of Aging: Social and Psychological Perspectives, 1*, 299–320.

Health Service Executive. (2011). *Time to move on from congregated settings – A strategy for community inclusion: Report of the Working Group on Congregated Settings*. Dublin: Health Service Executive. http://www.fedvol.ie/_fileupload/Next%20Steps/Time%20To%20Move%20On%20From%20Congregated%20Settings.pdf

Hernández, B., Reilly, R. B., & Kenny, R. A. (2019). Investigation of multimorbidity and prevalent disease combinations in older Irish adults using network analysis and association rules. *Scientific Reports, 9*(1), 14567. https://doi.org/10.1038/s41598-019-51135-7

Kamiya, Y., & Sofroniou, N. (2011). Socio-demographic characteristics of older people in Ireland. In A. Barrett, G. Savva, V. Timonen, & R. A. Kenny (Eds.), *Fifty plus in Ireland 2011*. The Irish Longitudinal Study on Ageing. https://www.ucd.ie/issda/t4media/0053-01_TILDA_Master_First_Findings_Report_2011.pdf

Kelly, M. P., Bonnefoy, J., Morgan, A., & Florenzano, F. (2006). *The development of the evidence base about the social determinants of health*. World Health Organization. https://www.who.int/social_determinants/resources/mekn_paper.pdf?ua=1

Kenny, R. A., Turner, N., & Donoghue, O. (2018). Introduction. In N. Turner, O. Donoghue, & R.-A. Kenny (Eds.), *Wellbeing and health in Ireland's over 50s 2009–2016* (pp. 9–16). The Irish Longitudinal Study on Ageing.

Laslett, P. (1991). *A fresh map of life: The emergence of the third age*. Harvard University Press.

McCallion, P., Burke, E., Swinburne, J., McGlinchey, E., Carrol, R., & McCarron, M. (2013). Influence of environment, predisposing, enabling and need variables on personal health choices of adults with intellectual disability. *Health, 5*(4), 749–756. https://doi.org/10.4236/health.2013.54099

McCallion, P., Swinburne, J., Burke, E., McGlinchey, E., & McCarron, M. (2013). Understanding the similarities and differences in aging with an intellectual disability: Linking Irish general population and intellectual disability datasets. In R. Urbano (Ed.), *Using secondary datasets to understand persons with developmental disabilities and their families (IRRDD-45)*. Academic Press.

McCarron, M., Haigh, M., & McCallion, P. (2017). *Health, wellbeing and social inclusion: Ageing with an intellectual disability in Ireland, Evidence from the first ten years of the intellectual disability supplement to the Irish Longitudinal Study on Ageing (IDS-TILDA)*. https://www.tcd.ie/tcaid/assets/pdf/wave3report.pdf

McCarron, M., Swinburne, J., Burke, E., McGlinchey, E., Carroll, R., & McCallion, P. (2013). Patterns of multimorbidity in an older population of persons with an intellectual disability: Results from the intellectual disability supplement to the Irish Longitudinal Study on Aging (IDS-TILDA). *Research in Developmental Disabilities*, 34, 521–527. https://doi.org/10.1016/j.ridd.2012.07.029

McCarron, M., Swinburne, J., Burke, E., McGlinchey, E., Mulryan, N., Andrews, V. ... McCallion, P. (2011). *Growing older with an intellectual disability in Ireland 2011: First results from the Intellectual Disability Supplement of the Irish Longitudinal Study on Ageing*. School of Nursing & Midwifery, Trinity College Dublin. https://www.hrb.ie/uploads/media/Growing_Older_with_an_Intellectual_Disability_in_Ireland_2011.pdf

McCausland, D. (2016). *Social participation for older people with an intellectual disability in Ireland* (PhD). Trinity College Dublin, Unpublished Thesis.

McCausland, D., Carroll, R., McCallion, P., & McCarron, M. (2020). The nature and quality of friendship for older adults with an intellectual disability in Ireland. [Manuscript submitted for publication]. Trinity College Dublin.

McCausland, D., McCallion, P., Brennan, D., & McCarron, M. (2018a). The exercise of human rights and citizenship by older adults with an intellectual disability in Ireland. *Journal of Intellectual Disability Research*, 62(10), 875–887. https://doi.org/10.1111/jir.12543

McCausland, D., McCallion, P., Brennan, D., & McCarron, M. (2018b). Interpersonal relationships of older adults with an intellectual disability in Ireland. *Journal of Applied Research in Intellectual Disabilities*, 31(1), e140–e153. https://doi.org/10.1111/jar.12352

McCausland, D., McCallion, P., Brennan, D., & McCarron, M. (2020). In pursuit of meaningful occupation: Employment and occupational outcomes for older Irish adults with an intellectual disability. *Journal of Applied Research in Intellectual Disabilities*, 33(3), 386–397. https://doi.org/10.1111/jar.12681

McCausland, D., Stancliffe, R. J., McCallion, P., & McCarron, M. (2019). Longitudinal use and factors associated with public transport and other travel options for older people with an intellectual disability in Ireland. *Journal of Applied Research in Intellectual Disabilities*, 33, 442–456. https://doi.org/10.1111/jar.12686

McCrory, C., Leahy, S., & McGarrigle, C. (2014). What factors are associated with change in older people's quality of life? In A. Nolan, C. O'Regan, C. Dooley, D. Wallace, A. Hever, H. Cronin, E. Hudson, & R. A. Kenny (Eds.), *The over 50s in a changing Ireland: Economic circumstances, health and well-being*. The Irish Longitudinal Study on Ageing.

McLoughlin, S., & Scarlett, S. (2018). Living conditions of adults in Ireland. In N. Turner, O. Donoghue, & R. Kenny (Eds.), *Wellbeing and health in Ireland's over 50s 2009–2016* (pp. 65–88). The Irish Longitudinal Study on Ageing.

McMunn, A., Breeze, E., Goodman, A., Nazroo, J., & Oldfield, Z. (2006). Social determinants of health in older age. *Social Determinants of Health*, 2, 267–298.

McNicholas, T., & Laird, E. (2018). Change in chronic disease prevalence and health behaviours over the first four waves of TILDA. In N. Turner, O. Donoghue, & R. Kenny (Eds.), *Wellbeing and health in Ireland's over 50s 2009–2016* (pp. 89–116). The Irish Longitudinal Study on Ageing.

Middleton, S., Hancock, R., Kellard, K., Beckhelling, J., Phung, V., & Perren, K. (2007). *Measuring resources in later life: A review of the data*. Joseph Rowtree Foundation.

Nolan, A., O'Regan, C., Dooley, C., Wallace, D., Hever, A., Cronin, H., & Hudson, E. (2014). *The over 50s in a changing Ireland: Economic circumstances, health and well-being*. Economic & Social Research Institute. https://www.esri.ie/publications/the-over-50s-in-a-changing-ireland-economic-circumstances-health-and-well-being

O'Dwyer, M., Peklar, J., McCallion, P., McCarron, M., & Henman, M. C. (2016). Factors associated with polypharmacy and excessive polypharmacy in older people with intellectual disability differ from the general population: A cross-sectional observational nationwide study. *BMJ Open*, 6(4), e010505. https://doi.org/10.1136/bmjopen-2015-010505

OECD. (2008). *Growing unequal? Income distribution and poverty in OECD countries*. Organisation for Economic Cooperation Development (OECD). https://www.oecd.org/els/soc/growingunequalincomedistributionandpovertyinoecdcountries.htm

Office of Disease Prevention and Health Promotion. (2014). *Social determinants of health*. https://www.healthypeople.gov/2020/topics-objectives/topic/social-determinants-of-health#five

Ramsay, H., Mulryan, N., McCallion, P., & McCarron, M. (2016). Geographical barriers to mental health service care among individuals with an intellectual disability in the Republic of Ireland. *Journal of Policy and Practice in Intellectual Disabilities*, 13(4), 261–268. https://doi.org/10.1111/jppi.12182

Raphael, D. (2006). Social determinants of health: Present status, unanswered questions, and future directions. *International Journal of Health Services*, 36(4), 651–677. https://doi.org/10.2190/3MW4-1EK3-DGRQ-2CRF

Robertson, D. A., King-Kallimanis, B. L., & Kenny, R. A. (2016). Negative perceptions of aging predict longitudinal decline in cognitive function. *Psychology and Aging, 31*(1), 71. https://doi.org/10.1037/pag0000061

Robertson, D. A., Savva, G. M., King-Kallimanis, B. L., & Kenny, R. A. (2015). Negative perceptions of aging and decline in walking speed: A self-fulfilling prophecy. *PLoS ONE, 10*(4), e0123260. https://doi.org/10.1371/journal.pone.0123260

Rodrigues, R., Huber, M., & Lamura, G. (Eds.) (2012). *Facts and figures on healthy ageing and long-term care*. Europe and North America, Occasional Reports Series 8. European Centre. https://www.euro.centre.org/publications/detail/403

Rowe, J. W., & Kahn, R. L. (1997). Successful aging. *The Gerontologist, 37*(4), 433–440. https://doi.org/10.1093/geront/37.4.433

Salive, M. E. (2013). Multimorbidity in older adults. *Epidemiology Reviews, 35*, 75–83. https://doi.org/10.1093/epirev/mxs009

Sheerin, F., Carroll, R., Mulryan, N., McCallion, P., & McCarron, M. (2017). Mental health, well-being, vitality and life events. In M. McCarron, M. Haigh, P. McCallion (Eds.), *Health, wellbeing and social inclusion: Ageing with an intellectual disability in Ireland* (Vol. 3, pp. 87–100). The Intellectual Disability Supplement to the Irish Longitudinal Study on Ageing.

Shokouh, S. M. H., Mohammad, A., Emamgholipour, S., Rashidian, A., Montazeri, A., & Zaboli, R. (2017). Conceptual models of social determinants of health: A narrative review. *Iranian Journal of Public Health, 46*(4), 435.

Solar, O., & Irwin, A. (2010). *A conceptual framework for action on the social determinants of health* (Vol. Discussion Paper 2 (Policy and Practice). World Health Organization.

Swedish National Institute of Public Health. (2007). *Healthy ageing: A challenge for Europe: Swedish National Institute of Public Health*. The Swedish National Institute of Public Health. https://ec.europa.eu/health/ph_projects/2003/action1/docs/2003_1_26_frep_en.pdf

United Nations. (2006). *Convention on the Rights of Persons with Disabilities*. New York: United Nations. https://www.un.org/development/desa/disabilities/convention-on-the-rights-of-persons-with-disabilities.html

United Nations. (2014). *The right to adequate housing* (Vol. Fact Sheet No. 21 (Rev.1)). Geneva: United Nations, Office of the High Commissioner for Human Rights. https://www.ohchr.org/documents/publications/fs21_rev_1_housing_en.pdf

Wolbring, G. (2011). People with disabilities and social determinants of health discourses. *Canadian Journal of Public Health, 102*(4), 317–319. https://doi.org/10.1007/bf03404058

World Health Organization. (2015). *World report on ageing and health*. World Health Organization. https://www.who.int/ageing/events/world-report-2015-launch/en/

World Health Organization. (2018). *Ageing and health*. World Health Organization. https://www.who.int/news-room/fact-sheets/detail/ageing-and-health

Zimmer, Z., & Das, S. (2014). The poorest of the poor: Composition and wealth of older person households in Sub-Saharan Africa. *Research on Aging, 36*(3), 271–296.

Suggested Readings

Emerson, E., Madden, R., Graham, H., Llewellyn, G., Hatton, C., & Robertson, J. (2011). The health of disabled people and the social determinants of health. *Public Health, 125*(3), 145–147. https://doi.org/10.1016/j.puhe.2010.11.003

McCallion, P., Burke, E., Swinburne, J., McGlinchey, E., Carrol, R., & McCarron, M. (2013). Influence of environment, predisposing, enabling and need variables on personal health choices of adults with intellectual disability. *Health, 5*(4), 749–756. https://doi.org/10.4236/health.2013.54099

McCarron, M., Swinburne, J., Burke, E., McGlinchey, E., Carroll, R., & McCallion, P. (2013). Patterns of multimorbidity in an older population of persons with an intellectual disability: Results from the intellectual disability supplement to the Irish Longitudinal Study on Aging (IDS-TILDA). *Research in Developmental Disabilities, 34*, 521–527. https://doi.org/10.1016/j.ridd.2012.07.029

McCausland, D., McCallion, P., Brennan, D., & McCarron, M. (2020). In pursuit of meaningful occupation: Employment and occupational outcomes for older Irish adults with an intellectual disability. *Journal of Applied Research in Intellectual Disabilities, 33*(3), 386–397. https://doi.org/10.1111/jar.12681

21
RETIREMENT FOR PEOPLE WITH INTELLECTUAL DISABILITY
Policy, Pitfalls, and Promising Practices

Christine Bigby

Introduction

It is no longer news that people with intellectual disabilities are living longer or that they need to think about retirement and their later life lifestyle. Retirement has been on the policy agenda of disability service systems since the pioneering work of Janicki and colleagues in the late 1980s (Janicki & Wisniewski, 1985). Back then, questions were posed about the relevance of retirement for people with intellectual disabilities as so few were in full-time paid employment. Which raised a further question about what, exactly, older people with intellectual disabilities might be retiring from. The answer, for most, was from some form of segregated program that offered centre-based day activities, training, or low paid sheltered employment. Proponents of normalisation also asked about the desirability of replicating the social norm of retirement that was associated with a devalued status and which rendered many older people vulnerable to social isolation and poverty (Wolfensberger, 1985).

A life course perspective suggests contextual and individual factors influence choices and experiences of retirement (Hareven, 2001). The historic time during which a person lives, their individual biography, as well as prevailing ageing and disability policies, service systems, and socio-economic factors determine the meaning of retirement for people with intellectual disabilities – what they are retiring from – what they might retire to – whether retirement is relevant to their lifestyle.

This chapter reviews issues of retirement for people with intellectual disabilities by tracing the debates over the past 40 years from the 1980s to 2020s. It is chiefly concerned with exploring the experiences and perspectives of people with intellectual disabilities on retirement and the challenges retirement has posed for policy and service systems. Finally, this chapter considers current policy directions and promising practices that might support a socially inclusive later life lifestyle.

Mainstream Approaches to Retirement

Polices and expectations about ageing and retirement of the general population have evolved since the 1980s, when these first became issues for people with intellectual disabilities. Mainstream policies reflect increasing expectations that retired people will remain active and socially engaged; living and contributing to their communities. The 2002 World Health Organisation (WHO) framework for *Active Ageing* emphasised processes of 'optimising opportunities for health, participation and security in order to enhance quality of life as people age' (World Health Organization, 2002). The shift to individualism as part of neo-liberalism, put a greater emphasis on each individuals' responsibility to maintain their own health, physical function and cognitive capacity in order to have a good old age. This was illustrated by the 2015 revised and renamed WHO framework *Healthy Ageing*, which defined the concept of healthy ageing as a process of 'developing and maintaining the functional ability that enables wellbeing in older age' (World Health Organization, 2015).

Since the 1980s, the age of retirement has become more flexible in many developed economies. Older workers are encouraged to stay at work longer or work on a part time basis. At the same time, the focus on older adults' rights and anti-discrimination measures has helped to address negative stereotypical attitudes towards ageing. Moreover, as life expectancy in most countries with developed economies has increased, retirement has become a longer and proportionally more significant part of the life course (Barbosa, Monteiro, & Murta, 2016).

Over the past 40 years, the challenges associated with retirement for people with and without intellectual disabilities have remained fairly similar. However, for people with intellectual disability, these challenges have tended to occur in a more staggered fashion and over a longer period of time. They can be summarised as 'adjusting to the loss of the worker role, establishing meaningful new daily activities, avoiding the potential decrease in social relationships, being a contributing member of society, and minimising the health risks of aging' (Fesko, Hall, Quinlan, & Jockell, 2012, p. 497). However, as stated above, for people with intellectual disabilities, retirement more often involves adjusting to the loss of connection to regular structured activities at a day centre rather than the loss of a worker role. A growing body of mainstream research suggests the predictors of a successful adjustment to retirement are physical health, finances, psychological health and personality-related attributes, leisure activities in and outside the home, voluntary retirement, and social integration (Barbosa et al., 2016). As this chapter will show, many of these features do not map well onto the characteristics of adults with intellectual disabilities approaching retirement.

Retiring from a Distinctive and Disadvantaged Position

The early research about retirement and people with intellectual disabilities in the USA, the UK, and Australia focused on people in their 50s and 60s. These cohorts had been born in the 1930s and 1940s (Ashman, Suttie, & Bramley, 1995; Bigby, 1992; Hogg, Moss, & Cooke, 1988; Janicki & Wisniewski, 1985). Some researchers ventured to suggest that the characteristics of future generations facing retirement might look quite different, as they would have lived through a different historic period. For example, in the future, ageing adults might never have been institutionalised, would have been employed and have stronger expectations about living inclusive lives. Yet the available data suggest that characteristics of older people with intellectual disabilities have changed very little over time. The characteristics of today's 50- and 60-year-olds (born in the 1960s and 1970s) are quite similar to those of earlier generations. Which means that despite living through very different historic times, the present generation are contemplating retirement from a similarly distinctive and disadvantaged position as their peers in earlier generations.

Available data suggest that those who retired in the 1980s – and those who will retire in the 2020s – have not been socially or economically included in their younger years. They have not lived healthier lifestyles, nor have they had access to quality health care. Across many countries with developed economies, adults with intellectual disabilities, compared to the general population, continue to have lower levels of physical activity, smaller social networks, less engagement in social relationships, and a smaller proportion of these adults have married or have children (Brotherton, Stancliffe, Wilson, & O'Loughlin, 2020; Hatton, Glover, Emerson, & Brown, 2016; McCausland, McCallion, Cleary, & McCarron, 2016). Their employment rates remain low (approximately 6% in the UK in 2015) and appear to be dropping. In countries such as Ireland, the USA and Australia, adults with intellectual disabilities continue to rely heavily on day centres for engagement in regular activities and social connections (Stancliffe, Kramme, & Nye-Lengerman, 2018). Evidence, particularly from the UK, suggests that although the differences in life expectancy for people with and without intellectual disabilities have reduced since the 1980s, the gap has closed less than expected (Heslop et al., 2014). Meanwhile, the higher mortality rates of people with intellectual disabilities are associated with adverse social determinants of health, such as unresponsive health care systems and lack of relationships with others to act as health advocates. For instance, Heslop and colleagues estimate that 49% of the deaths of people with intellectual disabilities are avoidable (i.e. amenable to good quality health care) compared to 24% among the general population.

The numbers of people with intellectual disabilities facing retirement have continued to increase since the 1980s. This demographic trend will remain as the impact of the post-World War II baby boom plays itself out over the next ten years. In Germany, for example, a six-fold increase in older people with intellectual disabilities is predicted from 2010 to 2030, as the baby boomer generation reaches retirement age (Dieckmann & Giovis, 2014). Nevertheless, older people with intellectual disabilities form a very small group within the general aged population (approximately 0.04% of 55 plus age group) and remain invisible in mainstream retirement research and policy (Heller, Gibbons, & Fisher, 2015). Older people are also a small minority of people with intellectual disabilities (approximately 3.3% of 55 plus age group). In some types of services however, they form a large proportion of people supported. For example, over half of all employees in Australian Business Enterprises (often large-scale segregated employment programs) are expected to be aged over 50 by 2025 (McDermott, Edwards, Abello, & Katz, 2010).

Perspectives of Older People with Intellectual Disabilities about Retirement

Early studies found that retirement was not something that appealed to many people with intellectual disabilities. Most did not want to stay at home and put their feet up, contrary to prevailing stereotypes among younger staff (Bigby, Wilson, Balandin, & Stancliffe, 2011). A sense of fear about what the losses of retirement might entail is a continuous thread in studies reporting perspectives of people with intellectual disabilities from different countries with developed economies. People facing retirement expressed concerned about multiple losses – income, social connections, and engagement in regular activities (Bigby & Knox, 2009; Bigby et al., 2011; David, Duvdevani, & Doron, 2015; Ellison & White, 2017; Fesko et al., 2012; Heller, 1999; Lövgren & Bertilsdotter Rosqvist, 2015; Mahon & Mactavish, 2000; McDermott & Edwards, 2012; Newberry et al., 2014; Rogers, Hawkins, & Eklund, 1998; Sutton, Sterns, & Roberts, 1992). They have also consistently expressed preferences for continuity; to remain active and engaged in work, learning or leisure and other structured activities as they age. As one woman put it, she wanted to 'keep on keeping on' (Bigby & Knox, 2009). Most of this research has also identified that people with intellectual disabilities have little knowledge about ageing and limited expectations about what retirement might entail.

There are some contrasting views. Several studies suggest that some people hold positive views, anticipating retirement as a time when they will become more like other people. For example, Edgerton's study of deinstitutionalisation (Edgerton & Gaston, 1991) suggests that as people with mild intellectual disabilities aged they became less dependent on benefactors, more competent than at any other stage of their lives and wanted the freedom to exercise control, even if this meant opting out day services. A more recent Australian study argued that people working in open employment, or who had definite offers of alternatives to work – such as activity-based retirement programs – were more positive towards retirement (Brotherton, Stancliffe, Wilson, & O'Loughlin, 2016, Brotherton et al., 2020). Overall, the body of research exploring perspectives on retirement points to anxiety and uncertainty. It also suggests there are significant gaps in education for people with intellectual disabilities about the possibilities of retiring or finding alternatives to their existing day time occupation as they age.

Experiences of Retirement of Older People with Intellectual Disabilities

Pushed Towards Retirement

Retirement is more likely to be a sudden, unplanned, and involuntary event for people with intellectual disabilities (Engeland, Kittelsaa, & Langballe, 2018; McDermott & Edwards, 2012) and not the type of planned and voluntary transition associated with good outcomes (Barbosa et al., 2016). Analysis of US data from 2014 to 2015 shows, for example, that as they aged, people with intellectual disabilities were more likely to stop work altogether rather than gradually reduce their hours (Stancliffe, Nye-Lengerman, & Kramme, 2019). One reason for this is the high proportion of people with intellectual disabilities already working part-time. There are also indications in these data that people with intellectual disabilities may retire from employment at a younger age than the average of 62 years for the US workforce. Interestingly, these data also show that some people do continue to work past the age of 65, and that in the 70–74 year old age group, a higher proportion of people with intellectual disabilities (though a small number) compared to the general population were still working. The reasons behind this pattern have not yet been explored, although it has been argued that finances are seldom a determining factor in retirement decisions of people with intellectual disabilities (Stancliffe et al., 2018).

A push towards retirement comes from both individual and structural factors. The idea of 'retirement as a solution' to a mismatch between the demands associated with being employed and personal circumstances emerged as a core theme in a qualitative study of Australians with intellectual disabilities who had retired from mainstream employment (Brotherton et al., 2020). The people in this study had been advised by health practitioners that continued employment was 'too risky', primarily in terms of their health or the likelihood of falls. Retirement was something 'they needed to do rather than wanted to do' (p. 6). These findings align with those in the US that show a substantial decrease in rates of employment for people with intellectual disabilities who also have mobility impairments as they age, as a result of increased difficulties with travel or undertaking work tasks (Stancliffe et al., 2019).

From a structural perspective, in some countries, the push comes from a mandatory retirement age being applied to users of services such as day centres as well as the workforce. For example, in Norway, funding for sheltered employees ceases when they reach the age of 67, and in Scotland, people must retire from day services at the age of 65. However, it seems that in both countries, 'informal' attendance, albeit part-time, may be facilitated post retirement (Engeland et al., 2018; Judge, Walley, Anderson, & Young, 2010).

The necessity for older people with intellectual disabilities attending day services to retire or change the type of service they use has been a core theme in the literature since the 1980s. Though couched as responding to changing needs, the drivers for change originate from economic imperatives, rigid funding or models of service and negative stereotypical misconceptions about ageing. Very simply, the rationale for change is a perceived misalignment between the aims and nature of services designed for younger people and the characteristics of older people (often classified as aged 40 years and over). Ageing is characterised as a deficit – deterioration in health, stamina, and functional capacity, and, particularly in the case of sheltered employees, declining productivity. During the 1990s in the UK, for example, it was argued that older people should retire from leisure and activity-based day centres, or that specialist programs should be created within these centres, to take account of older peoples' needs. This included their need for flexible hours, increased support needs, declining skill levels, preferences for a quieter environment, incompatibility with younger people, and staffs' lack of skills and knowledge about supporting older people (Bigby, 2004; Department of Health, 1997; Lambe & Hogg, 1995). Similarly, in the USA, the impetus for retirement was based on assumptions that older people would no longer benefit from the developmental programs or vocational training at the core of the day centres' activities (Janicki, 1992; Seltzer & Krauss, 1987).

Not surprisingly, this deficit perspective of being older dominated some of the early specialist retirement programs created in Australia, where service providers perceived that, 'older people are less active, more passive, require more harmony, more physical assistance, need more support and their individual fixed behaviour becomes magnified' (Bigby, Balandin, Fyffe, McCubbery, & Gordon, 2004, p. 247). Interestingly, despite ageing being the justification for change, many of these early 'retirement' programs included younger people with high complex needs and staff with little knowledge about ageing.

Engagement and Participation in Retirement

The fears of people with intellectual disabilities that retirement will mean a loss of social connections and regular activities are not entirely without foundation. There are, however, limited population level data about their everyday lives, and some differences exist between countries and groups of people with intellectual disabilities. Early US studies conducted in the 1980s and 1990s indicated that in general, older people with intellectual disabilities were less likely to participate in formal programmes than their younger peers, and that they participated in few regular activities, and that those activities were predominantly more passive leisure pursuits (Anderson, Lakin, Bruininks, & Hill, 1987; Janicki & MacEarchron, 1984; Seltzer & Krauss, 1987). One study suggested that 'retirees' days were often filled with diversionary activity, rather than leisure that was valued and meaningful to participants. Furthermore, they were not provided with opportunities to retain contact with previous friends or develop new social contacts' (Rogers et al., 1998, p. 127). Australian studies found a similar situation and showed that older people with intellectual disabilities had limited participation in day programs or in recreation and leisure activities outside their place of residence (Ashman, Hulme, & Suttie, 1990; Community Services Victoria, 1992).

The most comprehensive and recent data are from the USA and Norway. These show similar patterns of activity for people with intellectual disabilities as they age; an increased use of facility-based day programs and more people without any form of structured out of home activities (Engeland, Strand, Innstrand, & Langballe, 2020; Stancliffe et al., 2019). Norwegian data show that despite greater use of day centres by people aged over 64 years (10%), 82.6% of those with mild intellectual disabilities in this age group are neither employed nor using a day centre. Similarly, in the USA, more older people than younger people use facility-based day programs (approximately 50% of people over 65 years), that unpaid community activities (such as volunteering) decreases among older age groups, and approximately 32% of people over 65 do not have any regular out of home activities (Stancliffe et al., 2019). Though less comprehensive, studies from Ireland and the UK also suggest that day centres are the most common type of service used by older people with intellectual disabilities (McConkey, Kelly, Craig, & Keogh, 2019; Newberry, Martin, & Robbins, 2015). Notably, however, in the UK there has been an overall decline of around 5% in number of adults using day centres since 2010, which has not been replaced with other types of day support (Hatton, 2017).

These figures suggest the continuing relevance of early Australian research that highlighted the centrality of day centres to older people's wellbeing, and the risks of losing friends and regular activities if they were forced to retire (Bigby, 2000). For example, one participant in a Scottish study said of the day centre he attended, 'if I wasn't coming here I would just be staying in my bed' (Judge et al., 2010). The significance of day centres in terms of social connections for older people is reinforced by data from a representative sample of older people with intellectual disabilities in Ireland. More than two in five older people had no friends outside their own home, and although most had some contact with family, they did not participate with them in social activities, and relied on support staff for engagement in social activities (McCausland et al., 2016).

Small qualitative studies, from Norway and Australia of people with intellectual disabilities who had reluctantly retired from work for health reasons, provide glimpses of more positive possibilities. Both studies describe retirees as having positive experiences and greater self-determination. As one participant in the Norwegian study put it: 'I couldn't decide much at work. I can decide a lot more now, after retirement' (Engeland et al., 2018, p. 77). This study also found beneficial impacts on health and life satisfaction for the seven retirees interviewed for the study. The Australian study found that retirees missed the social contact associated with work but felt a greater sense of freedom. Significantly, however, they lacked the support to make the most of their newfound freedom, or to follow through on ideas about activities of interest, and were stuck at the point of 'planning how to plan' (Brotherton et al., 2020, p. 7).

Service Models to Support Retirement

As suggested earlier, people with intellectual disabilities contemplate retirement from a distinctive and disadvantaged position. The legacy of segregation and social exclusion of their earlier years means they live in a 'distinct social space' of family, peers with intellectual disabilities and paid staff. Their limited social networks mean they lack informal networks to facilitate participation in community activities. Possibilities for participation are also hampered by low expectations and the negative attitudes of others. Much of the earlier research on retirement suggested that staff in disability services did not expect older people with intellectual disabilities to be active or to participate in generic programs for older adults. Compounding such attitudes, staff in senior programs as well as the older people who use such programs are often reluctant and feel ill prepared to consider including people with intellectual disabilities. For example, Norwegian and Australian studies found trepidation, verging on discrimination, about including people with intellectual disabilities in mainstream older adult groups. This was summed up by comments such as, 'here at our centre a person with intellectual disability could not take part in discussions. They couldn't play bridge and couldn't participate or get anything out of a lecture' (Ingvaldsen & Balandin, 2011, p. 588). The participant of another study suggested staff were not trained for such eventualities. 'It's also a case of knowing what to do when things go wrong…Our volunteers would have had to have special training to deal with these sort [of people]' (Bigby et al., 2011, p. 171). Overall, these and other studies suggest a willingness by members of mainstream older adults' groups to include people with intellectual disabilities if appropriate support for inclusion – in the form of training or additional staff – could be made available (Bigby & Balandin, 2005).

In later life, as in earlier parts of their life course, people with intellectual disabilities require support to live a good life and communities require support to be inclusive. The challenge is finding the best ways of organising support.

Models for Retirement Services and Outcomes Sought

Overall, the development of retirement services for people with intellectual disabilities has been uneven and ad hoc. Few countries have developed a retirement service system or adopted a particular model of services. A 1990 international survey demonstrated that a range of innovative programs had been developed (Moss, 1993), and in the UK, for example, that considerable variation existed across different regions (Fitzgerald, 1998; Department of Health, 1997; Robertson, Moss, & Turner, 1996). Similarly, developments in Australia have been characterised by the ad hoc reconfiguration of programs and uneven development of pilot initiatives.

Debates about models for retirement service are influenced by local context and evaluative research. An early typology of services was derived from a US national survey (Seltzer & Krauss, 1987). This typology reflected the dominant way of thinking about services, at that time, as being group and place based. All three models identified involved attendance by older people with intellectual disabilities at some type of group-based program be it; (1) Age integrated – being included in programs with younger people with intellectual disabilities, such as continued attendance at day activity centres (2) Generic integration – being included in programs for the general aged population, such as senior citizens centres or day centres for the frail aged or (3) Specialist programs – attending new programs developed specifically for older people with intellectual disabilities either stand alone or within existing age integrated day centres (Seltzer & Krauss, 1987). Table 21.1 considers the strengths and weaknesses of each of these three models, citing examples from some of the early services. A later survey in Australia identified several

Table 21.1 Traditional models of retirement programs

Program model	Strengths	Weaknesses	Comments
Age integration For example, sheltered workshops, day activity centres, supported employment	• Minimises change and disruption • More varied social experience, cross age peers • Avoids labelling people as 'old' (Seltzer, 1988; Walker, Walker, & Ryan, 1996)	• Activities not age appropriate, not attuned to health needs, too pressured, not sensitive to age related changes, inflexible • Lack of age peer group with similar interests and levels of energy (Bigby et al., 2004; Seltzer, 1988)	• Model most commonly found in Australia and UK in 1990s (Ashman et al., 1993; Buys & Rushworth, 1997; Department of Health, 1997; Moss, 1993)
Specialist or age specific programs For example, dedicated day centres for older people with disability, non centre-based community access programs	• Staff specialist in ageing and disability • Less pressured to skill acquisition, foster peer relationships based on age and skill (Seltzer, 1988)	• Potential to isolate and segregate from both younger people with intellectual disability and old people in the community • Disruptions to previous friendships • Reduced choice and lower expectations (Moss 1993; Seltzer, 1988)	• Few examples in Australia • Specialist programs within age integrated service are a variant of this model
Generic integration For example, use of senior citizens centres, adult day centres, generic community leisure and recreation programs	• Age appropriate activities, possibilities of new friendships, wider range of activities and choice, fosters links into the community (Robertson et al., 1996; Seltzer, 1988)	• Barriers to access, poor understanding by staff of lifelong disability, inappropriate programs, geared to too high cognitive level • Not always available or accessible, cost may be prohibitive (Janicki, 1990) • Use of poor-quality services, with already devalued groups (Bigby et al., 2004; Le Pore & Janicki, 1997; Seltzer, 1988; Walker & Walker, 1998; Wolfensberger, 1985)	• Dominant model pursued in US, mandated joint planning (Moss, 1993) • Integration often requires support and development from specialist disability services at individual and system levels (Le Pore & Janicki, 1997)

Source: Adapted from Bigby (2005).

variations of these three models and an emerging brokerage approach for providing individualised support to participate in disability specific or age integrated groups (Bigby, 2005).

Thinking about the outcomes retirement services might achieve for older people with intellectual disabilities, Bigby (2004) proposed that they should support their 'sense of belonging, continuity and purpose'. From the literature and policy directions for older people both with and without intellectual disabilities, she identified six key objectives that could also be used as evaluative criteria: (1) Promotion of choice and use of person-centred planning (2) Maintenance and strengthening of social networks (3) Participation in the community (4) Maintenance of skills (5) Opportunities for self-expression and sense of self; and (6) Promotion of health and a healthy lifestyle. A comparison of seven exemplar retirement service models found they shared similar objectives. All models emphasised choice, planning, building social networks, and participation more than maintaining skills, finding opportunities for self-expression, or promoting a healthy lifestyle. However, services operationalised objectives quite differently. For example, choice in one service amounted to an annual program booklet of activities on offer from which a person might choose, while in another service choice involved experimenting with different types of activities and a detailed assessment of preferences-based observation and discussion with the individual and others who knew them well (Bigby, 2005). This study demonstrated the value looking beyond the rhetoric of service documentation and the danger of using service models as a proxy for quality of outcomes. Both traditional age-integrated day centres and newer brokerage models demonstrated a capacity to deliver tailored support to individual older people that enabled their participation in a range of activities without reinforcing age-related stereotypes. By highlighting variable ways of achieving key objectives, the study pointed to the significance of frontline practice, suggesting that 'structural arrangements or program models may be less important than the micro operationalization of objectives' (p. 84). It also questioned the value of devising specific service models for older people, as the practices used to support younger people, such as support for decision making and person-centred planning, were successfully applied to working with older age groups.

Individualised Approaches to Support in Retirement

The brokerage programs identified by Bigby in 2005 were precursors of a shift from block funding of services to an individualised approach. This was seen as a means to provide people with disabilities with greater flexibility, and choice and control in the provision of support (Bigby & Ozanne, 2001). Reforms of disability service systems over the last 30 years have seen many countries transition, at least partially, to individualised funding schemes. Such schemes potentially address the rigidity of funding for day centres that has been one of the drivers for retirement. They also enable support to be adapted to individuals' needs as they change with age. Individualised funding has also opened greater possibilities for supporting older people with intellectual disabilities to participate in a similar range of activities, groups and voluntary roles to that are available to older people in the general community. However, the capacity of individualised funding schemes to enable community participation and provide support that leads to a greater sense of belonging, continuity, and purpose for older people with intellectual disabilities depends on the level of funding available, the market, and the quality of support available for purchase.

Access and linkage work has to be done at individual and group levels. It involves identifying an individual's interests, locating and negotiating access to mainstream activities or groups, and providing orientation or mentoring to allay fears and build the confidence of other participants to include people with intellectual disabilities. Participation is more than simply being present at a group or activity but marked by sharing in activities and friendly interactions with other participants or group members (Craig & Bigby, 2015). Support for both the individual and the group must be long-term and episodic, varying in intensity as either the group or the needs of the person change. Several researcher-led demonstration programs in Australia have trialled this type of access and linkage work. Such programs illustrate not only the success of supporting older people with intellectual disabilities to be volunteers or to participate in mainstream community groups, but also the processes and practice skills involved in this type of support (Bigby et al., 2014; Craig & Bigby, 2015; Stancliffe, Bigby, Balandin, Wilson, & Craig, 2015).

The *Transition to Retirement Program* developed by Stancliffe and colleagues in Australia was designed for older workers transitioning from sheltered employment. The first stage was 'promoting retirement' to people and their families through examples of positive alternatives to work. The second stage, 'laying the groundwork', involved building trust and knowledge about the project among community groups and organisations in a locality. And a third stage, 'constructing the reality', tailored support to each participant, and involved person centred planning, locating a suitable group, mapping new routines, recruiting and training members of the group as mentors, and monitoring and providing ongoing support when necessary to the individual, group members or others involved in the person's life. Drawing on support practices from co-worker training (Storey, 2003) and person-centred Active Support, Stancliffe et al. (2015, p. 704) used the term 'active mentoring' as an approach to teaching community group members the necessary skills for enabling inclusion. Both this, and another study of older people with higher support needs, identified group features associated with successful inclusion such as; a willingness from leaders and other members, acceptance of specialist advice or training about engaging a person with intellectual disability, having an integrating activity or common group goal, and meeting regularity (Craig & Bigby, 2015; Stancliffe et al., 2015).

These studies and others involving a broader range of age groups identify the practice skills and 'behind the scenes' work required. Different but complementary skills are needed; micro skills for direct support of individuals 'in the moment' (primarily person centred Active Support); meso level skills for identifying, understanding and negotiating with organisations, groups and communities (community development skills); and skills for supporting decision making and working with individuals and their families around planning (most commonly seen as social work or casework and supported decision making skills).

Access and linkage programs are not a panacea for all aspects of retirement. Despite success in facilitating regular participation, the friendly interactions and acquaintances developed within groups were not transferred to settings outside the group or volunteer role, and did not provide a catalyst for participation in a wider range of social activities (Craig & Bigby, 2015; Stancliffe et al., 2015). Much more action research of this nature is needed to explore additional strategies for developing social connections and friendships between people with and without disabilities.

Progress on Policy and Laying the Foundations for Retirement into the Future

A final thread in debates about retirement concerns the issue responsibility and raises the question about which sector – Ageing or Disability – should be responsible for funding services for this group. There are no definitive answers, although the ideal type of 'mainstreaming approach', advocated by the 2007 United Nations Convention on the Rights on Persons with Disabilities, would suggest that funding should be the responsibility of the Ageing sector. These issues must be resolved in each jurisdiction, in the context of local policy, funding and service systems. In some jurisdictions attempts to do just that has involved time consuming and ultimately fruitless attempts to disentangle age related support needs from disability related support needs. Meanwhile, the continuing absence in many countries of any policy or settled systems for addressing issues of funding and support models for older people with intellectual disabilities is quite remarkable.

For example, early surveys in the UK suggested that few policy initiatives and little comprehensive service development was occurring. Analysis of Local Government community care plans for 1993/94, found that 18% of authorities had policies in relation to older people with disabilities (Robertson et al., 1996). 17 years later, Turner and Cooper Ueki (2015) drew attention to the lack of underpinning principles and limited progress made in the UK to include older people with intellectual disabilities in national policy and plans about ageing. She found that only 11% of the joint plans used by local government/NHS (Joint Strategic Needs Assessment and Joint Health and Wellbeing Strategies) gave any attention to this group.

Perhaps more than any other country, the USA has tried to bridge the ageing and disability services systems by sharing knowledge, expertise and relevant services while also mandating joint planning

(Factor, Heller, & Janicki, 2012; Janicki, 1992). An enduring approach has been to foster the inclusion of older people with intellectual disabilities in mainstream day programs for older people, with some provision of specialist support and resources. Nevertheless, there are considerable disparities between States and localities in approaches and responsibility to support for older people with intellectual disabilities.

In Australia, the introduction of the National Disability Insurance Scheme (NDIS, 2013), which provides individualised funding packages for people with severe disabilities, has begun to settle which sector has responsibility for funding support for retirement. Funding for participants in the Scheme continues past the age of 65 years, until a point where they might enter residential aged care (NDIS, 2013, s. 29). Approximately 1.1% of adults with intellectual disabilities aged over of 25 years fall into the category of being 65 years or over, and 7.6% are in the category of being aged 55 years or over (NDIS, 2019). The NDIS provides a clear distinction, for the first time in Australia, between support for people ageing into disability and those ageing with a disability by restricting disability funding and initial entry to the Scheme to people aged under 65 years. Alongside individualised funding, the Scheme also has a mandate to build the capacity of mainstream services to be inclusive of people with disabilities. As yet, little has occurred in this regard.

Last Words

In many countries, a disturbing trend continues whereby a significant proportion of older people with intellectual disabilities remain socially isolated and without regular activities. This trend cannot be easily divorced from the limited policy development that has occurred in the area of retirement for people with intellectual disability. This bleak picture points to the relative failure of several decades of disability policies aiming to further the social and economic inclusion of younger adults with intellectual disabilities. The social and economic inclusion of younger adults with intellectual disabilities should lay strong foundations for later life. Without such foundations, future generations will continue to face the prospect of ageing and retirement from a distinctive and disadvantaged position unless their individual biographies change. However, retirement is likely to become even less relevant in the 2020s to people with intellectual disabilities who are not employed. The disability policy context has changed since the 1980s and the forces that propelled people with intellectual disabilities towards retirement have weakened. For instance, some funding and service models are no longer quite so rigid today as they were in the 1980s. Meanwhile, negative and stereotypical views of ageing have also diminished over time.

Retirement in 2020 and beyond will be viewed through new lenses of disability rights, individualised funding schemes and markets. Access and linkage approaches to supporting community participation and social inclusion will replace day centres. The concept of retirement will have little relevance for people who are not employed when support for regular activities and inclusion in community groups is flexible and individualised. As they age, what will be necessary is to adjust individual plans and type of support to take account of changed support needs, and where necessary draw in supplementary knowledge about ageing. Similar types of support will be available to those who are employed as they chose to reduce their hours or retire from work. Looking further beyond the 2020s, individual biographies, the scope and adequacy of individualised funding, quality of support practice, and inclusive capacity of communities are likely to be the primary determinants of the sense of belonging continuity, and purpose of older people with intellectual disabilities.

References

Anderson, D., Lakin, K., Bruininks, R., & Hill, B. (1987). *A national study of residential and support services for elderly persons with mental retardation.* University of Minnesota, Department of Educational Psychology. https://conservancy.umn.edu/handle/11299/203384

Ashman, A. F., Hulme, P., & Suttie, J. (1990). The life circumstances of aged people with an intellectual disability. *Australia and New Zealand Journal of Developmental Disabilities, 16*(4), 335–347. https://doi.org/10.1080/07263869000034151

Ashman A.F., Suttie J. N. & Bramley J. (1993) *Older Australians and an Intellectual Disability*. Fred and Eleanor Schonell Special Education Research Centre, St Lucia, Qld.

Ashman, A., Suttie, J., & Bramley, J. (1995). Employment, retirement and elderly persons with developmental disabilities, *Journal of Intellectual Disability Research*, 39(2), 107–115. https://doi.org/10.1111/j.1365-2788.1995.tb00478.x

Barbosa, L. M., Monteiro, B., & Murta, S. G. (2016). Retirement adjustment predictors—A systematic review. *Work, Aging and Retirement*, 2(2), 262–280. https://doi.org/10.1093/workar/waw008

Bigby, C. (1992). Access and linkage: Two critical issues for older people with an intellectual disability in utilising day activity and leisure services. *Australia and New Zealand Journal of Developmental Disabilities*, 18(2), 95–109. https://doi.org/10.1080/07263869200034851

Bigby, C. (2000). *Moving on without parents: Planning, transitions and sources of support for older adults with intellectual disabilities*. Sydney: MacLennan and Petty.

Bigby, C. (2004). *Ageing with a lifelong disability: A guide to practice, program, and policy issues for human services professionals*. London: Jessica Kingsley Publishers.

Bigby, C. (2005). Comparative programs for older people with intellectual disabilities. *Journal of Policy and Practice in Intellectual Disability*, 2(2), 75–85. https://doi.org/10.1111/j.1741-1130.2005.00019.x

Bigby, C., & Balandin, S. (2005). Another minority group: A survey of the use of aged care day programs and community leisure services by older people with lifelong disability. *Australasian Journal on Aging*, 24(1), 14–18. https://doi.org/10.1111/j.1741-6612.2005.00061.x

Bigby, C., Balandin, S., Fyffe, C., McCubbery, J., & Gordon, M. (2004). Retirement or just a change of pace: An Australian national survey of disability day services used by older people with disabilities. *Journal of Intellectual and Developmental Disability*, 29(3), 239–254. https://doi.org/10.1080/13668250412331285145

Bigby, C., & Knox, M. (2009). "I want to see the Queen": Experiences of service use by ageing people with an intellectual disability. *Australian Social Work*, 62(2), 216–231. https://doi.org/10.1080/03124070902748910

Bigby, C., & Ozanne, E. (2001). Shifts in the model of service delivery in intellectual disability in Victoria. *Journal of Intellectual and Developmental disability*, 26(2), 177–190. https://doi.org/10.1080/13668250020054495

Bigby, C., Wilson, N. J., Balandin, S., & Stancliffe, R. J. (2011). Disconnected expectations: Staff, family, and supported employee perspectives about retirement. *Journal of Intellectual and Developmental Disability*, 36(3), 167–174. https://doi.org/10.3109/13668250.2011.598852

Bigby, C., Wilson, N. J., Stancliffe, R. J., Balandin, S., Craig, D., & Gambin, N. (2014). An effective program design to support older workers with intellectual disability to participate individually in community groups. *Journal of Policy and Practice in Intellectual Disabilities*, 11(2), 117–127. https://doi.org/10.1111/jppi.12080

Brotherton, M., Stancliffe, R. J., Wilson, N. J., & O'Loughlin, K. (2016). Supporting workers with intellectual disability in mainstream employment to transition to a socially inclusive retirement. *Journal of Intellectual and Developmental Disability*, 41(1), 75–80. https://doi.org/10.3109/13668250.2015.1078878

Brotherton, M., Stancliffe, R. J., Wilson, N. J., & O'Loughlin, K. (2020). Australians with intellectual disability share their experiences of retirement from mainstream employment. *Journal of Applied Research in Intellectual Disabilities*, 1–12. https://doi.org/10.1111/jar.12712

Buys, L. R., & Rushworth, J. S. (1997). Community services available to older adults with intellectual disabilities. *Journal of Intellectual and Developmental Disability*, 22(1), 29–37. https://doi.org/10.1080/13668259700033271

Community Services Victoria. (1992). *Services for older people with an intellectual disability*. Melbourne: Community Services Victoria.

Craig, D., & Bigby, C. (2015). "She's been involved in everything as far as I can see": Supporting the active participation of people with intellectual disability in community groups. *Journal of Intellectual and Developmental Disability*, 40(1), 12–25. https://doi.org/10.3109/13668250.2014.977235

David, N., Duvdevani, I., & Doron, I. (2015). Older women with intellectual disability and the meaning of aging. *Journal of Women & Aging*, 27(3), 216–236. https://doi.org/10.1080/08952841.2014.933608

Department of Health. (1997). *Services for older people with learning disabilities*. London: Department of Health.

Dieckmann, F., & Giovis, C. (2014). Demographic changes in the older adult population of persons with intellectual disability in Germany. *Journal of Policy and Practice in Intellectual Disabilities*, 11(3), 226–234. https://doi.org/10.1111/jppi.12087

Edgerton, R. B., & Gaston, M. A. (1991). *I've seen it all!: Lives of older persons with mental retardation in the community*. Paul H Brookes Publishing Company.

Ellison, C. J., & White, A. L. (2017). Exploring leisure and retirement for people with intellectual disabilities. *Annals of Leisure Research*, 20(2), 188–205. https://doi.org/10.1080/11745398.2015.1122535

Engeland, J., Kittelsaa, A. M., & Langballe, E. M. (2018). How do people with intellectual disabilities in Norway experience the transition to retirement and life as retirees?. *Scandinavian Journal of Disability Research*, 20(1), 72–81. https://doi.org/10.16993/sjdr.41

Engeland, J., Strand, B. H., Innstrand, S. T., & Langballe, E. M. (2020). Employment and attendance in day care centres for people with mild intellectual disabilities–do age, gender, functional level or hospital admissions matter?. *Journal of Intellectual Disability Research, 64*(3), 197–208. https://doi.org/10.1111/jir.12709

Factor, A., Heller, T., & Janicki, M. (2012). *Bridging the aging and developmental disabilities services networks: Challenges and best practices.* Illinois Institute on Disability and Human Development, University of Illinois at Chicago. https://www.aucd.org/docs/publications/bridging_aging_dd_2012_0419.pdf

Fesko, S. L., Hall, A. C., Quinlan, J., & Jockell, C. (2012). Active aging for individuals with intellectual disability: Meaningful community participation through employment, retirement, service, and volunteerism. *American Journal on Intellectual and Developmental Disabilities, 117*(6), 497–508. https://doi.org/10.1352/1944-7558-117-6.497

Fitzgerald, J. (1998). *Time for freedom?: Services for older people with learning difficulties: Good practice in the aftermath of long-stay hospital closure.* Centre for Policy on Ageing and Values into Action. http://hdl.handle.net/10068/379026

Hareven, T. (2001). Historical perspectives on aging and family relations. In R. Binstock & L. George (Eds.), *Handbook of aging and the social sciences* (pp. 141–159). Academic Press.

Hatton, C. (2017). Day services and home care for adults with learning disabilities across the UK. *Tizard Learning Disability Review, 22*(2), 109–115. https://doi.org/10.1108/TLDR-01-2017-0004

Hatton, C., Glover, G., Emerson, E., & Brown, I. (2016). *People with learning disabilities in England 2015: Main report.* Public Health England. http://www.improvinghealthandlives.org.uk/publications/313925/People_with_Learning_Disabilities_in_England_2015

Heller, T. (1999) Emerging models. In S. Herr & G. Weber (Eds.), *Ageing, rights and quality of life.* Brookes.

Heller, T., Gibbons, H. M., & Fisher, D. (2015). Caregiving and family support interventions: Crossing networks of aging and developmental disabilities. *Intellectual and Developmental Disabilities, 53*(5), 329–345. https://doi.org/10.1352/1934-9556-53.5.329

Heslop, P., Blair, P. S., Fleming, P., Hoghton, M., Marriott, A., & Russ, L. (2014). The confidential inquiry into premature deaths of people with intellectual disabilities in the UK: A population-based study. *The Lancet, 383*(9920), 889–895. https://doi.org/10.1016/S0140-6736(13)62026-7

Hogg, J., Moss, S., & Cooke, D. (1988). From mid-life to old age. Ageing and the nature of specific life transitions of people with mental handicaps. In G. Horobin & D. May (Eds.), *Living with menial handicap: Transitions in the lives of people with mental handicap* (pp. 148–165). Jessica Kingsley.

Ingvaldsen, A. K., & Balandin, S. (2011). If we are going to include them we have to do it before we die: Norwegian seniors' views of including seniors with intellectual disability in senior centres. *Journal of Applied Research in Intellectual Disabilities, 24*(6), 583–593. https://doi.org/10.1111/j.1468-3148.2011.00636.x

Janicki, M. (1992). *Integration experiences casebook: Program ideas in aging and developmental disabilities.* New York State Office of Mental Retardation and Developmental Disabilities. https://files.eric.ed.gov/fulltext/ED350729.pdf

Janicki, M., & MacEarchron, A. (1984). Residential, health and social service needs of elderly developmentally disabled persons. *The Gerontologist, 24*, 128–137. https://doi.org/10.1093/geront/24.2.128

Janicki, M. P., & Wisniewski, H. (1985). *Aging and developmental disabilities: Issues and approaches.* Brookes. https://doi.org/10.1093/geronj/40.6.769b

Janicki, M., (1990). Growing old with dignity: On quality of life for older persons with lifelong disability. In R. Schalock (ed) *Quality of life perspectives and issues.* Washington: American Association of on Mental Retardation

Judge, J., Walley, R., Anderson, B., & Young, R. (2010). Activity, aging, and retirement: The views of a group of Scottish people with intellectual disabilities. *Journal of Policy and Practice in Intellectual Disabilities, 7*(4), 295–301. https://doi.org/10.1111/j.1741-1130.2010.00279.x

Lambe, L., & Hogg, J. (1995). *Their face to the wind: Service developments for older people with learning difficulties in Grampian region.* Enable.

Le Pore, P., & Janicki, M. (1997). *The wit to win. How to integrate older persons with developmental disabilities into community aging programs* (3rd ed.). New York State Office of Aging. https://files.eric.ed.gov/fulltext/ED345390.pdf

Lövgren, V., & Bertilsdotter Rosqvist, H. (2015). 'More time for what?' Exploring intersecting notions of gender, work, age and leisure time among people with cognitive disabilities. *International Journal of Social Welfare, 24*(3), 263–272. https://doi.org/10.1111/ijsw.12135

Mahon, M., & Mactavish, J. (2000). A sense of belonging. In M. Janicki & E. Ansello (Eds.), *Community supports for aging adults with lifelong disabilities* (pp. 41–53). Brookes.

McCausland, D., McCallion, P., Cleary, E., & McCarron, M. (2016). Social connections for older people with intellectual disability in Ireland: Results from wave one of IDS-TILDA. *Journal of Applied Research in Intellectual Disabilities, 29*(1), 71–82. https://doi.org/10.1111/jar.12159

McConkey, R., Kelly, F., Craig, S., & Keogh, F. (2019). Changes in the provision of day services in Ireland to adult persons with intellectual disability. *Journal of Policy and Practice in Intellectual Disabilities, 16*(1), 13–20. https://doi.org/10.1111/jppi.12261

McDermott, S., & Edwards, R. (2012). Enabling self-determination for older workers with intellectual disabilities in supported employment in Australia. *Journal of Applied Research in Intellectual Disabilities, 25*, 423–432. https://doi.org/10.1111/j.1468-3148.2012.00683.x

McDermott, S., Edwards, R., Abello, D., & Katz, I. (2010). Community services and indigenous affairs. *Occasional Paper No 27: Ageing and Australian Disability Enterprises*. https://www.dss.gov.au/sites/default/files/documents/05_2012/op27.pdf

Moss, S. (1993). *Aging and developmental disabilities: Perspectives from nine countries*. The International Exchange of Experts and Information in Rehabilitation.

Newberry, G., Martin, C., Robbins, L. (2015). How do people with learning disabilities experience and make sense of the ageing process. *British Journal of Learning Disabilities, 43*, 285–292

NDIS. (2013). National Disability Insurance Scheme Act 2013. No. 20. https://www.legislation.gov.au/Details/C2013A00020

NDIS. (2019). National Disability Insurance Scheme. *COAG Disability Reform Council Quarterly Report for Q4*. https://www.ndis.gov.au/about-us/publications/quarterly-reports/archived-quarterly-reports-2018-19#th-quarterly-report-2018-19-q4

Newberry, G., Martin, C., & Robbins, L. (2015). How do people with learning disabilities experience and make sense of the ageing process?. *British Journal of Learning Disabilities, 43*(4), 285–292. https://doi.org/10.1111/bld.12149

Robertson, J., Moss, S., & Turner, S. (1996). Policy, service and staff training for older people with intellectual disability in the UK. *Journal of Applied Research in Intellectual Disabilities, 9*(2), 91–100. https://doi.org/10.1111/j.1468-3148.1996.tb00100.x

Rogers, N. B., Hawkins, B. A., & Eklund, S. J. (1998). The nature of leisure in the lives of older adults with intellectual disability. *Journal of Intellectual Disability Research, 42*(2), 122–130. https://doi.org/10.1046/j.1365-2788.1998.00103.x

Seltzer, M., & Krauss, M. (1987). *Aging and mental retardation. Extending the continuum*. American Association on Mental Retardation.

Seltzer, M. (1988). Structure and patterns of service utilisation by elderly persons with mental retardation. *Mental Retardation, 26*, 181–185

Seltzer, M. (1988). Structure and patterns of service utilisation by elderly persons with mental retardation. *Mental Retardation, 26*, 181–185

Stancliffe, R., Bigby, C., Balandin, S., Wilson, N., & Craig, D. (2015). Transition to retirement and participation in inclusive community groups using active mentoring: An outcomes evaluation with a matched comparison group. *Journal of Intellectual Disability Research, 59*(8), 703–718. https://doi.org/10.1111/jir.12174

Stancliffe, R. J., Kramme, J. E., & Nye-Lengerman, K. (2018). Exploring retirement for individuals with intellectual and developmental disabilities: An analysis of National Core Indicators data. *Intellectual and Developmental Disabilities 56*(4), 217–233. https://doi.org/10.1352/1934-9556-56.5.217

Stancliffe, R. J., Nye-Lengerman, K. M., & Kramme, J. E. (2019). Aging, community-based employment, mobility impairment, and retirement: National Core Indicators–Adult Consumer Survey Data. *Research and Practice for Persons with Severe Disabilities, 44*(4), 251–266. https://doi.org/10.1177/1540796919882921

Storey, K. (2003). A review of research on natural support interventions in the workplace for people with disabilities. *International Journal of Rehabilitation Research, 26*(2), 79–84.

Sutton, E., Sterns, H., & Roberts, R. (1992). 'Retirement' for older persons with developmental disabilities. *Generations: Journal of the American Society on Aging, 16*(1), 63–64.

Turner, S., & Cooper Ueki, M. (2015). Current policy and legislation in England regarding older people – What this means for older people with learning disabilities: A discussion paper. *British Journal of Learning Disabilities, 43*(4), 254–260. https://doi.org/10.1111/bld.12150

Walker, A., & Walker, C. (1998). Normalisation and 'normal' ageing: The social construction of dependency among older people with learning difficulties. *Disability and Society, 13*(1), 125–142.

Walker, A., Walker, C., & Ryan, T. (1996). Older people with learning difficulties leaving institutional care—A case of double jeopardy. *Ageing & Society, 16*(2), 125–150. https://doi.org/10.1017/S0144686X00003263

Wolfensberger, W. (1985). An overview of social role valorisation and some reflections on elderly mentally retarded persons. In M. Janicki & H. Wisniewski (Eds.), *Aging and developmental disabilities: Issues and approaches*. Paul Brookes Publishing.

World Health Organization. (2002). *Active ageing: A policy framework*. Geneva: World Health Organization. https://www.who.int/ageing/publications/active_ageing/en/

World Health Organization. (2015). *World report on aging and health*. Geneva: World Health Organization. https://www.who.int/ageing/events/world-report-2015-launch/en/

Suggested Readings

Bigby, C., Wilson, N. J., Stancliffe, R. J., Balandin, S., Craig, D., & Gambin, N. (2014). An effective program design to support older workers with intellectual disability to participate individually in community groups. *Journal of Policy and Practice in Intellectual Disabilities*, *11*(2), 117–127. https://doi.org/10.1111/jppi.12080

Craig, D., & Bigby, C. (2015). "She's been involved in everything as far as I can see": Supporting the active participation of people with intellectual disability in community groups. *Journal of Intellectual and Developmental Disability*, *40*(1), 12–25. https://doi.org/10.3109/13668250.2014.977235

Kåhlin, I., Kjellberg, A., Nord, C., & Hagberg, J. (2013) Lived experiences of ageing and later life in older people with intellectual disabilities. *Ageing and Society*, 1–27. https://doi.org/10.1017/S0144686X13000949

Stancliffe, R., Wilson, N., Gambin, N., Bigby, C., & Balandin, S. (2013). *Transition to retirement: A guide to inclusive practice*. Sydney University Press.

22
FAMILY CAREGIVING FOR ADULTS AGEING WITH INTELLECTUAL AND DEVELOPMENTAL DISABILITIES

Tamar Heller, Sumithra Murthy, and Catherine Keiling Arnold

Introduction

Families play an important role in providing physical, emotional, and material support to people with intellectual and developmental disabilities (IDD) across the lifespan (Braddock, Hemp, Tanis, Wu, & Haffer, 2017; Heller & Schindler, 2009). This includes providing informal help that supplements any formal support received by the person. Currently, family caregiver responsibilities are lasting longer than in prior decades because of factors such as increased average life expectancy for people with IDD (as well as for caregivers themselves) and in the United States (U.S.), the limited availability of formal services for persons with IDD (Heller & Schindler, 2009).

The number of caregivers for persons ageing with IDD is growing as the older adult population with IDD increases. In the U.S., the number of adults 60 and older with IDD is expected to reach an estimated 1.4 million adults by 2030 (Factor, Heller, & Janicki, 2012). Braddock et al. (2017) estimated that in 2015, approximately 3.6 million of the 5.1 million people with IDD in the U.S. were receiving residential care and supports from family caregivers; Only 13% of adults with IDD were living in supervised residential settings. They estimated that 71% of individuals with IDD live with a family caregiver, with 35% of those caregivers being between the ages of 41 and 59 and 24% being aged 60 or older (Braddock et al., 2017). It is not uncommon for adults with IDD to live with ageing parents until their parents are no longer able to care for them or pass away. The importance of unpaid caregivers in providing support to persons with IDD in the U.S. is significant as nearly 75% of individuals with IDD do not receive any substantive formal or paid supports (Hewitt, 2014). For those who qualify for services, there may be long waiting lists for community-level state supports resulting in people with IDD being more likely to rely mainly on their families for support for long periods of time (Larson et al., 2017).

Issues for Family Caregivers

The impact of long-term family caregiving on the financial, health, and social well-being of caregivers is a public health concern (Taggart, Truesdale-Kennedy, Ryan, & McConkey, 2012). Some families can experience poorer health, psychosocial, and economic outcomes because of their life-long caregiving activities and unmet needs for supports to assist them in their caregiving roles (Heller, Caldwell, & Factor, 2007). Often there is a change in relationship dynamics as families grow older together that can create new issues or exacerbate issues for family caregivers (Grossman & Webb, 2016). It is easiest to understand this by considering families of persons with IDD from an Ecological Framework perspective, which views the needs of caregivers and care recipients as interlinked so supports and services related to health, economics, and psychosocial concerns can be viewed as affecting both care recipients and caregivers (Eckenwiler, 2007; Shogren, 2013). Within this framework, the concept of Family Quality of Life (FQOL) is relevant. FQOL measures the well-being of the family and considers how individual and family-level needs interact (Zuna, Summers, Turnbull, Hu, & Xu, 2010). FQOL recognises positive adaptation and family strengths (Chiu et al., 2013). It supports the development of strategies to provide services and supports to families, not just individuals, that improve health, psychosocial, and economic outcomes.

Financial Outcomes

FQOL is impacted by many factors as family caregivers provide support to persons with IDD over a lifetime. Principal among those are employment and financial issues. Family caregiving can have significant economic impacts on caregivers and the family unit as a whole. Although it is common for caregivers in general to be employed (National Alliance for Caregiving, 2009), they often make employment changes in response to their caregiving responsibilities including reducing work hours, changing jobs, stopping work entirely, and taking a leave of absence (National Alliance for Caregiving, 2009). Caregivers of individuals with IDD in particular, are less likely to be employed than non-caregivers and even if employed, often miss more days of work (Bronheim, Goode, & Jones, 2006). Studies also report lower savings and lower income in families of people with IDD (Heller et al., 2007; Parish, Seltzer, Greenberg, & Floyd, 2004) as well as greater family related work role strain (Heller & Schindler, 2009). Obstacles to career advancements leading to economic losses have been found to increase in midlife for parents of children with IDD (Parish, Rose, & Swaine, 2010). Lost or missed opportunities in employment due to the constraints of family caregiving contributions to retirement plans and Social Security, thereby affecting long-term financial well-being as well (MetLife, 2011). These kinds of long-term economic losses are typically compounded for members of racial and ethnic minority groups (AARP, 2013). In sum, family caregivers often experience employment challenges over their work lives related to workplace flexibility and earnings that can result in less money available to them in retirement and later life.

Health and Social Outcomes

A study by Totsika, Hastings, and Vagenas (2017) showed that after controlling for demographics, caregivers of people with ID reported a similar quality of life to all other caregivers but worse physical health status. Health and well-being of families of adults with disabilities, especially adults with IDD, can be influenced by factors such as the characteristics of the family member with IDD, the family's socio-economic status, the extent of a family's social support network and the minority cultural context the family lives within (Heller et al., 2007; Heller & Schindler, 2009). Common mental health concerns for caregivers of persons with IDD include stress, depression, and isolation (Feinberg, Reinhard, Houser, & Choula, 2011; Pinquart & Sörensen, 2003) as well as physical health concerns such as heart disease, hypertension, stroke, poor immune function, and impaired sleep (Pinquart & Sörensen, 2007; Piazza, Floyd, Mailick, & Greenberg, 2014; Seltzer, Floyd, Song, Greenberg, & Hong, 2011). Compared to non-caregivers, caregivers of persons with IDD in general are more likely to report health problems (Ho, Collins, Davis, & Doty, 2005), a higher number of chronic conditions (Bronheim et al., 2006; Heller et al., 2007; Heller & Schindler, 2009; Lunsky, Tint, Robinson, Gordeyko, & Kuntz, 2014; Seltzer et al., 2011) and are less likely to see a general practitioner, see or afford a mental health professional, or afford prescription medicines (Heller & Schindler, 2009). Racial and ethnic minority caregivers of persons with IDD are at a higher risk for negative health outcomes (Magaña, Greenberg, & Seltzer, 2004; Magaña & Smith, 2006, 2008). In general, caregivers' elevated stress predicts nursing home placement of individuals with disabilities (Spillman & Long, 2007). For persons ageing with IDD, caregiver health is an important FQOL issue that can have consequences for their self-determination and independent living now and in the future.

Family Caregiving in Later Life

Compound Caregiving

Caregiving for individuals with IDD is usually life-long but the intensity of caregiving may vary at different periods of time. In later life, many caregivers face dual responsibilities of balancing caregiving of an ageing family member with IDD with caregiving for another family without IDD. This is termed compound caregiving. According to Perkins and Haley (2010), compound caregiving increased the total number of hours of caregiving, with parents of adults with IDD adding 12 more hours each week on top of their average 39-hour caregiving schedule. A study by Lunsky et al. (2014) showed that compound caregivers reported significantly higher burden, lower mastery, and higher family distress, especially when their child with IDD had medical support needs or a dual diagnosis of IDD and a mental health concern. Compound caregiving can lead to greater demands and greater unmet needs for family support. This situation heightens the need to plan for the needs of the family as a whole (Jokinen, 2006).

Reciprocity and Meaning

For many caregivers, providing care can be a source of fulfilment and meaningfulness. Some caregivers have been shown to experience better mental health outcomes, improved life satisfaction and positive well-being than their non-caregiving peers (Grossman & Webb, 2016). Caregivers often gain social networks, feel needed and useful, and, also have an opportunity to learn something about themselves in their role. They may also find that family members with disability form a bond of goodwill with them and that they benefit from mutual interdependence (Li, Shaffer, & Bagger, 2015). In some cases, a person with IDD also provides support to other family members, including to ageing parents, with tasks such as offering companionship and help with household chores (Heller & Factor, 2008).

Non-Traditional Caregivers

While most research on family caregiving for adults with IDD focuses on mothers, other family members, including fathers, siblings, and grandparents often provide substantial support to individuals with IDD as well. While fathers are less likely to be primary caregivers than mothers, those fathers who are involved in childhood are more likely to stay involved throughout the life cycle (Flippin & Crais, 2011). While the father is less likely to provide direct caregiving tasks, fathers still play a large role in providing support, such as in financial support (Heller, Hsieh, & Rowitz, 1997). Often fathers take on a larger caregiving role after their wife is no longer able to due to failing health or death (Gordon, Seltzer, & Krauss, 1996).

Siblings of people with IDD provide support throughout the life course (Arnold, Heller, & Kramer, 2012) often becoming caregivers for their brothers and sisters with IDD later in life (Hodapp, Sanderson, Meskis, & Casale, 2017). Siblings may experience compound caregiving (Perkins & Haley, 2010) as parents' age and they juggle care for their ageing parents, their own children, and their adult brothers and sisters with IDD. However, siblings do not seem to be as affected by compound caregiving as parents and spouses (Namkung, Greenberg, & Mailick, 2016). Predictors of future caregiving by siblings includes closer geographic proximity, having a sister with IDD, having more sibling contact and providing more support to their brother/sister with disabilities, and having a more positive feeling about the rewards of caregiving (Heller & Kramer, 2009). Siblings have indicated their support needs include peer support groups, information about financial as well as future planning, and education and training related to caregiver transitions (Arnold et al., 2012).

In the United States, a growing number of grandparents are living with grandchildren, as the numbers have risen from 5.8 million in 2000 to more than 7.2 million in 2018 (U.S. Census Bureau, 2018). More than one million children have a grandparent as their sole care provider. These grandchildren are more likely to have a disability than the general population. The role of grandparents of individuals with IDD can be quite distinct from that of grandparents of children without disabilities (Yang, Artman-Meeker, & Roberts, 2018) as they provide critical instrumental or socio-emotional supports to individuals with IDD and their families (Hornby & Ashworth, 1994; Lee & Gardner, 2010). Grandparents raising children with disabilities have many needs for services and supports that are often unmet. A study conducted in New York City found that grandparents serving as guardians for children with disabilities were less likely to receive social supports, had higher depression rates, and more role and financial strain than other caregivers (McCallion, Janicki, Grant-Griffin, & Kolomer, 2000).

Supports for Long-Term Caregivers

Unmet Formal Service and Supports Needs

In the U.S. all states and territories fund some level of supports for persons with IDD and their families through cash subsidies or direct service, although the amount allocated to these programs varies substantially. Supports include services like respite care, family counselling, future planning, home modification, in-home training, sibling support programs, education and behaviour analysis, and specialised equipment. However, it is estimated that only about 30% of people with IDD are known to or served by the state IDD agencies and are receiving services through the formal system (Larson et al., 2017). For this reason, among others, unmet need for services and supports is hard to measure.

There are few policies that support families in their roles as family caregivers. Most of these were obtained through activism by people with IDD and their families (Arnold & Nuchtern, 2018). Often these federal policies lack adequate funding. For example, Title II of the Developmental Disabilities Assistance and Bill of Rights Act of 2000 (DD Act) is specific to family support; however, no funding has ever been appropriated for its implementation (Hewitt, Agosta, Heller, Williams, & Reinke, 2013). In another example, funding has remained flat for the Lifespan Respite Care Program created in 2006 even though the size of the eligible population has grown substantially since that time (Administration for Community Living, 2017). Other federal programs including the National Family Caregiver Support Program, the Family and Medical Leave Act, and the Recognize, Assist, Include, Support, and Engage (RAISE) Family Caregiver Act hold the promise of support for caregivers of persons ageing with IDD, but to date none of them are funded at a level to begin to address unmet needs. There are patches of regional and local family support programs across the United States; however, they are inconsistent in their eligibility criteria and availability. Still, innovation has been occurring through activities such as the state-level Family Support 360 projects which developed unique family support demonstration programs and the Family Support Research and Training Center which has been bridging ageing and disability through cutting edge research.

Recognition of Family Support Needs

Family supports are a set of strategies directed to the family unit that benefit the individual with IDD with an overall goal of maximising the family's strengths and capabilities (Hecht, Reynolds, Agosta, McGinley, & Moseley, 2011). These strategies ideally are designed, implemented, and funded in a flexible manner that addresses the emotional, physical, and material well-being of the entire family (Wingspread Family Support Summit, 2011). Family support is intended to focus on the entire family unit (Heller, Gibbons, & Fisher, 2015). An example of this is future planning, which consists of engaging the family in discussions and planning in major life areas including financial and legal planning, where to live and work, and how to spend leisure time (Heller et al., 2007). Family decision-making benefits the person with DD (Neely-Barnes, Marcenko, & Weber, 2008) and future planning provides an opportunity for people with IDD to exercise self-determination (Heller et al., 2011) in the choices they make about what to do with their time, where to live, who will provide support to them, and much more. Heller and colleagues developed a future planning intervention that specifically includes siblings of adults with DD. *The Future is Now* is an evidence-informed curriculum that uses a peer support model which incorporates people with DD and families to be co-facilitators in the training (Factor et al., 2010). This intervention has shown success in helping families make plans, including completing a letter of intent, taking action on residential planning, and creating a special needs trust. Positive outcomes of this intervention included a decrease in caregiver burden as well as increased opportunities for the person with DD to participate in choice-making (Heller & Caldwell, 2006). Future planning is an ongoing process that continues throughout a person's lifespan (Coyle, Kramer, & Mutchler, 2014).

A study by Resch et al. (2010) showed that lack of family support was one of the most important barriers to caregiver well-being. The most promising and effective family supports (such as future planning) are family and person-centred and based on the culture, values, preferences, and needs of the family and the person with a disability (Bronheim et al., 2006), however less than 10% of state-level IDD funding goes to family support services (Braddock et al., 2015). Only 15% of families caring for a member with IDD receive family supports (Braddock et al., 2017). In general family caregivers of persons with IDD report respite services, case coordination, transportation, recreational activities, and information on housing, guardianship, and financial plans as being significant unmet needs. Families with individuals with IDD with lower levels of function and families with lower socio-economic status have reported more unmet needs (Burke & Heller, 2017). A recent study examined the impact of unmet needs longitudinally on families of people with disabilities (including IDD) found that higher unmet family support needs were associated with increased caregiving burden, decreased caregiving satisfaction and decreased self-efficacy in providing care to the person with a disability (Crabb, Owen, Stober, & Heller, 2019).

Conclusion

Families play a major role in providing care for adults ageing with IDD and will continue to do so in the future. Better efforts need to be made to improve family quality of life within an ecological framework that considers how the lives of caregivers and care recipients inter-connect and the impact of those connections over time. Supporting family caregivers of people with IDD will enhance outcomes for people ageing with IDD and the ageing family as a whole.

References

AARP. (2013). *Staying ahead of the curve 2013: AARP multicultural work and career study*. AARP. https://www.aarp.org/content/dam/aarp/research/surveys_statistics/general/2014/Staying-Ahead-of-the-Curve-2013-The-Work-and-Career-Study-AARP-res-gen.pdf

Administration for Community Living. (2017). *Support to caregivers*. Department of Health and Human Services. https://www.acl.gov/programs/support-caregivers

Arnold, C. K., Heller, T., & Kramer, J. (2012). Support needs of siblings of people with developmental disabilities. *Intellectual and Developmental Disabilities, 50*(5), 373–382. https://doi.org/10.1352/1934-9556-50.5.373

Arnold, C. K., & Nuchtern, C. (2018). Family support movements. In T. Heller, S. Parker Harris, C. Gill, & R. Gould (Eds.), *Disability in American life: An encyclopedia of concepts, policies, and controversies*. ABC-CLIO.

Braddock, D., Hemp, R., Rizzolo, M. C., Tanis, E. S., Haffer, L., & Wu, J. (2015). *The state of the states in intellectual and developmental disabilities: Emerging from the Great Recession*. American Association on Intellectual and Developmental Disabilities.

Braddock, D., Hemp, R., Tanis, E. S., Wu, J., & Haffer, L. (2017). *The state of the states in intellectual and developmental disabilities*. American Association on Intellectual and Developmental Disabilities. https://www.aaidd.org/publications/bookstore-home/product-listing/state-of-the-states-in-intellectual-and-developmental-disabilities-11th-edition

Bronheim, S., Goode, T., & Jones, W. (2006). *Policy brief: Cultural and linguistic competence in family supports*. National Center for Cultural Competence, Georgetown University Center for Child Development. https://nccc.georgetown.edu/documents/FamilySupports.pdf

Burke, M. M., & Heller, T. (2017). Disparities in unmet service needs among adults with intellectual and other developmental disabilities. *Journal of Applied Research in Intellectual Disabilities: JARID, 30*(5), 898–910. https://doi.org/10.1111/jar.12282

Chiu, C., Kyzar, K., Zuna, N., Turnbull, A., Summers, J. A., & Gomez, V. A. (2013). Family quality of life. In Wehmeyer, M. L. (Ed.), *The Oxford handbook of positive psychology and disability* (pp. 365–392). Oxford University Press. 10.1093/oxfordhb/9780195398786.013.013.0023

Coyle, C. E., Kramer, J., & Mutchler, J. E. (2014). Aging together: Sibling carers of adults with intellectual and developmental disabilities. *Journal of Policy and Practice in Intellectual Disabilities, 11*(4), 302–312. https://doi.org/10.1111/jppi.12094

Crabb, C., Owen, R., Stober, K., & Heller, T. (2019). Longitudinal appraisals of family caregiving for people with disabilities enrolled in Medicaid managed care. *Disability and Rehabilitation,* Advance online publication. https://doi.org/10.1080/09638288.2018.1557266

Eckenwiler, L. A. (2007). An ecological framework for caregiving [Letter to the editor]. *American Journal of Public Health, 97*(11), 1930–1931. https://doi.org/10.2105/AJPH.2007.117390

Factor, A., DeBrine, E., Caldwell, J., Arnold, K., Kramer, J., Nelis, T., & Heller, T. (2010). *The Future is Now: A future planning training curriculum for families and their adult relative with developmental disabilities* (3rd ed.). Rehabilitation Research and Training Center on Aging with Developmental Disabilities, University of Illinois at Chicago. https://fsrtc.ahslabs.uic.edu/the-future-is-now/

Factor, A., Heller, T., & Janicki, M. (2012). *Bridging the aging and developmental disabilities service networks: Challenges and best practices.* Institute on Disability and Human Development, University of Illinois at Chicago. https://www.aucd.org/docs/publications/bridging_aging_dd_2012_0419.pdf

Feinberg, L., Reinhard, S. C., Houser, A., & Choula, R. (2011). *Valuing the invaluable: 2011 update, the growing contributions and costs of family caregiving.* AARP Public Policy Institute. https://assets.aarp.org/rgcenter/ppi/ltc/i51-caregiving.pdf

Flippin, M., & Crais, E. R. (2011). The need for more effective father involvement in early autism intervention: A systematic review and recommendations. *Journal of Early Intervention, 33*(1), 24–50. https://doi.org/10.1177/1053815111400415

Gordon, R. M., Seltzer, M. M., & Krauss, M. W. (1996). The aftermath of parental death: Changes in the context and quality of life. In R. L. Schalock (Ed.), *Quality of life: Its applications to persons with disabilities* (pp. 23–40). American Association on Mental Retardation.

Grossman, B. R., & Webb, C. E. (2016). Family support in late life: A review of the literature on aging, disability, and family caregiving. *Journal of Family Social Work, 19*(4), 348–395. https://doi.org/10.1080/10522158.2016.1233924

Hecht, E., Reynolds, M., Agosta, J., McGinley, K., & Moseley, C. (2011). Building a national agenda for supporting families with a member with intellectual and developmental disabilities. *Wingspread Family Support Summit.* https://www.aucd.org/docs/publications/wingspread2012_supporting_families.pdf

Heller, T., & Caldwell, J. (2006). Supporting aging caregivers and adults with developmental disabilities in future planning. *Mental Retardation, 44,* 189–202. https://doi.org/10.1352/0047-6765(2006)44[189:SACAAW]2.0.CO;2

Heller, T., Caldwell, J., & Factor, A. (2007). Aging family caregivers: Policies and practices. *Mental Retardation and Developmental Disabilities Research Reviews, 13*(2), 136–142. https://doi.org/10.1002/mrdd.20138

Heller, T., & Factor, A. (2008). Family support and intergenerational caregiving: Report from the State of the science in aging with developmental disabilities Conference. *Disability and Health Journal, 1*(3), 131–135. https://doi.org/10.1016/j.dhjo.2008.04.004

Heller, T., Gibbons, H. M., & Fisher, D. (2015). Caregiving and family support interventions: Crossing networks of aging and developmental disabilities. *Intellectual and Developmental Disabilities, 53*(5), 329–345. https://doi.org/10.1352/1934-9556-53.5.329

Heller, T., Hsieh, K., & Rowitz, L. (1997). Maternal and paternal caregiving of persons with mental retardation across the life-span. *Family Relations, 46,* 407–415. https://doi.org/10.2307/585100

Heller, T., & Kramer, J. (2009). Involvement of adult siblings of persons with developmental disabilities in future planning. *Intellectual and Developmental Disabilities, 47*(3), 208–219. https://doi.org/10.1352/1934-9556-47.3.208

Heller, T., & Schindler, A. (2009). Family support interventions for families of adults with intellectual and developmental disabilities. *International Review of Research in Mental Retardation, 37,* 299–332. https://doi.org/10.1016/S0074-7750(09)37009-3

Heller, T. H., Schindler, A., Palmer, S. B., Wehmeyer, M. L., Parent, W., Jenson, R., ... O'Hara, D. M. (2011). Self-determination across the life span: Issues and gaps. *Exceptionality, 19*(1), 31–45. https://doi.org/10.1080/09362835.2011.537228

Hewitt, A. (2014). Presidential address, 2014—Embracing complexity: Community inclusion, participation, and citizenship. *Intellectual and Developmental Disabilities, 52,* 475–495. https://doi.org/10.1352/1934-9556-52.6.475

Hewitt, A., Agosta, J., Heller, T., Williams, A. C., & Reinke, J. (2013). Families of individuals with intellectual and developmental disabilities: Policy, funding, services, and experiences. *Intellectual and Developmental Disabilities, 51*(5), 349–359. https://doi.org/10.1352/1934-9556-51.5.349

Ho, A., Collins, S. R., Davis, K., & Doty, M. M. (2005). A look at working-age caregivers' roles, health concerns, and need for support. *Issue Brief (Commonwealth Fund), 854*, 1–12. https://www.commonwealthfund.org/publications/issue-briefs/2005/aug/look-working-age-caregivers-roles-health-concerns-and-need

Hodapp, R. M., Sanderson, K. A., Meskis, S. A., & Casale, E. G. (2017). Adult siblings of persons with intellectual disabilities: Past, present, and future. *International review of research in developmental disabilities* (Vol. 53, pp. 163–202). Academic Press. http://dx.doi.org/10.1016/bs.irrdd.2017.08.001

Hornby, G., & Ashworth, T. (1994). Grandparents' support for families who have children with disabilities. *Journal of Child and Family Studies, 3*(4), 403–412. http://dx.doi.org/10.1007/BF02233999

Jokinen, N. J. (2006). Family quality of life and older families. *Journal of Policy and Practice in Intellectual Disabilities, 3*(4), 246–252. https://doi.org/10.1111/j.1741-1130.2006.00086.x

Larson, S. A., Eschenbacher, H. J., Anderson, L. L., Taylor, B., Pettingell, S., Hewitt, A., Fay, M. L. (2017). *In-home and residential long-term supports and services for persons with intellectual or developmental disabilities: Status and trends through 2014*. University of Minnesota, Research and Training Center on Community Living, Institute on Community Integration. https://risp.umn.edu/publications

Lee, M., & Gardner, J. E. (2010). Grandparents' involvement and support in families with children with disabilities. *Educational Gerontology, 36*(6), 467–499. http://dx.doi.org/10.1080/03601270903212419

Li, A., Shaffer, J., & Bagger, J. (2015). The psychological well-being of disability caregivers: Examining the roles of family strain, family-to-work conflict, and perceived supervisor support. *Journal of Occupational Health Psychology, 20*(1), 40. https://doi.org/10.1037/a0037878

Lunsky, Y., Tint, A., Robinson, S., Gordeyko, M., & Kuntz, H. (2014). System-wide information about family carers of adults with intellectual/developmental disabilities—A scoping review of the literature. *Journal of Policy and Practice in Intellectual Disabilities, 11*(1), 8–18. https://doi.org/10.1111/jppi.12068

Magaña, S. M., Greenberg, J. S., & Seltzer, M. M. (2004). The health and well-being of black mothers who care for their adult children with schizophrenia. *Psychiatric Services, 55*(6), 711–713. https://doi.org/10.1176/appi.ps.55.6.711

Magaña, S., & Smith, M. J. (2006). Psychological distress and well-being of Latina and non-Latina white mothers of youth and adults with an autism spectrum disorder: Cultural attitudes towards coresidence status. *American Journal of Orthopsychiatry, 76*(3), 346–357. https://doi.org/10.1037/0002-9432.76.3.346

Magaña, S., & Smith, M. (2008). Health behaviors, service utilization and access to care among older mothers of color who have children with developmental disabilities. *Intellectual and Developmental Disabilities, 46*(4), 267–280. https://doi.org/10.1352/1934-9556(2008)46[267:HBSUAA]2.0.CO;2

McCallion, P., Janicki, M. P., Grant-Griffin, L., & Kolomer, S. R. (2000). Grandparent caregivers II: Service needs and service provision issues. *Journal of Gerontological Social Work, 33*(3), 63–90.

MetLife. (2011). *The MetLife study of caregiving costs to working caregivers: Double jeopardy for baby boomers caring for their parents*. MetLife Mature Market Institute. https://www.caregiving.org/wp-content/uploads/2011/06/mmi-caregiving-costs-working-caregivers.pdf

Namkung, E. H., Greenberg, J. S., & Mailick, M. R. (2016). Well-being of sibling caregivers: Effects of kinship relationship and race. *The Gerontologist, 57*(4), 626–636. https://doi.org/10.1093/geront/gnw008

National Alliance for Caregiving. (2009). *Caregiving in the U.S. 2009*. National Alliance for Caregiving. https://www.caregiving.org/wp-content/uploads/2020/05/Caregiving_in_the_US_2009_full_report.pdf

Neely-Barnes, S., Marcenko, M., & Weber, L. (2008). Does choice influence quality of life for people with mild intellectual disabilities? *Intellectual and Developmental Disabilities, 46*(1), 12–26. https://doi.org/10.1352/0047-6765(2008)46[12:DCIQOL]2.0.CO;2

Parish, S. L., Rose, R. A., & Swaine, J. G. (2010). Financial well-being of US parents caring for coresident children and adults with developmental disabilities: An age cohort analysis. *Journal of Intellectual and Developmental Disability, 35*(4), 235–243. https://doi.org/10.3109/13668250.2010.519331

Parish, S. L., Seltzer, M. M., Greenberg, J. S., & Floyd, F. J. (2004). Economic implications of caregiving at midlife: Comparing parents of children with developmental disabilities to other parents. *Mental Retardation, 42*(6), 413–426. https://doi.org/10.1352/0047-6765(2004)42<413:EIOCAM>2.0.CO;2

Perkins, E. A., & Haley, W. E. (2010). Compound caregiving: When lifelong caregivers undertake additional caregiving roles. *Rehabilitation Psychology, 55*(4), 409–417. https://doi.org/10.1037/a0021521

Piazza, V. E., Floyd, F. J., Mailick, M. R., & Greenberg, J. S. (2014). Coping and psychological health of aging parents of adult children with developmental disabilities. *American Journal on Intellectual and Developmental Disabilities, 119*(2), 186–198. https://doi.org/10.1352/1944-7558-119.2.186

Pinquart, M., & Sörensen, S. (2003). Differences between caregivers and noncaregivers in psychological health and physical health: A meta-analysis. *Psychology and Aging, 18*(2), 250–267. https://doi.org/10.1037/0882-7974.18.2.250

Pinquart, M., & Sörensen, S. (2007). Correlates of physical health of informal caregivers: A meta-analysis. *The Journals of Gerontology Series B: Psychological Sciences and Social Sciences, 62*(2), P126–P137. https://doi.org/10.1093/geronb/62.2.P126

Resch, J. A., Mireles, G., Benz, M. R., Grenwelge, C., Peterson, R., & Zhang, D. (2010). Giving parents a voice: A qualitative study of the challenges experienced by parents of children with disabilities. *Rehabilitation Psychology, 55*(2), 139–150. https://doi.org/10.1037/a0019473

Shogren, K. A. (2013). Considering context: An integrative concept for promoting outcomes in the intellectual disability field. *Intellectual and Developmental Disabilities, 51*(2), 132. https://doi.org/10.1352/1934-9556-51.2.132

Seltzer, M. M., Floyd, F., Song, J., Greenberg, J., & Hong, J. (2011). Midlife and aging parents of adults with intellectual and developmental disabilities: Impacts of lifelong parenting. *American Journal on Intellectual and Developmental Disabilities, 116*(6), 479–499. https://doi.org/10.1352/1944-7558-116.6.479

Spillman, B. C., & Long, S. K. (2007). *Does high caregiver stress lead to nursing home entry?*. Urban Institute. https://aspe.hhs.gov/system/files/pdf/74886/NHentry.pdf

Taggart, L., Truesdale-Kennedy, M., Ryan, A., & McConkey, R. (2012). Examining the support needs of ageing family carers in developing future plans for a relative with an intellectual disability. *Journal of Intellectual Disabilities, 16*(3), 217–234. https://doi.org/10.1177/1744629512456465

Totsika, V., Hastings, R. P., & Vagenas, D. (2017). Informal caregivers of people with an intellectual disability in England: Health, quality of life and impact of caring. *Health & Social Care in the Community, 25*(3), 951–961. https://doi.org/10.1111/hsc.12393

U.S. Census Bureau. (2018). American Community Survey: Selected social characteristics in the United States, Table DP02. https://data.census.gov/cedsci/table?y=2018&d=ACS%205-Year%20Estimates%20Data%20Profiles&tid=ACSDP5Y2018.DP02&hidePreview=true

Wingspread Family Support Summit. (March 6-8, 2011). Building a National Agenda for Supporting Families with a Member with Intellectual and Developmental Disabilities. https://www.aucd.org/docs/publications/wingspread2012_supporting_families.pdf

Yang, X., Artman-Meeker, K., & Roberts, C. A. (2018). Grandparents of children with intellectual and developmental disabilities: Navigating roles and relationships. *Intellectual and Developmental Disabilities, 56*(5), 354–373. https://doi.org/10.1352/1934-9556-56.5.354

Zuna, N., Summers, J. A., Turnbull, A. P., Hu, X., & Xu, S. (2010). Theorizing about family quality of life. In R. Kober (Ed.), *Enhancing the quality of life of people with intellectual disabilities* (pp. 241–278). Springer.

Acknowledgments

This chapter is funded by the National Institute on Disability, Independent Living and Rehabilitation Research, Administration for Community Living, grant # 90RT5012-01-03 to the Rehabilitation Research and Training Center on Developmental Disabilities and Health, and grant # 90RT5032-01-00 to the Family Support Research and Training Center, University of Illinois at Chicago. The contents of this article do not necessarily represent the policy of the US federal government.

Suggested Readings

Grossman, B. R., & Webb, C. E. (2016). Family support in late life: A review of the literature on aging, disability, and family caregiving. *Journal of Family Social Work, 19*(4), 348–395. https://doi.org/10.1080/10522158.2016.1233924

Heller, T., & Arnold, C. K. (2010). Siblings of adults with developmental disabilities: Psychosocial outcomes, relationships, and future planning. *Journal of Policy and Practice in Intellectual Disabilities, 7*, 16–25. https://doi.org/10.1111/j.1741-1130.2010.00243.x

Heller, T., Gibbons, H. M., & Fisher, D. (2015). Caregiving and family support interventions: Crossing networks of aging and developmental disabilities. *Intellectual and Developmental Disabilities, 53*(5), 329–345. https://doi.org/10.1352/1934-9556-53.5.329

Hewitt, A., Agosta, J., Heller, T., Williams, A. C., & Reinke, J. (2013). Families of individuals with intellectual and developmental disabilities: Policy, funding, services, and experiences. *Intellectual and Developmental Disabilities, 51*(5), 349–359. https://doi.org/10.1352/1934-9556-51.5.349

23
AGEING WITH INTELLECTUAL DISABILITY IN SWEDEN
Participation and Self Determination

Mia Jormfeldt and Magnus Tideman

Introduction

As in many other countries, the Swedish population is getting older (Socialstyrelsen – The National Board of Health and Welfare, 2016). By 2030, every fourth person in Sweden is estimated to be 65 or older. The expected increase in life expectancy also applies to people with intellectual disability who are more and more likely to live until later life (Coppus, 2013). This means that society's responsibilities to older adults with intellectual disability will need to increase in quantity and improve in quality.

Sweden has a history of being at the forefront of disability policies, and support and service to people with disability. The construction of the Swedish welfare system during the 20th century included raising the standard of living for people with disability. Special legislation that gave rights to individuals was introduced in the 1960s and was later combined with decisions to close institutions and replace them with housing and support within the community. Updated and expanded rights legislation came into force in 1994 and the closure of institutions was completed in 2003. In principle, this means that since the 1970s all children and young people with intellectual disability grow up with their parents, and as adults live in their own apartment or group home in the same residential areas as other citizens. Also, that older adults, who have spent most of their lives in an institution, now live in their own accommodation with support or in a group home.

Sweden has ratified the UN Convention on the Rights of Persons with Disability (Ds 2008:23, 2008). The Convention prescribes core areas such as health services, social security programmes, housing, and self-determination, which have a significant bearing on society's responsibilities to older adults with intellectual disability. Rules concerning support in Sweden are divided into two laws, the Social Services Act (SoL), which applies to all citizens and the Law Concerning Support and Services to Certain People with Disability (LSS) that give persons with disability certain 'extra' rights. Support measures under the Social Services Act shall, according to §1 'promote human economic and social security, equality and living conditions as well as active participation in society based upon democracy and solidarity'. Social services must, with respect to both their own and other people's social situations focus upon liberating and developing the individual's and groups' own resources. All actions are to be based upon respect for people's right to self-determination and integrity (SFS 2001:453, 2001). When actions according to SoL are not considered sufficient, the needs of persons with disability can be met through LSS. Support according to LSS shall 'promote equality in living conditions and full participation in social life [.......] and the goal required shall be that the individual is given the opportunity to live as others' (SFS 1993:387, 1993).

In the case of older persons, with or without disability, their support needs must primarily be met according to the Social Services Act through provision of ageing care, either via home care or in the form of a nursing home for older adults. It is home-help staff who carry out the support, which is organised as part of ageing care regardless of whether or not the person has an intellectual disability. In addition to personal care and cleaning, home care can provide daytime activities, meal on wheels and transportation services. Older people with intellectual disability can, when needed, additionally or instead receive support according to LSS. This might be support through accommodation in a group home or a personal assistant. In terms of support for older people with intellectual disability, the legal responsibility for assistance is thus twofold, they are entitled to help via SoL and if it is not enough also via LSS.

Both ageing care and disability care are financed through taxes and the individual pensioner pays fees for home care services based on income. Help through LSS is, in principle, free of charge, with the exception that the individual pays rent for living in a group home. Previously, in principle, all group homes were completely run by public authorities, with the municipalities being the main actor; however, a number are now being run by private actors (for detailed analysis and discussion see Meagher & Szebehely, 2013). Today, private companies account for more than 20% of non-disability ageing care and for almost 30% of disability care (National Board of Health and Welfare, 2017). The idea is that everyone should be able to choose whether they want private or municipal care, but in practice there are great differences in the possibilities for choice, especially in relation to place of residence. For older people with intellectual disability, choices, especially regarding group homes, are virtually non-existent (Urbas, Mineur, Arvidsson, & Tideman, 2015). There are few residences and what is offered is usually the only option.

Older Adults with Intellectual Disability in Sweden

The number of older people with intellectual disability in Sweden who receive support via LSS is increasing; however, knowledge of this growing group of older adults is very limited (SOU State Public Reports, 2008, p. 113). In 2017, there were 3,752 persons in Sweden over 65 (of whom 367 were over 80) with either developmental disorder, autism or an autism-like condition and who had some form of support according to LSS (National Board of Health and Welfare, 2017). There were slightly more men than women (52% men and 48% women, respectively). According to the National Board of Health and Welfare (2016), the largest increases have occurred in the age group 65 years and older. Between 2010 and 2014, this group increased by 16%. Housing with special services which, in principle, is available to everyone was the most common form of support among older people. There is, most likely, an unaccountable number of older people with mild intellectual disability who live in ordinary housing and can cope with everyday tasks themselves or with assistance via the Social Services Act (SFS 2001:453, 2001) or from relatives. The number of older people with intellectual disability who only have home help services according to SoL is not known since no statistics are available.

Current figures from the National Patient Register show a prevalence of 444 older persons (+55) with intellectual disability per 100,000 inhabitants (Ahlström, Sandberg, & Ng, 2016). This is 0.44% of the population, which is considered unrealistically low and shows that intellectual disability is not always documented in medical records. For many years, older persons with intellectual disability in Sweden have been 'invisible' in documents and policies in the field of ageing care. In the current national quality plan concerning care for older adults, older persons with intellectual disability were mentioned and the requirements needed for their support were discussed for the first time (SOU 2017:21, 2017). In particular, the need to strengthen skills of nursing staff and for more research was emphasised. It was found that scientific knowledge of what it means to age and live as an older person with intellectual disability and the best ways of designing support and service were very limited.

Current Research

Current Swedish research on living conditions and participation for older persons with intellectual disability concerns the group who live in group homes. The research is based on the perspectives of older adults and the staff about ageing and participation (Kåhlin, 2015), about opportunities and barriers in everyday life for self-determination for older people in group homes (Jormfeldt, 2016) as well as perspectives of managers and staff about healthy ageing of persons with intellectual disability (Johansson, 2017). In addition to these studies, there is also some register-based research on older people with intellectual disability from a health science or medical perspective, such as utilisation of health care services, causes of death, disease incidence and prevalence, and medication. The latter shows, for example, that older people with intellectual disability, in comparison with their peers in the general population, are more likely to have psychiatric diagnosis (Axmon, Björne, Nylander, & Ahlström, 2018a, 2018b), more likely to be prescribed antipsychotic medication (Axmon, Kristensson, Ahlström, & Midlöv, 2017) and people with mild or moderate intellectual disability were associated with higher chances of psychiatric diagnosis than people with severe or profound intellectual disability (Axmon et al., 2017). Overall, it can be concluded that Swedish research on older adults with intellectual disability and their living conditions as well as on society's efforts for this group is very limited, but that interest is growing as more and more people reach old age.

Participation and Self-Determination

The right to total participation and self-determination is strongly emphasised in Swedish society. For people with disability this is expressed in several laws (The Swedish Code of Statutes SFS 1993: 387; SFS 2001:453, 2001) and in international policy documents such as the UN Convention on the Rights of Persons with Disability (Ds 2008:23, 2008). This chapter focuses on participation and self-determination for older persons with intellectual disability with a focus on everyday life in group homes and the areas that emerge in Swedish research as important to improve possibilities for group's participation and self-determination.

Older Adult Perspectives of Ageing and Participation

Older adults with intellectual disability in Sweden today belong to the last generation with experience of living in large institutions and, thus, largely have had different experiences of self-determination and participation than younger persons with intellectual disability. Having grown up and lived in the institutions has meant a life of limited experience in exercising self-determination (Andersson, 2011). These large institutions, where many of today's older people with intellectual disability have spent most of their lives, can be likened to what Goffman (1961/2004) calls 'total institutions'. Places where staff controlled all activities which generally occurred in groups and where self-determination was virtually non-existent.

Older people with intellectual disability experience similar ageing related health conditions as persons without intellectual disability. Questions are raised about what support older people in Sweden get when handling issues such as ageing, failing abilities and diseases, deaths in the family as well as about their own inevitable death. Kåhlin (2015) shows that there are differences between how ageing is perceived by the staff of the group homes and older people themselves. The staff describe ageing mainly as physical changes in the body, while older adults themselves have broader perspectives about ageing. Older people also speak not only about the noticeable physical changes of ageing, such as wrinkles and grey hair, but also mental changes in the form of fatigue and reduced motivation to do things (Kåhlin, Kjellberg, Nord, & Hagberg, 2013). Older adults describe an adaptation of activities, which activities are possible to perform and where they can be performed (Jormfeldt, 2016; Kåhlin et al., 2013). This is due not only to fatigue and a reduced motivation but also an increased dependence on support to be able to perform desired activities (Kåhlin et al., 2013). The absence of simple aids such as glasses or difficulty in finding the, is also described as something that complicates participation (Jormfeldt, 2016; Kåhlin et al., 2013).

In order to support participation and self-determination of older adults in the best possible way, knowledge of both experiences of ageing and the more positive aspects, highlighted by the older people themselves, is required. Some argue that ageing has given them knowledge and experience that has made them more competent, which has led to an increased involvement and participation in activities as well as having found new areas of interest to become involved in. Ageing also means, according to older adults themselves, possibilities of becoming increasingly similar to ageing non-disabled people (Kåhlin et al., 2013). Those who have lived a life without disability become increasingly dependent upon the support of others in the latter part of their lives in the same way that people with intellectual disability have often been dependent throughout their lives.

Staff and Managers' Perspectives Concerning Ageing and Participation

Several different aspects affect older people's participation and possibilities for self-determination. In the context of the group homes, in addition to the individual's characteristics such as the severity of intellectual disability, previous life experience and the consequences of ageing, these include the physical design of the residence and adaptation to the needs of the ageing person. Furthermore, there is knowledge of and access to support technology/aids and the necessary support to use them. Finally, the attitude of the staff (and relatives) and the organisational aspects of the group home are influential. The most common way to consider older adults' possibilities for self-determination is expressed through interaction with the staff in everyday situations.

Knowledge about ageing is often lacking in staff who work in disability care. The opposite applies to staff within the non-disability ageing care; they usually lack knowledge of intellectual disability (SOU State Public Reports, 2017: 21). One of the group homes in Jormfeldt's study (2016) is located in a retirement home consisting of six wards. Two wards were for older people with intellectual disability. The criterion for moving into this accommodation is that the person is in need of help and supervision at night or has medical needs that are difficult to meet in a 'regular' group home. Half of the staff at these group homes are required to have education or experience in disability care and half are required to have education or experience from non-disability ageing care. The idea is that they will, thus, complement each other in terms of competence. When the staff themselves talk about education, they state that they have not received much further education since they started their basic education. Staff agree upon what sort of education they require – more knowledge of mental impairments and, in some cases, dementia in persons with intellectual disability (Jormfeldt, 2016).

Management and staff describe the ageing of people with intellectual disability mainly from a physical and mental perspective (Johansson, Björne, Runesson, & Ahlström, 2017; Kåhlin, Kjellberg, & Hagberg, 2016). They see that older adults become more dependent upon staff the older they become and that healthy ageing requires taking into account the wishes of older adults and the competence of staff to make decisions (Johansson et al., 2017). According to staff neither they, nor the older people, speak about the importance of ageing and its consequences. The staff believe that it is more important for older people to be regarded as adults and that the persons with intellectual disability live more in the present and find it difficult to imagine or consider the future and the consequences of ageing (Kåhlin et al., 2016). An explanation for staff's opinions may be that people with intellectual disability tend not to be associated with the characteristics that characterise different age groups, i.e. childhood, youth, and adult life. They are deprived of the indicators that signify different phases of life and according to Priestley (2003) and Sandvin (2008) disability overshadows everything else in the individual's life. Another example is that many people with intellectual disability risk being regarded as 'eternal children' (Bjarnason, 2005) throughout their lives and, thus, never thought of as adults. One consequence of this is that they are not considered 'older adults'. The few occasions when ageing was discussed in the group homes were mostly about changes in the residents' health conditions. These were changes that affected the work of the staff (Kåhlin et al., 2016) who had to be prepared for deterioration in residents health or ability to communicate and associated increasing support.

Ageing is an important factor that impacts on the ability to participate and experience self-determination; based on the fact that it is increasingly difficult to carry out activities on one's own. Over people become more and more dependent upon the staff and the staff's approaches, commitment, and knowledge. Managers of group homes and adult day care centres believe that self-determination and the possibility to make independent choices are important for healthy ageing to be experienced (Johansson, 2017). Staff are also important in interpreting and understanding the choices and desires of older people especially when their verbal communication ability is limited. Lack of knowledge regarding the older adult's own experiences of ageing and its consequences can lead to the staff having too high and sometimes too low expectations of the older person's competence and wishes.

Access or lack of access to assistive support aids is also something that affects not only the opportunity to participate in activities but also the opportunity to stay informed (Jormfeldt, 2016). Failure to provide adequate aids, for example, proper glasses can result in 'losing' previous abilities. If a person has been used to reading the newspaper and watching TV, the lack of proper glasses can lead to an individual becoming less inclined to stay informed and using their reading ability, which may over time disappear. When testing support aids such as glasses and hearing aids, time, knowledge, and information are needed to get older adults to participate as much as possible (Johansson, 2017).

The Importance of Housing for Participation and Self-Determination

Housing with special services (commonly known as group homes) is the most common form of housing for adults and older persons with intellectual disability in Sweden. Those who live in a group home today have their own apartment with one or two rooms, kitchen and bathroom. There are common areas such as a shared kitchen and living room. The group home also contains areas for the staff such as offices and overnight rooms.

The National Board of Health and Welfare (2011/2018) has stipulated that a group home should contain 3–5 apartments. This was changed after a ruling by the Supreme Administrative Court of Sweden 2007 stating that as a maximum of six people may live in a group home (Socialstyrelsen, 2011). Today, however, there are examples of larger group homes (this is also a trend in the other Nordic countries, Tössebro et al., 2012). In a recent study in Sweden (Johansson et al., 2017), group homes with 6–8 residents are described and Kåhlin (2015) describes group homes where between 6 and 9 people live.

In a group home there must be access to staff 24/7. Another form of special accommodation is an assisted living residence. Those who live there usually have a higher degree of independence than those who live in group homes. What mainly distinguishes a group home from an assisted living residence is the number of apartments that are included in the unit. In an assisted living residence, the number of apartments is more and they can be designed in different ways. They can be located in an 'ordinary' apartment building or in a detached building. They usually have an apartment that provides some common areas.

The possibilities for participation and self-determination are influenced by an older person's own abilities as well as their living arrangements (Jormfeldt, 2016; Kåhlin, 2015). For example, physical environments of group home, particularly common areas are often perceived as poorly adapted for older residents (Kåhlin, 2015). They are described as cramped and not suitable for the use of walkers and wheelchairs that older residents may need. Group homes may be located on the second floor of a building with access only by means of narrow stairs or small lifts For older persons who require walking frames or wheelchairs for mobility, this means that they spend more time inside the four walls of the group home as more support is required from the staff before they can actually get outside (Kåhlin, 2015. Group homes may also be on two floors with no lift to second floor apartments. While ageing care recipients who live on the second floor can be moved to a more adapted accommodation if they find it difficult to walk up and down the stairs, such a move may not be their preference.

When people with intellectual disability age, they become increasingly dependent upon staff whose attitude can be crucial for where older adults spend their time. Jormfeldt (2016) shows that there are organisational prerequisites concerning how much support the staff can give for activities outside the group home. When older persons become more mobile thanks to support aids, more staff are required to go out with them, while at the same time, it is often necessary that some staff remain in the group home.

Participation and Self-Determination: The Importance of Interaction

This part of the chapter is based upon a study which focussed on possibilities and obstacles for older people's participation and self-determination (Jormfeldt, 2016). Through observations in three group homes, situations were identified where self-determination (and its opposite) took place in the interaction with staff. These situations were video recorded and the analysis was based upon Goffman's interaction order (Goffman, 1967/2005, 1983).

Participation and self-determination deal with a complex interaction between different factors. It is influenced by age, past experiences, capacity and willingness to decide for oneself and the situation. From an interactionist perspective, the environment has great significance. Staff are the most important environmental element in a group home context, the support they provide and in which way it is given. Self-determination for older people with intellectual disability is not just about being able to decide upon issues of importance, such as where to live and with whom, but also about more basic everyday decisions such as what to eat or what clothes to buy (Jormfeldt, 2016). Analysis of the interaction between care recipients and staff at group homes showed that self-determination is not something that is clear-cut and stable. Rather, it can be understood as a continuum from self-determination to paternalism with some v events, interactions and actions closer to one or the other side of the continuum, or, midway between these two end-points. As the following examples illustrate, the result is, therefore, self-determination, paternalism, and self-determination between the extremes.

Self-Determination

Hasse is 71 years old and, besides having a moderate level of intellectual disability, also has communication difficulties and mobility disability. His most important project is to go out into the immediate area in his electric wheelchair. It is something that Hasse does most of the day. It is only when the weather is too bad that he stays at home. The fact that Hasse, despite having a considerable physical impairment, can independently go out is dependent upon partly the season, but also the availability of assistive aids. When it is winter, he needs help with dressing (footmuff, jacket, hat, and gloves) and due to his restrictions requires help for this from a member of staff. If the staff are busy helping one of the other residents, he has to wait until they have time. In the summer, however, Hasse can go out without such garments when the weather permits. He has an electric door opener in the form of a button on his wheelchair table (aid) which means that he is independent of the staff's help to open the front door and can go out whenever he wants. Hasse creates new social relationships when he goes out. In this way, he has come to know some people in the immediate area that he sometimes associates with. He can also let visitors into his apartment by using the door opener.

Another example of self-determination is buying food where Hasse chooses between different varieties of, for example, cheese, bread, cakes or apples. When it comes to apples, he also chooses the variety and how many apples he wants to buy. This is possible because Karin S (S = staff) asks, shows and informs him about the different varieties, their texture and how they taste. This happens every time Hasse makes food purchases. Therefore, Hasse is usually seen as a competent and selective person who can make his own choices.

Paternalism

The following example is an illustration of how paternalism is expressed in the interaction between a care recipient and staff. The example is from the transcription of a video recorded in a store where Hasse, with the help of the staff Karin S, is going to buy the blue t-shirts that he uses when he sleeps.

Hasse usually communicates through speech synthesiser with images on the computer that he points to. On this occasion, Hasse does not have the computer with him as it is being repaired; therefore, Hasse has to communicate with gestures and some sounds.

In the beginning of the situation, Karin S is busy finding the right size of blue t-shirts that Hasse needs to purchase. She has, at times, her back turned to Hasse and is busy looking in the piles of shirts that are folded on a shelf. Karin S stands in an aisle between two shelves. It is a narrow aisle where Hasse cannot drive in with his electric wheelchair, which results in him being stuck in a larger area between the different aisles. The distance between Hasse and Karin S is approximately two meters and what happens next is that Hasse tries to catch Karin S's attention.

1. (Hasse lifts his right arm and pulls at his sleeve at the same time he says Er. Er. and looks at Karin S)
2. KS: *There's one, we will have to take S* (small)
3. (KS stands and looks for the correct size among the different garments. She is out of the view of the camera and partly has her back turned to Hasse. It is only her voice that can be heard)
4. (KS is now back in view)
5. (H continues to put his arm on his sleeve and says)
6. H: *Er...Er.*
7. (KS looks up from pile of shirts, looks Hasse in the eyes and says,)
8. KS: *But you don't need any long-sleeved shirts, do you?* ((same time as she bends down and starts looking through the shirts))
9. H: *Yah*
10. KS: *Do you need long-sleeve shirts...there is L* (large)
11. KS: *Where were they now...yah, here they are*
12. KS: *one, two, three, four...we can get these*
13. (KS turns to Hasse and says)
14. KS: *four T-shirts for sleeping?*
15. (Hasse doesn't reply. He looks down at his sleeve. Karin nods and goes towards the till where Hasse follows)

In the above example, it is Hasse who initiates the decision making by showing that he wants something. The physical distance is relatively large and there is no 'taking turns' in the first part of the interaction (lines 1–4). Karin S speaks to herself. When Hasse, at his second attempt, succeeds in catching Karin's attention for a short while, the interaction becomes somewhat more focused and a short period of 'a two-way communication' occurs (lines 5–10). This is broken by Karin S when she returns to looking among the shirts while, at the same time, talking to herself. Karin S gives Hasse a brief moment of attention but without going into any real discussion. When Hasse is not heard, he repeats the wish until he catches Karin's attention, but Hasse has no explanation to why he cannot buy a long-sleeved shirt.

Distancing oneself from interaction can be done in a visible and direct way via actions of the physical body or parts of it (Goffman, 1967/2005). When Hasse looks down and does not answer Karin's question at the end (lines 14 and 15) it can be interpreted as being a reaction and not wanting to participate in any interaction. At the same time, he denies Karin's acceptance of her interpretation of the situation by not responding. He creates a distance to what is going on and one interpretation is that he gave up in his attempts to achieve his wishes. Hasse's wishes are ignored and he does not show any further interest in the events taking place and the purchases are then made without his involvement. It is Karin S who has the power of the situation and makes the decisions concerning what to buy.

Self-Determination between the Extremes

Ellen is 81 years old and has a mild to moderate level of intellectual disability. She communicates verbally. Previously, she could read and write but now her vision has deteriorated, and she says she can no longer do it. She usually needs support from a member of staff when she moves around indoors.

Outdoors she uses a wheelchair. The following example takes place late afternoon at the group home. Ellen sits in her armchair with her hands in front of her face and the television is on. Staff member Sofia S enters the kitchen. Sofia S stops and reads the menu that hangs on the refrigerator.

In the transcript below, the arrow indicates that something is said in an elevated pitch or intonation (which indicates a question, but it is not necessary so).

1. Sofia S: *pancakes for supper this evening Ellen*↑
2. (Ellen takes her hands away from her face when she answers Sofie S)
3. Ellen: *No, I don't want that*
4. SS: *You don't* ↑ *What do you want then*↑
5. E: *Porridge*
6. SS: *Porridge* ↑ *What sort of porridge*↑
7. E: *Rice pudding*
8. SS: *Rice pudding, there is some here so that should be OK.*
9. (Kajsa S comes into the kitchen)
10. SS: *(she wants) rice pudding*
11. (Kajsa S puts down her cup of coffee on the kitchen table and turns to Sofia S. Kajsa S whispers something that cannot be heard on film)
12. (Sofia S walks from the kitchen area, sighs and walks towards Ellen)
13. Kajsa S: *It doesn't say that it is for another day either*
14. SS: *No, do you fancy rice pudding then Ellen*
15. Kajsa S: *So, it's OK with Santa's porridge*[1] *then*
16. E: *Santa's porridge*↑
17. SP: *Yes*

Ellen and Sofia S share the same definition of the situation as they have the goal of finding out what Ellen wants for supper. When Sofia S informs Ellen about the menu for the evening, she does not offer Ellen any choice, but Ellen perceives it as a question. She can answer yes or no to the question which cannot be considered a real choice as a real choice means a minimum of two options (Stancliffe, 2001). When Ellen replies that she does not want pancakes, she initiates a partially new situation. When Sofia answers Ellen's statement, a focused conversation arises (Goffman, 1967/2005). Because Sofia S asks open questions, Ellen is given choices. She can in the first stage wish any dish she wants and when she wants to have porridge, she is offered more options in the form of which kind of porridge she would like to have. In line 8, Sofia expresses that, after all, there is one condition for Ellen's choice when she says, 'Rice pudding, there is some here so that should be OK'.

Had there not already been some ready-made rice pudding available, Ellen would, most likely, not have been able to have it, and made to choose something else. This means that Ellen's choice must fit into the current routine of the group home. This is in line with how Harnett (2010) describes how older persons have the greatest opportunity to get their wishes met if they know it fits into the routines of the ageing care home.

To summarise, there are differences in the situations described. In situations where self-determination was strongly noticeable, actions were characterised by a focused interaction of a two-way dialogue of words/sounds as well as gestures and looks. The participants were close to each other and both focused on reaching the desired goal. The situations were also characterised by the participants defining the current event in the same way and, if the common definition was threatened, both resident and staff made efforts to return to the original definition (Goffman, 1967/2005). In the situations characterised by paternalism, as in the example of the long-sleeved shirt, there was no common focus on the situation.

Between the extremes of self-determination and paternalism there are a number of situations where these opposites are not so clear-cut. In these situations, the individual makes decisions based on a limited number of choices. The person is offered or asked about their own personal wishes, i.e. the initiative or desire is expressed by someone else but the individual is given the opportunity to choose (within certain limits).

When the member of staff shows and informs about the alternative possibilities and choices, the stronger the care recipient's self-determination is. The situations between the extremes of self-determination and paternalism have traits of negotiation, conditions and a common or shared way of making decisions. These situations were commonplace in all group homes and for older persons with intellectual disability. If they had themselves initiated a decision-making situation by expressing their wishes, some form of negotiation often took place. It was common for the staff to initiate the situations and then it was about asking for requests or offering options, but this was often a request to which the care recipient could only reply yes or no.

Conclusion

Citizens' rights to participation and self-determination are strongly emphasised in today's Swedish society and is particularly relevant in disability policy discussions. The UN Convention on the Rights of Persons with Disability (Ds 2008:23, 2008) has strengthened this as a central goal for society's efforts in the area of disability. However, despite this, there are still significant shortcomings in the possibility of participation and self-determination for both younger and older persons with intellectual disability. The limited research available shows that staff are an importance influence determining the possibilities and conditions for participation and self-determination for older adults (Jormfeldt, 2016; Kåhlin, 2015).

In recent years, the issue of requirements for formal competence of staff in the form of a higher level of education has been discussed as a way to increase the quality of work with people with intellectual disability (Dunér & Olin, 2011) and, thereby, improve participation and self-determination. Today, there are no formal requirements for education in order to work in Sweden with older people with intellectual disability. It would be an important part of a professionalisation process within the field of disability to require a specific level of education about disability. An increased professionalisation and competence of staff working with older adults with intellectual disability is believed to increase the quality of treatment and care; however, this also risks further strengthening the staff's position of power in relation to the care recipients (Waerness, 1984).

Many of the growing proportion of older people in society have good health, good finances, and live active lives. As society focuses its interest on this resource-rich group, often referred to as the third age, older people with intellectual disability risk further marginalisation. In the wake of reforms that emphasise choice and 'all older adults' want to live by themselves and are conscientious consumers, the focus is moved even further away from the groups with disadvantaged economic and social conditions or who have functional limitations. Creating dignified and good living conditions for older adults with intellectual disability is not high on the political agenda. The lack of political interest has been made clear during the increasingly rigorous and restrictive interpretation and application of current legislation in recent years, which, in turn, has made it more difficult to get the support people with disability need.

Research and experience show considerable shortcomings in participation and self-determination for older people in their everyday lives which makes it difficult to participate and experience self-determination in other contexts, such as choosing where to live or exercise democratic rights to vote in elections. As more and more people with intellectual disability live longer, more scientific knowledge and service system developments are required to ensure the right to self-determination and full participation for everyone.

Note

1 Santa's porridge is another name for rice pudding in Sweden.

References

Ahlström, G., Sandberg, M., & Ng, N. (2016). Aging with intellectual disability: A prevalence study of older people in Sweden. *Journal of Intellectual Disability Research*, 60(7–8), 628–628. https://doi.org/10.1111/jir.12305

Andersson, O. (2011). *Den tredje kraften: Om påverkanskrafter under avvecklingsprocessen av de svenska vårdhemmen för personer med utvecklingsstörning* [The third force: On influencing forces during the decommissioning process of the Swedish nursing homes for people with intellectual disabilities]. Halmstad: Högskolan i Halmstad, Sektionen för hälsa och samhälle (HOS), Centrum för forskning om välfärd, hälsa och idrott (CVHI), Wigforss-gruppen [Halmstad University, School of Social and Health Sciences (HOS), Center for Research on Welfare, Health and Sport (CVHI), the Wigforss group]. http://hh.diva-portal.org/smash/get/diva2:482616/FULLTEXT01.pdf

Bjarnason, D. S. (2005). Students voices: How does education in Iceland prepare young disabled people for adulthood? *Scandinavian Journal of Disability Research*, 7(2), 109–128. https://doi.org/10.1080/15017410510032217

Coppus, A. M. (2013). People with intellectual disability: What do we know about adulthood and life expectancy? *Developmental Disability Research Reviews*, 18(1), 6–16. https://doi.org/10.1002/ddrr.1123

Ds 2008:23. (2008). FN:s konvention om rättigheter för personer med funktionsnedsättning, Ds 2008:23 [UN Convention on the rights of persons with disabilities]. https://www.regeringen.se/rattsliga-dokument/departementsserien-och-promemorior/2008/04/ds-200823/

Dunér, A., & Olin, E. (2011). En begynnande professionalisering? Om gränsarbete och kompetenskrav inom funktionshinderverksamhet och äldreomsorg [A beginning professionalization? About boundary work and competence requirements in the area of disability and elderly care]. *Socialvetenskaplig tidskrift [Social Science Journal]*, 4, 336–353. https://journals.lub.lu.se/svt/article/view/15722

Goffman, E. (1961/2004). *Totala institutioner* [Total institutions]. P.A. Nordstedt & Söner.

Goffman, E. (1967/2005). *Interaction ritual. Essays in face-to-face behavior*. Aldine Transaction Publishers.

Goffman, E. (1983). The interaction order. *American Sociological Review*, 48, 1–17. http://links.jstor.org/sici?sici=0003-1224%28198302%2948%3A1%3C1%3ATIOASA%3E2.0.CO%3B2-X

Harnett, T. (2010). Seeking exemptions from nursing home routines: Residents' everyday influence attempts and institutional order. *Journal of Aging Studies*, 24(4), 292–301. https://doi.org/10.1016/j.jaging.2010.08.001

Johansson, M. (2017). *Åldrande hos personer med intellektuell funktionsnedsättning – ur ledares perspektiv* [Aging in people with intellectual disabilities – From a leader's perspective. [PhD, Lund University, Faculty of Medicine]. https://portal.research.lu.se/ws/files/35070811/_ldrande_hos_personer_med_intellektuell_funktionsneds_ttning.pdf

Johansson, M., Björne, P., Runesson, I., & Ahlström, G. (2017). Healthy ageing in people with intellectual disabilities from managers' perspective: A qualitative study. *Healthcare*, 5(3), 45. https://doi.org/10.3390/healthcare5030045

Jormfeldt, M. (2016). *Tid, rum och självbestämmande: Möjligheter och hinder i vardagen för äldre personer med intellektuell funktionsnedsättning på gruppboende* [Time, space and self-determination: Opportunities and obstacles in everyday life for older people with intellectual disabilities on group housing]. Doktorsavhandling, Högskolan i Jönköping, Hälsohögskolan [PhD, Jönköping University, School of Health]. http://hj.diva-portal.org/smash/record.jsf?pid=diva2%3A1045873&dswid=-4703

Kåhlin, I. (2015). *Delaktig (även) på äldre dar: åldrande och delaktighet bland personer med intellektuell funktionsnedsättning som bor i gruppbostad* [Participating (even) in older days: aging and participation among persons with intellectual disabilities living in group housing]. Doktorsavhandling, Linköpings universitet. Institutionen för samhälls- och välfärdsstudier [PhD, Linköping University, Department of Social and Welfare Studies]. http://liu.diva-portal.org/smash/record.jsf?pid=diva2%3A781377&dswid=-4703

Kåhlin, I., Kjellberg, A., & Hagberg, J.-E. (2016). Ageing in people with intellectual disability as it is understood by group home staff. *Journal of Intellectual & Developmental Disability*, 41(1), 1–10. https://doi.org/10.3109/13668250.2015.1094038

Kåhlin, I., Kjellberg, A., Nord, C., & Hagberg, J.-E. (2013). Lived experiences of ageing and later life in older people with intellectual disability. *Ageing & Society*, 1–27. http://www.diva-portal.org/smash/get/diva2:620635/FULLTEXT01.pdf

Meagher, G., & Szebehely, M. (Eds.). (2013). *Marketisation in Nordic eldercare: a research report on legislation, oversight, extent and consequences* [Marketisation in Nordic eldercare: a research report on legislation, oversight, extent and consequences] (Stockholm Studies in Social Work 30), Stockholm University. https://www.mq.edu.au/about/about-the-university/faculties-and-departments/faculty-of-arts/departments-and-centres/department-of-sociology/documents/Marketisation-in-nordic-eldercare-webbversion-med-omslag1.pdf

Priestley, M. (2003). *Disability. A life course approach*. Blackwell Publishing.

Sandvin, J. T. (2008). Ålder och funktionhinder. In I. Söder, & M. Grönvik (Eds.), *Bara funktionshindrad. Funktionhinder och intersektionalitet*. Malmö: Gleerups Utbildning [Age and disability. In M. Söder & L. Grönvik (Eds.), *Only disabled: Disability and intersectionality*. Malmö: Gleerups Education].

SFS 1993:387. (1993). *Lagen om stöd och service till vissa funktionshindrade* [The Act on support and service for some disabled people]. Stockholm, Socialdepartementet [Stockholm, Ministry of Social Affairs]. https://www.riksdagen.se/sv/dokument-lagar/dokument/svensk-forfattningssamling/lag-1993387-om-stod-och-service-till-vissa_sfs-1993-387

SFS 2001:453. (2001). *Socialtjänstlagen* [The Social Services Act]. Stockholm, Socialdepartementet [Stockholm, Ministry of Social Affairs]. https://www.riksdagen.se/sv/dokument-lagar/dokument/svensk-forfattningssamling/socialtjanstlag-2001453_sfs-2001-453

Socialstyrelsen [National Board of Health and Welfare]. (2016). *Vård och omsorg om äldre – lägesrapport 2016* [Care for the elderly – Progress report 2016]. Stockholm, Socialstyrelsen [Stockholm, The National Board of Health and Welfare]. http://www.anhoriga.se/Global/Nyheter/Nyhetsdokument%202016/VardOmsorgOmAldre_lagesrapport_2016.pdf

Socialstyrelsen [National Board of Health and Welfare]. (2011). *Bostad med särskild service och daglig verksamhet. En forskningsöversikt. [Gouphomes and daily activities. A literature review]*. Stockholm: Socialstyrelsen.

Socialstyrelsen [National Board of Health and Welfare]. (2017). *Vård och omsorg om äldre. Lägesrapport 2017* [Care for the elderly – Progress report 2017]. Stockholm, Socialstyrelsen [Stockholm, The National Board of Health and Welfare]. https://www.socialstyrelsen.se/globalassets/sharepoint-dokument/artikelkatalog/ovrigt/2017-2-2.pdf

Socialstyrelsen [National Board of Health and Welfare]. (2018). *Bostad med särskild service för vuxna enligt LSS* [Housing with special service for adults according to LSS]. Stockholm, Socialstyrelsen. [Stockholm, The National Board of Health and Welfare]. https://www.socialstyrelsen.se/globalassets/sharepoint-dokument/artikelkatalog/handbocker/2018-6-12.pdf

SOU 2008:113. (2008). *Bo bra hela livet* [Stay well all your life]. Stockholm, Socialdepartementet. [Stockholm, Ministry of Social Affairs]. https://www.regeringen.se/rattsliga-dokument/statens-offentliga-utredningar/2008/12/sou-2008113/

SOU 2017:21. (2017). *Nationell kvalitetsplan för vård och omsorg om äldre personer* [National quality plan for care and care for the elderly]. Stockholm, Socialdepartementet [Stockholm, Ministry of Social Affairs]. https://www.regeringen.se/rattsliga-dokument/statens-offentliga-utredningar/2017/03/sou-201721/

Stancliffe, R. J. (2001). Living with support in the community: Predictors of choice and self-determination. *Mental Retardation and Developmental Disabilities Research Reviews*, 7(2), 91–98.

Tøssebro, J, Bonfils, I, S, Teittinen, A, Tideman, M, Traustadottir, R & Vesala, H (2012). Normalization Fifty Years Beyond – Current Trends in the Nordic Countries. *Journal of Policy and Practice in Intellectual Disabilities*, 9, 2, pp. 134-146.

Urbas, A., Mineur, T., Arvidsson, J., & Tideman, M. (2015). Valfrihetssystem inom primärvården och personer med intellektuell funktionsnedsättning – en kunskapsöversikt [Election system in primary care and people with intellectual disabilities – A knowledge overview]. *Nordisk Administrativ Tidsskrift [Nordic Administrative Journal]*, 2(95), 19–36. https://www.diva-portal.org/smash/get/diva2:865718/FULLTEXT01.pdf

Waerness, K. (1984). The rationality of caring. *Economic and Industrial Democracy*, 5, 185–211.

Suggested Readings

Harnett, T. (2010). Seeking exemptions from nursing home routines: Residents' everyday influence attempts and institutional order. *Journal of Aging Studies*, 24(4), 292–301. https://doi.org/10.1016/j.jaging.2010.08.001

Johansson, M., Björne, P., Runesson, I., & Ahlström, G. (2017). Healthy ageing in people with intellectual disabilities from managers' perspective: A qualitative study. *Healthcare*, 5(3), 45. https://doi.org/10.3390/healthcare5030045

Priestley, M. (2003). *Disability. A life course approach*. Blackwell Publishing.

United Nations. (2008). *Convention on the rights of persons with disabilities*. United Nations. https://www.un.org/development/desa/disabilities/convention-on-the-rights-of-persons-with-disabilities.html

24

TOWARDS UNTANGLING THE AGEING RIDDLE IN PEOPLE WITH INTELLECTUAL DISABILITIES

An Overview of Research on Frailty and Its Consequences

Josje D. Schoufour, Dederieke Maes-Festen, Alyt Oppewal, and Heleen M. Evenhuis

Frailty as a Measure of Ageing in the General Population

One of the biggest challenges Western society is currently facing is the shift in age distribution towards older age groups. These trends are accompanied by a greater burden of chronic diseases, social isolation, hospitalisation, disabilities, and healthcare costs. Research is required to better understand the process of ageing and methods to preserve health as long as possible. Several methods have been proposed to study ageing and age-related conditions. One such method is frailty. Frailty is the accumulation of age-related conditions in many physiological systems that eventually lead to increased vulnerability to adverse health outcomes including falls, disabilities, hospitalisation, and mortality (Clegg, Young, Iliffe, Rikkert, & Rockwood, 2013). Frailty has been shown a very useful concept in research to study ageing and has even been proposed a measure for biological age (Mitnitski et al., 2015). In the general population, the interest in frailty has led to increased knowledge about the risk factors and consequences of frailty, resulting in a broad range of screening instruments and preventative strategies. For example, an incredible amount of knowledge has been gathered about lifestyle factors that contribute to frailty leading to interventions aiming to prevent or slow onset (Apóstolo et al., 2018; Brinkman et al., 2018; Tieland, Trouwborst, & Clark, 2018). Furthermore, several screening instruments are being used in among others in hospitals to identify frail older adults (Rocha, Marmelo, Leite-Moreira, & Moreira-Gonçalves, 2017; Theou, Campbell, Malone, & Rockwood, 2018; Walston, Buta, & Xue, 2018).

Frailty can be measured using different operationalisations and methods. The two most frequently used approaches internationally to measure frailty (Bouillon et al., 2013) are the frailty 'phenotype' developed by Fried and colleagues (Fried et al., 2001), and the frailty index developed by Rockwood and Mitnitski (Mitnitski, Mogilner, & Rockwood, 2001). The frailty phenotype is based on five clinical core features (unintended weight loss, weakness, slowness, low physical activity, and poor endurance or exhaustion). People with at least three of these features are defined as frail, people with one or two are considered pre-frail and people with none are called robust. In contrast, the frailty index is a quantitative measure of frailty, based on non-specific accumulation of health impairments, also called deficits. These deficits can be symptoms, signs, diseases, disabilities, or laboratory data (Mitnitski et al., 2001; Rockwood, Abeysundera, & Mitnitski, 2007). Although the content of a frailty index is flexible, deficits need to adhere to several rules to be included in it. A deficit can only be included if (1) The deficit can be considered an aspect of health (2) The deficit is associated with age (3) The deficit does not saturate too early or is very rare (4) Together, the deficits must cover different health aspects and (5) At least 20–30 deficits must be included (Middleton, Kirkland, Mitnitski, & Rockwood, 2010; Mitnitski et al., 2001). In addition to these commonly used operationalisations of frailty, many others exist. They differ in content but all aim to identify people at risk for deterioration of health.

Frailty as a Measure of Ageing in People with Intellectual Disabilities

There is a lack of comprehensive insight into the effect of ageing on health and independence of people with ID (Reppermund & Trollor, 2016). Although premature ageing and its genetic basis have been established in people with Down syndrome (Horvath et al., 2015), there is little evidence indicating a more rapid ageing process in those with other causes of ID. Frailty could be a very useful method to better understand the ageing process of people with ID to understand if they experience premature ageing.

Methods to measure frailty from the general population may not be applied to older adults with ID. Indeed, given the characteristics of the population of older adults with ID, it could be that when you apply a diagnostic measure developed for the general population, the majority of people with ID would be found frail. In that case, frailty would not appear to be a distinctive concept in this population. Additionally, the relationship between frailty and age-related disability, intensively discussed for the general older population (Fried, Ferrucci, Darer, Williamson, & Anderson, 2004; Theou, Rockwood, Mitnitski, & Rockwood, 2012), seems even more complicated for a population with lifelong disabilities. Where disabilities are life-long they are more likely to result in frailty than be a result of frailty, as is usually the case in the general population (Abellan van Kan et al., 2008; Fried et al., 2004; Theou et al., 2012).

Although frailty measures from the general population cannot be simply implemented in people with ID, several research groups used the frailty approach to better understand ageing in people with ID. In this chapter we review the approaches that were applied, how the results help to better understand ageing and frailty in this population and discuss future research directions (Figure 24.1). More specifically, within this chapter we will address the following questions:

1. Is it feasible to measure frailty in older adults with ID?
2. How frail are older people with ID compared to older people from the general population?
3. Does frailty predict deterioration of health and (relative) independence in the same way as it does in the general population?
4. Which characteristics are associated with frailty?
5. Which recommendations can be made for future research and clinical practice?

Is It Feasible to Measure Frailty in Older People with ID and How Frail Are People with ID Compared to People from the General Population?

Until now, three measures of frailty have been applied in the ID population. First, Brehmer and Weber investigated frailty in older people with ID. They developed an experience-based questionnaire specially for people with ID that classified over a quarter (27%) of 50 included adults aged 50 years and over as frail (Brehmer-Rinderer, Zeilinger, Radaljevic, & Weber, 2013). This scale has not yet been validated in terms of predictive value for adverse health outcomes, and the uniqueness of the questionnaire makes direct comparison with the general population not yet possible.

Second, the frailty 'phenotype' developed by Fried and colleagues (Fried et al., 2001), was applied in the HA-ID study (Table 24.1). According to the frailty phenotype of Fried, 11% of those aged 50–64 years, and 18% of those aged 65 years and over were frail (Evenhuis, Hermans, Hilgenkamp, Bastiaanse, & Echteld, 2012). Compared to the general population in which 7–9% of those aged 65 years and over

> **The Healthy Aging and Intellectual Disability Study (HA-ID)**
>
> Most frailty research among people with ID so far has been performed in the HA-ID study, a population-based study on the health of 1050 people with ID, aged 50 years and over. All clients receiving care or support from three care organizations were invited to participate. The participation rate was 45% (1050/2332). Assessments included physical examinations, nutritional diaries, screening questionnaires and standardized psychiatric interviews for depression and anxiety, questionnaires on quality of life, IADL, ADL, mobility, dementia, social circumstances, and laboratory tests as well as the collection of data from the medical files. Detailed information has been published elsewhere (Hilgenkamp et al., 2011). Three years after the baseline measurements, all participants were invited for a follow-up study. To limit the burden of participation, information was gathered from medical files or by proxy questionnaires, without client involvement. From the 1050 participants, 19 had moved and 120 had died. From the 911 that were invited, 84% (n = 763) provided informed consent for participation. The HA-ID study was undertaken with the understanding and written consent of participants or the participant's legal representative. The ethical boards of the Erasmus MC University Medical Center Rotterdam and the participating care organizations reviewed and approved the HA-ID study, and the study conforms with the guidelines of the Helsinki declaration from 1975.
>
> Frailty was measured with the two internationally most frequently used approaches to measure frailty (Bouillon et al., 2013): the frailty 'phenotype' developed by Fried and colleagues (Fried et al., 2001), and the frailty index developed by Rockwood and Mitnitski (Mitnitski et al. 2001). For the frailty phenotype the diagnosis was based on established cut off values according to the Cardiovascular Health Study criteria. For the frailty index, 51 deficits were included that fulfilled all the frailty index criteria (Schoufour et al., 2013). The deficits included a broad spectrum of objective measurements (e.g. grip strength, walking speed, serum glucose), informer reports (e.g. fatigue, depression symptoms, dressing), and medical information (e.g. medication use, general hospital admission, asthma).

Figure 24.1 Frailty measures in *The Healthy Ageing and Intellectual Disability Study* (HA-ID).

are found to be frail, these percentages are rather high, especially for those aged 50–64 years (de Vries et al., 2011; Fried et al., 2001; Syddall et al., 2010).

Third, a frailty index was twice developed and applied in people with ID. These studies show that characteristics of the frailty index for people with ID appeared comparable to those in the general population: similar distribution, correlation with age and an observed maximum score around 0.7 (Drubbel et al., 2013, Mitnitski et al., 2001, Rockwood et al., 2007). Furthermore, the index's correlation with age was not influenced by the choice of the deficits, which indicates structural validity (Schoufour, Erler, et al., 2017). The score is represented on a continuous scale, which means that it is not designed to be used with a cut-off value to determine the prevalence of frailty. Schoufour et al. showed that the average frailty index score for people with ID aged 50 years and over in the HA-ID study was 0.27, equivalent to having an average of 14 out of 51 deficits. Results from general older populations (generally 65 years and over) usually show a mean score between 0.08 and 0.17 (Drubbel et al., 2013, Mitnitski et al., 2001; Rockwood et al., 2007, Romero-Ortuno & Kenny, 2012). Finding of the HA-ID

Table 24.1 HA-ID study's frailty phenotype (based on criteria in Fried et al., 2001)

	Characteristics matched to health measures
A	**Characteristics of frailty**
1	Shrinking: weight loss; loss of muscle mass (sarcopenia)
2	Weakness
3	Poor endurance; exhaustion
4	Slowness
5	Low activity
B	**Cardiovascular health measure**
1	Baseline: > 10 lbs loss unintentionally in prior year
2	Grip strength: lowest 20% (by gender, body mass index)
3	'Exhaustion' (self-report)
4	Walking time/15 feet: slowest 20% (by gender, height)
5	kcal/week: lowest 20%: males: <383 kcal/week; females: <270 kcal/week
C	**Presence of frailty**
	Positive for frailty phenotype: ≥ 3 criteria
	Intermediate or pre-frail: 1 or 2 criteria present

study were directly compared to findings in the general population and it was observed that people with ID accumulate more deficits at a younger age than observed in the general population (Romero-Ortuno & Kenny, 2012; Schoufour, Echteld, & Evenhuis, 2017) (Figure 24.2). Although the frailty index was clearly able to show differences in frailty levels, from the almost 1000 participants included there was not one person that had no deficits at all, in other words belonged to the so-called zero-state (Schoufour, van Wijngaarden, et al., 2014). Additionally, only few (6.6%) could be classified as 'least frail' (FI ≤ 0.10), whereas in the general population this percentage ranges between 43% (70 years and over) and 76% (50 years and over) (Rockwood & Mitnitski, 2011; Romero-Ortuno & Kenny, 2012; Schoufour, van Wijngaarden, et al., 2014). In addition, McKenzie et al., constructed a frailty index for almost 8000 people with ID, aged 18–99 years old. This frailty index was very similar to the HA-ID index, but also included people aged <50 years. They found already relatively high frailty index scores for people aged below the age of 30 and a high association with frailty index score and age (McKenzie, Ouellette-Kuntz, & Martin, 2015). The average score for the total population was 0.22 (SD = 0.13).

We conclude that frailty can be measured in people with ID, using existing instruments. The distribution of frailty of the 50+ ID population is comparable to that of the 70+ general population. Compared to the general 50+ population, high frailty scores are more prevalent. There is an increased health risk from a young age onwards compared to the general population (Figure 24.3).

Does Frailty Predict Deterioration of Health and Independence?

The question remained whether frailty would show the same predictive validity as observed in the general population, because lifelong impairments could have led to early rehabilitations or habituation.

The most frequently used adverse outcome against which to validate frailty instruments is mortality. Results from the HA-ID study showed that frailty measured with the frailty phenotype and the frailty index predicts mortality in people with ID. However, the frailty index showed a much stronger relation with mortality than the frailty phenotype, especially after adjustment for motor disability (Schoufour, Echteld, Boonstra, Groothuismink, Evenhuis, 2015; Schoufour, Echteld, et al., 2017). People classified as pre-frail or frail according to the frailty phenotype, were respectively 2.4 (CI = 1.26–4.6) and 5.2 (CI = 2.5–10.5) times more likely to die within three years. People classified by the frailty index as vulnerable (score 0.2–0.3), mildly (score 0.3–0.4), moderately (score 0.4–0.5) or severely frail (score >0.5)

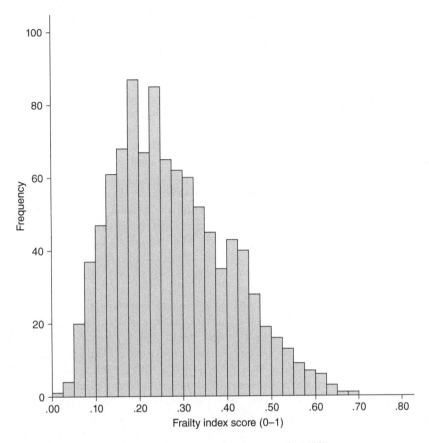

Figure 24.2 Frailty index distribution (HA-ID study) (Schoufouret et al., 2013)

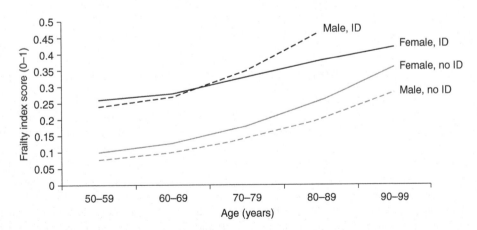

Figure 24.3 Frailty index and the association with age. Upper lines represent the average frailty index per age category and the corresponding trend line in people with intellectual disabilities. The lower grey lines represent the average frailty index per age category and the corresponding trend line from a large general European population aged 50 years and older (Schoufour et al., 2013).

were respectively 2.2 (CI = 0.9–5.0), 8.0 (CI = 3.7–17.3), 20 (CI = 9.1–41.2), or 33 (CI = 14.8–73.9) times more likely to die than those classified as relatively fit (FI < 0.2) (Figure 24.4).

In the introduction, we mentioned that frailty could be influenced by lifelong disabilities, such as motor disabilities. Indeed, we found that, if adjusted for motor disability, the frailty phenotype lost much of its predictive value, whereas the frailty index remained strongly related to mortality (Schoufour, Echteld, et al., 2017). This is likely explained because the phenotype of frailty is highly driven by motor disabilities, whereas the frailty index is a much broader concept. In people with ID, it has been hypothesised that, frailty, defined by the physically oriented frailty phenotype, seems to be over determined by (childhood) motor disabilities in this population (Evenhuis, Schoufour, & Echteld, 2013). This limits its predictive ability, because the strength of motor disabilities by themselves as a predictor of mortality is weaker than seen in the general population (Feeny et al., 2012; Majer, Nusselder, Mackenbach, Klijs, & van Baal, 2011). Lifelong or early onset motor disabilities appeared less predictive than motor disabilities acquired in later life. Furthermore, it was found that people with higher frailty index scores were more likely to deteriorate in their activities of daily living (ADL), instrumental activities of daily living (IADL), and mobility (Schoufour, Mitnitski, et al., 2014) than people with lower frailty index scores. For example, an individual with a rather high frailty index score (FI = 0.5) was estimated to lose 3.6 ADL points more during three years than an individual with a low frailty index score (FI = 0.1).

Also, higher frailty index scores were related to an increasing number of chronic comorbid conditions and medication prescriptions during follow-up (Schoufour, Echteld, Bastiaanse, & Evenhuis, 2015) in line with results from the general population (Crentsil, Ricks, Xue, & Fried, 2010; Gnjidic et al., 2012). Additionally, it was observed that the risk of increased care need was exponentially associated with frailty index scores (Martin, McKenzie, & Ouellette-Kuntz, 2018; McKenzie, Ouellette-Kuntz, & Martin, 2016; Schoufour, Evenhuis, & Echteld, 2014), which is also comparable to results in the general population (Jones, Song, & Rockwood, 2004; Rockwood et al., 2005). Contrary to results from the general population, no relation was found between high frailty index scores and hospital referrals (Ensrud et al., 2009; Ensrud et al., 2008; Fang et al., 2012; Hogan et al., 2012; Schoufour, Echteld, Bastiaanse, et al., 2015). The latter might be explained by missed diagnosis of conditions that normally require hospitalisation, or by the situation that that family/caregivers decide that hospitalisation is not in the best interest of the individual. Neither did we find a relation between the score on the frailty index and falls and fractures. In conclusion, both the frailty phenotype and the frailty index are able to predict early mortality. The frailty index is able to predict deterioration of health and independence in the same way as found in the general population. It can therefore be concluded that the frailty index is a valid measure for frailty in people with ID who present disabilities early in life.

Which Characteristics Are Associated with Frailty?

As to be expected on a basis of comorbidity risk, it was found that frailty in ID is associated with higher age, more severe ID, and Down syndrome (Brehmer-Rinderer et al., 2013; McKenzie et al., 2015; Schoufour et al., 2013). After adjustment for the level of ID, women had higher frailty index scores than men, but seem to cope with these deficits better, shown by a higher survival probability (Schoufour, Echteld, Boonstra, et al., 2015). These results are in line with results from the general population (Mitnitski et al., 2005; Song, Mitnitski, & Rockwood, 2010) and underline that women have, somehow, a higher capability, or more physiological reserves, to cope with a higher deficit load (Hubbard & Rockwood, 2011). Laboratory results showed that frailty in people with ID is associated with increased inflammation markers (CRP and IL-6), anaemia, metabolic markers (glucose, cholesterol, and albumin), and decreased renal functioning (Schoufour, Mitnitski, Rockwood, Evenhuis, & Echteld, 2015). Furthermore, the least frail participants (frailty index score ≤ 0.10) were characterised by better mobility and physical fitness, relative independence, less signs of depression or

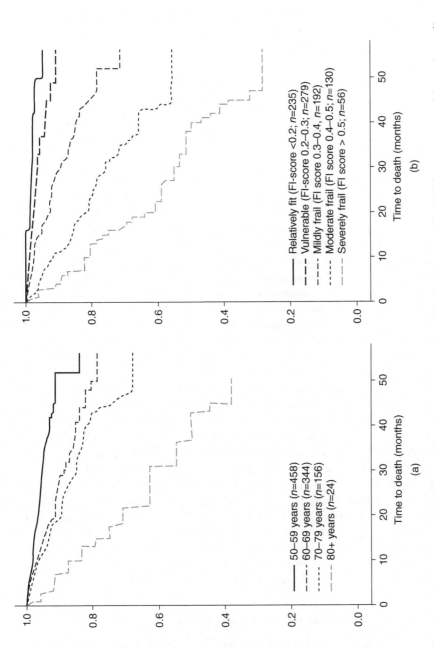

Figure 24.4 Kaplan-Meier survival curves stratified according to age categories (a) and frailty subgroups (b). (A) The youngest participants (upper line, solid black; 50–59) had the highest survival, the oldest participants (lowest line, long hash, light gray; ≥80) had the lowest, and the other age categories were in between. (B) Relatively fit participants (upper line, solid black; FI score < 0.20) had the highest survival, severely frail (lowest line, long dash light gray, FI score ≥0.50) had the lowest, and vulnerable (FI score 0.20–0.29), mildly frail (FI score 0.30–0.39), and moderately frail (FI score 0.40–0.49) were in between.

dementia, less chronic comorbidity (Schoufour, van Wijngaarden, et al., 2014) and with few feelings of distress (McKenzie et al., 2015). Living with a family member was observed to be protective for frailty, compared to living alone? (McKenzie et al., 2015).

Reflection: Understanding the Mechanisms of Frailty in People with ID

In a recent review by Clegg et al., frailty is said to be the result of lifelong accumulation of molecular and cellular damage, influenced by genetic and environmental factors. Up to a certain point, the human body can resist and repair this damage, but eventually, physiological reserves are depleted and a person becomes frail (Clegg et al., 2013). We have found that, in people with ID, frailty is more prevalent and starts at a younger age. McKenzie et al., already found high frailty index scores in people with ID aged between 18 and 50 years old (McKenzie et al., 2015). The question is why, and how this can be prevented. We point out several important aspects that could reduce the early onset of frailty.

As proposed by Clegg et al., genetic factors, environmental factors, and the interaction between the two are the origin of frailty. Starting with the former, healthy ageing and life expectancy are partially explained by genetic predisposition. It has been estimated that genetic factors explain around one third of the variation in life expectancy in the general population (Palombaro et al., 2009; Sirola & Rikkonen, 2005; Walter et al., 2012). In the ID population, genes might have a more pronounced effect as the impaired brain development resulting in intellectual disability could have a genetic origin (Gilissen et al., 2014). Congenital or early childhood disorders that originate from either genetic/chromosomal abnormalities or pre-natal errors could, in addition to their effect on childhood cognitive impairment, also determine frailty status in late adulthood. First of all, common conditions may themselves add to frailty, for example early mobility limitations, visual impairments, ADHD, and autism. Second, these problems are not isolated, but could lead to other problems, such as fatigue, pain, reduced fitness, decreased health literacy, inadequate health behaviour, and social isolation. Third, genetic predisposition could lead to decreased defence mechanisms, reduced physiological reserves, or altered physiological processes (e.g. deviant autonomic control during exercise). Furthermore, as a result of childhood cognitive impairment, environmental factors may differ from those in the general population (Douma, Dekker, de Ruiter, Tick, & Koot, 2007). It could be that people living within residential settings, receiving professional care and support, are less exposed to certain stressor events, such as financial problems, or neglect. On the other hand, it has been shown that, starting at young age, physical activity and nutritional quality can be substantially improved in the ID population) (Bastiaanse et al., 2020; Hilgenkamp, van Wijck, & Evenhuis, 2010; Humphries, Traci, & Seekins, 2009; Lotan, Henderson, & Merrick, 2006; Oppewal, Hilgenkamp, van Wijck, & Evenhuis, 2013; Temple, Frey, & Stanish, 2006). An additional remark needs to be made for people with borderline or mild levels of ID, who are usually living independently, with no specific support. It is very likely that lifestyle contributes more to frailty than genetic predisposition in this subpopulation. Indeed, results from the HA-ID study show that participants with borderline and mild ID have worse nutritional habits and higher risk for cardiovascular risk factors than people with more severe ID. Results from the general population also show that social-economic status is important for healthy ageing (Andrew, Mitnitski, Kirkland, & Rockwood, 2012; Guessous et al., 2014; Hoogendijk et al., 2014; St John, Montgomery, & Tyas, 2013; Szanton, Seplaki, Thorpe, Allen, & Fried, 2010).

Recommendations for Research and Clinical Practice

To identify frail people there is a need to develop predictive screening instruments that are applicable in clinical practice. The frailty index can be used as a basis for such a screening instrument. Nevertheless, several steps are necessary before clinical applicability is justified. First, our frailty index contained items from validated instruments, but when items from such instruments are taken out of the context of the full instruments, the known psychometric characteristics do not necessarily apply. As such, the validity of these individual items in the context of the frailty index remains unknown. Second, some items might be relevant for frailty but measurement is difficult in clinical settings, such as the fitness battery and expensive biochemical tests. An important question for further research is whether the frailty index remains valid after the removal of clinically less feasible measures. Third, to evaluate the stability of the frailty index, the test-retest reliability should be determined. Fourth, the ability of the frailty index to measure change should be evaluated in order to monitor the frailty status closely. Last, the sensitivity and specificity of the screening instrument needs to be evaluated, providing validity on an individual level. Another way to examine frailty would be via biochemical markers. This would be of special interest for people with communication difficulties. We showed that several biochemical markers are associated with frailty. It should be further studied whether a combination of biochemical measures could form an objective frailty index, as has been recently done for the general population (Howlett, Rockwood, Mitnitski, & Rockwood, 2014).

Frailty can be a slowly progressive state that involves the accumulation of health problems, of which many by themselves are no reasons for major concern. Therefore there is unlikely to be one simple intervention that prevents or even reverses frailty for a whole population. Furthermore, congenital disabilities and comorbidities, related to the ID, influence frailty but are complicated, if not impossible, to prevent. Hence, it is of paramount importance to closely monitor individuals at risk and develop an individual healthcare plan that takes into account all health aspects (social, physical, and physiological) and that aims at the highest quality of life. We recommend that more knowledge about frailty is provided to care givers, including physicians and daily care givers. One should be aware of the slowly progressing decline in health that could eventually lead to the clinical manifestation of frailty.

Screening and monitoring of frailty should be broadly implemented. Recovering from a very frail state is complicated, especially at an advanced age (Rockwood, Song, & Mitnitski, 2011). It is therefore important to be able to recognise people at risk to develop frailty. In the long run, it would be very beneficial if, using routinely collected data, a frailty index is calculated automatically every year for each individual. This would enable care givers to notice small changes in health status and intervene at an early stage.

Furthermore, there are several recommendations for clinical practice that could positively influence the overall frailty status in the ID population. In recent years, results from the HA-ID study and others, showed many aspects of health of people with ID that need improvement. Some examples: (1) Levels of physical fitness and physical activity are extremely low (Hilgenkamp, Reis, van Wijck, & Evenhuis, 2012; Oppewal et al., 2013), and dietary habits are poor (Bastiaanse et al., 2020), both offer much room for improvement (2) Depression and anxiety symptoms are often present but inadequately recognised (Hermans, Beekman, & Evenhuis, 2013; Hermans & Evenhuis, 2012). Early detection, the limitation of life events, sufficient social support, and proper treatment are therefore important (3) To limit the severe side-effects of antipsychotics, discontinuation should be considered (de Kuijper, Evenhuis, Minderaa, & Hoekstra, 2014; de Kuijper, Mulder, Evenhuis, Visser, & Hoekstra, 2013; Newcomer, 2007) and regular medication reviews are advised to limit the number of prescription errors (Zaal, van der Kaaij, Evenhuis, & van den Bemt, 2013) (4) Cardiovascular risk factors (e.g. high serum triglyceride, elevated blood pressure) are frequently present but often undiagnosed (de Winter, Bastiaanse, Hilgenkamp, Evenhuis, & Echteld, 2012; de Winter, Magilsen, van Alfen, Penning, & Evenhuis, 2009; de Winter, Magilsen, van Alfen, Willemsen, & Evenhuis, 2011). Pro-active screening and treatment are therefore recommended.

These recommendations suggest many opportunities to improve the care of people with ID. Nevertheless, in large and complex organisations for people with ID, the implementation of lifestyle interventions is complex, and several aspects need to be taken into account. First of all, as mentioned before, it is of paramount importance to create awareness of the problem of frailty and possible solutions throughout the care organisation. Without understanding, care givers will not be motivated to implement interventions, or adapt their everyday care. Second, screening for the areas that scientific research suggests need improvement needs to be implemented (e.g. nutrition, physical activity, depression). Third, effective interventions, with corresponding protocols need to be readily accessible. Fourth, time and money need to be made available to actually offer the required care. A clear sense is required therefore about who is responsible for what in the ID sector.

These points are already complicated within specialised ID organisations but may be even more complicated outside such organisations. People with borderline or mild ID who do not use any form of formal services will not benefit from interventions offered by care organisation. This group will increase further in years to come because of recent changes in healthcare legislation in the Netherlands that assigns the care for this group to general practitioners, geriatricians and informal caregivers in the community. In addition, a large degree of self-management among this group of older people with ID is now expected. Education about frail older people with ID and related problems for physicians and other formal and informal caregivers is essential to raise awareness about frailty. Furthermore, it is important that physicians can discuss their cases with specialised ID physicians. In the Netherlands, this has been dealt with by specialised ID outpatient clinics. But this option needs to be implemented widely, as is apparent from indications from general practitioners that they lack knowledge about this specific group (Bekkema, Veer de, & Francke, 2014). Additionally, people with ID who do not use any form of formal care or support, need to be educated themselves about a healthy lifestyle. This will require specific and carefully designed programs, because it is known that people from disadvantaged groups are difficult to reach with interventions.

Conclusion

Frailty should have a more central role in the care for people with an ID. In concordance with others, we predict that frailty is, and will increasingly become a major healthcare concern, that not only threatens the quality of life of older people with ID but also leads to increased healthcare costs. People with ID are already the most costly diagnostic group in the Netherlands (Slobbe, Smit, Groen, Poos, & Kommer, 2011) for whom costs have been growing since (2007–2012) (Kwartel, 2013). Therefore, greater awareness about the accumulation of age-related health problems must be created. It is important to realise that several age-related problems are more frequently observed and more severe in people with ID and that these problems might start before 'old age'.

References

Abellan van Kan, G., Rolland, Y., Bergman, H., Morley, J. E., Kritchevsky, S. B., & Vellas, B. (2008). The I.A.N.A Task Force on frailty assessment of older people in clinical practice. *The Journal of Nutrition, Health & Aging, 12*(1), 29–37. https://doi.org/10.1007/BF02982161

Andrew, M. K., Mitnitski, A., Kirkland, S. A., & Rockwood, K. (2012). The impact of social vulnerability on the survival of the fittest older adults. *Age and Ageing, 41*(2), 161–165. https://doi.org/10.1093/ageing/afr176

Apóstolo, J., Cooke, R., Bobrowicz-Campos, E., Santana, S., Marcucci, M., Cano, A., ... Holland, C. (2018). Effectiveness of interventions to prevent pre-frailty and frailty progression in older adults: A systematic review. *JBI Database of Systematic Reviews and Implementation Reports, 16*(1), 140–232. https://doi.org/10.11124/JBISRIR-2017-003382

Bastiaanse, L. P., Evenhuis, H. M., Odekerken, M., Vriend-Asscheman, B., Steenselen van, W., & Echteld, M. A. (2020). Inadequate dietary intake in older people with intellectual disabilities: Results of the HA-ID study. Manuscript submitted for publication.

Bekkema, N., Veer de, A., & Francke, A. (2014). Zorgen over patiënten met verstandelijke beperking [Concerns about patients with intellectual disabilities]. *Huisartsenzorg in Cijfers [General Practice Care in Figures], 57*, 259.

Bouillon, K., Kivimaki, M., Hamer, M., Sabia, S., Fransson, E. I., Singh-Manoux, A., & Batty, G. D. (2013). Measures of frailty in population-based studies: An overview. *BMC Geriatrics, 13*, 64. https://doi.org/10.1186/1471-2318-13-64

Brehmer-Rinderer, B., Zeilinger, E. L., Radaljevic, A., & Weber, G. (2013). The Vienna frailty questionnaire for persons with intellectual disabilities, revised. *Research in Developmental Disabilities, 34*(6), 1958–1965. https://doi.org/10.1016/j.ridd.2013.03.004

Brinkman, S., Voortman, T., Kiefte-de Jong, J. C., van Rooij, F., Ikram, M. A., Rivadeneira, F., & Schoufour, J. D. (2018). The association between lifestyle and overall health, using the frailty index. *Archives of Gerontology and Geriatrics, 76*, 85–91. https://doi.org/10.1016/j.archger.2018.02.006

Clegg, A., Young, J., Iliffe, S., Rikkert, M. O., & Rockwood, K. (2013). Frailty in elderly people. *Lancet, 381*(9868), 752–762. https://doi.org/10.1016/S0140-6736(12)62167-9

Crentsil, V., Ricks, M. O., Xue, Q. L., & Fried, L. P. (2010). A pharmacoepidemiologic study of community-dwelling, disabled older women: Factors associated with medication use. *The American Journal of Geriatric Pharmacotherapy, 8*(3), 215–224.

de Kuijper, G., Evenhuis, H., Minderaa, R. B., & Hoekstra, P. J. (2014). Effects of controlled discontinuation of long-term used antipsychotics for behavioural symptoms in individuals with intellectual disability. *Journal of Intellectual Disability Research: JIDR, 58*(1), 71–83. https://doi.org/10.1111/j.1365-2788.2012.01631.x

de Kuijper, G., Mulder, H., Evenhuis, H., Visser, F., & Hoekstra, P. J. (2013). Effects of controlled discontinuation of long-term used antipsychotics on weight and metabolic parameters in individuals with intellectual disability. *Journal of Clinical Psychopharmacology, 33*(4), 520–524. https://doi.org/10.1097/JCP.0b013e3182905d6a

de Vries, N. M., Staal, J. B., van Ravensberg, C. D., Hobbelen, J. S., Olde Rikkert, M. G., & Nijhuis-van der Sanden, M. W. (2011). Outcome instruments to measure frailty: A systematic review. *Ageing Research Reviews, 10*(1), 104–114. https://doi.org/10.1016/j.arr.2010.09.001

Douma, J. C., Dekker, M. C., de Ruiter, K. P., Tick, N. T., & Koot, H. M. (2007). Antisocial and delinquent behaviors in youths with mild or borderline disabilities. *American Journal of Mental Retardation: AJMR, 112*(3), 207–220. https://doi.org/10.1352/0895-8017(2007)112[207:AADBIY]2.0.CO;2

Drubbel, I., de Wit, N. J., Bleijenberg, N., Eijkemans, R. J., Schuurmans, M. J., & Numans, M. E. (2013). Prediction of adverse health outcomes in older people using a frailty index based on routine primary care data. *The Journals of Gerontology, Series A, Biological Sciences and Medical Sciences, 68*(3), 301–308. https://doi.org/10.1093/gerona/gls161

Ensrud, K. E., Ewing, S. K., Cawthon, P. M., Fink, H. A., Taylor, B. C., Cauley, J. A., ... Osteoporotic Fractures in Men Research Group. (2009). A comparison of frailty indexes for the prediction of falls, disability, fractures, and mortality in older men. *Journal of the American Geriatrics Society, 57*(3), 492–498. https://doi.org/10.1111/j.1532-5415.2009.02137.x

Ensrud, K. E., Ewing, S. K., Taylor, B. C., Fink, H. A., Cawthon, P. M., Stone, K. L., ... Cummings, S. R. (2008). Comparison of 2 frailty indexes for prediction of falls, disability, fractures, and death in older women. *Archives of Internal Medicine, 168*(4), 382–389. https://doi.org/10.1001/archinternmed.2007.113

Evenhuis, H. M., Hermans, H., Hilgenkamp, T. I., Bastiaanse, L. P., & Echteld, M. A. (2012). Frailty and disability in the older population with intellectual disabilities: Results from the Healthy Aging and Intellectual Disability Study (HA-ID). *Journal of the American Geriatrics Society, 60,* 934–938.

Evenhuis, H., Schoufour, J., & Echteld, M. (2013). Frailty and intellectual disability: A different operationalization? *Developmental Disabilities Research Reviews, 18*(1), 17–21. https://doi.org/10.1002/ddrr.1124

Fang, X., Shi, J., Song, X., Mitnitski, A., Tang, Z., Wang, C., ... Rockwood, K. (2012). Frailty in relation to the risk of falls, fractures, and mortality in older Chinese adults: Results from the Beijing Longitudinal Study of Aging. *The Journal of Nutrition, Health & Aging, 16*(10), 903–907. https://doi.org/10.1007/s12603-012-0368-6

Feeny, D., Huguet, N., McFarland, B. H., Kaplan, M. S., Orpana, H., & Eckstrom, E. (2012). Hearing, mobility, and pain predict mortality: A longitudinal population-based study. *Journal of Clinical Epidemiology, 65*(7), 764–777. https://doi.org/10.1016/j.jclinepi.2012.01.003

Fried, L. P., Ferrucci, L., Darer, J., Williamson, J. D., & Anderson, G. (2004). Untangling the concepts of disability, frailty, and comorbidity: Implications for improved targeting and care. *The Journals of Gerontology, Series A, Biological Sciences and Medical Sciences, 59*(3), 255–263. https://doi.org/10.1093/gerona/59.3.m255

Fried, L. P., Tangen, C. M., Walston, J., Newman, A. B., Hirsch, C., Gottdiener, J., ... Cardiovascular Health Study Collaborative Research Group. (2001). Frailty in older adults: Evidence for a phenotype. *The Journals of Gerontology, Series A, Biological Sciences and Medical Sciences, 56*(3), M146–M156. https://doi.org/10.1093/gerona/56.3.m146

Gilissen, C., Hehir-Kwa, J. Y., Thung, D. T., van de Vorst, M., van Bon, B. W., Willemsen, M. H., ... Veltman, J. A. (2014). Genome sequencing identifies major causes of severe intellectual disability. *Nature, 511*(7509), 344–347. https://doi.org/10.1038/nature13394

Gnjidic, D., Hilmer, S. N., Blyth, F. M., Naganathan, V., Cumming, R. G., Handelsman, D. J., ... Le Couteur, D. G. (2012). High-risk prescribing and incidence of frailty among older community-dwelling men. *Clinical Pharmacology and Therapeutics, 91*(3), 521–528. https://doi.org/10.1038/clpt.2011.258

Guessous, I., Luthi, J. C., Bowling, C. B., Theler, J. M., Paccaud, F., Gaspoz, J. M., & McClellan, W. (2014). Prevalence of frailty indicators and association with socioeconomic status in middle-aged and older adults in a Swiss region with universal health insurance coverage: A population-based cross-sectional study. *Journal of Aging Research, 2014,* 198603. https://doi.org/10.1155/2014/198603

Hermans, H., Beekman, A. T., & Evenhuis, H. M. (2013). Prevalence of depression and anxiety in older users of formal Dutch intellectual disability services. *Journal of Affective Disorders, 144*(1–2), 94–100. https://doi.org/10.1016/j.jad.2012.06.011

Hermans, H., & Evenhuis, H. M. (2012). Life events and their associations with depression and anxiety in older people with intellectual disabilities: Results of the HA-ID study. *Journal of Affective Disorders*, *138*(1–2), 79–85. https://doi.org/10.1016/j.jad.2011.12.025

Hilgenkamp, T. I., Reis, D., van Wijck, R., & Evenhuis, H. M. (2012). Physical activity levels in older adults with intellectual disabilities are extremely low. *Research in Developmental Disabilities*, *33*(2), 477–483. https://doi.org/10.1016/j.ridd.2011.10.011

Hilgenkamp, T. I., van Wijck, R., & Evenhuis, H. M. (2010). Physical fitness in older people with ID-Concept and measuring instruments: A review. *Research in Developmental Disabilities*, *31*(5), 1027–1038. https://doi.org/10.1016/j.ridd.2010.04.012

Hogan, D. B., Freiheit, E. A., Strain, L. A., Patten, S. B., Schmaltz, H. N., Rolfson, D., & Maxwell, C. J. (2012). Comparing frailty measures in their ability to predict adverse outcome among older residents of assisted living. *BMC Geriatrics*, *12*, 56. https://doi.org/10.1186/1471-2318-12-56

Hoogendijk, E. O., van Hout, H. P., Heymans, M. W., van der Horst, H. E., Frijters, D. H., Broese van Groenou, M. I., & Huisman, M. (2014). Explaining the association between educational level and frailty in older adults: Results from a 13-year longitudinal study in the Netherlands. *Annals of Epidemiology*, *24*(7), 538–544.e2. https://doi.org/10.1016/j.annepidem.2014.05.002

Horvath, S., Garagnani, P., Bacalini, M. G., Pirazzini, C., Salvioli, S., Gentilini, D., ... Franceschi, C. (2015). Accelerated epigenetic aging in Down syndrome. *Aging Cell*, *14*(3), 491–495. https://doi.org/10.1111/acel.12325

Howlett, S. E., Rockwood, M. R., Mitnitski, A., & Rockwood, K. (2014). Standard laboratory tests to identify older adults at increased risk of death. *BMC Medicine*, *12*, 171. https://doi.org/10.1186/s12916-014-0171-9

Hubbard, R. E., & Rockwood, K. (2011). Frailty in older women. *Maturitas*, *69*(3), 203–207. https://doi.org/10.1016/j.maturitas.2011.04.006

Humphries, K., Traci, M. A., & Seekins, T. (2009). Nutrition and adults with intellectual or developmental disabilities: Systematic literature review results. *Intellectual and developmental disabilities*, *47*(3), 163–185. https://doi.org/10.1352/1934-9556-47.3.163

Jones, D. M., Song, X., & Rockwood, K. (2004). Operationalizing a frailty index from a standardized comprehensive geriatric assessment. *Journal of the American Geriatrics Society*, *52*(11), 1929–1933. https://doi.org/10.1111/j.1532-5415.2004.52521.x

Kwartel, A. J. J. van der. (2013). *Branch report Disability Care 2012*. Disability Care Association Netherlands.

Lotan, M., Henderson, C. M., & Merrick, J. (2006). Physical activity for adolescents with intellectual disability. *Minerva Pediatrica*, *58*(3), 219–226.

Majer, I. M., Nusselder, W. J., Mackenbach, J. P., Klijs, B., & van Baal, P. H. (2011). Mortality risk associated with disability: A population-based record linkage study. *American Journal of Public Health*, *101*(12), e9–e15. https://doi.org/10.2105/AJPH.2011.300361

Martin, L., McKenzie, K., & Ouellette-Kuntz, H. (2018). Once frail, always frail? Frailty transitions in home care users with intellectual and developmental disabilities. *Geriatrics & Gerontology International*, *18*(4), 547–553. https://doi.org/10.1111/ggi.13214

McKenzie, K., Ouellette-Kuntz, H., & Martin, L. (2015). Using an accumulation of deficits approach to measure frailty in a population of home care users with intellectual and developmental disabilities: An analytical descriptive study. *BMC Geriatrics*, *15*, 170. https://doi.org/10.1186/s12877-015-0170-5

McKenzie, K., Ouellette-Kuntz, H., & Martin, L. (2016). Frailty as a predictor of institutionalization among adults with intellectual and developmental disabilities. *Intellectual and Developmental Disabilities*, *54*(2), 123–135. https://doi.org/10.1352/1934-9556-54.2.123

Middleton, L. E., Kirkland, S. A., Mitnitski, A., & Rockwood, K. (2010). Proxy reports of physical activity were valid in older people with and without cognitive impairment. *Journal of Clinical Epidemiology*, *63*(4), 435–440. https://doi.org/10.1016/j.jclinepi.2009.06.009

Mitnitski, A., Collerton, J., Martin-Ruiz, C., Jagger, C., von Zglinicki, T., Rockwood, K., & Kirkwood, T. B. (2015). Age-related frailty and its association with biological markers of ageing. *BMC Medicine*, *13*, 161. https://doi.org/10.1186/s12916-015-0400-x

Mitnitski, A. B., Mogilner, A. J., & Rockwood, K. (2001). Accumulation of deficits as a proxy measure of aging. *The Scientific World Journal*, *1*, 323–336. https://doi.org/10.1100/tsw.2001.58

Mitnitski, A., Song, X., Skoog, I., Broe, G. A., Cox, J. L., Grunfeld, E., & Rockwood, K. (2005). Relative fitness and frailty of elderly men and women in developed countries and their relationship with mortality. *Journal of the American Geriatrics Society*, *53*(12), 2184–2189. https://doi.org/10.1111/j.1532-5415.2005.00506.x

Newcomer, J. W. (2007). Antipsychotic medications: Metabolic and cardiovascular risk. *The Journal of Clinical Psychiatry*, *68*(Suppl 4), 8–13.

Oppewal, A., Hilgenkamp, T. I., van Wijck, R., & Evenhuis, H. M. (2013). Cardiorespiratory fitness in individuals with intellectual disabilities – A review. *Research in Developmental Disabilities*, *34*(10), 3301–3316. https://doi.org/10.1016/j.ridd.2013.07.005

Palombaro, K. M., Hack, L. M., Mangione, K. K., Barr, A. E., Newton, R. A., Magri, F., & Speziale, T. (2009). Gait variability detects women in early postmenopause with low bone mineral density. *Physical Therapy*, *89*(12), 1315–1326. https://doi.org/10.2522/ptj.20080401

Reppermund, S., & Trollor, J. N. (2016). Successful ageing for people with an intellectual disability. *Current Opinion in Psychiatry*, *29*(2), 149–154. https://doi.org/10.1097/YCO.0000000000000228

Rocha, V., Marmelo, F., Leite-Moreira, A., & Moreira-Gonçalves, D. (2017). Clinical utility of frailty scales for the prediction of postoperative complications: Systematic review and meta-analysis. *Revista Portuguesa de Cirurgia Cardio-toracica e Vascular: Orgao Oficial da Sociedade Portuguesa de Cirurgia Cardio-Toracica e Vascular [Portuguese Journal of Cardio-thoracic and Vascular Surgery: Official Body of the Portuguese Society of Cardio-Thoracic and Vasculus Surgery]*, *24*(3–4), 132.

Rockwood, K., Abeysundera, M. J., & Mitnitski, A. (2007). How should we grade frailty in nursing home patients? *Journal of the American Medical Directors Association*, *8*(9), 595–603. https://doi.org/10.1016/j.jamda.2007.07.012

Rockwood, K., & Mitnitski, A. (2011). Frailty defined by deficit accumulation and geriatric medicine defined by frailty. *Clinics in Geriatric Medicine*, *27*(1), 17–26. https://doi.org/10.1016/j.cger.2010.08.008

Rockwood, K., Song, X., MacKnight, C., Bergman, H., Hogan, D. B., McDowell, I., & Mitnitski, A. (2005). A global clinical measure of fitness and frailty in elderly people. *CMAJ: Canadian Medical Association Journal = Journal de l'Association Medicale Canadienne*, *173*(5), 489–495. https://doi.org/10.1503/cmaj.050051

Rockwood, K., Song, X., & Mitnitski, A. (2011). Changes in relative fitness and frailty across the adult lifespan: Evidence from the Canadian National Population Health Survey. *CMAJ: Canadian Medical Association journal = Journal de l'Association Medicale Canadienne*, *183*(8), E487–E494. https://doi.org/10.1503/cmaj.101271

Romero-Ortuno, R., & Kenny, R. A. (2012). The frailty index in Europeans: Association with age and mortality. *Age and Ageing*, *41*(5), 684–689. https://doi.org/10.1093/ageing/afs051

Schoufour, J. D., Echteld, M. A., Bastiaanse, L. P., & Evenhuis, H. M. (2015). The use of a frailty index to predict adverse health outcomes (falls, fractures, hospitalization, medication use, comorbid conditions) in people with intellectual disabilities. *Research in Developmental Disabilities*, *38*, 39–47.

Schoufour, J. D., Echteld, M. A., Boonstra, A., Groothuismink, Z. M., & Evenhuis, H. M. (2015). Biochemical measures and frailty in people with intellectual disabilities. *Age and Ageing*, *45*(1), 142–148.

Schoufour, J. D., Echteld, M. A., & Evenhuis, H. M. (2017). Comparing two frailty concepts among older people with intellectual disabilities. *European Journal of Ageing*, *14*(1), 63–79. https://doi.org/10.1007/s10433-016-0388-x

Schoufour, J. D., Erler, N. S., Jaspers, L., Kiefte-de Jong, J. C., Voortman, T., Ziere, G., ... Franco, O. H. (2017). Design of a frailty index among community living middle-aged and older people: The Rotterdam study. *Maturitas*, *97*, 14–20. https://doi.org/10.1016/j.maturitas.2016.12.002

Schoufour, J. D., Evenhuis, H. M., & Echteld, M. A. (2014). The impact of frailty on care intensity in older people with intellectual disabilities. *Research in Developmental Disabilities*, *35*(12), 3455–3461. https://doi.org/10.1016/j.ridd.2014.08.006

Schoufour, J. D., Mitnitski, A., Rockwood, K., Evenhuis, H. M., & Echteld, M. A. (2013). Development of a frailty index for older people with intellectual disabilities: Results from the HA-ID study. *Research in Developmental Disabilities*, *34*(5), 1541–1555. https://doi.org/10.1016/j.ridd.2013.01.029

Schoufour, J. D., Mitnitski, A., Rockwood, K., Evenhuis, H. M., & Echteld, M. A. (2015). Predicting 3-year survival in older people with intellectual disabilities using a Frailty Index. *Journal of the American Geriatrics Society*, *63*(3), 531–536. https://doi.org/10.1111/jgs.13239

Schoufour, J. D., Mitnitski, A., Rockwood, K., Hilgenkamp, T. I., Evenhuis, H. M., & Echteld, M. A. (2014). Predicting disabilities in daily functioning in older people with intellectual disabilities using a frailty index. *Research in Developmental Disabilities*, *35*(10), 2267–2277. https://doi.org/10.1016/j.ridd.2014.05.022

Schoufour, J. D., van Wijngaarden, J., Mitnitski, A., Rockwood, K., Evenhuis, H. M., & Echteld, M. A. (2014). Characteristics of the least frail adults with intellectual disabilities: A positive biology perspective. *Research in Developmental Disabilities*, *35*(1), 127–136. https://doi.org/10.1016/j.ridd.2013.10.016

Sirola, J., & Rikkonen, T. (2005). Muscle performance after the menopause. *The Journal of the British Menopause Society*, *11*(2), 45–50. https://doi.org/10.1258/136218005775544561

Slobbe, L. C. J., Smit, J. M., Groen, J., Poos, M. J. J. C., & Kommer, G. J. (2011). *Kosten van Ziekten in Nederland 2007, Trends in de Nederlandse zorguitgaven 1999–2010* [Costs of Diseases in the Netherlands 2007, Trends in Dutch healthcare expenditure 1999–2010]. Centraal Bureau voor de Statistiek [Central Bureau of Statistics].

Song, X., Mitnitski, A., & Rockwood, K. (2010). Prevalence and 10-year outcomes of frailty in older adults in relation to deficit accumulation. *Journal of the American Geriatrics Society*, *58*(4), 681–687. https://doi.org/10.1111/j.1532-5415.2010.02764.x

St John, P. D., Montgomery, P. R., & Tyas, S. L. (2013). Social position and frailty. *Canadian Journal on Aging = La Revue Canadienne du Vieillissement*, *32*(3), 250–259. https://doi.org/10.1017/S0714980813000329

Syddall, H., Roberts, H. C., Evandrou, M., Cooper, C., Bergman, H., & Aihie Sayer, A. (2010). Prevalence and correlates of frailty among community-dwelling older men and women: Findings from the Hertfordshire Cohort Study. *Age and Ageing, 39*(2), 197–203. https://doi.org/10.1093/ageing/afp204

Szanton, S. L., Seplaki, C. L., Thorpe, R. J. Jr, Allen, J. K., & Fried, L. P. (2010). Socioeconomic status is associated with frailty: The Women's Health and Aging Studies. *Journal of Epidemiology and Community Health, 64*(1), 63–67. https://doi.org/10.1136/jech.2008.078428

Temple, V. A., Frey, G. C., & Stanish, H. I. (2006). Physical activity of adults with mental retardation: Review and research needs. *American Journal of Health Promotion: AJHP, 21*(1), 2–12. https://doi.org/10.1177/089011710602100103

Theou, O., Campbell, S., Malone, M. L., & Rockwood, K. (2018). Older adults in the emergency department with frailty. *Clinics in Geriatric Medicine, 34*(3), 369–386. https://doi.org/10.1016/j.cger.2018.04.003

Theou, O., Rockwood, M. R., Mitnitski, A., & Rockwood, K. (2012). Disability and co-morbidity in relation to frailty: How much do they overlap? *Archives of Gerontology and Geriatrics, 55*(2), e1–e8. https://doi.org/10.1016/j.archger.2012.03.001

Tieland, M., Trouwborst, I., & Clark, B. C. (2018). Skeletal muscle performance and ageing. *Journal of Cachexia, Sarcopenia and Muscle, 9*(1), 3–19. https://doi.org/10.1002/jcsm.12238

Walston, J., Buta, B., & Xue, Q. L. (2018). Frailty screening and interventions: Considerations for clinical practice. *Clinics in Geriatric Medicine, 34*(1), 25–38. https://doi.org/10.1016/j.cger.2017.09.004

Walter, S., Mackenbach, J., Vokó, Z., Lhachimi, S., Ikram, M. A., Uitterlinden, A. G., ... Tiemeier, H. (2012). Genetic, physiological, and lifestyle predictors of mortality in the general population. *American Journal of Public Health, 102*(4), e3–e10. https://doi.org/10.2105/AJPH.2011.300596

de Winter, C. F., Bastiaanse, L. P., Hilgenkamp, T. I. M., Evenhuis, H. M., & Echteld, M. A. (2012). Cardiovascular risk factors (diabetes, hypertension, hypercholesterolemia and metabolic syndrome) in older people with intellectual disability: Results of the HA-ID study. *Research in Developmental Disabilities, 33*(6), 1722–1731.

de Winter, C. F., Magilsen, K. W., van Alfen, J. C., Penning, C., & Evenhuis, H. M. (2009). Prevalence of cardiovascular risk factors in older people with intellectual disability. *American Journal on Intellectual and Developmental Disabilities, 114*(6), 427–436. https://doi.org/10.1352/1944-7558-114.6.427

de Winter, C. F., Magilsen, K. W., van Alfen, J. C., Willemsen, S. P., & Evenhuis, H. M. (2011). Metabolic syndrome in 25% of older people with intellectual disability. *Family Practice, 28*(2), 141–144. https://doi.org/10.1093/fampra/cmq079

Zaal, R. J., van der Kaaij, A. D., Evenhuis, H. M., & van den Bemt, P. M. (2013). Prescription errors in older individuals with an intellectual disability: Prevalence and risk factors in the Healthy Ageing and Intellectual Disability study. *Research in Developmental Disabilities, 34*(5), 1656–1662. https://doi.org/10.1016/j.ridd.2013.02.005

Suggested Readings

Apóstolo, J., Cooke, R., Bobrowicz-Campos, E., Santana, S., Marcucci, M., Cano, A., ... Holland, C. (2018). Effectiveness of interventions to prevent pre-frailty and frailty progression in older adults: A systematic review. *JBI Database of Systematic Reviews and Implementation Reports, 16*(1), 140–232. https://doi.org/10.11124/JBISRIR-2017-003382

Evenhuis, H., Schoufour, J., & Echteld, M. (2013). Frailty and intellectual disability: A different operationalization?. *Developmental Disabilities Research Reviews, 18*(1), 17–21. https://doi.org/10.1002/ddrr.1124

Schoufour, J. D., Echteld, M. A., Bastiaanse, L. P., & Evenhuis, H. M. (2015). The use of a frailty index to predict adverse health outcomes (falls, fractures, hospitalization, medication use, comorbid conditions) in people with intellectual disabilities. *Research in Developmental Disabilities, 38*, 39–47.

Schoufour, J. D., Evenhuis, H. M., & Echteld, M. A. (2014). The impact of frailty on care intensity in older people with intellectual disabilities. *Research in Developmental Disabilities, 35*(12), 3455–3461. https://doi.org/10.1016/j.ridd.2014.08.006

25
HOW TO AVOID EARLY FRAILTY IN PEOPLE WITH INTELLECTUAL DISABILITIES?

Heleen M. Evenhuis, Josje D. Schoufour, Alyt Oppewal, and Dederieke Maes-Festen

Introduction

Why Research on Frailty?

Since the 1960s, it has been generally noted that people with intellectual disabilities showed signs of ageing at an earlier age than other people: formerly enthusiastic and active persons lost their interest in hobbies, activities, work, had difficulties walking, fell and broke hips, sat disengaged in a corner, stopped communicating, refused food, got recurrent pneumonias and died. Nobody understood why, therefore it had to be accepted as early ageing – and so it was. As a young doctor in long-term intellectual disability care, the lead author of this chapter, called this for herself 'the geriatric sequence' and was at a loss about how to prevent it. Decades later, at a geriatric congress, she first heard of the concept 'frailty', and realised that this was her former geriatric sequence: an increased vulnerability to severe health problems, disability, dependence, and death in the near future. In the general population, frailty is a phenomenon of people in their late 80s and 90s. And in the stage described above, practically unstoppable. But why so early in people with intellectual disabilities? And how to avoid it? This experience inspired the design and start of the Healthy Ageing and Intellectual Disability study in the Netherlands, followed by intervention studies.

Development of a Knowledge Base

Insights into causes of early decrease of health and independence in this population have grown, mostly during the 1990s and 2000s, starting with small-scale clinical inventories by pioneers of their own patient groups. That people with intellectual disabilities could get dementia on top of their lifelong disabilities, has trickled down in the literature since the 1980s, specifically – but not only – focused on people with Down syndrome. Outcomes of these pioneer studies provided arguments for the financing of larger-scale epidemiological studies in populations with intellectual disabilities since around 2000, followed by research into public health aspects: multimorbidity, polypharmacy, frailty. This primarily concerns three ongoing large-scale, broad epidemiological studies into health and ageing of persons with intellectual disabilities: the Dutch Healthy Ageing in Intellectual Disability (HAID) study among 1050 adult clients of formal intellectual disability support and care, aged 50 years and over (Hilgenkamp et al., 2011), the Intellectual Disability Supplement to the Irish Longitudinal Study on Aging (IDS-TILDA) among 753 adults receiving intellectual disability support and care, aged 40 years and over (McCarron et al., 2013), and the study of administratively held clinical data of 7,863 individuals with cognitive levels matching intellectual disability, aged 18–99 years, admitted to home care in Ontario, Canada (McKenzie et al., 2015), which we will refer to as the Canadian study.

This has led to better underpinning knowledge and partially surprising new insights into health and the persistent idea of early ageing of this population group. Based on these insights, we could determine that in general, persons with intellectual disabilities are not prematurely old – on a level of genetic processes regulating repair of DNA damage – but unhealthy. Only in people with Down syndrome, and a few other very rare syndromes, does early ageing have a genetic basis. The concept of frailty has been defined by geriatric pioneers and studied with validated measures. Insight into causes of frailty in people with intellectual disabilities may show the way how to avoid or postpone it.

Frailty and Intellectual Disability

The definition of frailty as an accumulation of mental and physical health deficits, and an index to measure that accumulation, has been developed in a Canadian geriatrics group (Rockwood & Mitnitski, 2007). Under the guidance of the authors, a specific intellectual disability index for people with intellectual disabilities was constructed and evaluated (Schoufour, Mitnitski, Rockwood, Evenhuis, & Echteld, 2013). This was interesting for the Canadian investigators, too, because it was the first frailty index for a disabled population.

In prospective evaluations, this index appeared as valid as in general populations: it is independently predictive for a decrease of independence and mobility (Schoufour, Evenhuis, & Echteld, 2014), increase of medication use and numbers of chronic disease (Schoufour, Echteld, Bastiaanse, & Evenhuis, 2015), increased intensity and costs of care and admission to long-term care facilities (Schoufour, Mitnitski, et al., 2014), and death within 3 and 5 years (Schoufour, Mitnitski, Rockwood, Evenhuis, & Echteld, 2015; Schoufour, Echteld, & Evenhuis, 2017; Schoufour et al., 2018). In comparison with large-scale frailty index studies in general populations, it became apparent that on average, people with intellectual disabilities are as frail at age 50–59 years as other people at age 75–80 years and become even frailer (Romero-Ortuno & Kenny, 2012; Schoufour et al., 2013) (Figure 25.1). A comparable frailty index for intellectual disability has been developed by a Canadian group in Ontario (McKenzie, Ouellette-Kuntz, & Martin, 2015), which is very interesting, because in this study, participants are followed from the age of 18 years onwards (Figure 25.2). In Figure 25.2, we see that Canadian adults with intellectual disabilities show an increase of mean frailty indexes from 0.1 to 0.2 already before age 50 years. This increase is comparable to figures for European men aged 50–70 years in the general population (Figure 25.1). As a conclusion, levels of frailty in adults with intellectual disabilities are comparable to those in much older people in the general population. This raises the question, Why so early?

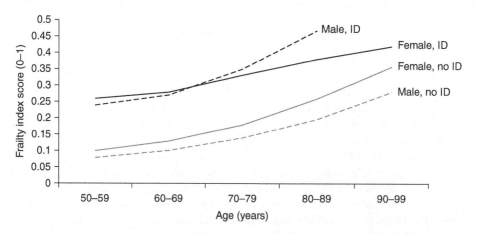

Figure 25.1 Frailty index and the association with age. Upper lines represent the average frailty index per age category and the corresponding trend line in people with intellectual disabilities. The lower grey lines represent the average frailty index per age category and the corresponding trend line from a large general European population aged 50 years and older. Score 0 = not frail to 1 = maximally frail (Schoufour et al., 2013)

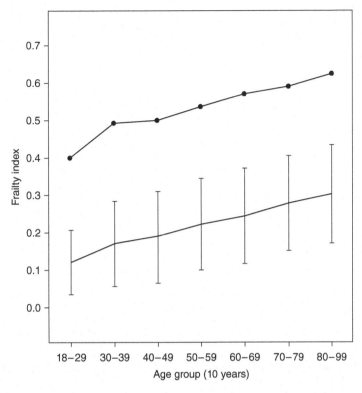

Figure 25.2 Frailty index vs age in the Canadian Study. (FI versus age plot: Average FI (bottom) and 99th percentile of the FI (top), against 10-year age groups. (McKenzie et al., 2015)).

A Pyramid of Accumulating Health Problems

Based on available epidemiological information and clinical experience with this specific population, we constructed a hypothetical model of potential underlying causes of frailty, appearing during the course of life and leading – through multimorbidity and polypharmacy – to frailty (Figure 25.3).

Based on this model, we will address opportunities to avoid or postpone frailty in people with intellectual disabilities, following the domains from childhood to old age. Because of word limits, we had to make a selection, and chose to focus on health risks that have been studied in high-quality epidemiological studies, and specifically on themes with which as a research group we have a specific expertise.

Genetic Factors, Syndromes, Congenital Motor and Sensory Disabilities

Genetic conditions as well as other congenital disabilities and health conditions should be recognised early to inform treatment, rehabilitation, and anticipation of secondary effects. Knowledge of syndromes, other genetic conditions, and syndrome-related conditions appearing during childhood, as well as diagnostic techniques has increased considerably and is now routinely applied in paediatric and clinical genetic clinics in high-income countries. Down syndrome is the most frequent and best recognised syndrome and has been studied extensively. Guidelines have been developed for the detection, diagnosis, and treatment of specific childhood conditions in this group, as well as for specific conditions occurring in adulthood, leading to early deterioration and a shortened life expectation. The wide-spread multidisciplinary Down syndrome outpatient clinics, with regular checks of expected

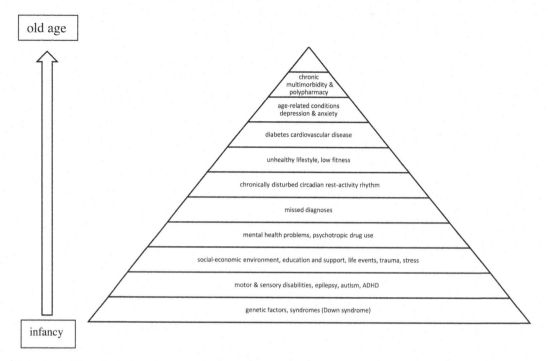

Figure 25.3 Hypothetical model of accumulation of factors threatening health of people with intellectual disabilities during their lifetime. Based on Evenhuis (2014).

health conditions, are a well-known example of the effectiveness of systematic pro-active, early identification and intervention. For other syndromes or congenital disabilities, longitudinal data collection by practice-driven syndrome-clinics has occurred, mostly on a limited scale, for several years, and should be set up broadly, systematically, and uniformly. At the time of writing, evidence-based knowledge into syndrome- or disability-related comorbidity, occurring in adulthood, and its underlying mechanisms, is gradually increasing, but still far from complete. As a result, such comorbidity may remain unidentified or not effectively treated until a late stage.

Psychotropic Drug Use

It has been known since the 1990s that persons with schizophrenia using antipsychotics have a strongly increased risk of diabetes and obesity. In psychiatry, systematic attention for prevention of this risk by specific lifestyle interventions has increased. But in the population with intellectual disabilities, the prevalence of psychotropic medication continues to be high. In the IDS-TILDA study, 59% of those using at least one drug had psychotropic prescriptions (O'Dwyer et al., 2017), whereas in the 50-plus HA-ID population, 43% had used psychotropic drugs and 29% antipsychotics for many years, which is comparable to the prevalence found in younger Dutch adults with intellectual disabilities (de Kuijper et al., 2010). A large majority of prescriptions are not based on psychotic symptoms, but on severe aggression, auto-mutilation, and other behavioural problems, for which the effectiveness of antipsychotics has not been established (de Kuijper et al., 2010).

Long-term antipsychotic drug use may have detrimental health effects, including extrapyramidal symptoms and metabolic and hormonal dysregulation. Therefore, control of antipsychotic drug use is of paramount importance. However, in practice, discontinuation is often hampered by fear of recurring behavioural problems by patients, parents, professional carers, and physicians. That it should be tried nevertheless became apparent in a discontinuation study among 99 Dutch adults with intellectual disabilities who had used antipsychotics because of challenging behaviour for over a year. Controlled discontinuation during 14 weeks resulted in significant improvements of mean scores on the Aberrant Behaviour Checklist and on most of its subscales for those who achieved complete as well as partial discontinuation (de Kuijper, Evenhuis, Minderaa, & Hoekstra, 2014). It also led to substantial decreases of waist circumference, body mass index, and systolic blood pressure within 12 weeks after both complete and incomplete discontinuation (de Kuijper et al., 2014). Apparently, even partial dose reductions may be of benefit.

Missed Diagnoses

It is a well-known fact that diagnoses are often missed in adults with intellectual disabilities because they either don't seek medical advice or have difficulty effectively communicating symptoms that may not be noticed by others, such as pain, dyspnoea, fatigue, heartburn, visual and hearing problems, anxiety, and depression. Further, many of them are unconcerned with long-term consequences of risk factors, whereas others actively avoid healthcare, fearing that a disease might become apparent. As an example, in the 18+ Dutch Visual and Hearing Impairment study of people with intellectual disabilities, visual impairment had been missed in 43% of cases, blindness in 36%, hearing impairment in 48%, and combined visual and hearing impairment in 88% (Meuwese-Jongejeugd et al., 2006; Meuwese-Jongejeugd et al., 2008; van Splunder, Stilma, Bernsen, & Evenhuis, 2006). As a result, unidentified visual and hearing problems may be interpreted as a person having a more severe level of intellectual disability, depressive symptoms, dementia, or challenging behaviour. This fact per se may have explained much of the behaviour, described at the start of this chapter in that 'geriatric sequence', which was wrongly accepted as signs of – unavoidable – ageing. It not only illustrates difficulties of physicians with communication, but also problems with the applicability of routine diagnostic methods, time constraints, reimbursement of costs, and multidisciplinary collaboration. Therefore, systematic screening of visual and hearing functions, both in children and in adults with intellectual disabilities aged 45 years and over – in Down syndrome from age 30 years and over – if necessary using specific diagnostic methods, has been recommended in an IASSID-guideline developed by the Special Interest Group on Health Issues in 2007. The continuing international lack of screening shows that there are barriers to implementation. As a result, glasses and hearing aids, optimal light and acoustics at home, in schools, at work and in day activity centres, cataract surgery, and educated teachers and professional carers, to this day are not available to a majority of people with intellectual disabilities.

Chronically Disturbed Circadian Rest-Activity Rhythm

In clinical practice and from published research, based on personal history taking as well as observations by others, it is known that the sleep-wake rhythm of people with intellectual disabilities is often disturbed. In the HA-ID study, one or more sleeping problems were established with actigraphy in 72% of participants who completed the measurements. This is considerably more than found by asking participants or caregivers (van de Wouw, Evenhuis, & Echteld, 2013). However internationally, there still is uncertainty about the definition of sleeping problems, diagnostic methods, and criteria in this population group, leading to diverging prevalence rates.

With actigraphy, quality of the circadian rest-activity rhythm over 24 hours can be studied, too. This is very relevant, because in fundamental sleep research, it has become increasingly apparent that the biological clock influences the regulation of metabolic processes on multiple levels. It appeared that the circadian rest-activity rhythm of older persons with intellectual disabilities is significantly less stable and more fragmented than in older persons without intellectual disability (Maaskant, van de Wouw, van Wijck, Evenhuis, & Echteld, 2013). A chronically disturbed 24-hour circadian rhythm has been found earlier in people with Alzheimer's dementia, too (Witting, Kwa, Eikelenboom, Mirmiran, & Swaab, 1990). This suggests a role of brain damage, but further research is necessary to answer that question. Light is the strongest stimulator of the circadian rhythm. Bright daylight during the day and dark during the night improves the sleep-wake rhythm even in patients with Alzheimer dementia (van Someren, Kessler, Mirmiran, & Swaab, 1997). For 'resetting' the biological clock, apart from more daylight, sufficient physical activity during the day, and a structured day-and-night rhythm appear to be most effective. It is self-evident that sleep-disturbing factors such as light and noise, burning gastric reflux, pain, psychotropic medication and even sleep medication, should be remedied.

Unhealthy Lifestyle, Low Fitness

Unhealthy nutrition and (extremely) low physical activity and fitness of people with intellectual disabilities are increasing gaining attention in the scientific literature. 'They are just like other people' is a frequent, shrugging reaction if you tell someone about this. Indeed, improvement of physical activity and fitness from a young age onwards is relevant for everyone, but it needs special attention in adults with intellectual disability. Individual barriers to joining movement and sports activities may be higher for this group than for other people: fear of not understanding what is required, fear of the unknown, fear to fail, fear to fall. Motor or sensory disabilities may further complicate participation as do attentional barriers. Many would love to go for a walk or go cycling but are not able or not allowed to do that alone in current traffic circumstances (van Schijndel-Speet, Evenhuis, van Wijck, van Empelen, & Echteld, 2014). Such barriers may be enhanced by anxiety and worries of family and staff of homes, limiting the amount and intensity of activities (negative support) (Frey, Buchanan, & Rosser Sandt, 2005). As a result, motor development and activities of daily life may be delayed in childhood, followed by impaired mobility, independence, social contacts, and work opportunities in their adult years. And, of course, impaired health. Over the age of 50 years, people with intellectual disabilities have fitness levels that are comparable on average to fitness levels of non-disabled people who are 20–30 years older. Their fitness may be too low to participate in regular sports or movement activities. Of course, this will discourage further participation in such activities, and limit participation in daily activities, too (Hilgenkamp, van Wijck, & Evenhuis, 2012; Oppewal, Hilgenkamp, van Wijck, Schoufour, & Evenhuis, 2014; Oppewal, Hilgenkamp, van Wijck, Schoufour, & Evenhuis, 2015).

Apart from that, research into the suitability of international physical activity and training guidelines in people with intellectual disabilities is in progress: there are scientific clues that they should be adapted because of an altered physiological response to exercise, resulting in a limited maximal cardiorespiratory capacity in this group. For example, lower peak heart rates are found (around 10–15 beats/minute lower) than in the general population, specifically but not only in people with Down syndrome (Fernhall et al., 2001). Since heart rate is controlled by the autonomic nervous system, this might be a result of underlying autonomic dysfunction. Indeed, blunted parasympathetic withdrawal and reduced sympathetic activation during exercise is seen in people with Down syndrome (Mendonca, Pereira, & Fernhall, 2010). Research on this topic is still in progress, but is pointing in the direction of the need for population-specific activity and training guidelines, because the existing guidelines for the general population are based on peak heart rate and maximal oxygen uptake estimations that are probably not suited for people with intellectual disabilities.

Diabetes and Cardiovascular Disease

Although cardiovascular risk factors (overweight, hypertension, cholesterol, glucose) can be easily diagnosed in adults with intellectual disabilities, with regular methods used in general practice, in this group such risks remain unidentified twice as much as in the general population. 50% of HA-ID participants with hypertension, 45% of those with diabetes, 45% of hypercholesterolemia cases, and 97%

of persons with peripheral arterial disease had not been diagnosed before the HA-ID study (de Winter, Bastiaanse, Evenhuis, Evenhuis, & Echteld, 2012; de Winter et al., 2013).

In this population group, an unhealthy lifestyle is not the only risk factor for diabetes and cardiovascular disease. As has been elucidated, the use of psychotropic drugs, specifically antipsychotics, contributes considerably to the risk.

Adverse metabolic effects of sleep disturbance, increasing the risk of type 2 diabetes mellitus, obesity, and cardiovascular disease, have been established in the general population by fundamental research as well as epidemiological studies (Nedeltcheva & Scheer, 2014). However, the chronically unstable and fragmented circadian rest-activity rhythm, found in older people with intellectual disabilities might not have the same impact as sleep disturbance caused by frequent jetlag, shift-work, or lights and noises during the night, so such metabolic effects need further evaluation in this specific population. Specific additions to existing diagnostic and therapeutic guidelines on diabetes and cardiovascular disease, including pro-active screening of risk factors, e.g. from age 40 onwards, and attention for specific underlying causes, might be a first step towards early identification and prevention in people with intellectual disabilities. We have shown earlier above that controlled discontinuation of antipsychotics in 14 weeks, prescribed for challenging behaviour, is often accepted by patients and carers, and on average does not lead to increase of behavioural problems (may even diminish them), and leads to improvement of cardiovascular risk factors, even in case of partial discontinuation (de Kuijper et al., 2010, 2014).

In cases of a very low fitness, discouraging participation in movement and sports, a careful step-by-step trajectory with progressive increase of the dose of activities, is required to improve fitness before participation in regular activities is feasible. For an HA-ID effect study (RCT) into improvement of movement and fitness in day care facilities, a program was developed based on behavioural change strategies that are relevant to this specific population (van Schijndel-Speet et al., 2014). The results showed that a progressively dosed exercise program offering a wide variation of activities, guided by movement experts and day activity professionals, was much appreciated by participants and staff and – even in 8 months – led to first significant improvements of objective measures of fitness and health (van Schijndel-Speet, Evenhuis, van Wijck, van Montfort, & Echteld, 2017).

Depression and Anxiety, Life Events

Although symptoms are often overlooked in people with intellectual disabilities, they may be prone to depression and anxiety for a range of psychological, social, and physical reasons. Over the age of 55 years, the risk of anxiety disorders is lower in older persons with intellectual disabilities than in the general population, but the risk of major depression is five times higher (Hermans, Beekman, & Evenhuis, 2013). Optimal support of independence and mental and physical wellbeing, proactive screening and rehabilitation of visual and hearing problems, support of social relationships, and sensible work or other day activities are extremely relevant to preventing depression and anxiety in this group. Because depressive symptoms are seldom recognised as such by the persons themselves, and are often missed by carers, screening with valid questionnaires may be considered in case of impairment of daily functioning which is not fully understood, or routinely applied over age 50 years.

Further, it has become increasingly apparent in fundamental sleep research that chronic sleep disturbance, through disturbance of, among others, the serotonin metabolism, is associated with depression. So, depression might be partially explained by disturbance of the sleep-wake rhythm, too. At the time of writing, two Dutch effect studies (placebo-controlled RCTs) of light exposure in adults with intellectual disabilities are being completed. In the one study optimal light exposure was applied in the daily living environment of older adults (Böhmer, Aarts, & Valstar, 2017) and in the other, adults with depressive symptoms were exposed to bright light lamps (10,000 lux) for 30 minutes in the morning (Hamers, Evenhuis, & Hermans, 2017; Hamers, Festen, Hermans, & Bindels, 2018). In both studies, modest effects on depressive symptoms were found, but not on the circadian rhythm (publications in preparation). So, is there another mediating path between light and depression?

Life events are an often-overlooked source of mental health problems. In the HA-ID study, a checklist was developed, based on internationally available life events questionnaires as well as on specific experiences of professionals working with people with intellectual disabilities. It had to be completed by carers who had known the participants for a long time. As much as possible, they discussed with the participant which events had been experienced as negative. It appeared that 72% of the participants reported at least one negative life event during the past year. This was significantly associated with symptoms of depression and anxiety and self-reported quality of life (Hermans & Evenhuis, 2012). Most frequently reported were problems with co-residents, structural changes of staff, mild physical diseases, loss or decrease of mobility, and severe disease of family, carer, or friend.

A 35-year old man with Down syndrome came with his father to our outpatient clinic. Staff of his group home suspected early dementia, but his father didn't believe that. The patient appeared an open, courteous, interested man with a relatively mild intellectual disability, who could very well answer my questions, whereas the father sketched the larger picture. After his mother died, this young man became impassive and sometimes incontinent, so he had been moved to another home, for persons needing more intensive support, where his functioning deteriorated further. Because his new room was less spacious than that in the former home, he couldn't keep his electric organ. When I asked what bothered him most, he silently said: 'My organ.' His mother, his home, his organ. Three major life events.

Heleen Evenhuis

So, life events, in our eyes even minor events, may be experienced as threatening and disturbing by people, even those with mild intellectual disabilities, and may lead to depressive symptoms and anxiety. Group life, including problematic co-residents, staff changes, and transfers, is a relevant source of such life events. Their impact, however, may not be recognised as such by carers, as illustrated by the above case. In our opinion, this is a relevant challenge for the organisation of formal care and support.

Multimorbidity and Polypharmacy

Multimorbidity and polypharmacy (as well as frailty) are relevant public health measures. Both multimorbidity and polypharmacy appeared, independently as strong predictors of death within 3 and 5 years (Schoufour, Mitnitski, et al., 2015; Schoufour et al., 2018).

Multimorbidity

Multimorbidity is generally defined as two and more chronic conditions that negatively influence daily functioning. In the HA-ID study, based on a list of 20 conditions diagnosed during the study, its prevalence was 80% (Hermans & Evenhuis, 2014). This was comparable to the outcomes of the IDS-TILDA study, based on 12 chronic conditions measured, where 71–75.8% of participants had two or more chronic health conditions (McCarron et al., 2013; O'Dwyer, Peklar, McCallion, McCarron, & Henman, 2016). It is comparable, too, to the 82% prevalence of multimorbidity in the Dutch nursing home population: a highly selected, frail population with considerable health problems (Schram et al., 2008). As a matter of fact, 47% of the HA-ID study population had four or more chronic conditions.

Although general practitioners and geriatricians have increasing experience with multimorbidity in older people, multimorbidity in the population with intellectual disabilities may require specific experience. This is illustrated in Table 25.1, showing high frequencies of conditions that in this population may remain undiagnosed, may require specific diagnostic methods, or may be difficult to treat.

Multimorbidity may be a manifestation of comorbidity clusters. A recent, unpublished, inquiry among Dutch intellectual disability physicians showed, that the most frequent indications for referral to intellectual disability outpatient clinics are: challenging behaviour, functional deterioration, syndrome-related

Table 25.1 Occurrence rates (%) of most frequent chronic health conditions over age 50 years

Most frequent chronic health conditions over age 50 years	Occurrence %
Dysphagia	52
Chronic constipation	43
Severe challenging behaviour	32
Hearing impairment	30
Visual impairment	25
Epilepsy	22
Peripheral arterial disease	20
Gastroesophageal reflux disease	20
Thyroid dysfunction	18
Autism	18

Source: Based on Hermans and Evenhuis (2014).

checks, overweight and underweight, swallowing problems, sleeping problems, epilepsy, and transfer by paediatricians of their patients with complex multiple problems after age 18 years.

Based on scientific evidence and shared longstanding clinical expertise, a working party consisting of representatives of all professional disciplines involved in intellectual disability healthcare established that nearly all of these referral indications could be categorised into a series of high-risk morbidity clusters, requiring interdisciplinary collaboration: (1) Challenging behaviour, psychologic and psychiatric problems (2) Syndromes and other genetic conditions (3) 'Unidentified syndromes' (4) Feeding, swallowing, and weight problems (5) Systematic medication reviews (6) Cerebral palsy (7) Visual and Hearing impairments (8) Lifestyle (9) Sleeping problems and (10) Ageing and functional deterioration.

Polypharmacy

Polypharmacy, defined as the permanent use of five or more drugs, was found in 40% of the HA-ID study population (Zaal, van der Kaaij, Evenhuis, & van den Bemt, 2013). Only 11% of the participants did not use any drugs, whereas, on the other hand, 6% had 10 or more permanent prescriptions at the start of the study. In Ireland, 31.5% of IDS-TILDA participants had polypharmacy (5–9 permanent drugs) and 20% excessive polypharmacy (≥10 drugs) (O'Dwyer et al., 2016).

In order to increase oversight and correct intake of prescribed drugs by persons with intellectual disabilities, specific support, and monitoring systems may be very useful. An example, appreciated by patients and carers, is Managing Own Medication (Beheer Eigen Medicatie), developed by the Dutch Institute for Rational Use of Medicine.

Support systems to advance appropriate prescriptions by physicians and prevention of unnecessary medication and side effects, are equally relevant. Over several decades, guidelines and systems for multidisciplinary medication reviews in older people have been developed internationally. In the Netherlands, a Systematic Tool to Reduce Inappropriate Prescribing (STRIP), which includes the Screening Tool to Alert doctors to Right Treatment (START) and the Screening Tool of Older People's Prescriptions (STOPP), has been developed as part of a guideline for older people with polypharmacy in the general population. Active involvement of the patient is part of this systematic multidisciplinary medication review.

In spite of the frequent polypharmacy in persons with intellectual disabilities, general practitioners rarely apply systematic reviews in this group, and if they do, it is usually without actively involving patients or their representatives. Recently, an implementation pilot project was completed in the South-West Netherlands by 11 triads, consisting of a general practitioner, a pharmacist, and an intellectual disability physician (Boot, Mulder-Wildemors, Voorbrood, & Evenhuis, 2019). After a one-day course into polypharmacy in persons with intellectual disabilities and the STRIP-method, the general practitioners and pharmacists found the method applicable in these patients. They were impressed by the numbers of pharmaceutical problems, identified by the pharmacists (on average five), and enthusiastic about the recommended interventions. The triads concluded the essential nature of multidisciplinary collaboration. Input by intellectual disability physicians was considered specifically relevant in cases of antipsychotic or antiepileptic prescriptions or communication problems with patients or carers. General practitioners were positively surprised about the active and useful contribution of the patients, whereas the patients (and their representatives) were happy about being involved.

Barriers experienced to implementation were the planning of multidisciplinary meetings, time investment required, and the lack of appropriate reimbursement. Time investment was high because of incomplete medical files, specifically the absence of reasons for psychotropic prescriptions, often dating back many years. If regular reviews became normal, files would be up-to-date and practitioners more experienced, reducing the time investment required. We conclude that multidisciplinary systematic reviews in this patient group are applicable and result in identification of some very relevant pharmaceutical problems and interventions, even in case of highly developed and well-organised medical care systems as in the Netherlands.

So, How to Avoid or Postpone Frailty?

Although we are aware that our selection was far from complete – mental health, and specifically challenging behaviour, were hardly mentioned in this chapter, it seems that 'pro-active', 'special knowledge', 'interdisciplinary', as well as 'development and implementation', are central notions in policies to structurally improve public health of people with intellectual disabilities.

Pro-active diagnosis and intervention, that is: without relying on the person or his carer taking the initiative, is increasingly being introduced in general practice, specifically around frail older people. As we have argued above, for people with intellectual disabilities, pro-active action is critically important for timely diagnoses of syndrome-related and motor disability-related health conditions, and conditions that are not easily visible, specifically if they occur more frequently than in other people. General practitioners normally deal with risks in order of their frequency in the general population, but sometimes the risks have a different order in people with intellectual disabilities. For example, gastroesophageal reflux (heartburn) should be high on the list in case of sleeping problems. We recommend screening of increased health risks that are frequently missed, such as visual and hearing impairment, depression, and cardiovascular risk factors. Use of diagnostic methods with proven validity is required; for example, just asking the person, or his carers, if he sees or hears well, is not a good screening method.

Special knowledge, of the person with an intellectual disability, his family, and involved healthcare professionals, will improve early recognition of symptoms: if you are aware of what to expect, you notice. You know what to ask (or require from) professionals. So provide concrete information about specific health risks, possible prevention, applicable diagnostic and therapeutic methods, methods for daily support and care, on all levels, in personal contacts, in handouts, on internet, in educational courses for all disciplines involved.

Interdisciplinary healthcare: disciplines make and evaluate their screening, diagnostic and intervention plans together, specifically in case of (clustered) multimorbidity.

Development and implementation: to support pro-active healthcare, special knowledge, and an interdisciplinary approach, national or international policies to develop valid tools for specialist healthcare and their reimbursement are essential. We specifically mention the development and implementation of evidence- and practice-based professional guidelines (or additions to general population guidelines), of systematic multidisciplinary medication reviews, of effective prevention and intervention programs, of interdisciplinary intellectual disability out-clinics as well as specific syndrome clinics, and of professional training programs. This is the most difficult part to accomplish, requiring vision, leadership, perseverance, and financing. In the Netherlands, after two decades of development and perseverance by the Dutch Association of Intellectual Disability Physicians, together with the specialist training school and the research group at the Erasmus MC, we are on our way now, but only partially. Development and implementation of healthcare improvement would be a good central theme for the International Association for the Scientific Study of Intellectual Disability (IASSID).

References

Böhmer, M. N., Aarts, M. J. P., & Valstar, M. J. (2017). *Bright-study: Morning light exposure and circadian rhythm in elderly with intellectual disabilities*. Berlin: Society of Light Therapy and Biological Rhythms.

Boot, F., Mulder-Wildemors, L., Voorbrood, V., & Evenhuis, H. (2019). Medicatiebeoordeling bij verstandelijke beperking [Medication review in intellectual disability]. *Huisarts en wetenschap [General Practitioner and Science]*, 62(1), 50–53.

de Kuijper, G., Evenhuis, H., Minderaa, R. B., & Hoekstra, P. J. (2014). Effects of controlled discontinuation of long-term used antipsychotics for behavioural symptoms in individuals with intellectual disability. *Journal of Intellectual Disability Research*, 58(1), 71–83. https://doi.org/10.1111/j.1365-2788.2012.01631.x

de Kuijper, G., Hoekstra, P., Visser, F., Scholte, F. A., Penning, C., & Evenhuis, H. (2010). Use of antipsychotic drugs in individuals with intellectual disability (ID) in the Netherlands: Prevalence and reasons for prescription. *Journal of Intellectual Disability Research*, 54(7), 659–667. https://doi.org/10.1111/j.1365-2788.2010.01275.x

de Winter, C. F., Bastiaanse, L. P., Evenhuis, T. I. M., Evenhuis, H. M., & Echteld, M. A. (2012). Cardiovascular risk factors (diabetes, hypertension, hypercholesterolemia and metabolic syndrome) in older people with intellectual disability: Results of the HA-ID study. *Research in Developmental Disabilities*, 33(6), 1722–1731. https://doi.org/10.1016/j.ridd.2012.04.010

de Winter, C. F., Bastiaanse, L. P., Kranendonk, S. E., Hilgenkamp, T. I., Evenhuis, H. M., & Echteld, M. A. (2013). Peripheral arterial disease in older people with intellectual disability in The Netherlands using the ankle-brachial index: Results of the HA-ID study. *Research in Developmental Disabilities*, 34(5), 1663–1668. https://doi.org/10.1016/j.ridd.2013.02.007

Evenhuis, H. M. (2014). Niet eerder oud, maar eerder ongezond, de kwetsbaarheid van mensen met verstandelijke beperkingen. [Not earlier old, but earlier unhealthy. Frailty of people with intellectual disabilities]. *Ned Tijdschr Geneeskd [The Netherlands Journal of Medicine]*, 158, A8016.

Fernhall, B., McCubbin, J. A., Pitetti, K. H., Rintala, P., Rimmer, J. H., Millar, A. L., & De Silva, A. (2001). Prediction of maximal heart rate in individuals with mental retardation. *Medicine & Science in Sports & Exercise*, 33(10), 1655–1660. https://doi.org/10.1097/00005768-200110000-00007

Frey, G. C., Buchanan, A. M., & Rosser Sandt, D. D. (2005). "I'd Rather Watch TV": An examination of physical activity in adults with mental retardation. *Mental Retardation*, 43(4), 241–254. https://doi.org/10.1352/0047-6765(2005)43[241:IRWTAE]2.0.CO;2

Hamers, P. C., Evenhuis, H. M., & Hermans, H. (2017). A multicenter randomized controlled trial for bright light therapy in adults with intellectual disabilities and depression: Study protocol and obstacle management. *Research in Developmental Disabilities*, 60, 96–106. https://doi.org/10.1016/j.ridd.2016.10.012

Hamers, P., Festen, D., Hermans, H., & Bindels, P. (2018, July). *A multicenter RCT with bright light therapy in adults with intellectual disability and depressive symptoms: First results*. Fifth IASSID Europe Congress, Athens.

Hermans, H., & Evenhuis, H. M. (2012). Life events and their associations with depression and anxiety in older people with intellectual disabilities: Results of the HA-ID study. *Journal of Affective Disorders*, 138(1–2), 79–85. https://doi.org/10.1016/j.jad.2011.12.025

Hermans, H., & Evenhuis, H. M. (2014). Multimorbidity in older adults with intellectual disabilities. *Research in Developmental Disabilities*, 35(4), 776–783. https://doi.org/10.1016/j.ridd.2014.01.022

Hermans, H., Beekman, A. T., & Evenhuis, H. M. (2013). Prevalence of depression and anxiety in older users of formal Dutch intellectual disability services. *Journal of Affective Disorders*, 144(1–2), 94–100. https://doi.org/10.1016/j.jad.2012.06.011

Hilgenkamp, T. I., Bastiaanse, L. P., Hermans, H., Penning, C., van Wijck, R., & Evenhuis, H. M. (2011). Study healthy ageing and intellectual disabilities: Recruitment and design. *Research in Developmental Disabilities*, 32(3), 1097–1106. https://doi.org/10.1016/j.ridd.2011.01.018

Hilgenkamp, T. I., van Wijck, R., & Evenhuis, H. M. (2012). Low physical fitness levels in older adults with ID: Results of the HA-ID study. *Research in Developmental Disabilities*, 33(4), 1048–1058. https://doi.org/10.1016/j.ridd.2012.01.013

Maaskant, M., van de Wouw, E., van Wijck, R., Evenhuis, H. M., & Echteld, M. A. (2013). Circadian sleep–wake rhythm of older adults with intellectual disabilities. *Research in Developmental Disabilities*, 34(4), 1144–1151. https://doi.org/10.1016/j.ridd.2012.12.009

McCarron, M., Swinburne, J., Burke, E., McGlinchey, E., Carroll, R., & McCallion, P. (2013). Patterns of multimorbidity in an older population of persons with an intellectual disability: Results from the intellectual disability supplement to the Irish longitudinal study on aging (IDS-TILDA). *Research in Developmental Disabilities, 34*(1), 521–527. https://doi.org/10.1016/j.ridd.2012.07.029

McKenzie, K., Ouellette-Kuntz, H., & Martin, L. (2015). Using an accumulation of deficits approach to measure frailty in a population of home care users with intellectual and developmental disabilities: An analytical descriptive study. *BMC Geriatrics, 15*(1), 170. https://doi.org/10.1186/s12877-015-0170-5

Mendonca, G. V., Pereira, F. D., & Fernhall, B. O. (2010). Reduced exercise capacity in persons with Down syndrome: Cause, effect, and management. *Therapeutics and Clinical Risk Management, 6*, 601. https://doi.org/10.2147/TCRM.S10235

Meuwese-Jongejeugd, A., van Splunder, J., Vink, M., Stilma, J. S., van Zanten, B., Verschuure, H., ... Evenhuis, H. (2008). Combined sensory impairment (deaf–blindness) in five percent of adults with intellectual disabilities. *American Journal on Mental Retardation, 113*(4), 254–262. https://doi.org/10.1352/0895-8017(2008)113[254:CSIDIF]2.0.CO;2

Meuwese-Jongejeugd, A., Vink, M., van Zanten, B., Verschuure, H., Eichhorn, E., Koopman, D., ... Evenhuis, H. (2006). Prevalence of hearing loss in 1598 adults with an intellectual disability: Cross-sectional population-based study. *International Journal of Audiology, 45*(11), 660–669. https://doi.org/10.1080/14992020600920812

Nedeltcheva, A. V., & Scheer, F. A. (2014). Metabolic effects of sleep disruption, links to obesity and diabetes. *Current Opinion in Endocrinology, Diabetes, and Obesity, 21*(4), 293. https://doi.org/10.1097/MED.0000000000000082

O'Dwyer, M., Peklar, J., McCallion, P., McCarron, M., & Henman, M. C. (2016). Factors associated with polypharmacy and excessive polypharmacy in older people with intellectual disability differ from the general population: A cross-sectional observational nationwide study. *BMJ Open, 6*(4), e010505. https://doi.org/10.1136/bmjopen-2015-010505

O'Dwyer, M., Peklar, J., Mulryan, N., McCallion, P., McCarron, M., & Henman, M. C. (2017). Prevalence, patterns and factors associated with psychotropic use in older adults with intellectual disabilities in Ireland. *Journal of Intellectual Disability Research, 61*(10), 969–983. https://doi.org/10.1111/jir.12391

Oppewal, A., Hilgenkamp, T. I., van Wijck, R., Schoufour, J. D., & Evenhuis, H. M. (2014). Physical fitness is predictive for a decline in daily functioning in older adults with intellectual disabilities: Results of the HA-ID study. *Research in Developmental Disabilities, 35*(10), 2299–2315. https://doi.org/10.1016/j.ridd.2014.05.027

Oppewal, A., Hilgenkamp, T. I., van Wijck, R., Schoufour, J. D., & Evenhuis, H. M. (2015). Physical fitness is predictive for a decline in the ability to perform instrumental activities of daily living in older adults with intellectual disabilities: Results of the HA-ID study. *Research in Developmental Disabilities, 41*, 76–85. https://doi.org/10.1016/j.ridd.2015.05.002

Rockwood, K., & Mitnitski, A. (2007). Frailty in relation to the accumulation of deficits. *The Journals of Gerontology Series A: Biological Sciences and Medical Sciences, 62*(7), 722–727. https://doi.org/10.1093/gerona/62.7.722

Romero-Ortuno, R., & Kenny, R. A. (2012). The frailty index in Europeans: Association with age and mortality. *Age and Ageing, 41*(5), 684–689. https://doi.org/10.1093/ageing/afs051

Schoufour, J. D., Echteld, M. A., & Evenhuis, H. M. (2017). Comparing two frailty concepts among older people with intellectual disabilities. *European Journal of Ageing, 14*(1), 63–79. https://doi.org/10.1007/s10433-016-0388-x

Schoufour, J. D., Echteld, M. A., Bastiaanse, L. P., & Evenhuis, H. M. (2015). The use of a frailty index to predict adverse health outcomes (falls, fractures, hospitalization, medication use, comorbid conditions) in people with intellectual disabilities. *Research in Developmental Disabilities, 38*, 39–47. https://doi.org/10.1016/j.ridd.2014.12.001

Schoufour, J. D., Evenhuis, H. M., & Echteld, M. A. (2014). The impact of frailty on care intensity in older people with intellectual disabilities. *Research in Developmental Disabilities, 35*(12), 3455–3461. https://doi.org/10.1016/j.ridd.2014.08.006

Schoufour, J. D., Mitnitski, A., Rockwood, K., Evenhuis, H. M., & Echteld, M. A. (2015). Predicting 3-year survival in older people with intellectual disabilities using a frailty index. *Journal of the American Geriatrics Society, 63*(3), 531–536. https://doi.org/10.1111/jgs.13239

Schoufour, J. D., Mitnitski, A., Rockwood, K., Evenhuis, H. M., & Echteld, M. A. (2013). Development of a frailty index for older people with intellectual disabilities: Results from the HA-ID study. *Research in Developmental Disabilities, 34*(5), 1541–1555. https://doi.org/10.1016/j.ridd.2013.01.029

Schoufour, J. D., Mitnitski, A., Rockwood, K., Hilgenkamp, T. I., Evenhuis, H. M., & Echteld, M. A. (2014). Predicting disabilities in daily functioning in older people with intellectual disabilities using a frailty index. *Research in Developmental Disabilities, 35*(10), 2267–2277. https://doi.org/10.1016/j.ridd.2014.05.022

Schoufour, J. D., Oppewal, A., van der Maarl, H. J., Hermans, H., Evenhuis, H. M., Hilgenkamp, T. I., & Festen, D. A. (2018). Multimorbidity and polypharmacy are independently associated with mortality in older people with intellectual disabilities: A 5-year follow-up from the HA-ID study. *American Journal on Intellectual and Developmental Disabilities*, *123*(1), 72–82. https://doi.org/10.1352/1944-7558-123.1.72

Schram, M. T., Frijters, D., van de Lisdonk, E. H., Ploemacher, J., de Craen, A. J., de Waal, M. W., ... Schellevis, F. G. (2008). Setting and registry characteristics affect the prevalence and nature of multimorbidity in the elderly. *Journal of Clinical Epidemiology*, *61*(11), 1104–1112. https://doi.org/10.1016/j.jclinepi.2007.11.021

van de Wouw, E., Evenhuis, H. M., & Echteld, M. A. (2013). Objective assessment of sleep and sleep problems in older adults with intellectual disabilities. *Research in Developmental Disabilities*, *34*(8), 2291–2303. https://doi.org/10.1016/j.ridd.2013.04.012

van Schijndel-Speet, M., Evenhuis, H. M., van Wijck, R., van Empelen, P., & Echteld, M. A. (2014). Facilitators and barriers to physical activity as perceived by older adults with intellectual disability. *Journal of Intellectual and Developmental Disability*, *52*(3), 175–186. https://doi.org/10.1352/1934-9556-52.3.175

van Schijndel-Speet, M., Evenhuis, H. M., van Wijck, R., van Montfort, K. C. A. G. M., & Echteld, M. A. (2017). A structured physical activity and fitness programme for older adults with intellectual disabilities: Results of a cluster-randomised clinical trial. *Journal of Intellectual Disability Research*, *61*(1), 16–29. https://doi.org/10.1111/jir.12267

van Someren, E. J., Kessler, A., Mirmiran, M., & Swaab, D. F. (1997). Indirect bright light improves circadian rest-activity rhythm disturbances in demented patients. *Biological Psychiatry*, *41*(9), 955–963. https://doi.org/10.1016/S0006-3223(97)89928-3

van Splunder, J. A., Stilma, J. S., Bernsen, R. M. D., & Evenhuis, H. M. (2006). Prevalence of visual impairment in adults with intellectual disabilities in the Netherlands: Cross-sectional study. *Eye*, *20*(9), 1004–1010. https://doi.org/10.1038/sj.eye.6702059

Witting, W., Kwa, I. H., Eikelenboom, P., Mirmiran, M., & Swaab, D. F. (1990). Alterations in the circadian rest-activity rhythm in aging and Alzheimer's disease. *Biological Psychiatry*, *27*(6), 563–572. https://doi.org/10.1016/0006-3223(90)90523-5

Zaal, R. J., van der Kaaij, A. D., Evenhuis, H. M., & van den Bemt, P. M. (2013). Prescription errors in older individuals with an intellectual disability: Prevalence and risk factors in the Healthy Ageing and Intellectual Disability Study. *Research in Developmental Disabilities*, *34*(5), 1656–1662.

Suggested Readings

Hermans, H., & Evenhuis, H. M. (2014). Multimorbidity in older adults with intellectual disabilities. *Research in Developmental Disabilities*, *35*(4), 776–783. https://doi.org/10.1016/j.ridd.2014.01.022

McCarron, M., Swinburne, J., Burke, E., McGlinchey, E., Carroll, R., & McCallion, P. (2013). Patterns of multimorbidity in an older population of persons with an intellectual disability: Results from the intellectual disability supplement to the Irish longitudinal study on aging (IDS-TILDA). *Research in Developmental Disabilities*, *34*(1), 521–527. https://doi.org/10.1016/j.ridd.2012.07.029

Ouellette-Kuntz, H., Martin, L., & McKenzie, K. (2018). Rate of deficit accumulation in home care users with intellectual and developmental disabilities. *Annals of Epidemiology*, *28*(4), 220–224.

van Schijndel-Speet, M., Evenhuis, H. M., van Wijck, R., van Montfort, K. C. A. G. M., & Echteld, M. A. (2017). A structured physical activity and fitness programme for older adults with intellectual disabilities: Results of a cluster-randomised clinical trial. *Journal of Intellectual Disability Research*, *61*(1), 16–29. https://doi.org/10.1111/jir.12267

26
DEMENTIA CARE FOR PERSONS AGEING WITH INTELLECTUAL DISABILITY

Developing Non-Pharmacological Strategies for Support

Karen Watchman and Kate Mattheys

Overview

Textbooks, academic articles, and information guides about dementia often give suggestions to carers about adapting the home environment, reinforcing the importance of music or reminiscence, and strategies that may lessen symptoms associated with dementia. Television programmes and media articles are taking an increased interest in such interventions in practice. However, such resources or features rarely, if ever, have clear application for people who also have an intellectual disability. This demonstrates the importance of conducting non-pharmacological (non-drug) intervention studies with participants who have an intellectual disability and who continue to remain excluded from mainstream dementia research (Watchman, 2016). Non-drug interventions represent a broad array of environmental, psychosocial, and non-medical approaches aiming to reduce the impact of behavioural and psychological changes that can be associated with dementia (Jokinen, 2014). This chapter discusses findings from a study in Scotland, UK on the effects of implementation of non-drug interventions with people who have an intellectual disability and dementia, specifically focusing on the examples of two individuals where a design change to the home environment, music playlist and reminiscence activity were implemented.

A focus on dementia is warranted due to increased prevalence in people with an intellectual disability, particularly among people with Down syndrome who are more susceptible to developing the condition at a younger age. At least one-third of individuals with Down syndrome in their 50s, and more than half of those who live to 60 or over, will develop dementia (Strydom, 2017). This compares to dementia prevalence rates of 7.1% of those aged over 65 who do not have an intellectual disability (Prince et al., 2014). People with other intellectual disabilities are also more likely to develop dementia than the general population, although this is not as prevalent as in people with Down syndrome (Royal College of Psychiatry, 2015).

Discussion of Literature

Findings from the available evidence suggest that non-pharmacological interventions may have potential benefits on some of the behavioural and psychological symptoms of dementia. Woods, O'Philbin, Farrell, Spector, and Orrell's (2018) systematic review of reminiscence with people who have dementia (not Down syndrome) identified some positive impacts on cognitive function, communication/interaction, quality of life, and mood. However, the effects are inconsistent across different types of reminiscence work and different contexts (for example, care home or community). It is argued that there may be little benefits beyond 'in the moment' enjoyment of the activity (Woods et al., 2018). Reminiscence-type activities have been incorporated into several pilot projects for use with people with intellectual disability and dementia. This includes a pilot support group that used life story books and cognitive games (Rosewarne, 2001) and a pilot memory café (Kiddle, Drew, Crabbe, & Wigmore, 2016).

There is a dearth of research exploring how support providers respond to changing needs in people with intellectual disability and dementia. Staff burden was a common theme in Courtenay, Jokinen, and Strydom's (2010) study, alongside concerns around availability of staff training and models of care. Iacono, Bigby, Carling-Jenkins, and Torr (2014) found that staff experienced difficulty in responding to the unpredictability of behaviour change in clients. This included struggling to identify whether the behaviour change related to symptoms or progression of dementia. Staff were uncertain about what changes to expect in the person, and when these were likely to occur. This was translated in their practice into 'taking each day as it comes', use of ad-hoc strategies to respond to changing needs, and being proactive rather than reactive.

Crook, Adams, Shorten, and Langdon (2016) explored the impact of reminiscence activities with a group of five participants with intellectual disabilities and dementia. Participants took part in three 30-minute sessions of life story books, rummage/memory boxes, and no intervention (no structured activity), with each participant trying all three activities (nine in total) over nine consecutive days. The researchers delivered the sessions and used 'dementia care mapping' as a method to record mood and engagement (via a 'mood engagement value') and behaviour. These were combined to provide an overall well-being/ill-being score. The reminiscence options led to improved wellbeing compared to no intervention for all the participants. Use of memory boxes and life story books led to an increase in communication, expressive and intellectual behaviours. Overall association was made with increased well-being and positive changes in behaviour, although there was variation in findings from different interventions: for one participant the memory box led to higher well-being scores, for another the life story book had the largest well-being impact.

In the UK, there has been a growth in the use of music-based activities including singing groups, personalised music playlists, and music therapy. Whilst many memories can be lost as dementia progresses, it has been suggested that 'musical memory' can be retained (Jacobsen et al., 2015). This ability to reconnect with music, and the memories that familiar music can evoke, has been linked to people with dementia connecting with their sense of self, feelings of belonging, increased engagement, communication, improved mood, and enhanced relationships (Mendes, 2015). However, the evidence base on the impact of music is inconclusive with Baird and Samson (2015) suggesting that music activities may be little more beneficial than other pleasant activities. One systematic review suggested a positive impact, although the evidence was considered low (Ueda, Suzukamo, Sato, & Izumi, 2013).

The role of music has been considered in two pilot projects with people with intellectual disabilities and dementia. Ward and Parkes (2017) explored the potential benefits of Singing for the Brain, a service developed by the Alzheimer's Society, UK that uses singing as a way in which people can take part in a stimulating, fun activity (Alzheimer's Society, 2012). Staff reported that the groups helped lift participants' mood and gave them more energy, and participants themselves enjoyed the singing. Singing as a group helped participants to bond with each other. A number of staff members felt that the intervention had a lasting impact on mood, over the whole day on occasions. The sessions were reported as having a calming effect on participants who were agitated, and to impact on memory. Some participants reminisced about songs and their links to family members. Bevins, Dawes, Kenshole, and Gaussen (2015) undertook a pilot of a music therapy group for five people with intellectual disability and dementia. Whilst some longer-term changes were observed, including changes in communication and mood, it was difficult to determine whether these changes came about as a result of taking part in the music therapy group, or from other factors in that person's life.

More literature is available that suggests strategies to improve the design of the built environment for people with dementia in the population generally, including for instance the impact of the spatial layout of buildings, increased levels of lighting, reduced noise levels, use of colour and contrasts, and personalised living environments: these have suggested a therapeutic effect that helps well-being, independence and behaviour (Marquardt, Buetker, & Motzek, 2014). Janicki, Dalton, McCallion, Baxley, and Zendell (2005) explored the provision of small group home care for people with intellectual disabilities, considering the physical characteristics of the homes, and the environmental adaptations that had been made in response to changes in behaviour as a result of dementia. The homes that had been specifically built for people with dementia tended to include fenced yards, paths that could be used to walk freely, increased lighting, signage, and universal design features that would allow wheelchair accessibility. The authors argue that dementia friendly homes have a universal benefit, regardless of whether people have an intellectual disability alongside the dementia. De Vreese et al. (2012) explored a combination of related environmental and psychosocial interventions for people with intellectual disabilities and dementia. Interventions included staff-oriented interventions such as training; environment-oriented interventions including lighting and signage; and client-oriented interventions such as daily individual and group activities, music, physical activities, and animal assisted activities.

The experiences of two anonymised participants from the study in Scotland of non-drug interventions are presented here to illustrate the effect and challenges of the different personalised non-pharmacological interventions faced during the UK study. The study included 16 participants with intellectual disability and dementia, 22 social care support staff and involved 5 co-researchers with intellectual disability (Watchman, Mattheys, McKernon, Strachan, Andreis & Murdoch, 2020). Ethical approval was provided by the appropriate human participants committee with informed consent provided by all participants. A multi-method approach to data collection was taken involving pre, mid and post testing:

- Goal attainment scales (linked to personal goals) to determine individualised interventions and subsequent rating with participants to determine if goals were achieved
- Semi-structured interviews with staff
- Neuropsychiatric Inventory Questionnaire with staff (NPI-Q) (Cummings et al., 1994). The NPI-Q is a measure of behavioural and psychological symptoms of dementia.
- Bespoke behaviour change tool to observe in the moment effects on the participants
- Photovoice to visually record perceptions of people with an intellectual disability
- Researcher field notes
- Intervention diary completed by staff to record the date, time, duration and frequency of interventions

Jim

Jim was a 69-year-old man living in supported accommodation with three other people with intellectual disability, and 24-hour staff support. Jim had a diagnosis of vascular dementia. Jim's care plan was heavily focused on issues relating to his behaviour, which was identified by staff as a key challenge; staff attributed changes in his behaviour to dementia. Jim could become very unsettled and agitated, which led to shouting, swearing, aggression, and self-harm. This was distressing for Jim and upsetting for the other residents living in the flat. Jim had difficulties with maintaining his morning routines, in particular around personal care. Staff tried to use 'de-escalation techniques', such as giving Jim time alone and a different staff member providing support, however these were rarely effective.

In consultation with Jim, use of a personalised music playlist and reminiscence memory box were agreed. His personal goals included remembering family and important memories, and not feeling anxious and worried. Jim's support team were initially unsure about whether the interventions would have a positive impact, expressing concern that if Jim was agitated then the interventions would not help him. Jim was provided with an mp3 player and headphones for his music (intervention two times per week over the 6-month period, and 'as required' if he became agitated), and a box with which staff could support him to create his own memory box (also twice week, on different days to the music, and 'as required').

> I went to Jim's flat to offer him the activities and we sat together and put together the box (it was flat-packed). Jim engaged with me in holding the box and putting it together and repeating back to me when I talked about things he could put in it... It was genuinely surprising how much he liked it. He held it, looked at it, he was smiling and his face was relaxed, after a little while he went off to show other people his new box.
>
> Researcher field notes

Jim's team had limited knowledge of his life before he moved into his current home and found it challenging initially to identify things that he might like to keep in his box, and to select songs that were meaningful to him. This was often a process of trial and error. A lack of Internet access in the flat posed further barriers as the support worker had to download songs remotely before Jim was able to play them. Jim tried in-ear headphones but did not like these, he subsequently tried over-the-ear headphones before settling on using a small speaker. Television theme tunes worked well and were meaningful for him, he enjoyed listening to them and identifying the television show that the song came from, and this initiated conversations about the programmes. Jim talked about other songs and memories they evoked, including songs that made him think about his mum:

> Sometimes there'll be a song, and he'll be like 'oh my mum liked that song', and then he'll start telling me about his mum, and how she used to play the records, and have a dance and things like that.
>
> Support Worker, transcribed interview notes

Jim listened to his playlist with one of his flatmates and they chatted together about the music. This had a positive impact on their relationship (which could otherwise be fraught) although on some occasions there was tension, for instance if Jim wanted to listen to his music and his flatmate sang too loudly over the songs. Sometimes he found it difficult to remember the songs or to get his words out. Jim was very specific about who he wanted to do the interventions with; by the end of the project he only chose to do them with his key worker Katherine and refused other members of staff. Key positive impacts of the music playlist included helping him at times when he was feeling unsettled. There were two reported occasions when Jim was becoming very agitated and the music helped him to feel calmer and more relaxed.

> Jim's mood was becoming very elevated, he was stuttering, and his speech was very fast and loud. I asked would he like to listen to his music. I played some music for him. He became relaxed, his speech slowed down, his mood was less elevated.
>
> Support Worker, intervention log

Jim remained very proud of his memory box. He personalised it himself and enjoyed looking through it, talking about the items in his box, and arranging them. This included childhood story books, television show memorabilia, photos, and artwork.

> Katherine (support worker) advised that Jim had been excited about me coming out as he was looking forward to showing me the new things he had put in his box. His body language suggested he was proud of it, he showed me the tv book he has in it, he was interested in this and enjoyed looking through the pictures and pointing people out. He showed me his items but did not pass me them to look at – staff said afterwards he likes the box so much he doesn't want other people holding the items.
>
> Researcher field notes

Jim's support worker learned more about Jim in the process of helping him put together the memory box. It led to increased conversation and communication between them as Jim talked about the items in his box and this triggered memories; this was also the case with his music playlist. Using both interventions led to improved relationships with his key worker as she learned more about Jim and spent time doing the interventions with him.

> It's good to get an insight, because we didn't know. Like the Mr Men, or holidays, or music his mum liked, we're finding out now. Now we have a tiny idea of things that he done in the past. And what he liked to do.
>
> Support Worker, transcribed interview notes

Key benefits of the memory box and music combined included improved mood, engagement, communication, and observed behaviour during the times that Jim took part in the interventions. These positive effects of both interventions could last for several hours. Jim enjoyed the interventions and was happier and more relaxed when he was doing them. He engaged with the activities, sitting up straight, talking about the songs or the items in his memory box. Sometimes he could become a little frustrated if he could not find an appropriate word or was struggling to remember a memory. In these instances, he would change the track on his mp3 player or move onto another item in his memory box.

At the start of the 6-month intervention period, Jim was on a high dose of the anti-psychotic medication quetiapine, alongside 'as required' benzodiazepine medication for use when he was agitated. By the end of the project Jim's anti-psychotic medication was significantly reduced and his support worker was unable to recall the last time staff needed to give him 'as required' medication. She attributed this directly to the impact of the interventions. The positive impact for Jim had a beneficial wider impact on the flat as everyone was more settled as a result.

> It's absolutely amazing I think, just something that's so so simple. I'm amazed with psychiatrists, it's like 'we'll try this drug, we'll up that drug', but why are they not suggesting this? Before you we didn't really know, we knew with the dementia training they talked about the music and that, but we didn't really have any insight into how changing this can be for a person, make their quality of life so much better.
>
> Support Worker, transcribed interview notes

Lucy

Lucy was a 55-year-old woman with Down syndrome who lived in her own flat with support three times a day, alongside additional support to help her with housework, shopping, and to enable her to meet up with her best friend once a week. She had a cat at home. Lucy described having lots of interests, including a season ticket to watch the local football team, going to discos, swimming, and watching soap operas. She worked at a café one day a week and attended a drop-in centre once a fortnight. Her support worker felt that music was very important to Lucy and that it helped both her mood and to feel less confused. She had been diagnosed with dementia a year previously, type unspecified. When Lucy was confused, she could become upset about the loss of her parents. Sometimes Lucy could be forgetful, but staff reported that she had 'good days and bad days'. Prior to her diagnosis, she was very independent and on a good day was still able to manage most tasks independently with just a little support, although she was reported as needing increasing help with her everyday activities. Lucy had some difficulties with the design in her flat. This included environmental problems with crossing the threshold into the bathroom; the bathroom flooring was very shiny, which Lucy struggled to walk on. The lighting in the bedroom was also an issue, as it was very dark and hard for Lucy to see properly.

Two interventions were agreed with Lucy as part of the study: a music playlist (two times per week on a planned basis or 'as required' if she became upset or confused) and one-off design changes, which consisted of changes to the bathroom floor (to make it more accessible and to the bedroom lighting. Staff changes led to significant delays in implementing the interventions but after recruitment Lucy's new support worker helped her to create a music playlist. Although this had a largely positive impact on her mood, communication and interaction (she often started singing and dancing to the music with the staff member, enjoying listening to it with her), there was one occasion where the music had a negative impact, and six occasions when it had both a positive and negative impact. Although Lucy's favourite group had been Abba, this music led to her becoming upset and tearful and staff needed to adapt her playlist:

> I don't put Abba on anymore… sometimes she will go down, you know, but it's hard to tell… Westlife, that dropped her right down, and it wasn't a sad song, it was quite an up beat one. But it had that effect, and I thought I won't do that one again. It's trial and error.
>
> Support Worker, transcribed interview notes

Once the most appropriate music had been identified for Lucy's playlist, this helped to raise her mood when she was feeling upset, and at times reduced confusion. She sang along to the songs, danced with staff, and enjoyed the music. This positive impact lasted throughout the time that the staff member was present in Lucy's flat.

> Played iPod through kitchen cd player, trying to sing along, giggling and improved mood, after lunch was dancing +++, still wandering around the house but kept coming back giving whoops of delight, very animated. Hugging and kissing me saying 'I love you'. Ask Lucy if she wanted music every day, replied 'Yes yes yes everyday'.
>
> Support Worker, intervention log

Although the music was experienced positively by Lucy, there were on-going difficulties with engaging the wider staff team in this process. Issues around staff confidence in using mp3 players alongside motivation and other time issues, acted as barriers.

> You will see quite a big gap on the last lot [of recording], there is not as many pages because I was off or I haven't been supporting her… It takes a while for people to understand how important it is. I will do more memos and stuff because it needs to be done properly, it's not about just putting a radio on.
>
> Support Worker, transcribed interview notes

Delays and problems with the proposed changes to the lighting and bathroom flooring lasted throughout the entire intervention period. Within this timeframe, Lucy experienced a significant progression in dementia, becoming increasingly restless, confused and distressed. Her support package was increased however not to the level that her support worker felt she needed. The lighting was installed eight months behind schedule, but within a few weeks Lucy had been admitted to an assessment centre. The bathroom floor was installed whilst Lucy was at the assessment centre, however the multidisciplinary team subsequently made the decision that it was unsafe for her to return home, and she moved permanently into a care home for people with intellectual disabilities.

Study Implications

Co-researchers with intellectual disability engaged in photovoice methodology during the study and pictorially recorded their perspectives on reminiscence, music playlists, and design changes (Watchman, Mattheys, Doyle, Boustead, & Rincones, 2020). Photovoice combines photography with social action, typically providing a tool for underrepresented populations to raise awareness of aspects affecting their own communities (Wang & Burris, 1994). Co-researchers understood the aims of the interventions and believed that their peers benefitted from them. A co-researcher who observed design changes discussed how they helped with being safer at home; his subsequent photographs and discussion of his images reflected the security he observed and that he also felt in his own home.

There were key 'in the moment' impacts of the interventions for both Jim and Lucy, as there were for other participants over the 12-month period. 75% of individualised goals set were considered by the participants with intellectual disability and dementia to have been met, or to have exceeded expectations by the end of the implementation period. Analysis suggests that there were consistently more goals achieved by participants living in smaller group homes with up to three peers with intellectual disability, than when living alone or in a larger group home including a residential care home for older people. Individualised interventions were appropriate both as regular activities for participants to enjoy independently or with staff and peers, plus as tools to help with distress, agitation, and confusion. The importance of 'in-the-moment' behaviour changes was recognised with a consistent positive effect (81%) recorded on behaviour, mood, and agitation, an increase in communication, and positive changes noted in body language. Engagement and interaction increased during the activities, including talking more about memories, about songs and singers, and singing. The interventions had an impact on mood, with the majority of reporting suggesting that participants were happier during the interventions. However, there were also a small number of occasions when participants could become upset, particularly in relation to reminiscence and music. Staff commonly spoke about the interventions as a 'distraction' that they used as tools with which to take participants' minds off an issue that was causing them to be upset or agitated. This was not always effective but often helped.

There was no global change in NPI-Q scores over the intervention period. The severity of symptoms associated with dementia rose slightly to the midpoint of each 6-month cycle and decreased towards the end, a similar trajectory to other studies and associated with decreasing mobility and progression towards more advanced stage of dementia (Tolea et al., 2015). However, there was wide variation between participants and recognising the limitation of the small sample makes it difficult to make inferences. The findings from the combined data collection measures suggest that whilst there were a small number of occasions in which interventions had a variable impact, broadly they had a positive immediate and short-term effect with potential for reduction in medication.

This has a wider reach beyond the study due to the high rates of prescriptions of antipsychotic medications, and over-medication experienced by people with intellectual disabilities (Sheehan et al., 2015). National guidance recommends prioritising the use of non-pharmacological interventions for the behavioural and psychological changes that can be associated with dementia (NICE, 2018; US Department of Health and Human Services, 2011) with recognition of the importance of non-pharmacological interventions for people with dementia. However, in reality medication is often prescribed; this often includes anti-psychotic drugs which carry serious risks of side effects including increased mortality (Ma et al., 2014).

Study findings support research identifying positive impacts of non-pharmacological interventions. This includes the beneficial impact of reminiscence on well-being and communication for people with intellectual disabilities and dementia (Crook et al., 2016; Kiddle et al., 2016). Findings also support research identifying music as an enjoyable activity that has a positive impact on mood (Bevins et al., 2015), alongside a calming effect on people who are agitated (Ward & Parkes, 2017). However, alongside the positive impacts of the music and reminiscence interventions, the small number of occasions when participants became upset indicates the need for caution when planning these types of interventions. Some of the participants in the study grew up in long-stay hospitals or institutions; periods of their life that they did not have positive memories of and did not wish to recall. This reflects the very different life trajectories faced by many older people with intellectual disability. Interventions need to be tailored to the individual with, for instance, reminiscence focusing on an area of the person's life that would most promote their well-being; this may actually be around their current life rather than previous experiences.

Key Issues

- People with intellectual disability remain over-medicated with changes in behaviour often attributed to progression of dementia without considering the effect of polypharmacy. Many types of psychotropic medicines have been used to manage behaviour or reduce agitation, including antipsychotics, antidepressants, mood stabilisers, and sedatives despite limited evidence for efficacy in people with intellectual disability. Changes in behaviour or an increase in agitation should not automatically be attributed to dementia – the effect of medication, in addition to staff approaches and communication, should be investigated.
- Individualised person-centred interventions (in which the person with intellectual disability has control and choice as far as possible), if safely implemented, can be appropriate both as regular activities for participants to enjoy, and as tools to help with distress, agitation, and confusion. The importance of 'in-the-moment' behaviour changes should be recognised with a consistent positive effect noted on observed behaviour and agitation, an increase in communication, positive changes in body language and potential decrease in psychotropic medication.
- People with intellectual disability and dementia remain a digitally excluded population. Although the intention was to implement the most appropriate intervention based on individual goals and preferences, this is not always possible due to a lack of Internet access or lack of digital awareness of support staff, for example, downloading music or reminiscence apps online. Future planning, and indeed future-proofing, social care services must take this into account and plan for a more digitally adept population.
- Participants enjoyed the interventions as stand-alone pleasurable activities including both the one-to-one nature of engaging with staff members or peers and for individual enjoyment. Staff reflected on how involvement in the project had enabled them to learn more about the participants, thus leading to improved relationships. Participants learnt new skills around technology (using mp3 players and tablets) and re-engaged with previous interests and skills. Participants took ownership of their interventions and this gave a sense of pride.

Conclusion

An emphasis on non-pharmacological interventions is not currently extended to people with intellectual disability and dementia, nor is it yet widely included in staff training or organisational induction activities. A culture change is required in health and social care services to avoid starting again, or 'reinventing the wheel' whenever a new diagnosis of dementia is made, so that organisations have strategies for supporting their ageing population, many of whom may have dementia in mid-later life. The example of this study identified that staff teams faced a number of challenges around implementing non-drug interventions; this included 'finding the time' to do the interventions, new support teams and lack of staff confidence or motivation. Implementation was most effective when whole teams engaged with the process and saw the benefits of the interventions in practice, when managers gave active support to the process, and staff were given time within their roles to undertake the interventions. Key recommendations for practice therefore include the need for specifically allocated staff members or key workers to take a lead in the implementation process and ensure regular use; training for staff teams to develop required skills, knowledge and confidence around non-drug interventions; and the incorporation of interventions into individual care plans, to ensure these are recognised strategies to support the person with intellectual disability and dementia rather than an addition to every day support.

References

Alzheimer's Society. (2012). *Singing for the brain: Results of an evaluation of three Alzheimer's society services in England and Wales*. London: England.

Baird, A., & Samson, S. (2015). Music and dementia. *Progress in Brain Research*, *217*, 207–235.

Bevins, S., Dawes, S., Kenshole, A., & Gaussen, K. (2015). Staff views of a music therapy group for people with intellectual disabilities and dementia: A pilot study. *Advances in Mental Health and Intellectual Disabilities*, *9*(1), 40–48.

Crook, N., Adams, M., Shorten, N., & Langdon, P. E. (2016). Does the Well-being of individuals with Down syndrome and dementia improve when using life story books and rummage boxes? A randomized single case series experiment. *Journal of Applied Research in Intellectual Disabilities*, *29*(1), 1–10.

Courtenay, K., Jokinen, N. S., & Strydom, A. (2010). Caregiving and adults with intellectual disabilities affected by dementia. *Journal of Policy & Practice in Intellectual Disabilities*, *7*(1), 26–33.

Cummings, J. L., Mega, M., Gray, K., Rosenberg-Thompson, S., Carusi, D. A., & Gornbeing, J. (1994). The neuropsychiatric inventory: Comprehensive assessment of psychopathology in dementia. *Neurology*, *44*(12), 2308–14.

De Vreese, L. P., Mantesso, U., De Bastiani, E., Weger, E., Marangoni, A. C., & Gomiero, T. (2012). Impact of dementia-derived nonpharmacological intervention procedures on cognition and behavior in older adults with intellectual disabilities: A 3-year follow-up study. *Journal of Policy and Practice in Intellectual Disabilities*, *9*(2), 92–102.

Iacono, T., Bigby, C., Carling-Jenkins, R., & Torr, J. (2014). Taking each day as it comes: Staff experiences of supporting people with Down syndrome and Alzheimer's disease in group homes. *Journal of Intellectual Disability Research*, *58*(6), 521–533.

Jacobsen, J. H., Stelzer, J., Fritz, T. H., Chételat, G., La Joie, R., & Turner, R. (2015). Why musical memory can be preserved in advanced Alzheimer's disease. *Brain*, *138*(8), 2438–2450.

Janicki, M., Dalton, A. J., McCallion, P., Baxley, D. D., & Zendell, A. (2005). Group home care for adults with intellectual disabilities and Alzheimer's disease. *Dementia*, *4*(3), 361–385.

Jokinen, N. S. (2014). Non-pharmacological interventions. In K. Watchman (Ed.), *Intellectual disability and dementia: Research into practice*. London: Jessica Kingsley Publishers.

Kiddle, H., Drew, N., Crabbe, P., & Wigmore, J. (2016). A pilot memory café for people with learning disabilities and memory difficulties. *British Journal of Learning Disabilities*, *44*(3), 175–181.

Ma, H., Huang, Y., Cong, Z., Wang, Y., Jiang, W., Gao, S., & Zhu, G. (2014). The efficacy and safety of atypical antipsychotics for the treatment of dementia: A meta-analysis of randomized placebo-controlled trials. *Journal of Alzheimer's Disease*, *42*, 915–937.

Marquardt, G., Buetker, K., & Motzek, T. (2014). Impact of the design of the built environment on people with dementia: An evidence-based review. *Health Environments Research & Design Journal*, *8*(1), 127–157.

Mendes, A. (2015). Unlocking' people with dementia through the use of music therapy. *Nursing and Residential Care*, *17*(9), 512–514.

National Institute of Health and Care Excellence. (2018). *Dementia: assessment, management and support for people living with dementia and their carers*. Retrieved from https://www.nice.org.uk/guidance/ng97/chapter/recommendations

Prince, M., Knapp, M., Guerchet, M., McCrone, P., Prina, M., Comas-Herrera, A., … Salimkumar, D. (2014). *Dementia UK: Update*. Alzheimer's Society. Retrieved from www.alzheimers.org.uk/sites/default/files/migrate/downloads/dementia_uk_update.pdf

Rosewarne, M. (2001). Learning disabilities and dementia: A pilot therapy group. *Journal of Dementia Care*, *9*(4), 18–20.

Royal College of Psychiatry. (2015). *Dementia and people with intellectual disabilities*. Leicester: The British Psychological Society.

Sheehan, R., Hassiotis, A., Walters, K., Osborn, D., Strydom, A., & Horsfall, L. (2015). Mental illness challenging behaviour, and psychotropic drug prescribing in people with intellectual disability: UK population based cohort study. *BMJ*, *351*, 4326.

Strydom, A. (2017). Defining cognitive decline in individuals with Down syndrome. *Alzheimer's and Dementia*, *13*(7), P1211–P1212. https://doi.org/10.1016/j.jalz.2017.07.378

Tolea, M. I., Morris, J. C., & Galvin, J. E. (2016). Trajectory of Mobility Decline by Type of Dementia. *Alzheimer disease and associated disorders*, *30*(1), 60–66. https://doi.org/10.1097/WAD.0000000000000091

Ueda, T., Suzukamo, Y., Sato, M., & Izumi, S. (2013). Effects of music therapy on behavioural and psychological symptoms of dementia: A systematic review and meta-analysis. *Ageing Research Reviews*, *12*(2), 628–641.

US Department of Health and Human Services. (2011). *National Alzheimer's Project Act (NAPA)* Retrieved from https://aspe.hhs.gov/system/files/pdf/105066/cmtach-JP1.pdf

Wang, C., & Burris, M. A. (1994). Photovoice: Concept, methodology and use for participatory needs assessment. *Health Education and Behaviour*, *24*(3), 369–87.

Watchman, K. (2016). Investigating the lived experience of people with Down syndrome with dementia: Overcoming methodological and ethical challenges. *Journal of Policy and Practice in Intellectual Disabilities*, *13*(2), 190–198.

Watchman, K., Mattheys, K., McKernon, M., Strachan, H., Andreis, F. & Murdoch, J. (2020) A person-centred approach to implementation of psychosocial interventions with people who have an intellectual disability and dementia-A participatory action study. *Journal of Applied Research in Intellectual Disabilities*. https://doi.org/10.1111/jar.12795

Watchman, K., Mattheys, K., Doyle, A., Boustead, L. & Rincones, O. (2020) Revisiting Photovoice: Perceptions of Dementia among Researchers with Intellectual Disability. *Qualitative Health Research*, 30 (7), pp. 1019–1032. https://doi.org/10.1177/1049732319901127

Ward, A. R., & Parkes, J. (2017). An evaluation of a singing for the brain pilot with people with a learning disability and memory problems or a dementia. *Dementia*, *16*(3), 360–374.

Woods, B., O'Philbin, L., Farrell, E. M., Spector, A. E., & Orrell, M. (2018). Reminiscence therapy for dementia. *Cochrane Database of Systematic Reviews* (3). https://doi.org/10.1002/14651858.CD001120.pub3

Suggested Readings

Burke, C., & Charlesworth, P. (2018). *Hidden in Plain sight – Dementia and learning disability*. London: Foundation for People with Learning Disabilities.

National Down Syndrome Society. (n.d.). *Aging and Down syndrome: a health and well-being guide*. Retrieved from http://www.ndss.org/wp-content/uploads/2017/11/Aging-and-Down-Syndrome.pdf

Watchman, K. (2014). *Intellectual disability and dementia: Research into practice*. London: Jessica Kingsley Publishers.

Watchman, K., & Janicki, M. (2019). The intersection of intellectual disability and dementia: Report of the International summit on intellectual disability and dementia. *The Gerontologist*, *59*(3), 411–419.

Wilkinson, H., Watchman, K., & Hare, P. (2018). *Supporting people with learning disabilities and dementia self-study guide: A self-study guide for support staff*. London: Pavilion Publishers.

27
END-OF-LIFE CARE FOR ADULTS WITH INTELLECTUAL DISABILITIES

Teresa Moro and Jacqueline McGinley

Introduction

Case Example

Sophia is a 55-year-old woman with intellectual disability (ID) who also has congestive heart failure. Sophia has lived in the same small community agency residence with three other adults for the last 15 years. She initially moved in after her father died because her then 70-year-old mother could not care for Sophia at home. While there is frequent staff turn-over, two female residential staff caregivers are close to Sophia. One woman has been at the home for 16 years and another woman has been there for three years. These women support Sophia's physical and emotional needs, and they think of her as part of their families. After Sophia's mother died, these women took her to the funeral and have helped her grieve the loss.

These women were the first to notice when Sophia began coughing frequently and became more confused. They took Sophia to her doctor appointments, and explained to her what was going on and asked her what she wanted to do. According to her cardiologist, Sophia would continue to get sicker and need more help. Sophia is becoming more often confused and no longer attends day program.

The issue of where to care for Sophia at the end of life has become a crisis because she does not have an advance care plan and there is no existing agency protocol about caring for residents at the end of life. Sophia wants to stay in her home. The staff members want to care for her in her home because they feel she will be most comfortable surrounded by her agency family. The agency administrators have said that they cannot provide the staff with any additional support and that Sophia may be moved out of her home due to potential liability and a lack of resources. There is the possibility of bringing in home hospice, but none of the local agencies have any experience supporting people with ID.

If Sophia is transferred out of the community agency residence, she will either have to go to a family caregiver's home, an intermediate care facility for adults with developmental disabilities (ICF/DD), a nursing home, or an in-patient hospice. Everyone involved in her care is concerned about Sophia being moved because transitions have always been difficult for her. Sophia's brother/guardian is angry because he assumed that once Sophia was in the community agency residence she would be cared for forever. Her brother hopes that she can stay in the agency, because he is 67-years-old and does not have the resources to care for Sophia in his home which is four hours away. The nearest ICF/DD with an open bed is two hours away, so neither her agency family nor her brother/guardian will be able to visit. Local nursing homes have no experience caring for people with ID.

Broad Overview

Increasingly, people with ID in economically advanced nations are living long enough to acquire the same chronic and life-limiting health conditions, e.g. cancer and cardiovascular disease, as the general population (Hosking et al., 2016; Stankiewicz, Ouellette-Kuntz, McIsaac, Shooshtari, & Balogh, 2018; Tuffrey-Wijne et al., 2016). Due to the increased likelihood of acquiring these conditions caregivers in community agencies and family homes need to plan for what happens when adults with ID age, experience advanced illness, and die. End-of-life decision making for adults with ID is complicated because they often do not have any advance care plans and have historically been omitted from conversations about healthcare and end-of-life decision making (Kirkendall, Linton, & Farris, 2016).

End-of-life care is that which is provided when death is soon anticipated because an individual has a progressive and irreversible condition from which recovery is not expected and/or withdrawal of life-sustaining treatment is an option (American Association of Intellectual and Developmental Disabilities [AAIDD], 2012). Quality end-of-life care must include physical comfort and emotional support for the person who is dying; emotional support for the family or caregivers; open communication; shared decision making; and timely access to care (Teno, 2005). Conversely, adults with ID encounter healthcare disparities and multiple systemic barriers to quality end-of-life care (Friedman, Helm, & Woodman, 2012; Northway et al., 2018).

Service systems are often ill-equipped to adequately meet the needs of adults with ID at the end of life (Burke & Heller, 2017). Adults with ID may experience poor medical care, including a lack of pain recognition or proper symptom management (Tuffrey-Wijne et al., 2016). Some adults with ID are overtreated while others do not receive any medical intervention for highly treatable conditions, such as urinary tract infections, that become worse when left untreated (Hosking et al., 2016; Hunt et al., 2019).

As their care needs increase, adults with ID may experience transitions into skilled care in hospitals, hospices, and nursing homes where the healthcare providers generally have minimal experience or training in supporting them (Havercamp et al., 2016). If adults with ID remain in their community agency residences, there is often no protocol, training, or resources available to staff for providing end-of-life care (Bigby, Bowers, & Webber, 2011). In the United States, some community agencies run ICF/DDs, which offer 24-hour skilled nursing care. Not all agencies have this level of care, and, even when they do, a resident can only be moved from a community residence into an ICF/DD if there is an available bed. If there are no free beds or the agency does not have an ICF/DD, then the transition involves leaving the agency and entering another system of care, such as a nursing home.

The literature on end-of-life care for adults with ID in nursing homes is limited; however, there is evidence to suggest that adults with ID are admitted to nursing homes at an earlier age and remain in them longer than members of the general population (Kerins, Price, Broadhurst, & Gaynor, 2010). Adults with Down syndrome may also experience more relocations and are more likely to die in a nursing home than other peers with ID (Patti, Amble, & Flory, 2010). Staff in nursing homes lack training in caring for adults with ID and may not understand their unique needs and communication styles.

Overall, the systemic barriers to quality end-of-life services for adults with ID have contributed to a piecemeal system that relies heavily on untrained agency staff or family caregivers (McGinley, 2016). In the long-term, it is imperative that practice professionals and scholars determine how and where to best focus care interventions and policy change. However, it is also important to focus on ways to improve end-of-life care for adults with ID in the here and now.

Transparency and Planning for End-of-Life Care

The main idea of this chapter is that greater transparency and planning in all aspects of care are critical to improving the quality of end of life for adults with ID. Specifically, healthcare and residential systems need to provide greater clarity about what services they provided, the experience of those providing the services, and the likelihood of late-life transitions. With greater transparency and planning adults with

ID, their caregivers and/or guardians, and their providers in hospices, hospitals, and nursing homes will be better prepared to provide care.

Clinical and research literature exploring the nature and quality of end-of-life care for adults with ID has become more prevalent in the last decade (Tuffrey-Wijne et al., 2016). We are only beginning to understand where people with ID die and who provides care at the end of life (Moro, Savage, & Gehlert, 2017). While end-of-life care and residential services will differ greatly based on geographical location, most of the literature comes from nations with advanced economies (Kirkendall et al., 2016). This section will explore this literature to describe the current state of decision making, healthcare, hospice care, and community agency residence care for adults with ID at the end of life.

Healthcare Decision Making at the End of Life

Healthcare decision making for adults with ID is complicated and involves multiple stakeholders, including: healthcare providers; families and/or guardians; community agency residence staff; and providers in other settings such as nursing homes, on-site hospice, and ICF/DDs. Too often, decisions for adults with ID are made by a proxy who is either a family member or friend, or a court-appointed guardian. End-of-life care planning for adults with ID is often precipitated by a health crisis, such as a cardiac arrest. Thus, an already stressful time is made more so as decisions are made quickly while dealing with acute illness. Family members may make decisions for adults with ID without eliciting the individual's preferences or may decide that the individual should not be informed about their illness to be protected from distress (Kirkendall et al., 2016).

Suggestions for Improvement

Families, guardians, agency caregivers, or trusted others need to openly discuss death with adults with ID in order to find out what they want when they become ill (see recommended readings for resources). Ideally, advance care planning occurs before someone is diagnosed with a life-limiting illness. An advance care plan for adults with ID should be tailored to their needs and include information about what the illness means to them; what they want to do when their condition changes; who should make decisions for them if they are unable to; what living well means to them; and what they want, including where they wish to be, if they become ill (Kingsbury, 2010; Voss et al., 2019). In Ireland, the Future Care Road Map pilot study program proved successful in assisting families in establishing future care plans for adults with ID (McCausland, Brennan, McCallion, & McCarron, 2019).

Many adults with ID want to be informed about their life-limiting medical conditions and can participate in healthcare decision making (Ryan, Guerin, Dodd, & McEvoy, 2011). Stress may be compounded if adults with ID who are ill are not given information about their diagnosis or the support they need to participate in their healthcare (Flynn, Hulbert-Williams, Hulbert-Williams, & Bramwell, 2016). A supported decision-making model encourages the participation of adults with ID in decision making by receiving support and working with trusted others to understand the decisions to be made and to articulate their preferences (Douglas & Bigby, 2020). Adults with ID should be encouraged to express their wishes in their preferred communication mode because verbal and nonverbal communication can illicit important insights regarding end-of-life care preferences (American Association of Intellectual and Developmental Disabilities [AAIDD], 2012). Plans should be revisited annually or when someone experiences significant changes.

Healthcare at the End of Life

Adults with ID and advanced illness will interface with healthcare providers who have little or no training or experience working with them (Havercamp et al., 2016). Communication barriers arise when an adult with IDD cannot articulate their pain and symptoms, or if providers are unable to understand them and no support person is present (Flynn et al., 2016; Gates, 2011; Iacono, Bigby, Unsworth, Douglas, & Fitzpatrick, 2014). Thus, providers may give inadequate information about prognosis and treatment options (Friedman et al., 2012). When adults with ID are hospitalised, they have poorer outcomes and more hospital-acquired complications, such as infections, skin breakdown, and medication errors, than members of the general population and other adults with disabilities (Ailey, Johnson, Fogg, & Friese, 2015). Misdiagnosis may also be due to diagnostic overshadowing, which occurs when providers incorrectly attribute symptoms to a trait associated with ID and not the underlying medical condition (Kinley, Denton, & Scott, 2018; Moro et al., 2017). A family or agency staff caregiver may need to be present most of the time during hospitalisation in order to guarantee that basic needs are met and that appropriate assessments and interventions are completed.

Suggestion for Improvement

Clinical and research scholars have offered several suggestions for improving medical communication. First, medical and other allied healthcare educational programs need to include disability content in their courses (Havercamp et al., 2016; Northway et al., 2018). It is optimal for programs to offer stand-alone courses in working with adults with disabilities; in addition, instructors can require articles, use illustrative examples, or integrate simulation labs about people with disabilities within existing courses. In their practice, healthcare providers must consider the individual's level of functioning and understanding when delivering information (Gates, 2011; Tuffrey-Wijne et al., 2016). Medical information should be presented in whatever format (written, sign language, pictures, sound board) best meets the needs of the individual with ID. Information should be broken down into small chunks and delivered gradually in a slow, ongoing process (Tuffrey-Wijne et al., 2016). Adults with ID should be asked who they want present during appointments because a trusted person can facilitate communication when providers do not understand what is being conveyed. Providers should also take time to build rapport and speak directly to adults with ID and not talk down to them, direct all communication towards caregivers, or make assumptions about what the individual should want (McNeil et al., 2018).

Healthcare providers must adapt their care and be knowledgeable about what services their hospital offers for adults with ID. In the United States, Rush University Medical Center (Rush) has implemented some initiatives tailored to meet the needs of adults with ID (Berthold, 2014; Wirtz, Ailey, Hohmann, & Johnson, in press). Once a person with ID has been identified at Rush, providers receive prompts through the electronic medical record (EMR) to collect information about their preferred means of communication; physical and behavioral challenges; eating habits; and environmental preferences and needs. Rush also has an *Adults with Intellectual and Developmental Disabilities Committee*, which is an interprofessional collaboration devoted to improving healthcare provision for adults with ID. This group created educational materials using plain language and pictures to explain common medical procedures, such as having blood drawn. They also provide education to hospital staff, including the security department. Rush also supports an initiative called *Neurodiversity Allies*, which is a group of graduate students who provide on-call assistance helping adults with ID feel more comfortable when they are in the emergency department or hospital.

Hospice Care at the End of Life

Adults with ID may be placed in an in-patient hospice or receive in-home hospice care in a family or a community agency residence. While there is a need for these supports, adults with ID often underutilise palliative care services (Bailey, Doody, & Lyons, 2016). Palliative care providers generally have limited or no experience working with adults with ID (Ryan et al., 2011). When an adult with ID receives in-home hospice, the family may incorrectly assume that hospice caregivers provide the majority of the care (Farmer, 2020). However, most hospice providers offer routine home care which is not intensive and they only provide continuous home care for someone in a crisis who needs 8–24 hours of care (Berry, Connor, & Stuart, 2017). Thus, much of the hands-on care, including medication and pain management, is provided by family members, usually women (Seaman, Bear, Documet, Sereika, & Albert, 2016). Often family members are not prepared for the physical and emotional toll of caring for someone at the end of life. Even in countries that offer universal healthcare, caregivers are rarely paid, and they may experience emotional and financial hardship related to providing care (Rowland, Hanratty, Pilling, van den Berg, & Grande, 2017). Caring for an adult with ID at the end of life may be more difficult for ageing parents or siblings who may also be experiencing late-life disability or their own chronic health conditions.

Suggestions for Improvement

In-home hospice providers need to be transparent about what services they provide and how often hospice providers will be at the home. This may mean repeating the information several different times using written and verbal mediums. It is critical that family or community agency residence administrators and staff understand that either they are responsible for providing much of the hands-on care or they will need to hire and pay privately for a professional caregiver. Hospice providers need training on working with adults with ID. They also need to offer ongoing support to families dealing with the emotional and financial toll caregiving takes. Given the rapidly ageing population of adults with ID, hospice providers should make an effort to reach out to community agencies serving adults with ID in order to form care networks (Bailey, Doody, & Lyons, 2016).

In the United States, the Erie County Medical Center provides a unique palliative care program that trains medical students and community volunteers about the process of natural dying, stages of grief, spirituality through end of life, and compassionate caregiving (Grimm et al., n.d.). These trainees serve as *mercy doulas*, or companions, to people who are dying and do not have an established network of family and friends. Recently, this program partnered with local community agency residences and the mercy doulas now provide comfort and support to adults with ID, any involved family, roommates and friends, and agency staff caregivers. Although there is little research regarding the efficacy of doulas at the end of life, this emerging model addresses some of the gaps within existing community-based, end-of-life care for adults with ID (Rawlings, Tieman, Miller-Lewis, & Swetenham, 2019).

Community Agency Residence Care at the End of Life

Many adults with ID who are cared for in family homes will experience a transition into a community agency residence as their family caregivers age, become ill, or die (Bigby, 2010; Brennan, Murphy, McCallion, & McCarron, 2018). While this transition may be initially difficult, many families assume that once an adult with ID is in agency care they will remain there forever (Bigby et al., 2011). There is often no discussion about what will happen when an adult with ID experiences functional decline or has advanced illness. Prior discussions about end of life may be lacking because agency staff are either reluctant to discuss death or because this may not be perceived as part of their role (Tuffrey-Wijne, Rose, Grant, & Wijne, 2017). As the case example illustrates, end-of-life care for adults with ID living in community agency residences may become a crisis for everyone involved because difficult, life-changing decisions must be made quickly.

Staff caregivers in community agency residences may become like family and want to provide end-of-life care (Hunt et al., 2019). However, most agency staff are untrained, have no or limited resources, and are unprepared for the emotional and physical challenges of providing end-of-life care (Kingsbury, 2010; Tuffrey-Wijne et al., 2017). When in-home hospice is received in the community agency residence, there may be some confusion between agency staff and palliative care providers about their specific role.

Suggestions for Improvement

Administrators in community agencies need to decide whether or not the agency is equipped to provide end-of-life care in their residences. Once a decision is made, this policy should be clearly articulated to adults with ID and their families, guardians, and trusted others. They should be informed about what services are provided when someone experiences functional decline or becomes ill. There also needs to be transparency about under what conditions they will transfer someone out of their agency residence and the likely features of the transfer process, including where the adult with ID might be transferred to.

Agencies that provide end-of-life care in community agency residences should designate a staff person, e.g. social worker, to reach out to local hospices and hospitals to form professional networks. These agencies should also identify staff willing to be involved in end-of-life care and seek the advice of hospice providers on establishing end-of-life protocols. Agency staff who provide end-of-life care need training about how to support the adult with ID, their family, other adults with ID in the day and residential programs, and other staff at the community agency residence (Hunt et al., 2019). Recently, a one-day training course developed for community agency staff on discussing dying was shown to decrease their self-reported worry and increase their knowledge about conveying bad news to people with ID who are ill (Tuffrey-Wijne et al., 2017). Ideally, all staff should receive some training on end-of-life care; however, that may not be feasible given limited resources and workforce challenges. A small end-of-life committee may be sufficient for providing support and training as needs arise. Given the increased ageing population of adults with ID, staff in community agency residences will at some point support someone at the end-of-life and the quality of their and the dying person's experience will depend largely on their preparedness for these scenarios. Agency staff who provide direct end-of-life care need on-going support and referrals to bereavement services.

Key Issues

Below are some key actions that can be implemented in the here and now:

1. Medical and allied healthcare educational programs need to include disability content in their courses.
2. Healthcare providers need to actively seek out available resources on how to effectively provide care to adults with ID at both their own and other institutions (see Addendum for resources).
3. Families, guardians, staff caregivers, and trusted others need to talk to adults with ID about death and engage them in advance care planning (see Addendum for resources).
4. At community agencies, long-term planning needs to begin when adults with ID first enter the system, and there needs to be a clear articulation of what services the agency provides when someone in residential care experiences functional decline or has advanced illness.
5. Community agencies, hospices, and hospitals need to form professional networks to support interprofessional collaboration when caring for adults with ID at the end of life.

Conclusion

While improving end-of-life care for adults with ID is increasingly becoming a research and clinical priority, there is still work to be done. Some of the most pressing issues for further research, policy, and practice are presented below.

Research

Disability researchers must continue to compile large-scale tracking data on where adults with ID live when they have advanced illness, where they die, and who is providing their care (Tuffrey-Wijne et al., 2017). This research will provide the critical information that is needed in order to determine where interventions are best placed. Scholars must also continue to partner with people with ID when conducting research or designing clinical protocols that impact their lives (Savage, Moro, Boyden,

Brown, & Kavanaugh, 2015). Ideally, research will begin to include adults with severe ID, who have been historically unrepresented within the existing literature (Kirkendall et al., 2016). Although there has been limited collaboration to date, future research must also bridge the ageing and disability research networks (Bigby, 2010). More information is needed in order to determine whether established interventions focused on improving healthcare for older adults or adults at the end of life are applicable to adults with ID, and, if not, what modifications are needed (Heller, Gibbons, & Fisher, 2015). For example, in England, the Steps to Success Palliative Care Programme was successfully adapted for adults with ID from a program designed for frail older adults (Kinley et al., 2018).

Policy

People with ID experience healthcare disparities and are more likely than the general population to die from conditions that are treatable (Williamson, Contreras, Rodriguez, Smith, & Perkins, 2017). Adults with ID also experience high rates of hospitalisation and readmissions, which contributes to higher annual healthcare costs than the general population (Balogh et al., 2018; Lunsky, De Oliveira, Wilton, & Wodchis, 2019). One possible explanation for the increased hospitalisations and death from conditions that are treatable is poor access to or acquisition of primary care and a lack of care coordination (Glover, Williams, Heslop, Oyinlola, & Grey, 2017; Hosking et al., 2016). It is important to implement hospital-wide policies about care coordination, which include at-home services for adults with ID and their family or agency staff caregiver. Better care coordination has the potential to decrease rates of readmission and overall costs of caring for adults with ID (Ruiz, Giuriceo, Caldwell, Snyder, & Putnam, 2019). Post-discharge care coordination that includes the perspectives of adults with ID and their caregivers may also serve to decrease caregiver stress and reduce risk for readmission. Adapting services to meet the needs of adults with ID is additionally important because there is evidence to suggest that hospitals with these programs have lower costs per day when caring for adults with ID than do hospitals without (Wirtz et al., in press).

Practice

Social workers are involved in the care of adults with ID at the end of life in hospitals, hospices, nursing homes, and community agencies. Social workers are instrumental in connecting adults with ID and their caregivers with financial, legal, educational, medical, and family services. Thus, it is important that these systems of care form relationships before an adult with ID has advanced illness (Kirkendall et al., 2016; Tuffrey-Wijne et al., 2016). Community agency staff are often overloaded, thus social workers from area hospitals, nursing homes, and hospices should actively reach out to community agencies. These social workers might run free informational services about hospital resources and best practices in ageing and end-of-life care. Informational events serve to support reciprocal resource and knowledge sharing across systems of care. This is mutually beneficial because community agency staff and family caregivers will learn what end-of-life care looks like, and healthcare providers will learn how to work with adults with ID. Ultimately, this may be financially efficacious because adults with ID and their caregivers may be more likely to seek services from providers that are familiar.

References

Ailey, S. H., Johnson, T. J., Fogg, L., & Friese, T. R. (2015). Factors related to complications among adult patients with intellectual disabilities hospitalized at an academic medical center. *Intellectual and Developmental Disabilities*, *53*(2), 114–119. https://doi.org/10.1352/1934-9556-53.2.114

American Association of Intellectual and Developmental Disabilities [AAIDD]. (2012). *Caring at the end of life: Position Statement of AAIDD*. AAIDD. http://aaidd.org/news-policy/policy/position-statements/caring-at-the-end-of-life#.UmN-jHDihwg

Bailey, M., Doody, O., & Lyons, R. (2016). Surveying community nursing support for persons with an intellectual disability and palliative care needs. *British Journal of Learning Disabilities, 44*(1), 24–34. https://doi.org/10.1111/bld.12105

Balogh, R., Lin, E., Dobranowski, K., Selick, A., Wilton, A. S., & Lunsky, Y. (2018). All-cause, 30-day readmissions among persons with intellectual and developmental disabilities and mental illness. *Psychiatric Services, 69*(3), 353–357. https://doi.org/10.1176/appi.ps.201600534

Berry, L. L., Connor, S. R., & Stuart, B. (2017). Practical ideas for improving the quality of hospice care. *Journal of Palliative Medicine, 20*(5), 449–452. https://doi.org/doi:10.1089/jpm.2017.0016

Berthold, J. (2014). *Remembering, and respecting, the most vulnerable: Hospitals seek to improve care for patients with intellectual, developmental disabilities*. ACP Hospitalist. https://acphospitalist.org/archives/2014/12/disabilities.htm

Bigby, C. (2010). A five-country comparative review of accommodation support policies for older people with intellectual disability. *Journal of Policy and Practice in Intellectual Disabilities, 7*(1), 3–15. https://doi.org/10.1111/j.1741-1130.2010.00242.x

Bigby, C., Bowers, B., & Webber, R. (2011). Planning and decision making about the future care of older group home residents and transition to residential aged care. *Journal of Intellectual Disability Research, 55*(8), 777–789. https://doi.org/10.1111/j.1365-2788.2010.01297.x

Brennan, D., Murphy, R., McCallion, P., & McCarron, M. (2018). "What's going to happen when we're gone?" Family caregiving capacity for older people with an intellectual disability in Ireland. *Journal of Applied Research in Intellectual Disabilities, 31*(2), 226–235. https://doi.org/10.1111/jar.12379

Burke, M. M., & Heller, T. (2017). Disparities in unmet service needs among adults with intellectual and other developmental disabilities. *Journal of Applied Research in Intellectual Disabilities, 30*, 898–910. https://doi.org/doi:10.1111/jar.12282

Douglas, J., & Bigby, C. (2020). Development of an evidence-based practice framework to guide decision making support for people with cognitive impairment due to acquired brain injury or intellectual disability, *Disability and Rehabilitation, 42*(3), 434–441, https://doi.org/10.1080/09638288.2018.1498546

Farmer, B. (2020). Morning Edition [Daily Radio Program]. In *Patients Want To Die At Home, But Home Hospice Care Can Be Tough On Families*. National Public Radio. https://www.npr.org/sections/health-shots/2020/01/21/789958067/patients-want-to-die-at-home-but-home-hospice-care-can-be-tough-on-families?utm_term=nprnews&utm_medium=social&utm_campaign=npr&utm_source=facebook.com&fbclid=IwAR3h23B_LLMLBFGGje2EXRxYP98V-Fls8whMEoUGH2AwCdhf6hXhkaUQ7r8&fbclid=IwAR1P2wTPbLg6Tj_jS2f20lBP3SDPlkAYKEful_zG6tZZzZp6TF2KEs3crlE

Flynn, S., Hulbert-Williams, N. J., Hulbert-Williams, L., & Bramwell, R. (2016). "You don't know what's wrong with you": An exploration of cancer-related experiences in people with an intellectual disability. *Psychooncology, 25*(10), 1198–1205. https://doi.org/10.1002/pon.4211

Friedman, S. L., Helm, D. T., & Woodman, A. C. (2012). Unique and universal barriers: Hospice care for aging adults with intellectual disability. *American Journal on Intellectual and Developmental Disabilities, 117*(6), 509–532. https://doi.org/10.1352/1944-7558-117.6.509

Gates, B. (2011). The valued people project: Users' views on learning disability nursing. *British Journal of Nursing, 20*(1), 15–21. https://doi.org/10.12968/bjon.2011.20.1.15

Glover, G., Williams, R., Heslop, P., Oyinlola, J., & Grey, J. (2017). Mortality in people with intellectual disabilities in England. *Journal of Intellectual Disability Research, 61*(1), 62–74. https://doi.org/10.1111/jir.12314

Grimm, K. T., Lauer, S., & Wiggins, M. (n.d.). *Education strategies: Mercy doula training for medical students*. Center to Advance Palliative Care. https://www.capc.org/seminar/poster-sessions/mercy-doula-training-for-medical-students/

Havercamp, S. M., Ratliff-Schaub, K., Macho, P. N., Johnson, C. N., Bush, K. L., & Souders, H. T. (2016). Preparing tomorrow's doctors to care for patients with Autism Spectrum Disorder. *Intellectual and Developmental Disabilities, 54*(3), 202–216. https://doi.org/10.1352/1934-9556-54.3.202

Heller, T., Gibbons, H. M., & Fisher, D. (2015). Caregiving and family support interventions: Crossing networks of aging and developmental disabilities. *Intellectual and Developmental Disabilities, 53*(5), 329–345. https://doi.org/10.1352/1934-9556-53.5.329

Hosking, F. J., Carey, I. M., Shah, S. M., Harris, T., DeWilde, S., Beighton, C., & Cook, D. G. (2016). Mortality among adults with intellectual disability in England: Comparisons with the general population. *American Journal of Public Health, 106*(8), 1483–1490. https://doi.org/10.2105/AJPH.2016.303240

Hunt, K., Bernal, J., Worth, R., Shearn, J., Jarvis, P., Jones, E., … Todd, S. (2019). End-of-life care in intellectual disability: A retrospective cross-sectional study. *BMJ Supportive & Palliative Care*, 1–9. https://doi.org/10.1136/bmjspcare-2019-001985

Iacono, T., Bigby, C., Unsworth, C., Douglas, J., & Fitzpatrick, P. (2014). A systematic review of hospital experiences of people with intellectual disability. *BMC Health Services Research, 14*, 1–8. https://doi.org/https://doi.org/10.1186/s12913-014-0505-5

Kerins, G. J., Price, L. C., Broadhurst, A., & Gaynor, C. M. (2010). A pilot study analyzing mortality of adults with developmental disabilities residing in nursing homes in Connecticut. *Journal of Policy and Practice in Intellectual Disabilities, 7*(3), 177–181. https://doi.org/10.1111/j.1741-1130.2010.00262.x

Kingsbury, L. A. C. (2010). Use of person-centered planning for end-of-life decision making. In S. L. Friedman & D. T. Helm (Eds.), *End-of-life care for children and adults with intellectual and developmental disabilities* (pp. 275–290). American Association on Intellectual and Developmental Disabilities.

Kinley, J., Denton, L., & Scott, S. (2018). Development and implementation of the steps to Success palliative care programme for learning disability residential care homes in England. *International Journal of Palliative Nursing, 24*(10), 428–436. https://doi.org/https://doi.org/10.12968/ijpn.2018.24.10.492

Kirkendall, A. M., Linton, K., & Farris, S. (2016). Intellectual disabilities and decision making at end of life: A literature review. *Journal of Applied Research in Intellectual Disabilities, 30*(6), 982–994. https://doi.org/doi:10.1111/jar.12270

Lunsky, Y., De Oliveira, C., Wilton, A., & Wodchis, W. (2019). High health care costs among adults with intellectual and developmental disabilities: A population-based study. *Journal of Intellectual Disability Research, 63*(2), 124–137. https://doi.org/10.1111/jir.12554

McCausland, D., Brennan, D., McCallion, P., & McCarron, M. (2019). Balancing personal wishes and caring capacity in future planning for adults with an intellectual disability living with family carers. *The Journal of Intellectual Disabilities, 23*(3), 413–431. https://doi.org/10.1177/1744629519872658

McGinley, J. M. (2016). From nonissue to healthcare crisis: A historical review of aging and dying with an intellectual and developmental disability. *Intellectual and Developmental Disabilities, 54*(2), 151–156. https://doi.org/https://doi.org/10.1352/1934-9556-54.2.151

McNeil, K., Gemmill, M., Abells, D., Sacks, S., Broda, T., Morris, C. R., & Forster-Gibson, C. (2018). Circles of care for people with intellectual and developmental disabilities: Communication, collaboration, and coordination. *Canadian Family Physician, 64*(Suppl 2), S51–S56.

Moro, T. T., Savage, T. A., & Gehlert, S. (2017). Agency, social and healthcare supports for adults with intellectual disability at the end of life in out-of-home, non-institutional community residences in Western nations: A literature review. *Journal of Applied Research in Intellectual Disabilities*, 1–12. https://doi.org/10.1111/jar.12374

Northway, R., Todd, S., Hunt, K., Hopes, P., Morgan, R., Shearn, J., ... Bernal, J. (2018). Nursing care at end of life: A UK-based survey of the deaths of people living in care settings for people with intellectual disability. *Journal of Research in Nursing, 24*(6), 366–382. https://doi.org/10.1177/1744987118780919

Patti, P., Amble, K., & Flory, M. (2010). Placement, relocation and end of life issues in aging adults with and without Down's syndrome: A retrospective study. *Journal of Intellectual Disability Research, 54*(6), 538–546. https://doi.org/10.1111/j.1365-2788.2010.01279.x

Rawlings, D., Tieman, J., Miller-Lewis, L., & Swetenham, K. (2019). What role do death doulas play in end-of-life care? A systematic review. *Health and Social Care in the Community, 27*(3), e82–e94. https://doi.org/10.1111/hsc.12660

Rowland, C., Hanratty, B., Pilling, M., van den Berg, B., & Grande, G. (2017). The contributions of family care-givers at end of life: A national post-bereavement census survey of cancer carers' hours of care and expenditures. *Palliative Medicine, 31*(4), 346–355. https://doi.org/doi:10.1177/0269216317690479

Ruiz, S., Giuriceo, K., Caldwell, J., Snyder, L. P., & Putnam, M. (2019). Care coordination models improve quality of care for adults aging with intellectual and developmental disabilities. *Journal of Disability Policy Studies, 30*(4), 191–201. https://doi.org/10.1177/1044207319835195

Ryan, K., Guerin, S., Dodd, P., & McEvoy, J. (2011). Communication contexts about illness, death and dying for people with intellectual disabilities and life-limiting illness. *Palliative and Supportive Care, 9*, 201–208. https://doi.org/10.1017/s1478951511000137

Savage, T. A., Moro, T. T., Boyden, J. Y., Brown, A. A., & Kavanaugh, K. L. (2015). Implementation challenges in end-of-life research with adults with intellectual and developmental disabilities. *Applied Nursing Research, 28*(2), 202–205. https://doi.org/10.1016/j.apnr.2014.10.002

Seaman, J. B., Bear, T. M., Documet, P. I., Sereika, S. M., & Albert, S. M. (2016). Hospice and family involvement with end-of-life care: Results from a population-based survey. *The American Journal of Hospice & Palliative Care, 33*(2), 130–135. https://doi.org/doi:10.1177/1049909114550392

Stankiewicz, E., Ouellette-Kuntz, H., McIsaac, M., Shooshtari, S., & Balogh, R. (2018). Patterns of mortality among adults with intellectual and developmental disabilities in Ontario. *Canadian Journal of Public Health, 109*, 866–872. https://doi.org/10.17269/s41997-018-0124-8

Teno, J. M. (2005). Measuring end-of-life care outcomes retrospectively. *Journal of Palliative Medicine, 8*(Suppl 1), S42–S49. https://doi.org/10.1089/jpm.2005.8.s-42

Tuffrey-Wijne, I., McLaughlin, D., Curfs, L., Dusart, A., Hoenger, C., McEnhill, L., ... Oliver, D. (2016). Defining consensus norms for palliative care of people with intellectual disabilities in Europe, using Delphi methods: A white paper from the European association of palliative care. *Palliative Medicine, 30*(5), 446–455. https://doi.org/10.1177/0269216315600993

Tuffrey-Wijne, I., Rose, T., Grant, R., & Wijne, A. (2017). Communicating about death and dying: Developing training for staff working in services for people with intellectual disabilities. *Journal of Applied Research in Intellectual Disabilities, 30*(6), 1099–1110. https://doi.org/10.1111/jar.12382

Voss, H., Vogel, A., Wagemans, A. M. A., Francke, A. L., Metsemakers, J. F. M., Courtens, A. M., & de Veer, A. J. E. (2019). Advance care planning in the palliative phase of people with intellectual disabilities: Analysis of medical files and interviews. *Journal of Intellectual Disability Research, 63*(10), 1262–1272. https://doi.org/10.1111/jir.12664

Williamson, H. J., Contreras, G. M., Rodriguez, E. S., Smith, J. M., & Perkins, E. A. (2017). Health care access for adults with intellectual and developmental disabilities: A scoping review. *OTJR: Occupation, Participation and Health,* 1–10. https://doi.org/10.1177/1539449217714148

Wirtz, J., Ailey, S. H., Hohmann, S., & Johnson, T. (2020). Patient outcomes associated with tailored hospital programs for intellectual disabilities. *American Journal of Managed Care, 26*(3), e84–e90. https://doi.org/10.37765/ajmc.2020.42640

Suggested Readings

American Association of Intellectual and Developmental Disabilities Board of Directors. (2012). Caring at the end of life: Position statement of AAIDD [Website]. http://aaidd.org/news-policy/policy/position-statements/caring-at-the-end-of-life#.UmN-jHDihwg

Coalition for Compassionate Care of California. (2015). Thinking ahead matters: Supporting and improving healthcare decision-making and end-of-life planning for people with intellectual and developmental disabilities [Website]. https://coalitionccc.org/wp-content/uploads/2015/10/thinking_ahead_matters_final.pdf

Sunderland People First. (n.d.). *When I Die*. UK: Sunderland People First [Website]. https://www.pcpld.org/wp-content/uploads/when_i_die_2_0.pdf

The ARC Center for Future Planning. (2020). Build your future plan [Website]. https://futureplanning.thearc.org/

Tuffrey-Wijne, I. (2013). *How to break bad news to people with intellectual disabilities: A guide for careers and professionals.* Jessica Kingsley Publishers.

Wiese, M. Y., Stancliffe, R. J., Wagstaff, S., Tieman, J., Jeltes, G., & Clayton, J. (2018). TEL Talking End of Life [Website]. https://www.caresearch.com.au/TEL/

PART V

Policies to Support Persons Ageing with Disability

PART V

28
RESPONDING TO CHANGING WORKFORCE REALITIES
One Profession's Experience

Fintan Sheerin, Philip McCallion, and Mary McCarron

Introduction

Intellectual disability service provision has seen significant changes over the past 50 years. Initially, this was principally marked by a movement towards greater individualisation, both in terms of service configuration and living situation. Thus, in the United States, Australia, and the United Kingdom, the 1970s saw the emergence of community group homes and, thereafter, independent living options. Similar developments took place in Ireland, albeit somewhat later. The movement of people with intellectual disability to the community has not been a particularly smooth one and has been marked, in many cases, by incomplete transitioning, with mainstream health and social services being unprepared to respond to the individual and diverse needs of these people. Recent evidence has also demonstrated changes in survival rates, longevity and health status among people with intellectual disability, leading to arguably greater health and social care complexities, including increased mortality (Shavelle & Strauss, 1999; Strauss, Shavelle, Baumeister, & Anderson, 1998). It is against such a backdrop that this chapter is set. In it, we seek to describe the professional profile of those staff groups that provide direct services, and how dynamic policies and paradigms have resulted in a major overhaul of staffing which has left services ill prepared to meet the emerging health and social concerns. Tracing the history of staffing, primarily in the United Kingdom and Ireland, we will consider how one profession in Ireland, intellectual disability nursing, has responded to the challenges being posed and has redirected itself towards ensuring that positive health and social outcomes can be maintained for people with intellectual disability.

Staffing Intellectual Disability Services

The history of intellectual disability service provision has been recounted many times elsewhere (Sheerin, 2000) but it is important to note that in Ireland and the United Kingdom, from the mid-1800s to the 1950s, many people with intellectual disability found themselves congregated in institutions, often based on models which sought to contain or manage the problem of intellectual disability. They offered accommodation, sustenance and basic activation and the staffing models reflected their 'long-stay hospital' nature, with nurses and nursing assistants abounding, overseen by matrons and medical officers. Whilst intellectual/learning disability nursing has existed in some form for 100 years in the United Kingdom, it did not emerge in Ireland until the 1940s, under the supervision of the Royal Medico-Psychological Association (Sweeney & Mitchell, 2009). It was not until the late 1950s, though, that the nursing profession was brought under the auspices of the nursing board (Sweeney & Mitchell, 2009).

This branch of nursing quickly became the predominant direct care provider in Ireland for the second half of the 20th century, providing for the everyday health and social needs of those in intellectual disability services. Nursing assistants worked under their authority. Whilst the need for a specialist intellectual disability nurse was questioned from the outset, particularly from within the nursing profession (Sweeney & Mitchell, 2009), it was to again come under scrutiny as service changes in the 1980s saw a movement from the largely biomedical model, characterised by segregation, and reductionism (Barr, 1996; Sheerin & McConkey, 2008), towards a more humanistic paradigm (Gates & Wilberforce, 2003; Mercer, 1992) embodying holism and integration. This development was driven by policy changes (Department of Health, 1990), and resulted in a questioning of the focus on the physical processes of disease and its management which had hitherto been the basis upon which much of intellectual disability nursing practice had been built (Richardson, 1997).

The growing dissonance that was developing between service and nursing philosophies led to the adoption of the bio-psycho-social model (Engel, 1977) as the basis for intellectual disability nursing provision (Eastern Regional Health Authority, 2003). This model, albeit innately medical, had previously been taken on by learning disability nurses in the UK, following the release of the *Report of the Committee of Enquiry into Mental Handicap Nursing and Care* (Department of Health, 1979), a report which, amongst other things, suggested that learning disability nurse training should be discontinued and that all those involved in the provision of residential care be amalgamated into one generic, commonly trained 'residential care staff' (p. 86). It was in response to this that learning disability nursing refocused itself on supporting the health of people with intellectual disability who were now increasingly situated in community settings (Barr, 1996). *The Learning Disability Nursing Project* (Department of Health, 1995) was crucial in restructuring the nursing role, for it used as its reference point the needs of people with learning disability.

The changes to learning disability nursing in the United Kingdom, which sought to respond to the new realities of people with intellectual disability, led to an affirmation of the relevance of the nursing role. Such changes did not, however, occur in Ireland where desegregation and movement to the community had lagged behind significantly. This was despite the fact that stated government policy supported such developments (Department of Health, 1990); it also said little about the nursing role but referred increasingly to the need for generic social care workers and educators with an emphasis on practical home making skills. Social care work became regulated in Ireland under the Health and Social Care Professionals Act (Government of Ireland, 2005) and was tasked with planning and providing care to vulnerable persons across the lifespan. The place of social care work, as part of the multidisciplinary team, was set out in the above act and facilitated greater engagement of other (non-nursing) professions allied to medicine in community settings whilst, at the same time resulting in a significant reduction in the number of nurses working within community settings. This brought with it a refocusing of service, in those settings, away from health.

Whilst there had been some attempts to examine the intellectual disability nurse role, these did not really take account of the new realities that were taking root in Irish services. Thus, a Department of Health commissioned working group remained firmly based in a biomedical perspective and failed to provide any clarity on the contribution or relevance of nursing to intellectual disability services (Department of Health, 1997). The first significant attempt to explore the role of intellectual disability nursing in Ireland was undertaken by (Sheerin, 2006). Concerned at the fact that such nurses had become increasingly localised in residential services where only a third of people with intellectual disabilities were located (Barron & Mulvany, 2004), he sought to find out what nurses understood their unique interventional role to be. Unfortunately, nothing unique was found, bar a small number of clinical practices. No further evaluation of the nursing role in Ireland was undertaken, until the *Shaping the Future of Intellectual Disability Nursing in Ireland* (hereafter referred to as *Shaping the Future*) study was commenced in 2014, following emerging data from health statistics and longitudinal studies demonstrating that the health outcomes of people with an intellectual disability were significantly different to others in the population (Burke, McCallion, & McCarron, 2014) as well as anecdotal reports that health needs of those in community settings were not being met.

Changing Demographics

The last years of the 20th century saw the Republic of Ireland slowly moving towards what was to be called the *Celtic Tiger* economy. This led to improving standards of living and population health mirroring those of other western European countries, with reduced infant mortality and increasing longevity. Whereas national censuses provided statistics to verify this in respect of the overall population (Central Statistics Office, 2012), limited data existed in respect of people with intellectual disabilities. The National Intellectual Disability Database (NIID) (Hourigan, Fanagan, & Kelly, 2018) reported that more than 35% or the intellectual disability population was under the age of 20 years. This growth was due to increased life expectancy, and improvements in medical care and services (Health Service Executive, 2009; McCarron et al., 2011; McConkey, Barr, & Baxter, 2007; Nakken & Vlaskamp, 2007; Simkiss, 2012). The Department of Health and Children and the Irish Hospice Foundation (Department of Health and Children & Irish Hospice Foundation, 2005) undertook a needs assessment in respect of the palliative needs of children living with life-limiting conditions, defined as an incurable illness sometimes concurrent with I/DD, likely to require on-going and significant healthcare support. They projected the prevalence rate of such conditions to rise from 1,369 in 2005 to 1,610 by 2021, whilst noting that this was likely to be an underestimate. This rising prevalence has been noted more recently by Fraser and Parslow (2018) in their national cohort, data-linkage study across paediatric intensive care units across the United Kingdom and Ireland. The Irish Hospice Foundation and Laura Lynn (2013) also carried out a needs assessment based on detailed analysis of Central Statistics Office (2012) data. Noting a year-by-year increase in numbers of children dying from life-limiting conditions over the period 2005–2010, they suggested that more were surviving to (and dying during) childhood who previously would have died at, or shortly after birth. Furthermore, the recent *Model of Care for Transition from Paediatric to Adult Healthcare Providers in Rare Diseases* (Health Service Executive, 2018. p. 6) noted that some children are achieving greater longevity with 'conditions previously considered fatal have now reached over 90% survival ... and now survive into adult life with complex chronic rare diseases that previously did not survive past infancy'. The increased likelihood of parents supporting their children with intellectual disabilities and life-limiting illness at home, as well as the greater emphasis on community models of living, has meant that there is a need for skilled health professionals who can assist these families with health concerns and liaison with health services.

Increased longevity has also been noted in the Irish population, with a mean life expectancy of 81.5 reported by the World Health Organization (2018). This has also been described amongst people living with an intellectual disability with the NIID report demonstrating annual increases in the number of people over the age of 35 years, from 45.6% in 2004 to 49.1% in 2017 (Hourigan et al., 2018). The Intellectual Disability Supplement to the Irish Longitudinal Study on Ageing (McCarron et al., 2017) has, through its first three waves, provided further important insights into the realities of people with an intellectual disability who are achieving ages that have not been seen previously in Ireland. Recent findings and perspectives suggest that continued growth in longevity has stalled over the last 10 years, despite there being more older adults with intellectual disability (McCallion & McCarron, 2014; McCarron et al., 2017), and that deaths from manageable health conditions could be prevented through more concerted and skillful healthcare (Heslop et al., 2014). What is clear is that advancing age carries with it increased complexity, as age-related health issues have become more prevalent in this population leading to challenges that are not being adequately addressed (McCarron et al., 2017). Many older people continue to live in community-based homes well into their senior years but, as has been noted, such settings are predominantly staffed by social care workers whose focus is not on the complex health issues that have become prevalent. This posed a challenge to health professionals, and particularly intellectual disability nursing as it combines both a health and social focus (McCarron, Sheerin, et al., 2018)

Policy

It has been noted that policy changes were afoot in the late 1990s in respect of how Irish services could best address the needs of people with an intellectual disability. The focus was still largely on 'needs' rather than lives and so service models remained somewhat static, albeit with a greater emphasis on community living. As the first decade of the 21st century progressed, though, there was an increasing move away from any vestige of institution culminating in the 2011 report, *Time to Move on From Congregated Settings* (Health Service Executive, 2011) which set out the health service's policy on future service developments, grounded in a strong affirmation of the 'social model' and a clear rejection of the 'medical model', including any core role for highly-skilled staff, such as intellectual disability nurses, in meeting day-to-day 'basic care needs' (p. 126). This sought to mirror service patterns in other countries where the focus was on access to common, rather than specialised health, social, or other services. It also coincided, though, with emerging evidence from those jurisdictions that the aforementioned demographic changes were presenting challenges for the achievement of positive health and social outcomes, particularly as there had been an inadequate response from mainstream health and social services (Bigby, 2002; MacArthur et al., 2015; Robertson, Hatton, Emerson, & Baines, 2014).

Over the same period, policy developments increasingly grounded themselves in a philosophy of person-centeredness (National Disability Authority, 2005), with an impetus in government towards achieving personalised budgets to support the person with an intellectual disability to build the life of his or her choosing, availing of an individually-determined configuration of services and supports (Department of Health, 2018). However, as discovered by Higgins et al. (2013), many people with an intellectual disability and their families found it difficult to navigate the available services and sought the assistance of a facilitator/intermediary who could assist in a liaison role.

The economic downturn of 2008 left public services particularly compromised in Ireland, struggling to meet mainstream need, never mind accommodating people with intellectual disabilities. It was against this policy background, changing landscape, emerging health inequities and financial constraints that the Health Service Executive, in 2014, sought to reaffirm the role and contribution of the Registered Nurse in Intellectual Disability (RNID) within a health and social model of care aimed at meeting the health needs of people with intellectual disabilities and their families/carers.

Re-tasking a Profession

The review of intellectual disability nursing (McCarron, Sheerin, et al., 2018) was undertaken over a two-year period and brought together the contributions and perspectives of a broad range of stakeholders. It was overseen by a steering committee comprising representation from the regulatory authority for nursing, unions, self-advocacy groups, the chief nurse, health and social service leadership, service providers, academics, state bodies, and practitioners. Signoff by such a widespread group has been instrumental in ensuring that recommendations have moved swiftly to implementation.

From the beginning of the resultant project, the team was conscious that for very many years intellectual disability nursing in Ireland had been caught in a loop of self-doubt, fuelled by repeated failures to clearly establish what the role of the discipline actually was (Sheerin, 2012). This lack of direction needed to be acknowledged but it was decided that it would not be used to frame the narrative of the study. Indeed, the team looked with hope towards the future, as reflected in the name of the resultant report: *Shaping the Future of Intellectual Disability Nursing in Ireland* (McCarron, Sheerin, et al., 2018) and grounded itself in person-centeredness with its focus on supporting people to live ordinary lives in ordinary places. The initial stage in the study design sought to engage with intellectual disability nurses as well as key stakeholders, so as to ascertain the scope of nurses' service delivery as well as identifying how they viewed their contribution in the future. This information was gleaned through the employment of a 21-item survey tool, administered across a random sample of 1,500 RNIDs, yielding a 26.3% ($n = 394$) return. Further perspectives on the nursing role were obtained through the conduct of 17 focus groups with a diversity of groups: family members; RNIDs; people with intellectual disability; RNID educators; service managers; RNID students; and interface staff. This was further enhanced through key informant interviews with national and international experts ($n = 6$) and receipt of submissions ($n = 32$). After each round of data collection, findings were presented to a stakeholder convening for consideration and consultation. Four main themes emerged from the data which were to provide a basis for framing the future role of intellectual disability nursing. These were:

- Person-centeredness and person-centred planning
- Supporting individuals with an intellectual disability with their health, well-being, and social care
- Developing nursing capacity, capability, and professional leadership
- Improving the experience and outcomes for individuals with an intellectual disability

Person-Centeredness and Person-Centred Planning

'Person-centeredness' and 'person-centred care' are terms that have been used a lot over the past 10–20 years. As such, they became somewhat trendy concepts, often as a challenge to the perceived positivism and deindividualisation of health and social care provision. Person-centeredness is about putting the person in the centre, finding out how that person wants to live his/her life – what his/her hopes and dreams are – and working as a support to facilitate the realisation of these. It is best fulfilled through acceptance of and respect for the uniqueness of the other person (McCarron et al., 2013). Sanderson (2000) describes it as 'a process of continual listening, and learning; focussed on what is important to someone now, and for the future; and acting upon this in alliance with their family and friends. It is based on a completely different way of seeing and working with people with intellectual disabilities, which is fundamentally about sharing power and community inclusion' (p. 2). It is about equalising the relationship between service user and service provider and must be grounded in true human engagement (Sheerin, 2019). The service response has often been one of implementing person-centeredness in a unit or house but person-centeredness goes much, much farther than that. In fact, if really understood and properly implemented, it cannot be anything other than a game changer for service provision.

The importance of such an approach was regularly highlighted in the findings of the report with one family member noting that it could transform a situation, *opening the gate* to new possibilities. It was recognised that intellectual disability nursing must continue to have, at its core, the values inherent in person-centeredness. Recognising the centrality of this, it is incumbent on nursing to develop enhanced skills in human interaction, with capability to understand meaning in both verbal and non-verbal communication, with an emphasis on becoming attuned to the person, as well as developing mutual understanding of each person's cognitive and affective states (Griffiths & Smith, 2016).

Such intensive engagement is also vital to maximising self-advocacy, particularly in respect of people with severe, profound and multiple disability. It was considered that the RNID is ideally positioned to facilitate the person's voice being heard but that this requires spending time with the person to be considered as a valued activity through which true empathic communication can be achieved. Intellectual disability nurses were recognised as being highly skilled in such approaches and it was recommended that they will play an important role in supporting the achievement of personal autonomy, as ensconced in the Assisted Decision Making (Capacity) Act (Government of Ireland, 2015).

In recognition of their 'pivotal role in communication and understanding of the perspectives of the person' (McCarron, Sheerin, et al., 2018, p. 18), it was recommended that further relevant education and training in person-centeredness, autonomy, self-advocacy/advanced advocacy, and assisted decision-making would be made available to RNIDs, both as part of continuing professional development and within modified nursing curricula. This was to be complemented by the introduction of clinical supervision to ensure best practice is supported. In this way, by reaffirming the focus, enhanced knowledge, and advanced skills of the RNID, their competence will be augmented, such that they will take lead roles, alongside their interdisciplinary colleagues, in the delivery of community-based service for people with an intellectual disability.

Supporting Individuals with an Intellectual Disability's Health, Well-Being, and Social Care

It has been noted that previous studies pointed to RNIDs having difficulty when attempting to describe the uniqueness of their contribution to the lives of people with an intellectual disability (Sheerin & McConkey, 2008). In this study, however, when presented with 21 prioritised areas of practice (Alaszewski, Motherby, Gates, Ayer, & Manthorpe, 2001; Sheerin, 2006), their prioritised responses did describe a strong health focus with some similarities to those reported in Sheerin and McConkey's (2008) findings, and included: health-related care; promotion of optimal physical health; psycho-social support; and promotion of optimal mental health across the life-span. Such a focus is timely, considering the inadequacies in mainstream services, particularly in respect of access and screening, that have resulted in considerable health disparities for people with an intellectual disability (Bigby, McCallion, & McCarron, 2014; Emerson & Baines, 2011; Emerson et al., 2001; McCarron et al., 2011). This is an issue which emerged strongly from focus groups with family members who highlighted not just the disparities but also the fragmentation between various health services and agencies, particularly around times of transition. They noted that they were often unable to assimilate information during consultation with healthcare professionals, whilst concurrently supporting the person with an intellectual disability. Noting the recent enactment of capacity legislation (Government of Ireland, 2015), they indicated that they were being increasingly excluded from such interactions where the person with an intellectual disability is an adult.

Both family members and people with an intellectual disability spoke of the importance of the RNID in bridging gaps between services, in communication and support. One parent noted that such nurses have a fundamental role in advocating and ensuring quality for both families and people with an intellectual disability by helping them *to navigate the system and gain access to the relevant services/experts*. Indeed, the nurse was seen to be the linchpin who could bring disparate services together and promote coherency.

The priority areas that were highlighted for practice in the future clearly reflected the changing landscape (Table 28.1), as did their identification of future training needs, which focused on, for example, managing comorbidities, palliation, person-centeredness, facilitation, dementia assessment, risk management, and assessment of capacity.

The development of specialist and advanced roles in intellectual disability nursing has been somewhat limited, due to the difficulties in identifying relevant specialties. It may also have arisen from a fear that the discipline might become 'over medicalised' if explicitly health-related specialisms provided the foci. And so, quite 'non-specific specialisms' were identified, for example, clinical nurse specialist in community care. *Shaping the Future of Intellectual Disability Nursing in Ireland* identified the development of generalist, specialist and advanced practice roles throughout the entire life-span of the person with an intellectual disability (Figure 28.1).

The aim of this development is that people with an intellectual disability will have access the specialist RNID skills across all healthcare settings, primary, secondary, and tertiary. The implications of

Table 28.1 Priority areas for future nursing provision

Area of practice	Rank
Services for older people, including retirement	1
Services for managing complex medical needs	2
Communication skills	3
Services to support children with complex disability	4
Specialist services to support people with dementia including specialist memory clinics	5
Services to support people with autism	6
Services to support people with mental health concerns	7

Pregnancy
- Generalist offering support and advice in Primary Care
- Specialist Liaison in Maternity Services

Infancy
- Generalist providing health screening, assessment, and promotion in Primary Care
- Specialist (Early Interventions) in Primary Care liaising with health, social care, disability services, and multidisciplinary team

Childhood
- Generalist providing health screening, assessment, and promotion in Primary Care
- Generalist in Intellectual Disability Services
- Specialist Liaison in Childrens Secondary and Tertiary Health Care and Schools
- Specialist/RANP (e.g. epilepsy, autism, behaviour support, augmentated communication)

Adolescence
- Generalist providing health screening, assessment, and promotion in Primary Care
- Generalist in Intellectual Disability Services
- Specialist Liaison in Childrens Secondary and Tertiary Health Care and Schools
- Specialist/RANP (e.g. epilepsy, autism, behaviour support, relationships & sexuality)

Young Adulthood
- Generalist providing health screening, assessment, and promotion in Primary Care
- Generalist in Intellectual Disability Services
- Specialist Liaison and Specialists/RANPs in Adult Secondary and Tertiary Health Care
- Specialist/RANP (e.g. epilepsy, autism, behaviour support, relationships & sexuality, work support)

AduLthood
- Generalist providing health screening, assessment, and promotion in Primary Care
- Generalist in Intellectual Disability Services
- Specialist Liaison and Specialists/RANPs in Adult Secondary and Tertiary Health Care
- Specialist/RANP (e.g. epilepsy, autism, behaviour support, relationships & sexuality, work support)

Middle Age
- Generalist providing health screening, assessment, and promotion in Primary Care
- Generalist in Intellectual Disability Services
- Specialist Liaison and Specialists (dementia, etc.)/RANPs in Adult Secondary and Tertiary Health Care
- Specialist/RANP (e.g. epilepsy, autism, behaviour support, relationships & sexuality, mental health)

Older Adult
- Generalist providing health screening, assessment, and promotion in Primary Care
- Generalist in Intellectual Disability Services
- Specialist Liaison and Specialists (dementia, etc.)/RANPs in Adult Secondary and Tertiary Health Care
- Specialist/RANP (e.g. epilepsy, ageing, behaviour support, relationships & sexuality, bone health)

End of Life
- RNID Generalist providing health screening and promotion in Primary Care
- RNID Generalist in Intellectual Disability Services
- RNID Specialist Liaison and Specialists/RANPs (end of life) in Palliative Care
- RNID Specialist/RANP (e.g. bereavement, counselling)

Figure 28.1 The roles of the RNID through the life-span. (Adapted from McCarron, Sheerin, et al., 2018).

this go well beyond the discipline of intellectual disability nursing as there is a requirement that liaison roles will be set up to bridge the gaps between acute health and disability services. This has been a challenge in other jurisdictions where the roles of liaison intellectual disability nurses have been trialled (Brown et al., 2016; MacArthur et al., 2015). *Shaping the Future* identifies the need for such liaison nurses at all stages throughout the life span of the person, both within disability services and in health services (Figure 28.1) such that these nurses can work in tandem at transition points to ensure that common health services can be delivered in a way that will meet the person-centred needs of the individual with an intellectual disability. An example of one such service-based role, has been in place in north county Dublin for some years (Psychiatric Nurses' Association, 2013), and whereas no mainstream health-based equivalent has been in operation in Ireland, one model applied in the National Health Service, in the United Kingdom, is the employment of a consultant learning disability nurse in an major children's hospital (National Health Service, 2018). The Irish Health Service Executive has commenced piloting of liaison intellectual disability nurses within acute hospital services.

It also implies that specialist and advances practitioners in intellectual disability nursing may be located in a range of health and social locations frequented by people with an intellectual disability, including community agencies, acute hospitals, day services, schools, and other educational facilities, legal; and business services, and the criminal justice system. In these situations, RNIDs will take on leadership and governance roles, as integral members of the multidisciplinary team, employing their unique skills and knowledge to support the health of people with an intellectual disability.

Developing Nursing Capacity, Capability, and Professional Leadership

Until recently, the education and training of intellectual disability nurses in Ireland was grounded in a model that has been surpassed by demographic and policy changes. While the discipline has attempted to respond to these changes through curriculum modifications, student placements have traditionally been organised in association with formerly institutional services that were home to the original schools of nursing, prior to their movement into academia in 2002. This has arguably meant that, whereas RNIDs have been educated to find employment across service areas, they may, in fact, be socialised and trained to work in more traditional situations where people have more medical needs (McCarron, Sheerin, et al., 2018). This concern was previously highlighted by service managers in Sheerin's (2006) study. Of those RNIDs who responded to *Shaping the Future* study survey (McCarron, Sheerin, et al., 2018), 30.9% were working in residential services or group homes, 10.5% in day services with 15.3% in community group homes and only 2% in care coordination of people living independently. This suggests that, at the time of the study, RNIDs had themselves become congregated around congregated settings.

The findings of the current report recognise the need for nursing capacity to be developed so that RNIDs can be better prepared to meet the needs of people with an intellectual disability. Nurses identified a large number of areas for upskilling and education and those that were prioritised are presented in Table 28.2.

Other areas for development included health promotion skills, psychosocial interventions, counselling, epilepsy care, and supporting sexuality/parenting. These developments are becoming embedded in new intellectual disability nursing curricula that are being implemented from 2018 and changes are also taking place in respect of experiential placements which are increasingly community-based.

Historically, there have been limited options for intellectual disability nurses to undertake taught post-graduate programmes, with most offerings being generic programmes in, for example, age-related healthcare, dementia, and palliative care. New programmes have developed more recently, grounded in evidence emerging from research studies and in the findings of the *Shaping the Future* report. For example, the Intellectual Disability Supplement to The Irish Longitudinal Study on Ageing (McCarron et al., 2017) has provided the grounding for the commencement of an MSc in Ageing, Health and Wellbeing in Intellectual Disability as well as a Centre for Ageing and Intellectual Disability at one

Table 28.2 Priority areas for additional education and upskilling

Area of upskilling and education	Rank
Management of multiple health conditions	1
Palliative and end of life care	2
Person-centred planning	3
Evidence-based practice and programmes	4
Dementia assessment and care	5
Educational skills	6
Care planning	7
Advocacy support	8
Assessment of capacity	9
Community development and supporting family carers	10

location. These graduate programmes, as well as continuing professional development will be crucial in enhancing the skill complement of intellectual disability nurses and will further support the creation of clinical nurse specialist (CNS) and advanced nurse practitioner (ANP) roles in areas of identified need: dementia; behaviour support; epilepsy; palliative and end of life care; autism; mental health; older person care; forensics; health promotion; and complex needs.

In identifying the central role of RNIDs in health and social care provision, it is acknowledged that they will be required to be leaders and to support people with an intellectual disability to take on leadership in their own lives. Deficiencies in leadership were highlighted in the reports that emanated from two widely publicised scandals in the United Kingdom and Ireland: Winterborne View and Áras Attracta. They pointed to the failure or absence of leadership (Áras Attracta Swinford Review Group, 2016a, 2016b; Department of Health, 2012; Mencap, 2014) and called for the development of such leadership at all levels, including those who avail of services. The *Shaping the Future* report therefore recommended that leadership development programmes be embedded in all intellectual disability nursing programmes as well as being provided through in-service education and training. Excellence will be further enhanced through the creation of formal links between Irish nursing leadership and their counterparts on the *Strengthening the Commitment* steering group in the United Kingdom.

Improving the Experience and Outcomes for Individuals with an Intellectual Disability

The identification of *person centeredness* as the backdrop for addressing the re-alignment of this nursing discipline demands that the person with an intellectual disability must be at the centre of everything that falls within its focus and sphere of action. This is a profound statement for, arguably, it moves the lens away from service-centred to person-centred outcomes. Ratti et al. (2016), in a systematic review examining the effectiveness of person-centred planning (PCP) on outcomes for people with an intellectual disability, noted primary outcome areas to include: quality of life; life satisfaction; daily choice-making; self-determination; participation in activities; community participation; and social networks/relationships. Whereas the effectiveness of PCPs was not proven, these outcome areas may provide guidance for where nursing, through its health and social care actions, may seek to improve the life experiences and outcomes of the people they serve.

The achievement of such outcomes for people will require the nurse to be able to work collaboratively, with other members of the team, with those working in social and community agencies and, most importantly, in partnership with the person with an intellectual disability and their family. Such an approach may contribute positively to the person's quality of life (Brown, Schalock, & Brown, 2009; National Disability Authority, 2010; Schalock et al., 2002).

The success of this re-shaping process will be dependent upon the timely and effective implementation of the report recommendations. At the time of writing this chapter, there is evidence that higher education institutes have been adapting their course offerings and are seeking to further develop relationships with their partner service sites, with the aim of enhancing nursing education and training. Formal implementation has also commenced, bridging health and social care sectors and some of the key roles recommended in the report are now being piloted. Whether these changes do in fact lead to improvements people with an intellectual disability will only be seen in the future when outcomes and experiences can be measured and explored. Some innovations were, however, in place before the study was commenced and these provided important insights into what the future of intellectual disability nursing might be. The person-centred outcomes of such work initiated by expert intellectual disability nurses have been hugely positive, demonstrating key roles in, for example, the development of memory clinics for people with an intellectual disability and concomitant dementia (McCarron, McCallion, et al., 2018; McCarron & Reilly, 2010).

Challenge in Providing Service

It has been noted that demographic changes within the intellectual disability population have occurred concurrently with paradigmatic changes that saw a refocusing of service provision away from largely medical understandings of disability towards perspectives grounded in social theory (Finkelstein, 2004). Whereas former responses to intellectual disability were often characterised by congregation and de-individualisation and provided away from mainstream services, more recent perspectives have called for something quite different. Thus, there is an expectation that health, social, and other service responses should now be provided in spaces and facilities that are common to all citizens, echoing the concept of *universal design* that is embedded in the United Nations Convention on the Rights of Persons with Disabilities (United Nations, 2006). Furthermore, individualisation and person-centeredness should be fundamental to such services, promoting self-direction and choice, with greater integration between health, social, and other services (National Disability Authority, 2010).

The call for integrated, person-centred practice demands close interaction between both professional and other members of the interdisciplinary team. Whilst it is acknowledged that such integration is characteristic of the relationship between a number of the allied health professions, nursing was typically positioned elsewhere, perhaps due to the nature of its roles. It may also have been related to a lack of clarity with regard to nursing's contribution both within the discipline and in allied health professions (Sheerin, 2012). The *Shaping the Future* report has sought to address this and has highlighted the need for nursing to engage actively and positively as part of the team. Whereas the nursing role was, heretofore, one of providing 24 hour direct care, it is now acknowledged that the skills of these nurses will be used in a focused way, to meet individual needs of people with an intellectual disability. On the surface, this may not seem to be a significant change. It is, however, ground-breaking, as it represents, not just a re-focussing of intellectual disability nursing practice, but rather a redefinition of a discipline which had found security in identifying (perhaps entrenching) itself in the role of *key care provider* (Bruton, 2003). The vision of intellectual disability nursing in Ireland is arguably now one of being a highly-skilled member of the interdisciplinary team, alongside its allied health profession partners, and in partnership with people with an intellectual disability, their families and carers (McCarron et al., 2018).

Conclusion

Since its inception in the mid-1900s, the journey of intellectual disability nursing has been a difficult one. Through its early decades, it was positioned precariously on the margins of the nursing profession, and as perspectives changed, it was similarly positioned in respect of the people it sought to serve. It has had to contend with the possibility that it had become a *disabling profession* (Illich, 2011) and consider how it might best meet the needs and expectations of people with an intellectual disability. The resultant movement away from being solely a direct care provider, has not, however, seen it become distant from those people; rather, it has refined the nature of its interactions with them. It is, therefore, clearly committed to supporting people with an intellectual disability and their family to obtain high quality health and social services, through skilled partnership and engagement (Sheerin, 2019). Furthermore, such partnering will ensure that it is their voices that be the primary ones guiding ongoing service developments.

References

Alaszewski, A., Motherby, E., Gates, B., Ayer, S., & Manthorpe, J. (2001). *Diversity and change: The changing roles and education of learning disability nurses*. English National Board for Nursing, Midwifery and Health Visiting.

Áras Attracta Swinford Review Group. (2016a). *Time for action: Priority actions arising from national consultation*. http://13.94.105.41/eng/services/publications/disability/easyreadtimeforaction.pdf

Áras Attracta Swinford Review Group. (2016b). *What matters most*. https://www.lenus.ie/handle/10147/622679

Barr, O. (1996). The challenges for learning disability nurses. *Professional Nurse, 12*, 231–233.

Barron, S., & Mulvany, F. (2004). *Annual report of the National Intellectual Disability Database Committee*. Health Research Board.

Bigby, C. (2002). Ageing people with a lifelong disability: Challenges for the aged care and disability sectors. *Journal of Intellectual & Developmental Disability, 27*(4), 231–241. https://doi.org/10.1080/1366825021000029294

Bigby, C., McCallion, P., & McCarron, M. (2014). Serving and elderly population. In M. Agran, F. Brown, C. Hughes, C. Quirk, & D. Ryndak (Eds.), *Equality and full participation for individuals with severe disabilities: A vision for the future* (pp. 319–348). Paul H. Brookes.

Brown, M., Chouliara, Z., MacArthur, J., McKechanie, A., Mack, S., Hayes, M., & Fletcher, J. (2016). The perspectives of stakeholders of intellectual disability liaison nurses: A model of compassionate, person-centred care. *Journal of Clinical Nursing, 25*(7-8), 972–982. https://doi.org/10.1111/jocn.13142.

Brown, R. I., Schalock, R. L., & Brown, I. (2009). Quality of life: Its application to persons with intellectual disabilities and their families—Introduction and overview. *Journal of Policy and Practice in Intellectual Disabilities, 6*(1), 2–6. https://doi.org/10.1111/j.1741-1130.2008.00202.x

Bruton, M. (2003). *Final report of the special working group on the RMHN*. Health Service Employers Agency. https://www.lenus.ie/handle/10147/44452

Burke, E., McCallion, P., & McCarron, M. (2014). *Advancing years, different challenges: Wave 2 IDS-TILDA*. Trinity College Dublin. https://www.tcd.ie/tcaid/assets/pdf/Wave_2_Report_October_2014.pdf

Central Statistics Office. (2012). *Vital statistics*. Government of Ireland. https://www.cso.ie/en/media/csoie/releasespublications/documents/vitalstats/2012/annualreport2012.pdf

Department of Health. (1979). *Report of the committee of inquiry into mental handicap nursing*. H.M. Stationery Office.

Department of Health. (1990). *Report of the review group on mental handicap services*. Government of Ireland.

Department of Health. (1995). *Continuing the commitment: The report of the Learning Disability Nursing Project*. Great Britain.

Department of Health. (1997). *Report of the working group on the role of the mental handicap nurse*. Government of Ireland.

Department of Health. (2012). *Transforming care: A national response to Winterbourne View Hospital*. Great Britain. https://assets.publishing.service.gov.uk/government/uploads/system/uploads/attachment_data/file/213215/final-report.pdf

Department of Health. (2018). *Towards personalised budgets for people with a disability in Ireland*. Government of Ireland. https://www.gov.ie/en/publication/4ea89a-task-force-on-personalised-budgets/

Department of Health and Children, & Irish Hospice Foundation. (2005). *Palliative care for children with life-limiting conditions in Ireland: A national policy*. Government of Ireland. http://hospicefoundation.ie/wp-content/uploads/2012/04/Palliative-care-needs-assessment-for-children-2005.pdf

Eastern Regional Health Authority. (2003). *Looking into the future: Maximising the nursing contribution to a comprehensive intellectual disability service*. Government of Ireland.

Emerson, E., & Baines, S. (2011). Health inequalities and people with learning disabilities in the UK. *Tizard Learning Disability Review, 16*(1), 42–48. https://doi.org/10.5042/tldr.2011.0008

Emerson, E., Kiernan, C., Alborz, A., Reeves, D., Mason, H., Swarbrick, R., ... Hatton, C. (2001). The prevalence of challenging behaviors: A total population study. *Research in Developmental Disabilities, 22*(1), 77–93. https://doi.org/10.1016/s0891-4222(00)00061-5

Engel, G. L. (1977). The need for a new medical model: A challenge for biomedicine. *Science, 196*(4286), 129–136. https://doi.org/10.1126/science.847460

Finkelstein, V. (2004). Representing disability. In J. Swain, S. D. French, C. Barnes, & T. C. (Eds.), *Disabling barriers – Enabling environments* (2nd ed., pp. 13–20). Sage.

Fraser, L. K., & Parslow, R. (2018). Children with life-limiting conditions in paediatric intensive care units: A national cohort, data linkage study. *Archives of Disease in Childhood, 103*(6), 540–547. https://doi.org/10.1136/archdischild-2017-312638

Gates, B., & Wilberforce, D. (2003). The nature of learning disabilities. In B. Gates (Ed.), *Learning disabilities: Towards inclusion* (pp. 3–19). Churchill Livingston.

Government of Ireland. (2005). Health and Social Care Professionals Act, 2005.

Government of Ireland. (2015). Assisted Decision Making (Capacity) Act, 2015.

Griffiths, C., & Smith, M. (2016). Attuning: A communication process between people with severe and profound intellectual disability and their interaction partners. *Journal of Applied Research in Intellectual Disabilities: JARID, 29*(2), 124–138. https://doi.org/10.1111/jar.12162

Health Service Executive. (2009). *Report of the national reference group on multidisciplinary disability services for children aged 5–18.* Government of Ireland. https://www.hse.ie/eng/services/publications/disability/multidisciplinarydisabilityserviceschildren.html

Health Service Executive. (2011). *Time to move on from congregated settings.* Government of Ireland. https://www.hse.ie/eng/services/list/4/disability/congregatedsettings/time-to-move-on-from-congregated-settings-%E2%80%93-a-strategy-for-community-inclusion.pdf

Health Service Executive. (2018). *Model of care for transition from paediatric to adult healthcare providers in rare diseases.* Government of Ireland. https://www.hse.ie/eng/about/who/cspd/ncps/rare-diseases/resources/model-of-care-for-transition-from-paediatric-to-adult-healthcare-providers-in-rare-diseases.pdf

Heslop, P., Blair, P. S., Fleming, P., Hoghton, M., Marriott, A., & Russ, L. (2014). The confidential inquiry into premature deaths of people with intellectual disabilities in the UK: A population-based study. *Lancet, 383*(9920), 889–895. https://doi.org/10.1016/s0140-6736(13)62026-7

Higgins, A., Sheerin, F., Daly, L., Sharek, D., Griffiths, C., Vries, de, & McBennett, J., P. (2013). *Evaluation report of four family-focus initiatives funded by GENIO.* Government of Ireland. https://www.genio.ie/system/files/publications/Evaluation_of_family_support_programmes_Genio__March_2013.pdf

Hourigan, S., Fanagan, S., & Kelly, C. (2018). *Annual report of the National Intellectual Disability Database Committee 2017.* Government of Ireland. https://www.hrb.ie/fileadmin/2._Plugin_related_files/Publications/2018_pubs/Disability/NIDD/NIDD_Annual_Report_2017.pdf

Illich, I. (2011). *Disabling professions.* Boyars.

Irish Hospice Foundation & Laura Lynn. (2013). *Respite services for children with life-limiting conditions and their families in Ireland.* http://hospicefoundation.ie/wp-content/uploads/2012/05/RESPITE-SERVICES-FOR-CHILDREN-WITH-LIFE-LIMITING-CONDITIONS-IN-IRELAND-A-NATIONAL-NEEDS-ASSESSMENT.pdf

MacArthur, J., Brown, M., McKechanie, A., Mack, S., Hayes, M., & Fletcher, J. (2015). Making reasonable and achievable adjustments: The contributions of learning disability liaison nurses in 'Getting it right' for people with learning disabilities receiving general hospitals care. *Journal of Advanced Nursing, 71*(7), 1552–1563. https://doi.org/10.1111/jan.12629

McCallion, P., & McCarron, M. (2014). Deaths of people with intellectual disabilities in the UK. *Lancet, 383*(9920), 853–855. https://doi.org/10.1016/s0140-6736(13)62190-x

McCarron, M., McCallion, P., Carroll, R., Burke, E., McGlinchey, E., O'Donovan, M., … Ryan, J. (2017). *Health, wellbeing and social inclusion: Ageing with an intellectual disability in Ireland.* Trinity College Dublin. https://www.tcd.ie/tcaid/assets/pdf/wave3report.pdf

McCarron, M., McCallion, P., Coppus, A., Fortea, J., Stemp, S., Janicki, M., & Watchman, K. (2018). Supporting advanced dementia in people with Down syndrome and other intellectual disability: Consensus statement of the International summit on intellectual disability and dementia. *Journal of Intellectual Disability Research, 62*(7), 617–624. https://doi.org/10.1111/jir.12500

McCarron, M., McCausland, D., Keenan, P., Griffiths, C., Hynes, G., & McCallion, P. (2013). *Collaborative initiatives to implement person centred practice.* Trinity College Dublin.

McCarron, M., & Reilly, E. (2010). *Supporting persons with intellectual disability and dementia: Quality dementia care standards. A guide to practice.* Trinity College Dublin. http://www.docservice.ie/Uploads/Userfiles/Files/Dementia%20Publication%202011.pdf

McCarron, M., Sheerin, F., Roche, L., Ryan, A. M., Griffiths, C., Keenan, P., … McCallion, P. (2018) *Shaping the future of intellectual disability nursing in Ireland.* Health Services Executive, Ireland. https://www.inmo.ie/tempDocs/shaping-the-future-of-intellectual-disability-nursing-in-ireland-2018.pdf

McCarron, M., Swinburne, J., Burke, E., McGlinchet, E., Mulryan, N., Andrews, V., … McCallion, P. (2011). *Growing older with an intellectual disability in Ireland in 2011.* Trinity College Dublin. https://www.tcd.ie/tcaid/assets/pdf/idstildareport2011.pdf

McConkey, R., Barr, O., & Baxter, R. (2007). *Complex needs. The nursing response to children and young people with complex physical healthcare needs*. Department of Health, Social Services and Public Safety, University of Ulster, Belfast.

Mencap. (2014). *Out of sight: Stopping the neglect and abuse of people with a learning disability*. Mencap. https://www.mencap.org.uk/sites/default/files/2016-08/Out-of-Sight-Report.pdf

Mercer, J. (1992). The impact of changing paradigms of disability on mental retardation in the year 2000. In L. Rowitz (Ed.), *Mental retardation in the year 2000* (pp. 15–39). Springer-Verlag.

Nakken, H., & Vlaskamp, C. (2007). A need for a taxonomy for profound intellectual and multiple disabilities. *Journal of Policy and Practice in Intellectual Disabilities*, 4(2), 83–87. https://doi.org/10.1111/j.1741-1130.2007.00104.x

National Disability Authority. (2005). *Guidelines on person centred planning in the provision of services for people with disabilities in Ireland*. http://nda.ie/nda-files/Person-Centred-Planning-Guidelines.pdf

National Disability Authority. (2010). *Developing services for people with disabilities: A synthesis paper summarising the key learning of experiences in selected jurisdictions*. http://nda.ie/nda-files/Developing-Services-for-People-with-Disabilities-A-Synthesis-Report1.pdf

National Health Service. (2018). *@NHS shines a spotlight on Intellectual (Learning) Disabilities*. Great Ormond Street Hospital Charity. https://www.gosh.org/news/NHS-shines-spotlight-on-Intellectual-Learning-Disabilities

Psychiatric Nurses' Association. (2013). *Improving acute healthcare access for people with intellectual disabilities*. PNA. http://www.pna.ie/images/291113.pdf

Ratti, V., Hassiotis, A., Crabtree, J., Deb, S., Gallagher, P., & Unwin, G. (2016). The effectiveness of person-centred planning for people with intellectual disabilities: A systematic review. *Research in Developmental Disabilities*, 57, 63–84. https://doi.org/10.1016/j.ridd.2016.06.015

Richardson, M. (1997). Addressing barriers: Disabled rights and the implications for nursing of the social construct of disability. *Journal of Advanced Nursing*, 25(6), 1269–1275. https://doi.org/10.1046/j.1365-2648.1997.19970251269.x

Robertson, J., Hatton, C., Emerson, E., & Baines, S. (2014). The impact of health checks for people with intellectual disabilities: An updated systematic review of evidence. *Research in Developmental Disabilities*, 35(10), 2450–2462. https://doi.org/10.1016/j.ridd.2014.06.007

Sanderson, H. (2000). *Person centred planning: Key features and approaches*. York: Joseph Rowntree Foundation. http://www.familiesleadingplanning.co.uk/documents/pcp%20key%20features%20and%20styles.pdf

Schalock, R. L., Brown, I., Brown, R., Cummins, R. A., Felce, D., Matikka, L., … Parmenter, T. (2002). Conceptualization, measurement, and application of quality of life for persons with intellectual disabilities: Report of an international panel of experts. *Mental Retardation*, 40(6), 457–470. https://doi.org/10.1352/0047-6765(2002)040<0457:CMAAOQ>2.0.CO;2

Shavelle, R., & Strauss, D. (1999). Mortality of persons with developmental disabilities after transfer into community care: A 1996 update. *American Journal of Mental Retardation: AJMR*, 104(2), 143–147. https://doi.org/10.1352/0895-8017(1999)104<0143:MOPWDD>2.0.CO;2

Sheerin, F. (2000). Mental handicap nursing. In J. Robbins (Ed.), *Nursing and midwifery in Ireland in the twentieth century* (pp. 163–175). An Bord Altranais.

Sheerin, F. (2006). *Employing standardised language to define the unique interventions of intellectual disability nursing* [PhD, University of Ulster, Belfast]. http://www.tara.tcd.ie/handle/2262/91403

Sheerin, F. (2012). *Describing intellectual disability nursing an exploration of nurse and non-nurse caring in intellectual disability service provision*. Lambert Academic Publishing.

Sheerin, F. (2019). The cloaked self: Professional decloaking and its implications for human engagement in nursing. *International Journal of Nursing Knowledge*, 30(2), 99–105. https://doi.org/10.1111/2047-3095.12211

Sheerin, F. K., & McConkey, R. (2008). Frontline care in Irish intellectual disability services: The contribution of nurses and non-nurse care staff. *Journal of Intellectual Disabilities: JOID*, 12(2), 127–141. https://doi.org/10.1177/1744629508090984

Simkiss, D. E. (2012). Community care of children with complex health needs. *Paediatrics and Child Health*, 22(5), 193–197. https://doi.org/10.1016/j.paed.2011.09.006

Strauss, D., Shavelle, R., Baumeister, A., & Anderson, T. W. (1998). Mortality in persons with developmental disabilities after transfer into community care. *American Journal of Mental Retardation: AJMR*, 102(6), 569–581. https://doi.org/10.1352/0895-8017(1998)102≤0569:mipwdd≥2.0.co;2

Sweeney, J., & Mitchell, D. (2009). A challenge to nursing: An historical review of intellectual disability nursing in the UK and Ireland. *Journal of Clinical Nursing*, 18(19), 2754–2763. https://doi.org/10.1111/j.1365-2702.2009.02889.x

United Nations. (2006). *Convention on the rights of persons with disabilities*. United Nations. https://www.un.org/development/desa/disabilities/convention-on-the-rights-of-persons-with-disabilities.html

World Health Organization. (2018). *World Health Statistics 2018*. https://apps.who.int/iris/bitstream/handle/10665/272596/9789241565585-eng.pdf?ua=1

Suggested Readings

McCarron, M., Sheerin, F., Roche, L., Ryan, A. M., Griffiths, C., Keenan, P., ... McCallion, P. (2018) *Shaping the future of intellectual disability nursing in Ireland.* Health Services Executive, Ireland. https://www.inmo.ie/tempDocs/shaping-the-future-of-intellectual-disability-nursing-in-ireland-2018.pdf

Burke, E., McCallion, P., & McCarron, M. (2014). *Advancing years, different challenges: Wave 2 IDS-TILDA.* Trinity College Dublin. https://www.tcd.ie/tcaid/assets/pdf/Wave_2_Report_October_2014.pdf

McCarron, M., McCallion, P., Coppus, A., Fortea, J., Stemp, S., Janicki, M., & Watchman, K. (2018). Supporting advanced dementia in people with Down syndrome and other intellectual disability: Consensus statement of the International summit on intellectual disability and dementia. *Journal of Intellectual Disability Research, 62*(7), 617–624. https://doi.org/10.1111/jir.12500

McCarron, M., McCallion, P., Carroll, R., Burke, E., McGlinchey, E., O'Donovan, M., ... Ryan, J. (2017). *Health, wellbeing and social inclusion: Ageing with an intellectual disability in Ireland.* Trinity College Dublin. https://www.tcd.ie/tcaid/assets/pdf/wave3report.pdf

29
AGEING IN PLACE IN GROUP HOMES
An Australian Context

Tal Araten-Bergman and Christine Bigby

Introduction

The past several decades have seen dramatic increases in life expectancy of people with intellectual disabilities. Thanks to medical advances and socioeconomic developments, many of this group now live and age in the community at rates similar to the general population (Coppus, 2013; Strydom, Dodd, Uchendu, & Wilson, 2020). However, there is still disparity between mortality rates of people with intellectual disabilities and the general population, with some figures suggesting people with intellectual disabilities die an average of 20 years earlier than the general population (O'Leary, Cooper, & Hughes-McCormack, 2018). Nevertheless, people ageing with intellectual disabilities make up a small but significant proportion of all disability service users in most countries with advanced economies. For example, in Australia, 7.6% (11,306) of all adult participants with intellectual disabilities (53,328) in the National Disability Insurance Scheme (NDIS) are aged 55 years and older (NDIS, 2019).

Ageing of people with intellectual disabilities emerged as a pressing social phenomenon in the 1980s, when researchers and advocacy groups began calling on public policy and service providers to adapt to the age associated support needs of this population (Anderson, Lakin, Bruininks, & Hill, 1987; Bigby, 2000, 2002, 2008; Janicki & MacEarchron, 1984; Monahan & Wolf, 2014). Researchers explored the unique age associated health and social support needs of people with intellectual disabilities, and proposed policy aims, funding mechanisms and an array of services necessary to address such needs. However, since these issues were first raised, the context of debates about policy, funding and services for older people with intellectual disabilities has shifted significantly, reflecting changing conceptualisations of both ageing and disability, public policy trends and philosophies of service delivery and practice.

Since the 1980s, theoretical conceptualisations of ageing and disability have evolved from individual models focusing on deficit and pathology to a broader social gaze that embraces a socio-ecological framework focused on person/environment fit (Agmon, Sa'ar, & Araten-Bergman, 2016). This framework now understands that quality of life is determined by physical, mental and genetic dispositions combined with living circumstances, health status, lifestyle and formal and informal support networks across the life course, and the availability of supports to meet needs (Kattari, Lavery, & Hasche, 2017).

In parallel, public policy in Australia has embraced a rights-based approach that puts greater emphasis on community living, consumer choice and quality of life as desirable outcomes. These trends have been manifested by the ratification of the Convention on the Rights of Persons with Disabilities (UNCRPD), the development of the National Disability Strategy 2010–2020, and the adoption of Active Ageing as a guiding principle for age care policy (World Health Organisation, 2002, 2015).

Taken together, Australian ageing and disability policies now stress expectations that all citizens, regardless of their age or impairment, should have equal opportunities for healthy and active ageing, and access to support necessary to achieve this goal (Bigby, 2008). However, despite such clear aims, progress has been slow in responding to support needs of ageing people with intellectual disabilities. The introduction of the NDIS in 2013 reformed the entire disability service system by ceasing block, or program-based, funding of services and introducing individualised funding packages (Commonwealth Government of Australia, 2013). The NDIS provides the logical point from which to explore policy and service system issues for meeting the needs of older people with intellectual disabilities. The focus of this chapter is on ageing in place of those who live in shared supported disability accommodation, or small group homes as they are referred to in Australia. People with intellectual disabilities are a very large proportion of the 17,000 people who live in groups homes and many of them are in their 50s and 60s. This chapter reviews knowledge about the needs of this group. First, it reflects back on progress made and obstacles encountered to ageing in place prior to the NDIS. Then it looks forward to explore the potential of the NDIS to more effectively enable ageing in place, while also exploring some early indicators of the extent to which this is already being realised.

People Ageing with Intellectual Disabilities in Group Homes

A growing body of evidence suggests that people with intellectual disabilities experience a complex combination of disability and age-related changes. Epidemiological studies demonstrate some subgroups of this population experience health issues associated with ageing at an earlier age and many have poorer health compared to the general population. Some of these disparities are explained by genetic predisposition, such as the link between Down Syndrome and increased likelihood and early onset of Alzheimer's disease and heart conditions (Navas, Llorente, García, Tassé, & Havercamp, 2019; Rubenstein, Hartley, & Bishop, 2020; Strydom et al., 2020).

Contextual factors also contribute to a higher prevalence of chronic health conditions among this group, including for example, a lifetime of poor access to healthcare, dismissive attitudes of healthcare providers, diagnostic overshadowing, low rates of screening and communication challenges (Coppus, 2013; Haveman et al., 2010). Similarly, research suggests that people with intellectual disabilities residing in group homes have heightened risks of developing age-related conditions due to lifestyle and factors associated with quality of care such as poor nutrition, low physical activity and high rates of medication (García-Domínguez, Navas, Verdugo, & Arias, 2020). Other aspects of their life experiences mean people with intellectual disabilities age from a disadvantageous position. For example, many will not have married or have had children and thus will have very limited informal support networks as their parents age and die (Bigby, 2002, 2004). As many will not have been employed, they will have accumulated limited wealth and will have been reliant on poverty level state income support during their adult years (Bigby, 2004, 2008). Finally, although exact figures are not available, the history of deinstitutionalisation and patterns of family care in Australia mean that many group home residents were relocated from institutions between the 1970s and early 2000s. Others were moved from their family home when parents could no longer provide care (Bigby, 1999; Bowers, Webber, & Bigby, 2014; Wiesel & Bigby, 2015). Their life histories will have provided few opportunities to develop the skills or experiences required to exercise choice and control over their lives. Consequently, many are reliant on staff to manage long-term (sometimes complex) health and social issues, and enable decision making and access to services (Webber, Bowers, & McKenzie-Green, 2010).

While social factors play a role for all people independent of age, they accumulate over a person's lifetime and have a greater impact on health and quality of life as people age (Bigby, 2004; García-Domínguez et al., 2020; Northway, Jenkins, & Hart, 2017). Scholars suggest that the overarching areas for which people with intellectual disabilities need support are not substantially affected by age and include the same quality of life domains identified for the general population including personal development, self-determination, interpersonal relations, social inclusion, rights, emotional, physical and material wellbeing (Factor, Heller, & Janicki, 2012; Janicki & Wisniewski, 1995). Similarly, it is clear that older people with intellectual disabilities continue to require some specialist disability services such as accommodation, advocacy, assistance in their daily living activities and support for decision-making (Lin, Lin, & Hsu, 2016; Schepens, Van Puyenbroeck, & Maes, 2019). However, accommodating age related changes means adapting the nature and intensity of these supports, and in some cases, it necessitates additional supports. For example, as they age people may need increased support to navigate mainstream health systems and manage their health-related needs, as well as access home modification, assistive devices such as hearing aids, dementia assessment services and age appropriate recreational activities. In thinking of the broad aims of services and supports for older people with intellectual disabilities, Heller and Sorensen (2013) proposed three key objectives: (1) Providing supports to meet people's psychosocial needs (2) Possibilities for fostering physical, social, material, and cognitive health and well-being, and (3) Prospects for realising a sense of stability, predictability, and control.

Aged Care and Disability Policies to Support Ageing in Place

Historically, at the federal level, disability and aged care service systems have been divided according to age; access to aged care services for those aged 65 years and older, and access to disability services restricted to those aged under 65 years. Both systems are complemented by services from other sectors such as health and income security.

Ageing in place has been a central element of age care policies, which is evident in the Steering Committee for the Review of Government Service Provision's Report (SCRGSP, 2018) stating that the aim of the aged care sector is to promote the wellbeing and independence of older people – and their carers – by enabling them to stay in their own homes, or by supporting their care needs in residential care. The Australian government has adopted the World Health Organisation's broad perspective on ageing in place, which goes beyond physical space of residence to encompass social relationships with others, psychological identity and a sense of belonging (Gitlin, 2003). The World Health Organisation defines the concept of ageing in place as: 'Meeting the desire and ability of people, through the provision of appropriate services and assistance, to remain living in the community in his or her current home or an appropriate level of housing'. As such, ageing in place is 'designed to prevent or delay a move to a dependent facility, such as a nursing home' (WHO, 2004, p. 109).

The WHO definition emphasises the retention of a person's choice and control over their environment as their care needs increase. For the general population, ageing in place offers significant benefits such as less disruption to their lives, and is associated with greater quality of life, health, social inclusion and longevity (Vanleerberghe, De Witte, Claes, Schalock, & Verté, 2017). Beside these individual positive outcomes, ageing in place is also cost-effective in terms of public expenditure (Marek, Stetzer, Adams, Popejoy, & Rantz, 2012).

Australia's policy focus on ageing in place has led to a significant rebalancing of residential and community-based care. For example, between 2008/9 and 2015/6 admissions to permanent residential care decreased significantly, from 23.8 per 1000 people over 70 years to 19.6/1000 and home care packages increased from 8.04/1000 to 12.0/1000 (Khadka et al., 2019).

Prior to the NDIS, Australian government responses to the phenomena of older people with disabilities reflected a sense of shared responsibility by the aged care and disability sectors. The federal government's stated aim was that 'the disability and aged care systems should be flexible, streamlined and aligned to ensure that older people with disability, people with younger onset dementia or people with disability whose needs change as they age receive the services they need from the most appropriate system' (Productivity Commission Inquiry Report, 2011a). Thus, the expectation was that all older people would be enabled to stay in the community as long as possible, including people with intellectual disabilities living in group homes. This was evident from the government's ratification of the UNCPRD, article 19 of which states that 'persons with disabilities have the opportunity to choose their place of residence and where and with whom they live on an equal basis with others', and that they 'have access to a range of in-home, residential and other community support services, including personal assistance necessary to support living' (UNCRPD article 19 A and B, 2006).

References to the specific situation faced by older people with intellectual disabilities in group homes featured in various policy documents alongside aims of avoiding inappropriate admission to residential aged-care facilities (Bigby, 2010). However, no firm policies stipulated which sector, aged care or disability, had responsibility for funding or service delivery. Policy remained at the level of general statements that neglected to define the meaning of ageing in place in group homes or reasonable expectations about adjustments to be made. This ultimately meant that there were no mechanisms to translate high level policy intent about ageing in place for people with intellectual disabilities into practice, and thus ensure adequate resources for adjusting support in group homes and access to mainstream services as their needs changed (Bigby, 2004, 2008, 2010).

The consequence of this was that people ageing with intellectual disabilities and their families or paid carers were left to navigate a complex pathway between two systems to find appropriate services to meet their support needs. They experienced inconsistency and uncertainty about access, and failure by disability, aged and health care schemes to respond adequately to their unique combination of support needs (Bigby, 2002; Foster & Boxall, 2015; Innes, McCabe, & Watchman, 2012; Weber & Wolfmayr, 2006; WHO, 2011). Such failures too often resulted in people with intellectual disabilities in their 50s and 60s admitted prematurely and inappropriately to residential aged care facilities (Bigby & Knox, 2009; Webber et al., 2010).

Complexity of Ageing in Place in Group Homes

Since the late 1980s, government inquiries, reports and advocacy groups have articulated strong support for the right of people with intellectual disabilities to age in place and remain in their preferred environment. For example, the Productivity Commission Report on Disability Care and Support (2011a) that provided the blueprint for the NDIS, noted: 'many people with a disability want the capacity to stay in their own home (including a group home) and to stay with the support workers and service providers they like as they grow older' (vol. 1, Ch. p.179). However, ageing in place has been a slippery concept for people with intellectual disabilities in group homes, involving an array of complex and diverse policy and service issues. First and foremost, there has been a lack of clarity about how ageing in place is understood for this group. For example, in 2007, an Australian survey of disability service providers revealed a strong commitment to ageing in place, but considerable inconsistencies about what it actually meant. Interpretations ranged from a person remaining in the same group home until death, or until they needed a certain level of medical or complex care, or until the service provider could not or would not provide support any longer, to moving from ones disability group home to another better tailored to age-related needs (Fyffe, Bigby, & McCubbery, 2007). Similar variability of understanding was found in a qualitative exploration of the perspectives of 10 group home supervisors (Webber et al., 2010) who held two very different philosophies about the role of group homes and their staff. The first posited that residents should remain in the group home and staff should coordinate a range of disability, health and community services to support the residents' changing needs. The second philosophy was based on the premise that group home services were ill-prepared to support age-related needs of residents who would be better supported by experts in nursing homes. As such, it was thought that residents should transfer into aged care residential services when they could no longer participate in the daily group home routine.

A second complexity has been defining necessary strategies, since ageing in place is a much more complex endeavour in a group home compared to a family home. Accommodating changing support needs of older group home residents is not easily codified because their support needs are likely to change at different rates and require ongoing reorganisation of resources. This may include changed organisational policies or informal practices, a redesign of support worker roles, or a regrouping of residents across services within an organisation (Fyffe et al., 2007; Wilkinson, Kerr, Cunningham,

& Rae, 2004). Things to be considered include the impact on co-residents' wellbeing as the needs of one resident changes, role delineation between disability and visiting allied health or nursing staff, training for required changes in staff practice such as supporting people with dementia (Bigby, 2010). Some of the unique issues confronting disability service organisations were outlined by Fyffe and colleagues (2007), including: managing multiple medical appointments as a result of increased health related needs; negotiating with hospital and specialist and allied health care services; managing new resident dynamics; sustaining demands for extra resources such as active night staff; and accessing appropriate external advice on management of age related conditions. A Delphi project conducted prior to the introduction of the NDIS sought the views of disability support workers in rural Australia and identified 29 issues they considered as problematic in supporting older people with intellectual disabilities. These were captured in three broad themes: (1) Barriers to accessing disability, health and aged care services (2) Time constraints on staff having to balance contradicting demands such as coordinating services and managing paperwork required by funding bodies (3) Lack of adequate government funding for appropriate staffing levels, staff training or meeting increasing age-related needs (Wark, Hussain, & Edwards, 2014a, Wark, Hussain, & Edwards, 2014b, Wark, Hussain, & Edwards, 2015).

A third complexity has been that despite expectations that people in group homes should age in place, there has been little funding to accommodate their additional support needs. For example, a 2009 report from the New South Wales Ombudsman (2009) stated that 'Services generally have to try to meet the changing needs of their ageing clients from within their existing resources, with no increase in funding to take account of increased support needs' (p. 64). In the few instances where additional funding has been allocated, it has been through short term pilot programs which, even when successful – as many were – were not then funded programmatically. For example, one significant pilot program demonstrated the feasibility of 'topping up' group home services with aged care expertise and creating working alliances between aged care and disability services to enable residents to age in place despite their meeting eligibility criteria for residential aged care (AIHW, 2006; Bigby, 2008). The cost differentials between the two sectors may account for government failure to act on pilots such as this. For example, a 2005 report found residential aged care cost approximately $44,000 per person per year compared to $84,000 for disability accommodation (Senate Community Affairs Reference Committee, 2005, 2007). Topping up an already more expensive place in a group home to avoid a move to a much cheaper aged care place might makes sense in terms of quality of life, but it might not appeal to government.

Most commonly the commitment of disability services providers to support their ageing clients has been ad hoc and within existing resources. Reliance on individual organisations reconfiguring their resources leads to inconsistent or unpredictable responses across the service system and has been critiqued as unsustainable given the differing capacity of providers to absorb increased costs (Bigby, 2008). Ad hoc approaches also mean there is no shared understanding of circumstances that might warrant proposing a resident move from a group home, nor any guide to the decision processes involved to ensure respect for rights of choice and control (Bigby, 2010).

Bigby brought these issues together in a critical review of Australian policy and existing service provision for ageing people with intellectual disabilities between 1999 and 2010. In a series of publications, she observed that in the absence of consistent policy guiding service provision, debates often narrowed into issues around the intersection of, and interrelationship between, the disability and age care sectors and around which of these should be responsible for meeting the needs of this population. She identified that policy was structured in such a way that implied support needs were either disability or age related but not both, and that three broad issues often led to unmet need that ultimately prevented ageing in place.

The first issue Bigby identified was the problem of knowledge gaps in existing services, which meant neither the aged care or the disability sector had appropriate services or skills to provide quality support (Bigby, 1999, 2002, 2004, 2008, 2010). For example, staff in disability services lacked knowledge of ageing processes and felt ill prepared to provide care to people with age associated health needs.

Similarly, staff in aged care services such as residential aged care, dementia and aged care assessment services, lacked knowledge and experience in assessing working with people with intellectual disabilities.

The second issue was the rigid demarcation between sectors that restricted access to aged care programs by group home residents under the age of 65, which prevented access to aged related expertise and supplementary support for residents to age in place. For example, people in group homes could not access Home and Community Care (HACC) packages designed to support older people living in their own homes to age in place and had difficulties accessing aged care and dementia assessment services. The split of funding responsibilities and rigid boundaries also hampered inter and intra-sector collaboration (Australian Government Productivity Commission, 2011a, 2011b; Bigby, 2010; Thill, 2015).

And a third issue was the lack of agreement about whether there was a need to determine if a certain need was age or disability related in order determine which sector should pay. One position argued that any increased costs associated with the ageing of people with intellectual disabilities should be borne by the aged care sector, and that specialist disability services should complement services available to other older Australians. For example, a person with Down syndrome living in a group home who experienced early onset dementia had an age-related problem that required access to aged care expertise (such as memory clinics) in addition to existing disability supports (such as support with decision-making or participation in the community). Thus, aged care dementia specific services should be made available as well as disability services in a partnership between the two sectors. The contrasting position argued that either one sector or other should meet the costs of anyone in an accommodation support service, be it disability or aged care, as such services – including health services – should be sufficient to meet all needs. A person was either someone with a disability or someone in need of aged care but could not be both at the same time, otherwise they were 'double dipping'. Thus, the person with Down syndrome living in a group home with early onset dementia had a disability related problem and a health problem, and should be supported by the group home service in conjunction with the health system (or move to residential aged care). The argument underpinning this position is, of course, that this person already has substantial support from the disability system, which costs much more per capita than the aged care services available to other older people, and disability services must organise their resources to take account of any change to support needs. Implicit in this position is an assumption that residential aged care can simply replace disability services. Yet this position ignores the very narrow focus of residential aged care on personal or nursing care, its lack of expertise in working with people with intellectual disabilities, and need of people with intellectual disabilities for broader support to assist with issues such as life planning, maintaining contact with family, advocacy and community access.

The NDIS Promising Policy and Emerging Issues

In the 15 years since Bigby's review, the aged care and disability sectors have both undergone significant reform that has fundamentally changed the Australian policy and funding landscape. The reforms are marked by a move away from block funded service delivery towards individualised funding and person-centred approaches and also by shifts to a more competitive, market-based service system.

In the aged care arena, policy has shifted, though less dramatically than in disability, towards more individualised and consumer directed services. The Federal government continues to fund residential aged care services but the balance is shifting towards home care, which is known as the Home Care Package (HCP) Program. This program enables individuals to purchase subsidised in-home care supports with funding levels determined by the person's needs, which are assessed through Aged Care Assessment Team/Services (ACAT/S) (My Aged Care, n.d).

More radical reform occurred in the disability sector with the implementation of the NDIS, which consolidated a fragmented system into a demand driven market model, in which services are funded from individuals' packages rather than through block funding or commissioning. Responsibility for funding disability services is centralised and rests with the federal government. The NDIS is a complex scheme based on insurance rather than welfare principles, but to put it very simply, the Scheme provides individualised funding packages to eligible people with severe and permanent disabilities to purchase services according to their needs and self-defined goals. Although entry to the NDIS is restricted to people aged 65 or under, the legislation provides for existing participants to remain in the scheme past the age of 65 or choose to transfer into the aged care system at the age 65 or older. Importantly, if a person remains an NDIS participant after the age of 65, they may purchase supports to meet their age-related support needs from private or non-government organisations registered as NDIS providers. However, if an NDIS participant aged over 65 enters a residential aged care facility or receives an aged care HCP on a permanent basis, they are automatically transferred to the aged care system and from that time will be unable to access NDIS funding (National Disability Insurance Scheme, 2013, section 29 (1)).

At face value, the NDIS offers people with intellectual disabilities the potential for much greater choice and control over the nature and delivery of their support across their life course. It holds significant promise of enabling people ageing with intellectual disabilities to age in place in groups homes. This has yet to be fully tested as the rollout of the Scheme across Australia will only be completed in 2020. Its implementation has been widely critiqued and characterised by relentless and rapid change to its operating procedures, rules and policies, and pricing structures, all of which make analysis and robust conclusions about its impact difficult (Bigby, 2020). However, early analysis suggests that overall, the Scheme has not taken good account of issues specific to adults with intellectual disabilities, who experience poorer outcomes compared to other participant groups (Wilson et al., 2020). They undoubtedly fall into the group found to be at risk of receiving lower levels of service than previously because they are largely unable to advocate for themselves and struggle to navigate NDIS processes (Dowse & Wiese, 2016). In this last section we tentatively explore the changed disability policy landscape and how NDIS legislative provisions are being interpreted. We consider early indications about the effectiveness of the reformed system through the lens of ageing in place for people with intellectual disabilities. While it is too early to evaluate the effects of the new policy, our analysis considers the possibilities for surmounting previous obstacles to ageing in place and the challenges ahead.

Realities of Purchasing Additional Support to Age in Place

The NDIS provides a participant with choice and control over the support they can purchase with their funding package, but it effectively denies simultaneous access to aged care services while they reside in group homes. As indicated earlier, an NDIS participant can purchase support associated with age related changes using their NDIS funds. For example, a group home resident could purchase an assessment from an occupational therapist or a home modification or active night-time support to take account of changed support needs, if it is deemed to be a reasonable and necessary disability related cost, and included in their NDIS plan. Making this happen relies on making a claim or knowing what is possible, on the NDIS' agreement to review and change a plan as well as finding suitable providers registered to provide NDIS funded services. A survey of 21 disability support providers suggested the limited knowledge of people with intellectual disabilities or their families, providers themselves and planners makes this almost impossible in practice. NDIS participants and their families had almost no awareness of the potential resources available or restrictions that applied to accessing aged care services (Araten-Bergman & Bigby, 2020). Similar findings were evident in an early evaluation of the NDIS trial sites that revealed continuing uncertainties and confusion about service provision for people ageing with intellectual disabilities. The interfaces between disability, aged care and health sectors were seen as unclear and NDIS planners were seen as ill equipped to assist people with disabilities and their carers to explore age-related needs and services (Mavromaras et al., 2018).

Research does suggest that the NDIS had increased the level and types of supports available to older people with disability (Araten-Bergman & Bigby, 2020). The reliance on an individualised support plan with attached funding and the opportunity to review the plan regularly does indeed provide flexibility and opportunities to adjust services as support needs change. However, it now quite clear that realising the potential benefits of the NDIS' individualised approach relies on having the capability to articulate, either directly or through an advocate, one's needs and goals, and to identify and engage with adequate services once required support funding is agreed (Bigby, 2020; Mavromaras et al., 2018). Ageing people with intellectual disabilities, particularly those who previously lived in institutions frequently lack informal supports and are reliant on group home staff or relatively unskilled support coordinators to assist them in articulating their needs and to develop and manage support plans. Service providers, who may have known their clients for many years often take on such roles. However, this entails considerable unfunded work and raises concerns around the potential conflict of interest (Mavromaras et al., 2018). A major issue for older people with intellectual disabilities in maximising the potential of the NDIS to support ageing in place is the absence of independent government-funded advocacy or brokerage services to assist people with intellectual disability to appropriately articulate their needs and build their support plan across the lifespan. (Dowse & Wiese, 2016; Fleming et al., 2019). This is compounded by the absence of a supported decision-making scheme to enable them to gain independent support for decision making (Bigby, 2020).

Supporting older people with intellectual disabilities and developing support plans requires time, skills in identifying support needs and articulation of those needs to services. It requires a strong relationship, lengthy commitment and trust between the person with intellectual disabilities, planners and services. Research has highlighted concerns about the superficial nature of NDIS planning processes, including planners' limited understanding of the unique combination of age-related disability and health needs, the reality in group home living conditions as well as gaps in their knowledge about available community services and support outside of the disability service system (Araten-Bergman & Bigby, 2020; Mavromaras et al., 2018). Preliminary research also indicates that in some cases, NDIA planners' lack of knowledge had led to inconsistent types and levels of support to older people through the NDIS. Similarly, service providers and advocates reported challenges in getting NDIS plans reviewed in a timely manner to accommodate changing needs as people age.

Making a Decision to Transition from Disability to Aged Care

The decision whether to leave the NDIS in order to transfer to a permanent aged care package and move to aged care residential services is a critical one, with significant implications for a person's rights and quality of life. Not the least of which is the fundamental differences between the funding and access rights of these two systems. The NDIS is a rights-based system, not means tested and access to funding to meet assessed needs is legally guaranteed if eligibility requirements are met. By contrast, the aged care system is means tested and rationed by availability of government funding (i.e. demand is capped) (Hodgkin, Savy, Clune, & Mahoney, 2020).

For people living in group homes, transferring into the aged care system will mean loss of their home and the support system they may have had for many years. In order to make such life changing decisions, they need access to accurate information and independent advice about availability and quality of care and support in both disability and aged care systems. There are to date no clear NDIS rules that translate the meaning of high-level legislative provisions about shifting from one system to another. Nor is there any clear guidance about the issues that should be considered before making such shift. A compounding issue is the lack of any guidance about the circumstances that might mean a person with intellectual disabilities can no longer stay in the group home. Indeed, there are no service standards for how, or by whom, such a decision will be made. Finally, there are currently no protocols for referral from the NDIS to the aged care system, nor for monitoring the transition process and outcomes.

Potential Impact of Pressures on Disability Service Providers from Individualised Funding

The NDIS' shift from block to individualised funding has led to significant changes at the group home and organisational levels for disability support providers. These new funding arrangements have prompted some organisations to develop new services to better meet the needs and interests of older residents. For example, disability service providers report on a range of strategies they employ to allow residents to use their NDIS funding and provide them with adequate services as part of their support plans. These include developing new group homes that focus on serving residents with early onset of dementia, providing staff with trainings and support on ageing and intellectual disability, and forming new relationships with health and community services including palliative care and dementia services (Araten-Bergman & Bigby, 2020).

On one hand, individualised funding is perceived as having increased the accountability of group homes for delivering positive outcomes for residents. On the other hand, the cessation of block funding and NDIS pricing[1] may also restrict the ability of service providers to support residents. For example, block funding allowed for flexible use of funds between residents; hours of allied health professionals were assigned to a service rather than a specific resident and their time could be shared among a number of residents and they could provide training and guidance to staff across services. In the context of individualised funding, where funded hours are attached to an individual, this cross subsidisation is not possible.

In addition, initial evidence from the NDIS evaluation (Mavromaras et al., 2018) showed that inadequate pricing meant some organisations were considering withdrawing from some areas of service. Furthermore, service providers indicated the pricing provided few incentives to support participants with multiple and complex needs, such as those ageing with intellectual disabilities for whom ageing in place requires innovative strategies and complex coordination as well as highly skilled workforce. The hourly basis of NDIS pricing fails to take adequate account of the non-face to face costs associated with quality services, such as administrative costs, internal planning to adjust supports as needs change, professional development, advocacy, and building partnerships with other services and sectors (Mavromaras et al., 2018). It seems that organisations may confront market disadvantages in providing services for ageing people with intellectual disabilities, and there may be hidden drivers that push older group home residents towards the aged care system. Alternatively, organisations may interpret ageing in place narrowly as providing people the opportunity to age in the disability sector, but not necessarily in their current group home. Until there are some changes in the approach to pricing by the NDIS, it's funding mechanisms are likely to constrain development of partnerships and knowledge transfer between disability and aged care professionals. This will directly disadvantage older people with intellectual disabilities and jeopardise the availability and quality of their accommodation services.

Conclusion

The policy implications of the increased life expectancy of older people with intellectual disability, recognised almost four decades ago, have inspired policy debates in Australia and around the world. And during the following decades, major reforms have occurred for older people and people with disabilities in Australia. These reforms have addressed some of the tensions between the aged care and disability sectors by assigning uncapped federal funding to the disability sector. In hindsight, this assigned the responsibility for addressing the needs of older people with disabilities solely to the disability sector and ostensibly provided them with control over which sector better addresses their needs. In theory, people with intellectual disabilities can now purchase a wide array of services to accommodate their needs and allow them to age in place within their group home. The support is available until a point in time where the person makes an informed choice to move into aged care residential care. This process logic is based on three assumptions: first that the disability service system has the capacity, knowledge, skills and expertise to adequately respond to the changing needs of people with intellectual disability as they age. Second, that people with intellectual disabilities can articulate, claim and manage their own age-related support services within a disability system; and third, that the aged care system can adequately accommodate older people with intellectual disabilities complex needs. None of these assumptions are supported by evidence. Research discussed earlier in the chapter suggests that disability staff have little knowledge and few skills in respect of ageing and the evidence also points to the relative disadvantage of people with intellectual disabilities in the NDIS (Bigby, 2020). And finally, Australian research indicates that although residential aged care providers may be more skilled than disability support providers in meeting the health needs of older people with intellectual disabilities, their capacity to meet their social needs or ensure their human rights is limited (Bigby, Webber, McKenzie-Green, & Bowers, 2008; Webber et al., 2014).

The inherent systems segmentation and split funding mechanism between the aged care and disability sectors continues to hamper cross sector partnerships and knowledge and skills transfer. Despite significant reforms, the indications are that people ageing with disabilities in group homes remain disadvantaged. Moving forward, it will be important that the NDIS gives attention to translating legislative intentions about the interface of disability and aged care systems into clear rules and guidance for people with intellectual disabilities, their families, planners, advocates and service providers. In this context it is crucial to provide people with intellectual disabilities avenues to gain independent advice, accurate information and support for decision making about the life changing decisions they are likely to confront as they age. It will also be important for both the NDIS and the disability sector to clearly define what ageing in place means for older people with intellectual disabilities in group homes, develop a clear guidance on how to best support their changing needs within the disability system, and maximise choice and control over their environment. Finally, if the desirable policy aim is to allow people with intellectual disabilities to age in place in their group homes, critical consideration is required in the development and adjustment of NDIS pricing. This is necessary to ensure that appropriate funding is available for group home providers to adequately support the changing needs of people with intellectual disabilities as they age.

Note

1 Though based on market principles the National Disability Insurance Agency sets the price that disability support providers can charge for every items of service they deliver and which are purchased by participants from their NDIS funding package.

References

Agmon, M., Sa'ar, A., & Araten-Bergman, T. (2016). The person in the disabled body: A perspective on culture and personhood from the margins. *International Journal for Equity in Health*, 15(1), 1–11. https://doi.org/10.1186/s12939-016-0437-2

Anderson, D. J., Lakin, K. C., Bruininks, R. H., & Hill, B. K. (1987). *A national study of residential and support services for elderly persons with mental retardation (Report No. 22).* University of Minnesota, Department of Education Psychology.

Araten-Bergman, T., & Bigby, C. (2020). Aging with intellectual disability: Exploring the impact of the NDIS on service provision. *Living with Disability Research centre,* La Trobe University.

Australian Government Productivity Commission. (2011a). *Disability care and support.* http://www.pc.gov.au/projects/inquiry/disability-support/report

Australian Government Productivity Commission. (2011b). *Caring for older Australians.* http://www.pc.gov.au/projects/inquiry/aged-care

Australian Institute of Health and Welfare. (2006). *National evaluation of the aged care innovative pool disability aged care interface pilot: Final report.* Aged Care Series No.12, Cat. No. AGE 50. Canberra, AIHW. https://www.aihw.gov.au/reports/aged-care/national-evaluation-aged-care-pilot-final-report/contents/table-of-contents

Bigby, C. (1999). Policy and programs for older people with an intellectual disability. In E. Ozanne, C. Bigby, S. Forbes, C. Glennen, M. Gordon, & C. Fyffe (Eds.), *Reframing opportunities for people with an intellectual disability* (Chapter 7). University of Melbourne.

Bigby, C. (2000). *Moving on without parents: Planning, transitions and sources of support for older adults with intellectual disabilities.* Maclennan and Petty.

Bigby, C. (2002). Ageing people with a lifelong disability: Challenges for the aged care and disability sectors. *Journal of Intellectual and Developmental Disability*, 27(4), 231–241. https://doi.org/10.1080/1366825021000029294

Bigby, C. (2004). *Ageing with a lifelong disability: A guide to practice, program, and policy issues for human services professionals.* Jessica Kingsley Publishers.

Bigby, C. (2008). Beset by obstacles: A review of Australian policy development to support ageing in place for people with intellectual disability. *Journal of Intellectual and Developmental Disability, 33*(1), 76–86. https://doi.org/10.1080/13668250701852433

Bigby, C. (2010). A five-country comparative review of accommodation support policies for older people with intellectual disability. *Journal of Policy and Practice in Intellectual Disabilities, 7*(1), 3–15. https://doi.org/10.1111/j.1741-1130.2010.00242.x

Bigby, C. (2020). Dedifferentiation and people with intellectual disabilities in the Australian National Disability Insurance Scheme: Bringing research, politics and policy together. *Journal of Intellectual & Developmental Disability,* 1–11. https://doi.org/10.3109/13668250.2020.1776852

Bigby, C., & Knox, M. (2009). "I want to see the queen": Experiences of service use by ageing people with an intellectual disability. *Australian Social Work, 62*(2), 216–231. https://doi.org/10.1080/03124070902748910

Bigby, C., Webber, R., McKenzie-Green, B., & Bowers, B. (2008). A survey of people with intellectual disabilities living in residential aged care facilities in Victoria. *Journal of Intellectual Disability Research, 52*(5), 404–414. https://doi.org/10.1111/j.1365-2788.2007.01040.x

Bowers, B., Webber, R., & Bigby, C. (2014). Health issues of older people with intellectual disabilities in group homes. *Journal of Intellectual and Developmental Disability, 39*(3), 261–269. http://hdl.handle.net/11343/230779

Commonwealth Government of Australia. (2013). *National Disability Insurance Scheme.* http://www.ndis.gov.au/

Coppus, A. M. W. (2013). People with intellectual disability: What do we know about adulthood and life expectancy? *Developmental Disabilities Research Reviews, 18*(1), 6–16. https://doi.org/10.1002/ddrr.1123

Dowse, L., & Wiese, M. (2016). Cognitive disability and complex support needs: Challenges in the National Disability Insurance Scheme. In E. Moore (Ed.), *Case management: Inclusive Community practice* (pp. 417–437). Oxford University Press.

Factor, A., Heller, T., & Janicki, M. (2012). *Bridging the aging and developmental disabilities services networks: Challenges and best practices.* Institute on Disability and Human Development, University of Illinois at Chicago.

Fleming, P., McGilloway, S., Hernon, M., Furlong, M., O'Doherty, S., Keogh, F., & Stainton, T. (2019). Individualised funding interventions to improve health and social care outcomes for people with a disability: A mixed-methods systematic review. *Campbell Systematic Reviews, 3.* https://doi.org/10.4073/csr.2019.3

Foster, L., & Boxall, K. (2015). People with learning disabilities and 'active ageing'. *British Journal of Learning Disabilities, 43*(4), 270–276. https://doi.org/10.1111/bld.12144

Fyffe, C., Bigby, C., & McCubbery, J. (2007). *Exploration of the population of people with disabilities who are ageing, their changing needs and the capacity of the disability and age care sector to support them to age positively.* Canberra: National Disability Administrators Group.

García-Domínguez, L., Navas, P., Verdugo, M.Á, & Arias, V. B. (2020). Chronic health conditions in aging individuals with intellectual disabilities. *International Journal of Environmental Research and Public Health, 17*(9), 3126. https://doi.org/10.3390/ijerph17093126

Gitlin, L. N. (2003). Conducting research on home environments: Lessons learned and new directions. *The Gerontologist, 43*(5), 628–637. https://doi.org/10.1093/geront/43.5.628

Haveman, M., Heller, T., Lee, L., Maaskant, M., Shooshtari, S., & Strydom, A. (2010). Major health risks in aging persons with intellectual disabilities: An overview of recent studies. *Journal of Policy and Practice in Intellectual Disabilities, 7*(1), 59–69. https://doi.org/10.1111/j.1741-1130.2010.00248.x

Heller, T., & Sorensen, A. (2013). Promoting healthy aging in adults with developmental disabilities. *Developmental Disabilities Research Reviews, 18*(1), 22–30. https://doi.org/10.1002/ddrr.1125

Hodgkin, S., Savy, P., Clune, S., & Mahoney, A. M. (2020). Navigating the marketisation of community aged care services in rural Australia. *International Journal of Care and Caring.* https://doi.org/10.1332/239788220X15875789936065

Innes, A., McCabe, L., & Watchman, K. (2012). Caring for older people with an intellectual disability: A systematic review. *Maturitas, 72*(4), 286–295. https://doi.org/10.1016/j.maturitas.2012.05.008

Janicki, M., & MacEarchron, A. (1984). Residential, health and social service needs of elderly developmentally disabled persons. *The Gerontologist, 24,* 128–137. https://doi.org/10.1093/geront/24.2.128

Janicki, M., & Wisniewski, H. (1995). *Aging and developmental disabilities: Issues and approaches.* Brookes.

Kattari, S. K., Lavery, A., & Hasche, L. (2017). Applying a social model of disability across the life span. *Journal of Human Behavior in the Social Environment, 27*(8), 865–880. https://doi.org/10.1080/10911359.2017.1344175

Khadka, J., Lang, C., Ratcliffe, J., Corlis, M., Wesselingh, S., Whitehead, C., & Inacio, M. (2019). Trends in the utilisation of aged care services in Australia, 2008–2016. *BMC Geriatrics, 19*(1), 213. https://doi.org/10.1186/s12877-019-1209-9

Lin, J. D., Lin, L. P., & Hsu, S. W. (2016). Aging people with intellectual disabilities: Current challenges and effective interventions. *Review Journal of Autism and Developmental Disorders*, *3*(3), 266–272. https://doi.org/10.1007/s40489-016-0082-0

Marek, K. D., Stetzer, F., Adams, S. J., Popejoy, L. L., & Rantz, M. (2012). Aging in place versus nursing home care: Comparison of costs to Medicare and Medicaid. *Research in Gerontological Nursing*, *5*(2), 123–129. https://doi.org/10.3928/19404921-20110802-01

Mavromaras, K., Moskos, M., Mahuteau, S., Isherwood, L., Goode, A., Walton, H., ... Flavel, J. (2018). *Evaluation of the NDIS*. Final report. National Institute of Labour Studies, Flinders University. https://www.dss.gov.au/sites/default/files/documents/04_2018/ndis_evaluation_consolidated_report_april_2018.pdf

Monahan, D. J., & Wolf, D. A. (2014). The continuum of disability over the lifespan: The convergence of aging with disability and aging into disability. *Disability and Health Journal*, *1*(7), S1–S3.

My Aged Care. (n.d.). *Types of care*. Retrieved June 22, 2020, from https://www.myagedcare.gov.au/

National Disability Insurance Scheme. (2013). National disability insurance scheme act. https://www.legislation.gov.au/Details/C2018C00276

National Disability Insurance Scheme. (2019). *COAG Disability Reform Council Quarterly Report for Q4*. https://www.ndis.gov.au/about-us/publications/quarterly-reports/archived-quarterly-reports-2018-19#th-quarterly-report-2018-19-q4

Navas, P., Llorente, S., García, L., Tassé, M. J., & Havercamp, S. M. (2019). Improving healthcare access for older adults with intellectual disability: What are the needs?. *Journal of Applied Research in Intellectual Disabilities*, *32*(6), 1453–1464. https://doi.org/10.1111/jar.12639

Northway, R., Jenkins, R., & Hart, D. (2017). Training of residential social care staff to meet the needs of older people with intellectual disabilities who develop age-related health problems: An exploratory study. *Journal of Applied Research in Intellectual Disabilities*, *30*(5), 911–921. https://doi.org/10.1111/jar.12283

NSW Ombudsman. (2009). *Annual report 2008–2009*. Retrieved June 30, 2020, from: www.ombo.nsw.gov.au/news-and-publications/publications/annual-reports/reviewable-deaths-vol-1/report-of-reviewable-deaths-in-2008-and-2009-volume-1-deaths-of-people-with-disabilities

O'Leary, L., Cooper, S. A., & Hughes-McCormack, L. (2018). Early death and causes of death of people with intellectual disabilities: A systematic review. *Journal of Applied Research in Intellectual Disabilities*, *31*, 325–342. https://doi.org/10.1111/jar.12417

Rubenstein, E., Hartley, S., & Bishop, L. (2020). Epidemiology of dementia and Alzheimer disease in individuals with Down syndrome. *JAMA Neurology*, *77*(2), 262–264. https://doi.org/10.1001/jamaneurol.2019.3666

Schepens, H. R., Van Puyenbroeck, J., & Maes, B. (2019). How to improve the quality of life of elderly people with intellectual disability: A systematic literature review of support strategies. *Journal of Applied Research in Intellectual Disabilities*, *32*(3), 483–521. https://doi.org/10.1111/jar.12559

SCRGSP (Steering Committee for the Review of Government Service Provision) 2018, *Report on Government Services 2018*, Productivity Commission, Canberra.

Senate Community Affairs Reference Committee (SCARC). (2005). *Access and equity in aged care*. Commonwealth of Australia.

Senate Community Affairs Reference Committee (SCARC). (2007). *The funding of the Commonwealth States/Territories Disability Agreement*. Canberra: Commonwealth of Australia. https://www.aph.gov.au/Parliamentary_Business/Committees/Senate/Community_Affairs/Completed_inquiries/2004-07/cstda/report/index

Strydom, A., Dodd, K., Uchendu, N., & Wilson, S. (2020). Dementia and other disorders associated with ageing in people with intellectual disability. In S. Bhaumik, & R. Alexander (Eds.), *Oxford textbook of the psychiatry of intellectual disability* (pp. 83–89). Oxford University Press.

Thill, C. (2015). Listening for policy change: How the voices of disabled people shaped Australia's National Disability Insurance Scheme. *Disability & Society*, *30*(1), 15–28. https://doi.org/10.1080/09687599.2014.987220

United Nations Convention of the Rights of Persons with Disabilities. (2006). United Nations. http://www.un.org/disabilities/convention/conventionfull.shtml

Vanleerberghe, P., De Witte, N., Claes, C., Schalock, R. L., & Verté, D. (2017). The quality of life of older people aging in place: A literature review. *Quality of Life Research*, *26*(11), 2899–2907. https://doi.org/10.1007/s11136-017-1651-0

Wark, S., Hussain, R., & Edwards, H. (2014a). Impediments to community-based care for people ageing with intellectual disability in rural New South Wales. *Health & Social Care in the Community*, *22*(6), 623–633. https://doi.org/10.1111/hsc.12130

Wark, S., Hussain, R., & Edwards, H. (2014b). The training needs of staff supporting individuals ageing with intellectual disability. *Journal of Applied Research in Intellectual Disabilities*, *27*, 273–288. https://doi.org/10.1111/jar.12087

Wark, S., Hussain, R., & Edwards, H. (2015). Assisting individuals ageing with learning disability: Support worker perspectives. *Tizard Learning Disability Review, 20*(4), 213–22. https://doi.org/10.1108/TLDR-02-2015-0008

Webber, R., Bowers, B., & Bigby, C. (2014). Residential aged care for people with intellectual disability: A matter of perspective. *Australasian Journal of Ageing. Advanced online publication. 33*(4), E36–E40. https://doi.org/10.1111/ajag.12086

Webber, R., Bowers, B., & McKenzie-Green, B. (2010). Staff responses to age-related health changes in people with an intellectual disability in group homes. *Disability & Society, 25*(6), 657–671. https://doi.org/10.1080/09687599.2010.505736

Weber, G., & Wolfmayr, F. (2006). The Graz declaration on disability and ageing. *Journal of Policy and Practice in Intellectual Disabilities, 3*(4), 271–276. https://doi.org/10.1111/j.1741-1130.2006.00090.x

WHO Centre for Health Development. (2004). *A glossary of terms for community health care and services for older persons* (p. 109). World Health Organisation.

Wiesel, I., & Bigby, C. (2015). Movement on shifting sands: Deinstitutionalisation and people with intellectual disability in Australia, 1974–2014. *Urban Policy and Research, 33*(2), 178–194. http://dx.doi.org/10.1080/08111146.2014.9809

Wilkinson, H., Kerr, D., Cunningham, C., & Rae, C. (2004). *Home for good? Models of good practice for supporting people with a learning disability and dementia.* Pavilion. https://www.issuelab.org/resources/17290/17290.pdf

Wilson, N. J., Riches, V. C., Riches, T., Durvasula, S., Rodrigues, R., & Pinto, S. (2020). Complex support needs profile of an adult cohort with intellectual disability transitioning from state-based service provision to NDIS-funded residential support. *Journal of Intellectual & Developmental Disability,* 1–10. https://doi.org/10.3109/13668250.2020.1717069

World Health Organisation. (2002). *Active aging: A policy framework.* World Health Organisation. https://www.who.int/ageing/publications/active_ageing/en/

World Health Organisation. (2011). *World report on disability.* Available at: http://www.who.int/disabilities/world_report/2011/en/index.html

World Health Organisation. (2015). *World report on aging and health.* Geneva: World Health Organisation. https://www.who.int/ageing/events/world-report-2015-launch/en/

30
SUPPORT, SERVICE POLICIES, AND PROGRAMS FOR PERSONS AGEING WITH DISABILITIES IN KOREA

Kyung Mee Kim and Seung Hyun Roh

Introduction

The ageing population in Korea is growing very rapidly; those aged 65 years and over have increased from 7.2% in 2005 to 13.8% in 2017. However, the population of people ageing with disabilities in Korea is increasing even more rapidly than the general ageing population (Ministry of Health & Welfare, 2018). Those with disabilities aged 65 years and increased more dramatically from 32.5% (2005) to 46.6% (2017) while those aged 50 years and over increased from 62.7% (2015) to 76.9% (2017).

Despite the increase in the population of people ageing with disabilities, support for them is extremely under-developed. Policies for people with disabilities and older adults were developed separately from each other which resulted in neither of the fields that serve people with disabilities and older adults taking interest in the policies and services for people ageing with disabilities. Furthermore, the desire for services by people with disabilities as they age tends to increase but the types of services this group uses tending to decrease. Among the people ageing with disabilities, individuals with developmental disabilities are experiencing extreme difficulties using local community services due to the changes in their support systems that occur after the age of 40, such as their parents' deaths (Kim, Shin, & Hwang, 2018).

This chapter reviews issues surrounding the disconnect between policies for people with disabilities and older adults in Korea, the deficiencies in community services for people ageing with disabilities, and the inadequate community residential services for people with developmental disabilities and suggests approaches to resolving these issues.

The Concept of People Ageing with Disabilities

Korea's Welfare of the Aged Act defines the aged as persons of 65 years or over. The Act on Prohibition of Age Discrimination in Employment and Aged Employment Promotion defines the aged as persons of 55 years or over. However, considering the health gap between the population with disabilities and those without disabilities and their rapid loss of social role, it is sometimes argued that there is a need to lower the age definition. Many studies define persons with disabilities who are 50 years or over as people ageing with disabilities (Hwang et al., 2014; Kim, Lee, Roh, & Jeong, 2011; Roh, 2006; Roh, 2012b). On the other hand, because people with developmental disabilities experience changes in their support systems that occur after the age of 40 due to their parents' ageing and/or deaths, 40 years or over is sometimes considered to the definition of people ageing with disabilities (Roh, Jung, & Hwang, 2018; Roh, Kim, & Jee, 2014; Roh, Kim, & Jee, 2017).

A study was conducted that compared the difference between 'ageing with disability' and 'disability with ageing' in people ageing with disabilities who are 50 years or over in Korea, established these population categories for analysis (Roh, 2006). A later study explored the duration of disability and age of onset using these categories. It examined the differences between individuals who had had a disability for 20 years or more and those who had a disability for less than 20 years. Findings showed that the 'ageing with disability' population with longer duration of disability and early onset of disability had relatively satisfactory levels of health status, social participation, life satisfaction, and household income. However, they experienced high levels of discrimination, and had fewer household assets than persons who did not acquire disability until later life. In contrast, the 'disability with ageing' population with shorter periods of disability and later onset of disability had relatively higher household assets than persons ageing with disability but lower levels of health status, social participation, life satisfaction, and household income, and higher medical expenses (Hwang et al., 2014; Kim et al., 2011).

Income, Health, and Changes to One-Person Households for Persons Ageing with Disabilities

Data from the 2014 Census for the Disabled in Korea were analysed for this chapter and compared to 2014 data for people without disabilities from the Korean National Health and Nutrition Examination Survey. Results analysing perceptions of health for the population with disabilities and the total population in Korea are as shown below (Figure 30.1). The percentage of people stating their self-perceived health condition is good is presented. Both the total population and the population with disabilities showed a decline in their perceptions of good health as they aged. However, there were more rapid changes in the population with disabilities as they aged.

Analysis of the rate of unmet healthcare needs based on age, which indicates the rate of persons who have not been treated despite needing medical treatment, is shown in Figure 30.2. Compared to the total population, the population with disabilities had relatively higher rates of unmet healthcare needs. The age group in their 50s showed the greatest gap between the population with disabilities and the total population in unmet healthcare needs.

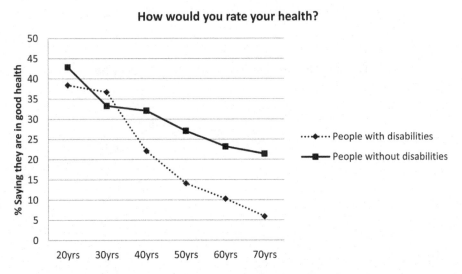

Figure 30.1 Self-rated perception of good health. (Korean National Health and Nutrition Examination Survey, 2014).

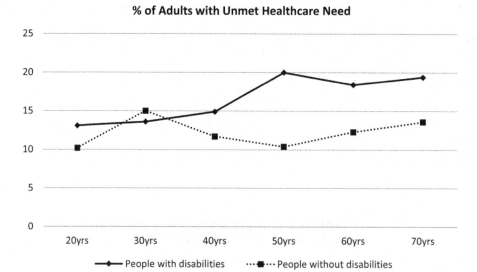

Figure 30.2 Self-reported unmet healthcare need. (Korean National Health and Nutrition Examination Survey, 2014).

The household income of the population with disabilities by age (equalised household income = household income/square root of #household members) is shown in Figures 30.3 and 30.4. Household income decreased as age increased; earned income, in particular, dropped sharply. Business income was high in the age group in their 50s but declined as age increased; however, public transfer income increased with age but only to an insignificant degree – it did not counterbalance the decrease in earned income.

Analysis of one-person households for the population of persons with disabilities by age showed an increase in one-person households in older age groups. This was especially prominent in the female population with disabilities. Support is likely to be needed by households with just one-person for people with disabilities in their 60s and 70 with 22.1% and 36.4% living alone, respectively (see Figure 30.5).

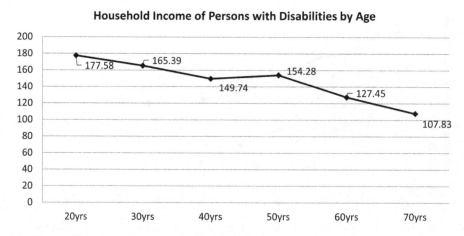

Figure 30.3 Household income of persons with disabilities by age. (2014 Census for the Disabled in Korea).

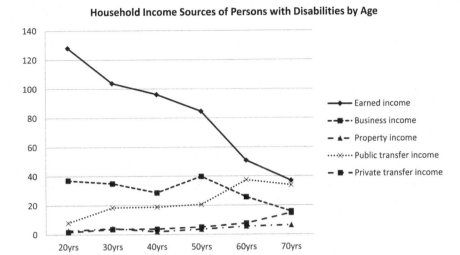

Figure 30.4 Household income sources of persons with disabilities by age. (2014 Census for the Disabled in Korea).

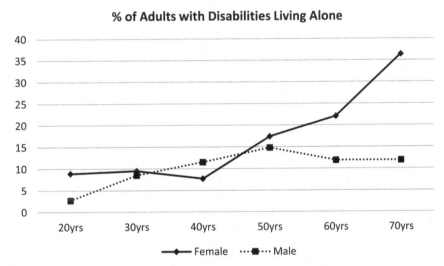

Figure 30.5 Conditions on one-person households for population with disabilities by age. (2014 Census for the Disabled in Korea).

Key Issues

Separate Policies for People with Disabilities and Older Adults and Difficulties in Linking Policies: A Focus on Long-Term Care

Korea's care policies for people with disabilities and older adults are operated separately from each other. Long-Term Care Insurance was introduced in 2008 to provide public health care services to elders. The policy targets adults 65 years and over or those under 65 years of age who have geriatric conditions such as dementia or vascular dementia but excludes people with disabilities. Personal Assistance Services for the Disabled in Korea were launched in 2007 as a pilot project and formally introduced in 2011 with the goal of improving care, social participation, and independent living for people with disabilities. Service recipients are people with severe disabilities between the ages of 6 and 65 and services are provided taking account of activities of daily living (ADL), instrumental activities of daily living (IADL), the characteristics of disability, and the social environment.

The common features of Personal Assistance Services and Long-Term Care Insurance are the eligibility determination and assessment methods, support for the independence of an individual, an emphasis on services that support the individual and household to continue living within the community rather than institutionalisation. The difference, on the other hand, is that because Personal Assistance Services emphasise an independent living paradigm that highlights social participation and independent living, it only provides homecare services and not facility care.

With the implementation of the separate Long-Term Care Insurance, the most critical issue at hand is the problem surrounding the continuity of services. In other words, multiple problems occur when a person with disabilities who has been using Personal Assistance Services turns 65 and is transferred into the services provided by the Long-Term Care Insurance.

First, the users of Personal Assistance Services receive drastically decreased benefits when transferred over to Long-Term Care Insurance. The benefit package for Personal Assistance Services is calculated by adding additional benefits (environmental factors considered) to the basic benefit package (degree of disability), but Long-Term Care evaluates the degree of disability based on only the basic benefit package. Thus, fewer supports and services are available. Second, a difference in co-payment occurs with persons paying much more for services under Long-Term Care Insurance. For Personal Assistance Services, the co-payment is proportional to 6–15% of the average household income based on the basic benefits derived from the national average household income. Then, 2–5% of the co-payment is added as additional benefits. For Long-Term Care Insurance, users pay 15% of the total cost for homecare services and 20% of facility care services. Third, there is a difference between the philosophies behind the systems. The home visiting care under the Long-Term Care Insurance can only be used up to 4 hours a day, which inevitably limits the availability usage of service hours for things such as hospital visits or social participation. Personal Assistance Services, however, aim to provide services that enable everyday activities, social participation, and independent living, therefore, can be used as much as the user wishes to within the limits of the benefits. Fourth, some local governments provide additional benefits along with Personal Assistance Services that do not continue when the user is transferred over to Long-Term Care Insurance; the users are put in a situation in which they have to give up the additional benefits provided by their local governments. Fifth, when a Personal Assistance Service user turns 65 years but is determined as ineligible for Long-Term Care Insurance (or is determined ineligible after 65), they are able to use Personal Assistance Services again. This causes issues surrounding fair distribution of benefits regarding the general ageing population and people ageing with disabilities that occurred after the age of 65 (Ku et al., 2014; Seon et al., 2016; Yun, 2015).

Absence of Community Services

Roh et al. (2014) describe the issues surrounding Korea's services for people ageing with disabilities as a paradox. The needs for services increased as people grew older, but the actual use of services decreased. The number of times people with disabilities in general and adults with developmental disabilities used disability-related site-based services showed a rapid decrease for people in their 30s and thereafter. In other words, adults with developmental disabilities were using less and less of welfare centres for people with disabilities, vocational rehabilitation facilities, and daycare centres for people with disabilities the older they were (Figures 30.6–30.7).

Roh et al. (2014) identified the reasons for decreases in community welfare service use by people ageing with disabilities as: first, the focus of these services on school-aged children and young adults and middle-aged adults. In other words, the supply availability of services for people with disabilities of 40 years or older was extremely limited. In particular, an important factor contributing to service usage

Persons Ageing with Disabilities in Korea

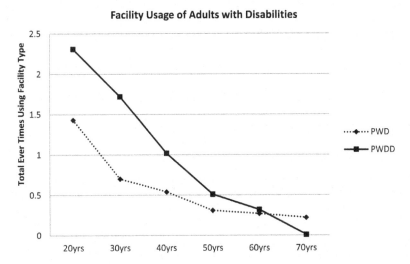

Figure 30.6 Adults with disabilities' facility experiences (use experiences). (2014 Survey on the Current Status of People with Disabilities).

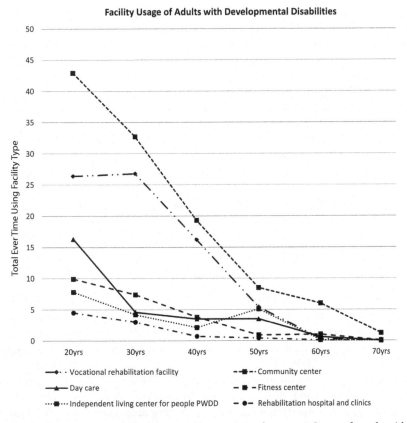

Figure 30.7 Facility usage of adults with disabilities. (2014 survey on the current Status of people with disabilities).

difficulty was the ageing of primary caregivers for people with developmental disabilities and changing support systems. Second, it was difficult to link services for people with disabilities and older adults. This was due to the differences in the identities of people with disabilities and older adults, cultural differences, and differences in service needs (Kim et al., 2011; Roh, 2006).

Absence of Various Residential Service Models

After the independent living model was introduced to Korea in 2000, there was a movement towards deinstitutionalisation (Lee, Kim, & Yoon, 2007). A limit was put on new admissions into residential facilities, and support for independent living was provided for people who would have been previously admitted to residential facilities. Furthermore, existing large-scale facilities started phase downsizing to smaller scale facilities as resident populations declined.

Among people ageing with developmental disabilities, those with Down's syndrome, severe brain lesions, and severe developmental disabilities showed higher health risks due to premature ageing (World Health Organization (WHO), 2000). At this time, there are not enough community supports for older people with developmental disabilities who are deinstitutionalised. The current system of support services is rudimentary. Because of this, residential facilities are contemplating developing supports for people ageing with disabilities but these are efforts made by individual practitioners or institutions. There is not enough social awareness about the need for residential services for people ageing with developmental disabilities or adequate welfare policies to address these needs. Community support is urgently needed for older people with developmental disabilities who do not have a strong familial support system due to the death of their parents – who are usually their primary caregivers. Research on how people with developmental disabilities are living as one-person households after their parents' deaths and how to support them is limited.

According to a study on group home support for middle and older-aged people with developmental disabilities (Roh, Jung, et al., 2017; Roh et al., 2014; Roh, Kim, et al., 2017), health risks such as chronic diseases increased among this population between their 20s to 40s but health risks actually decreased among residents in their 50s and thereafter. This decrease was due to the high discharge rate of people with developmental disabilities in their 50s or older who had high health risks. This evidence supports the case that current group homes cannot adequately provide services related to ageing issues and have difficulty in providing continued support for people ageing with developmental disabilities. Policy measures are needed to help people ageing with developmental disabilities spend their later lives in familiar environments within their communities through various residential services.

Discussion

Discussions about the need for a connection between policies for persons with disabilities and older adults have gained more interest recently for two reasons. First, the wide spread awareness of dual experiences and shared common ground. People ageing with disabilities experience ageing and disability together. This kind of dual experience expands the common ground across ageing and disability constituencies (Roh, 2006). Considering the challenging experiences with disabilities noted earlier, these need to be resolved through disability policies. However, when considering the challenging experiences related to ageing, these need attention from policies regarding older adults. However, the shared common ground suggests that disability and ageing needs should be tackled together by both policies regarding people with disabilities and older adults.

The second reason for the need of a link between policies on disabilities and the elderly is policy efficiency. When both policies work separately, it causes unnecessary costs in administrative and financial resources. From a macro perspective, linking policies can be an efficient alternative. Putnam (2002) suggested that a change in perspective from a needy person to needs is necessary to make this link. When emphasis is put on the person, policies on older adults and policies on disabilities differ greatly. When emphasis is put on the needs, rather than differentiating between people with disabilities and older adults, Putnam suggests that a solution that includes all of their needs can be developed.

Link between Policies for Disabilities and Older Adults

In Korea, issues focused on policies for care and services have been under discussion. For care policies, the future for links based on the commonalities between Personal Assistance Services and Long-Term Care Insurance are being discussed. Creating a link based on the commonalities between community services for older adults and people with disabilities are being discussed as well (Hwang, et al., 2014; Kim et al., 2011; Roh, 2006). These are described below.

Personal Assistance Services and Long-Term Care Insurance

There are many problems that accompany the separation of Personal Assistance Services and Long-Term Care Insurance. However, realistically, combining the two systems under current conditions has its limitations. Other countries that have separated systems like Korea are Japan and France. Both countries transfer people ageing with disabilities over to Long-Term Care Insurance when they reach a certain age but have exceptions to keep system flexibility (Seon et al., 2016). Combining both systems in Korea can be achieved through creating flexible services that are based on self-determination of the people with disabilities regardless of age. In addition, it would be necessary to guarantee people with disabilities under the age of 65 the use of services through Long-Term Care Insurance so that they have access to facility care if needed. Taking a long-term perspective, the increase of people ageing with disabilities will further complicate the various issues that arise from the currently separated systems; therefore, discussions on ways to link the two systems need to continue.

A Community service model for active ageing

Korea's community services for people ageing with disabilities need to be based on the social model of disability and active ageing model. The World Health Organization (2002) defined 'active ageing' as a process of optimising opportunities for health, social participation, and security in order to enhance quality of life as people age.

Roh, Kim, & Jee (2017) suggested the following four future directions for active ageing for people ageing with disabilities. First, policies need to be founded on human rights. The disability service model has changed to a human rights paradigm, representative of the independent living model, and is based on self-determination and emphasises social participation. The active ageing model aims for active social participation founded on human rights of people ageing with disabilities. Second, policies should be based on a positive model regarding disabilities and ageing (Cameron, 2011). The active ageing theory is complementary to the positive model for disabilities in that it reflects a positive perspective on ageing. Third, policies require different services that take the experience of disability into account. Fourth, active ageing services for people ageing with disabilities should emphasise networks within communities. In other words, although separate services specifically for people ageing with disabilities need to be developed, there is a need to seek a network delivery system that could provide services through cooperation between disability policies, policies for the elderly, and healthcare policies. Services for people ageing with disabilities need to critically consider the connection with community.

Community Service Development for People Ageing with Disabilities

There is a need for the development and supply of community services for people ageing with disabilities who are 50 years and over that continue on as persons reach age 65. Personnel responsible for disability policies within the community tend to think older adult welfare programs and policies should be responsible for all people 65 years and over with disabilities. This is due to the age classification that segments policies on disabilities and those for older adults. Therefore, even when people ageing with disabilities seek support, they argue that if individuals are 65 years or older, older adult welfare programs and policies should take responsibility in providing support. However, people ageing with disabilities wish to continue with their disability services even after they turn age 65. People ageing with disabilities who have lived as people with disabilities for a long period of time desire to use disability services within their communities. People who were experiencing 'disability with ageing' also show interest in receiving disability services rather than services for older adults. The problem is that disability related services – those that have an independent living and human rights orientation and permit service use to support community-based engagement are limited for older adults.

Numerous seminars on linking disability services and services for older adults have been held over the past 10 years but those who were interested and participated were limited to professionals in the field of disability. This is problematic as community services that are provided to people ageing with disabilities who are 50 years or over need to continue to support them when they are 65 years or over, so the investment of professionals in the field of ageing is critical. In order to develop community services, the needs of people ageing with disabilities need to be understood and the field of disability consulted. For example, in Gyeonggi Province, a project on opening senior community centres for people ageing with disabilities is being discussed. This would be done through the establishment of regulations developed in cooperation with organisations for people with disabilities. Additionally, the field of developmental disabilities is making efforts to develop specialised services for middle and old-aged people with developmental disabilities. Linking disability services and services for older adults are important tasks but the service supply model that connects with community healthcare resources must also be in place.

Providing Various Residential Services within the Community

Research on Korea's residential services for people ageing with disabilities has been centred on 'ageing in place'. Ageing in place provides support to help individuals age in their original place of residence which means they preferably avoid living in residential facilities and are able to maintain existing social relationships. Previous research related to people with developmental disabilities (Bigby, Webber, McKenzie-Green, & Bowers, 2008b; Janicki, 2004) defined 'ageing in place' as maintaining community residential services including living in their original homes or maintaining similar disability services within the community. Suggestions on various residential services for people ageing with disabilities are as follows.

First, there is a need for instructions on the future direction of residential services for people ageing with disabilities on the national level. The policy should include the entire life cycle and aim to maintain familiarity of residence. People with disabilities who are living in their original homes should be supported to maintain the original home life. The continuance of current services for users of group homes or other community residential services need to be supported as well. In addition, self-determination of the individuals and familiarity of residential services for people deinstitutionalised, and those who self-support themselves, need to be considered.

Second, specialist residential services for older adults need to be developed. Roh et al. (2014) studied practitioners and individual users and suggested the need for specialised group homes for people ageing with developmental disabilities. However, since there are advantages to cohabitating with various age groups, age-specific services based on the user's choice should be introduced. Furthermore, Roh et al. (2014) also suggested introducing care-intensive group homes for people ageing with disabilities. Analysis of group home conditions in the past 3 years has revealed that the number of people who left group home services in and after their 50s was increasing. In other words, this means that it was difficult for people with disabilities who have high health risks to maintain long-term group home living. Care-intensive group homes for older adults that specialises in supporting prematurely ageing people with developmental disabilities who have high health risks should be considered. Care-intensive group homes need to be located at the centre of the community. Roh et al. (2014) suggests that the group homes should consist of 10 or less inhabitants and need to be supported by healthcare and welfare resources.

Third, residential services need to complement day activity services. In order to do this, welfare services, employment services, activity support services, and social networks need to collaborate with each other. In other words, meaningful social activities for people ageing with disabilities are essential. Fourth, there needs to be a network of health support. Providing residential services to people ageing with disabilities from solely the field of welfare has limitations. Rather, it is important to have a connection with community healthcare services. Partnership between residential services and healthcare services is a fundamental task. Fifth, there needs to be workforce support for providing residential services for people ageing with disabilities. The current residential services put all pressures that arise from health risks associated with caused by ageing on practitioners and families. The workforce for supporting people ageing with disabilities needs to be adjusted and development of educational resources are needed to professionalise the practitioners' services for people ageing with disabilities.

Conclusion

The population of people ageing with disabilities is rapidly growing. People ageing with disabilities experience both disabilities and ageing at the same time. However, access to both disability services and services for older adults are limited for this population. This is a particular problem for people with developmental disabilities who experience significant life changes when parental, primary caregivers die and community residential services are unable to meet their needs. Research, policymaking, and service development related to supporting persons ageing with disability are still rudimentary. This chapter, has therefore, discussed the direction Korea should take in supporting people ageing with disabilities by investigating the linkage of policies for disability and for older adults, methods to increase community services, and ways to support residential services.

It is a promising change to see the recent intense increase in discussions related to this topic in Korea. Policies and services for people ageing with disabilities require multidisciplinary partnerships and collaboration. A future that provides a viable alternative through collaboration between each fields' professionals, practitioners, and families with the people with disabilities at the centre, seems very promising.

References

Bigby, C., Webber, R., McKenzie-Green, B., & Bowers, B. (2008b). A survey of people with intellectual disabilities living in residential aged care facilities in Victoria. *Journal of Intellectual Disability Research, 52*, 404–414. https://doi.org/10.1111/j.1365-2788.2007.01040.x

Cameron, C. (2011). Not our problem: Impairment as difference, disability as role. *Journal of Inclusive Practice in Further and Higher Education, 3*(2), 10–25.

Hwang, J. H., Kim, S. H., Roh, S. H., Kang, M. H., Jung, H. K., Lee, J. Y., & Lee, M. K. (2014). *Political implications of providing integrated public services for disabled elderly*. Korea Institute for Health and Social Affairs.

Janicki, M. (2004). Provision of "dementia capable" care in group homes for adults with intellectual disabilities. *Journal of Intellectual Disability Research, 48*(4), 426.

Kim, K., Shin, Y., & Hwang, S. (2018). Psychosocial experiences of the ageing of middle-aged people with intellectual disabilities in South Korea. *International Journal of Developmental Disabilities*, 1–8.

Kim, S. H., Lee, S. H., Roh, S. H., & Jeong, I. G. (2011). *A study on service linkage plan for the disabled elderly people*. Korea Institute for Health and Social Affairs.

Ku, C. H., Kim, J. W., and Kim. D. K. (2014). *Converging between personal assistance services for people with disabilities above 65 years old and long-term care*. Korean Ministry of Health & Welfare.

Lee, I., Kim, K., & Yoon, J. (2007). The evaluation of the demonstration program of centers for independent living and the future direction in Korea. *Korean Journal of Social Welfare*, 59(2), 197–222 [in Korean].

Ministry of Health & Welfare. (2018). *2017 Survey on the current status of people with disabilities*. Korean Ministry of Health & Welfare.

Putnam, M. (2002). Linking aging theory and disability models: Increasing the potential to explore aging with physical impairment. *The Gerontologist*, 42(6), 799–806. https://doi.org/10.1093/geront/42.6.799

Roh, S. H. (2006). *A study on constructing the model of the people with physical disabilities' subjective quality of life according to aging*. [Unpublished doctoral dissertation]. Seoul Korea: Soongsil University.

Roh, S. H. (2012b). The longitudinal study on the factors of the employment and employment types among disabled elderly. *Disability & Employment*, 22(3), 51–82. https://doi.org/10.15707/disem.2012.22.3.003

Roh, S. H., Jung, D. J., & Hwang, H. (2018). *Supporting active aging for aging with disabilities in Gyeonggi-do*. Gyeonggi-do Associations of Persons with Physical Disabilities.

Roh, S. H., Kim, S. J., & Jee, Y. K. (2014). *Supporting group homes for aging with developmental disabilities*. Seoul Group Home Supporting Center.

Roh, S. H., Kim, S. J., & Jee, Y. K. (2017). *Supporting group homes and current status for aging with developmental disabilities*. Seoul Group Home Supporting Center.

Seon, W. D., Kang, E, N., Hwang, J. H., Lee, Y. K., Kim, H. S., Choi, I. D., Han, E. J., Nam, H. J., Seo, D. M., & Lee, S. H. (2016). *Performance evaluation and improvement on long-term care insurance*. Korea Institute for Health and Social Affairs.

World Health Organization. (2000). *Ageing and intellectual disabilities – Improving longevity and promoting healthy aging: Summative report*. Switzerland. https://www.who.int/mental_health/media/en/20.pd

World Health Organization. (2002). *Active Ageing: A policy framework*. Geneva, Switzerland. https://www.who.int/ageing/publications/active_ageing/en/

Yun, S. Y. (2015). *Revising the assessment tools for long-term care for the elderly and personal assistance services for people with disabilities*. Korean Ministry of Health & Welfare.

Suggested Readings

Hwang, J. H., Kim, S. H., Roh, S. H., Kang, M. H., Jung, H. K., Lee, J. Y., & Lee, M. K. (2014). *Political implications of providing integrated public services for disabled elderly*. Korea Institute for Health and Social Affairs.

Kim, S. H., Lee, S. H., Roh, S. H., & Jeong, I. G. (2011). *A study on service linkage plan for the disabled elderly people*. Korea Institute for Health and Social Affairs.

Seon, W. D., Kang, E, N., Hwang, J. H., Lee, Y. K., Kim, H. S., Choi, I. D., Han, E. J., Nam, H. J., Seo, D. M., Lee, S. H. (2016). *Performance evaluation and improvement on long-term care insurance*. Korea Institute for Health and Social Affairs.

Shin, Y. R., Kim, K. M., Yoo, D. C., & Kim, D. K. (2016). Exploring the experience to be old from the perspectives of people with disabilities. *Journal of Critical Social Policy*, 50, 200–240.

Shin, Y. R., Kim, J. S., & Kim, K. M. (2016). On the cross of disability and old age. *Korean Journal of Social Welfare*, 68(4), 143–167.

31

TRENDS IN INTEGRATING LONG-TERM SERVICES AND SUPPORTS IN THE UNITED STATES

Michelle Putnam and Caitlin E. Coyle

Introduction

Within the traditional study of ageing, disability onset has been characterized as a common feature of later life – that is, disability happens within the context of growing older. Alternatively, the field of disabilities studies and those who focus their work on specific disabilities such as cerebral palsy, arthritis, traumatic brain injury, autism, or down's syndrome consider disability as a context within which a person ages. These different perspectives about how to think about disability have profoundly influenced the historical development of ageing and disability-related long-term service and support policies in the United States (U.S.) – or lack thereof (Putnam, 2014). At this time, however, these more philosophical perspectives about how to understand ageing and how to understand disability are overshadowed by the practical aspects of persons with disabilities obtaining and affording the long-term services and supports (LTSS) they need to live successfully in the community.

The group of individuals who first experience sustained disability in later life as older adults can be referred to as persons *ageing into disability*. This is the population that U.S. long-term care policy was originally designed for with an emphasis on institutional nursing care at the end of life. Those who experience onset of disability in early or mid-life can be referred to as persons *ageing with disability*. The growth of the ageing with disability population represents tremendous success across research, practice and policy and by individuals and families, professionals, and advocates to improve longevity and advance quality of life for persons living with long-term disability. However, later life needs of this population have received only minimal attention in the policy arena. That said, as human longevity continues to increase, we are beginning to see the emergence of a support and service population that includes both persons ageing into and ageing with disability. This blended population raises questions about how the historically segmented ageing and disability service systems in the U.S., with their different perspectives on ageing and disability, will adapt to meet the needs of this broad consumer group. This includes issues of how supports and services will be paid for, regulated, or delivered given the growing size of the population needing assistance and ongoing changes in the health and social care systems in the U.S. In this chapter, we describe the systems of LTSS for the older adult population and the population of persons with disabilities in the U.S., detail the historical legal context that has generated a shift in policy and programs to focus on home and community-based supports and services, and highlight points at which the support needs and service delivery approaches of the ageing with disability and the ageing into disability populations converge as well as points at which they are less similar and continued segmentation of service delivery may be recommended.

Segmentation of Ageing and Disability LTSS

LTSS encompasses a wide range of health, health-related, social, and independent living supports and services. LTSS is an umbrella term that refers to supports and services provided in community settings and institutional settings – such as skilled nursing facilities (Hado & Komisar, 2019). In the U.S., programs and policies that fund and provide LTSS to people disabilities are usually segmented by age (children and youth, working age adults, and older adults) and nature of disability (developmental/intellectual, physical, and psychiatric). This segmentation has created public policy silos dividing ageing and disability programs from each other bureaucratically and financially and has institutionalised fields of professional practice with specialties in ageing/older adults, physical disability, intellectual/developmental disability, and mental health/illness (Putnam, 2014). The system of delivering LTSS is not formally organised, but is made up of private and public providers, who loosely comprise a network. Oftentimes these LTSS organisations specialize in one or more population groups – limiting their pool of potential partnerships. The nature of these relationships is often fluid and can take the shape of formal contractual, memorandum of understanding (MOU), or referral pathways and many are not linked in any way. Not surprisingly then, this conglomeration of LTSS providers and policymakers are hardly considered a system at all, from a professionals or health insurers standpoint, and may specialize in one or more population groups. Tensions around which set of support and service providers have responsibility for specific groups of persons with disabilities or types of disability-related needs, has historically resulted in service gaps and neglect of support and service needs for persons ageing with disability. A fairly simple example being that lack of inclusion of persons with intellectual disability in typical programs for older adults.

Segmentation is reinforced by distinct service cultures, the use of specialised language and vocabulary, and population-specific fields of professional training which has been discussed in detail by scholars working in this area (see Factor, Heller, & Janicki, 2012; Putnam, 2007, 2011). This approach to LTSS represents a collective thinking that historically has categorized individuals first, then determined what supports and services they need second. This prioritisation based on age and disability type is directly linked to federal and state level legislation and program eligibility criteria that categorically define consumers – people with disabilities, older adults, persons with severe mental illness – as a means of both identifying and justifying public supports for specialised groups of citizens.

Segmenting by age has served the purpose of developing specialised areas of research, professional practice, and program development for older adults and for adults with different types of disabilities considered to be of working age. The resultant fields of science, practice, and policy have quickly developed impressive knowledge bases and have contributed to improved population health, social welfare conditions, as well as reduced marginalisation of older adults and persons with disabilities. As the separate ageing and disability systems developed, it is likely that most consumers and their families moved within them, rarely bumping into their borders or seeing these silos. Thus, it might be the case that these ageing and disability silos played a positive role in advancing research, practice, and policy. That said, these silos have limited work across age groups and across disability categories. The silos aggregated all older adults into a single group for which disability is equated with loss, and for younger people with disability focused initiatives on gain through rehabilitation, employment and independence without consideration for later life. This juxtaposition has resulted in LTSS being provided to older adults to prevent loss and LTSS being provided to persons of working age to support gains. Therefore, the frame of LTSS and its outcomes for individuals has historically been fundamentally different.

The increasing population size of persons ageing with disability challenge this siloed system of LTSS based on age and segmented by disability type and suggests a need to rethink how we structure eligibility and provide services and supports as well as what they consist of and how they are paid for. This demographic trend is occurring in the U.S. at the same time that the delivery of LTSS has pivoted away from defaulting to care provision in institutional settings to preferring home and community-based settings (HCBS) (Friedman, Caldwell, Rapp Kennedy, & Rizzolo, 2019). This shift is a result of federal policy changes aimed at "re-balancing" the location that care is provided in and eliminating the historical bias for public funding to pay only for institutional care. As the shift towards home and community-based care has occurred, related initiatives have followed, focusing on increasing participant-direction,[1] providing person-centred care,[2] and increasing program flexibility (Kaye, 2014). Additionally, over the past decade, managed care as a modality of cost management of insurer costs and care coordination as the operational model within managed care that facilitates consumer navigation of service providers has been widely adopted for LTSS. Thus, the environment within which initiatives forwarding integration of ageing and disability services and recognition of shared interests in LTSS in the U.S. is complex and, in many ways, particular to how the U.S. structures its health and social care. Many other countries have equally complex and siloed systems, making it important learn both about details within national systems and trends national in policy in order to be able to better understand LTSS needs of persons ageing with disability globally.

Long-term Services and Supports in the U.S.

In the U.S., health insurance for adults under age 65 is obtainable through an employer, in the private marketplace, or through public insurers including Medicaid (health insurance for low income individuals), Medicare (health insurance for adults 65 and older or persons under age 65 receiving federal disability unemployment insurance, Social Security Disability Insurance), and Tricare (health insurance for persons with a qualified military service record). LTSS is typically not covered under private health insurance policies obtained through an employer, or if it is, service provision is limited to a few weeks of home care after an acute injury or hospitalisation. Medicare covers some LTSS, but it is typically limited to 90 days following a hospitalisation. Medicaid does cover LTSS for as long as it is prescribed, thus it offers the strongest insurance coverage for persons with disabilities of any age. Medicaid, however, as noted above, insures low-income individuals who fall at or below the federal poverty line – the amount of income at which a person is considered poor. Medicaid insurance is offered through a federal-state partnership, and eligibility varies state by state. Federal guidelines for the traditional Medicaid program set an income cap for individuals at the annually determined individual federal poverty level, however states are allowed to offer Medicaid insurance to persons above that rate but the federal-state cost share changes based on the piece of the insurance program the state decides to expand. Income qualification criteria for Medicaid insurance can be less than the federal poverty line. Some states seek to reduce their spending on the Medicaid program by setting the income eligibility as low as 30% of the federal poverty line, which is a fairly harsh qualification criterion. Persons who do not qualify for Medicaid and do not otherwise have health insurance, or who only hold Medicare or private insurance that does not cover LTSS, pay for LTSS privately if they can afford it. If they are not able to privately pay for LTSS, they often go without care and have substantial unmet needs or they rely primarily on informal support – family and friends. State Medicaid programs can also set criteria for level of disability severity an individual is required to have to qualify for the state's program. Medicaid LTSS benefits can vary state to state as well. All states offer home and community-based care, but some states have waiting lists for certain types of services, and some states offer more generous benefits and coverage than others.

In addition to Medicaid LTSS, many older adults receive support from the Older Americans Act (OAA) funded programs including meals, home care services, respite care, transportation, and information and referral services which are administered through the Administration for Community Living, a federal agency that includes both ageing and disability units. Eligibility for OAA programs is based primarily in income-level and need, as federal funding for the OAA is quite limited. OAA programs are delivered through Area Agencies on Aging (AAAs). AAAs can be a public or private nonprofit agency designated by its state to address the needs and concerns of all older persons at the regional and local levels. AAA is a general term – names of local AAAs may vary. Within states, an individual AAA is primarily responsible for a designated geographic area and is funded through a combination of OAA funds, Medicaid funds, state support, contracts with other organisations, and private donations. There are over 600 AAAs and 256 Native American ageing programs (which parallel AAA's) in the U.S.

Sources of support outside of Medicaid for persons with disabilities include Centers for Independent Living (CIL). There are more than 400 CILs throughout the nation, many funded in part through the federal 1974 Rehabilitation Act. State departments, county units and city departments may also provide assistance to persons with developmental disabilities, persons with severe mental illness, and persons with sensory impairments. In addition, at the local level there are often a wide range of community-based organisations that provide assistance with employment, home modifications, housing, transportation, caregiver supports, home care, and other areas. These programs have limited funding, relying primarily on grants and private donations, but they are important providers of LTSS, particularly for persons who do not qualify for Medicaid insurance.

As persons with disabilities with onset in early and mid-life grow older, this loose network of LTSS has only just begun the process of adapting to their evolving needs. As a new service population, LTSS providers have limited experience working with individuals ageing with disabilities – those that do may be more concentrated in urban areas where population density increases the likelihood of regular contact with these consumers. Additionally, service providers who have traditionally worked with a specific category of consumers may need to engage in capacity building to adequately meet the needs persons ageing with disability. Because many people with LTSS experience more than one type of disability (e.g. a person with serious mental illness may also have a mobility impairment and several chronic health conditions), there is a need for the LTSS network in general to integrate services and move out of the historical program silos. Starting in the 1970s, disability and ageing advocates pushed for change in the long-term care culture that tended to medicalise disability and warehouse older adults, however culture change was slow and process was unsteady. A critical ruling in 1999 by the Supreme Court changed the trajectory of LTSS in the United States and set up a new environment for considering the LTSS needs of persons ageing with disability.

The Shift from Institutional to Home and Community-Based Care

The U.S. Supreme Court's ruling in the case of Olmstead v L.C. (Olmstead v. L.C., 527 U.S. 581, 1999), known as the Olmstead decision directed that people with disabilities (of all ages) must be offered community-based options for service receipt, within certain feasibility parameters. The case originated in the state of Georgia and the plaintiffs sued the state government for discrimination under the Americans with Disabilities Act claiming that the refusal of the state to provide community-based LTSS through its Medicaid program and requirement that the plaintiffs receive care in an institutional setting violated their civil rights. The case rose from the state level to the federal level through the appeals process and resulted in a decision in favour of the plaintiffs. Importantly, President George W. Bush proactively enforced implementation of this ruling through his 2001 New Freedom Initiative (NFI), an Executive Order mandating demonstrated compliance by entities receiving federal funds (Executive Order No. 13217, 3 C.F.R., Sect. 13217, 2001). Thus, the Olmstead ruling combined with the NFI had the effect of immediately forcing Medicaid programs in every state to work towards providing more equitable offerings of institutional and home and community-based care LTSS options. The Olmstead decision and the NFI occurred in a LTSS marketplace heavily disposed to institutional care, with limited consumer directed decision-making, and without ready consumer portals into home and community-based services. Additionally, most programs and services for adults were targeted to distinct consumer markets based on program eligibility criteria typically marked by age (e.g. adults age 60 or 65 and older, adults age 18–59 or 18–64) and/or by category of disability (e.g. physical disabilities, developmental or intellectual disabilities, psychiatric disabilities, sensory and/or communication disabilities). In order to comply with the Olmstead decision, structural change was required.

In response to the NFI, starting in 2001, the Centers for Medicaid and Medicare Services (CMS) which oversees the Medicaid program, in collaboration with other federal partners including a principal partner – the Administration on Ageing, began offering competitively awarded grant funds to states supporting "systems change" programs to facilitate compliance with the Olmstead decision. In addition to these grants, the Administration on Ageing provided grant funds for states to open Ageing and Disability Resource Centers in 2003. CMS funded initiatives that permitted persons currently in skilled nursing facilities to move to community settings through a program titled Money Follows the Person in 2005, Person-Centered Planning grants in 2007 and it permitted states to offer Self-Directed Personal Assistant Services in 2007 and other self-direction options have become options since that time. There have been additional advancements in offering home and community-based services (HCBS), self-directed services and community-based options including the codification of balancing of HCBS and institutional care in the Affordable Care Act of 2010 (Harrington, Ng, LaPlante, & Kaye, 2012). Most recently there has been administrative clarification about what a home and community-based setting is that articulates the requirement that the individual receiving services has chosen to live in the residence, that it is integrated into the community, that is ensures rights to privacy, dignity, and respect, provide autonomous and independent decision making, and facilitates choice among possible service providers (U.S. Department of Health & Human Services, 2014).

Medicaid is the primary LTSS insurer in the U.S. In 2018, Medicaid spending accounted for 52% of all LTSS payments with the rest being paid by private insurance (11%) and other public and private sources (20%), and individual out-of-pocket (16%) making up the rest (Watts, Musumeci, & Chidambaram, 2020). Total LTSS spending in 2018 was 379 billion dollars. Data on the distribution of spending between home and community-based services and institutional care is not yet reported for 2018, but the latest data available shows that in 2016, 57% of Medicaid spending was for HCBS and 43% for institutional care. This is markedly different than the distribution of funding in prior years. In 2005, only 37% of Medicaid LTSS spending was on HCBS and in 1995, it was just 18% (Eiken, Sredl, Burwell, & Amos, 2018). This significant shift in LTSS delivery can be traced directly to the Olmstead decision and the NFI.

Prior to the NFI, states were able to offer HCBS if they chose to by applying for a Medicaid program waiver that permitted paying for services outside of institutions. However, the NFI effectively increased usage of the HCBS waivers as they were the readiest vehicles for Olmstead compliance (Musumeci & Claypool, 2014). Because such a large systems change was enacted in every state, advocates for disability and ageing constituencies became heavily engaged in long-term care redesign. Disability advocates pushed strongly for a complete elimination of institutional settings and default self-direction in LTSS. Ageing advocates supported HCBS but were wary about having older individuals direct their own care or live in the community if persons were felt to be unsafe at home. These tensions existed prior to the NFI and in some cases were heighted in the systems redesign process that CMS facilitated. That said, federal bureaucrats purposefully attempted to address these disparate perspectives and wrote into the balancing initiatives directives that were designed to help dismantle the silos of ageing and disability and form bridges across them. State governments were usually the primary grantees for all of these balancing grants and work in partnership with local governments, other federal government agencies, or non-governmental organisations. The grants typically required some level of collaboration between ageing and disability service networks and/or service providers in order to obtain the funding. Most of the grants focused on the redevelopment of HCBS infrastructure and increased offerings of programs that met the needs of both older and younger adults with LTSS needs. These actions helped formalize partnerships between ageing and disability non-profits, service providers, and consumer advocates and began a national trend towards the integration of ageing and disability in LTSS. This integration is far from complete and the partnerships are not always equitable, but the idea that shared interests in LTSS may overcome the bifurcation that categorisation by age established is a reasonable one. The population of persons who experienced early and mid-life onset of disability and are ageing with disability are likely to most keenly feel this transition. Below we briefly describe and discuss several of these integration initiatives.

Program Integration Initiatives that Hold Promise for Persons Ageing with Disability

As noted earlier, LTSS encompasses a wide range of services and supports and can be delivered in a range of community settings. Because there is no universal health insurance in the U.S., Medicaid insurance differs across states, payment for LTSS is sometimes private and there is no visible network of LTSS providers, supports and services to consumers, it can be difficult for persons with and without prior experience interacting with service systems and support providers to obtain affordable and adequate LTSS. As such, integration of ageing and disability programs and services has strongly focused on helping consumers access supports and services and advancing mechanisms for coordinating supports and service delivery across traditional ageing and disability silos. These goal of these first steps have mainly been to help consumers get to the services that already exist and to divert them from institutional care through implementation of mechanisms that increase HCBS capacity.

Ageing and Disability Resource Centers

Aging and Disability Resource Centers (ADRCs) demonstration grants were first awarded to individual states in 2003 by the federal Administration on Ageing to develop programs that improved consumer access to information and referrals to LTSS including independent living supports and services and institutional care. ADRC grants were offered through 2016, at which time they became permanently authorised in the Older American's Act (OAA) as programs that states could offer using OAA funds (Older Americans Act Reauthorization Act of 2016, Pub. L. 114-144, 2016). Some states have also passed legislation institutionalising ADRCs as a part of their LTSS networks. Both the original ADRC grants and the legislated ADRC programs require collaboration across ageing and disability entities. At the state level, typically the state unit on ageing partners with one or more disability-related units to administer and implement the ADRC such as a department of rehabilitation, mental and behavioural health, or intellectual and developmental disability. Although these partnerships are required, they greatly vary in their strength and seem to have only scratched the surface of the capacity that is needed to serve cross-populations (Coyle, Putnam, Mutchler, & Kramer, 2016). ADRCs themselves exist in local communities as portals for information and referral assistance. A state may have several ADRCs located in different regions. Often, local ADRCs have lead agencies and organisations, commonly a local Area Agency on Aging (AAA) and a CIL. Additional ADRC partners often include other public agencies and non-profit organisations ranging from university centres to LTSS provider organisations. ADRCs are not physical centres, but virtual ones. The ADRC model is known as the No Wrong Door approach meaning that any partnering agency or organisation can act as a single point of entry into the LTSS system. The main structure of the ADRC is a set of operational protocols that attempt to move a consumer smoothly across the LTSS network using tools and mechanisms such as universal assessments, standardised data collection to determine eligibility for Medicaid and other services, and access to shared databases. Technical assistance is offered to ADRCs by the federal government drawing on best practices from the field.

Money Follows the Person (MFP) & Nursing Home Transition Programs

Money Follows the Person (MFP) grants were first awarded by CMS in 2007 for the purpose of helping states identify Medicaid beneficiaries who would like to transition from institutional to home and community-based care. MFP grants were intended to actively engage states in complying with the Olmstead ruling by offering additional federal funding for these individuals and paying for the costs of transition from institutional to community-based care including assisting with rent payments, obtaining furnishings and securing technology needed to live independently. MFP has its roots in MiCASA (Medicaid Community Attendant Services Act), a program heavily championed by disability rights activists in the 1990s and 2000s to permit choice over where long-term care services are provided – at home or in an institution (Hayashi, 2007). MFP embeds the disability philosophy of self-determination in its program aims. The MFP program has resulted in the creation of procedures of how to adhere to consumer choices and has been linked to the adoption of the philosophies of consumer-direction and person-centred care. All U.S. states participated in MFP which succeeded in moving over 90,000 individuals from institutional to community-based care between 2007 and 2018 (Musumeci, Chidambaram, & Watts, 2019). Federal funding for the MFP program ended in 2020, however many states have already, or are intending to, add the MFP program to their Medicaid LTSS program and continue with this work. While the MFP program has been a success, known and existing challenges include extensive waiting lists for HBCS slots in most states as federal regulations permit states to cap the number of Medicaid beneficiaries receiving HCBS instead of institutional care (Musumeci, Watts, & Chidambaram, 2020).

Lifespan Respite Care Program (LRCP)

The Lifespan Respite Care Program (LRCP) is intended to expand and streamline access to respite care services for family caregivers of persons of all ages (children and adults) with special needs. Administered by the federal Administration for Community Living, grant funds were first awarded funds in 2009 to states to establish Lifespan Respite Care systems. While the program is authorised in statute, annual funds are quite limited (only $3.5 million in 2019). Funds are designated primarily for the coordination of existing ageing and disability-related respite programs, improving operational procedures that increase access to respite, and improving the overall quality of respite services (Administration for Community Living, 2019a) Additionally LRCP seeks to coordinate a respite care network across local, state, and federal levels, develop new respite services where needed, and train respite providers. The Administration for Community Living supports these efforts by providing technical assistance to states through the Lifespan Respite Technical Assistance Center (see https://archrespite.org). In 2020, about three-quarters of all states have had LRCP funding. The integration of ageing and disability in the LRCP, like in the ADRC program, emphasises infrastructure development. State grantees must focus on and include in the LRCP respite needs of caregivers who support persons of any age. LRCP are not required, however, as ADRCs are, to have formal partnerships between ageing and disability state units or community-based organisations. It is not uncommon, however, for LRCPs to be affiliated or part of a state's ADRC network where these partnerships do exist.

Alzheimer's Disease Programs Initiative (ADPI)

The Alzheimer's Disease Program Initiative (ADPI) is a small federal program funded through the Administration for Community Living intended to assist states and communities in developing dementia-capable home and community-based care service systems by increasing capacity of care providers and providing services to consumers and their families. The ADPI emphasises the use of evidence-based dementia care and requires states to incorporate the needs of persons ageing with intellectual/developmental disability in their programming (ACL, 2019b). ADPI evolved from an earlier set of dementia-related program grants that focused on both coordination of local public and private supports and organisation providing supports and services to persons with dementia and their families and translation of evidence-based dementia practices into home and community-based care settings. Much like the LRCP program, ADPI provides technical assistance to states and communities through a national centre – the National Alzheimer's and Dementia Resource Center. It provides assistance to consumers through the National Alzheimer's Call Center.

All of these examples of integrated LTSS initiatives have their origins within the federal government and the move away from institutional care and towards home and community-based care. All were initiated after the Olmstead decision and are rooted in the Americans with Disability Act's framework of access to equal opportunity that is the heart of all civil rights laws in the U.S. The program described here, along with others not described, relies on very limited federal funding to leverage substantial LTSS infrastructure and program changes at the state level. The initiatives focus primarily on improving coordination across and access to traditional ageing and disability service network silos through program linkages rather than increasing the funding for LTSS itself or access to Medicaid insurance. However, the structural changes they have been put into place are consequential. They have strengthened the formal bonds between government levels and community-based organisations – in sum, service providers.

The challenge for consumers is that most of these infrastructure changes are invisible to them. The changes may be much appreciated by consumers, as they will benefit persons in need of LTSS by helping them to understand the services and supports available to them, determine if their insurance will pay for the services or if they will have to pay for them on their own (if they can afford them), and set up and manage services. In these ways, the LTSS network in a local community becomes easier to navigate for persons with disabilities of any age. What these programs do not do is address the lack of insurance benefit for LTSS outside of Medicaid, state-to-state differences in LTSS benefits through Medicaid insurance, or the affordability of privately paid LTSS. In addition, they have minimal focus on persons ageing with disability – the programs coordinated through these initiatives are still categorized in traditional ways – for older adults, persons with physical disability, persons with intellectual/development disability, or persons with serious mental illness. Which means that few recognise any unique needs of persons ageing with disability or offer specific programming for this population. If they do, they typically add ageing-related components to disability programs – for example adding retirement services for persons with intellectual/developmental disability within this population specific program stream. But there are few services for older adults that have been widened to ensure they are inclusive for persons with severe mental illness, persons with long-term physical or sensory disability, or those with intellectual/developmental disabilities.

That said, there are changes in how supports and services are being delivered that have the potential to sidestep these categorical boxes younger and older persons with disabilities are often placed in. These are modalities such as person-centred care and self-direction, that overtly focus on consumer preference, need, and choice as compared to a prescribed menu of supports that previously may have been assigned to a consumer through a case management model that relied heavily on what the professional believed was relevant and important. Additionally, LTSS offered within managed care models of Medicaid that rely on private insurers to coordinate needed services provide some flexibility for consumers that previously did not exist in state-delivered, case-management models. Some Medicaid managed care programs are also addressing social determinants of health that go far beyond traditional LTSS. For example some Medicaid state contracts require managed care companies to make sure LTSS consumers have adequate housing, access to employment or job training or education, access to transportation, are food secure, facilitate development of social networks and to provide health and wellness promotion options in addition to other traditional LTSS services (Hinton, Rudowitz, Diaz, & Singer, 2019). A critique of these requirements of managed care providers is that states are medicalising basic social welfare needs by moving this responsibility to health insurers instead of the state itself. The positive view on including social determinant of health in managed care models is that for persons with disabilities of all ages, LTSS begins to address a wider set of needs including solving root issues of problems – for example not being able to bath oneself might be addressed with the provision of an accessible shower, paid for through insurance.

From Integrated LTSS to Inclusive Communities

The distance between LTSS and inclusive communities that welcome persons with disabilities of all ages, remains pretty wide, but there is potential to close the gap. There have been efforts at the national level to develop measures and indicators for LTSS and HCBS that provide information about whether persons with LTSS services and supports are meeting their needs, respecting their choices, and helping them to do the things they would like to do (National Quality Forum, 2016). However only some of these indicators are being put into use (Centers for Medicare & Medicaid Services, 2019). This matters for persons ageing with disability in particular as it will provide new information about how services and supports perform over time, particularly as an individual grows older. Combined with the person-centred model of care and participant-direction, it also allows the individual to more responsively modify the LTSS as their needs change over time.

The distance that still needs to be covered between LTSS and community inclusion is the bridge to interventions that support persons ageing with disability live to actively engage and be a part of their communities. One example of this is the age friendly/liveable community framework for community planning. The Age-Friendly framework was developed by the World Health Organization (WHO) (WHO, 2007). According to WHO, an age-friendly community is one where people participate, are connected, remain healthy and active, and feel they belong – no matter their age. Through assessment, planning, action, and evaluating progress, communities all over the world are taking steps to improve their social and physical environments as a strategy for promoting health and well-being throughout the life course.

The Age-Friendly model includes a conceptual framework (domains) for describing areas for communities to focus on. It also lays out a process intended to ensure repeated consultation with the community, collective reflection, action and evaluation. The Age-Friendly framework includes eight domains of community life that intersect with liveability, accessibility, and the ability to thrive within the community. These include transportation, housing, social participation, respect and social inclusion, civic participation and employment, communication and information, community support and health services, and outdoor space and buildings. Within each domain, elements are identified relevant to affordability, appropriateness, and accessibility. These "three A's" of age-friendly are the levers by which the model can effect meaningful change for older adults and persons ageing with disability. For example considering the dimensions of a domain like respect and social inclusion can ensure that an action such as improving accessibility of local government meeting is not only accessible for persons with physical or sensory impairments, but also for persons with intellectual or developmental disabilities. Thus, we posit that a truly inclusive process of becoming an age friendly community would include three additional "A's": adaptability, acceptability, and advocacy. The process that this model is intended to be applied to is one that is community-driven. Ensuring that persons with disabilities, their families, and their advocates are included in the development and implementation of such initiatives can increase the likelihood that this framework becomes linked to LTSS so that the integration initiatives discussed earlier take as their farthest aim the inclusion of persons with disabilities in their communities.

Perhaps one of the most crucial elements of creating authentically inclusive communities is the availability, accessibility, and affordability of housing for older people with disabilities. Persons with disabilities often rely on income supports like Supplemental Security Income to make ends meet; and that level of income causes these individuals to be priced out of nearly every housing market in the nation. Although housing subsidies exist (Section 811), the lack of availability results in wait-lists that may take years. For persons who have always lived with family support systems, those support systems are ageing too (Coyle, Kramer, & Mutchler, 2014) and a later-life residential transition is required. If other family members cannot step in, these people face high risk of institutionalisation or homelessness. Other individuals may have lived in group homes; but as these residents age, their needs for care increase and their mobility may change. Oftentimes, these group homes are not equipped to accommodate the residents and their age-related needs, not to mention the increasing number of professional caregivers that need to be inside the home at one time.

Ageing with disability as a population trend breaks through our historical categorizations of older and younger people with disabilities. Changing the way LTSS is coordinated and delivered and linking it to larger goals of social inclusion can further leverage the shift from policies and programs that categorize people based on whom they are, to what they are about and what they would like to do as community members. The speed of these two parallel trends – which arguably have moved forward independently – have outpaced research and practice-based knowledge about how to support individuals ageing with disability at their intersection. This means that people ageing with disabilities in need of LTSS and are too easily excluded from society when affordable and adequate LTSS is not available. Rebalancing initiatives have leveraged tremendous policy change at state and local levels, in many cases employing innovative strategies to implement these changes. However, these policy advancements remain new and somewhat delicately perched in tense federal and state budget climates where changes in executive and legislative leadership hold great sway over how programs are shaped and to the extent to which programs become embedded and sustained. That said, their shared timing provides opportunities to integrate historically siloed ageing and disability programs and to redefine how we conceptualize the ultimate goals of LTSS.

Notes

1 Participant-directed services permit the individual to determine for themselves the types of LTSS they need to successfully live in the community. See Sciegaj et al. (2016).
2 Person-centred care is a multi-modal engagement model where the health care professional and care recipient co-design personalized care based on the needs and preferences of the recipient. See Santana et al. (2018).

References

Administration for Community Living. (2019a). *Lifespan Respite Care Program.* https://acl.gov/programs/support-caregivers/lifespan-respite-care-program
Administration for Community Living. (2019b). *Alzheimer's Disease Programs Initiative.* https://acl.gov/programs/support-people-alzheimers-disease/support-people-dementia-including-alzheimers-disease
Centers for Medicare & Medicaid Services. (2019). *Measures for Medicaid managed long term services and supports plans: Technical specifications and resource manual.* https://www.medicaid.gov/media/3396
Coyle, C. E., Kramer, J., & Mutchler, J. E. (2014). Aging together: Sibling carers of adults with intellectual and developmental disabilities. *Journal of Policy and Practice in Intellectual Disabilities, 11*(4), 302–312. https://doi.org/10.1111/jppi.12094
Coyle, C., Putnam, M., Mutchler, J., & Kramer, J. (2016). The role of Aging and Disability Resource Centers in serving adults aging with intellectual disabilities and their families: Findings from seven states. *Journal of Aging & Social Policy, 28*(1), 1–14. https://doi.org/10.1080/08959420.2015.1096142
Eiken, S., Sredl, K., Burwell, B., & Amos, A. (2018). *Medicaid expenditures for long-term services and supports in FY 2016.* IBM Watson Health. http://www.advancingstates.org/sites/nasuad/files/ltssexpenditures2016.pdf
Executive Order No. 13217, 3 C.F.R., Sect. 13217. (2001).
Factor, A., Heller, T., & Janicki, M. (2012). *Bridging the aging and developmental disability service networks: Challenges and best practices.* Institute on Disability and Human Development, University of Illinois at Chicago, Associate of University Centers on Disabilities. https://www.aucd.org/template/news.cfm?news_id=8557&parent=295&parent_title=AUCD%20Publications&url=/template/page.cfm?id%3D295
Friedman, C., Caldwell, J., Rapp Kennedy, A., & Rizzolo, M. C. (2019). Aging in place: A national analysis of home-and community-based Medicaid services for older adults. *Journal of Disability Policy Studies, 29*(4), 245–256. https://doi.org/10.1177/1044207318788889
Hado, E., & Komisar, H. (2019). *Long-term services and supports [fact sheet].* AARP Policy Institute. https://www.aarp.org/ppi/info-2017/long-term-services-and-supports.html
Harrington, C., Ng, T., LaPlante, M., & Kaye, H. S. (2012). Medicaid home-and community-based services: Impact of the affordable care act. *Journal of Aging & Social Policy, 24*(2), 169–187. https://doi.org/10.1080/08959420.2012.659118
Hayashi, R. (2007). MiCASSA—My home. *Journal of Social Work in Disability & Rehabilitation, 6*(1–2), 35–52.
Hinton, E., Rudowitz, R., Diaz, M., & Singer, N. (2019). *10 things to know about Medicaid managed care.* Kaiser Family Foundation. https://www.kff.org/medicaid/issue-brief/10-things-to-know-about-medicaid-managed-care/
Kaye, H. S. (2014). Toward a model long-term services and supports system: State policy elements. *The Gerontologist, 54*(5), 754–61. https://doi.org/10.1093/geront/gnu013

Musumeci, M., & Claypool, H. (2014). *Olmstead's role in community integration for people with disabilities under Medicaid: 15 years after the Supreme Court's Olmstead decision*. Kaiser Family Foundation. https://www.kff.org/medicaid/issue-brief/olmsteads-role-in-community-integration-for-people-with-disabilities-under-medicaid-15-years-after-the-supreme-courts-olmstead-decision/

Musumeci, M., Chidambaram, P., & Watts, M. O. (2019). *Medicaid's Money Follows the Person program: State progress and uncertainty pending federal funding reauthorization*. Kaiser Family Foundation. https://www.kff.org/medicaid/issue-brief/medicaids-money-follows-the-person-program-state-progress-and-uncertainty-pending-federal-funding-reauthorization/

Musumeci, M., Watts, M. O., & Chidambaram, P. (2020). *Key state policy choices about Medicaid home and community-based services*. Kaiser Family Foundation. https://www.kff.org/report-section/key-state-policy-choices-about-medicaid-home-and-community-based-services-issue-brief/

National Quality Forum. (2016). *Quality in home and community-based services to support community living: Addressing gaps in performance measurement*. http://www.qualityforum.org/Publications/2016/09/Quality_in_Home_and_Community-Based_Services_to_Support_Community_Living__Addressing_Gaps_in_Performance_Measurement.aspx

Older Americans Act Reauthorization Act of 2016, Pub. L. 114-144.

Olmstead v. L.C. (1999). 527 U.S. 581.

Putnam, M. (2007). Moving from separate to crossing aging and disability service networks. In M. Putnam (Ed.), *Aging and disability: Crossing network lines* (pp. 5–17). Springer Publishing Company.

Putnam, M. (2011). Perceptions of difference between aging and disability service systems consumers: Implications for policy initiatives to rebalance long-term care. *Journal of Gerontological Social Work, 54*(3), 325–342. https://doi.org/10.1080/01634372.2010.543263

Putnam, M. (2014). Bridging network divides: Building capacity to support aging with disability populations. *Disability and Health Journal, 7*, S51–S59. https://doi.org/10.1016/j.dhjo.2013.08.002

Santana, M. J., Manalili, K., Jolley, R. J., Zelinsky, S., Quan, H., & Lu, M. (2018). How to practice person-centred care: A conceptual framework. *Health Expectations: An International Journal of Public Participation in Health Care and Health Policy, 21*(2), 429–440. https://doi.org/10.1111/hex.12640

Sciegaj, M., Mahoney, K. J., Schwartz, A. J., Simon-Rusinowitz, L., Selkow, I., & Loughlin, D. M. (2016). An inventory of publicly funded participant-directed long-term services and supports programs in the United States. *Journal of Disability Policy Studies, 26*(4), 245–251. https://doi.org/10.1177/1044207314555810

U.S. Department of Health & Human Services. (2014). *Summary of key provisions of the home and community-based services (HCBS) settings final rule (CMS 2249-F/2296-F)*. [Fact sheet]. https://www.medicaid.gov/sites/default/files/2019-12/hcbs-setting-fact-sheet.pdf

Watts, M. O., Musumeci, M., & Chidambaram, P. (2020). *Medicaid home and community-based services enrollment and spending*. Kaiser Family Foundation. http://files.kff.org/attachment/Issue-Brief-Medicaid-Home-and-Community-Based-Services-Enrollment-and-Spending

World Health Organization. (2007). *Global age-friendly cities: A guide*. https://www.who.int/ageing/publications/age_friendly_cities_guide/en/

Suggested Readings

Coyle, C., Putnam, M., Mutchler, J., & Kramer, J. (2016). The role of Aging and Disability Resource Centers in serving adults aging with intellectual disabilities and their families: Findings from seven states. *Journal of Aging & Social Policy, 28*(1), 1–14. https://doi.org/10.1080/08959420.2015.1096142

Friedman, C., Caldwell, J., Rapp Kennedy, A., & Rizzolo, M. C. (2019). Aging in place: A national analysis of home-and community-based Medicaid services for older adults. *Journal of Disability Policy Studies, 29*(4), 245–256. https://doi.org/10.1177/1044207318788889

Hado, E., & Komisar, H. (2019). *Long-term services and supports [Fact sheet]*. AARP Policy Institute. https://www.aarp.org/ppi/info-2017/long-term-services-and-supports.html

Putnam, M. (2014). Bridging network divides: Building capacity to support aging with disability populations. *Disability and Health Journal, 7*, S51–S59. https://doi.org/10.1016/j.dhjo.2013.08.002

32
ACCESS TO ASSISTIVE TECHNOLOGY IN CANADA

Rosalie H. Wang and Michael G. Wilson

Introduction

Assistive technology (AT) is considered a universal need that supports participation and inclusion of persons of all ages and abilities in all aspects of life (World Health Assembly, 2018). However, the system of AT access in Canada is characterised by high complexity, lack of integration, access barriers and inequities, coverage disparities, and unmet needs (Mattison, Wilson, Wang, & Waddell, 2019; Schreiber, Wang, Durocher, & Wilson, 2017).

Issues of AT access exemplify challenges in policy and practice situated in both ageing and disability domains. The Toronto Declaration states that it is an imperative to bridge ageing and disability knowledge, policies, and practices to address challenges associated with the increasing proportion of seniors and concurrently, persons with chronic health conditions in the population (Bickenbach et al., 2012). These challenges are multi-sectoral, and include, for example, the need to prevent and manage chronic health conditions, build health and social care-provider capacity, and enable healthy ageing and community-based and long-term care living. Bridging explicitly emphasises continuity while acknowledging complexity in the life-course, and serves the goals of enhancing efficiency and care equity, and promotes participation and inclusion at individual and societal levels (Bickenbach et al., 2012). To realise the goal of more equitable AT access, we need to bridge knowledge, policies, and practices in the ageing and disability fields and sectors by identifying areas of challenge, intersection, and synergy and fostering collaboration to arrive at a clear vision and set of priorities to enable integrated systems.

This chapter includes four focus areas. We first describe AT and its importance to seniors and persons with disabilities, emphasising the universality of AT in its purpose and outcomes, and thus an exemplar for improving equitable access through bridging knowledge, policies, and practices. Second, we outline the Canadian legislative and policy context relevant to understanding the state of services for seniors, persons with disabilities, and AT access, highlighting the underlying complexity and challenges for bridging. Third, we report findings from aspects of an integrated knowledge translation research initiative we have undertaken to enhance equitable AT access in Canada. We present findings that illustrate the current problematic state of AT access and draw on several examples of AT programs that illustrate differences in how seniors ageing into disability and persons ageing with disabilities are viewed and how their needs are addressed within programs. Finally, to illustrate how concepts and mechanisms of bridging align with and advance our research initiative's goal, our activities are summarised in relation to key focus areas for bridging the fields and sectors of ageing and disability – *advancing the bridging cause, theoretical frameworks, consumer engagement, knowledge transfer,* and *long-term supports and services and AT* (Naidoo, Putnam, & Spindel, 2012).

Universality of Assistive Technology

While variably defined, AT generally refers to the diversity of technology that can help with daily living and activity participation, which involves products (e.g. devices, software) and services related to AT delivery such as training. Common ATs include wheelchairs, hearing aids, communication devices, or mobile computers. AT benefits people of all ages, including those who are ageing well, ageing into disability, or ageing with a disability, people with diverse conditions and abilities, and caregivers (Madara Marasinghe, 2016; Mortenson et al., 2012; World Health Assembly, 2018). AT can assists people with physical, sensory, cognitive, or psychological/mental health concerns by supporting participation in daily self-care activities, mobility and transport, communication, education, and employment (Baldassin, Shimizu, & Fachin-Martins, 2018; Barbosa et al., 2018; Brims & Oliver, 2019; Charters, Gillett, & Simpson, 2015; Gillespie, Best, & O'Neill, 2012; Jamieson, Cullen, McGee-Lennon, Brewster, & Evans, 2014; Khasnabis, Mirza, & MacLachlan, 2015; Perelmutter, McGregor, & Gordon, 2017; Sauer, Parks, & Heyn, 2010).

Owing to the established universality of the purpose and beneficial outcomes of AT and the detriments associated with the lack of access, recent global priorities for health and social development have called for universal access to AT. The World Health Organizations' World Health Assembly passed a resolution on 'Improving access to AT', noting that AT is a means of enabling and promoting social, economic, and political inclusion and participation of older people and persons with disabilities, and that universal access can help to achieve the Sustainable Development Goals and support the United Nations Convention for Persons with Disabilities (UN CRPD) (World Health Assembly, 2018).

Legislative and Policy Context Relevant to Ageing, Disability, and Assistive Technology Access

Canada is a federation with federal, provincial, and territorial legislation and policies that direct and guide its activities and programs and services for eligible residents. Some challenges for bridging knowledge, policies, and practices are rooted in system complexity ascribed to the nature of federated systems and their distributed governance, and bureaucratic and practical issues with navigating and communicating between government levels and sectors towards common agendas and goals. As described below, federal disability-related legislation is highly dispersed across multiple government sectors and there is no comprehensive federal policy framework to address the needs of persons with disabilities or seniors, or to provide universal AT access.[1]

Health Systems

Health systems are the responsibility of provincial and territorial governments, and the federal government primarily plays a financing and regulatory role. The majority of financing comes from provinces and territories. There is some direct federal provision of services for select groups (e.g. veterans, First Nations and Inuit people). The federal government regulates the provincial and territorial health systems through the *Canada Health Act* which provides the 'criteria and conditions related to insured health services and extended health care services that the provinces and territories must fulfil to receive the full federal cash contribution under the Canada Health Transfer' (Government of Canada, 2018). The Act outlines five broad principles (public administration, comprehensiveness, universality, portability, and accessibility), which requires that care be free at the point of use in hospitals or when provided by physicians (Lavis & Mattison, 2016). This arrangement means that care provided by health professionals other than physicians (e.g. nurses, physical or occupational therapists) and other types of services (e.g. AT, prescription drugs) that are not provided in hospitals or long-term care settings, are left at the discretion of the provinces and territories. As a result, there are differences in the nature and extent of coverage for these services across the country.

Social Care

Publically-funded social care services for seniors, persons with disabilities, and other population groups in Canada are not comprehensively addressed by federal legislation and do not have national overarching principles or minimum standards compared to health services (Moscovitch & Thomas, 2018). Funding to the different provinces and territories is provided through the Canada Social Transfer (*Federal-Provincial Fiscal Arrangements Act* 1985). The majority of the social services budget is covered by provinces and territories, and each jurisdiction has its own legislation and policies to direct the services and programs that are publicly financed. Further, how health and social care services interface with each other differs across provinces and territories, adding to the coverage variability across the country.

Disability-Related Legislation and Policy

The issue of overarching federal legislation specific to persons with disabilities has been a topic of debate for decades. The inclusion of persons with disabilities under the *Canadian Charter of Rights and Freedoms* in the *Constitution Act* (1982) was considered a significant advance for disability rights (McColl, Jaiswal, Jones, Roberts, & Murphy, 2017). The Charter protects the rights of citizens to be treated equally in its laws and programs, regardless of race, religion, national or ethnic origin, colour, sex, age or physical or mental disability. Within the Charter's equality rights, provisions are also made for laws, programs, or activities directed at affirmative action to improve the conditions of individuals or groups that are disadvantaged. The *Canadian Human Rights Act* (1985) and the human rights acts within each province and territory protects Canadians from discrimination of various forms including disability and age. Federal legislation relevant to Canadians with disabilities in specific contexts, such as the *Employment Equity Act, Air Transportation Regulation, or Broadcasting Act*, is numerous and complex. No less than 38 acts and regulations have direct relevance to persons with disabilities, with various other legislation having consequences for persons with disabilities (McColl et al., 2017). Adding further complexity, provincial and territorial governments, and often municipal governments, have disability-related legislation (McColl et al., 2017).

Broad federal legislation concerning Canadians with disabilities came into force in July 2019. The *Accessible Canada Act* aims to proactively support full participation and equality of Canadians, and in particular, persons with disabilities (Government of Canada, 2019). Accessibility standards and regulations created seek to ensure federally governed sectors (e.g. banking, telecommunications, transportation, and federal government services) are accessible through barrier identification, removal, and prevention. Accessibility legislation addressing barriers for persons with disabilities for specific jurisdictions are in place only for Ontario, Manitoba, and Nova Scotia only.

Canada also has a legal responsibility to promote and protect the human rights and fundamental freedoms of persons with disabilities since ratifying the CRPD and recently acceding the Optional Protocol (Government of Canada, 2014, 2019; United Nations, 2006). A recent review by the UN Rapporteur on the rights of persons with disabilities indicated that Canada does not have a comprehensive policy framework and has fallen behind in putting into place the plans needed to meet its obligations under the CRPD (Devandas-Aguilar, 2019).

Assistive Technology-Related Legislation and Policy

There is no overarching federal legislation or policy that stipulates universal access to AT for Canadians even though Article 4 of the CRPD stipulates obligations to make AT available and affordable, and to support use of AT that helps to achieve the CRPD's objectives (Schreiber et al., 2017). Federal programs offering funding or services for AT have associated legislation that outlines specific population groups that are eligible for coverage, such as veterans or refugees. Provincial or territorial legislation and policies for health and social services may outline coverage for AT but conditions such as resident eligibility criteria, what AT may be covered, and other details vary widely.

Enhancing Equitable Access to Assistive Technology

Our research initiative focuses on enhancing equitable access to AT through an integrated knowledge translation approach that prioritises engagement with citizens (including seniors, persons with disabilities, caregivers, and others), policymakers, stakeholders, and researchers to steer all research phases (Canadian Institutes of Health Research, 2015). The initiative includes projects aimed at comprehensively understanding the:

- Landscape of Canadian AT programs
- Research evidence related to the problem, options for addressing the problem, and implementation considerations; and
- Values and preferences of citizens and insights from policymakers and stakeholders about what needs to be done to enhance equitable AT access.

Our initiative ultimately aims to co-create a vision for enhancing equitable AT access in Canada with principles to underpin policy action, short- and long-term policy priorities, and targeted action plans to address these priorities. We present general findings on the AT system, along with specific examples of access issues for seniors and persons with disabilities to illustrate current equity challenges which emphasise the need to bridge at knowledge, policy, and practice levels. Our activities are summarised using the focus areas for bridging ageing and disability fields and sectors, which illustrate the alignment of bridging concepts and mechanism with our initiative.

Overview of Assistive Technology System

The AT access system in Canada is complex, fragmented, and uncoordinated. AT funding and services are offered by multiple sources – government, charity, worker's safety (e.g. provincially/territorially legislated employer programs), automobile insurance (e.g. provincial crown corporations), or other private insurance (e.g. employment benefits) programs. Our scan of government programs offering funding and services for AT to adults and older adults in 14 jurisdictions (national, provincial, and territorial) revealed seven federal programs and between two to 10 programs in individual provinces or territories (Schreiber et al., 2017). Federal programs cover different population subsets in different government ministries, departments, or agencies. At the time of the scan these included the Ministry of Veterans Affairs; Ministry of Immigration, Refugees and Citizenship; Ministry of Health (for First Nations and Inuit peoples); Ministry of Public Safety and Emergency Preparedness (for correctional services); Department of National Defence and Canadian Armed Forces; and Employment and Social Development Canada. In provinces and territories, AT may be offered by programs under several or combinations of ministries or departments, such as health, social services, community services, seniors and housing, active living and wellness, children and family services, human resources and skills development, labour, education, justice, or finance. Further, there is no minimum standard for who should be covered and what should be provided (Durocher, Wang, Bickenbach, Schreiber, & Wilson, 2017).

The scan found significant contributions to AT programs from charities. 16 national charity programs were identified. Some national charities have divisions to serve specific jurisdictions, and some charities operate joint programs with provincial or territorial governments. For each province or territory, there were between two to 19 charity programs. Many of the programs cover individuals with specific conditions (e.g. Muscular Dystrophy), while others provide more general coverage (e.g. Red Cross). There is collaboration between government and charitable programs to enhance coverage, but such collaborations can also make the process of accessing AT complex for citizens.

Government and charity programs are unique in many ways with respect to providing AT access. Differences include eligibility criteria, the types of devices or services offered, funding arrangements (e.g. co-funding, top-up funding, free loan pools), and provider and documentation requirements to receive funding. Some programs include rules which require access to programs in a certain sequence (e.g. having to secure coverage from applicable private insurance first before applying for supplemental funding from government or charities).

Considering the high variation in programs and absence of minimum standards, it is evident that bridging is lacking in policies and practices for AT and service delivery for seniors and persons with disabilities. It is also unsurprising that citizens, policymakers, and other stakeholders report access barriers, system navigation concerns, inequitable access, and coverage disparities (Mattison, Waddell, Wang, & Wilson, 2017; Mattison, Waddell, & Wilson, 2017; Mattison, Wilson, Wang, & Waddell, 2017; Waddell, Wilson, & Mattison, 2017). Unmet AT needs were also reported in the 2012 Canadian Survey on Disability, where approximately 27% of persons with disabilities reported in need of at least one assistive device that they currently did not have (Arim, 2017).

Access Issues for Seniors and Persons with Disabilities

Further analysis of government AT programs in the scan reveal multiple examples of potential inequity of access to funding and services for seniors and persons with disabilities. Identifying inequities between and within programs offer insight into the assumptions about seniors and persons with disabilities that underlie current policies and practices, and how the needs of these groups are prioritised and addressed. Table 32.1 presents select areas of potential inequity alongside example programs.[2]

While program characteristics resulting in inequities are often complex and intersecting, we highlight characteristics that pertain to eligibility criteria that exclude according to age and place of residence and productivity goals, which often relate to age and life-course.

These examples of AT access inequities illustrate the lack of bridging of policies and practices, especially in government divisions within jurisdictions serving seniors and persons with disabilities. The examples demonstrate how a lack of bridging can manifest as inequities for those who may have similar needs or who may benefit from specific AT. The program criteria also do not consider users at transition points where changes in age can result in abrupt losses or gains in services. The examples highlight assumptions and expectations regarding service needs and the life-course of younger and older persons with disabilities, such as if only seniors are offered AT that can address acute health conditions. These discrepancies often focus on minimising risks associated with community living and with critical health conditions that may result in hospitalisation and high resource utilisation by seniors. The same AT may not be offered to younger persons with disabilities, though they may equally benefit. The examples also point to underlying assumptions about what younger and older people can contribute to society in their productivity pursuits. While the productivity-oriented programs focus on younger people, with trends in deferring retirement or seeking alternative productive activities after retirement, needs are shifting and greater demand for equity and age inclusion in these productivity-oriented programs may arise. The inequities outlined corroborate other findings from our citizen panels whereby citizens with and without lived experiences of disability and AT use reported that ATs are not allocated fairly, access is not driven by citizens' needs, and integration of AT and other support services is lacking (Mattison, Waddell, Wang, et al., 2017; Mattison, Waddell, & Wilson, 2017; Mattison, Wilson, Wang, et al., 2017). The examples also confirm what has been previously cited, which is that younger and older persons with disabilities are treated differently with respect to what is provided or expected in care and support services (Naidoo et al., 2012). Identifying, comparing, and understanding areas that can result in inequities stimulate discussions to systematically bridge policies and practices.

While Table 32.1 highlights potential inequities related to age criteria for eligibility, several government programs offer AT programs that cover all ages. Federally, this includes the Non-Insured Health Benefits program through Health Canada for First Nations and Inuit peoples. At the provincial level, examples include the Alberta Aids to Daily Living, Manitoba's Home Care Services – Supplies and Equipment, and Ontario's Ministry of Health and Long Term Care Assistive Devices programs. While being inclusive with respect to age criteria for eligibility, these programs may present other inequities such as having criteria related to disability type or maximum income thresholds.

Table 32.1 Programs offering funding and services for assistive technology[a] and equity concerns

Eligibility criterion with equity concerns	Example program	Program description and eligibility criteria	Equity concerns (possible inequities generated) and bridging-related issues
Age	Jurisdiction: Alberta Government ministry/department: Ministry of Seniors and Housing Program name: Special Needs Assistance for Seniors (SNAS)	For residents who are - aged 65+ - in financial need - enrolled in Seniors Benefits Program or eligible for Seniors Financial Assistance Program has categories of funded supports, each with own criteria and funding limits; allows recipients to purchase lift chair (maximum one/ lifetime), and install/maintain personal response service	Equity concerns: - Program restricts access according to age, no coverage for under age 65 - Comparable but non-equivalent program (Assured Income for the Severely Handicapped [AISH]) for residents not eligible for Old Age Security Pensions and in financial need, through Ministry of Community and Social Services - Differences in eligibility criteria beyond age and supports covered, e.g. SNAS program covers some services (personal support) and equipment (e.g. appliances, furniture), but options restricted to certain covered AT compared to AISH Bridging-related issues: - Different supports for AT offered to different age groups for potentially similar needs, not aligning with life-course needs - Programs overseen by different government ministries, different priorities and budgets
	Jurisdiction: Nova Scotia Government ministry/department: Department of Health and Wellness Program name: Personal Alert Service	For residents who are - aged 65+ - considered to be low income - living alone - using mobility aid - having recent history of falls Provides personal alert device/personal alert emergency response system, reimburses initial cost and maximum service fee/year	Equity concerns - Program restricts access according to age, no coverage or equivalent program for under age 65 Bridging-related issues: - Supports offered to only one age group for potentially similar needs, not aligning with life-course needs, more benefits after transition to aged 65 - Program criteria may imply that younger persons with disability benefit less from this specific AT
	Jurisdiction: New Brunswick Government ministry/department: Department of Social Development Program name: Disability Support	For residents who are - aged 19–64 - having long-term disability (services for mental health/addictions are through other programs) Provides disability-related supports for community living/participation, e.g. support workers, respite, living-skills training, transportation, assistive devices not covered under other programs; resources to enable self-management or have social-work support to develop/ execute community living plan	Equity concerns: - Program restricts access according to age, no coverage or equivalent program for aged 65+ Bridging-related issues: - Supports offered to only one age group for potentially similar needs, not aligning with life-course needs, fewer benefits after transition to aged 65 - Priority for provision of supports for transition to/maintenance of community living for younger persons but not for seniors with similar goals - Program criteria may imply that seniors are already established in their living arrangements or have supports in place for community living, or that life-course transitions for seniors may be to seniors' residences where supports are available

(Continued)

Table 32.1 Programs offering funding and services for assistive technology[a] and equity concerns *(Continued)*

Eligibility criterion with equity concerns	Example program	Program description and eligibility criteria	Equity concerns (possible inequities generated) and bridging-related issues
	Jurisdiction: Prince Edward Island *Government ministry/department:* Department of Family and Human Services *Program name:* Disability Support	For residents who are younger than 65 years Provides recycled or new devices such as mobility, bathroom, bedroom, or household aids, communication devices, hearing or visual aids	Equity concerns – Program restricts access according to age, no equivalent government program for residents with long-term disability who are aged 65+ – Red Cross (charity) provides short term equipment loans of some AT (mostly mobility/bathroom aids) Bridging-related issues: – Supports offered to only one age group for potentially similar needs, not aligning with life-course needs, fewer benefits after transition to age 65 – Priority for provision of supports for younger persons – Program criteria may imply that seniors can pay out-of-pocket or already have access to AT (e.g. in residential care)
Place of residence	*Jurisdiction:* British Columbia *Government ministry/department:* Ministry of Social Development and Social Innovation *Program name:* Medical Equipment and Devices	For residents who are – 18 years + – meeting financial eligibility criteria Not for residents of care facilities funded by Ministry of Health Funds walking, transferring, and toileting aids, wheelchairs, scooters, hospital beds, other medically essential aids	Equity concerns: – Program restricts access according to place of residence, no equivalent program for facility-dwelling residents – While no age criterion for facility admission, residents tend to be seniors with low income or with living expense subsidies from government programs (Cohen et al., 2009; Mackenzie, 2015) – Facilities have some AT, but AT availability varies, so residents may not get what they need (e.g. depends on what is facility-purchased or donated) Bridging-related issues: – Supports offered to one group but not another for potentially similar needs, not aligning with life-course needs, fewer benefits after transition to care facility – Programs overseen by different government ministries, different priorities and budgets
Productivity goals	*Jurisdiction:* Canada *Government ministry/department:* Employment and Social Development Canada jointly with some provinces/territories *Program name:* Canada Student Grant for Services and Equipment for Students with Permanent Disabilities	For students who are – in post-secondary institution – having severe permanent disability that prevents work/participation in studies for the rest of life – in financial need Provides grants for hearing, vision, communication devices; equipment up to $8000/school year	Equity concerns: – Program restricts access according to higher education goals – While no age criterion for eligibility, programs tend to benefit younger adults as over 90% of Canadian university students are under 40 years (Dale, 2010) Bridging-related issues: – Program availability highlights priorities for pursuit of higher education goals, often more relevant to younger adults in their life-course for establishing careers – Productivity goals of seniors (and persons with disabilities) who may benefit from AT and who are not pursuing formal post-secondary education are not supported

(Continued)

Table 32.1 Programs offering funding and services for assistive technology[a] and equity concerns *(Continued)*

Eligibility criterion with equity concerns	Example program	Program description and eligibility criteria	Equity concerns (possible inequities generated) and bridging-related issues
	Jurisdiction: Canada *Government ministry/department:* Agreements between Employment and Social Development Canada and provinces/territories (expired in 2018, new consolidated agreements forthcoming) *Program name:* Labour Market Agreement for Persons with Disabilities	Federal government contributes costs to programs/services delivered by province/territory towards enabling employability of persons with disabilities and increasing employment opportunities through employers Variable implementation in each province/ territory, eligibility criteria dependent on specific programs. e.g. for some programs under Manitoba's Department of Families – services and AT for training/employment delivered by charities (e.g. Society for Manitobans with Disabilities)	Equity concerns: - Program restricts access according to employment goals - While no age criterion for eligibility, programs often benefit younger adults in their life-course towards gainful employment - E.g. in Manitoba several programs/services were delivered under three government departments: Families; Health, Seniors and Active Living; and Education and Training, 12% of users were aged 55+ and 87% of users aged 15 – 54 (Government of Manitoba, 2017) Bridging-related issues: - Program availability highlights priorities for pursuit of training to seek and maintain gainful employment, and for supports through employers for persons with disabilities to attain gainful employment - Productivity goals of seniors (and persons with disabilities) who may benefit from AT and who are not pursuing gainful employment are not supported

[a] *Program details are subject to change at any time. Refer to Schreiber et al. (2017) for sources.*

Bridging Ageing and Disability to Enhance Equitable Access to Assistive Technology

Bridging knowledge, policies, and practices in AT is sensible and serves the goals of enhancing efficiency and equity of care, and promoting participation and inclusion broadly. Our findings offer program-level evidence that illustrates the lack of bridging of knowledge, policies, and practices in ageing and disability, which contribute to AT system access challenges and equity issues. To demonstrate how our initiative is striving to bridge these areas to advance our goals, we summarise in Table 32.2 our research and knowledge translation activities according to focal areas for bridging-related activities as outlined in Naidoo et al. (2012) – *advancing the bridging cause, theoretical frameworks, consumer engagement, knowledge transfer,* and *long-term supports and services and AT.*

Key Issues

Several core findings have emerged consistently across projects comprising the initiative. These findings include:

- AT is universally beneficial for participation and inclusion regardless of age or abilities
- Bridging knowledge, policies, and practices in AT and the services associated with AT delivery is sensible and serves the goals of enhancing efficiency and equity of care, and promoting participation and inclusion of seniors and persons with disabilities
- Many examples exist that illustrate a lack of bridging in the Canadian context that can result in inequity of AT access and
- Proactive steps are being taken to advance the bridging cause to enhance equity of AT access in Canada, such as through our integrated knowledge translation based initiative

Table 32.2 Key focal areas for bridging ageing and disability to enhance equity of assistive technology access

Focal area and description	Activities
Advancing the bridging cause - Emphasises need to advance cause of bridging, actively put bridging concepts/activities on agendas - Underscores need to foster understandings of similarities in fields/sectors and collaborative opportunities to support rights, participation, and inclusion and improve efficiency and equity - Leverages collective strength to advocate for human rights	We engaged stakeholders in ageing and disability sectors nationally as members of steering committees, citizen panels, and a stakeholder dialogue to create common understandings and advance the goal of enhancing equitable AT access (Mattison, Waddell, Wang, et al., 2017; Mattison, Waddell, & Wilson, 2017; Mattison, Wilson, Wang, et al., 2017). Specifically, we engaged: - citizens with/without lived experiences of disability/AT use and caregiving - leaders from ageing and disability-related consumer/caregiver groups - leaders from professional/service provider/industry organisations - federal, provincial, or territorial policymakers - researchers studying ageing, disability, and technology
Theoretical frameworks - Two applicable models for bridging: life-course perspective on ageing and biopsychosocial model of disability	We incorporated the life-course perspective and biopsychosocial model in understanding AT users' experiences of ageing and disability and their interactions within society.
Consumer engagement - Active participation of consumers/families - Ensures needed voices are heard and values/goals are included in any knowledge, policy, and practice development and implementation	We actively involved consumers (citizens) and their caregivers from seniors and disability communities in integrated knowledge translation research by convening citizen panels across Canada to identify citizens' values and preferences for enhancing equitable AT access.
Knowledge transfer - Knowledge refers to ideas, concepts and information - Transferring knowledge necessitates synthesis/exchange of knowledge between stakeholders (researchers, practitioners, policymakers, industry, and public) - Goal is application of knowledge by stakeholders to achieve benefits - In bridging, knowledge transfer aims to identify common needs/outcomes for shared vision, language and agreed upon approaches for research, policy, and practice	We used an integrated knowledge translation approach, which prioritises meaningful engagement of stakeholders throughout the initiative. This included: - engaging stakeholders in an interdisciplinary steering committee to guide projects; - convening citizen panels and a stakeholder dialogue with system leaders to identify values, preferences and insights about enhancing equitable AT access; - conducting interviews with system leaders to develop/refine short- and long-term policy priorities for enhancing equitable AT access and principles to underpin policy action; - conducting a national survey of citizens to refine/rank priorities and principles; and - convening a policy symposium with stakeholders to identify actions to address priorities which will be included in a vision document to be shared across fields/sectors and stakeholder groups.
Long-term supports and services and assistive technology - Delivery of long-term supports and services and AT is focal area whereby bridging ageing and disability sectors makes inherent sense	Each phase of our initiative has focused on AT and its associated delivery services in our process to enhance equitable AT access, e.g. we focus on integration of health/social systems and enhancing collaboration/coordination among governments, charitable organisations, and industry.

Conclusion

Our initiative to enhance equitable AT access in Canada is a work in progress, though much work has been completed to comprehensively understand the challenges. Our next steps involve responding to recommendations from stakeholders to co-create short- and long-term priorities and principles to underpin policy actions. Our policy symposium will take a proactive approach with stakeholders to create targeted action plans to address priorities. These activities will advance bridging across ageing and disability through knowledge, policies, and practices in AT access.

Notes

1 A comprehensive survey of all relevant legislation and policies is beyond the scope of this chapter.
2 The examples are intended to highlight access differences to enrich dialogue for knowledge exchange and policy/practice development, rather than to criticise or endorse any governing body or program, or to judge for whom or what purposes funding/services should increase/decrease. The examples are not exhaustive (e.g. examples pertain to adult/older adult cohorts as these were the research foci).

References

Arim, R. (2017). *Canadian survey on disability, 2012: A profile of persons with disabilities among Canadians aged 15 years or older, 2012*. Statistics Canada. https://www.statcan.gc.ca/pub/89-654-x/89-654-x2015001-eng.pdf

Baldassin, V., Shimizu, H. E., & Fachin-Martins, E. (2018). Computer assistive technology and associations with quality of life for individuals with spinal cord injury: A systematic review. *Quality of Life Research, 27*(3), 597–607. https://doi.org/10.1007/s11136-018-1804-9

Barbosa, R., de Oliveira, A., de Lima Antão, J., Crocetta, T. B., Guarnieri, R., Antunes, T., ... de Abreu, L. C. (2018). Augmentative and alternative communication in children with Down's syndrome: A systematic review. *BMC Pediatrics, 18*(1), 160. https://doi.org/10.1186/s12887-018-1144-5

Bickenbach, J., Bigby, C., Salvador-Carulla, L., Heller, T., Leonardi, M., Leroy, B., ... Spindel, A. (2012). The Toronto declaration on bridging knowledge, policy and practice in aging and disability: Toronto, Canada, March 30, 2012. *International Journal of Integrated Care, 12*, e205. https://doi.org/10.5334/ijic.1086

Brims, L., & Oliver, K. (2019). Effectiveness of assistive technology in improving the safety of people with dementia: A systematic review and meta-analysis. *Aging & Mental Health, 23*(8), 942–951. https://doi.org/10.1080/13607863.2018.1455805

Canadian Institutes of Health Research. (2015). *Guide to knowledge translation planning at CIHR: Integrated and end-of-grant approaches*. CIHR. http://www.cihr-irsc.gc.ca/e/45321.html

Charters, E., Gillett, L., & Simpson, G. K. (2015). Efficacy of electronic portable assistive devices for people with acquired brain injury: A systematic review. *Neuropsychological Rehabilitation, 25*(1), 82–121. https://doi.org/10.1080/09602011.2014.942672

Cohen, M., Tate, J., & Baumbusch, J. (2009). *An uncertain future for seniors: BC's restructuring of home and community health care, 2001–2008*. Ottawa: Canadian Centre for Policy Alternatives. Retrieved from http://www.policyalternatives.ca/publications/reports/uncertain-future-seniors

Dale, M. (2010). *Trends in the age composition of college and university students and graduates*. Statistics Canada. https://www150.statcan.gc.ca/n1/pub/81-004-x/2010005/article/11386-eng.htm

Devandas-Aguilar, C. (2019). *End of mission statement by the United Nations Special Rapporteur on the rights of persons with disabilities, Ms. Catalina Devandas-Aguilar, on her visit to Canada. April 12, 2019*. United Nations. https://www.ohchr.org/en/NewsEvents/Pages/DisplayNews.aspx?NewsID=24481&LangID=E

Durocher, E., Wang, R. H., Bickenbach, J., Schreiber, D., & Wilson, M. G. (2017). 'Just access'? Questions of equity in access and funding for assistive technology. *Ethics & Behavior, 29*(3), 172–191. https://doi.org/10.1080/10508422.2017.1396461

Gillespie, A., Best, C., & O'Neill, B. (2012). Cognitive function and assistive technology for cognition: A systematic review. *Journal of the International Neuropsychological Society, 18*(1), 1–19. https://doi.org/10.1017/S1355617711001548

Government of Canada. (2014). *Convention on the rights of persons with disabilities: First report of Canada*. Government of Canada http://www.ccdonline.ca/media/international/Convention%20on%20the%20Rights%20of%20Persons%20with%20Disabilities%20-%20First%20Report%20of%20Canada.pdf

Government of Canada. (2018). *Canada Health Act. 2018-12-27*. Retrieved from https://www.canada.ca/en/health-canada/services/health-care-system/canada-health-care-system-medicare/canada-health-act.html

Government of Canada. (2019). *Making an accessible Canada for persons with disabilities. 2019-06-28.* https://www.canada.ca/en/employment-social-development/programs/accessible-people-disabilities.html

Government of Manitoba. (2017). *Labour Market Agreement for Persons with Disabilities (LMAPD) Report 2016–2017.* https://www.gov.mb.ca/wd/ites/pubs/lmapd/lmapd_2016_17.pdf

Jamieson, M., Cullen, B., McGee-Lennon, M., Brewster, S., & Evans, J. J. (2014). The efficacy of cognitive prosthetic technology for people with memory impairments: A systematic review and meta-analysis. *Neuropsychological Rehabilitation, 24*(3–4), 419–444. https://doi.org/10.1080/09602011.2013.825632

Khasnabis, C., Mirza, Z., & MacLachlan, M. (2015). Opening the GATE to inclusion for people with disabilities. *The Lancet, 386*(10010), 2229–2230. https://doi.org/10.1016/S0140-6736(15)01093-4

Lavis, J. N., & Mattison, C. A. (2016). Introduction and overview. In J. N. Lavis (Ed.), *Ontario's Health System: Key insights for engaged citizens, professionals and policymakers* (pp. 15–43). McMaster Health Forum.

Madara Marasinghe, K. (2016). Assistive technologies in reducing caregiver burden among informal caregivers of older adults: A systematic review. *Disability and Rehabilitation: Assistive Technology, 11*(5), 353–360. https://doi.org/10.3109/17483107.2015.1087061

Mackenzie, I. (2015). *Seniors' housing in BC: Affordable, appropriate, available.* British Columbia, Canada: Office of the Seniors Advocate. Retrieved from https://www.seniorsadvocatebc.ca/app/uploads/sites/4/2015/05/Seniors-Housing-in-B.C.-Affordable-Appropriate-Available.pdf

Mattison, C. A., Waddell, K., Wang, R. H., & Wilson, M. G. (2017). *Citizen brief: Enhancing equitable access to assistive technologies in Canada.* McMaster University. https://macsphere.mcmaster.ca/handle/11375/21911

Mattison, C. A., Waddell, K., & Wilson, M. G. (2017). *Panel summary: Enhancing equitable access to assistive technologies in Canada.* McMaster University.

Mattison, C. A., Wilson, M. G., Wang, R. H., & Waddell, K. (2017). *Evidence brief: Enhancing equitable access to assistive technologies in Canada.* McMaster University.

Mattison, C. A., Wilson, M. G., Wang, R. H., & Waddell, K. (2019). Enhancing equitable access to assistive technologies in Canada: Insights from citizens and stakeholders. *Canadian Journal on Aging/La Revue Canadienne du Vieillissement,* 1–20. https://doi.org/10.1017/S0714980819000187

McColl, M. A., Jaiswal, A., Jones, S., Roberts, L., & Murphy, C. (2017). *A review of disability policy in Canada.* Canadian Disability Policy Alliance. http://www.disabilitypolicyalliance.ca/wp-content/uploads/2018/01/A-Review-of-Disability-Policy-in-Canada-3rd-edition-Final-1-1.pdf

Mortenson, W. B., Demers, L., Fuhrer, M. J., Jutai, J. W., Lenker, J., & DeRuyter, F. (2012). How assistive technology use by individuals with disabilities impacts their caregivers: A systematic review of the research evidence. *American Journal of Physical Medicine & Rehabilitation, 91*(11).

Moscovitch, A., & Thomas, G. (2018). *A new social care act for Canada: 2.0.* Canadian Association of Social Workers. https://www.casw-acts.ca/sites/default/files/documents/A_New_Social_Care_Act_for_Canada_2.0.pdf

Naidoo, V., Putnam, M., & Spindel, A. (2012). Key focal areas for bridging the fields of aging and disability: Findings from the growing older with a disability conference. *International Journal of Integrated Care, 12,* e201. https://doi.org/10.5334/ijic.1082

Perelmutter, B., McGregor, K. K., & Gordon, K. R. (2017). Assistive technology interventions for adolescents and adults with learning disabilities: An evidence-based systematic review and meta-analysis. *Computers & Education, 114,* 139–163. https://doi.org/10.1016/j.compedu.2017.06.005

Sauer, A. L., Parks, A., & Heyn, P. C. (2010). Assistive technology effects on the employment outcomes for people with cognitive disabilities: A systematic review. *Disability and Rehabilitation: Assistive Technology, 5*(6), 377–391.

Schreiber, D., Wang, R. H., Durocher, E., & Wilson, M. G. (2017). *Access to assistive technology in Canada: A jurisdictional scan of programs.* AGE-WELL NCE. https://agewell-nce.ca/wp-content/uploads/2019/01/agewell_jurisdictional-scan_2017_June-30_FINAL.pdf

United Nations. (2006). *Convention on the rights of persons with disabilities.* United Nations. http://www.un.org/disabilities/documents/convention/convoptprot-e.pdf

Waddell, K., Wilson, M. G., & Mattison, C. A. (2017). *Dialogue summary: Enhancing equitable access to assistive technologies in Canada.* McMaster University. https://www.mcmasterforum.org/docs/default-source/product-documents/stakeholder-dialogue-summary/asst-tech-sds.pdf?sfvrsn=4

World Health Assembly. (2018). *Improving access to assistive technology: Report by the Director-General.* WHO. http://apps.who.int/gb/ebwha/pdf_files/WHA71/A71_21-en.pdf

Suggested Readings

Mattison, C. A., Wilson, M. G., Wang, R. H., & Waddell, K. (2020). Enhancing equitable access to assistive technologies in Canada: Insights from citizens and stakeholders. *Canadian Journal on Aging = La Revue Canadienne du Vieillissement, 39*(1), 69–88. https://doi.org/10.1017/S0714980819000187

Naidoo, V., Putnam, M., & Spindel, A. (2012). Key focal areas for bridging the fields of aging and disability: Findings from the growing older with a disability conference. *International Journal of Integrated Care, 12*, e201. https://doi.org/10.5334/ijic.1082

Schreiber, D., Wang, R. H., Durocher, E., & Wilson, M. G. (2017). *Access to assistive technology in Canada: A jurisdictional scan of programs.* AGE-WELL NCE Canada. https://agewell-nce.ca/wp-content/uploads/2019/01/age-well_jurisdictional-scan_2017_June-30_FINAL.pdf

United Nations. (2006). *Convention on the rights of persons with disabilities.* United Nations. http://www.un.org/disabilities/documents/convention/convoptprot-e.pdf

33
AGEING WITH DISABILITY
Using Financial Mechanisms to Facilitate Intersectoral Collaboration

David McDaid and A-La Park

Introduction

The deaf-blind author and pioneering advocate for people with disabilities, Helen Keller, has been attributed as saying *'alone we can do so little. Together we can do so much'*. Too often governmental and non-governmental organisations working in ageing and disability can be isolated within the high walls of the castles in their fiefdoms meaning that opportunities to improve ageing with disability are lost. Intersectoral activity may be resisted if it is perceived almost like a hostile attempt by one organisation to scale the ramparts of another castle for their own purposes without considering the implications for the other sector.

A consensual approach maybe more productive with different organisations in the ageing and disability spheres lowering their respective drawbridges and facilitating collaboration to provide better services and supports. Collaboration across sectors and agencies is of critical importance. As individuals age they are increasingly likely to acquire the sudden onset of a disability or just experience symptoms of gradual functional decline. At the same time more and more people with disabilities acquired earlier in life are reaching older age. If collaboration leads to better outcomes this not only benefits people as they age, it also potentially has benefits for governments and society.

Measures that protect and promote quality of life and wellbeing for people ageing with disability may help to reduce or delay the need for substantial care and support. Even small improvements in health and/or in ability to maintain independent living, as well as achieving synergies in the provision of services, eliminating duplication of effort, are likely to have positive downward impacts on these future costs (Zingmark, Norstrom, Lindholm, Dahlin-Ivanoff, & Gustafsson, 2019). For example, there is potential to improve outcomes and reduce the costs of delayed discharges from hospital by increased collaboration between the health and housing sectors in the provision of reablement services for frail older people with disabilities that can help in their rehabilitation (Kjerstad & Tuntland, 2016; McDaid, Park, Eliot, Livsey, & Swan, 2014). Early action to identify chronic health problems in people with physical and intellectual disabilities can also help ensure that longer life expectancy means more time spent in good quality health (Garcia-Dominguez, Navas, Verdugo, & Arias, 2020).

These potential benefits are not restricted to reducing the need for health, social care, and other services. There are also benefits from maintaining health, wellbeing, and independence. Older people are consumers whose spending power can help stimulate the economy, something that is particularly important in the current global economic climate. For example, in 2015 the UK government estimated that all 10.4 million households with one or more disabled members had a combined income of £249 billion ($360 billion USD), or £23,900 ($34,600 USD) after housing costs had been paid (Department for Work and Pensions, 2016). Similarly, the average annual income for UK pensioner couples in 2017 was £23,500 ($33,600 USD) (Department for Work and Pensions, 2018), while an earlier study calculated that they made a positive net contribution to the UK economy (even accounting for higher health and social care costs of £40 billion ($57 billion USD) in 2010 rising to £77 billion ($110 billion USD) by 2030 (Royal Voluntary Service, 2011).

There is thus a business and economic case to foster better outcomes in this population. It also has policy resonance, potentially relieving some of the increased pressure on welfare systems. Policy makers have, for example, spoken of the importance of better integration across sectors, as well as more direct involvement of ageing with disability service users in co-producing health and social care services (Ouellette-Kuntz et al., 2019). Already there has been a shift in some long-term care policies towards ageing in place, with more co-production of care services through collaboration between stakeholders from the private, public, and voluntary sectors (Alders & Schut, 2019). These approaches need, however, to do more to include populations with specific needs, including people ageing with or into disability.

In this chapter we argue that financial mechanisms should be more widely used to stimulate collaboration between sectors that can support ageing with disability. We focus on these issues because funding issues can present major impediments to collaboration. In different sectors, funding streams may have tight restrictions on their use and be subject to different financial incentives and cost-containment concerns. A predominance of vertical policy-making structures and funding silos may reduce the prospects for intersectoral work (Corbin, Jones, & Barry, 2018; Rantala, Bortz, & Armada, 2014; Wong et al., 2017).

This challenge is compounded when one sector is disproportionally financially responsible for the delivery of any action, for example, protecting health and wellbeing, but does not perceive that it will enjoy many of the benefits of the action (McDaid & Wismar, 2015). This will be particularly relevant if a sector perceives that it must take on a substantial extra workload without receiving adequate additional resources. For example, social care budget holders may be reluctant to fund activities to promote community leisure and other activities to reduce risks of social isolation and loneliness in people ageing with disability unless benefits such as reduced future demand for home and community-based care can be identified.

Given the centrality of resources to policy implementation, well-designed approaches that ensure appropriate funding may help to overcome barriers and disincentives to intersectoral collaboration. These mechanisms can help facilitate genuine co-production of strategies across sectors. They can also be designed to better involve different stakeholders, such as the voluntary sector, as well as informal carers in different welfare regimes. To look at these issues we draw on literature on how different funding mechanisms and financial incentives have helped facilitate joint actions between the health and social care sectors and the consider whether and how they can be used to support people ageing with or into disability.

What Do We Know About Using Financing Mechanisms to Facilitate Intersectoral Collaboration?

There remains a very limited literature specifically on financing mechanisms used for ageing with or into disability. This literature focuses on barriers to collaboration between these sectors rather than solutions. Much of the discussion concerns measures to influence individual behaviour rather than the behaviour of organisations, most notably empowering older people and those with disabilities through the use of different forms of cash transfer or vouchers that have been introduced to purchase services and supports from different sectors, agencies and the private sector that they feel best meet their needs (Carbone & Allin, 2020; Roets et al., 2020; Woolham, Daly, Sparks, Ritters, & Steils, 2017). Social prescribing, a mechanism whereby health system funds are used to purchases activities and services outside of the health system to support groups, such as people with mental health problems, chronic illness and disability, are another mechanism that stimulates intersectoral thinking targeted at individuals (McDaid, Damant, & Park, 2019). Other examples aimed at individual behaviour include the use of financial, tax and other incentives to encourage continued participation in work (Laun, 2017) or even physical activity (Harkins, Kullgren, Bellamy, Karlawish, & Glanz, 2017).

There are, in contrast, few examples of structural approaches to encourage sectors to work together on ageing with or into disability, but that may be because these issues do not have great prominence within the portfolios of health, social care, housing, and other agencies that may provide relevant services. We can however draw on the growing evidence base on the use of financing mechanisms for intersectoral collaboration involving the health sector that could be applied to ageing with disability (Jakovljevic et al., 2019; Johansson & Tillgren, 2011; McDaid & Park, 2016; McGuire et al., 2019; Rantala et al., 2014).

Previously we reviewed the role of financial and regulatory measures in encouraging collaboration across sectors to promote better health and wellbeing. This review was not specifically focused on any age group or condition but different mechanisms that are helpful to better collaboration and co-production were identified (McDaid & Park, 2016). The most frequently used of these mechanisms were earmarked funding, delegated financing, and joint budgeting.

Earmarked Funding

Earmarked funding conditional on collaborative activity can be allocated to multiple organisations for a shared project or goal. The process for allocating funding may be prescriptive, stipulating that funding is linked to use of a specific cross-sectoral programme to address an issue, or it may allow for innovation in the way in which that priority issue is addressed. It can also be a competitive process where organisations from two or more sectors may have to collaborate to develop a proposal regarding how funds will be used to any specific issue.

Example that are particularly relevant include earmarked funding from the Population Health Fund (PHF) (Public Health Agency of Canada, 2007) and latterly the Innovation Strategy of the Public Health Agency of Canada (Office of Evaluation, 2015). Under the PHF national and regional projects resulted from a competitive bidding process in which applications had to demonstrate that intersectoral work would be undertaken, for example, linking academic, community, educational, and voluntary sector organisations within and outside the health sector. Evaluation found that the PHF facilitated intersectoral actions, with some projects sustained beyond the lifetime of the grant through the successful acquisition of funding from other sources. A limitation was that many smaller one-off projects had insufficient time to generate evidence on which activities had worked, with limited project funding for evaluation and did not share lessons learnt. When the PHF was replaced by an Innovation Strategy the programme structure changed to adopt a phased longer-term funding approach, focused on projects of larger scale. This financing model for intersectoral partnership working led to the development of sustained and expanded intersectoral programmes across Canada.

Delegated Financing

Another approach to consider is delegated financing (Schang & Lin, 2012). This involves allocating funding to an independent statutory organisation, such as a public health foundation, frequently from multiple budgetary sources, not just health budgets (Schang, Czabanowska, & Lin, 2012). If properly independent of government, organisations operating through this financing mechanism may be more sustainable as they can be less vulnerable to government budgetary and electoral cycles (Greaves & Bialystok, 2011). They can decide which projects and activities to fund, with many projects being intersectoral.

Joint Budgeting

Joint budgeting (also known as resource pooling) is a third approach to funding intersectoral collaboration in which two or more sectors share their resources to address a specific issue (McDaid, 2012). It is perhaps the most frequently used of these three approaches and has been used for specific health and social care service projects for different client groups, including older people in England through the

Better Care Fund which brings to together health care system funds with local government social care funds, 'with the intention of better, more joined-up services to older and disabled people, to keep them out of hospital and avoid long hospital stays' (Harlock et al., 2020).

Pooling funds from health and social care services may help to reduce administration and transaction costs, thus generating economies of scale through shared staff, resources and purchasing power while facilitating more rapid decision-making (Mason, Goddard, Weatherly, & Chalkley, 2015). Under this mechanism, financial resources can be shared in a number of ways, including budget alignment. For example, shared budgets between the health sector and a local municipality can be arranged to meet agreed health promotion aims. Funds are often time limited and sometimes there may be an agreement to jointly fund a post for an individual who will be responsible for providing services and/or attaining objectives relevant to both sectors. Budgets across organisations might also become fully integrated, with resources and the workforce fully coming together; however, most initiatives stop short of fully pooling resources.

An important point is that joint budgeting can be either mandatory or voluntary. It may be accompanied by legislation, regulatory instruments, and detailed legal agreements between sectors. Some have, for example, included specifying a host/lead partner for the budget and clarifying the functions, agreed aims and outcomes and levels of financial contributions by different sectors, as well as relevant accountability issues. In the short term, mandatory budget pooling and a de facto requirement for different sectors to collaborate may facilitate intersectoral actions and provide opportunities for mutual learning across sectors. However, the imposition of mandatory schemes may lead to resistance to collaboration from different sectors, which may threaten the long-term sustainability of schemes.

Evidence from partnerships between health and social welfare services in the United Kingdom suggests that there may also be a reluctance to collaborate beyond what is stated in specific contracts and detailed legal partnership agreements; good accountability mechanisms, as well as clear legal and financial frameworks, need to be in place (Glendinning, 2003; Mitchell, Tazzyman, Howard, & Hodgson, 2020). Tensions have also been seen in some local Better Care Fund programmes in England where there was a lack of agreement on how money should be spent, nor on how the risk of any financial losses from programmes should be shared (Harlock et al., 2020). If mutual learning or trust does not develop between sectors, then mandatory partnerships may be difficult to sustain if mandatory joint funding ceases. In contrast, although voluntary partnerships may take longer to develop, they may be more sustainable as a result of the trust that evolves between sectors over time.

Using Economic Arguments to Strengthen the Case for Enhanced Intersectoral Working

Partners need to perceive collaboration to be in their own interests by adding value to what they can achieve in isolation. Too often, stakeholders from one sector do not look at the consequences of an action for their partners. Economic arguments can be used to address this issue. This is done by identifying and placing a monetary value on outcomes of interest to each sector in any collaboration, even if these outcomes appear tangential to the primary goal, in this case of better ageing with disability. It is particularly helpful to present cogent arguments indicating that the collaboration will be a win-win for all partners (McDaid & Wismar, 2015).

Consider a hypothetical voluntary arrangement between health care budget holders and local government leisure service budget holders to pool funds to tackle social isolation and loneliness in frail older people. There is increasing evidence that loneliness has an adverse impact on the physical health of vulnerable populations (Leigh-Hunt et al., 2017), and that leisure and other social activities can help to reduce the risk of loneliness (Gao et al., 2018). Demands for future expensive health care services may thus be reduced if health care budget holders invest resources in this type of non-clinical activity. Similarly, local governments may be more prepared to invest resources in tackling loneliness, something that may not see as a core activity, if they are presented with the growing evidence base that high levels of loneliness are a risk factor for cognitive decline (Luchetti et al., 2020). The costs of providing social and long-term care for dementia account for a large share of expenditure for local governments in many countries; relatively low-cost investment in measures to tackle loneliness may then appear more attractive.

Overcoming Barriers and Seizing the Opportunity

We believe that there is a real opportunity to use financial mechanisms to stimulate interaction and bridge the ageing and disability sectors to allow for better ageing with disability. There are potentially substantial benefits, not just to the health and social care sectors, but to the wider economy of promoting better ageing and the maintenance of independence in this population group. Historically, responsibility for ageing and disability has often rested with multiple agencies, potentially in different sectors with different hierarchical and administrative structures. This may make collaboration difficult, but there is evidence broadly in the health, social care and public health sectors that financial mechanisms can incentivise collaboration between sectors.

Options to consider include earmarking funding for activities to support ageing with disability conditional on an intersectoral approach being taken. Ongoing financing of intersectoral activities could also be made conditional on effective monitoring and achievement of defined outputs and outcomes. This could include phased funding that could eventually lead to replication and/or scaling up, as has been used by the Innovation Strategy of the Public Health Agency of Canada.

Funding may also be delegated to a specific independent agency that has a remit to work across the ageing and disability sectors; much can be learnt from health promotion foundations that operate along these lines, such as the Victorian Health Promotion Foundation in Australia. Pooling budgets across sectors, to support the needs of people ageing with disability is another option. In England, the Better Care Fund allows local health budget holders to pool some funds with local government to promote healthy ageing and reduce the need for crisis interventions. This English model also provides an example of how establishing a legal and regulatory framework for these partnerships can help in the way they function, for instance by allowing staff from either organisation to be paid in a comparable way. It also promotes accountability and transparency on how funds are spent.

The literature has also identified many different potential barriers to implementation of financing mechanisms. They can include poor leadership, a lack of buy-in from different stakeholders, organisational resistance to change, worries over impacts on core function, insufficient resources, imbalanced hierarchical structures and differences in work culture (McGuire et al., 2019). Many of these issues boil down to the concept of trust. Intersectoral collaboration requires trust to be built between partners regardless of the financing mechanism. Building trust is particularly important when different sectors voluntarily come together to collaborate and share resources. This necessarily relies more heavily on trust and open discussion; in turn, mutual learning and innovation is enhanced by the development of trusting relationships. Creating collaboration champions and co-location of ageing and disability organisation personnel may also have a positive impact on establishing trust. Shared targets and rewards, flexibility in planning, and access to external mediation if necessary can also help (McDaid & Park, 2016; McGuire et al., 2019).

It is also clear that identifying outcomes of interest to all potential intersectoral partnerships, as well as the economic costs and payoffs, can help to facilitate partnerships. This requires creative thinking recognising that sectors may have very different priorities. However, it also means that there may also be a need for compensation mechanisms, i.e. the additional transfer of funds across sectors may be helpful when it is not possible to generate economic win-wins for all sectors (Johansson & Tillgren, 2011). Even where there are economic win-wins, these may not be realised for some years, so it is important that these financing mechanisms are adequately resourced.

Reviews also suggest that many successful experiences in the use of financial mechanisms are more likely to operate at a local rather than national level, with local government often central to intersectoral activities identified. This may be because local governments are usually well positioned to lead intersectoral processes by influencing several sectors that can be fundamental to health, such as land use, transportation, environmental protection, leisure services, education, and community development.

Conclusion

Potentially there is a wealth of innovative practice on the use of financing mechanisms to stimulate intersectoral collaboration; this may include examples of good practice that support ageing with disability that have not come to the fore. A first step is to have platforms in place where existing expertise and knowledge on financing mechanisms from different local and national contexts can be shared to help services collaborate to support people ageing with or into disability. Going forward it is also important to formally evaluate the effectiveness and cost-effectiveness of these financial mechanisms in different contexts, including the use of different strategies to help smooth their use, such as creating the conditions for mutual learning and trust. In this way the aspiration of Helen Keller that *'together we can do so much'*, perhaps through more joined-up, integrated care and support that meets the needs of all of those ageing with disability might be realised.

References

Alders, P., & Schut, F. T. (2019). Trends in ageing and ageing-in-place and the future market for institutional care: Scenarios and policy implications. *Health Economics, Policy, and Law*, *14*(1), 82–100. https://doi.org/10.1017/s1744133118000129

Carbone, S., & Allin, S. (2020). Advancing direct payment reforms in Ontario and Scotland. *Health Reform Observer–Observatoire des Réformes de Santé*, *8*(1). https://doi.org/10.13162/hro-ors.v8i1.4154

Corbin, J. H., Jones, J., & Barry, M. M. (2018). What makes intersectoral partnerships for health promotion work? A review of the international literature. *Health Promotion International*, *33*(1), 4–26. https://doi.org/10.1093/heapro/daw061

Department for Work and Pensions. (2016). *The spending power of disabled people and their families in 2014/15, and changes since 2012/13*. Government of the United Kingdom. https://assets.publishing.service.gov.uk/government/uploads/system/uploads/attachment_data/file/572187/spending-power-of-disabled-people-and-their-families-2014-15.pdf

Department for Work and Pensions. (2018). *Pensioners' Incomes Series: An analysis of trends in pensioner incomes*: 1994/95–2016/17. Government of the United Kingdom. https://assets.publishing.service.gov.uk/government/uploads/system/uploads/attachment_data/file/693324/pensioners-incomes-series-2016-17-report.pdf

Gao, M., Sa, Z., Li, Y., Zhang, W., Tian, D., Zhang, S., & Gu, L. (2018). Does social participation reduce the risk of functional disability among older adults in China? A survival analysis using the 2005-2011 waves of the CLHLS data. *BMC Geriatrics*, *18*(1), 224. https://doi.org/10.1186/s12877-018-0903-3

Garcia-Dominguez, L., Navas, P., Verdugo, M. A., & Arias, V. B. (2020). Chronic health conditions in aging individuals with intellectual disabilities. *International Journal of Environmental Research and Public Health*, *17*(9). https://doi.org/10.3390/ijerph17093126

Glendinning, C. (2003). Breaking down barriers: Integrating health and care services for older people in England. *Health Policy*, *65*(2), 139–151. https://doi.org/10.1016/s0168-8510(02)00205-1

Greaves, L. J., & Bialystok, L. R. (2011). Health in all policies-all talk and little action? *Canadian Journal of Public Health*, *102*(6), 407–409. Retrieved from http://www.ncbi.nlm.nih.gov/pubmed/22164546

Harkins, K. A., Kullgren, J. T., Bellamy, S. L., Karlawish, J., & Glanz, K. (2017). A trial of financial and social incentives to increase older adults' walking. *American Journal of Preventive Medicine*, *52*(5), e123–e130. https://doi.org/10.1016/j.amepre.2016.11.011

Harlock, J., Caiels, J., Marczak, J., Peters, M., Fitzpatrick, R., Wistow, G., ... Jones, K. (2020). Challenges in integrating health and social care: The better care fund in England. *Journal of Health Services Research & Policy*, *25*(2), 86–93. https://doi.org/10.1177/1355819619869745

Jakovljevic, M., Jakab, M., Gerdtham, U., McDaid, D., Ogura, S., Varavikova, E., ... Getzen, T. E. (2019). Comparative financing analysis and political economy of noncommunicable diseases. *Journal of Medical Economics*, *22*(8), 722–727. https://doi.org/10.1080/13696998.2019.1600523

Johansson, P., & Tillgren, P. (2011). Financing intersectoral health promotion programmes: Some reasons why collaborators are collaborating as indicated by cost-effectiveness analyses. *Scandinavian Journal of Public Health*, *39*(6 Suppl), 26–32. https://doi.org/10.1177/1403494810393559

Kjerstad, E., & Tuntland, H. K. (2016). Reablement in community-dwelling older adults: A cost-effectiveness analysis alongside a randomized controlled trial. *Health Economics Review*, 6(1), 15. https://doi.org/10.1186/s13561-016-0092-8

Laun, L. (2017). The effect of age-targeted tax credits on labor force participation of older workers. *Journal of Public Economics*, 152, 102–118. https://doi.org/10.1016/j.jpubeco.2017.06.005

Leigh-Hunt, N., Bagguley, D., Bash, K., Turner, V., Turnbull, S., Valtorta, N., & Caan, W. (2017). An overview of systematic reviews on the public health consequences of social isolation and loneliness. *Public Health*, 152, 157–171. https://doi.org/10.1016/j.puhe.2017.07.035

Luchetti, M., Terracciano, A., Aschwanden, D., Lee, J. H., Stephan, Y., & Sutin, A. R. (2020). Loneliness is associated with risk of cognitive impairment in the survey of health, ageing and retirement in Europe. *International Journal of Geriatric Psychiatry*, 35(7), 794–801. https://doi.org/10.1002/gps.5304

Mason, A., Goddard, M., Weatherly, H., & Chalkley, M. (2015). Integrating funds for health and social care: An evidence review. *Journal of Health Services Research & Policy*, 20(3), 177–188. https://doi.org/10.1177/1355819614566832

McDaid, D. (2012). Joint budgeting: Can it facilitate intersectoral action? In D. McQueen, M. Wismar, V. Lin, C. Jones, & M. Davies (Eds.), *Intersectoral governance for health in all policies. Structure, actions and experiences*. Copenhagen World Health Organization. https://www.euro.who.int/__data/assets/pdf_file/0005/171707/Intersectoral-governance-for-health-in-all-policies.pdf

McDaid, D., Damant, J., & Park, A. L. (2019). *Identifying the potential value of sustained participation in community activities arising from referral through social prescribing*. Greater London Authority. https://www.london.gov.uk/sites/default/files/activitiesguide.pdf

McDaid, D., & Park, A.-L. (2016). *Evidence on financing and budgeting mechanisms to support intersectoral actions between health, education, social welfare and labour sectors*. World Health Organization Regional Office for Europe. https://www.euro.who.int/__data/assets/pdf_file/0004/318136/HEN-synthesis-report-48.pdf

McDaid, D., Park, A.-L., Eliot, J., Livsey, L., & Swan, A. (2014). *Prescription for success – A guide to the health economy*. London, UK: National Housing Federation. https://www.housing.org.uk/about-us/

McDaid, D., & Wismar, M. (2015). Making an economic case for intersectoral action. In D. McDaid, F. Sassi, & S. Merkur (Eds.), *Promoting health, preventing disease: The economic case*. Open University Press.

McGuire, F., Vijayasingham, L., Vassall, A., Small, R., Webb, D., Guthrie, T., & Remme, M. (2019). Financing intersectoral action for health: A systematic review of co-financing models. *Globalization & Health*, 15(1), 86–86. https://doi.org/10.1186/s12992-019-0513-7

Mitchell, C., Tazzyman, A., Howard, S. J., & Hodgson, D. (2020). More that unites us than divides us? A qualitative study of integration of community health and social care services. *BMC Family Practice*, 21(1), 1–10. https://doi.org/10.1186/s12875-020-01168-z

Office of Evaluation. (2015). *Evaluation of the innovation strategy 2009–2010 to 2013–2014*. Health Canada and Public Health Agency of Canada. https://www.canada.ca/content/dam/phac-aspc/migration/phac-aspc/about_apropos/evaluation/reports-rapports/2014-2015/eis-sie/assets/pdf/eis-sie-eng.pdf

Ouellette-Kuntz, H., Martin, L., Burke, E., McCallion, P., McCarron, M., McGlinchey, E., ... Temple, B. (2019). How best to support individuals with IDD as they become frail: Development of a consensus statement. *Journal of Applied Research in Intellectual Disabilities: JARID*, 32(1), 35–42. https://doi.org/10.1111/jar.12499

Public Health Agency of Canada. (2007). *Crossing sectors: Experiences in intersectoral action, public policy and health*. Public Health Agency of Canada. https://www.ottawapublichealth.ca/en/index.aspx

Rantala, R., Bortz, M., & Armada, F. (2014). Intersectoral action: Local governments promoting health. *Health Promotion International*, 29(suppl_1), i92–i102. https://doi.org/10.1093/heapro/dau047

Roets, G., Dermaut, V., Benoot, T., Claes, C., Schiettecat, T., Roose, R., ... Vandevelde, S. (2020). A critical analysis of disability policy and practice in Flanders: Toward differentiated manifestations of interdependency. *Journal of Policy and Practice in Intellectual Disabilities*. https://doi.org/10.1111/jppi.12336

Royal Voluntary Service. (2011). *Gold age pensioners: Valuing the socio-economic contribution of older people in the UK*. WRVS. https://www.royalvoluntaryservice.org.uk/Uploads/Documents/gold_age_report_2011.pdf

Schang, L. K., Czabanowska, K. M., & Lin, V. (2012). Securing funds for health promotion: Lessons from health promotion foundations based on experiences from Austria, Australia, Germany, Hungary and Switzerland. *Health Promotion International*, 27(2), 295–305. https://doi.org/10.1093/heapro/dar023

Schang, L. K., & Lin, V. (2012). Delegated financing. In D. McQueen, M. Wismar, V. Lin, C. Jones, & M. Davies (Eds.), *Intersectoral governance for health in all policies. Structure, actions and experiences*. Copenhagen World Health Organization. https://www.euro.who.int/__data/assets/pdf_file/0005/171707/Intersectoral-governance-for-health-in-all-policies.pdf

Wong, S. T., MacDonald, M., Martin-Misener, R., Meagher-Stewart, D., O'Mara, L., & Valaitis, R. K. (2017). What systemic factors contribute to collaboration between primary care and public health sectors? An interpretive descriptive study. *BMC Health Services Research*, 17(1), 796. https://doi.org/10.1186/s12913-017-2730-1

Woolham, J., Daly, G., Sparks, T., Ritters, K., & Steils, N. (2017). Do direct payments improve outcomes for older people who receive social care? Differences in outcome between people aged 75+ who have a managed personal budget or a direct payment. *Ageing & Society, 37*(5), 961–984. https://doi.org/10.1017/S0144686X15001531

Zingmark, M., Norstrom, F., Lindholm, L., Dahlin-Ivanoff, S., & Gustafsson, S. (2019). Modelling long-term cost-effectiveness of health promotion for community-dwelling older people. *European Journal of Ageing, 16*(4), 395–404. https://doi.org/10.1007/s10433-019-00505-1

Suggested Readings

Harlock, J., Caiels, J., Marczak, J., Peters, M., Fitzpatrick, R., Wistow, G., ... Jones, K. (2020). Challenges in integrating health and social care: The better care fund in England. *Journal of Health Services Research & Policy, 25*(2), 86–93. https://doi.org/10.1177/1355819619869745

Johansson, P., & Tillgren, P. (2011). Financing intersectoral health promotion programmes: Some reasons why collaborators are collaborating as indicated by cost-effectiveness analyses. *Scandinavian Journal of Public Health, 39*(6 Suppl), 26–32. https://doi.org/10.1177/1403494810393559

Mason, A., Goddard, M., Weatherly, H., & Chalkley, M. (2015). Integrating funds for health and social care: An evidence review. *Journal of Health Services Research & Policy, 20*(3), 177–188. https://doi.org/10.1177/1355819614566832

McDaid, D., & Park, A.-L. (2016). *Evidence on financing and budgeting mechanisms to support intersectoral actions between health, education, social welfare and labour sectors.* World Health Organization Regional Office for Europe. https://www.euro.who.int/__data/assets/pdf_file/0004/318136/HEN-synthesis-report-48.pdf

McDaid, D., & Wismar, M. (2015). Making an economic case for intersectoral action. In D. McDaid, F. Sassi, & S. Merkur (Eds.), *Promoting health, preventing disease: The economic case.* Open University Press.

McGuire, F., Vijayasingham, L., Vassall, A., Small, R., Webb, D., Guthrie, T., & Remme, M. (2019). Financing intersectoral action for health: A systematic review of co-financing models. *Globalization & Health, 15*(1), 86–86. https://doi.org/10.1186/s12992-019-0513-7

34
ENABLING A GOOD OLD AGE FOR PEOPLE AGEING WITH DISABILITY
Reflections on Progress

Christine Bigby and Michelle Putnam

The Handbook has presented a snapshot of current scholarship about people ageing with disability. This last chapter aims to draw out some of the dominant themes from the collection, reflect on progress made since ageing with disability first emerged as a public issue in the early 1980s, and consider future priorities for research and service system development. 'Defying all odds', coined by Moll and Cott (2020) about people with cerebral palsy, might also characterise more generally the field of ageing with disability. Mainstream scholarship has taken little heed of people ageing with disability; gerontological research rarely includes this group and they have been excluded, for example, from key constructs such as 'successful ageing'. Neither have disability or ageing policies and service systems taken good account of this group. Nevertheless, a small group of scholars continue to explore theories that interrogate the complex experiences of people ageing with a disability and investigate the responses of health and social care systems to them. Their work is important and should receive more attention than it does. As the size of the ageing with disability population grows, increasing the number of scholars and researchers in the field of ageing with disability is crucial for advancing knowledge and practice. Public and private funders should take note of the real and immediate need to invest in research related to ageing with disability.

As the balance of chapters in this book suggest, current research agendas are primarily focused on health and social care, finding ways for service systems to be more inclusive and better respond to the often unique combinations of needs of people ageing with disability. There remains limited basic research on health and functioning seeking to identify and compare risk factors for disease of people ageing with a disability with the general population, as is often done for other minority population groups. This is likely due in large part to the continued general perception of disability as normative in later life, abnormal in earlier life, and the lack of imagination regarding life course trajectories of people with disabilities. In the US, for example, it has long been permissible – and even scientifically justifiable – to exclude persons with disabilities from research studies based on their disability status alone – citing concerns about the difficulty of including persons with disabilities in the research process and the difficulty in interpreting data when disability is present (Rios, Magasi, Novak, & Harniss, 2016).

Despite this, over the last 30 years pioneering work at some of the US research centres on Ageing and Disability funded by the National Institute of Disability, Independent Living, and Rehabilitation Research (NIDILRR) have explored a wide range of health and wellness issues related to ageing with physical disability, establishing foundational knowledge about persons ageing with polio, multiple sclerosis and spinal cord injury. However, NIDILRR funding for those centres has decreased over time. Contributions from these centres include identifying cross-disability ageing-related symptoms and conditions including chronic pain, fatigue, and depression as noted in Campbell and Putnam (2020) and the unpacking of associated secondary health conditions, and the significance of time since injury on health and function particularly in groups such as persons with spinal cord injury and those with cerebral palsy (Kemp & Mosqueda, 2004). Similarly, the Institute on Disability and Human Development in Chicago led by Tamar Heller for many years played a very significant role in research about people with intellectual and developmental disabilities as well as translating knowledge about health and family issues into training programs and practice guides. A strong international group of scientists in the UK and US, led work related to health of ageing people with intellectual disability through IASSIDD (International Association for the Scientific Study of Intellectual and Developmental Disabilities) and in collaboration with the WHO (World Health Organization) (see, for example, Davidson, Prasher, & Janicki, 2003; WHO, 2000). Several of the authors in this Handbook are extending the parameters of ageing with disability research including exploring issues of ageing among persons with serious mental illness, autism, and deafblindness. In doing so, they move ageing and life course issues farther into the disability population which is positive for the field.

It may be the case that early health related research shaped current study by sharply identifying the impact of social and contextual factors rather than individual characteristics on health risks in later life. An outstanding example of this was the Netherlands group that showed the different pattern of ageing among people with intellectual disabilities was largely due to reversible lifestyle factors rather than early onset of ageing. This work connected high levels of frailty at a younger age in people with intellectual disabilities with their very low levels of physical activity, social relationships, and community participation. In many ways, factors such as these can be tied back to the quality of support provided in supported accommodation and other services earlier in the life course (Evenhuis, Schoufour, Oppewal, & Festen, 2020). More recently, findings from the Intellectual Disability Supplement to the Irish Longitudinal Study on Ageing comparing a large representative sample of people with intellectual disabilities with the general population vividly illustrated how the poor health of ageing people with intellectual disabilities could be improved through social and health promotion measures, in future generations. It showed, for example, significant under diagnosis and failure to treat conditions such as osteoporosis, high levels of obesity and low levels of physical fitness (Burke, McCarron, & McCallion, 2014; McCarron et al., 2011). Similar research exploring the influence of social determinants of health and persons ageing with physical disability has yet to be conducted to any notable extent, but the work of intellectual disability researchers provides a roadmap for doing so.

This research on health supports the trend towards focusing on service systems. And while still very much an interdisciplinary field of research, the interest of social work scholars in issues of ageing with disability appears to be increasing relative to other disciplines. This explains the growing use of social models of disability and socio-ecological theories in the field. Building on earlier health research, these scholars put an emphasis on context; the impact of social, physical, and technological environments on experiences of people ageing with a disability. However, there remains much potential, as Yoshizaki-Gibbons (2020) suggests, to use critical disability or gerontological theories to understand and address the inequities of ageing with a disability, or rethink mainstream theories to be inclusive of this group, as Harnett, Jönson, and Taghizadeh Larsson (2020) do in proposing a *Scandinavian Model of Successful Ageing*.

Taken as a whole the chapters in this book point to the limited inroads of rights-based policies into the quality of life of people with disabilities and to the systemic disadvantages they experience earlier in their life course which are compounded as they age. This work suggests that applying the theory of cumulative advantage and disadvantage to the population ageing with a disability may be worthy of further exploration (Dannefer, 2003). Central to this theory is the 'the systemic tendency for inter individual divergence in a given characteristic (e.g., money, health, or status) with the passage of time' (Dannefer, 2003, p. S327) as a result of the interaction of complex forces. And, that this divergence and cumulative disadvantage is a property of populations rather than individuals. Although, the population of people ageing with a disability is made up of diverse sub-groups, they nevertheless bring to processes of ageing similar experiences of discrimination, stigma, and multiple adverse social determinants of health, such as poverty, unemployment, insecurity and stress. All of which impact on potential for healthy or active ageing and a good old age.

How Far Have We Come

Life expectancy for people with intellectual disabilities is indicative in many ways of the progress made to enable a good old age for people with disabilities in general, and how far there is still to go. 30 years ago the first sizeable cohort of people with intellectual disabilities survived into old age. The increases in life expectancy 'from average of 20 years in 1930s to 70 years in 1993…' (Bigby, 2004) were heralded as a success of medical science, public health and deinstitutionalisation. Although life expectancy remained less than general population at that time, especially for people with severe intellectual disabilities, there was optimism that the gap would progressively reduce and remaining differences only be due to genetics or medical frailty. However, the gap has closed less than expected – figures suggest, for example, in the US life expectancy from birth of between 50.4 and 58.5 years for people with intellectual disabilities compared to 78.5 years for the general population (Lauer & McCallion, 2015), and in the UK 64–68 years for people with intellectual disability compared to approximately 80 years in the general population (Heslop et al., 2014). Such differences are not inevitable but associated with social determinants of health and the responsiveness of health and social care systems. The UK data suggests, for example, there are twice as many avoidable deaths (amenable to receipt of good quality health care) among people with intellectual disabilities compared to the general population (37% of deaths compared to 13%). These data suggest that people with intellectual disabilities of all ages do not get appropriate health care; reducing life expectancy and comprising health earlier in the life course.

As many of the chapters in the Handbook illustrate the issues are twofold, early life course experiences mean good foundations for ageing are not laid and people with disabilities embark on ageing with multiple disadvantages, which are then compounded by neither the disability nor aged care service systems being well prepared to support their health and wellbeing as they age. Of most concern are the similarities between the individual biographies of people ageing with a disability in the 2000s with those of earlier generations despite significant changes in policy landscapes. More than a decade of rights based policies have largely failed to deliver promises of increased self-determination and more inclusive communities or mainstream service systems for people with disabilities. This lack of progress may be due in part to difficulties of enacting such policies in climates of austerity and neo liberalism based on individual consumers rather than collective social responsibilities. In countries like the United Kingdom this has meant tighter eligibility for disability services and reduced expenditure and in the US, shifting responsibility back to families to support people with disabilities in later life.

This example of persons ageing with intellectual disability is perhaps an early warning for other groups of persons with disabilities. The research on ageing with intellectual disability is much more extensive than it is for other groups and includes development of many evidence-based interventions. Persons with intellectual disabilities are often more recognised as having unique needs compared to persons with less identifiable conditions and disability experiences. From a practical perspective, it seems like there would be general agreement that issues of ageing for persons with intellectual disability are important to be proactive about, but it is rare when this is the case.

Emerging and Growing Sub-Groups of People Ageing with Disabilities

This book has included chapters on the life experiences of emerging groups of people ageing with disabilities – people who are deafblind, autistic people, and those with severe mental illness. Notably absent is research on ageing people with polio, a group whose size has diminished with the death of many of the ageing cohort and leading activists such as Australian Margaret Cooper (Cooper & Bigby,

2014; Frohmader, 2018). One of the largest groups of those ageing with disability remain those with intellectual disabilities, about whom there remains significant scholarship, although notably, there is a gradual change of leadership as early leaders such as Matthew Janicki and James Hogg retire. Despite its relative size, concerns most relevant to this group continue to gain little prominence in services systems. Evidence alone is often insufficient to influence policy, requiring advocacy and support from a wide base to gain attention. Limited progress around issues relevant to people with intellectual disabilities reflects their ongoing issue of challenges with self-advocacy and reliance on advocates or family members either to advocate on their behalf or support their self-advocacy. As initial research from the Australian National Disability Insurance Scheme indicates this is the group that fares worst in individualised funding schemes and for whom, in Australia at least there is no strong national advocacy voice (Bigby, 2020). Resolving 'what happens when parents die' remains a defining issue for both those who live at home and who live in other forms of supported accommodation, as it is predominantly parents who care about and often also care for adults with intellectual disabilities. The inherent tensions between self-determination and parental advocacy remain deeply embedded in discourses about planning for the future, which continues to be perceived as a parental responsibility bound up with securing future security and safety. The rights imperatives for supported decision making to enable people with cognitive impairment to exercise self-determination about their futures are only just being translated into practice, as demonstrated by the scholarship carefully reviewed by Carney and Then (2020).

Some progress has been made, in some places, in translating the large body of research that about people ageing with disability into policies and practice. Much of this aims to build bridges between ageing and disability knowledge and systems, particularly around issues of dementia. Examples related to intellectual disability include, the development of tools for diagnosis (Strydom et al., 2010), models for support and practice guidelines (US: Bishop et al., 2015; Ireland: McCarron & Reilly, 2010; Scotland: Watchman, 2014) which in Ireland meant that over half of people with Down syndrome are screened in memory clinics (Burke et al., 2014 and evaluation of the efficacy of mainstream dementia interventions such as memory boxes for people with intellectual disabilities (Crook, Adams, Shorten, & Langdon, 2015). In addition, programs and policies focused on home care and community living have begun to focus on personal need or functional need as initial criteria for program supports rather than chronological age alone. Examples of this related to physical disability include the Ageing and Disability Resource Centers in the United States (Putnam & Coyle, 2020) that attempt to seam together social care services for consumers and new supportive digital technologies that can be customised for an individual rather than built for a category or disability group (Sanford & Remillard, 2020).

Many dedicated bridging initiatives have been forwarded over the past few decades; however, they have struggled to gain traction. Since 2009, there have declarations calling for bridging from conferences in Graz (Weber, 2009), Barcelona (Salvador-Carulla, 2009), and Toronto (Bickenbach et al., 2012). The Bridging Aging and Disability International Network (BADIN) sponsored by the March of Dimes Ontario was a multi-year effort launched in 2012 attempting to launch the work of bridging, but had difficulty finding its own footing in the space between international scholarship and practice application and is now being re-envisioned. Still, work towards bridging ageing and disability remains an important need.

In regards to persons ageing with physical, sensory disability, serious mental illness, and acquired intellectual impairment, as noted earlier, researchers have made important contributions to these areas of study but overall the body of knowledge across these disability sub-groups remains quite modest. Central to moving the work forward is changing perceptions about the nature of disability – which is often viewed as static, and perceptions of supporting persons with these types of disabilities – which is often viewed solely in relation to obtaining, returning to, or sustaining employment. Rarely is a global view of the disability experience – including the experience over time – considered. Disability is still too often deemed a personal trait, an independent variable, rather than an integral experience. Given the heterogeneity of the disability experience, this assignment of disability is simply outdated. Moving forward, much more research is required related to the social determinants of health among all ageing with disability sub-groups. Included in that analysis must be issues of inclusion and exclusion – participation and engagement.

Moreover, much more attention must be given to how the experience of ageing with disability intersects with other traits, identities, roles, and factors including gender, sexual orientation, ethnicity, race and indigenous status, immigration and citizenship status, and more. To date ageing with disability scholarship and research has focused on establishing basic knowledge and/or developing more global interventions. The limited number of scholars has resulted in attention to core pieces of work at the expense of exploring and understanding the nuanced pieces of the ageing with disability experience known to exist. In the future, work must move forward in a broader way if an inclusive knowledge base is to be truly built.

The Research Landscape and Where to Next?

The landscape of ageing with disability research has changed little since it first emerged and with a few notable exceptions is characterised by small-scale one-off studies. Most notable is the absence of research from low- and middle-income countries where ageing with a disability remains an emerging issue.

The body of international scholars working remains small – perhaps no more than 200 or 300 across all disciplines by our estimation. Research in this field is fragmented and often fails to progress from exploratory to programmatic or theory testing studies. Much research is driven by practice experience, which fails to build from the outer most edges of knowledge. This tendency is not helped by the trend of conducting systematic reviews that go back 10 years or less, and in missing early foundational work, return new researchers to ground zero again and again. With small sub populations and issues distinct from mainstream ageing research funding for larger or programs of work is difficult to attract. Throughout this book scholars have flagged where new knowledge if needed to inform policy and practice, and returned to unresolved questions from the past. Research with people ageing with disability about their lived experiences is one area of critical importance, to ensure the application of the rights to practice is grounded in peoples wants and aspirations as well as expert defined needs. Translational research to identify the best ways of embedding knowledge about practice with populations ageing with disability in mainstream health and community care service systems should also be a priority in the future. But perhaps most important, the research landscape just needs to expand in breadth and depth across most areas. This field is still very young and the population of persons ageing with disability continues to grow in size. There is limited research-based knowledge to explain their experiences or to inform practice and policy. In general, this is problematic, but in cases of crisis – such as coping with the COVID 19 pandemic and its aftermath or balancing the economic costs of supporting ageing populations against pressing budgetary concerns of issues such as climate change and poverty alleviation, it is easy for gaps that people ageing with disabilities already fall into to become wider.

Despite all of these challenges, this Handbook is intended to offer readers a view into ageing with disability scholarship that helps them to identify where they can contribute to the field and work towards enabling a good old age for persons ageing with disability. We greatly appreciate all of the scholars who have contributed to it. The Handbook is not able to cover all of the topics or issues found in the existing body of knowledge, so we encourage readers to explore on their own outside of the Handbook to discover what else exists in this field of study. And whatever that area is, whether one this Handbook has highlighted or not, we encourage readers to engage with the material and the ageing with disability population and hope that in reading our book readers feel more able to do so.

References

Bickenbach, J., Bigby, C., Salvador-Carulla, L., Heller, T., Leonardi, M., Leroy, B., ... Spindel, A. (2012). The Toronto declaration on bridging knowledge, policy and practice in aging and disability: Toronto, Canada, March 30, 2012. *International Journal of Integrated Care, 12*, e205. https://doi.org/10.5334/ijic.1086

Bigby, C. (2004). *Aging with a lifelong disability: Policy, program and practice issues for professionals*. London: Jessica Kingsley.

Bigby, C. (2020). Dedifferentiation and people with intellectual disabilities in the Australian national disability insurance Scheme: Bringing research, politics and policy together. *Journal of Intellectual and Developmental Disability, 45*(3), 1–11.

Bishop, K. M., Hogan, M., Janicki, M. P., Keller, S. M., Lucchino, R., Mughal, D. T., & Wolfson, S. (2015). Guidelines for dementia-related health advocacy for adults with intellectual disability and dementia: National task group on intellectual disabilities and dementia practices. *Intellectual and Developmental Disabilities, 53*(1), 2–29. https://doi.org/10.1352/1934-9556-53.1.2

Burke, E., McCarron, M., & McCallion, P. (2014). *Advancing years, different challenges: Wave 2 IDS-TILDA findings of the ageing of people with intellectual disability* (pp. 1–178). Dublin: School of Nursing and Midwifery, Trinity College, Dublin.

Campbell, M., & Putnam, M. (2020). Reducing the shared burden of chronic conditions among persons aging with disability and older adults in the United States through bridging aging disability. In M. Putnam & C. Bigby (Eds.), *Handbook on ageing with disability* (pp. 57). Routledge.

Carney, T., & Then, S. (2020). Support for decision-making as people age with a cognitive impairment. In M. Putnam & C. Bigby (Eds.), *Handbook on ageing with disability* (pp. 186). Routledge.

Cooper, M., & Bigby, C. (2014). Cycles of adaptive strategies over the life course. *Journal of Gerontological Social Work, 57*(5), 421–437. https://doi.org/10.1080/01634372.2013.875972

Crook, N., Adams, M., Shorten, N., & Langdon, P. E. (2015). Does the well-being of individuals with down syndrome and dementia improve when using life story books and rummage boxes? A randomized single case series experiment. *Journal of Applied Research in Intellectual Disabilities, 29*(1), 1–10. https://doi.org/10.1111/jar.12151

Dannefer, D. (2003). Cumulative advantage/disadvantage and the life course: Cross-fertilizing age and social science theory. *The Journals of Gerontology Series B: Psychological Sciences and Social Sciences, 58*(6), S327–S337. https://doi.org/10.1093/geronb/58.6.S327

Davidson, P., Prasher, V., & Janicki, M. (2003). *Mental health, intellectual disabilities, and the aging process*. Oxford: Blackwell Publishing.

Evenhuis, H., Schoufour, J., Oppewal, A., & Festen, D. (2020). How to avoid early frailty in people with intellectual disabilities?. In M. Putnam & C. Bigby (Eds.), *Handbook on ageing with disability* (pp. 287–299). Routledge.

Frohmader, C. (2018). *Vale Dr Margaret Cooper OAM*. Women with Disabilities Australia. http://wwda.org.au/vale-margaret-cooper-oam/

Harnett, T., Jönson, H., & Taghizadeh Larsson, A. (2020). Rethinking the concept of successful aging: A disability studies approach. In M. Putnam & C. Bigby (Eds.), *Handbook on ageing with disability* (pp. 14–22). Routledge.

Heslop, P., Blair, P. S., Fleming, P., Hoghton, M., Marriott, A., & Russ, L. (2014). The confidential inquiry into premature deaths of people with intellectual disabilities in the UK: A population-based study. *The Lancet, 383*(9920), 889–895. https://doi.org/10.1016/S0140-6736(13)62026-7

Kemp, B. J., & Mosqueda, L. (2004). In B. J. Kemp & L. Mosqueda (Eds.), *Aging with a disability: What the clinician needs to know*. Baltimore, MD: The Johns Hopkins University Press. ISBN: 0-8019-7817-9.

Lauer, E., & McCallion, P. (2015). Mortality of people with intellectual and developmental disabilities from select US state disability service systems and medical claims data. *Journal of Applied Research in Intellectual Disabilities, 28*(5), 395–405. https://doi.org/10.1111/jar.12191

McCarron, M., & Reilly, E. (2010). *Supporting persons with intellectual disability and dementia: Quality dementia care standards, a guide to practice*. Dublin, Ireland: Daughters of Charity Service.

McCarron, M., Swinburne, J., Burke, E., McGlinchey, E., Mulryan, N., Andrews, V., … McCallion, P. (2011). *Growing older with an intellectual disability in Ireland 2011: First results from the Intellectual Disability Supplement of the Irish Longitudinal Study on Ageing (IDS-TILDA)*. Dublin: School of Nursing and Midwifery, Trinity College Dublin.

Moll, L., & Cott, C. (2020). Understanding the experience of growing older with cerebral palsy. In M. Putnam & C. Bigby (Eds.), *Handbook on ageing with disability* (pp. 83–96). Routledge.

Putnam, M., & Coyle, C. (2020). Trends in integrating long-term services and supports in the United States. In M. Putnam & C. Bigby (Eds.), *Handbook on ageing with disability* (pp. 361–372). Routledge.

Rios, D., Magasi, S., Novak, C., & Harniss, M. (2016). Conducting accessible research: Including people with disabilities in public health, epidemiological, and outcomes studies. *American Journal of Public Health, 106*(12), 2137–2144. https://doi.org/10.2105/AJPH.2016.303448

Salvador-Carulla, L., Balot, J., Weber, G., Zelderloo, L., Parent, A. S., McDaid, D., … Participants at the Conference. (2009). The Barcelona declaration on bridging knowledge in long-term care and support. Barcelona (Spain), March 7, 2009. *International Journal of Integrated Care, 10*, e042.

Sanford, J. A., & Remillard, E. T. (2020). Design for one is design for all: The past, present and future of universal design as a strategy for aging-in-place with disability. In M. Putnam & C. Bigby (Eds.), *Handbook on ageing with disability* (pp. 169–185). Routledge.

Strydom, A., Shooshtari, S., Lee, L., Raykar, V., Torr, J., Tsiouris, J., & Maaskant, M. (2010). Dementia in older adults with intellectual disabilities – Epidemiology, presentation, and diagnosis. *Journal of Policy and Practice in Intellectual Disabilities*, 7(2), 96–110. https://doi.org/10.1111/j.1741-1130.2010.00253.x

Watchman, K. (2014). *Learning disability and dementia*. London: Jessica Kingsley.

Weber, G. (2009). The Graz Declaration on Disability and Ageing 2006. *International Journal of Integrated Care*, 9(Suppl), e77.

World Health Organization. (2000). *Ageing and intellectual disabilities – Improving longevity and promoting healthy ageing: Summative report*. Geneva, Switzerland: World Health Organization.

Yoshizaki-Gibbons, H. (2020). Integrating critical disability studies and critical gerontology to explore the complexities of aging with disabilities. In M. Putnam & C. Bigby (Eds.), *Handbook on ageing with disability* (pp. 32–44). Routledge.

GLOSSARY

Acquired brain injury is a type of brain injury that is not hereditary, congenital, degenerative, or related to birth trauma.

Active ageing is a concept promoted by the World Health Organization and others focused on facilitating opportunities for good health, social engagement and participation, and financial security in later life.

Activities of daily living (ADLs) is a term used to describe skills required to independently take care of oneself. ADLs commonly evaluated to assess for home or social care service needs include personal hygiene or grooming, dressing, toileting, transferring or ambulating, and eating.

Age-friendly communities are a concept promoted by the U.S. organization AARP to create liveable communities for persons of all ages, particularly older adults. Specially developed planning guides and resources are provided to member cities, towns, and communities who seek Age-friendly certification.

Ageism is bias, stereotyping, and discrimination against individuals and groups on the basis of their age.

Ageing with disability is the phenomenon of persons growing older with disability that started in early life or adulthood and that continues into later life.

Ageing into disability is the phenomenon of persons experiencing disability for the first time in later life. Persons commonly considered ageing into disability are those 60 and older who did not experience sustained disability earlier in life.

Alzheimer's disease is a form of dementia that results in memory loss and impairment. Onset of Alzheimer's disease is most common in later life.

Assisted living facility is a type of group home that provides a range of daily care supports and services for persons with physical or cognitive impairments such as meal service, assistance with personal care, housekeeping, laundry, help with medications, and other items. Residents have their own rooms or apartments and share common areas.

Bipolar disorder is a mental health condition that causes extreme mood swings. Bipolar disorder is most often first diagnosed in late adolescence or early adulthood but can be diagnosed at any age.

Cerebral palsy (CP) is a group of conditions that affect body movement, muscle control, muscle coordination, muscle tone, reflex, posture, and balance. CP is mostly commonly diagnosed within the first year of life, often within a few months after birth.

Chronic conditions/chronic diseases are terms that refer to a broad range of health conditions and diseases that last more than 1 year, require medical care, and/or limit individual function. And individual may have multiple related or unrelated chronic conditions.

Cognitive function is an umbrella term that refers to the ability to learn, think, problem solve, reason, remember, make decisions, and pay attention. Facets of cognitive function are often individually assessed to determine the need for social care.

Cognitive impairment is assessed through evaluation of cognitive function. Presence of cognitive impairment can range from mild to severe and can influence an individual's ability to carry out mental tasks.

Community group home is a residential setting for persons with disabilities, commonly persons with intellectual or cognitive impairments. Community groups homes range in size from just a few residents to 20 or more and provide daily supports and services to residents to help them meet their daily living needs. Residents have their own rooms but may share common areas.

Community integration is a concept referring to the full inclusion of persons with disabilities into the daily life of the communities they choose to live in. Community integration efforts often include provision of supports and services designed to optimise the social, vocational, personal outcomes.

Community-based setting refers to the provision of supports and services or programmes to individuals in their own homes, small group homes, local community venues, or non-residential institutional facilities such as schools.

Comorbidity is the presence of one or more primary conditions or diseases that occur at the same time in an individual. For example, a person may have depression and heart disease.

Congregate setting is a space where multiple people reside, meet, or gather. Services and supports to persons with disabilities are often provided in congregate settings.

Convention on the Rights of Persons with Disabilities (CRPD) was adopted by the United Nations in 2006 and has been ratified by 181 nations. The CRPD sets out human rights for persons with disabilities through this treaty. Notably, the United States has not ratified the CRPD.

Deinstitutionalisation is a policy practice of moving persons with disabilities, of all types, out of large institutional settings such as nursing homes, psychiatric hospitals, and residential facilities into their own homes and/or small group residential living units.

Dementia-friendly communities are communities that support the needs of persons with dementia and their caregivers, empowers and includes them in society, recognizes their rights and seeks to realise their full potential in society.

Developmental disability (DD) is a term referring to a group of conditions that affect physical, language, learning, and behavioural development in children. Internationally, definitions of DD vary with some nations including intellectual disability under the umbrella of DD while other nations include DD under the category of intellectual disability. Those nations that consider DD as a category of intellectually tend to have a younger age cut-off for DD diagnosis (i.e. age 6 in Australia). Nations that view DD as a broad category may have age cut-offs for DD diagnosis of early adulthood (i.e. age 22 in the United States).

Diagnostic condition is the general term given to a medical diagnosis of a disease or chronic condition. Most impairments have an underlying medical diagnosis. Having a diagnostic condition does not equate to having a disability.

Disability onset is the point in time when disability first starts.

Disability rights movement is the term given to national and international social and political movements to secure equal rights for persons with disabilities.

Down syndrome is a diagnostic condition related to the presence of an extra chromosome in a person's DNA. Persons with Down syndrome experience developmental disability.

End-of-life care is a term used to describe care provided to an individual during the time surrounding death. End-of-life care is typically medical and/or palliative.

Frailty is a diagnosable condition characterised by decline in physical reserve and function. A clinical diagnosis of frailty is made by assessing items such as grip strength, energy level, walking speed, physical activity, and weight loss.

Group home see Community group homes.

Habitation is a process that helps persons with disabilities attain, keep, or improve skills for daily functioning.

Health inequality is a term given to differences in people's health across population groups that are avoidable. Health inequalities are due to differences in access to health care, resources, and social and economic conditions and can be addressed through policies and actions that promote equitable access to resources.

Home and community-based care services are provided in the home and community including home health aide, personal care, adult day health services, and respite care.

Home care is a service provided in an individual's home by a medical professional. It includes services such as wound care, nutritional therapy, injections, monitoring chronic conditions or illnesses, and patient and caregiver education.

Intellectual disability (ID) is a disability where individuals experience limitations in reasoning, learning, problem solving, and in adaptive behaviour. Severity of ID varies. Persons with ID typically experience disability in education, employment, and other domains where they may be marginalised or discriminated against based on their intellectual abilities. There is general agreement that to be diagnosed with ID, onset must be prior to age 18.

Intermediate care facility (ICF) is a type of institutional care that provides health and social care for persons with intellectual disabilities.

Independent living is a term associated with having choice and control over one's living situation. Independent living is sometimes used to describe a type of housing facility. Within the disability rights movement, independent living is associated with self-determination and the right and opportunity to make one's own decisions.

Independent Living Movement is a worldwide movement comprised of persons with disabilities and their allies working for equal rights and opportunities for all persons with disabilities. The movement advocates for the advancement of human rights including self-determination, societal and economic inclusion, removal of barriers and provision of resources to facilitate access to, and participation and engagement in, all domains of society.

Institutionalisation is the process of confining persons to institutional settings. Institutional care settings were historically the main locations where persons with disabilities received supports and services, and the only services for persons with disabilities that were publicly funded. Often persons with disabilities, who were institutionalised, lived in an institution their entire lives.

Instrumental activities of daily living (IADLs) are a set of activities associated with being able to live interpedently. IADLs include house cleaning and doing chores, managing money, preparing meals, shopping, taking prescribed medications, and being able to get out into the community. Ability to perform IADLs is often professionally assessed to determine disability and eligibility for support services.

Integrated health care combines primary health care and mental health care – including behavioural health care in one setting or in one health care practice.

Integrated setting is a setting where individuals with disabilities and individuals without disabilities who are not service providers interact. An integrated setting means a community-based setting.

Learning disability is a term most often used in the United Kingdom to classify disability that affects the way a person learns new things. In other nations, this same person may be classified as having a developmental disability or an intellectual disability. Persons with learning difficulties may have difficulty understanding new or complex information, experience challenges with physical and behavioural development.

Long-term supports and services (LTSS) include a wide range of health and social care supports and services ranging from assistance with bathing to provision of personal assistant services to adaptive technology. LTSS includes both institutional and home and community-based care.

Medical model of disability is a perspective that views disability as a biomedical condition of the person. In the medical model, disability is considered a disorder that requires the individual to adapt to the condition.

Mental health condition/illness is a condition or diagnosed illness that affects the way a person thinks, feels, behaves and their mood. Mental illness ranges from mild to severe. Mental illness can affect daily living.

Medicare is a federal health insurance programme in the United States for qualified workers age 65 and older or qualified workers with disabilities who may or may not be employed. Individuals qualify for Medicare insurance through attainment of work credits. Persons with disabilities under age 62 must have a qualifying disability to be eligible. Workers who qualify for Medicare health insurance may be able to insure family members through Medicare as well. Medicare does not cover most long-term care costs.

Medicaid is a federal-state health insurance programme in the United States for low-income individuals. Medicaid covers acute and long-term care. Income eligibility is at the federal poverty line, but states can set income eligibility at a lower level. Medicaid has several sub-programmes, each with their own eligibility criteria. Some states have more types of Medicaid programmes than others. The federal government cost shares Medicaid with states paying for between 50% and 95% of all Medicaid costs.

Mobility impairment refers to lower or upper body impairments that limit an individual's ability to use one or more of their arms or legs. Mobility impairments may be temporary or permanent and range from paralysis to difficulty with fine motor skills.

Multi-morbidity is a term similar to comorbidity. Multi-morbidity is generally used to describe the presence of more than two chronic conditions or diseases in the same person.

Multiple sclerosis (MS) is a disease of the central nervous system that is commonly degenerative. MS is characterised by symptoms such as pain, fatigue, muscle weakness, difficulty walking, and depression.

Normalisation principle is an approach to supporting persons with disabilities that insists on including persons with disabilities in the regular patterns and conditions of everyday life.

Nursing home is an institutional setting for long-term care that provides care for residents. Nursing homes may or may not be skilled nursing facilities.

Onset of impairment refers to the chronological time that an impairment is first identified.

Person-centred care is a care approach where health and social care professionals work collaboratively with people using services. Person-centred care values the opinions, beliefs, and knowledge of the individual and supports individuals to develop knowledge, skills, and confidence to manage their own care.

Person-centred planning is a range of planning processes employed by health and social care professionals that emphasise self-determination and decision-making control by the individual. Person-centred planning can be employed in a wide range of settings and most commonly employed in health and social care and education settings.

Personal assistance is a term used to describe a wide range of help and support provided by a personal assistant to a person with a disability. Personal assistance is a type of independent living support. Personal assistants do not provide medical care.

Personalisation/personalised support is a term used in the United Kingdom that is synonymous with person-centred planning.

Physical function is an umbrella term that refers to the ability of the individual to perform regular daily activities that involve mobility and use of the body. Facets of physical function are often individually assessed to determine the need for social care.

Polypharmacy is the concurrent use of multiple drugs or medications that medically necessary. Polypharmacy is most often a concern when five or more medications are being taken by an individual.

Rehabilitation is short-term care intended to support a person to regain, keep, or improve their physical or mental capabilities that have been lost.

Schizophrenia is a serious mental illness that affects how a person thinks, feels, and behaves. Schizophrenia is a life-long chronic condition.

Self-determination is a philosophy that argues for persons choosing and setting their own goals, making their own decisions, and being in charge of their own lives.

Self-realisation is synonymous with self-determination.

Severe mental illness is mental, emotional, or behavioural condition that can lead to serious functional impairment that interferes with or limits one or more major life activities.

Skilled nursing facility is an institutional setting for long-term care that provides advanced or skilled care to residents including rehabilitation.

Social and economic determinants of health are a range of personal, social, economic, and environmental factors that influence individual and population health.

Social care is a term used to describe personal care and practical assistance. Types of support provided under social care include help with activities of daily living, instrumental activities of daily living, assistance in the home and in activities outside of the home, home adaptations, and other supports.

Social disability is frequently associated with severe and complex mental health conditions. Social disability influences the development of social relationships, engagement with others, and may have an effect on daily living.

Social isolation is a lack of social connections and relationships. Social isolation can lead to loneliness, which is the feeling of being alone.

Social model of disability is a perspective that views disability as not an individual physiological condition but a product of physical, social, and institutional or societal structures. In the social model, disability is not inevitable and can be eliminated by changing the barriers that exclude persons with disabilities and limit their engagement and participation in society.

Successful ageing is a concept that emphasises growing older with strong physical health, social relationships, and meaningful personal experiences. As a model, successful ageing has been critiqued for viewing disability as unsuccessful ageing and its lack of consideration of variations in the ageing experiences.

Supported decision-making promotes individual self-determination, autonomy, and control through a set of relationships, practices, and agreements. Supported decision-making is an alternative to guardianship that emphasises the desires and choices of the person with disability.

Traumatic brain injury (TBI) is a change in brain function or other evidence of brain functional change caused by external force. A TBI is a type of acquired brain injury.

Universal design is a design process that aims to create environments and products that are usable and accessible to all individuals regardless of age, disability, or other factors.

INDEX

Note: *Italicized* page numbers refer to figures, **bold** page numbers refer to tables

ability-based design (ABD) 179–182; auto-personalisation in 180; benefits of 181–182; goals of 179–182; limitations of 182; in smart phones and tablets 179–180, *180*
ableism 38–40
accelerated ageing 100
accessible design 173
acquired brain injury, defined 399
Act on Prohibition of Age Discrimination in Employment and Aged Employment Promotion (Korea) 350
actigraphy 291–292
active ageing 16; adoption of 337; community service model for 357–358; defined 399; definition of 77, 357
active mentoring 248
activities of daily living (ADLs), defined 399
Activity Theory 229
ADA Accessibility Standards 173, 178
Adams, M. 301
Administration for Community Living (ACL) 62
Administration on Aging (AoA) 62, 225, 364
Administration for Community Living 225
Administration on Developmental Disability 225
adolescents with disability 46
advanced nurse practitioner (ANP) 331
Advocacy Coalition Framework 51
Affordable Care Act of 2010 365
Aged Care Assessment Team/Services (ACAT/S) 342
Age-Friendly City initiatives 9
age-friendly communities, defined 399
Age-Friendly framework 369
ageing 71–75; accelerated 100; bridging fields of disability and 11; and chronic conditions 59–60; definition of 73–74; and functional ability 74; and health 229–230; and intrinsic capacity 74; segmentation of 362–363; successful 14–20; theories 9–10; usual 15

ageing in place: emerging issues 342–343; gaps in existing services for 340–341; in group homes 340–342; individualised funding 344–345; lack of clarity 340; necessary strategies for 340–341; policies on 342–343; purchasing additional support 343–344; restricted access to services 341; sector to pay for services 341; support needs 341; transitioning from disability to aged care 344
ageing into disability 171, 361; versus ageing with disability 7–8; chronic conditions 58–61, *59*; defined 3, 399; nexus of 60–61
ageing policy 74
ageing with disability 3–11, 170, 361; versus ageing into disability 7–8; cerebral palsy 84; chronic conditions 58–61, *59*; congenital 84; consilience of disability and 71–75; defined 4–5, 161, 399; demographics 57; duration of disability 5; early-onset 84; financial mechanisms for intersectoral collaboration 384–389; foundational concepts 3–4; in Korea 350–359; life expectancy 57; nexus of 60–61, **62**; onset of impairment 4; overview 23; phenomenon 6–7; population 58; population size 5–6; prevalence of 5; research landscape 396; social models of disability for 8–9; status of scholarship 10–11; sub-groups 394–396
ageing with lifelong disability 23–28; experiences of 27–28; individual meanings 27–28; life course perspective 24–25; life stories 25–26; life story research 26–27
age-integration model of retirement **246**
ageism 38–40; defined 399
age-related chronic conditions 60
age-specific retirement programs **246**
Ageing and Developmental Disabilities (Janicki/Wisniewski) 219
Aging and Disability Evidence-based Programs and Practices (ADEPP) 62, 63

Index

Aging and Disability Resource Centers (ADRCs) 64, 65, 163, 366, 395
Ageing and Mental Retardation (Krauss/Seltzer) 219
Agree, E. M. 103
Alberta Aids to Daily Living 376
Alzheimer's disease 126, 151, 292, 399
Alzheimer's Disease Program Initiative (ADPI) 367–368
American Spinal Cord Injury Scale 7
Americans with Disabilities Act (ADA) 113, 164, 173
amnesia 126
amyloid precursor protein (APP) 222
Ansello, E. F. 224
anxiety 293–294
Area Agencies on Aging (AAAs) 163, 363–364
Arnstein, S. 213
arthritis 127
Ask Larsen, F. 100
Assisted Decision Making (Capacity) Act (Ireland) 327
assisted living facility, defined 399
assistive technology 165, 172, 372–381; access for persons with disabilities 376; access for seniors 376; equitable access to 375, 379; funding and services for **377–379**; key issues 379, **380**; legislation and policy on 374; overview 372, 375–376; universality of 373
audio accounts 27
Australia: discrimination against working age adults with disability 49–50; employment of adults with disabilities in 48; groups homes 338–346; housing of working adults with disabilities 48–49; National Disability Insurance Scheme 342–345; retirement of older people with intellectual disabilities 244; violence against working age adults with disability 49; working age adults with disabilities in 46
Australian Victorian Law Reform Commission 187
autism spectrum condition and ageing 148–154; adults with childhood diagnosis 149; adults with late diagnosis 149; ASC characteristics 150–151; brain development in 152–153; cognition in 152–153; co-occurring intellectual disabilities in 149–150; dementia in 152; general well-being/outcomes 149–150; mental health 151–152; overview 148–149; Parkinsonism in 152; physical health 151–152; prevalence 149; prevalence of 5; quality of life 149–150
auto-personalisation 180–181

Bach, M. 188
Baird, A. 301
Barnes, C. 8
Bass, S. A. 33
Baxley, D. D. 302
benefits, eligibility requirements 72
Berridge, C. 15
'best interests of the person' test 188
Better Care Fund 387
Bevins, S. 301
Bigby, C. 247, 301, 341

biography 26
bipolar disorder, defined 399
Blumenthal, J. A. 187
bone breakage 10
Borg, E. 97
brain 152–153
Brandt, E. N., Jr. 8
Brehmer-Rinderer, B. 274
Bridging Aging and Disability International Network (BADIN) 395
Bülow, P. 27

Cadbury, H. 27
Calasanti, T. 15
Campbell, M. 392
Canada: access to assistive technology in 372–382; assistive technology-related legislation and policy 374; disability-related legislation and policy 374; health systems 373; incidence of cerebral palsy in 83; social care 374
Canada Health Act 373
Canada Health Transfer 373
Canada Social Transfer 374
Canadian Charter of Rights and Freedoms 374
Canadian Human Rights Act 374
Capability Theory 73
capacity limitation 72
cardiovascular disease 292–293
caregivers and caregiving: compound caregiving 256; family caregivers 254–258; family support needs 257–258; fathers 256; financial outcomes 255; grandparents 257; health outcomes 255–256; intellectual and developmental disabilities (I/DD) 220–221, 254–258; in later life 256–257; multiple sclerosis 140; non-traditional 256–257; number of 254; reciprocity and meaning 256; siblings 256; social outcomes 255–256; supports for long-term caregivers 257; supports needs 257; traumatic brain injury 131; unmet formal services 257
Carey, G. 52
Carey, N. 100, 101, 102
Carling-Jenkins, R. 301
Carney, T. 190, 394
Center for Healthy Ageing 63
Center for Universal Design 174
Centers for Independent Living (CILs) 163, 364
Centers for Medicaid and Medicare Services (CMS) 179, 364
cerebral palsy and ageing 83–93; completing college/university 89–90; defined 399; *Defying the odds* narrative 84–92; disruption on self-regulation of disordered body 90; failure to display physical abilities 86; going to work 89–90; growing older 89–91; health care/rehabilitation inaccessibility 91; incidence of 78; learning to walk 87–88; living on their own 90; parents' responses 87; segregation to integration 88–89; slowing down and declines in functioning 90
child support payments 72

Index

children with disabilities: discrimination 47; harassment of 47; poverty 45–47; segregation 89; sense of belonging 89; socio-economic position 46–47
cholesterol 60
chronic conditions 58–61; age-related 59–60; cognitive disorders 60; defined 399; multiple 60; onset of 60; physical conditions 60; secondary conditions 58; shared burden of 61
Chronic Disease Self-Management Education Programs (CDSMP) 62
Chronic Disease Self-Management Program (CDSMP) 63
chronic traumatic encephalopathy 128
circadian rest-activity rhythm 291–292
citizen as consumer 39
citizen as labourer 39
Clarke, P. J. 100
Clegg, A. 280
clinical nurse specialist (CNS) 331
cognition 152–153
cognitive disability 187
cognitive function, defined 400
cognitive impairment and ageing 186–192; decision-making 189–192; defined 400; dementia 188, 191–192; individual rights 189; literature and inquiries 187; overview 186–187; relational autonomy 189; taxonomies 187–189
commodification 40–41
commodity culture 39
community agency residence care 314–315
Community Based Research Network (CBRN) 163
community engagement 234
community group homes 338–346; access restrictions in 341; complexity of ageing in place in 340–342; defined 400; and deinstitutionalisation 338; emerging issues 342–343; and family care 338; gaps in existing services 340–341; health conditions in 338; individualised funding 344–345; lack of clarity 340; life histories 338; National Disability Insurance Scheme (Australia) 342–345; necessary strategies for 340–341; overview 338–339; policies on 339–340, 342–343; purchasing additional support 343–344, 344; sector to pay 341; social factors 338–339; support needs 341
community integration, defined 400
Community Integration Index 129–130
community participation 161–166; environmental factors in 164–165; of people ageing with physical disability 161–163; role of personal factors and health in 163–164; role of supports and services in 165–166
community service development 358
community service model 357–358
community services, absence of 354–355
community-based care 364–365
community-based setting, defined 400
comorbidity, defined 400
Compeer Model 117

compound caregiving 256
compulsory systems 38–40
congregate setting, defined 400
Connaire, K. 224
consumer behaviour 39
consumer society 39
Continuity Theory 229
Convention on the Rights of Persons with Disabilities (CRPD), defined 400
Cooper, M. 394
Cooper Ueki, M. 248
Cott, C. A. 97
Courtenay, K. 301
Crabtree, J. 151
Crammond, B. 52
critical disability studies: versus critical gerontology 34; defined 33; integrating with critical gerontology 37
critical gerontology: versus critical disability studies 34; defined 32–33; integrating with critical disability studies 37
Croen, L. A. 152
Crook, N, 301

Dahlgren, G. 231
Dalton, A. J. 302
Damen, G. W. 100
Dawes, S. 301
De Leeuw, E. 52
De Vreese, L. P. 302
deafblindness 97–103; communication partners in 102; congenital versus acquired 99–100; definition of 97; hidden population 99–100; misrecognition of 101–102; multiple changes in 100–101; overview 97; studies on 97–98; unmet needs 101–102; as an unrecognized disability 97
decision-making 189–192
decrement in functioning 72
Defying the odds narrative 84–92; abandonment of disordered body 91; achieving sense of belonging 87; appearance of disordered body 86; components of 86; described 85–86; interpretation of 91–92; labelling the disordered body 87; living on their own 90; main threads 86, *86*; making a place for themselves 89–90; meta-narrative *86*, 86; normalisation of physical impairment 87–88; overview 84–85; struggling to fit in 88–89
deinstitutionalisation, defined 400
Delanty, N. 6
delegated financing 386
dementia: in autistic adults 151–152; care mapping 301; case examples 302–305; and cognitive impairment 188; decision-making in 191–192; key issues 306; music-based activities for 301; in people with I/DD 222–223, 300–308; prevalence rates 300; studies on 300–302; and successful ageing 19; in traumatic brain injury 126
dementia pugilistica 128
dementia-friendly communities, defined 400

depression 108, 109, 126, 293–294
Developmental Disabilities Assistance and Bill of Rights Act of 2000 (DD Act) 257
developmental disability (DD), persons with: caregiving for 220–221; defined 400; dementia in 222–223; Down syndrome 222–223; end-of-life care 224; family caregiving for 254–258; health and ageing era 220; life expectancy 6, 219, 394; number of 254; population size 5; views on 219–220; work and retirement 223
diabetes 60, 292–293
diagnostic condition 5; defined 400
disability 71–75, 196–203; bridging fields of ageing and 11; consilience of ageing and 71–75; defined 8; definition of 74; duration of 5; functional limitation 72; growing up with 45–47; versus impairment 8; onset of 9–10; social models of 8–9, 196; unrecognised 97
Disability Act 196
disability care: framework for 197–198; home care 200; living at home 200; nursing homes 198–199; overview 196–197; versus personal assistance 200–201; user gaze in 201–203
disability onset, defined 400
disability policy 73, 74
disability prevalence 6
disability rights movement 196, 400
discrimination, against working age adults with disability 49–50
Disease Prevention and Health Promotion Services (DPHPS) 62
disordered body 85; abandonment of 91; appearance of 86; disruption on self-regulation of 90; labelling 87
Dolan, E. 6
domestic violence 128
Donnely, M. 188
Down syndrome: defined 400; and dementia 222–223, 300; frailty in 287, 292
Draper, K. 126
Duggan, L. 38
duration of disability 5

early-life disability onset 9–10
earmarked funding 386
Education for all Handicapped Children Act 25
Ekuma, O. 142
eldercare 196–203; framework for 197–198; home care 200; living at home 200; nursing homes 198–199; overview 196–197; versus personal assistance 200–201; user gaze in 201–203
The Elderly Caregiver (Roberto) 221
electronic election ballots *181*, 182–183
eligibility requirements 72
employment: of people with cerebral palsy 89–90; of people with I/DD 223; of people with SMI 115–116; of senior citizens 209; of working age adults with disability 47–48
Employment Equity Act (Canada) 374

end-of-life care: case example 310; community agency residence care 314–315; defined 400; healthcare 312–313; healthcare decision making 312; hospice care 313–314; in integrated social planning 209; key issues in 315; literature on 311; overview 311; people with I/DD 224; for people with intellectual disabilities 310–316; planning for 311–312; policies 316; practices 316; transparency iu 311–312
Environmental Press Model 169–183
Equal Rights Framework 197–198
Estes, C. L. 33, 39
European Innovation Partnership on Active and Healthy Ageing 16
Evenhuis, H. 294
evidence-based practices (EBP) 61–62; needs and supply gap 63–65
EZ Ballot *181*, 182–183

Fahey-McCarthy, E. 224
falls 139–140
Family and Medical Leave Act 257
family caregivers and caregiving 254–258; compound caregiving 256; family support needs 257–258; fathers 256; financial outcomes 255; grandparents 257; health outcomes 255–256; in later life 256–257; non-traditional 256–257; reciprocity and meaning 256; siblings 256; social outcomes 255–256; supports for long-term caregivers 257; supports needs 257; unmet formal services 257
Family Quality of Life (FQOL) 255
Family Support 363 projects 257
Family Support Research and Training Center 257
Farrell, E.M. 300
Federal Healthy People 2020 231
Federal-Provincial Fiscal Arrangements Act (Canada) 374
financial mechanisms: delegated financing 386; earmarked funding 386; for intersectoral collaboration 384–389; joint budgeting 386–387
Finkelstein, D. 8
Finlayson, G. 142
Finlayson, M. 142
Foti, M. 109
frailty 273–282; avoidance of 287–297; avoiding 296–297; characteristics associated with 278–280; defined 401; and deterioration of health and independence 276–278; index 273–274, 274–276, *276*, 278, 287, *290*; and intellectual disability 287; Kaplan-Meier survival curves *279*; knowledge base 287; as measure of ageing in general population 273–274; as measure of ageing in people with intellectual disabilities 274–280; measurement of 273–274, 274; mechanisms of 280; phenotype 273, 274–275, **276**; postponing 296–297; recommendations 280–282
Fried, L. P. 273
functional ability 74
functional limitation 72
Future Care Road Map (Ireland) 312–313
The Future is Now 258

Gagne, J. 98
Gaussen, K. 301
generic integration model of retirement **246**
geographical information system (GIS) 211
geriatric syndromes 229
Gibbons, H. M. 33
Global Public Inclusive Infrastructure (GPII) initiative 180
Goffman, E. 112
gonadotropins 125
Goodley, D. 33
Gray, D. B. 162
Grossman, B. R. 39
Groulx, G. 98
group homes *see* community group homes
Gullacksen, A. 100, 102

habitation, defined 401
Hagberg, J. E. 27
Haley, W. E. 256
Harnett, T. 198, 269, 393
Harvey, D. 38
Hastings, R. P. 255
Haugland, G. 110
Hay, T. 110
health: and ageing 229–236; deterioration of 276–278; environmental determinants of 45; inequalities 230; of older adults with intellectual disabilities 232–236; and poverty 230; self/proxy rated 234; social determinants of 45, 230
Health and Retirement Study 64
Health Canada for First Nations and Inuit peoples 376
health frameworks, social determinants of 230–231
health inequality, defined 401
healthy ageing, definition of 77
Healthy Ageing in Intellectual Disability (HAID) study 275–276, 287
Heller, T. 258, 339, 393
Henwood, B. F. 114
Hersh, M. 102
Heslop, P. 242
Hickey, A. 151
Hills, G. 6
Hogg, J. 395
Hollingsworth, H. H. 162
Hollister, B. A. 39
home and community-based care, defined 401
home and community-based services (HCBS) 364–365
home care 200, 364–365; defined 401
Home Care Package (HCP) Program 342
homelessness 114–115
HOPES psychosocial skills training program 111, 117
Hopper, K. 110
hormones 125
hospice care 313–314
housing: integrated social planning 209; for people with mental illness 114–115; for working adults with disabilities 48–49
hypertension 60

Iacono, T. 301
ICF model of disability 205
ICF-Based Environmental Intervention Model 170, *170, 176*
identity politics 77
impairment 8; versus disability 8; onset of 4–5
independence, deterioration of 276–278
independent living, defined 401
Independent Living Movement 88, 401
individual rights 189
Individuals with Disabilities Education Act 25
Institut National d'excellence en Sante et en Services Sociaux (INESSS) 130
Institute on Disability and Human Development 392
institutionalisation: defined 401; and multiple sclerosis 141
instrumental activities of daily living (IADLs), defined 401
integrated health care, defined 401
integrated setting, defined 401
integrated social planning 205–214; accessibility 209; citizen participation 208; counselling and participation 209; designing participation 213; end of life care 209; funding 206–207; health and medical care 209; housing 209; importance of 205–206; key issues 213–214; local supply and everyday services 209; mobility 209; municipality's lead role in 207; neighborhood awareness 209; neighbourhood orientation 207–208; neighbourhood-oriented, GIS-based social reporting: 211; person-centred approach 208; person-oriented key objectives 211; planning areas 210; planning process 211–212; political mandate 210; political participation 210; prerequisites for 206–207; process model for *212*; scope of planning 208–210; service providers 206–207; shared principles of 207–208; social encounters and activities 209; social inclusion in 207; strategic planning elements 210–211; support services 209; volunteering 209; work and employment 209; work structures 210–211
intellectual and developmental disabilities (I/DD), persons with: caregiving for 220–221; dementia in 222–223; Down syndrome 222–223; end-of-life care 224; family caregiving for 254–258; health and ageing era 220; life expectancy 6, 219, 394; number of 254; population size 5; views on 219–220; work and retirement 223
intellectual disabilities, persons ageing with: anxiety 293–294; cardiovascular disease in 292–293; chronically disturbed circadian rest-activity rhythm 291–292; community engagement 234; congenital motor and sensory disabilities 288–290; dementia care for 300–308; depression 293–294; diabetes in 292–293; early frailty avoidance 287–297; employment rates 241; end-of-life care for 310–316; frailty of 273–282; genetic factors 288–290; group homes 337–346; health and wellness of 229–236; health problems 288–296; life events

293–294; living circumstances of 233; low fitness 292; missed diagnoses 291; mortality rates 242; multimorbidity 294–295; polypharmacy 295–296; psychotropic drug use 290–291; relationships 233–234; retirement 242–249; self/proxy rated health 234; social support 233–234; in Sweden 262–270; unhealthy lifestyle 292
intellectual disability (ID): defined 401; and frailty 287; taxonomy 187
intellectual disability nursing: capability 330–331; capacity 330–331; challenges in providing service 332; demographics 325; future roles of 327; and intellectual disability nursing 332; in Ireland 323–325; person-centered care 327; person-centeredness 327; person-centred planning 331; policies on 326; priority areas for education and upskilling **331**; priority areas for future provision **328**; professional leadership 330–331; re-tasking 326–327; roles of *329*; staffing 323–325; supporting individuals 328–330
Intellectual Disability Supplement to the Irish Longitudinal Study on Ageing (IDS-TILDA) 232–233, 288, 393
intermediate care facility (ICF), defined 401
International Association for the Scientific Study of Intellectual and Developmental Disabilities (IASSIDD) 393
International Classification of Functioning 8
International Classification of Functioning, Disability, and Health 161, 169–170, *170*
International Social Security Association (ISSA) 70
intersectionality 51, 186
intersectoral collaboration: delegated financing 386; earmarked funding 386; economic arguments for 387; joint budgeting 386–387
intimate partner violence (IPV) 128
intrinsic capacity 74
iPhone 180
Ireland 5; *Celtic Tiger* economy 325; intellectual disability services in 323
Irish Hospice Foundation 325
Irwin, A. 231

Janicki, M. 219, 224, 302, 395
Japan, employment rate 48
Jarry, J. 98
Jee, Y. K. 357
Jeppson Grassman, E. 28
Jiang, D. 142
jobs *see* employment
joint budgeting 386–387
Jokinen, N. S. 301
Jönson, H. 198, 393
Jormfeldt, M. 265, 266
Jost, J. 110
Journal of Deafblind Studies on Communication 99

Kahlin, I. 27
Kahn, R. L. 14

Kail, B. 38
Kane, R. A. 197
Kane, R. L. 197
Katz, S. 15
Keene, J. R. 38
Keller, H. 384
Kelley-Moore, J. A. 33
Kenshole, A. 301
Kerzner, L. 188
Kim, S. J. 357
Kjellberg, A. 27
Kohn, N. A. 187, 190
Kok, E. 213
Korea, people ageing with physical disabilities in 350–359; absence of community services 354–355; absence of residential service models 355–356; ageing population 350; changes to one-person households 351–352, *353*; community service development 358; community service model 357–358; facility usage of *356*; health *351*, 351–352, *352*; income 351–352, *352*, *353*; long-term care insurance 353–354, 357; overview 350–351; personal assistance services 353–354, 357; residential service with community 358–359
Krauss, M. 219
Kremer- Preiß, U. 208

Lane, J 6
Langdon, P. E. 301
Latham, K. 100
Laustrup, B. 100
Law Concerning Support and Services to Certain People with Disability (Sweden) 262–263
Lawton, M. P. 8, 169
learning disability, defined 401
Learning Disability Nursing Project 324
LeJeune, B. J. 102
life adjustment model 102
life courses 23–24; and ageing with disability 24–25
life events 293–294
life expectancy 57, 394
life history work 26
life review 26
life stories 25–26
life story research, adults with lifelong disability 26–27
Lifespan Respite Care Program (LRCP) 257, 367
Lifespan Respite Technical Assistance Center 367
lifestyle drift 51
Linton, S. 33
long-term care insurance 353–354, 357
long-term disability populations 219–225; caregiving 220–221; caregiving for 220–221; dementia in 222–223; health and ageing era 220; work and retirement 223, 224
long-term services and supports (LTSS) 40, 163, 165–166, 361–370, 402; Ageing and Disability Resource Centers 366; Alzheimer's Disease Program Initiative 367–368; versus inclusive communities 368–370; Lifespan Respite Care Program 367;

Money Follows the Person (MFP) 366–367; nursing home transition programs 366–367; overview 361; program integration initiatives 366; segmentation of 362–363; shift from institutional to home and community-based care 364–366; siloed system of 362; in United States 363–364
Lynn, L. 325

MacArthur model 14, 17
Mace, Ron 174
Malawi, employment rate 48
Manitoba's Home Care Services 376
March of Dimes Ontario 395
Marrie, R. A. 142
Martinson, M. 15
McCallion, P. 207, 224, 302
McCarron, M. 207, 224
McLoughlin, S. 230
Medicaid 40, 179, 365, 402
Medicaid Community Attendant Services Act 367
medical model of disability, defined 402
Medicare 179, 402
Meekosha, H, 38
memory box 27
memory loss 126
menstrual cycle 125
mental health condition/illness: autism spectrum condition in ageing 151–152; defined 402; recovery 110–111
mercy doulas 314
Merton, R. K. 197
Michell-Auli, P. 208
mid-life disability onset 9–10
Mitchell, D. 39
Mitchell, L. 208
Mitnitski, A. 273
mobility impairment 139–140; defined 402
Model of Care for Transition from Paediatric to Adult Healthcare Providers in Rare Diseases 325
Moll, L. R. 97
Molton, I. R. 33
Money Follows the Person (MFP) 364, 366–367
Morgan, K. A. 162
multimedia life stories 27
multi-morbidity, defined 402
multimorbidity 294–295
multiple chronic conditions 60
multiple sclerosis 138–139; causes of 138–139; diagnostic age range 138; factors in 138; life expectancy in 138; overview 138–139; prevalence of 5, 138; symptoms 138; types of 139
multiple sclerosis and ageing 139–144; health insurance 142; health promoting behaviours 143; home care 142; institutionalism 141; maintaining purpose 142–143; mobility and falls in 139–140; need for assistance in 140; participation in valued activities 142–143; quality of life 142–143; tangible supports 141–142
multiple sclerosis (MS), defined 402
Multiple Streams Approach 51

musculoskeletal issues 127
music 301
musical memory 301

Nahemow, L. 8, 169
narrative analysis 26
National Alzheimer's and Dementia Resource Center 367
National Alzheimer's Call Center 367
National Board of Health and Welfare (NBHW) 197
National Council on Aging (NCOA) 63
National Council on Disability 208
National Disability Insurance Scheme (Australia) 51, 188, 225, 249, 337–338, 342–345, 395
National Family Caregiver Support Program 257
National Health and Aging Trends Study (NHATS) 64
National Institute of Disability, Independent Living, and Rehabilitation Research (NIDILRR) 392
National Intellectual Disability Database (NIID) 325
National Patient Register 263
needs: assessment 73; disability-related 73; health-related 73
neighbourhood orientation 207–208
neoliberal capitalism 37–38
Nest Learning Thermostat 180
neuroendocrine system 124–125
new ageism 15
New Freedom Initiative 364–365
Nirje, B. 16
Non-Insured Health Benefits program (Canada) 376
Nord, C. 27
Nordic relational model of disability 196
normalisation principle: defined 402; Scandinavian 16
Norway, retirement of older people with intellectual disabilities 244
Novak, A. N. 207
nursing homes 41, 141, 198–199; defined 402; transition programs 366–367

Oberman, L. M. 152
occupational therapy 169
OECD countries 70; employment of adults with disabilities in 48
Older Americans Act (OAA) 62, 363–364, 366
older people 196–203; framework for analysing support for 197–198; home care 200; integrated social planning for 208–210; and internalised ageism 201–203; living at home 200; in nursing homes 198–199; overview 196–197; personal assistance 200–201; user gaze 201–203
older persons, global population of 57
Oliver, M. 8, 102
Olmstead decision 364
onset of impairment 4–5; age of 4–5; defined 402; early-life 9–10; mid-life 9–10
Ontario Neurotrauma Foundation 130
O'Philbin, L. 300
oral history 26
Orrell, M. 300
O'Toole, Corbett 35–37, 40–41

Padgett, D. K. 28, 114
Panel Study on Income Dynamics 64
Panhuizen, B. 213
Parkes, J. 301
Parkinson's disease 152
Parks, J. 109
Pascual-Leone, A. 152
paternalism, self-determination between extremes 268–270
Pathways' Housing First Program 115
Patient Protection and Affordable Care Act (ACA) 61
peer support 117
people ageing with physical disability (PAwPD): assistive technology for 165; cognitive changes in 164; community participation 161; enabling good old age for 392–397; long-term support services for 165–166; with mobility devices 163–164; personal factors and health in 163–164
Perkins, E. A. 256
person with disabilities: access to assistive technology 376; global number of 6
personal assistance 17, 200–201; defined 402
personal assistance services 354, 357
personalisation/personalised support, defined 402
person-centered care 327
person-centeredness 327
person-centred care, defined 402
person-centred planning, defined 402
person-centred planning (PCP) 331
person-environment fit theory 8
persons ageing into disability, defined 3
Phillipson, C. 33
photo albums 27
photovoice methodology 305
physical function, defined 402
polarised ageism 15
political economy 37–38
Pollington, C. 101
polypharmacy: defined 403; in persons with intellectual disabilities 295–296
Pope, A. M. 8
Population Health Fund (PHF) 386
Portacolone, E. 40
post-traumatic stress syndrome 109
poverty 45–47; and childhood disability 46–47; and disability 47; and health outcomes 230
Priestley, M. 265
Productivity Commission Report on Disability Care and Support 340
psychotropic drugs 290–291
Public Health Agency of Canada 387
punch drunk 128
Putnam, M. 98, 392

Quadagno, J. 38
quality of life, ageing with multiple sclerosis 142–143
Quick Ballot *181*, 183

Recognize, Assist, Include, Support, and Engage (RAISE) Family Caregiver Act 257
reference group theory 197
registered nurse in intellectual disability (RNID): capability 330–331; capacity 330–331; challenges in providing service 332; future roles of 327; in Ireland 323–325; person-centered care 327; person-centeredness 327; person-centred planning 331; policies on 326; priority areas for education and upskilling **331**; priority areas for future provision **328**; professional leadership 330–331; re-tasking 326–327; roles of *329*; supporting individuals 328–330
rehabilitation, defined 403
Rehabilitation Act 62
relational autonomy 189
relationships 233–234
reminiscence 26
Report of the Committee of Enquiry into Mental Handicap Nursing and Car 324
reproductive hormones 125
Resch, J. A. 258
residential service 355–359
residualistic conversion model 51
resilience 50–51, 143
resource pooling 386–387
retirement: access and linkage work in 247; active mentoring in 248; age of 241; from distinctive and disadvantaged position 241–242; engagement and participation in 244–245; experiences of older people with intellectual disabilities 243–245; individualised approaches to support in 247–248; mainstream approaches to 240–241; perspectives of older people with intellectual disabilities 242; policy initiatives on 248–249; service models for 245–248; traditional models of **246**; transition to 248
return to work policy 73
Roberto, K. 221
Rockwood, K. 273
Rogne, L. 39
Roh, S. H. 354, 357
Rönnberg, J. 97
Roosevelt, Franklin 35
Rowe, J. W. 14
Royal Commission Inquiry 187, 188
Royers, T. 213
Russell, M. 41

Samson, S. 301
Sandvin, J. T. 265
Scandinavian Model of Successful Ageing 16–17, 393
Scandinavian normalisation principle 16
Scarlett, S. 230
Schäper, S. 211, 213
schizophrenia 108, 109, 110, 112, 113; defined 403; prevalence of 5
Schreenberger, R. C. 219
Screening Tool of Older People's Prescriptions (STOPP) 295

Screening Tool to Alert doctors to Right Treatment (START) 295
secondary conditions 58
Selective Optimization with Compensation 229
self-determination 264–270; defined 403
self-realisation, defined 403
self-stigma 113, 116
Seltzer, M. 219
Sen, Amartya 73
serious mental illness (SMI) 108–118; cognitive factors 109; and employment 115–116; and homelessness 114–115; housing programs for people with 114–115; impact of policies on individuals 110; incidence of 108; in later life 108–109; mental health recovery 110–111; morbidity 109; mortality 109; narrative understanding of 111–112; overview 108; peer support 117; social disability 110; social factors 111–112; and social inclusion 113; and social relationships 116–117; and socio-economic status 110–111; stigma of 112–113; treatment factors 111
severe mental illness, defined 403
Shakespeare, T. 8
Shaping the Future of Intellectual Disability Nursing in Ireland 324, 328–330
shared burden of chronic conditions: evidence-based practices 61–62; reducing 61–62, 65–66
Sheets, D. J. 33
Shibusawa, T. 28, 114
Shogren, K. A. 187
Shorten, N. 301
Simcock, P. 98, 100, 101
Singer, P. 109
Singing for the Brain 301
skilled nursing facility, defined 403
Snyder, S. 39
social and economic determinants of health, defined 403
social care: in Canada 374; defined 403
social determinants: of health 230; of health frameworks 230–231; self/proxy rated health 234
social determinants of health 45, 50
social disability 110, 116; defined 403
social hierarchy 45
social inclusion 113–114, 207
social isolation, defined 403
social model of disability 8–9, 196; defined 403
social policy: defined 75; effectiveness of 75–76; equity 75–76; ethical requirements 75–77; reasons for failure of 76; relevance of 75–76
social relationships 116–117
Social Security Disability Insurance (SSDI) 36
Social Services Act (Sweden) 262
social stratification 45
social support 233–234
socio-economic position (SEP) 45–47
socio-economic status (SES): and childhood disability 45; and health outcomes 230; and mental health 110–111
Sok, K. 213
Solar, O. 231

Soldatic, K. 38
Solway, E. 39
Sorensen, A. 339
South Africa, employment rate 48
Southall, K. 98
specialised design 172–174; accessible design 173; assistive technology 172; benefits of 173; limitations of 173–174
specialist model of retirement **246**
Spector, A. E. 300
spinal cord injury 126; life expectancy 6; prevalence of 5
spousal abuse 128
Stancliffe, R. 207, 248
standard policy approach 70–71, 75–77
Stark, S. L. 162
Starkstein, S. 152
Stevenson, T. 27
Stiefel, D. H. 100
stigma 112–113
Stoffel, S. 101
Stott, J. 151
Straßbuger, G. 213
structural stigma 112
Strydom, A. 301
successful ageing 14–20, 77; activities with high level of functioning 17–18; defined 15, 403; and dementia 19; and disability policies 16; MacArthur model 14, 17; and normalisation principle 16; overview 14–15; Scandinavian model 16–17, 393
suicide 126–127
support services 40, 209
supported decision-making, defined 403
Svendsen, D. 109
Sweden: ageing with intellectual disability in 262–270; housing for participation and self-determination 266–267; older adult perspectives of ageing and participation 264–265; participation in 264; paternalism in 267–268; self-determination in 264, 267; staff and managers' perspectives on ageing and participation 264–266
Swedish Research Council for Health, Working Life and Welfare 197
Switzerland, employment rate 48
Systematic Tool to Reduce Inappropriate Prescribing (STRIP) 295

Taghizadeh Larsson, A. 393
Technology-Related Assistance for Individuals with Disabilities Act of 1988 172
TechSAge Model of Ageing and Disability 170, *171*
testosterone 125
Then, S. 394
Todd, S. 224
Toronto Declaration on Bridging Ageing and Disability 11
Torr, J. 301
Totsika, V. 255
traumatic brain injury (TBI) 123–131; caregivers 131; as chronic condition 129; and chronic traumatic

encephalopathy 128; classification of **124**; and community integration 129–130; defined 403; definition of 124; depression in 126; guidelines 130–131; long-term effects of 124; and mental health 126; mild 127–128; musculoskeletal outcomes 127; neuroendocrine disturbances 124–125; neurological outcomes 126–127; overview 123–124; prevalence of 5; rehabilitation 130–131; reproductive hormone disturbances 125; sex differences 123, 128–129
Tuffrey-Wijne, I. 224
Turner, S. 248
type of disability experience 5

United Kingdom: disabled children in 46; discrimination against working age adults with disability 49–50; employment of adults with disabilities in 48; housing of working adults with disabilities 49; income of households with disabled member 384; income of pensioner couples 385; violence against working age adults with disability 49; working age adults with disabilities in 46
United Nations Convention on the Rights of Persons with Disabilities (CRPD) 70, 76–77, 99, 186–192, 262, 346; 'best interests of the person' test 188; equality principle in 187; funding of retirement 248; and inclusive social planning 207; individual rights 189; relational autonomy 189; support for decision-making 188, 189–192
United States 5; ageing with disability population 58; disabled children in 46; employment of adults with disabilities in 48; long-term services and supports in 361–370; retirement of older people with intellectual disabilities 244; violence against working age adults with disability 49; working age adults with disabilities in 46
universal basic income 72
universal design, defined 403
universal design (UD) 169–183; ability-based design 179–182; accessible design 173; assistive technology 172; benefits of 178; definition of 172; design for all 174–176; design for one 179–183; evolution of 172–174; future of 182–183; limitations of 178–179; principles of 176–177, **177**; reasons for using 175–176; specialised design 172–174
universal policy 72

universalism 78
unrecognised disability 97
user gaze 197, 201–203
Usher syndrome 100
usual ageing 15

Vagenas, D. 255
vascular dementia 151
Verbrugge, L. M. 100
Victorian Health Promotion Foundation 388
video reports 27
violence, exposure to 49
volunteering 209
vulnerability 50–51

Ward, A. R. 301
Watson, N. 8, 39
Weber, G. 274
Welber, S. 110
Welfare of the Aged Act (Korea) 350
Westwood, S. 100, 101, 102
white matter 152
Whitehead, M. 231
Whitemore, M. 27
Wisniewski, H. 219
Wittich, W. 98, 101, 103
Woods, B. 300
work *see* employment
working age adults with disability: discrimination against 49–50; employment 47–48; exposure to violence 49; housing 48–49; living conditions 47; and poverty 47
World Federation of the Deafblind 101, 102
World Health Organization (WHO): Age-Friendly City initiatives 9; framework 231; framework for *Active Ageing* 241; framework for *Healthy Ageing* 241; *World Report on Aging and Health* 73–74
Wu, I. 224

Yorkston, K. M. 33
Yoshizaki-Gibbons, H. 33, 393

Zendell, A. 302
Zimring, C. 213
Zola, Irving 78

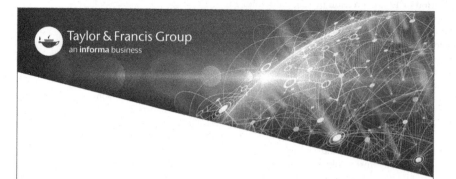